Life and Thought of Śaṅkarācārya

Life and Thought of Śaṅkarācārya

Govind Chandra Pande

MOTILAL BANARSIDASS PUBLISHERS
PRIVATE LIMITED • DELHI

First Indian Edition: Delhi, 1994
Reprint: Delhi, 1998, 2004

ISBN: 81-208-1104-6

Also available at:
MOTILAL BANARSIDASS
41 U.A. Bungalow Road, Jawahar Nagar, Delhi 110 007
8 Mahalaxmi Chamber, 22 Bhulabhai Desai Road, Mumbai 400 026
236, 9th Main III Block, Jayanagar, Bangalore 560 011
120 Royapettah High Road, Mylapore, Chennai 600 004
Sanas Plaza, 1302 Baji Rao Road, Pune 411 002
8 Camac Street, Kolkata 700 017
Ashok Rajpath, Patna 800 004
Chowk, Varanasi 221 001

Printed in India
BY JAINENDRA PRAKASH JAIN AT SHRI JAINENDRA PRESS,
A-45 NARAINA, PHASE-I, NEW DELHI 110 028
AND PUBLISHED BY NARENDRA PRAKASH JAIN FOR
MOTILAL BANARSIDASS PUBLISHERS PRIVATE LIMITED,
BUNGALOW ROAD, DELHI 110 007

Atulita-bala-dhāmaṁ hema-śailābha-dehaṁ
Danuja-vana-kṛśānuṁ jñāninām agra-gaṇyam/
Sakala-guṇa-nidhānaṁ vānarāṇām adhīśaṁ
Raghupati-priya-bhaktaṁ vāta-jātaṁ namāmi//

Contents

Preface

The celebration of the Twelfth Centenary of Śaṅkara's birth recently has sparked off a renewed interest in the study of the most important philosopher India has produced. Not that the interest in Śaṅkara had ever flagged, as witnessed by the unbroken continuity of Advaitic writings for more than a millennium; but the Śaṅkara Jayantī Mahotsava not only sought to pay homage to the best of Vedāntic teachers but also to rediscover him as a great historical figure of contemporary relevance. Indeed a centenary celebration cannot simply be yet another annual remembrance, a *puṇyasmṛti*; it cannot help being the celebration of a historical event of lasting significance, of which the echoes may still be heard after centuries. The celebration was bound to raise historical questions about the date and age of Śaṅkara. Despite the existence of several legendary biographies of Śaṅkara from medieval times and their disregard by historians, there has also been some interest in what could be described as the historical biography of the Master. A connected question which has assumed importance in recent years relates to the authenticity of the large number of writings which have been ascribed to him. The original character and development of Śaṅkara's ideas present closely related issues.

When did Śaṅkara live? What do we know of his history? Which works did he actually compose? Unless these questions are properly answered we cannot decide the relationship of Śaṅkara to his 'contemporaries' and would not be able to place his life, work and thought in a meaningful historical and cultural perspective. Nor would we be able to decide whether he was simply a dry philosophical commentator or also a saint-poet of no mean order who composed enchanting, popular as well as profound, hymns. Was he also a religious reformer and organiser? How many monastic centres and schools did he found, if any? What was his attitude to Yoga, Tantra or the new bhakti schools? Was he simply the last of the old Vedāntins seeking to keep close to the ancient form of the Vedic tradition, or was he one of the leaders of the new Smārta-Paurāṇika transformation who could be described as Ṣaṇmatasthāpanācārya, the real founder of medieval Hinduism?

The answer to such questions necessarily requires a reconsideration of his doctrines with reference to their textual sources, logical compulsions and development within his own writings. How was Śaṅkara able to reconcile his deep reverence of the Vedic tradition with the need for representing the essential truth of Vedānta so that it could meet the philosophical and religious challenges of his times? Do his commentaries help to unveil the hidden secret of the Vedāntic texts encrusted in 'lesser truth' or do they foist a new philosophy on them? Was he an orthodox theologian or an original philosopher, a genuine Vedāntin or a *"pracchanna-bauddha"*?

Thus although the historical and cultural significance of Śaṅkara is unquestioned, his historical biography is still a desideratum. Similarly although monastic schools have sought to standardize, clarify and refine his philosophical and spiritual doctrines over more than a millennium, the latter have never failed to inspire new enquiry and reflection. Nor can it be said that they have been finally defined and systematized. In fact, recently new doubts have been raised about what Śaṅkara actually taught and the inner tensions and variations within his ideas and interpretations have been noted.

It is in the background of these and similar questions that the present study has been conceived. It attempts to assess critically the present state of evidence on Śaṅkarācārya in the context of perennial as well as contemporary questions. It attempts to reconstruct the life and thought of Śaṅkara on historical principles, i.e., to determine the age and biography of Śaṅkara and also his original ideas and writings within this framework. It is primarily based on the first-hand study of the corpus of Śaṅkara's writings or writings attributed to him, in the original, and on a critical and comparative study of all of his available traditional biographies. The works of his near contemporaries like Dharmakīrti and Śāntarakṣita, Kumārila and Maṇḍana, as well as of his disciples like Sureśvara and Padmapāda have also been fully utilized as also those of others who like Gauḍapāda, Bhartṛhari or Bhāruci preceded him or who like Bhāskara, Vācaspati Miśra, and Sarvajñātma Muni came later but were not too far removed. The general literary works and epigraphic records of the Age have been used where relevant. Traditional and modern interpretations of savants, philosophers, scholars and historians have been duly considered. Indeed, Śaṅkara studies seem to be on the threshold of a new revolution of which the watchword may be said to be "Back to Śaṅkara". However, despite the claim of enthusiasts, no actual revolutionary breakthrough has so far occurred. My search for the original text, historical context and the real meaning of Śaṅkara, does not, therefore, discard the monastic tradition of Advaitic learning and creativity as irrelevant but it does seek to discover the original Śaṅkara rather than rest content with the Śaṅkara as interpreted by the medieval religious ethos and intellectual context. Correctly understood, the inspiration of Śaṅkara is perennial and refreshing and should provide a particular basis for a universal, philosophical religion today.

Among the many topics discussed in the present work may be mentioned the question of the authenticity of Śaṅkara's biographical sources or of the works traditionally ascribed to him, the mode of synthesis in his thought reconciling interpretation and independent reflection, orthodoxy and heterodoxy, conservatism and the revolutionary innovation of his attitude to the social and spiritual dimensions of ethics, and the question of his active organizational work.

While I hold the Śaṅkarite monasteries in high esteem, my examination of their historical traditions has not always led me to accept them. Indeed, since the traditions are at times mutually discrepant, one could not possibly agree with all of them. One can only hope that perhaps more evidence would be brought to light one day and the present state of doubt and disbelief would be modified to the satisfaction of all. Meanwhile, one must plead for the toleration of inevitable differences. Similarly although important questions have been raised and suggestions put forward in recent years by several historians and scholars, especially German and Japanese, their results still need critical assessment and constructive application.

That I became engaged at all in writing this book is largely due to my friend Prof. K.S. Murty who invited me to speak on Śaṅkara in the Brighton Philosophical Conference in 1988 and later suggested that I should write a historical biography of Śaṅkara. He also suggested that the history of Śaṅkarite monasteries needs to be critically examined. I am deeply beholden to him for his suggestions and for his interest in the writing of this book.

Many others have helped me with books, reprints and transcripts of unavailable books and manuscripts. Among these I must specially mention Mr. Bader of the National University, Australia, Dr. Antarkar of Bombay, Prof. Balasubramanian and Prof. Veezhinathan, Sri Kuppuswami Sastri of Kanchi, Prof. G.C. Tripathi of the Allahabad Sanskrit Vidyapitha, Prof. V.N. Misra and Dr. B.N. Misra of the Sanskrit University, Varanasi, Sri R.C. Tripathi, IAS of the Department of Culture, Government of India and Sri Munish Joshi of Archaeological Survey of India. I am also thankful to Prof. Irfan Habib, Chairman, ICHR for taking interest in the project initially. Lastly, my thanks are due to my Publishers for their kind interest and unfailing courtesy.

Allahabad G.C. PANDE
25.6.1992

Abbreviations

AA, AAG	=	Anantānandagiri, *Śaṅkara-Vijayam* (ed N. Veezhinathan, University of Madras, 1971)
AAS	=	Ānandāśrama Sanskrit Series, Pune
AS	=	V. Bhattacharya, *Āgama-śāstram* (Calcutta University)
AiUB	=	*Aitareyopaniṣadbhāṣyam* of Ś. (Īśādi/SG)
BUB	=	*Bṛhadāraṇyakopaniṣadbhāṣyam* of Ś. (Īśādi/SG)
BGB	=	*Bhagavad-gītā-bhāṣyam* (Motilal Banarsidass)
BSB	=	*Brahmasūtrabhāṣyam* (Nirnayasagar, text only; SG)
BUBV	=	*Bṛhadāraṇyakopaniṣadbhāṣya-Vārtikam* of Sureśvara (Mahesh Res. Inst., Varanasi)
BS	=	*Brahmasūtram*
Br	=	*Bṛhacchaṅkaravijayam*
Bra	=	Brahmānanda's *Bṛhacchaṅkaravijayam* (MS)
Bha	=	*Bhāmatī*, 2 Vols. (ed. Akhandananda, Varanasi)
Cid	=	Cidvilāsa, *Śaṅkara-vijaya-vilāsaḥ*, (ed. W.R. Antarkar, Bharatiya Vidya, 1973)
CUB	=	*Chāndogyopaniṣadbhāṣyam* (Īśadi/SG)
Go	=	Govindanātha, *Śaṅkarācārya-caritam* (Poona, 1931)
GV, GVK	=	K. Laksmana-sastri, *Guruvaṁśa-Kāvyam*, (Srirangam, 1972)
IUB	=	*Īśopaniṣad-bhāṣyam* (Īśadi/SG)
Īśādi	=	*Īśādidaśopaniṣadaḥ* with Śaṅkara's com. (Vanivilasagranthamala, Varanasi)
JSV	=	Rajagopal Sharma, *Jagadguru-Śāṅkara-maṭha-Vimarśa*
JUB	=	Journal of the University of Bombay
KUB (Pada/Vākya)	=	*Kenopaniṣad-pada/vākya-bhāṣyam* (Īśādi/SG)

Katha-B	=	*Kaṭhopaniṣad-bhāṣyam* (Īśādi/SG)
MUB	=	*Muṇḍakopaniṣadbhāṣyam* (Īśādi/SG)
MKB	=	*Māṇḍūkya-Kārikā-bhāṣyam* (Īśādi/SG)
MSB	=	Maṇḍana, *Brahmasiddhi* (Madras, 1937)
Mbh	=	*Mahābhāratam* (Critical ed.)
M	=	Mādhava, *Śaṅkara-digvijayam* (Poona, 1915)
MS	=	*Mārkaṇḍeya-Saṁhitā* (MS)
MKV	=	*Madhyamaka-Kārikā-Vṛtti* (ed. La Vallee Poussin)
ND	=	*Nyāyadarśanam* (*Bhāṣya-Vārtika-Tātparyaṭīkā-vṛttisahitam*), reprint of Calcutta Sanskrit Series ed. New Delhi, 1985)
NS	=	Sureśvara, *Naiṣkarmyasiddhi* (Poona, 1980)
NB	=	*Nyāyabindu* (with Dharmottara and Durveka Miśra's Commentaries, K.P. Jayaswal Inst., Patna, with Hindi commentary by G.C. Pande, Jaipur, 1972).
NSA	=	Nīlakaṇṭha, *Śaṅkarābhyudayam* (ed. W.R. Antarkar, JUB)
PC	=	*Patañjali-caritam/Vijayam* (Īśādi/SG)
PV	=	*Pramāṇavārtikam* (Varanasi, 1968)
PS	=	*Prapañcasāraḥ* (SG)
PSM	=	Sadāśiva Bodhendra, *Puṇya-śloka-mañjarī* (ed. Rama Sastri, 1961)
Pra	=	*Prācīna-Śaṅkara-Vijayam*
PP	=	*Pañca-pādikā* (*BS* with nine commentaries, Calcutta)
RCD	=	Rāja Cūḍāmaṇi Dīkṣita, *Śaṅkarābhyudayam* (Srirangam, 1986)
RM	=	Sadāśiva Brahmendra, *Jagad-guru-ratna-mālā-stavaḥ* with *Suṣamā* of Ātmabodha, Madras, 1962
SR	=	*Śiva-rahasyam* (*MS* in G.N. Jha Res. Institute, Allahabad)
SDS	=	Sadānanda, *Śaṅkara-Digvijaya-sāram*, Bombay, 1890
SS	=	*Saṅkṣepaśārīrakam* (ed. N. Veezhinathan, Madras)
SV	=	*Ślokavārtikam* (Varanasi, 1978)
SG	=	*Śaṅkara-granthāvali*, 10 Vols. (revised Samata ed.)

TMD	=	Tirumala Dīkṣita, *Śaṅkarābhyudayaḥ* (ed. W.R. Antarkar, JUB, 1965)
TUB	=	*Taittirīyopaniṣadbhāṣyam* (Īśādi/SG)
TUBV	=	*Taittirīyopaniṣadbhāṣya-Vārtikam* (ed. Balasubramanian)
V	=	Vyāsācala, *Śaṅkara-Vijayaḥ*, Madras, 1959
VP	=	*Vākyapadīyam*, ed. Raghunatha Sarma, S.S. University, Varanasi

1

Sources for the History of Śaṅkara

The sources for the historical reconstruction of Śaṅkara's life and work may be divided into five principal classes.

Contemporary or Near Contemporary Literature

This includes the works ascribed to Śaṅkara, his disciples and other contemporaries. Nearly four hundred works are found ascribed to Śaṅkara.[1] Several important works of his immediate disciples also survive. Kumārila and Maṇḍana Miśra are generally accepted as his near contemporaries and several of their works are known. Several other thinkers who are presupposed by Śaṅkara or who refer to him, could not be far removed from him. Among these could be mentioned Dharmakīrti, Bhartṛhari, Gauḍapāda, and Bhāskara.[2] From the critical examination of these works it is possible to reconstruct the structure and development of Śaṅkara's thoughts and their historical position.

Traditional Biographical Literature

In this category may be mentioned:

A. Supposedly lost biographies:
   (i) Padmapāda : *Vijaya-ḍiṇḍima*
   (ii) Citsukha : *Bṛhat-Śaṅkara-Vijaya*
   (iii) Ānandagiri : *Prācīna-Śaṅkara-Vijaya*

All of these have been lost except for references and quotations in later works. Whether these works ever existed has also been doubted, from a 'sectarian' as well as a strictly objective point of view.

B. Biographical accounts or references in 'Purāṇic' or semi-Purāṇic literature:
   (i) *Mārkaṇḍeya-saṁhitā* (unpublished)
   (ii) *Śiva-rahasya* (unpublished except for Canarese edn.)
   (iii) *Liṅga Purāṇa* (Bombay edn.)
   (iv) *Kūrma Purāṇa* (Kashi Raj Trust edn.)

(v) *Bhaviṣyottara Purāṇa* (Bombay, 1897)
(vi) *Skanda Purāṇa* (M.S. Mor, Calcutta edn.)
(vii) *Saura Purāṇa* (*ASS*, 1889)
(viii) *Padma Purāṇa* (M.S. Mor, Calcutta edn.)

C. Extant biographies:

(i) Mādhava: *Saṅkṣepa-Śaṁkara-Jaya* with its two commentaries—Dhanapati Sūri's *Ḍiṇḍima* and Acyutarāya Moḍaka's *Advaitarājya-Lakṣmī* (Anandasrama, Poona, 1915)
(ii) Vyāsācala, *Śaṅkara-vijaya* (GOML, Madras, 1954 edn.)
(iii) Brahmānandīya *Bṛhac-Chaṅkara-Vijaya* (unpublished)
(iv) Anantānandagiri, *Śaṅkara-vijaya* (ed. Veezhinathan, University of Madras, 1971)
(v) *Puṇya-Śloka-Mañjarī* (ed. Rama Saṣtri, 1961)
(vi) *Jagad-guru-ratna-mālā-stava* (Madras, 1962)
(vii) *Pariśiṣṭa, Makaranda,* and *Suṣamā* (As above)
(viii) Govindanātha, *Śaṅkarācārya-Carita* or *Keralīya Śaṅkara-Vijaya* (Poona, 1931)
(ix) Cidvilāsa, *Śaṅkara-Vijaya-Vilāsa* (Bharatiya Vidya, 1973)
(x) Rājacūḍāmaṇi Dīkṣita, *Śaṅkarābhyudaya* (Srirangam, 1987)
(xi) Tirumala Dīkṣita, *Śaṅkarābhyudaya* (*JUB*, 1965)
(xii) Parameśvara Kavi Kaṇṭhīrava, *Ācārya-Vijaya* (*JUB*, 1968)
(xiii) Puruṣottama Bhāratī, *Śaṅkara-Vijaya-Saṁgraha* (ed. W.R. Antarkar)
(xiv) Sadānanda, *Śaṅkara-Digvijaya-sāra* (Bombay, 1890)
(xv) Kāśī Lakṣamaṇa Śāstrī, *Guru-Vaṁśa-Kāvya* (Vani Vilas Press, Srirangam, 1927)
(xvi) Nīlakaṇṭha, *Śaṅkarābhyudaya* (*JUB*)
(xvii) Nīlakaṇṭha, *Śaṅkara-mandāra-saurabha** (unpublished)
(xviii) Kṛṣṇabrahmānanda, *Śaṅkara-Vijaya** (*quoted*)
(xix) Vallīsahāya, *Ācārya-digvijaya-campū** (*quoted*)
(xx) Bālagopālayati, *Śaṅkarācārya Mahimā** (*quoted*)

Monastic Traditions and Records

These include the succession lists of the heads of the five principal monasteries, their oral traditions and written records including grants, etc., made to them. It has been claimed that the earliest of these grants goes back to the 12th century or the 13th century but most of them belong to the late medieval period from the 14th century onwards. Of the old manuscripts available with these monasteries no exhaustive lists have been compiled or published. The so-called *Mahānuśāsana* ascribed to Śaṅkara is really a part of this monastic tradition. So also are the *Guru-Paramparā-stotras, Maṭhāmnāyopaniṣad, Maṭhāmnāya* or *Āmnāyasetu* which is referred to by Ātmabodha early in the 18th century. Several attempts have been made to reconstruct these from the different monastic traditions. Some manuscripts of the texts are said to exist in the Oriental Institute, Mysore, and BORI, Pune, as also with the monasteries. Selected inscriptions and documents too have been published. There are also a number of sculptures at Kāñcī and elsewhere which have been sought to be identified with Śaṅkara and some incidents of his legend. These sources would be discussed later.

Miscellaneous Literary Sources

(i) Rāmabhadra Dīkṣita, *Patañjali-Caritam* (Kavya-Mala, 1895)
(ii) *Darśana-Prakāśa** (quoted)
(iii) *Maṇimañjarī**
(iv) *Keralotpatti**
(v) *Śrīvidyārṇava* (Reprinted, Varanasi, 1986)
(vi) Belgaum Manuscript discovered by K.B. Pathak
(vii) Ānandānubhava, *Nyāya-ratna-dīpāvalī* (quoted)
(viii) Svayamprakāśa, *Tattvadīpana* (quoted)
(ix) *Jinavijaya** (quoted)
(x) Tāranātha, *History of Buddhism in India* (tr.)

Extant contemporary or near-contemporary sources directly relevant for the history of Śaṅkara consist principally of the works which may be ascribed to Śaṅkara himself and of those which may be attributed to his contemporaries or near-contemporaries. Which of the works traditionally ascribed to Śaṅkara are really his, needs to be critically ascertained in this context. Similarly, to ascertain the contemporaries of Śaṅkara, we need to ascertain the date of Śaṅkara critically. The date of Śaṅkara as well as the authenticity of the works ascribed to him will be considered below.

---

* Not examined personally.

However, although these works may tell us a lot about the ideas and Age of Śaṅkara as also about his position in the process of Indian cultural and philosophical development, they do not tell us much about his biography in the ordinary sense. In what may be termed philosophical despair, Prof. Belvalkar was thus led to declare that it is the works of Śaṅkara which constitute his best biography.[3] Insofar as the thoughts of a thinker constitute the essence of his life, this is undoubtedly true. Nevertheless the biography of a thinker requires information about him as a historical individual engaged in ordinary or original social activity. Definitely authentic and extant sources for Śaṅkara's biography in this sense are despairingly meagre. On the other hand, there is a fair extent of medieval literature containing the legendary biography of Śaṅkara. To what extent this legend of Śaṅkara is based on his history, remains a question for critical examination.

Many incidental attempts have been made by earlier scholars to examine the biographical sources of Śaṅkara in the course of their general works. Thus T.S. Narayana Sastri,[4] C.N. Krishnaswami Iyer,[5] N.K. Venkatesan,[6] K.T. Telang,[7] S.S. Surya Narayana Sastri,[8] N.Venkata Ramana,[9] Bhasyacarya,[10] N.Ramesan,[11] Rajendra Nath Ghosh,[12] Baldev Upadhyaya,[13] Tapasyananda,[14] T.M.P. Mahadevan,[15] K.G. Nateshan Sastri,[16] have given some thought to this question incidentally while sketching a general account of the life and works of Śaṅkara. However, the critique of the sources in these works tends to be summary and tentative and generally revolves round the same few facts. Most of these works were originally published between 1910 and 1930 although a few have been published or republished in the post-Independence period. Work of a different kind has been attempted by Dr. W.R. Antarkar for his Ph.D. from the University of Poona in 1961. His dissertation was entitled "Śaṅkara Vijayas: A Comparative and Critical Study."

Insofar as such enquiries reveal the origin and development of the legend of Śaṅkara they would facilitate the task of discovering the history of Śaṅkara to the extent possible.

The extant legendary biographies of Śaṅkara date from the 14th to the 18th centuries, i.e., they are posterior to the Ācārya by at least half a millennium to a millennium. Although they have certain broad similarities, they have numerous contradictions in detail, and they are full of miracles and exaggerations. Taken by themselves these works can only be regarded as the diverse versions of the medieval legend of Śaṅkara, which obscures and distorts his original history through the lavish exercise of a mythical imagination used for the purpose of authenticating and popularizing the influence of many medieval monastic institutions claiming to derive their several traditions from Śaṅkarācārya. This apparently required, among other things, the projecting of a god-like image of Śaṅkara who performs miracles freely and is regarded as a divine incarnation with a mission. Apart from the haze of exaggerations and miracles, it was also apparently felt necessary by some to invest Śaṅkara with a hoary antiquity which would defy ordinary historical disproof. This, however, overreached itself because the unquestioned works of Śaṅkara himself constitute the standing disproof of such claims of remote antiquity. Perhaps this happened because the Vedāntic scholars of the late medieval age were ignorant of the historical implications of Śaṅkara's Buddhistic allusions, the relevant Buddhistic works having disappeared from India by that time.

It needs to be kept in mind that the concept of a historical biography in the modern sense did not and could not exist significantly in ancient India. The modern tendency is to treat the historical individual as a product of his times and is strongly influenced by a philosophy of determinism, generally social and historical, sometimes even psychological. The traditional philosophy of history regarded the appearance of the great man in history as determined by providence. Thus the *Gītā* expressly formulates the concept of Incarnation in times of declining virtue. This model has continued in traditional thinking from the *Mahābhārata* to the present day.[17] There was, in ancient times however, a genre of writing which sought to commemorate the life and deeds of some great man, saint or ruler, in an idealistic and poetic manner. Such *caritakāvyas* or *ākhyāyikās* or *prabandhas* may be illustrated by *Buddhacarita*, *Harṣacarita*, *Prabandha Cintāmaṇi*, etc. There were also epics celebrating the victories of gods or rulers and called *vijaya-kāvyas* such as *Haravijaya* or *Gauḍavaho*, or *Pṛthvīrāja-vijaya*. The legendary biographies of Śaṅkara are modelled generally on the style of such ornate epic poetry and in their form combine the features of age-old hagiography and royal panegyrics. The life of Buddha provides a ready model and also the earliest example of this tendency. Beginning with the simple and fragmentary canonical accounts of certain parts of Buddha's life, we reach in about five to six hundred years the exaggerated epic accounts of the *Mahāvastu*, *Lalitavistara* and the *Buddhacarita* with their different sectarian affiliations and divergences. The human Buddha of the Canon is lost here in a veritable god in human form whose 'life' is now a part of devotional celebration. Similar appears to have been the case with Śaṅkara. The model of the *panegyrics* or royal *digvijaya* also took a hand in the shaping of this legend.* The medieval Abbots and Masters imitated the pomp of royal titles in the spiritual domain and compared their public debates or *Śāstrārtha* with royal *digvijaya*. So Śaṅkara was represented as conquering the whole world of spiritual and philosophical learning through debating. Hence most of these biographies are entitled *vijayas* or *digvijayas*.

Monasticism, scholasticism and devotionalism may be said to be the most prominent characteristics of the ethos reflected in these biographies of Śaṅkara but it is to be remembered that these tendencies had been growing over a long period of time. In fact, it is plausible to hold that they became much more pronounced later. Exaggeration in the service of these tendencies may, thus, be said to be the principal form of distortion to which the legend of Śaṅkara subjects his history. This legend was not a simple fabrication but the transformation of earlier historical traditions and legends which had been recorded in simpler, less poetic and more natural versions. After the new versions of the legends had found their finished expression in elegant poetry, the older texts tended to be neglected, not the least perhaps because they did not fully agree with the new standardized versions. Traditional Vedāntic scholarship had little interest in the mere history of Śaṅkara, though the monasteries were interested in preserving the deeds and records of the properties and rights gifted to them from time to time. The surviving records in this respect, however, do not go beyond the 12th century in any case.

The 12th century, indeed, forms a kind of watershed. The older, fragmentary and now largely lost biographical accounts of Śaṅkara belong to the period anterior to the 12th century. The next century is barren in this respect while from the 14th or the 15th century the new form of the legend is found to have already clearly emerged.

---

* The legend of Śaṅkara does not contain more miracles than the New Testament account of the life of Jesus. It does not make him mythical. For some recent discussions about Śaṅkara and myth see Bader's summary in his *Meditation in Sankara's Vedanta.* (1990), pp. 15-24.

According to an essentially oral tradition the earliest work which dealt with the life of Śaṅkara was the *Vijaya-ḍiṇḍima* of Padmapāda who was one of the four famous direct disciples of the Master.[18] Padmapāda is said to have composed a work in two parts on the Ācārya's commentary on the *Brahmasūtras*. The first part was a subcommentary and the second part was entitled *Vijaya-ḍiṇḍima* and it has been surmised within an oral tradition to have been anecdotal or narrative in character. Unfortunately the whole work is said to have been consumed by fire and only a portion of the first part was recovered through the marvellous memory of the Master himself who could recall what he had heard when the work was partly read out to him earlier. This surviving portion is known as *Pañcapādikā* and philosophical enquirers have always expressed the highest admiration for it. On the other hand, the very existence of the *Vijaya-ḍiṇḍima* is far from being established.

The other two ancient works are said to have been the *Bṛhat-Śaṅkara-Vijaya* of Citsukha and the *Prācīna-Śaṅkara-Vijaya* of Ānandagiri or Ānandajñāna. Citsukha is said to have been a direct disciple and a former fellow student of Śaṅkara by the name of Viṣṇuśarman.[19] His work consisted of three parts: *Pūrvācārya-satpatha, Śaṅkarācārya-satpatha* and *Sureśvarācārya-satpatha* and had 224 *prakaraṇas*. The first part dealt with the preceptors prior to Śaṅkara, the second with him and the third with his immediate successor. It appears to have been written in a simple and natural style and had regard for chronology. This work has been referred to by Ātmabodha in his famous commentary entitled *Suṣamā* which is said to have been composed in A.D. 1720 and it appears to have been used by Cidvilāsa and Sadānanda Yati. It has been referred to in Acyuta's *Advaitarājya-Lakṣmī* as a source of the *Mādhavīya* while commenting on it (17.16.103): '*etat kathā-jālam Bṛhacchaṅkara-vijaya evam Śrīmad Ānandajñānākhyānandagiri-viracite draṣṭavyam iti dik.*' Here Ānandajñāna rather than Citsukha is made the author, which makes one doubt if Acyuta had himself seen the work. That it survived till the present century has been averred by T.S. Narayana Sastri who claimed to have had in his possession a mutilated manuscript of the text. He has given a summary of its contents up to the meeting of Śaṅkara with Kumārila, giving copious excerpts and quotations purporting to be from the original text. Unfortunately he died before completing the biographical account. Nor has his manuscript been known to be personally available to anyone else. However a very hostile critic from Śṛṅgerī also admits the existence of a manuscript of the *Śaṅkarācārya-satpatha* in the Dvarika monastery.[20] Under the circumstances although scepticism about the genuineness of Narayana Sastri's account of Citsukha's work cannot be ruled out, still the fact that Citsukha has been quoted by earlier writers such as Ātmabodha has made researchers like Dr. Antarkar place full faith in him. It may be pointed out that the language of some of the verses attributed to Citsukha is simple to the point of appearing to lack classical sophistication. The fact that Citsukha attributes many works to Śaṅkara apart from the acknowledged commentaries, is also a circumstance which is highly significant and needs to be critically assessed. Above all, the reference to the date of Śaṅkara in hoary antiquity certainly shows that all the excerpts ascribed to Citsukha could not have been authentic and that these interpolations or fabrications are earlier than Ātmabodha. This is also shown by some other quotations in *Suṣamā.* Thus in an obvious quotation from the *Vyāsācalīya* (XII.82), it gives a version which does not agree either with the present *Vyāsācalīya* or with the present *Mādhavīya.* The version of *Suṣamā* contains a highly dubious reference to a *maṭha* of Kāñcī. The version of *Bṛhac-Chaṅkara-Vijaya* before Ātmabodha, thus, must have been already 'restructured' or 'reconstructed', or at least 'doctored' in parts with interpolations. Uncritical reliance cannot therefore be placed on its uncorroborated excerpts.

Prācīna-Śaṅkara-Vijaya is reputed to have been the source drawn upon by Mādhava's *Śaṅkara-digvijaya—'Prācīna-Śaṅkarajaye sāraḥ saṅgṛhyate sphuṭam.'* The commentator Acyutarāya remarks that *"Ye hi sūtra-bhāṣyādiṭīkākārāḥ 'śuddhānandabhagavatpūjyapāda-śiṣyā. bhagavadānand-ajñānākhyā Ānandagiritvena prasiddhāḥ tadracitaḥ prakṛta-granthāt prācīnaḥ cirantanaḥ Śaṅkara-vijayaḥ"*. Dhanapatisūri too says *'iti Prācīna-Vijayokteḥ'*. Both the commentaries of the *Mādhavīya*, viz., *Advaitarājya Lakṣmī* and *Ḍiṇḍima* quote numerous verses (in all 811 stanzas) apparently from the ancient work which is now no longer available. The author of the work was Ānandajñāna or Ānandagiri, a disciple of Śuddhānanda. Ānandagiri is known as the author of *Tātparyanirṇaya.* He has been placed as early as the 11th century and as late as the 14th century. The possibility of two persons with the same name cannot, however, be ruled out. There is some confusion about the name of his work which has also been called *Bṛhac-Chaṅkara-Vijaya.* T.S.

Narayan Sastri claimed to have a manuscript of the work with him.[21] He describes it as consisting of eleven *sargas* and as explicitly a summary of *Bṛhac-Chaṅkara-Vijaya*.[22] Dr. Antarkar has given information that the late Sri Balashastri Haridasa of Nagpur claimed to have seen a palm leaf manuscript of the text with the pontiff of Kāñcī. However, Dr. Antarkar himself has not succeeded in gaining access to the manuscript,[23] nor has the present writer been able to gain any information about it from Kāñcī.

Thus, of the three contemporary or ancient biographies of Śaṅkara one was destroyed in the author's very lifetime while the other two were definitely available till the 18th century and perhaps survived till recent times. Of these the work of Citsukha was seminal, that of Ānandajñāna being derived from it. But it remains a fact that none of the three is extant or known to be extant today. All that survives from them are certainly not insignificant fragments quoted by later writers. Their real importance lies in the fact that the probability of their existence provides some justification for the presumption of a lost ancient basis for the medieval legend of Śaṅkara. On the other hand, some followers of the Śṛṅgerī tradition are sceptical about the existence of these works and are inclined to believe that 'excerpts' from them are modern concoctions of the Kāñcī tradition. In view of the evidence of Ātmabodha and the commentators of the *Mādhavīya* who quote from these works such scepticism is unwarranted. Before considering later works we might consider at this stage a number of Purāṇic and Āgamic texts which give a highly mythologized account of Śaṅkara. Their importance lies in the fact that they supply a motif which is recurrent in later literature, viz., the idea that Śaṅkara was an incarnation of Śiva and that he was born to rescue the Vedic faith and social ethos from the hostile attacks launched on them by diverse varieties of heterodoxy. Thus *Kūrmapurāṇa* (Chap. I, 28, vv. 32-35), *Liṅgapurāṇa* (Chap I, 40, 20-22), *Saurapurāṇa*, *Bhaviṣyottara Purāṇa* (Chap. 36), *Skandapurāṇa* (II, 5, 24), and *Padmapurāṇa* (quoted by Vijñānabhikṣu) are said to contain references to Śaṅkara especially in the context of some of the *yugas* or the *tīrthas*. A manuscript of the *Skandapurāṇa* in the Gupta script has been dated in the 7th century. Usually however, the *Purāṇa* is identified with various *saṁhitās* of uncertain age.[24] Unfortunately the *Purāṇa* has never been critically edited and its printed text is known to contain a considerable and uncertain amount of interpolation. Its uncorroborated descriptions cannot consequently be considered authentic for the early post-Gupta period. The *Saurapurāṇa* too is not critically edited. It is an *upapurāṇa* quoted by Hemādri in the 13th century but could not be in its present form much earlier since it seems to attack the system of Madhva.[25] The *Liṅgapurāṇa* as a *mahāpurāṇa* is doubtless earlier than Alberuni but it is difficult to be more precise. Fortunately, the *Kūrmapurāṇa* has been critically edited by the Kashi Raj Trust. The *Bhaviṣyottara Purāṇa* is a continuation of the ancient *Bhaviṣyat Purāṇa* which is not available in its ancient form. The *Bhaviṣyottara* 'is more a handbook of religious rites'.[26] Fortunately the *Kūrmapurāṇa* has been critically edited by the Kashi Raj Trust in 1972 and is dated *c.* A.D. 800 in its present form.

These texts do suggest that by the 11th century Śaṅkara had been recognized in Purāṇic literature as the exponent of Advaita and as an incarnation of Śiva. More important are the texts called *Mārkaṇḍeya-Saṁhitā* (22nd *khaṇḍa*, 7th *parispanda*) and *Śiva-rahasya*. The latter is a voluminous text said to have been published in the Canarese script in 30 volumes in 1950.[27] Its manuscripts are found at various places but their textual variations have not been critically studied. It is devoted to the detailed exposition of Śaiva principles, myths and rituals. It gives in chap. XVI of the 9th *aṁśa* a brief account of Śaṅkara's incarnation, mission and achievements. It was regarded as an authority in the *Nirṇayasindhu* in the 17th Century. Whether this account of Śaṅkara in *Śiva-rahasya* consisted of 44 or 60 verses has been disputed by rival monastic claimants.[28] *Mārkaṇḍeyasaṁhitā* is not known to have been published. It consists of 100 *khaṇḍas*, each *khaṇḍa* consisting of several *parispandas*. An account of Śaṅkara occurs in the 7th and 8th *parispandas* of the 72nd *khaṇḍa* as also in part of 73rd *khaṇḍa*.[29] In these texts the Śaṅkara legend is more developed than in the *Purāṇas*. These various Purāṇic and Āgamic texts which might be placed between A.D. 900 and A.D. 1300 show how the life and thought of Śaṅkara came to be adopted within the Smārta-Paurāṇic and tantric tradition in the post-Classical period and came to form the nucleus of the legend of Śaṅkara as a divine incarnation.

Of the medieval biographies of Śaṅkara the most popular is the *Śaṅkara-digvijaya* of Mādhava. It is also called *Saṅkṣepa-Śaṅkara-Jaya*, which finds mention in *Suṣamā*. *Vyāsācalīya* too seems to have referred to the same or a similar text or its original (see below). The name of the author is also mentioned as Vidyāraṇya or Mādhava. If it were really the work of the great Mādhava-

Vidyāraṇya who is known to have played a prominent part in blessing the foundation of the Vijayanagara Empire, it would be the earliest of the medieval biographies and of high authenticity because Vidyāraṇya was not only an acknowledged master of Vedānta but also one of the principal organizers of the Śṛṅgerī tradition. Several modern scholars, however, have rejected the identity of the Mādhava who wrote the present work with Vidyāraṇya. Thus Bhasyacarya, S.S. Suryanarayana Sastri, T.S. Narayana Sastri, Baldeva Upadhyaya, and Dr. Antarkar have all held this Mādhava to be a much later minor poet.[30] Professor Suryanarayana Sastri pointed out that the *Mādhavīya* is guilty of gross anachronism by bringing together celebrated figures of different ages and making them the contemporaries of Śaṅkara.[31] T.S. Narayana Sastri expressed the opinion that the *Mādhavīya* is a modern fabrication by some supporters of the Śṛṅgerī Maṭha against the claims of the Kāñcī or Kumbhakonam *maṭha*.[32] Baldeva Upadhyaya gives several reasons to discredit the identity of the author with Vidyāraṇya, although he admits the undoubted value of the work in terms of its knowledge and insight into the philosophical disputations recorded. His arguments are:

(*a*) that Vidyāraṇya belonged to the Śṛṅgerī Maṭha but the *Mādhavīya* does not quite follow its tradition. One would like to comment that if this were to be granted, as indeed must be done at least in part, this would knock down the critique of T.S. Narayana Sastri and evoke the suspicion that the *Mādhavīya* has been the victim of modern sectarian criticism;

(*b*) that this work is not listed among the writings of Vidyāraṇya;

(*c*) that the author calls himself Nava-Kālidāsa; and

(*d*) that his style lacks the maturity of Mādhava.[33]

He surmises that this Mādhava may be the Mādhava-bhaṭṭa who wrote the *Bhārata-Campū* and bore the title of 'Nava-Kālidāsa'. He would be later than Rāja Cuḍāmaṇi Dīkṣita, and that would explain his plagiarism from the latter's work. Dr. Antarkar substantially agrees with Upadhyaya. He thinks that *Mādhavīya* has plagiarised earlier works to the extent of more than 50 per cent of its own bulk.* He thinks that this plagiarism is proved by repetitions and confusions in the *Mādhavīya*. There is undoubtedly a formidable case against the identity of Mādhava and Vidyāraṇya.

---

* See below note (35).

Although some scholars including Tapasyananda, Sri Rajgopal Sharma and others belonging to the Śṛṅgerī tradition have from time to time sought to argue forcefully in favour of the identity, it cannot be said that the question has been fully decided.[34] Nevertheless, they have brought out significant facts and the question does deserve a dispassionate review. That the author of the *Mādhavīya* lacks a sense of precise chronology may be readily granted but that does not prove anything definite about the identity of the author because such lack of historical or chronological knowledge was not uncommon among poets and philosophers of the age when they wrote about events which happened several centuries earlier. In this particular work the flight of fancy beyond information seems to have been regarded poetically legitimate by the author. On the other hand, from the colophon of the work itself we cannot conclusively determine the identity of the author. However, the claim of the author that his teacher was *Vidyātīrtha* cannot he dismissed without regarding the verse as interpolated for which there is no adequate reason, and both the commentators of the work identify its author with Mādhava Vidyāraṇya. The author has undoubted poetic capacity and philosophical scholarship. If he were the poet Mādhava-bhaṭṭa, one should have expected this fact to have come out quite clearly in his work. On the other hand, the identity with Vidyāraṇya is complicated by the multiplicity of Mādhavas at the same time. There was Mādhava, the brother of Sāyaṇa, Mādhava the son of Sāyaṇa, and Mādhava the Minister and General. It is possible that there was a fourth Mādhava who became Vidyāraṇya (see Rajgopal Sharma, *JUSVM*, pp. 354-67).

The relationship with Rāja Cūḍāmaṇi Dīkṣita has been said to be ambiguous in the sense that the latter could have been the borrower. This is certainly a possibility. The *Mādhavīya* has a large number of verses in common with *Vyāsācalīya* (475 stanzas), Rāja Cūḍāmaṇi (125 stanzas, actually 137 stanzas), Tirumala Dīkṣita (476 verses), and Rāmabhadra (11 stanzas). Thus out of its 1843 stanzas as many as 1100 are common to it and the works mentioned[35] above. These and other similarities in the *digvijayas* suggest common sources on which all the authors drew. The *Mādhavīya* clearly bases itself on *Prācīna-Śaṅkara-Jaya* and that should explain the common source of the different authors. In this uncertainty the *Mādhavīya* cannot be said to have been necessarily the borrower. As a result it could belong to a fairly extensive time bracket, viz., from the 14th to the 17th centuries. It could be referring to Vyāsācala as an earlier writer and if so and if the latter is the same as Mahādevendra Sarasvatī of Kāncī Kāmakoṭipīṭha, it could hardly be earlier than the middle of the 16th century. 'Vyāsācala' occurs in the 17th verse of the *Upodghāta* of the *Mādhavīya*. As to the verse '*Vyāsācala-pramukha-paṇḍita-pūrvika*' etc. its authenticity is doubtful. It is not to be traced in the Haridvara edn. Nor was it available to the commentators. On the other hand, Vyāsācala has also been identified with Vidyāśaṅkara or Śaṅkarānanda, a predecessor of Vidyāraṇya. Ātmabodha identifies *Vyāsācalīya* and *Mādhavīya* by implication.[36] It may also be noted that the first few verses of the *Mādhavīya* are reminiscent of some verses of Jagannātha Paṇḍitarāja who was a contemporary of Shah Jahan. But both may have been inspired by an earlier model. If the traditional authorship is rejected, it is difficult to understand how the work of a minor poet of the 17th century could be confused with that of the famous Vidyāraṇya and how this confusion came to be rampant, to be questioned only by criticism which was in the beginning not unconnected with sectarian differences. It has to be remembered that the *Suṣamā* refers to a *Saṅkṣepa-Śaṁkara-Vijaya*. It seems that during the 17th and 18th centuries there was a growing search for the biographical traditions of Śaṅkara, not as history, but as inspiring poetry and the *Mādhavīya* seems to have met this need most successfully.

Although from one point of view it might be possibly as late as the early 17th century, and poetic, the *Mādhavīya* cannot be by any means dismissed as valueless because it claims to be and is recognized by its commentators to be based on some earlier work known as *Prācīna-Śaṅkara-Jaya*. While it has been argued that the *Mādhavīya* was influenced by the *Vyāsācalīya* and Rāja Cūḍāmaṇi Dīkṣita's *Śaṅkarabhyudaya*, it seems more likely that it was itself the original *Vyāsācalīya*, from which the present work of that name would be derived. The first of these works was available to its commentators and they generally found it reliable. On the whole, it seems more likely that the present *Mādhavīya* is the creditor rather than the debtor of the works for which plagiarism has been alleged against it.[37] Thus, although questioned, the authenticity of the *Mādhavīya* has not been disproved.

It has been suggested by some scholars that the *Śaṅkara-vijaya* of Vyāsācala should be regarded as earlier than the *Mādhavīya*. On the other hand, as is more likely if the *Mādhavīya* were known as *Vyāsācalīya*, the present *Vyāsācalīya* would be its summary in part. According to Sri Ātreyakṛṣṇa Śāstri in his Tamil work *Śaṅkara-guru-paramparā*, Vyāsācala was the fifty-second guru in the line of sixty-five *gurus* beginning from Sarvajñātmendra Sarasvatī and ending with Mahādevendra Sarasvatī the Fifth. This Vyāsācala occupied the seat of Kāmakoṭipīṭha of Kāñcī from A.D. 1498-1507. His name is also found in a copper-plate of A.D. 1507 of the reign of Narasimhadeva Rai, the Vijayanagara King. Vyāsācala is said to have been born in Kāñcī and his original name was Kuppanna. When he ascended the Kāmakoṭi seat his name was changed to Mahādevendra Sarasvatī. In the mountain called Vyāsācala he performed severe penances and hence came to be popularly known as Vyāsācala Mahendra Sarasvatī, Vyāsādri, Vyāsagiri, etc. On the other hand, Vyāsācala has also been identified with Vidyāśaṅkara, the tenth head of the Śṛṅgerī monastery and the teacher of Mādhava Vidyāraṇya. These are the two contrasted versions of the spokesmen of Kāñcī and Śṛṅgerī traditions, though it has also been proposed to identify Vyāsācala with Vidyāśaṅkara, the 51st *ācārya* of Kāmakoṭi whose period is given as A.D. 1296 to 1384 (Narayana Sastri, *op. cit.*, pp. 228-29).

This *Śaṅkara-vijaya* ascribed to Vyāsācala too is highly poetic in style and has the declared aim of expounding doctrinal mysteries (*siddhānta-rahasya*). Its verse is simpler than that of the *Mādhavīya* and is at once lucid and elegant. This suggests in fact a much earlier date. Indeed, the editor of the text has a pertinent remark on the usually accepted identification proposed by Atreyakṛṣṇa Śāstri. He says, "If what Atreyakrishna Sastri says is correct, it is rather strange that Vyāsācala who was a head of the Kanchi Kamakoti Mutt, has not even mentioned by name that Mutt, the life of the founder of which is described in this work." If the Mutt revalries are not recent, the author of the *Vyāsācalīya* could have been a different person. In any case, the lists of succession of the pontiffs of the Mutts cannot be regarded as free from doubt especially for the earlier period in view of the repetition of names and the uncertainty of dates.

A comparison of the contents of the *Mādhavīya* and the *Vyāsācalīya* will show their relationship. The sixteen cantos of the former run thus: (I) Prologue (*Upodghāta*), (II) Birth (*Udbhava*), (III) Incarnations of Gods, (IV) Childhood up to Eight Years, (V) Renunciation, (VI) Restoration of the Tradition of *Ātmavidyā*, (VII) Meeting Vyāsa, (VIII) Debating with Maṇḍana, (IX) Claim to be the master of All Learning, (X) Study of Erotics, (XI) Econounter with *Bhairava*, (XII) Meeting new disciples, (XIII) Preaching of *Brahmavidyā*, (XIV) Pilgrimage of Padmapāda, (XV) Digvijaya, (XVI) Ascension to *Śāradāpīṭha*.

In the *Vyāsācalīya* the cantos are as follows: (I) About the parents of Śaṅkara, (II) About Upamanyu, (III) About the austerities of Upamanyu, (IV) Birth of Śaṅkara and his life up to the death of his mother, (V) Meeting with Kumārila and Maṇḍana, (VI) Debate with Viśvarūpa, (VII) About Sureśvara and Padmapāda, (VIII) About Padmapāda and some Myths, (IX) Padmapāda, Ugra Bhairava and Toṭaka, (X) Illness of the Master, (XI) Gods and Treatment, (XII) Various Journeys ending with *Sarvajña-pīṭhārohaṇa*. It needs to be mentioned that the text as edited under the orders of the Govt. of Madras in 1954 *does not* contain several verses at the end quoted by Ātmabodha or by T.S. Narayana Sastri on the basis of some manuscript from Kumbhakonam. These verses tend to support the claim that Śaṅkara died at Kāñcī and also give a fanciful date of his death. The verses have the appearance of being apocryphal.[38]

It will be obvious that Vyāsācala has introduced a great deal of utterly irrelevant material while compressing the central narrative. Mādhava is more elaborate but better organized. It seems that both depend on earlier works which themselves had certain characteristic differences especially about the order of Śaṅkara's itinerary and the location of the *Sarvajñapīṭha*. It would not appear sound to regard the *Mādhavīya* as based upon the *Vyāsācalīya* or the latter as a wholly original work even though a large part of its narrative 4th canto or the corresponding parts of the *Mādhavīya* could not be independent.

It also needs to be noted that although the *Vyāsācalīya* has been critically edited on the basis of existing manuscripts, its original text as available in the 17th century to Ātmabodha was apparently more elaborate. This is shown by the fact that only some of the verses quoted by Ātmabodha are available in the present text while several are found in the *Mādhavīya*, from which it has been reasonably surmised by some that the *Mādhavīya* was the original *Vyāsācalīya*.

If the *Vyāsācalīya* dresses up meagre facts with fanciful digressions and elaborations, the *Bṛhac Chaṅkara-Vijaya* of unknown authorship concentrates on doctrinal debates. The work is large in size and has remained unpublished. Although its transcript has been made available by the courtesy of Sri Mahadeva Sastri of

Kumbhakonam to some scholars as also to the present author, it has not been seen by most writers on the subject. Nor has the history of the manuscript been ascertained. It claims to be the exposition of Śaṅkara's life and deeds by Brahmānanda to his disciple Yogānanda. Brahmānanda is said to be the disciple of *Sarvajañātman.* The work is in two parts. The first briefly narrates the life story of Śaṅkara within the traditional framework of having been divinely inspired for the eradication of 72 kinds of false views. The second part concentrates on the debate against the wrong views.

Despite its size and claim of antiquity, the work is really of quite uncertain date. It seems to be an attempt by some anonymous author to reconstruct the lost *Bṛhat Śaṅkara-Vijaya* largely on the basis of traditions relating to Ānandagiri's work. Whether its basis was the original work of Ānandagiri or the existing version of Anantānandagiri, is difficult to determine. It has been surmised that its author was a native of Tanjore. The work is written in a simple language and its style is reminiscent of the *purāṇas.*

The contents of the work are as follows: It begins with a prayer to Ratnagarbha Gaṇeśa, Candramaulīśvara Śiva, Śaṅkarācārya and Sureśvara. Yogānanda asks his teacher Brahmānanda about the book that the latter constantly studied. Brahmānanda explains that the book contains the life of Śaṅkara which he gathered from his teacher Sarvajñātman, disciple of Sureśvara. This biography is described as *lokacaryā-caritrakam* or *avatāra-caritrakam.* Chap. I describes the Nature of Time and its various durations. Chap. II describes the four ages especially the Kali Age, Chap. III continues the topic and describes Śaṅkara as the teacher in the Kali Age which Buddha began and Kalki would end. Chap. IV deals with Buddhāvatāra which facilitated the Kali Yuga. In the Age of King Yaśovardhana India is said to have been Buddhist. Chap. V describes *Gauḍapāda-Caritra,* VI-VIII describe *Bhattapādacaritra,* IX-XXV describe the birth of Śaṅkara and relate his renunciation, meeting with Gauḍapāda, composing commentaries and *stotras,* gathering disciples, consecrating divine icons and *liṅgas* and the commencement of the *digvijaya.* There is considerable emphasis here on Tantra, Yoga, and worship. Then begins the second part of the work dealing with debates with various systems and schools. Chap. I with the *Vaikhānasa,* Chap. II with the *Gāṇapatyas,* VIII with *Vaiṣṇavas,* IX with still another variety of *Gāṇapatyas,* X with *Durgāmata,* XI with some other *Śāktas,* XII with the *Jainas,* XIV with *Vairājas*, XVII with *Hairaṇyagarbhas*, XVIII with *Īśvaramata* XIX with *Traimūrtamata*, XX with *Gāṇapatyas*, mentioning Moreśa Paṇḍita, XXI with Bhāgavatas following Rāmānuja, XXII with the worshippers of Rādhākṛṣṇa at Puri, XXIII with *Bhūtamata*, XXIV with *Manmathamata*, XXV with *Vīraśaivas*, XXVI with *Siddhamata*, XXVII with *Jñānamata*, XXVIII with *Gandhāramata*, XXIX with *Mahāgaṇapatimata*, XXX with *Mattārimata* and *Śaivādvaita*, XXXI with *Yakṣeśamata*, XXXII with *Rākṣasamata* XXXIII with *Raudramata*, XXXIV with *Sauramata*, XXXV with *Lakṣmīmata*, XXXVI with *Śrīkaṇṭha*. XXXVII with *Sauramata*, once again, XXXVIII with *Śiva-Sūryamata*, XXXIX with *Brahma-Sauramata*, XL with *Pārvatīmata*, XLI with *Gayāmāhātmya*, XLII with Theistic Buddhism beyond the Himalayas, XLIII with atheistic Buddhism, XLIV with *Vaivasvatamata*, XLV with *Śāṇḍilyamata*, XLVI with *Varunamata*, XLVII with *Somamata*, XLVIII with *Bhaumamata*, XLIX with *Bṛhaspatimata*, L with *Vahnimata*, LI with *Budhamata*, LII with *Śukramata*, LIII with *Purāṇamata*, LIV with *Siddhiārga*, LV with *Sāṅkhya*, LVI with *Mahāśāktas*, LVII with *Śanimata*, LVIII with *Indramata*, LIX with *Yamamata*, LX with *Vāyumata*, LXI with *Auḍulomimata*, LXII with *Śakaṭāyanamata*, LXIII with *Nyāyamata*, LXIV with *Karmamata*, LXV with *Smārtamata*. LXVI with *Vīrabhadramata*, LXVII with *Harihara*, LXVIII with the Command of Śiva about the correlation of diverse sects, LXIX with Journery to Kailāsa etc., LXX with Journey to Kāñcī, LXXI with Sureśvara, LXXII with Padmapāda, LXXIII with *Hastāmalaka*, LXXIV with Toṭaka, LXXV with *Girijāsuta-Gāṇapatamata*, LXXVI with *Paramatakālānala-Śaivamatasthāpana*, LXXVII with *Śāktamata-Sthāpana* LXXVIII with *Sauramatasthāpana*, LXXIX with *Vaiṣṇava-mata-sthāpana*, mentioning Rāmānanda, LXXX with Thirty-one Monasteries, LXXXI with the *Saundaryalaharī-stotra*, LXXXII with worship at Kanchi, LXXXIII with Vedic *Ṣanmatasthāpana*, LXXXIV with some *Stotras*, LXXXV with *Bhagavatapāda-siddhi*, LXXXVI with Sureśvara's going to *Śaradāmaṭha*, LXXXVII with *Sarvajñātmānusṭhānakaraṇa*, and the last chapter is a brief *Phalaśruti*.

From the contents it would be clear that the existing form of the work cannot be earlier than the 16th century. It surveys the Tantric and Purāṇic cults in detail and refers to the Theistic Buddhists, Siddhas, the Vīraśaivas, Rāmānuja and Rāmānanda explicitly. The older philosophical schools with which Śaṅkara was concerned in his commentaries are dealt with very briefly. Śaṅkara is emphasized as *Ṣaṇmatasthāpanācarya*. The ritual of worship at Kāñcī and the hymns of Śaṅkara are given a prominent place. If the present work had the ancient *Bṛhat Śaṅkara-Vijaya* as its inspiration, it has certainly succeeded in retouching it in the light of some later developments. Nevertheless, although the actual composition of the work is of an unknown late date, its general structure and atmosphere are reminiscent of older works especially of Ānandagiri's work as reported in the commentaries of the *Mādhavīya*.

Anantānandagiri's *Śaṅkara-vijaya* is acclaimed by some to be the earliest of the extant *Vijayas*. It was published from Calcutta twice, in 1868 by the Asiatic Society of Bengal and again in 1881 when it was edited by Jivananda. It has had the good fortune of having received a fully critical edition from the University of Madras in 1971. The editor's comparison of the various manuscripts and their variant readings helps to reveal how the ancient tradition tended to be changed in certain directions. The variants determined as more ancient tend to be in agreement with the tradition of *Śiva-rahasya* and *Mārkaṇḍeya-saṁhitā*. Acyutarāya Moḍak, the author of *Advaitarājya Lakṣmī* on the *Mādhavīya*, refers to the account in the *Śiva-rahasya* and observes that its details may be seen in the *Bṛhac Chaṅkara-Vijaya* of Ānandagiri also known as Ānandajñāna. Dhanapati Sūri, the author of *Diṇḍima* on the *Mādhavīya*, gives a detailed summary of an ancient account, apparently of the *Prācīna-* or *Bṛhat-Śaṅkara-Vijaya*, which has a close identity with the present work both in content and form. In spite of variations both the accounts agree 'almost completely with regard to (1) the order of the various stages of the tour; (2) the names of the opponents and also of the places where they were encountered; (3) the descriptions of the two; (4) arguments and citation on either side, (5) the period of Śaṅkara's stay at every place etc.[39] Some of the verses cited by Dhanapati Sūri are also to be found *verbatim* in Anantānandagiri. K.T. Telang also felt that the present *Śaṅkara-vijaya* is based on a more elaborated ancient one. This was also the opinion of the author of *Guru-vaṁśa-kāvya* as also of Sadānanda, the author of *Śaṅkara-digvijaya-sāra*. There are, thus, fair grounds for assuming that Anantānandgiri's *Śaṅkara Vijaya* is a kind of summary reproduction of the ancient work of Ānandagiri. On the other hand, some Śṛṅgerī partisans have questioned the antiquity and reliability of the work in the same manner in which the Kāñcī partisans have questioned the antiquity of the *Mādhavīya*.

Thus Dr. Dakshinamurthy has questioned the choice of manuscript and referred to the scarcely veiled references to Rāmānuja and Madhva in the text and to its dependence on *Vaiyāsika-nyāya-mālā* (Review Pamphlet, 1973). Interpolations, however, even within the critical text cannot be ruled out.[40]

Anantānandagiri calls himself a disciple of Śaṅkara, describing the latter as his *Parama-guru*. This has been taken by Telang to mean only that the author belonged to the *Advaita-paramparā*. On the other hand, the list of teachers according to the tradition of the Kāmakoṭipīṭha mentions Ānandajñāna as the seventh in succession from Śaṅkara. He was the disciple of Śuddhānanda and has been described by Acyutarāya as the author of the ancient and elaborate *Śaṅkara-jaya* which was apparently followed by Anantānandagiri.

The contents of the present *Śaṅkara-vijaya* are listed below and have an obvious similarity to those of the anonymous *Bṛhat-Śaṅkara-Vijaya* mentioned above *Prakaraṇas:* 1. *Śāstropakaraṇam*, 2. *Guroravatāra-kathā*, 3. *Advaitasvarūpa-kathanam*, 4. *Śaiva-mata-nirākaraṇam*, 5. *Śaivaikadeśa-mata-nirākaraṇam*, 6. *Bhakta-bhāgavata-mata-nirākaraṇam*, 7. *Vaiṣṇava-mata-nirākaraṇam*, 8. *Pāñcarātra-mata-nibarhaṇam*, 9. *Vaikhānasa-mata-nibarhaṇam*, 10. *Karma-hīna-Vaiṣṇava*, 11. *Hairaṇyagarbha°*, 12. *Agnivādi°*, 13. *Saura°*, 14. *Guru-stuti*, 15. *Gaṇapati-mata-nibarhanam*, 16. *Ganapatyaikadeśi°*, 17. *Ucchiṣṭagaṇapati°*, 18. *Gaṇapati-mata-traya*, 19. *Śakti-mata*, 20. *Śakti-mataikadeśa*, 21. *Śakti-mataikadeśa-śārada°*, 22. *Śakti-mataikadeśi-tritaya*, 23. *Kāpālika°*, 24. *Kāpāli-kaikadeśi°*, 25. *Cārvāka°*, 26. *Saugata°*, 27. *Jaina°*, 28. *Bauddha°*, 29. *Mattāri°*, 30. *Visvaksena°*, 31. *Manmatha°*, 32. *Kuvera°*, 33. *Indra°*, 34. *Yama°*, 35. *Varuna-Vāyu-bhūmyudaka°*, 36. *Kuvera°*, 37. *Varāha°*, 38. *Loka°*, 39. *Guṇa°*, 40. *Sāṅkhya°*, 41. *Yoga°*, 42. *Pīlu°*, 43. *Karma°*, 44. *Candra°*, 45. *Bhaumādīgrahapañcakamatasya°*, 46. *Kṣapaṇaka°*, 47. *Pitṛmata°*, 48. *Śeṣa-garuḍa°*, 49. *Siddha°*, 50. *Gāndharva°*, 51. *Bhūta-Vetāla°*, 52. *Vyāsa-darśanam°*, 53. *Brahma-deva-vara-pradānam*, 54. *Vyāsa-dattāyuh-prapañcanam*, 55. *Bhāṭṭa-darśanam*, 56. *Maṇḍana-miśra-jayaḥ*, 57. *Sarasavāṇyā saha yati-prasaṅga-prapañcaḥ*, 58. *Dehāntara-sañcāra-videha-kāma-śāstra-prapañcaḥ*, 59. *Śiṣyā-gamanam*, 60. *Nṛsiṁha-śākṣātkāraḥ*, 61. *Sarasvatī-jayaḥ*, 62. *Guroḥ sarasa-vāṇyāh ca Śṛṅga-giri-sthāna-nivaśanam*, 63. *Kāñcīnagara-nirmāṇam*, 64. *Śrī-Kāmākṣī-Prapañcanam*, 65. *Śrī-Cakra pratiṣṭhā-yoga-liṅga-sthāpanam*, 66. *Mokṣa-mārga-Prakaraṇam*, 67. *Śaiva-mata-sthāpanam*, 68. *Vaiṣṇava°*, 69. *Saura°*,

70. *Śakti°*, 71. *Gāṇapatya°*, 72. *Kāpālika°*, 73. *Gurustotram*, 74. *Saccidānandaikyam.*

From these contents which generally agree with those reported in the commentary of Dhanapati Sūri, it would seem that the original work of Ānandajñāna already showed that the life of Śaṅkara was conceived on the mythical pattern of divine incarnation, disputation with rival sects and schools, the establishment of new temple and monastic centres of worship, and the synthesis of Smārta-Purāṇic cults under the aegis of Advaita. The older philosophical debates as found in the writings of Śaṅkara himself follow the context of the ancient *Sūtras*, which appears to have partly changed. What is important now is the relationship of Śaṅkara to religious cults and sects. Already in Śaṅkara's times the Ṣaṇmatas had become important as is known from the Tamilian saints. Śaṅkara is thus conceived here primarily as a religious reformer and organizer and his life reflects the role which his monastic tradition certainly assumed gradually in medieval times as the ancient heterodoxies and their challenge disappeared and the atmosphere of faith and worship became ubiquitous. This 'restructuring' of the elements of Śaṅkara's biography in the original work of Ānandajñāna, possibly of the 10th or early 11th century, apparently relied on the more ancient echoes of debates which were still well known as well as the new Purāṇic mythological perspective, and it gave high relief to the 'religious' and 'synthetic' aspects of the life and work of Śaṅkara.

Puṇya-Śloka-Mañjarī and *Jagad-guru-ratna-mālā-stava* are said to be works of the 16th century and embody the tradition preserved in the Kāmakoṭipīṭha of Kāñcī. Some followers of Śṛṅgeri have disputed the authenticity of these works since they deny the very existence of any old Kāñcī tradition. It is believed that memorial verses containing the quintessential biographical facts of the founder and various pontiffs of the *Pīṭha* had been preserved orally from generation to generation. The fifty-fourth pontiff of the *Pīṭha* was Sarvajña Sadāśiva Bodha (1523-29) who was himself the grand-disciple of Mahādeva IV (1498-1507), some time believed the author of the *Vyāsācalīya*. Sadāśiva Bodha composed the *Puṇya-Śloka-Mañjarī* which is a collection of 109 memorial verses (*puṇya-ślokas*) relating to his predecessors. He says that most of these were old verses. This is quite probable because it is customary to compose such memorial verses of successive pontiffs after their demise giving details of their birth, initiation, enlightenment etc.

These verses were necessary for offering worship to the deceased teachers on their anniversaries. 'For this, a knowledge of the year, month and *tithi*, is necessary. The *Puṇya-Śloka-Mañjarī* is a collection of such verses which have come down from time to time; and Sarvajña Sadāśiva was only their editor. He arranged them in chronological order and probably supplied missing verses'.[41]

Jagad-guru-ratna-mālā-stava is said to have been composed by Sadāśiva Brahmendra who was a disciple of Parama Śivendram, the 55th head of the *Maṭha*. This work follows the one mentioned above. It consists of 86 verses of which the first 33 relate to Śaṅkarācārya. On the other hand, it has been argued that the famous Śadāśiva of Nerur belonged to the 18th century and hence could not have been the author of the work which is supposed to have been commented upon in 1720.

The commentary was written by Ātmabodha, the pupil of the 61st pontiff Mahādevendra Sarasvatī. The commentary called *Suṣamā* was written in A.D. 1720 and is a mine of information about works which have been lost since. Such are the *Prācīna-Śaṅkara-Vijaya*, the *Bṛhac- Chaṅkara-vijaya* of Citsukha, *Ācārya-vijaya* of Ānandagiri, *Śaṅkara-vijaya* of Vidyāraṇya. He also mentions the *Patañjali-vijaya* of Rāmabhadra, *Śaṅkara-vijaya* of Vyāsācala, *Keralīya-Śaṅkara-Vijaya*, *Āmnāya-setu* or *Maṭhāmanāya*, and *Saṅkṣepa-Śaṁkara-Vijaya*. Ātmabodha has also added a *Pariśiṣṭa* of 13 verses to the *Guru-ratna-mālā*.

Although the account in this tradition is distinguished by sobreity and restraint, it clearly records the (1) establishment of five monastic centres and (2) the *liṅgas*, as also (3) the *Sarvajña-pīṭhārohaṇa* and (4) *Niryāṇa* at Kāñcī. It portrays Śaṅkara as the teacher of Advaita and at the same time as the *Ṣaṇmata-guru* that is, as the author of a multi-sectarian harmony under the aegis of *Advaita*. Śṛṅgeri partisans doubt the authenticity of the work attributed to Ātmabodha, principally because of the four points mentioned above, but total scepticism is not really warranted. On the other hand, this tradition quotes a couple of older verses giving an impossibly early date for Śaṅkara.

Govindanātha's *Śaṅkarācārya-Carita* has been critically edited and its manuscript history goes back to the late 18th century. The date of the text itself is uncertain. It does appear to embody a Keralīya tradition and has been supposed by some scholars to be the same as *Keralīya-Śaṅkara-Caritam* which has been referred to by the author of the *Suṣamā*. On the other hand, the two works have also been distinguished. It has also been suggested that Govindanātha was the same as the disciple of Ram Variar, who bore the same name. The work was perhaps not later than the 17th century.

There can be no doubt of the simplicity, naturalness and restraint of Govindanātha's style. His work avoids poetic exaggeration and is sparing with respect to miracles. It has a marked brevity and gives the impression of being a summary of some more detailed work. It clearly acknowledges the priority of Vyāsācala. The work is in 9 chapters or *adhyāyas* in verse. The first *adhyāya* gives the history in brief—*Kathā-Saṅkṣepa*, the second mentions the story of Upamanyu and the birth of Śaṅkara. The third describes his education, renunciation, initiation, visit to Badarikāśrama, the composition of the commentary on the *Vedānta-sūtras* and the meeting with Vyāsa. The fourth *adhyāya* describes the death and last rites of Śaṅkara's mother, the fifth his visit to Kumārila Bhaṭṭa at Prayāga and disputation with Viśvarūpa. The sixth speaks of the gathering of disciples, the seventh and eighth of his peregrinations in the south and the ninth of his ascending the *Sarvajñapīṭha* and death at *Dakṣina-Kailāsa*.

Apart from style the narrative of Govindanātha is distinguished by several features. It makes Śaṅkara go to his native place from Badari to see his dying mother and places this event prior to the meeting of Śaṅkara with Kumārila. In the second place there is no mention of the *Digvijaya* in his poem. The explanation of this lies, however, not in the fictitious character of the *Digvijaya* but in the selective and summary character of the present work. Finally Govindanātha places the death of Śaṅkara at Vṛṣācala in the extreme south. It has been alleged by some that here the printed text diverges from the authentic manuscript but there are counter-allegations that the manuscript itself has been tampered with.

The *Śaṅkara-Vijaya-Vilāsa* of Cidvilāsamuni is another work of which the date cannot be precisely ascertained. The text has been critically edited by Dr. Antarkar.[42] The author of the work is said to be Cidvilāsa Yati or Muni who recounts the life story of Śaṅkara to his disciple Vijñākanda. Anantānanda has described both of these as the direct disciples of Śaṅkara. On the other hand, Cidvilāsācārya also figures as the twelfth pontiff in the succession list of the Śāradāpīṭha. It is, however, probable that these old names have been used by some later and anonymous writer.

T.S. Narayana Sastri believed that Cidvilāsa followed the work of Citsukha except that the original manuscript has been flouted in some printed edition in the interest of the Śṛṅgerī tradition. The Śṛṅgerī tradition tends to support the reliability of this work. Baldeva Upadhyaya has expressed the opinion that Cidvilāsa follows Anantānandagiri. Antarkar holds the view that Cidvilāsa should be held older than Mādhava, Rāja Cūḍāmani Dīkṣita and even Tirumala Dīkṣita, which would date Cidvilāsa in the 16th century or earlier. He also disputes the opinion of Bodas that Cidvilāsa like Mādhava-Vidyāraṇya belonged to the Śṛṅgeri tradition.[43] This would devalue Narayana Sastri's criticism also.

The work is entirely in verse and follows the Purāṇic style. The narrative 'is fairly lucid, straightforward and almost matter of fact'. The work is in thirty-two *adhyāyas* of which the first gives a summary of the whole. According to it Śivaguru, the father of Śaṅkara, performed his *upanayana* at the age of five and was contemplating his marriage when he passed away. Śaṅkara met Govindapāda at Badari and Kumārila at Ruddhanagara.He met Maṇḍana Miśra in Kashmir and ascended the *Sarvajñapīṭha* at Kāñcī. He passed away in the Himalayas.

There are some oddities in the work which look strange. Śaṅkara is made to challenge Maṇḍana's wife on his own. In the debate described in the 29th chapter the Cārvākas, the Ārhatas and the Saugatas have been rolled into one. In the second chapter the Jainas and the Buddhists have been ignored. In chapter 31 Śaṅkara is curiously described as shattered by old age.

The *Śaṅkarābhyudaya* of Rāja Cūdāmaṇi Dīkṣita is another work which has as many as 137 verses in common with the *Mādhavīya*, 131 belonging to the second, third and fourth cantos of the *Śaṅkarābhyudaya* and six to other cantos.[44] It has been suggested that Mādhava is the borrower. The possibility of Dīkṣita borrowing from the *Mādhavīya* or both drawing on some third source, however, remains equally plausible. Also, the arguments against the *Mādhavīya* tend to suffer from *petitio principii*.[45]

Happily the date of Rāja Cūḍāmaṇi Dīkṣita is more or less certain. He belonged to the Court of Raghunātha Nāyaka who ruled at Tanjore from A.D. 1614 to 1633. Rāja Cūḍāmaṇi Dīkṣita was the brother-in-law of the celebrated Appaya Dīkṣita and the son of Śrīnivāsa Dīkṣita who has been picturesquely described as '*Dantidyoti-divāpradīpāṅka*' since he was officially welcomed by illumination placed on the heads of elephants even during the day, a style of welcome which was normally the privilege of rulers only. Rāja Cūdāmaṇi was the author of twenty-seven works of which ten are known to survive. Of the present work only eight cantos have survived.

In the first canto the author relates how he dreamt of Gīrvāṇendra Sarasvatī and at his instance took up the composition of this work. He describes the birth, childhood, renunciation, initiation, and the literary activities of Śaṅkara up to his twelfth year. The second canto describes Śaṅkara's meeting with the sage Vyāsa, the acceptance of Sanandana as disciple, the meeting with Kumārila, the debate with Viśvarūpa, and the literary works of Sureśvara and Padmapāda. The third canto mentions the death and last rites of the mother of Śaṅkara, restoration of the *Pañcapādikā* and of the three plays of king Rājaśekhara, bestowal of grace of Toṭaka, acceptance of Hastāmalaka as disciple and the illness and treatment of Śaṅkara. The fourth canto refers to Śaṅkara's visit to Gokarna, *Hari-hara-kṣetra*, his raising a dead child on the way to *Mūkāmbikā-kṣetra*, adventure of *Parakāya-praveśa*, visit to the temple of Mūkāmbikā, and the incident of the Kāpālika. The fifth canto describes the visit to the temple of Anantaśayana and Madurā. The sixth canto mentions the visit to Rameśvara, the seventh visits to the banks of the Kaveri and to the temples of Srirangam, Cidambaram, Arunacala, Satyavrata and Kāñcī, ascending the *Sarvajñapīṭha* and singing some hymns in praise of the goddess. The eighth canto relates the worship of Kāmeśvari while residing at Kāñcī. The work as extant ends here. It is clear that at least one more canto should be expected to have existed.

The *Śaṅkarābhyudaya* of Tirumala Dīkṣita may naturally be considered at this place. The author belonged to the Bharadvājagotra and was the son of Tirumala Kāṇḍopādhyāya. He (the author) was the spiritual disciple of one Parama Śivendra. Now it is known that the 57th head of the Kāñcī Kāmakoṭipīṭha was known as Parama Śivendra and his traditional dates are between A.D. 1539 and A.D. 1587. This would place Tirumala Dīkṣita about the middle or later half of the 16th century A.D.

The present work has about 475 stanzas in common with Mādhava's *Śaṅkṣepa-Śaṁkara-Jaya* and it has often been supposed that the latter has borrowed from the former.[46] However, the present work refers to earlier poetic biographies and claims to be selective. It is obvious that it too is a kind of summary based on earlier works. Although briefer and simpler than Mādhava's, it also contains anachronistic stories like the meeting of Śaṅkara with Abhinavagupta and Nīlakaṇṭha.

The work has been edited from a single and incomplete manuscript.[47] The first canto describes the visit of the Gods to Śiva, the description of irreligion on earth, the decision of Śiva to incarnate himself for the restoration of the Vedic faith and order, the life and deeds of Kumārila and the birth of Śaṅkara. A large number of verses in this canto occur in the *Mādhavīya* also. It is most likely that the ultimate source of these verses is some old account of the kind in *Śiva-rahasya* or *Mārkaṇḍeya-saṁhitā.*

The second canto describes the childhood and studies of Śaṅkara and gives the stories of the golden *āmalaka,* the visit of King Rājaśekhara and the visit of the sages. It ends with the departure of Śaṅkara from home after persuading his mother. The third canto describes Śaṅkara's meeting with Govindapāda near the Narmada, the miracle of containing the flooded waters of the river, repairing to Kāśī, acquiring some disciples and meeting with the Caṇḍāla. The fourth canto describes the meeting of Śaṅkara with Vyāsa and later with Kumārila at Prayaga. From there Śaṅkara proceeds to Mahismati to meet Maṇḍana and debate with him. The fifth canto continues the debate at the end of which there is a fresh debate with the wife of Maṇḍana. Śaṅkara then seeks to learn erotics vicariously by entering the dead body of the King Amaruka. In the sixth canto Śaṅkara returns to win the debate and wanders to different places like Maharashtra, Mallikarjuna and the banks of the Kṛṣṇā river. He overcomes numerous sectaries in debates. The seventh canto proceeds to tell the story of the Kāpālika who persuaded Śaṅkara to agree to give up his head for the sake of the Kāpālikas gruesome ritual of human sacrifice. The Kāpālika, however, is frustrated by the intervention of Padmapāda. The extant manuscript breaks off at this point.

Another work available in similarly fragmentary condition is the *Ācārya-vijaya* or *Ācārya-Vijayākhyāna* by Sri Paramesvara Kavi Kanṭhirava. Only five cantos of the work appear to be available. The author was the son of Sri Devaraja of the Saṅkṛti gotra and devotee of Śrī Rāma. He refers explicitly to Mādhava and the *Mādhavīya* and to Appaya Dīkṣita. Since Appaya Dīkṣita belongs to the 17th century, the present work could not be earlier. The work is in mixed prose and verse and has the form of *Campū.* Its style resembles that of Vallīsahāya who is the author of another similar *Campū* entitled *Ācārya-vijaya-Campū.*

The first *taraṅga* describes how the gods decide to incarnate on earth to help the revival of the Vedic faith, with Śiva cast in the role of Śaṅkarācārya. It describes the deeds of Kumārila and the birth of Maṇḍana and of the disciples of Śaṅkara, Sudhanvā and Rājaśekhara and identified in this account. The second *taraṅga* describes Śaṅkara's studentship, renunciation of home, meeting with Govindapāda on the Narmadā and going to Kāśī. It also describes many stories relating to his childhood including the visit of King Rājaśekhara. The third *taraṅga* describes Śaṅkara's meeting with the Cāṇḍāla, his visit to Badarī and the composition of the commentaries, return to Kāśī, meeting with Vyāsa, visiting Kumārila and debate with Maṇḍana and his wife. The fourth *taraṅga* is devoted to Śaṅkara's acting the role of Amaruka. The fifth *taraṅga* is incomplete and deals with the attempt of Śaṅkara's disciples to remind him of his real nature. The canto has two beginnings and it seems that there might have been two drafts or versions.

On the whole, the present work seems to be essentially a literary exercise based on the *Mādhavīya*.

Śaṅkara-Vijaya-Saṁgraha or *Kūṣmāṇḍa-Śaṅkara-Vijaya* of Puruṣottama Bhāratī is a work of unknown date. It is brief and simple and has some interesting novelties. It is the only biographical version which traces the birth of Śaṅkara from a non-uterine source. He is said to have been born from a pumpkin of which the seed was divinely given, and which was nourished by a widow who became Śaṅkara's mother. The story was disbelieved by the people but that did not deter the affectionate mother. It describes various incidents of the Śaṅkara's life briefly but does not refer to Kumārila. At the end it describes Śaṅkara as establishing the *six* modes of worship, *Ṣaṇmatas*.

It may be recalled that stories of miraculous birth are not unknown for ancient saints and prophets such as Buddha or Jesus. Detractors such as some Mādhava authors have used them against the legitimacy of Śaṅkara's birth.

Several biographical works have been composed since the late eighteenth century on the basis of earlier works or tradition. *Śaṅkara-Digvijaya-sāra* of Sadānanda is one of these. Sadānanda is said to have belonged to West Punjab and to have come to Varanasi with a *Nānakpanthī*, holy man, Baba Ram Dayal. He (Sadānanda) recited the Purāṇas for a living and out of the proceeds of a gift had a temple of Śiva constructed on the Manikarṇikā Ghāt in A.D. 1796. He was also the father-in-law of Dhanapati Sūri mentioned above as the author of a well-known commentary on the *Mādhavīya* called *Ḍiṇḍima*. *Śaṅkara-Digvijaya-sāra* was composed in A.D. 1780. The work is a professed summary of the *Mādhavīya* and follows it closely. On the other hand, it has been regarded as the summary of the *Prācīna-Śaṅkara-Vijaya*. The author also wrote several other works many of which remain unpublished.

The *Guru-Vaṁśa-Kāvya* of Kāśī Lakṣmaṇa Śāstrī is the principal work expounding the biography of Śaṅkara from the standpoint of tradition preserved in the Śṛṅgeri Maṭha. This work is said to have been written under the inspiration of Sri Saccidananda Bharati who was the head of the Maṭha from A.D. 1772 to 1814 or his namesake who was the pontiff from 1705 to 1741. The Śṛṅgeri tradition puts the date of the work around A.D. 1730. The first part of the work was published from a manuscript in the Śṛṅgeri Maṭha by Rama Sastrigal from the Vani Vilas Press in seven cantos. The second part has not been published. The first three of these cantos relate to Śaṅkara. The rest are mainly concerned with Vidyāraṇya.

Some of the peculiarities of this account are as follows. The author says that he strictly follows older authors (*Prācām asammataṁ naiva*. . .). Among the older authors he mentions *Ānandagiri-yatīndrādi* (p. 6). The work begins with Nārada's observations to Brahmā, on the depraved conditions on earth. On Brahmā's prayer Śiva assures him that his *aṁśa* on earth as Śaṅkara will restore the true faith. The rest of the first canto narrates the birth of Śaṅkara. The second canto describes Śaṅkara as a child prodigy, mentions the plays of king Rājaśekhara as having the same name as the king (2 9), and describes Śaṅkara's renunciation after the crocodile episode. The crocodile is said to have been a *gandharva* in its previous life. Śaṅkara proceeded to Govindapāda and after receiving instruction composed his literary works. Then he went on a pilgrimage to Badarikāśrama and met Vyāsa. Sanandana-Padmapāda was initiated. On the Triveni, Śaṅkara met Kumārilabhaṭṭa who directs him to Viśvarūpa. Maṇḍanamiśra is clearly distinguished from Viśvarūpa. After the debate it is Viśvarūpa who became Sureśvara. The debate with Ubhayabhāratī is omitted. Śaṅkara then goes to Narmada and thence to his dying mother whose last rites he performed. The third canto describes the diverse peregrinations and organizational activities. Thus he established the five *maṭhas* as Varanasi, went to Kashmir to ascend the *Sarvajñapīṭha*, was challenged to show knowledge of *Kāmakalā*, which he did after entering the body of the dead King Amaruka.

The goddess Śāradā was pleased with him and he requested her to accompany him as a boon to the banks of the Tungabhadrā for being permanently located there in the *maṭha*. The goddess Śāradā was installed in the Śṛṅgerī Maṭha and Sureśvara was put in charge of her worship. Śaṅkara then proceeded to Kāñcī and founded there both Śiva-Kāñcī and Viṣṇu-Kāñcī and consecrated the goddess Kāmākṣī. He then established the Six Sects. From here the Master went to Badari and consecrated the image of Nārāyaṇa immersed in the Alakanandā. Padmapāda was sent to preside over the *maṭha* at Jagannatha in the east. Hastāmalaka was sent to the west to Dvārakā and Toṭaka was placed in charge of the Jyotirmaṭha near Badari. Śaṅkara then proceeded to Nepal to see the goddess Siddheśvarī. He then went to the abode of Dattātreya and stayed with him.

Nīlakaṇṭha, the author of *Śaṅkarābhyudaya*, indicates his reverence for Nṛsiṁha Bhāratī Svāmī and hence for the Śṛṅgeri tradition. Another work of apparently the same author is called *Śaṅkara-mandāra-saurabha*. The author's father composed a work in A.D. 1805 and the two Nṛsiṁha Bhāratīs of Śṛṅgerī span the periods A.D. 1817 to 1879 and from 1879 to 1912. Nīlakaṇṭha, thus, appears to have flourished after them in 19th century.

Śaṅkarābhyudaya is in six *sargas* or cantos. It generally follows the *Mādhavīya*, though it has some peculiarities. In canto I, stanza 26 it gives the date of Śaṅkara's birth as the Kali year 3889, *Vibhava saṁvat*, bright half of the 10th day which corresponds to A.D. 788, Vaiśākha Śukla Daśamī. In this respect it agrees completely with *Śaṅkara-mandāra-saurabha*. However, the ancient source whence this date is derived is not known. On Sureśvara, Maṇḍana and Viśvarūpa, the present work tends to hold the view that they were identical. The work also makes Śaṅkara actually revive the dying Kumārila and initiate him so that the latter may leave the body like a Yogin.

The work begins with the situation on earth demanding divine intervention to save orthodoxy and goes on to describe the birth and education of Śaṅkara and the visit of King Rājaśekhara. The second canto describes his renunciation, initiation by Govindapāda, the miracle of containing the flooded Narmadā and the instruction of his teacher that he should compose a commentary on the *Vedānta-sūtras* and proceed to Kāśī for it. In the third canto Śaṅkara meets Sanandana and the *Cāṇḍāla* in Kāśī and proceeds to Badarī to write the commentary. He composed the commentary not only on the *sūtras* but on the *Upaniṣads* and the *Gītā,* and also wrote a number of other works such as the *Upadeśa-sāhasrī.* Coming back to Kāśī and teaching his views he met Vyāsa and had a debate with him. He then meets Kumārila and is directed to Maṇḍana. In the fourth canto Śaṅkara meets Maṇḍana at Mahismati on the banks of Revā. He debates with Maṇḍana and his wife and is led to the adventure of learning erotics by entering another body. In the fifth canto he wins the debate, acquires more disciples, wanders around and manages to save the *Pañcapādikā.* In the sixth canto he goes round the country on *digvijaya,* goes to Kashmir to the *Sarvajñapīṭha,* and finally to Kailāsa.

The work has hardly any originality and as mentioned before, seems to follow the *Mādhavīya* generally, but the *Mādhavīya* does not give any date for the birth of Śaṅkara. It would be of great interest to know what the source of the present work was in giving a precise date. The *Maṭhāmnāya* of Puri was published as the *Śaṅkarācārya-jagadguru-maṭhāmnāya* by Yogendra Asthavadhana Sarma in 1930 from Puri. In the verses collected by Sri Baldeva Upadhyaya as belonging to that *Maṭhāmnāya* a list of 142 Heads has been given.[48] The present Śaṅkarācārya of Puri Śri Niranjanadeva, has supplied a list of 143 names to Śri Udayavīra Śāstrī, Śri Bhāraṭī Kṛṣṇa Tīrtha being the 143rd and Śri Niranjanadeva the 144th. Of these the actual dates are known of only the last five pontiffs, the first of whom became Head in 1849.[49] Among the 138 names there are many repetitions.

The tradition of the Jyotirmaṭha of Badarīnātha is incomplete and shows interruption in the succession. Of the earliest period, 21 names are recounted in verses as an Appendix to a manuscript of the *Mantra-rahasya* (Mayadatta Shastri, *Jyotishpiṭha-Paricaya,* p. 16). From the middle period there is a list of 21 names between A.D. 1497 and A.D. 1776. (Hari Krishna Raturi, *Garhwal Ka Itihas,* p. 55). After that it was only in 1941 that Brahmananda Sarasvati became the pontiff. In the meanwhile Nambudri Brāhmaṇas called Rawals have been appointed as priests of the Badrīnātha temple. There is no evidence for the current assumption that this practice goes back to the ancient period.

The succession list of the Śāradāpīṭha of Dvārakā contains 77 names up-to-date. The list has been published several times (cf. Upadhyaya. *op. cit.,* U.V. Shastri, *op.cit., Yatisandhyāsamuccaya pub.* Dvārakāpīṭha 1967, *Theosophist,* Vol. XVI nos. 3 & 5.) If the chronology of this list is accepted, the beginning of the list would go back to 491 B.C. This gives too long an average. The fault apparently is not so much with the duplication of names as with the attribution of long periods to too many Heads. The average for the first 24 pontiffs is 47 years, for the next 52 it is 19 years, while the overall average is 30 years only. The average for pontiffs between A.D. 664 and A.D. 1945, appears reasonable and based on real data, which supports the date of Śaṅkara in the 7th century A.D.

The tradition of succession at Śṛṅgeri may be gleaned from several publications such as *Guruvaṁśa Kāvyam, Śrīmajjagadguru-Śaṅkara-maṭha Vimarśa, Kashi men Kumbhagana mathavisayaka Vivada, Maṭhāmnāya* (Vani Vilas Press). The list of the *Ācāryas* at Śṛṅgerī is a short one of 35 names and within it similar names occur a dozen times. There is another list of the Heads of the Kudli Maṭha comprising 63 names in which distinct names are only 26. It has been supposed by some scholars that these lists are incomplete. It is more likely that these lists attest to the late beginning of the monastic tradition itself, at least in its pontifical form.

The succession list of the Kāmakoṭipīṭha mentions 68 pontiffs from Śaṅkara to the present incumbent. The list is comparable in length to that of Śāradāpīṭha. *Puṇya-Śloka-Mañjarī, Ratna-mālā-stava, Pariśiṣṭa, Jagadguru Paramparāstotra,* and *Maṭhāmnāya-setu* given the earliest lists based on memorial verses.

Apart from the *Maṭhāmnāyas* of the different monastic centres, there is also a text called *Mahānuśāsana* which claims to embody Śaṅkara's general instructions to the monastic heads. How far these monastic traditions are authentic and what light they actually throw on the date and history of Śaṅkara would be examined in detail later.

Miscellaneous Literary Sources: The Tradition of the Śrīvidyārṇava

Generally Śaṅkara is remembered only as the founder of an ascetic-monastic tradition. There is also, however, a little known tradition which maintains that there was a succession of householder disciples of Śaṅkara. The *Śrīvidyārṇava,* a Tantric text, is the most important old authority for this. It is said to have been composed by Vidyāraṇya Yati, a disciple of Pragalbhācārya who was in turn the disciple of Viṣṇuśarmā said to be one of the direct disciples of Śaṅkara. The famous Bhāskara Rāya is said to have belonged to this householder tradition.[30]

Of the other works listed in this section, *Patañjali-Caritam* gives a fanciful account of Gauḍapāda and Govinda, *Darśana-Prakāśa* and *Belgaum MS* are important for chonology and would be discussed below. *Maṇimañjarī* is sectarian and hostile, *Keralotpatti* late and *inauthentic* and *Jinavijaya* is totally unknown, perhaps fictitious. Tārānātha is unreliable except that it echoes Buddhist hostility.

Comparative Synopsis of the Biographical Sources

Some sources claim to give the date of Śaṅkara. The *Puṇya-Śloka-Mañjarī, Bṛhac Chaṅkara-Vijaya* and *Keralotpatti, Prācīna-Śaṅkara-Vijaya* as quoted in *Suṣamā, Śaṅkarapaddhati* as quoted in *Darśana-Prakāśa, Kṛṣṇabrahmānanda's Śaṅkara Vijaya*, the so-called *Jinavijaya, the Belgaum MS, Nīlkaṇṭha Dikṣita's Śaṅkarābhyudaya* and *Śaṅkara-mandārasaurabha*, and the monastic traditions give diverse dates for the birth of Śaṅkara. These dates range from 50 B.C. or 476 B.C., to A.D. 400, A.D. 688 or A.D. 788. The basis and cogency of these traditions will be analysed later.

About the place of Śaṅkara's birth the more pervasive tradition asserts it to have been Kaldi in Kerala while Anantānandagiri states it to have been Chidambaram.The name of Śaṅkara's father is generally given as Śivaguru and this is supported by the *Bṛhac-Caṅkara-Vijaya*. The name of the mother has been given as Āryāmbā, which may be an honorific rather than a name, as *Satī* (*Mādhavīya*) or as *Viśiṣṭā* (Anantānandagiri). *Manimanjari*, however, describes Śaṅkara as the son of a poor Brāhmaṇa widow. *Kūṣmāṇḍa-Śaṅkara-Vijaya* too describes him as a child miraculous obtained by a widow.

The death of Śaṅkara's father has been placed shortly before or after his *upanayana*. The first alternative has been mentioned by Āṇandagiri, Vyāsācala, Mādhava, Govindanātha, and *Guruvaṁśa-Kāvya*. The second has been followed in *Prācīna-Śaṅkara-Vijaya, Jagad-guru-ratna-mālā, Suṣamā* and *Cidvilāsīya*. The account of Śaṅkara's education varies in degrees of elaboration in the different texts. He is generally portrayed as a child prodigy. Several accounts relate childhood miracles of Śaṅkara. Two of these have attracted the fancy of the authors specially, viz., causing a rain of golden *āmalakas* in the house of a poor woman, and causing a shift in the course of the river Cūrṇi.

Śaṅkara's renouncing of home life is generally attributed to *āpat-saṁnyāsa* of the crocodile episode but a simpler version also exists which attributes it to the persuasion of Śaṅkara's mother by him or by the sages without the interventionof the crocodile. Some versions make the crocodile essentially supernatural. Śaṅkara's meeting Govindapāda and being initiated by him is common to all versions but the place of meeting is not the same in all. The usual version identifies it with the banks of the Narmada but occasionally Kāśī or even Badarī is mentioned, some versions mentioned the miracle of Śaṅkara's containing the waters of the flooded Narmada river.

The writing of the commentaries is generally described next and is either placed in Kāśī or in Badarī. Some texts name various other works and the occasions when they were composed. Some texts describes a meeting with Gauḍapāda but usually it is only a meeting with Vyāsa. The meeting with Vyāsa takes the form of a testing debate in some works like the *Mādhavīya*. In some other texts it is just a simple meeting where Vyāsa is not incognito.

The meeting with Kumārila is the next important event but its position in the course of events shows variation. In some versions the death of Śaṅkara's mother and the performance of her funeral rites come before the meeting with Kumārila. After meeting Kumārila Śaṅkara meets Maṇḍana or Viśvarūpa. Some texts distinguish the two. After the debate with Maṇḍana or Viśvarūpa as the case may be, there is again a difference of versions about the debate with his wife, which all do not mention. In some versions this debate with the wife leads to the incident of *Para-Kāya-praveśa*.

Beyond this point there are widely varying accounts of diverse journeys, pilgrimages, debates, and the founding of monastic centres and the installation of images, *yantras* and *liṅgas*. There is little consistency about the number, nature or order of these events.

The end is generally placed at the age of thirty-two and the place where it occurred is either identified with Kāñcī, or located in Kerala, or in the Himalayas.

About the disciples of Śaṅkara there is a large agreement but where each one was deputed, is a matter of dispute. There are some incidents narrated about the disciples and their earlier histories of which the versions are not wholly consistent. Some information is also vouchsafed about the literary activity of the disciples.

List of Major Episodes and Themes

I 1. Gods decide to incarnate to save the Vedic faith—*MS, SR, RM, M, AA,*

2. Kumārila, the Buddhists and King Sudhanvan—*M,*

II 3. Description of Kerala, Kalati. *GU.*
4. Studies, and marriage of Śaṅkara's father. *V,M.*
5. Śaṅkara's parents paractise penance and are blessed *V.M. Cid*
6. Illustrative story of Upamanyu *V,*
7. Birth and Infancy of Śaṅkara including learning as a prodigy and *Cūḍākarman M, Br, Pra, PSM, V, Gu, Cid, RcD,*
8. *Upanayana* and the death of Śaṅkara's father. *V, AA, M, Go, Gu; Pra, RM, Cid.*
9. Śaṅkara's education *AA, M, RcD,*
10. Childhood miracles
= Rain of golden *āmalakas M, TMD,*
= Changing the course of *cūrṇi. RCD, V,*
= Meeting King Rajaśekhara *RCD, TMD,*
= Rescuing the image of Kṛṣṇa *Go, V,*
11. Renunciation
= episode of the crocodile *Go, M.*
= Persuasion of the mother by sages *TMD,*
= Persuasion by Śaṅkara, *V* (after the crocodile
episode), *TMD* (after the sages),

III 12. (a) Meeting Govindapāda *RM, Pra, PC, M*
= Narmadā *M, TMD,*
= Kāśī
= Badarī. *PV*
(b) History of Govinda and Gauḍa - *PV,*
13. Miracle of Containing flood waters *M, TMD,*
14. (a) Writing of Commentaries and the literary activity, *RCD,*
(b) Acceptance of disciples *M, V,*
15. (a) Meeting Śiva as Cāṇḍāla, *Br, M, TMD, RM* (*Suṣamā*),
(b) Meeting Gauḍapāda, *Bra, M,*
(c) Meeting Vyāsa and being blessed with further years.
16. (a) Passing away of Govindapāda, *Br,*
17. Meeting Kumārila
= *K's* life *Br, AA,*
18. Meeting Maṇḍana, Go,
= Viśvarūpa *RCM, V*
= Debate *Go, V, Gu*
= Debate with Maṇḍana's wife *AA, M, Cid, TMD,*

= *Para-kāya-praveśa M, Gu, RM, RcM, TMD, V,*

19. Last rites of the mother *M, V, RcD,*

IV 20. (a) Digvijaya = *Cid, M, AA, BSV,*
(b) Pilgrimages *M, V, AA, Cid, Gv, RcD,*

21. Establishment of *maṭhas RM,*

22. Establishment of Images and *Liṅgas* Badarinātha—*Gu, RM*
Establishment of Six Schools—*AA, Gu, liṅgas-RM, MS, GU, SR,*

V 23. Sarvajñapīṭhārohana : Kāñcī, *RcD, RM*
: Kashmir, *Bra, M, V,*

24. (a) Śaṅkara's illness = *RcD, V, M,*
(b) Passing away : Kāñcī, *RcD, RM, V* (according to *Suṣamā*)
: Himalayas, *M, Cid.*
: Kerala. *GO.*

Conclusion

The original source of Śaṅkara's biography appears to have consisted principally of Citsukha's *Bṛhac-Chaṅkara-Vijaya* which is no longer extant but of which mutilated copies are said to have existed till recently and of which some excerpts are still available. Ānanda-Jñāna's *Prācīna-Śaṅkara-Vijaya* was presumably based on it and could have belonged to the eleventh century. In the meanwhile the Śaṅkara legend had been canonized in some Purāṇic or semi-Purāṇic texts. *Saṅkṣepa-Śaṅkara-Jaya* ascribed to Mādhava and presumably of the 14th century relied on *Prācīna-Śaṅkara-Jaya* but remodelled it as a poetical work instinct with doctrinal content. Anantānanda's *Śaṅkara-digvijaya* was another new work similarly deriving from the *Bṛhat-Śaṅkara-Vijaya,* and presumably datable around the 13th century. The major works of the Kāñcī tradition, *Puṇya-Śloka-Mañjarī, Jagad-guru-ratna-mālā-stava* and *Suṣamā,* belong to the period from the 16th to the 18th centuries. The older works were still accessible to Ātmabodha in the 18th century. In the same period a number of new and poetical biographies of Śaṅkara were composed by Rāja-Cūḍāmaṇi Dīkṣita, Tirumala Dīkṣita, Vyāsācala, Govindanātha, Cidvilāsa etc. Towards the end of the 18th century Sadānanda composed his *Śaṅkara-digvijaya-sāra* and several extensive commentaries replete with quotations from ancient works were composed on the *Mādhavīya.* The Śṛṅgerī tradition has produced the *Guru-Vaṁśa-Kāvya.*

From about the middle of the 19th century a most unfortunate dispute has divided the Kāñcī and Śṛṅgerī monasteries. The Kāñcī Maṭha claims to be the principal original *maṭha*, the Śṛṅgerī Maṭha declares it to be one of recent origin. In this dispute historical records have been questioned but not always without bias. In this controversy textual variation and dates have come for critical examination but not from a neutral or unbiased point of view. The controversialists suffer from the mistaken belief that to accept the antiquity or authenticity of a text in some sense warrants accepting the truth of all that it says. There are, in fact, no unimpeachable sources of Śaṅkara's biography or of the early history of the monasteries of which the rival claims cannot be categorically substantiated or refuted in the present state of knowledge.

A major difficulty with the assessment of the 'biographical' sources of Śaṅkara is the absence of critically edited texts containing a full history of the manuscripts used. As a result each party to the running monastic disputes relies on declaring any inconvenient text as an interpolation or forgery. Of the controversial texts Anantānandagiri's *Śaṅkara-vijaya* is perhaps the only one critically edited. Dr. Antarkar's editions are a welcome move making critically edited texts accessible. Sectarian controversies envelop almost all the biographical sources on which doubts have been cast from one side or the other. These doubts allege recent fabrication of the 'sources' in whole or part in favour of some monastic claims or the other. If all the older sources or their printed versions or particular manuscripts are to be subjected to radical scepticism, we are left only with monastic traditions and claims. Now since monastic records have never been fully accessible to objective historians and since oral traditions are not competent to establish anything of historical value relating to antiquity, it would follow that the search for Śaṅkara's biography is a quest for the Holy Grail. The exponents of Śṛṅgerī deny that Śaṅkara established the Kāñcī Maṭha of which the primacy is declared by its supporters. In this controversy a larger question arises, did Śaṅkara establish any monastery? It would, thus, seem that the legendary biography of Śaṅkara as well as the current traditions of monastic establishments, both are matters wholly open to scepticism and critical enquiry.

Actually a radical scepticism follows only if we concentrate on contradictions by taking modern exponents of the monastic traditions to be in possession of real past history apart from past literary records. Although many obscurities and contradictions in these records stem from indifference to history in their preservation and re-working, the extant literary sources going back to the 14th or 15th century and basing themselves on older works, do reveal the growth of the Śaṅkara legend which transformed old historical or semi-historical records of which some direct knowledge appears to have existed till at least the 18th century. That these old works have ceased to be traceable and that new works have been produced without sufficient respect for history, is unfortunate and needs to be remedied.

What we have, on the whole, is a bare biographical framework for Śaṅkara underlying his diverse legendary biographies. Whether anything more can be trusted will be examined below.

APPENDIX

Some Purāṇic and Semi-Purāṇic Excerpts

Liṅgapurāṇa I.40. 20-22:

Nindanti veda-vidyāṁ ca dvijāḥ karmāṇi vai khalu/
Kalau Rudro mahādevaḥ Śaṅkaro nīla-lohitaḥ//
Prakāśate pratiṣṭhārthaṁ dharmasya vikṛtākṛtiḥ/
Ye taṁ viprā niṣevante yena kenāpi Śaṅkaram//
Kali-doṣān vinirjitya prayānti paramam padam/

Kūrmapurāṇa, 28,32,35:

Kalau Rudro mahādevo lokānām īśvaraḥ paraḥ/
Sa devatā bhavennṛṇām devatānāñca daivatam//
Kariṣyat yavatārāṇi Śaṅkaro nīla-lohitaḥ//
Śrauta-smārta-pratiṣṭhārtham bhaktānāṁ hita-Kāmyayā//
Upadekṣyati taj jñānaṁ śiṣyāṇam brahma-sañjñitam/
Sarva-Vedānta-sāram hi dharmān veda-nidarśitām//
Vijitya Karmajān doṣān yānti te paramam padam//

Saurapurāṇa (as quoted by Baldeva Upadhyaya, *op.cit.*, p. 19):

Caturbhiḥ saha śiṣyaistu Śaṅkaro' vatariṣyati/
Vyākurvan Vyāsa-sūtrāṇi śruter arthaṁ yathocitam/
Sa evārthaḥ śruter grāhyaḥ Śaṅkaraḥ savitānanaḥ//

Śiva-rahasya, IX. 16:

Varṇāśrama-paribhraṣṭān adharma-pravaṇān janān/
Kalyabdhau majjamānān stān dṛṣṭvā nukrośato' mbike//11-16
Madaṁśa-jātaṁ Deveśi kalāvapi tapodhanam/

Keraleṣu tadā vipraṁ janayāmi Maheśvari// (7)
Tasyaiva Caritan te'dya Vakṣyāmi śṛṇu Śailaje/
Kalyādimemahādevi sahasra-dviṭayāt param/ (8)
Jainā Bauddhā buddhiyuktā mīmāṁsā-niratāḥ kalau/
Veda-bodhita-vākyānām anyathaivaprarocakāḥ(II)
Pratyakṣa-vāda-Kuśalāḥ śalyabhūtāḥ kalau śive (12)
Teṣām utpāṭanārthāya sṛjāīśe madaṁśataḥ// (14)
Kerale śaśala-grāme vipra-patnyām madaṁśataḥ/
Bhasviṣyati Mahādevi Śaṅkarākhyo dvijottamaḥ//(15)
Upanītatadā mātrā Vedān sāṅgān grahīṣyati/
Abdāvadhi tataḥ śabde vihatya sa tu tarkajām//(16)
Matim mīmāṁsamānb' sau kṛtvā śāstreṣu niścayam/
Vādimattadvipa-varān Śaṅkarottama-kesarī//(17)
Bhinattyev tadā Buddhān,siddha-vidyān api drutam/
Jainān vijigye tarasā tathānyān kumatānugān//(18)
Tadā mātaram ā mantrya parivrāṭ sa bhaviṣyati/
Parivrājaka-rūpeṇa Miśramāśrama-dūṣakān//(19)
Daṇḍa-hastastathā kuṇḍī kaṣāya-vasanojjvalaḥ/
Bhasma-divya-tripuṇḍrāṅko rudrākṣa-bharanojjvalaḥ//(20)
Tāra-rudrārtha-parīṇāḥ Śiva-liṅgārcana-priyaḥ/
Sva-śiṣyaistādṛṣairghuṣyan bhāṣya-vākyāni so'mbike//(21)
Maddatta-vidyayā Bhikṣur virājati Śaśāṅkavat/
Advaitam eva sūtrārtham prāmāṇyena kariṣyati/(22)
Avimukte samāsīnaṁ Vyāsaṁ vākyair vijitya ca//
Śiayaiś caturbhiḥ samyuktam bhasma-rudrākṣa-bhūṣaṇam/(26)
Madaṁśatastvaṁ Jāto' si bhuvi cādvaita-siddhaye// (37)
Tadbheda-giri-vajrastvam saṁjāto'si madaṁśataḥ/
Dvātriṁśatparamāyuṣṭe śīghram Kailāsam āvasa//(39)
Etat pṛatigṛhāṇa tvam pañca-liṅgaṁ supūjaya/(40)

Mārkaṇḍeya-saṁhitā(72/7/10):
Gatvā Kailāsa-śailaṁ jagad-akhila-guruḥ Śankarācārya-yogī
Dṛṣṭvā sāmbaṁ Śivaṁ taṁ svayamiti suciraṁ cintayannantaraṅge/
Labdhyā pañcātma-liṅgānyamala-tara-śubhā-liṅgit-anyaṅga-bhājām
Bhūtyai saundarya-sāram hima-giri-duhituḥ Prāpayan gām ayāsit/
Ibid.,72/7/ 11-18, *Ih*73/7/1-2: describe the establishment of the five *liṅgas* and the appointment of the pontiffs at Kāñcī and Śṛṅgerī (Vide, Veezhinathan, *op.cit.* pp. vi-vii)

Padmapurāṇa:

"Māyāvādam asac-chāstram pracchannam bauddhameva ca/
Mayaiva kathitaṁ Devi, Kalau Brāḥmaṇa-rūpine//
Vedārthaṁ mohaśāstram māyāvādam svaidikam/"

(Nakamura, *op.cit.*, p.125)

REFERENCES

1. This is the estimate of S.K. Belvalkar on the basis of the *Catalogus catalogorum* of Aufrecht, the Trienneal Reports and the Descriptive catalogues of the Govt. Oriental Library, Madras, the collected editions of Śaṅkara's works from Mysore, Srirangam, Poona etc. (*Shree Gopal Basu Mallik Lectures on Vedanta*, Poona, 1929, p. 217). M.M. Gopinatha Kaviraj refers to two hundred such works (*Bhumika*, Introduction to *B.S. Bhasya-Ratnaprabhā*, Hindi, Acyuta-grantha-mala, Kasi, p. 24). Of these the number of authentic works is generally considered to be limited e.g., Tangaswami lists 112 works among these (*A Bibliographical Survey of Advaita Vedanta Literature*, 1980, pp. 214-27). The *Samata* edition in ten volumes includes 118 works including small tracts and hymns. Cf. K. Potter (ed) *Encyclopaedia of Indian Philosophy*, Vol. III.
2. Cf. Hajime Nakamura, *History of Vedanta*, Vol. I, pp. 75 ff.
3. Belvalkar, *op.cit.*, p.240.
4. T.S. Narayana Shastri, *The Age of Sankara* (Madras 1916, 1971, 1980).
5. C.N. Krishnasvami Iyer, *Sankaracarya—His Life and Times*, (G.A. Natesaṅ, Madras).
6. N.K. Venkatesan, *Sankaracarya and His Kamakotipitha* (Kumbhakonam, 1915).
7. K.T. Telang, *Sankaracarya, Philosopher and Mystic* (Adyar, 1911).
8. S.S. Suryanarayana Sastri, *Sankaracarya* (G.A. Natesan, Madras).
9. N. Venkataraman, *Sankaracarya the Great and His Successors in Kanchi* (Madras, 1923).
10. Bhasyacharya, *Age of Sankara* (Adyar Library Series).
11. N. Ramesan, *Sri Sankaracarya* (Ponnur, 1959).
12. Rajendra Nath Ghosh, *Acarya Sankara of Ramanuja* (Referred to by Kaviraj).
13. Baldeva Upadhyaya, *Sri Sankaracarya* (Allahabad, 1963).
14. Tapasyananda, Introduction to his English Tr. of *Sankara-digvijaya.*
15. T.M.P. Mahadevan, *Adishankara—His Life and Times* (National Book Trust, 1960).
16. K.G. Nateshan Shastri, *Sri Sankaracarya* (Tiruchirapalli 1980).
17. Cf. Saradananda, *Sri Sri Ramakrishna Lila-Prasanga*, Vol. I, pp. 1-11; Cf. Butterfield, *Christianity and History*, on Providence in History as a kind of Master Director of the orchestra.
18. Cf. Rāja-Cūḍāmaṇi Dīkṣita, *Śaṅkarābhyudya*, 2.58-60, *Ibid.*, 3.24-34; Vyāsācala, *Śaṅkara-vijaya*, 7.71, B. Upadhyaya, *op.cit.*, p. 10, Antarkar, *Sahyādri*, Jan. 1967, p. 23, Rajgopal Sharma, *Jagadguru-Śaṅkara-matha-Vimarsa*, p.101.
19. T.S. Narayan Sastri, *op.cit.*, pp. 224-26; W.R. Antarkar, *op.cit.*, (Published in

parts); Antarkar, *Sahyadri*, Dec. 1966, pp. 3-4, *JUB*, Sept. 1960, XXIX (NS) pt. 2, pp. 113-19.

20. Rajgopal Sharma *op.cit.*, p.185, so also Dr. Antarkar about Kanchi Matha- *JUB*, 1960, p.114.
21. T.S. Narayana Shastri, *op.cit.*, p.265.
22. *Ibid.*, p.228.
23. Antarkar, *op.cit.*, p.119.
24. CF. Winternitz, *History of Indian literature*, Vol. I pp. 570-71.
25. *Ibid.*, pp. 535-36.
26. Winternitz, *op.cit.*, p.567.
27. Cf. Anantānandagiri, *Śaṅkara-Vijayam*, ed. N. Veezhinathan 1971, Preface, p. iv.
28. Cf. Rajgopal Sharma, *op.cit.*, pp. 123-25.
29. *RMS* (Madras, 1962), App. pp. 127-33.
30. N. Bhasyacharya, *op.cit.*, p. 10.
31. S.S. Suryanarayana Shastri, *Life and Teaching of Sankaracarya*, pp. 4-5.
32. T.S. Narayana Sastri, *op.cit.*, pp. 155 ff.
33. Baldeva Upadhyaya, *op.cit.*, pp. 14-16.
34. Tapasyananda (Tr.) *Śaṅkara-digvijaya*, pp. ix-xiv; Rajgopal Sharma, *Srimajjagadguru-Śaṅkara-maṭha-vimarśa* pp. 185-215.
35. Antarkar, Reprint, *JUB*, Arts no. Vol. XII, no. 77, Nov. 1972, p. 5.
36. Cf. Rajgopal Sharma, *op.cit.*, pp. 198 ff.
37. T. Chandrasekharan (ed.), *Śaṅkara Vijaya* by Vyāsācala, pp. 1-2, Narayana Sastri, *op.cit.*, pp. 230-31.
38. *Ibid.*, pp. 198-99. The identity of *Mādhavīya* and the original *Vyāsācalīya* comes but strikingly from the fact that according to Ātmabodha the description of Śaṅkara's meeting with the *caṇḍāla* may be seen in detail from *Vyāsācalīya*. Now the verse quoted and the details occur in the *Mādhavīya* rather than the present *Vyāsācalīya*.
39. Antankar, *JUB*, Sept: 1961, p. 74; cf. N. Veezhinathan (ed.), *Śaṅkara-Vijaya* of Anantānandagiri, Intr., p. iii.
40. Cf. Veezinathan (ed.), *op.cit.*, pp. 147-98.
41. Venkata Raman, *op.cit.*, pp. 6-7.
42. In *Bharatiya Vidya*, 1973.
43. *Ibid.*, Introduction.
44. The enumeration may be seen in *JSV*, pp. 202-203.
45. Ed. S.V. Radhakrishna Shastri, 1986.
46. Antarkar, Intr. to his edn. of *TDSA*, p. 139.
47. Ed. N.R. Antarkar, *JUB*, 1965.
48. Baldeva Upadhyaya, *op.cit.*, pp. 207-208; Udayavira Sastri, *Vedānta Darsana Ka Itihas* (1970), p.326.
49. Udayavira Shastri, *op.cit.*, l.c.
50. The text was edited by Kak and Shastri in 1941 from Kashmir. It has been reprinted from Varanasi in 1986. The work has been dated in the 11th century. The work describes the worship of Śrīvidyā and draws on earlier works. The author mentions the list of teachers and the circumstances under which it was composed—Vol. I, pp. 3-4.

2

The Date of Śaṅkara

The date of Śaṅkara has been discussed now for over a century by scholars. Although the views of historians have tended to narrow down the extent of controversy to within two centuries now, it cannot be said that the dispute has been finally settled. In particular it is worth noting that the traditional date or dates upheld by most of the Śaṅkarite monasteries even today widely diverge from the critical scholarly opinions which are not unanimous. It would, therefore, not be out of place to begin by examining the traditional view.

The traditional view is argued most forcefully by the proponents of the Kāñcī Maṭha tradition.[1] They argue that Śaṅkara lived from 508 B.C. to 476 B.C. The basis of their argument is twofold. In the first place they rely on the dates given in the *Bṛhacchaṅkara-Vijaya, Prācīna-Śaṅkara-Vijaya, Puṇya-Śloka-Mañjarī, Jagadguru-Ratnamālā* and Ātmabodha's commentary called *Suṣamā.* In the *Bṛhacchaṅkara-Vijaya* it is stated that Śaṅkara was born in the thirty-first year after 26 centuries of the Yudhiṣṭhira era had elapsed. It was the cyclic year Nandana, the month of 'Vaiśākha', the fifth lunar day of the bright fortnight and a Sunday.[2] The *Prācīna-Śaṅkara-Vijaya* as quoted by Ātmabodha says that Śaṅkara was born in the year Nandana when 2593 years of *Kali* era had gone by.[3] The *Puṇya-Śloka-Mañjarī* states that Śaṅkara died at the age of 32 in the *Kali* year 2625.[4] It was the year called *Raktākshī* and the *tithi* was the bright *Ekādaśī.*

The epoch of the *Kali* era has been determined to be 3102 B.C.[5] The Yudhiṣṭhira era began from the coronation of Yudhiṣṭhira which took place 37 years before the beginning of *Kali* i.e. to say in 3139 B.C. As a result the dates mentioned in these texts come to mean that Śaṅkara lived from 508 B.C. to 476 B.C. In confirmation of this the evidence of a Jaina text called *Jinavijaya* has also been adduced. It is said that according to *Jinavijaya* Śaṅkara died in the year 2157 of the Yudhiṣṭhira era.[6] Now the Yudhiṣṭhira era of the Jainas is said to be counted from 2624 B.C. and is later than the standard Yudhiṣṭhira era by 505 years. This gives the date of Śaṅkara's death as 474 B.C. That the same year is meant here as in the *Puṇya-Śloka Mañjarī* is clear from the fact that the Jaina text also designates the cyclic year as *Tāmrākshī.*

The tradition of the Śāradā Pīṭha at Dvārkā holds that Śaṅkara was born in the year 2631 of the Yudhiṣṭhira era on the fifth bright *tithi* of 'Vaiśākha' and died in the year 2663 of the same era on the full moon day of 'Kārtika'. This is said to be based on the traditional horoscope of *Guruvaṁśāvalī* in the Śāradā Pīṭha. According to another version the dates in the Dvārkā Śāradā Piṭha chronology are in the *Kali* era, with the result that there is a slight difference in the Kāñcī and Dvārkā traditions.[7] The tradition of the monastery of Puri is said to be similar to these two traditions.

The semi-Purāṇic text *Śīva Rahasya* has also been quoted in support of these traditions as the text states that the birth of Śaṅkara took place in the 3rd millennium of *Kali.*[8] The so-called copper-plate of king Sudhanvan has also been adduced as evidence. This copper-plate is supposed to have been issued in the year 2663 of the Yudhiṣṭhira era.[9] Another kind of evidence brought forward consists of the succession lists of the monastic heads. The Kāñcī Maṭha adduces the list of 66 pontiffs following Sureśvarācārya.[10] For each one of these, it is claimed, that tradition records their relevant cyclic year, month, *tithi* and the duration of headship. For some of them the year is specified in some known era which allows a complete chronological table of succession of the monastic heads from Śaṅkara to today. However, it gives for 11 *ācāryas* from Savajñātman to Saccidghana a period of 748 years with an impossible average of 68 years. Even for 53 *ācāryas* from Vidyāghana I to Candrasekhara VI occupying a period of 1636 years, the average of 30 years is too long. One cannot, therefore, avoid the impression that the actual period has been mistakenly expanded at least for the earlier period. Similarly the Śāradā Pīṭha of Dvārkā has a list of 76 pontiffs, which as explained before gives impossible averages. The list of Govardhana Pīṭha has an unusually large number of 142 successive heads explained on the basis of their adopting *sannyāsa* after *gārhasthya.*[11] Compared to these the lists of Jyotiṣ Pīṭha and Śṛṅgerī are much shorter. In the case of the former there is an acknowledged gap of four centuries. In the case of Śṛṅgerī there are only thirty-five names but Sureśvara is ascribed about 700 years.

This seems to be the result of the gap created by dating Śaṅkara in the 1st century B.C. on the assumption that the 14th year of Vikramaditya referred to the so-called Vikrama era, a view now given up by the spokesmen of Śṛṅgerī. The Kāñcī tradition postulates an interruption of eight centuries in the succession at Śṛṅgerī to explain it. The Śṛṅgerī Maṭha, however, not only repudiates the claims of Kāñcī but also the chronology more or less accepted by the other *maṭhas.*[12]

This monastic chronology which places Śaṅkara in the 6th and 5th centuries B.C., hardly needs detailed refutation because it contradicts the entire chronology of ancient India as determined by scientific history. It tends to make Śaṅkara a contemporary of Buddha whereas Śaṅkara, Kumārila and Sureśvara are clearly posterior to Dignāga and at least Sureśvara is clearly posterior to Dharmakīrti also. The chronology errs by antedating Śaṅkara by more than a millennium. The protagonists of this chronology argue that the title of Śaṅkarācārya was adopted by all the successive heads of the monasteries established by the founder and that there were a number of pontiffs who not only bore the general title of Śaṅkarācārya but who had also a remarkably similar career. In particular there was a 'recent' or Abhinava Śaṅkara who lived from A.D. 788 to A.D. 812. The Kāñcī tradition thus records five Śaṅkaras—Ādi, Kṛpā, Ujjwala, Mūka, and Abhinava: It is this last Śaṅkara who is said to be confused by modern historians with the original or Ādi Śaṅkara. The modern historian, on the other hand, cannot help feeling that this multiplication of Śaṅkaras and of other monastic pontiffs is only the consequence of the artificial gap created by an antedated chronology. The traditionist defence in terms of a differentiation of Abhinava from Ādi Śaṅkara will not really hold water because by Ādi Śaṅkara the historian means none else but the person who was the author of the *Brahmasūtrabhāṣya,* not some one who might have been known as 'Śaṅkarācārya' and lived about the same time. The historian has a precise characteristic for identifying Śaṅkara and that characteristic cannot belong to anyone who lived much before the 7th century A.D.

As for the traditional succession lists of monastic heads, there is little evidence of their authenticity beyond the earlier medieval period. This tradition seems to have arisen in the 14th and 15th centuries and has hardly any credibility for an earlier period far removed from it. The lists as they are, appear to contain confusions due to repetitions, omissions, and fictitious elaborations. As shown earlier where the lists are long they give unrealistic averages. As is well known in the case of ancient lists of kings and sages, such lists cannot be the independent basis of reliable chronological conclusions.

As for the dates of the Kali and Yudhiṣṭhira eras to be found in the *Bṛhat-* and *Prācīna-Śaṅkara-Vijaya* they only raise a problem—how are these impossible dates to be explained. Perhaps they were based on the mythical connection of Gauḍapāda and Patañjali and some lost tradition about the age of Patañjali. It is possible that when the virtually lost tradition of the *Mahābhāṣya* was revived by Bhartṛhari in the 5th century there could have been a tradition that Patañjali flourished a millennium back. In the light of this the memorial lunar birth data of Śaṅkara were perhaps sought to be fitted into some Kali or Yudhiṣṭhira era. This could only have been done a few centuries after Śaṅkara. It may be recalled that these eras were certainly not commonly used in the earlier period, that they owed their origin to astronomical hypotheses and varying calculations in the post-Classical period, and that, as may be seen from Kalhaṇa and Jain records there were differences about the beginning of the Yudhiṣṭhira era.[13] Al-beruni mentions the Kali and Pāṇḍava eras but says they were not commonly used.[14] The earliest epigraphic use of the Kali era is in fact to be found in the 7th century in the celebrated Aihole inscription. The fact is that the earlier practice was to record dates in terms of *tithi* and cyclic years. The use of fixed eras appears to have been inspired by the Indo-Greeks and the earliest Indian eras to be used were the Mālava and Śaka eras. As for the 'quotes' from *Jinavijaya* some concrete details are needed to specify its existence or whereabouts.

In this connection the tradition of the Śṛṅgerī Maṭha deserves consideration. It has been said that some palm-leaf manuscripts in the monastery dating from the 17th century and claiming to be copied from an original of the 15th century recorded a verse in which Śaṅkara was said to have been born in the 14th year of king Vikramāditya.[15] It has been suggested that this Vikramāditya could be the Badami-Cālukya Vikramāditya I son of Pulakesin II, who ascended the throne in A.D. 654-55. This would give Śaṅkara's dates as A.D. 668-700. It may be recalled, however, that Kalhaṇa speaks even of Harṣa Vikramāditya, which appears a later confusion.[16] There was also a Cālukya Vikramāditya II who ascended the throne about A.D. 733.[17] Although the Śṛṅgerī tradition is too vague to enable us to determine the precise date of Śaṅkara, it cannot be ruled out on the grounds of general historical improbability. On the other hand, it gives a plausible date for Śaṅkara. It is worth noting that this reasonable tradition eschews the mythical Kali era.

We may now turn to the view most popular among historians, viz., that Śaṅkara lived from A.D. 788 to A.D. 820. K.B. Pathak had argued for it on the basis of the evidence of a manuscript of three pages which he discovered in Belgaum. Its colophon states that the giver of salvation directly incarnated himself as Śaṅkarācārya on earth for the destruction of evil conduct. The rise of Śaṅkara took place in the year called Vibhava which was in the Kali year 3889. At the age of eight he studied the four Vedas; at twelve he was the author of all the *Śāstras*; at sixteen he composed the great commentary; at thirty-two the sage went away. In the Kali year 3921 was his entry into the Cave. On the full moon day of 'Vaiśākha' Śaṅkara attained to Śivahood.[18] This gives Śaṅkara's dates of birth and death precisely as equivalent to A.D. 788 and A.D. 820. Some other works also give a similar date. They are Nilakantha Bhatta's *Śaṅkara-mandāra-saurabha* and *Śaṅkarābhyudaya*,[19] Kṛṣṇabrahmānanda's *Śaṅkaravijaya*,[20] and *Āryavidyā-Sudhākara* of Yajñeśvara *Cimana*.[21]

The precision of these dates and their general agreement with probability has given great credibility to this view. Unfortunately, none of the texts which give these dates can be earlier than the 16th century. They cannot claim greater antiquity or authority than the other group of texts mentioned earlier. Whether these later dates are consistent with other known facts about Śaṅkara, has been debated. Thus Belvalkar has attempted to defend K.B. Pathak's view against several criticisms.[22] The brunt of these criticisms is that by placing Śaṅkara between 788 and 820 the gap between Gauḍapāda, Kumārila, and Maṇḍana, on the one hand, and Śaṅkara on the other becomes too great to permit any direct contact between them. At the same time, on the other hand, the gap between Śaṅkara and Vācaspati Miśra becomes too narrow to permit the interposition of Sureśvara, Padmapāda and Bhāskara between them.

Some of Śaṅkara's traditional biographies assert that although Gauḍapāda was the teacher of Śaṅkara's teacher and a Yogī of many years he was still alive to meet his grand pupil. While this could be doubted as a legendary exaggeration, a curious bit of evidence has been pointed out recently.[23] It consists of a passage in the *Chāndogyabhāṣya* which could be taken to suggest that

Gauḍapāda was still alive when Śaṅkara was writing.[24] Even if this is explained away somehow, it would still be unreasonable to suppose that the gap between Śaṅkara and Gauḍapāda was of more than half a century. Now Gauḍapāda is reputed to have been the author of *Sāṁkhya Kārikābhāṣya* which was translated into Chinese by Paramārtha between A.D. 546 and 569. It has also been argued by Walleser that Gauḍapāda was prior to Bhāvaviveka who appears to quote *Āgamaśāstra* (3.5) in his *Tarkajvālā* (8.13).[25] Now Bhāvaviveka was a senior contemporary of Dharmapāla and is generally placed between A.D. 490 and 570.[26] This would preclude Gauḍapāda from being later than the first half of the 6th century. If Gauḍapāda is to be placed between A.D. 500 and 550, it would not do to place Śaṅkara almost two centuries or more after him.

However, these arguments are far from being conclusive. Whether the Gauḍapāda of the *Śāṅkhya Kārikābhāṣya* is the famous Vedāntin of that name could be reasonably doubted. Nor can it be said that Bhāvaviveka 'quotes' Gauḍapāda even though he has some verses of which one is especially close to those of Gauḍapāda. *Āgamaśāstra* (3.5) and *Tarkajvālā* (8.13) could well be an older verse as Vijñāna Bhikṣu refers a similar verse to *Viṣṇupurāṇa* even though it is not available there. The verse in *AS'* is = *Yathaikasmin ghaṭākāśe rajodhūmādibhiryute / Na sarve samprayujyante tadvajjīvāḥ sukhādibhiḥ'* // Its idea is a fairly common idea.

The cases of Kumārila and Maṇḍana, however, are on a different footing and present real difficulties. Kumārila has been quoted by Śāntarakṣita in the *Tattvasaṅgraha* and a variety of facts from Tibetan sources attest to Śāntarakṣita having lived in the first half of the 8th century.[27] Since Kumārila is generally supposed to be familiar with Dharmakīrti he will have to be placed in the middle of the second half of the 7th century at the latest (Kaviraj, *op.cit.*, p. 27). However, it has to be remembered, as pointed out by Udayavira Sastri, that in his discussion of *Pratyakṣa* Kumārila seems to presuppose Dignāga rather than Dharmakīrti since he has in mind *Pratyakṣa* as *Kalpanābodha,* not as *abhrānta.* Commentators like Pārthasārathi Miśra, however, identify the *Pūrvapakṣa* with Dharmakīrti's (on Kumārila and Dignāga, see *IHQ, I,* pp. 603 ff). If Śaṅkara was born in A.D. 788 he would be about a century removed from Kumārila, which contradicts the unanimous belief of all the legendary biographies of Śaṅkara that he was a junior contemporary of Kumārila.

Now Maṇḍana has been regarded as a disciple of Kumārila and a contemporary and later disciple of Śaṅkara. This too would become virtually impossible if there is a gap of a century between Kumārila and Śaṅkara. Even if the equation of Maṇḍana and Sureśvara is rejected, the difficulty still remains concerning the contemporaneity of Viśvarūpa or some other disciple of Kumārila who became a disciple of Śaṅkara as Sureśvara.

Another argument used in this connection has been that Umveka was one of the disciples of Kumārila and that Umveka was identical with Bhavabhūti who was patronised by king Yaśovarman of Kannauj.[28] This would tend to place Bhavabhūti or Umveka in the first half of the 8th century. It has to be granted, however, that while suggestive, this argument cannot be said to be conclusive because the equation of Bhavabhūti and Umveka is not beyond dispute.

On the other side, it has been argued that Vācaspati Miśra, one of whose works is dated in A.D. 841 is clearly aware of the writings of Padmapāda, Sureśvara and Bhāskara who presuppose Śaṅkara. If Śaṅkara died in A.D. 820 the interval between him and Vācaspati will be too narrow to interpolate these three authors between them.

Belvalkar has tried to answer the question by saying that the interval is sufficient as far as the interposition of Padmapāda between Śaṅkara and Vācaspati is concerned. As for Bhāskara he doubts that there is sufficient evidence for placing him earlier than Vācaspati on the ground that the alleged citation in *Bhāmatī* from the *Bhāskara Bhāṣya* is itself a quotation in the latter work. This argument of Dr. Belvalkar, however, is not cogent because the basis for regarding Vācaspati later than Bhāskara is not confined to the citation of a stanza. It has been pointed out that there are several passages in *Bhāmatī* in which the views of Bhāskara have been rejected.[29] Bhāskara, moreover, has been attacked by the great Jain logician Prabhācandra who lived *c.* A.D. 800. This line of argument clearly militates against placing Śaṅkara between A.D. 788 and 820. A consideration of the date of Sureśvara, too, would strengthen this line of argument. Sureśvara is known to have been quoted by the Jain scholar Vidyānanda in the *Ashṭasāhasrī*. Vidyānanda is in turn referred to by Jinasena and is presupposed by Prabhācandra. The writings of Jinasena covered the years from A.D. 783 to A.D. 833. The priority of Vidyānanda to both Jinasena and Prabhācandra suggests that Vidyānanda should be placed in the second half of the 8th century. Sureśvara, thus, even if he were a contemporary of

Vidyānanda for some time, as supposed by Belvalkar, would still have to be credited with having composed the *Bṛhadāraṇyakavārtika* at least by the date which is being attributed to Śaṅkara for his birth.

Whether Hastāmalaka is believed to have been the son of Prabhākara and whether Prabhākara was the disciple or predecessor of Kumārila, does not substantially alter the situation. The dating proposed by Prof. K.B. Pathak does create too great a gap between Kumārila and Śaṅkara and too narrow a gap between Śaṅkara and Vācaspati. As for Prof. Belvalkar's argument that Kumārila presupposes Akalaṅka who should be placed in the 8th century, it has to be remembered that the dating of Akalaṅka is not at all certain (cf. Nemi Chandra Jain, *Tirthankara Mahavira Aur Unki Acharya Prampara,* Vol. II pp. 304-5).

By the side of the popular view discussed above there are several others which seek to place Śaṅkara in the 9th century or the 7th century. Nilakantha Shastri thus referred to an inscription from Cambodia, in which Śivasoma, the preceptor of Indravarman, the ruler of Campā, claims to have studied the *Śāstras* from Bhagavad Śaṅkara. (*JOR*, Vol. XI, 1937, p. 285) Now Indravarman ruled between A.D. 878 and 889 and Śivasoma himself was the grandson of the maternal uncle of Jayavarman II who belonged to A.D. 802 to 869. Śivasoma thus could hardly have studied in India earlier than the 9th century; nor could Śaṅkara be much earlier. The identification of Bhagavad Śaṅkara with Śankarācārya is, however, not established beyond doubt. In fact, since he is called '*Bhagavacchāṅkarāhvaya*' he could have been a successor to the great Śaṅkara. It is possible that Śivasoma served as pupil to some celebrated direct disciple of Śaṅkara and glorified the occasion duly by describing the teacher as one who was 'called Bhagavat Śaṅkara' (cf. my paper in *Prācya-Pratibhā*, South-east Asia number, 1991-92).

On the other hand, Rajendra Nath Ghosh has eloquently argued for the 7th century as the time when Śaṅkara was born. He relies on a quotation in a work called *Darśana-Prakāśa* belonging to the Mahānubhāva sect. This quotation is from a lost earlier work called *Śankarapaddhati* and declares that Śaṅkara died in the Śaka year 642.[30] This corresponds to the year A.D. 720 and gives Śaṅkara's date of birth as A.D. 688. Ghosh, however, aruged that the actual birth of Śaṅkara should be placed in the year A.D. 686 on astrological grounds. The whole argument depends on a quotation from a lost work of which the nature and authenticity are unknown. Nevertheless the view places Śaṅkara in a plausible time bracket. Much less probable is the view of the *Keralotpatti* which places Śaṅkara's birth in A.D. 400.[31]

Several scholars have tried to determine the date of Śaṅkara by considering a date of the ruler in whose time Sarvajñātman Muni composed the famous work *Saṁkṣepa-Śārīraka*. Since Sarvajñātman was a pupil of Sureśvara who was the direct disciple of Śaṅkara, the date of Sarvajñātman would give a fair indication of that of Śaṅkara. Now according to Sarvajñātman, his work was written while the ruler Manu-Kulāditya was still ruling: *Srīmatyakṣata-śāsane manu-kulāditye bhuvam śāsati.*[32] R.G. Bhandarkar surmised that this ruler could be either Vikramāditya I who reigned until A.D. 679 or Vikramāditya II who reigned until A.D. 747 both belonging to the Cālukya dynasty.[33] This would place Śaṅkara about the beginning or the end of the 7th century. Unfortunately neither is the reference to the dynasty clear nor is the proposed identification of the ruler indisputable.[34] However, if Śaṅkara were born in the years after the accession of Vikramāditya I, Sarvajñātman could have lived in the times of Vikramāditya II.

Again, Telang sought to identify the ruler Pūrṇavarman whom Śaṅkara mentions with the ruler of the same name mentioned by Hsuan Tsang.[35] Śaṅkara would thus be earlier than the middle of the 7th century A.D. Unfortunately the reference need not have been to a ruler contemporary or near contemporary of Śaṅkara. Recently Prof. V.S. Pathak has aruged that the context of the reference suggests that the coronation of Pūrṇavarman should have been a real or historical event. This would place Śaṅkara not earlier than A.D. 625.

Following a similar line of thought Dr. D.R. Bhandarkar identified the Balavarman mentioned by Śaṅkara with a person of the same name seen in an inscription of the Rāṣṭrakūṭa ruler Govinda III of the late 8th century.[36] This too has the same defect as the opinion of Telang cited before.[37]

It seems clear that the date of Śaṅkara cannot be fixed either in terms of the dates mentioned in different literary works which belong to much later times or on the basis of any definite historical synchronisms in the context of political history. The only fruitful method is to consider the dates of other authors and philosophers of whom Śaṅkara makes use or who make use of him.

There is clear evidence that Śaṅkara presupposes Gauḍapāda.

Dharmakīrti and Kumārila. On the other hand, Śaṅkara is clearly presupposed by Sureśvara, Bhāskara and Vācaspati Miśra. The last of these is the author of the famous commentary *Bhāmatī* on the *Śarīrakabhāṣya* of Śaṅkara and in this commentary Vācaspati clearly criticises some interpretations of Sureśvara who commented on Śaṅkara. Vācaspati also criticises Bhāskara who in turn criticises Śaṅkara.[38] Now Vācaspati wrote his *Nyāyasūcī-nibandha* in the year corresponding to A.D. 841. Since Sureśvara and Bhāskara thus lie between Vācaspati and Śaṅkara, the latter could not have lived later than the 8th century in any case. Sureśvara is quoted by Vidyānanda in his *Aṣṭasāhasrī*, a commentary on Samantabhadra's *Āptamīmāṁsā*.[39] Vidyānanda is referred to by Jinasena in the *Ādipurāṇa* which was written in A.D. 838.[40] Although his *Harivaṁśa Purāṇa* was written in A.D. 783. Jinasena also refers to Prabhācandra whose *Prameya-Kamalamārtaṇḍa* seems later than the *Aṣṭasāhasrī* of Vidyānanda. Vidyānanda, thus could hardly be later than A.D. 800 and Sureśvara would belong at the latest to the second half of the century. Śaṅkara should not then be placed much after the middle of the 8th century at the latest.

On the other hand, Śaṅkara clearly quotes from Dharmakīrti.[41] Now Hsuan Tsang is silent about Dharmakīrti in A.D. 634 while I-tsing records the fame of Dharmakīrti in 673.[42] The major period of Dharmakīrti then must have been about the middle of the 7th century. Again, while Kumārila probably presupposes Dharmakīrti he is certainly presupposed by Śānkarakṣita who belonged to the first half of the 8th century. Kumārila, thus, could not be later than the second half of the 7th century and since Śaṅkara seems to criticise Kumārila[43] and is generally regarded as his junior contemporary he should be placed at the earliest towards the end of the 7th and the beginning of the 8th century. This would agree with the tradition recorded in *Darśana-Prakāśa* and at Śṛṅgerī.

To sum up, in determining the date of Śaṅkara the following data need to the taken into account:

- (a) Śaṅkara was the grand-disciple of Gauḍapāda.
- (b) Śaṅkara was later than Dharmakīrti.
- (c) Śaṅkara was the junior contemporary of Kumārila.
- (d) Śaṅkara was the contemporary of Maṇḍana and Sureśvara who survived him.
- (e) Śaṅkara was earlier than Bhāskara.
- (f) Śaṅkara belonged to an age when there was no paramount sovereign.

Now the date of Gauḍapāda is not certain. From his indebtedness to Mahāyānic texts and Masters like *Laṅkāvatāra*, Nāgārjuna, Asaṅga and Vasubandhu, and from a probable quotation from him by Bhavya, he would appear to have lived between A.D. 500 and 600. Since it is not certain if Śaṅkara had any living contact with him and since Yogins like Vidyātīrtha, Tailanaga Svami or Devraha Baba may be exceptionally long-lived, the consideration of the possible date of Gauḍapāda does not help decide that of Śaṅkara except that it tends to support his date in the 7th century than in late 8th century.

Dharmakīrti has been placed about the middle of the 7th century on the ground of his non-mention by Hsuan Tsang and his mention by I-tsing.[44] This is a good reason but not wholly decisive since one cannot eliminate all possible causes of non-mention.[45] When Hsuan Tsang reached Nālandā in A.D. 637, Śīlabhadra was the abbot and his Master Dharmapāla had died many years ago. According to Tibetan tradition as a young man Dharmakīrti had met Dharmapāla who had directed him to Īśvarasena. It is Īśvarasena from whom Dharmakīrti studied the system of Dignāga. Now Dharmapāla and Īśvarasena are said to have been students of Dignāga, who was the student of Vasubandhu. Unfortunately the date of Vasubandhu has been a matter of much controversy. He has been placed in the 4th century as also in the 5th. Even two Vasubandhus have been postulated.[46] Hirakawa's opinion that there was only one Vasubandhu, that he was the contemporary of Skandagupta Vikramāditya and Narasinhagupta Baladitya, and that Vasubandhu may thus be placed between A.D. 400 and 480, appears the most plausible.[47] Dignāga then could be placed between A.D. 480 and 540. Dharmapāla and Īśvarasena would be datable in the later half of the 6th century and Dharmakīrti's dates would be approximately 580-650. On account of the difficult style of his writings and his Bhavabhūti-like response to his critics it is possible that it took time for his appreciation to grow but once begun it increased rapidly. This would account for Hsuan Tsang's failure to mention him.

Thus Śaṅkara's quoting from Dharmakīrti makes him not earlier than *c.* 650 and would agree with Śaṅkara's being a junior contemporary of Kumārila who appears to have been more or less a contemporary of Dharmakīrti. It has been said that Kumārila criticised Dharmakīrti and Akalaṅka.[48] What is definite is that Kumārila criticises Dignāga, Maṇḍana criticises Dharmakīrti and Akalaṅka's students criticise Kumārila. Besides Śāntarakṣita quotes from Kumārila and Śāntarakṣita has been placed in 680-740.[49] Kumārila could thus be placed in 600-670.

Thus 650 would appear to be the *terminus a quo* for Śaṅkara. The *terminus ad quem* is provided by the possible dates of Maṇḍana, Sureśvara and Padmapāda. Maṇḍana has been commented upon by Uṁveka who is quoted by Kamalaśīla.[50] Kamalaśīla has been placed in A.D. 700-750.[51] Even if Maṇḍana was not Sureśvara, he (Maṇḍana) was, despite opinions to the contrary, aware of Śaṅkara whose opinion he criticises in his *Brahmasiddhi*.[52] Thus Maṇḍana could be placed in A.D. 650-720. Sureśvara has been quoted by Vidyānanda who is referred to by Jinasena whose literary activity extended from 783 to 838. Similarly *Bhāmatī* refers to some views of Padmapāda and the author of *Bhāmatī* wrote the *Nyāyasūcī-nibandha* in A.D. 841. Thus the works of Śaṅkara's students appear to have become well known by the beginning of the 9th century. That Bhāskara criticises Śaṅkara and Vācaspati Miśra criticises Bhāskara also supports the belief that the literary activities of Śaṅkara's first generation supporters and critics could not be later than the second half of the 8th century. Thus we could regard *c.* 775 as the *terminus ad quem* for Śaṅkara.

The dates of Śaṅkara could, thus, range between 650 and 775. If we accept the unanimous tradition of Śaṅkara's meeting with Kumārila while the latter was dying, and his contemporaneity with Maṇḍana, whether Sureśvara or not, Śaṅkara would have to be placed between 650 and 700. This would agree with the date in *Darśanaprakāśa* and the Śṛṅgerī tradition.

REFERENCES

1. E.g., T.S. Narayana Sastri, *Age of Sankara* (2nd edn.) pp. 223 ff; H.H. Jagadguru Sri Candrasekharendra Sarasvati, *Adi Sankara—His Life and Times*, (Bombay, 1988), pp. 108 ff; N. Venkataramana, *Sankaracarya the Great and His Successors in Kanchi* (1923).
2. "*Ṣaḍviṁśe śatake Śrīmad Yaudhisthira-śakasya vai Ekatriṁśé thavarṣe tu hāyane nandane śubhe Meṣa-rāśiṁ gate sūrye vaiśākhe māsi śobhane Śuklapakṣe ca pañcamyāṁ tithyāṁ bhāskara-vāsare*"

It should be noted that *Bṛhacchaṅkaravijaya* is no longer available although T.S. Narayana Sastri, *op.cit.*, declared that he possessed a mutilated copy of the work. Ātmabodha too quotes profusely from the work. These verses are said to be from the 22nd *prakaraṇa* of the second section (*Śaṅkarācārya-satpatha*) of the *Bṛhat.* At another place, the same text says, "*Vahnyabda-śāstra nayanāṅka-Yudhisthirābde Dvātrinśatam hi śarade dharanim vibhūṣya* /" (quoted T.S. Narayana Sastri, *op.cit.*, p.226).

3. "*Tiṣye prayātyanala-śevadhi-bāṇa-netre (2593) yo nandane dinamaṇāvudagadhvabhāji/Rādhe diteruduni nirgatam aṅga-lagne 'pyāhūtavān- śiyaguruḥ sa ca Śaṅkareti//*" (*Suṣamā* quotes ad *Gururatnamala*, (17).
Kalyabdaiśca śare kṣarādhva-nayanaiḥ... dhā ma prapede param//" (quoted, Narayana Sastri, *op.cit.*, p.227)
4. "*Maheśāṁśājjāto madhuramupadiṣṭādvaya-nayomahāmohadhvānta-praśamana-raviḥ ṣaṇmata-guruḥ/Phale* (32) *svasmin svāyuṣyapi śara-carābde pi* (2625) *cakaleḥ vililye raktāṣiṇyadhi-vṛṣa-sitaikādaśi pare//*" (*Puṇyaślokamañjarī*, verse 4)
5. Thus *Al-biruni's India* (ed. Sachau), Vol. II, p.4
6. "*Rsir bāṇas tathā bhumih martyākṣau vāma-melanāt Ekatvena labhetānkah tamrākṣastatra vatsaraḥ//*" (Narayana Sastri quotes it from *Sanskrita-Candrikā*, Vol. IX nos. I-III 6, Sastri, *op.cit.*, p.233).
7. On the Dvārkā tradition see Govindadasa's article in the *Theosophist*, Vol. *XVI*, nos. 3, 5.
8. "*Kalyādime mahādevi sahasra-dvitayāt param*" (*Śivarahasya*, Aṁśa IX, Ch. XVI. Stanza 8). Cf. Venkatesa Iyer, '*Sri Sankaracarya and His Kamakoti Pitha*', T.S. Narayana Sastri, *op.cit.*, pp. 266-67.
9. T.S. Narayana Sastri, *op.cit.*, pp. 220-21.
10. *Ibid.*, pp. 195-97; Venkataraman, *op.cit.*, pp. 10 ff.
11. Udayavira Shastri has compiled these lists in his monograph on the date of Śaṅkara in English and his earlier work in Hindi quoted above. Baladeva Upadhyaya *Sri Sankaracarya*, pp. 190 ff., also gives these lists.
12. Cf. R.K. Aiyar and K.R. Venkataraman, *The Truth About the Kumbhakonam Mutt*, (1977), pp. 82 ff.
13. Cf. Kalhana, *Rājataraṅginī*, 1.49-56; T.S. Narayana *op.cit.*, p.22.
14. Sachau, *op.cit.*, Vol. II, pp. 1 ff.
15. Cf. Rajgopal Sharma *Srimajjagadguru-Sankaramatha-Vimarsa*, (1963), p.25.
16. Kalhana, *op.cit.*, 3. 125.
17. Nilkantha Sastri, *History of South India* (4th edn.) pp. 151-53.
18. "*Duṣṭācāra-vināśāya prādurbhūto mahītale/*
Sa eva Śaṅkarācāryaḥ Sākṣāt Kaivalya-nāyakaḥ//
Nidhi-nāgebha-vahnyabde (3889) *vibhave Śaṅkarāhvayaḥ/*
Aṣṭavarṣe Caturvedī Dvādaśe sarva-śāstrakṛt/
Śodaṣe krtavān bhāṣyam dvātriṁśe munirabhyagāt//
Kalyabde Candra-netrāṅka-vahnyabde (3921) *guhāpraveśaḥ/*
Vaiśākhe pūrṇimāyām tu Śaṅkaraḥ Śivatām iyāt//
(K.B. Pathak, *I.A.*, 1882, pp. 173-75).
19. *Śaṅkarābhyudaya*, 1.26 - "*Navādhikāśīti Yutāṣṭa - śaktyā Yukte sahasra tritaye vyatīte/*
Kaleḥ samānām vibhavābda-rādhā-site daśamyām udabhut maheśaḥ//"
cf. *Antarkar (ed) Śaṅkarābhyudaya* intr. p.2.
20. "*Nidhi-nāge-bha-vahnyabde vibhave Śaṅkarodayaḥ kalau tu Śālivāhasyasakhendu-śata-saptake//* (quoted, Kaviraj, *op.cit.*, p.26).
21. Cf. H. Nakamura, *A History of Early Vedanta Philosophy*, I. p.49.
22. S.K. Belvalkar, *S.G.B. Mallik Lectures on Vedanta.*
23. S.L. Pandey, *Pre-Samkara Vedanta*, p.30.
24. *Bhāṣya ad Cha VII* 12.1, "Tathānuśāsatyadyāpi ta eva *nānyā iti.*"

25. *Āgamaśāstra*, intr. p.45 according to Nakamura it is *8.12*.
26. Nakamura *op. cit.*, p.183.
27. Nakamura, *op.cit.*, pp. 81-85.
28. *Ibid.*, l.c.
29. Cf. *Ślokavārtika* (Madras), Intr.
30. Cf. Nakamura, *op.cit.*, pp. 68-72.
31. Kaviraj, *op. cit.*
32. *Saṅkṣepa-śārīraka*, 4.62.
33. Cited, Kaviraj, *op. cit.*
34. Cf. Bühler, *IA*. XIV p.64.
35. The reference to Pūrṇavarman occurs in Śaṅkara's Comm. on *BS*, 2.1.18 Cf. Telang, "The Date of Śaṅkarācārya", *IA, XIII*, pp.95 ff. Prof. V.S. Pathak has sought to revive the view recently.
36. The reference to Balavaraman-ad *BS* 2.4.1; 4.3.5. D.R. Bhandarkar, *IA* XII, 1912, p. 200.
37. Cf. *IA*, XIII, pp. 53-55.
38. E.g., vide Amalānanda's Vedanta Kalpataru ad *BSB* 1.2.26.
39. Cf. S.C. Vidyabhusana, *History of Indian Logic*, p. 187 fn. 4.
40. Cf. K.B. Pathak, *JBRAS*, 1894, pp. 227-28.
41. See below : Cf. Nakamura, *op.cit.*, pp. 75 ff. *Upadeśa*, 18, 141 is virtually identical a verse from *PV*, 2.355. The verse is also said to occur in *Pramāṇa-viniścaya*, La Vallé Poussin quoted Nakamura, *op.cit.*
42. *Ibid.*, p.77.
43. *Ibid.*, *Upadeśasāhasrī*, 18.139-41.
44. Taranatha places Dharmakīrti in the reign of king Sronbtsan-sgam-po (617-51), Taranatha, *History of Buddhism*.
45. Cf. Rahul Sankrityayana, *Vāda-nyāya*; intr. p.5.
46. Noel Peri *BEFEO*, XI, 1911; Takakusu, *JRAS*, 1905, Frauwallner, *On the Date of the Buddhist Master of Law Vasubandhu*.
47. Akira Hirakawa, *Index to the Abhidharmakośabhāṣya* (1973) Preface.
48. Belvalkar, *op.cit.*, p.210, Malvania (ed.) *Nyāyabindu* (1955), introd. p.xvii.
49. Nakamura, *op.cit.*, p.84.
50. Kunjunni Raja, Preface (p. viii) to *SV* (Madras, 1971).
51. Nakamura, *op.cit.*, l.c.
52. See below.

3

The Age of Śaṅkara

The epoch of Śaṅkara is the epoch which followed the death of the great king Harṣavardhana of Kannauj in the north and of his contemporary Pulakeśin II in the Deccan. After the fall of the Guptas and the Vākāṭakas the age of great and stable empires seemed to pass and the period from c. A.D. 650 onwards witnessed a ceaseless struggle for power and the rise and fall of numerous relatively short-lived empires having a distinct regional basis.[1] It was a period of perpetual strife when armies under different conquerors foraged and campaigned in quick succession. A new dimension was added to this strife by the expansionist threat of the Arabs in the first half of the 8th century. While imperial titles and boasts multiplied, the substance of imperial rule steadily declined. As the 8th century progressed, it saw the struggle between Kashmir, Kannauj and Gauḍa and the beginning of what has been called the Tripartite War between the Pālas, the Pratīhāras and the Rāṣṭrakūṭas. A similar dynastic conflict raged in the Deccan and the South. The Cālukyas, the Pallavas and the Pāṇḍyas were engaged in intermittent strife, with the Rāṣṭrakūṭas joining later. Each of these powers attained imperial status for a while and then lost it. The age of empires was increasingly substituted by what has been called a 'feudal-federal' polity.[2]

The empire itself instead of being an organized and stable unity became a loose federation of smaller states under subordinate rulers styled *sāmanta, mahāsāmanta, mahārāja* etc.[3] The system of cash payment to civil and military officials tended to fall into disuse.[4] Although outright landgrants were generally made for religious purposes, officials were usually paid by being allowed the right to appropriate in whole or part the revenue due from a village or villages.[5] This tended to produce in effect a system of *Zamindari.*[6] Coupled with the fact of a hierarchy among the vassals and their duty of supplying troops in times of need, this system came to resemble the 'feudal' system of medieval Europe in certain aspects. However, despite the practical fragmentation of sovereign power and the growing importance of a class of people whose influence rested on their rights over land, this system did not theoretically accept the equation of sovereignty with property. Nor were the rights of the peasant or the village community wholly superseded. The caste system too remained in force and was quite different from the feudal class system as known in the west.[7]

The existence of such a 'feudal-federal' polity corresponds to the descriptions we find in the writings of Śaṅkara. Thus commenting on *BS* 1.3.33. he says *'Idānīm iva nānyadā pi sārvabhaumaḥ kṣattriyostīti brūyāt'*. 'One might say that there never was any universal ruler just as there is none now.' It is clear that there was no real imperial ruler in Śaṅkara's age but the aspiration for one was not lost. Śaṅkara, again, clearly distinguishes between independent and subordinate rulers. Thus commenting on *Br.* 2.5.15 he says, *'Rājatva-viśeṣaṇam adhi-patir iti bhavati kaścid rājocitavṛttim āśritya rājā na tvadhipatih.'* 'Overlordship qualifies Kingship. One could be a ruler by following the livelihood proper to a king but without being an overlord.' He uses the administrative terminology which began from the Gupta age. Thus he says *'svatantraḥ na Kumārāmātyavat.'* 'Independent not like *Kumārāmātya.*' Again commenting on *Ch.* 2.1.2. he says *'rājānaṁ sāmantam copāgāt'*. 'He approached the king and the vassal.' It has to be remembered that while the older meaning of *sāmanta* was a neighbour, from the 6th century onwards it came to be used for subordinate rulers or feudatories. It is in this latter sense that Śaṅkara apparently uses the word.[8] He similarly uses the term *māṇḍalika* which had a similar import *'svatantraḥ patirna māṇḍalikaḥ'* (ad. *Br.* 4.3.33). 'Independent ruler, not *māṇḍalika.*'

Political anarchy over a period of time necessarily implied a growing disorder in the traditional social system. Śaṅkara thus, notes the decay of the *Varṇāśramadharma* in his times. Commenting on *BS* 1.3.33 he remarks, *'Idānīm iva Kālāntare pyavyavasthitaprāyān varṇāśramadharmān pratijānīta.'* 'One might suppose that *Varṇāśramadharma* was in disorder earlier also just as it is now.' It has been suggested, on the other hand, that this was an age when efforts were made to restore and liberalize the traditional *dharma.*[9] Thus Kumārila is said to represent the revival of orthodoxy. The *Devalasmṛti* and the *Manubhāṣya* of Medhātithi illustrate liberal tendencies in *Smṛti* literature. Though it is true that there was some attempt to adjust the *Smṛti* tradition to some of the new conditions created by foreign invasions, there is little evidence of the success of the kings in restoring the pristine form of the *Varṇāśrama* system which was in reality on the decline.[10] The age of the classical *Smṛtis* and *Purāṇas* was over. It was now an age of commentaries as well as of minor and apocryphal *Smṛtis* most of which have been lost except for quotations in later compendia. The earliest extant commentary is that of Bhāruci on Manu. Its special significance lies in the fact this Bhāruci was probably identical with the Vedāntin of that name and a predecessor of Śaṅkara. Bhāruci has been dated two to three centuries before Śaṅkara.[11] In his commentary Bhāruci is specially concerned with determining the status of the various pronouncements in Manu, whether they are examples of *Vidhi* or *Arthavāda* etc. His philosophical point of view is that of *Jñāna-Karma-Samuccaya* and his methodology that of *Mīmāṁsā*. As a result his commentary does not contain much new institutional data but is rather concerned with the precision and consistency of the text. Thus Manu 7/69 has *ānata-sāmantam* as a qualification of the kingdom. Derrett translates *sāmanta* as feudatory but the commentary has nothing to justify the translation. The fact is that *sāmanta* in Manu as well as Yājñavalkya has the older sense of 'neighbouring or frontier state'. This comes out quite clearly in the commentary of Kullūka which is much later. Although *sāmanta* meant 'feudatory' in the times of Kullūka, he preserves the old traditional meaning quite faithfully. As is well known, Manu admits as sources of law 'the laws of castes and districts, the laws of guilds, and the laws of families' (8.41). Bhāruci explains that *Jāti-dharmas* being based on the *śāstra* are eternal, not so the others, but they still deserve to be respected by the ruler. Thus laws of districts mean laws made by public bodies, relating to the grazing of cattle and protection of water. Laws of guilds are 'put into currency by merchants, artisans, and minstrels in order to further their respective businesses. These laws the king must uphold.' Although such laws are plainly empirical the King should uphold them if they are not repugnant to the scriptures.

Actually there was a vast and increasing body of non-scriptural laws based on custom, convention and enactment. We get epigraphic evidence of charters granted by local rulers for the regulation of local business.[12] There is also evidence of powerful guilds with their own regulations. It has been argued by some scholars that there was a marked decline in trade, guilds and use of money in northern India in the post-classical period.[13] This has been competently questioned.[14] Some decline is understandable owing to the blocking of north-western land-routes but oceanic trade continued to flourish especially towards the south-east. As a result trade and guilds in the Deccan and the south showed no decline.[15]

Nearer to Śaṅkara's time than Bhāruci, is Viśvarūpa's commentary on the *Yājñavalkyasmṛti*. Viśvarūpa has been identified by some scholars with Bhavabhūti and Sureśvara as also with Uṁveka and Maṇḍana.[16] Since Uṁveka comments on Maṇḍana their distinctness may be granted and since Bhavabhūti and Uṁveka are quoted as distinct they too may be reasonably distinguished. The relationship of Maṇḍana to Sureśvara and Viśvarūpa has been much debated. There is, however, no insuperable reason to question the identity of Viśvarūpa with Sureśvara or Bhavabhūti. Viśvarūpa, thus, would be a contemporary of Śaṅkara, unless we identify the King Pratāpaśīla he refers to with Prabhākaravardhana, which would place him about A.D. 600 and hence make him earlier than Śaṅkara as usually dated.[17]

Yājñavalkya mentions the procedure of making landgrants on cloth or copperplates marked with the King's seal. Viśvarūpa explains that *bhūrjapatra* is to be avoided. The grant should mention the earlier three generations including the women. It should be marked by the messenger, royal signature, seal, the name of the camp etc., and it should specify the gift 'such a village in such a region'. The name of the scribe should also be there. The grant should be in perpetuity.[18] Although it is not expressly stated, the grants seem to be contemplated in the context of religious gifts or charity to deserving Brāhmaṇas, learned men etc. There is no reference here to any connection with the grant of revenue to official functionaries. These grants are essentially free gifts in perpetuity made out of piety or for the promotion of learning.

The liberal social outlook of Viśvarūpa like that of Medhātithi comes out clearly in his interpretation of a verse of Yājñavalkya which was used by medieval commentators as the basis for justifying *Satī*.[19] There is a vast difference in attitude between Viśvarūpa and Medhātithi on one side and Aparārka and Mādhava on the other.

It needs to be emphasized that *Smṛti* law was not the only law regulating practical affairs. Local customs, charters given by powerful chiefs and the laws of guilds were important sources of actual laws and the *Smṛtis* advised the King to accept them except where they were contrary to canonical law. Canonical law, however, was itself subject to change. Yājñavalkya mentions twenty *Smṛtis* but most of them are not available in their ancient or pristine form. Even the *Viṣṇusmṛti* on which Bhāruci is said to have commented, shows evidence of interpolations.[20] Again it is difficult to always reconcile the available texts of most of these with the quotations attributed to them in medieval digests and compendia.

The fact is that during the centuries between Patañjali and Śaṅkara the social system of the ancient *sūtras* had become increasingly unreal. Old concepts remained like old bottles into which new meanings were added in practice.[21]

If politically the post-Gupta age represents a period of decline in organized power as well as centralized organisation, and shows at the same time the emergence of parochialism, regionalism, 'feudalism' and a new ruling class, culturally it is still an age of vigorous creativity.[22] It may be recalled that political anarchy is not incompatible with the efflorescence of a certain kind of culture as is illustrated by Renaissance Italy or the Period of the Contending States in China. The age of Śaṅkara is the age of Bāṇa and Mayūra, Bhavabhūti and Māgha; it is the age of the emergence of great spired temples with their riot of sculptures, of commentaries and sub-commentaries, of 'Ācāryas, Siddhas and Sāmantas.'[23] The Kailāśa temple represents not only the might of the Rāṣṭrakūṭas but also the climactic fusion of the rock-cut-style with the structural temple as also the harmonious vision of cosmic unity, an exquisite world emerging from he unmanifest core of solid rock. The culmination of the increasingly *rococo* age in the great shrine at Konark is symptomatic of the aspiration of the age as well as its unhappy end.

The religious culture of the age was marked by eclecticism, syncretism, broadminded tolerance and tantricism. Ample evidence of this is furnished by the *Purāṇas* and *Smṛtis,* art and architecture and the general literature of the period. Thus speaking of the court of Harṣavardhana, Bāṇa alludes to the presence of ascetics belonging to the Buddhist, Jaina, Pāśupata and Pārāśari sects ('*Jainairārhataiḥ Pāśupataiḥ Pārāśaribhiśca... upāsyamānam*).'[24] It may be recalled that long back Pāṇini had spoken of the *Bhikṣusūtras* of Pārāśarya who has been identified with Vyāsa.[25] Bāṇa also describes the Pārāśaris as '*Kamaṇḍalu-jala-śuciśaya-caraṇeṣu caitya-praṇati-pareṣu Pārāśariṣu*'.[26] The Pārāśaris could have been Vedāntins but their devotion to *Caitya*-worship suggests that they were not an orthodox sect. The Vedāntins are, however, definitely indicated by the term *Aupaniṣadas* or *Brahmavādinaḥ*.[27] The diversity of sects and their tolerant symbiosis is well brought out by Bāṇa in his description of the *āśrama* of Divākaramitra: *'ārhatair maskaribhiḥ śvetapaṭaiḥ Pāṇḍaribhikṣubhir bhāgavatair Varṇibhiḥ Keśaluñcanaiḥ Kāpilaiḥ Jainaiḥ lokāyatikaiḥ Kāṇādair Aupaniṣadair Aiśvarakāraṇikaiḥ Paurāṇikaiḥ Sāptatāntavaiḥ Śābdaiḥ Pāñcarātrikaiḥ anyaiśca'*.[28] We have here a reference to the *Ārhatas* or Jainas, *Maskarins* or Ājīvakas,[29] *Pāṇḍari Bhikṣus* who had abandoned the *Kāṣāyas*,[30] *Śvetapaṭas* or the *Śvetāmbara* Jains, *Keśaluñcanas* or some kind of Jain ascetics with shaven heads, the Buddhists called *Jainas* here apparently because Jina was one of the names of Buddha,[31] the *Bhāgavatas* as also the *Pāñcarātrikas*, the *Aiśvarakāraṇikas* who are explained as *Naiyāyikas* but could be Pāśupatas or Śaivas,[32] the Kāpilas or the followers of Sāṅkhya and the *Sāptatāntavas* who could be the ritualistic Mīmāṁsakas, the Vedāntins called *Aupaniṣadas* here, the *Śābdas* or grammarians, the *Paurāṇikas* who apparently followed that revised and syncretic version of the Vedic faith expounded in the *Purāṇas*, and the *Lokāyatas* or materialists. The views of most of these have been criticised by Śaṅkarācārya.

That these diverse sects lived peacefully together at the Court of Harṣa or the *Āśrama* of Divākaramitra, is not a fanciful description of Bāṇa and can be easily seen from the evidence of Hsuan Tsang.[33] Despite their personal preferences the rulers patronized diverse sects and it is this tolerant, secular ethos of the state which ensured the harmonious symbiosis of the sects.[34]

Although the king was supposed to maintain the *Varṇāśramadharma*, there is ample evidence to show that the *Āśrama* system had well-nigh broken down.[35] The *Vānaprastha Āśrama* had virtually ceased to exist. The Brāhmaṇical *sannyāsins* were overshadowed by all kinds of heretical or unorthodox mendicants. The common run of mendicants indeed received little esteem in society.[36] Although Agrahāra grants were made to maintain Vedic study and the daily ritual and although the kings did perform the great sacrifices from time to time, popular religion was governed by the *Purāṇas* and consisted of the worship of diverse gods and goddesses at home or in the temples and of the performance of *dāna, vratas, utsavas, yātrās,* and petty rites of a superstitious nature.[37] Charities on diverse occasions testified to the growing vogue of *Dāna-Dharma*. It is this mixture of heterogeneous *pūjā*, *vratas, dāna* and *saṁskāras* which had captured the popular mind. It was increasingly drawn by the superstitious search for 'invisible' gains or for marvels and miracles with the help of *Tantra* or alchemy. The sense of sin was nourished on the new religious texts which prescribed endless ritual for its expiation. At the same time eroticism was encouraged by Tantricism itself. It should not, however, he concluded that the Purāṇic literature shows religious decadence. It represented, on the other hand, a vigorous revival. The older Vedic religion, its myths, rites and ideas, were given a new form and this religion extended beyond the upper caste males to include all the castes and women. It substituted the abstractness of Vedic religion by concrete and visible symbols, the images of gods, which gave an endless opportunity to the artistic imagination. Temples with their lofty spires were the expression of an aspiration of the soul and their sculpture portrayed the wealth of creation. The religion of *Bhakti* came into prominence and culminated in the *Bhāgavata* which is the concentrated essence of what the Āḷvārs and Nāyanārs had been singing in the South and what had been foreshadowed in the *Gītā* and the Pāñcarātra Āgamas.

Indeed, the 7th and 8th centuries were the golden age of *Bhakti* in the South. It was the age of the Āḷvārs and the Nāyanārs and of a sharp conflict between the Hindu reform and revival which they represented and the heterodoxy of Jainism and Buddhism. Thus Appar himself turned from Jainism to Śaivism and is said to have converted the Pallava ruler Mahendravarman who had scoffed at false mendicants in his famous play *Mattavilāsa*. Another great Nāyanār was Jñānasambandhar who is said to have defeated the Jainas in a public debate and converted the Pāṇḍya ruler of Madura. It is said that the ruler then turned against the Jainas whom he persecuted. This story is reminiscent of the story in the *Mādhavīya* about Kumārila and Sudhanvan. Another famous Nāyanār was Sundaramūrti who was befriended by the Chera ruler Cheruman Perumal.[38] Among the Vaiṣṇava Āḷvars of the age may be mentioned Tirumalisai who was probably an elder contemporary of the Pallava ruler Mahendravarman I. Tirumalisai also turned from Jainism to Vaiṣṇavism. Another Āḷvar Tirumangai too attacks Jainism and Buddhism.

This *Bhakti* movement of which the Āḷvars and the Nāyanārs were the protagonists was a simple religion of the heart in which all sections of the people participated. Avoiding ritualistic and dogmatic subtlety, it was intensely emotional and tended to have a socially levelling effect.[39] If the Smārta texts sought to synthesize the Five Sects, the Āḷvārs saw harmony in the Six Schools (Ṣaṇmatas).[40]

The principal part of the popular *Smārta-Paurāṇic* religion consisted of the Five Sects or the Six Schools in which God was imaged in diverse anthropomorphic forms and worshipped in images and temples through a kind of stylized ritual appropriate to welcoming and honouring human guests, rulers, etc. This religion embraced practically all sections of society spreading from the lowly village shrines to the great temples created by royal munificence. The inscriptions of the Guptas, the Vākāṭakas, the Pallavas, the Cālukyas and Rāṣṭrakūṭas give vivid glimpses of these temples and the diverse faiths which they focused. There were famous sun temples, for example, at Mandsor during the Gupta period, at Mutton in Kashmir established by Lalitāditya or at Multan, referred to by the Arabs. The Śaivas and Śāktas had numerous holy places or *maṭhas* in different parts of the country from Śrīnagara and Kailāsa to Ujjain and Onkāreśvara, Kāñcī and Vṛṣācala. Similarly the worship of Viṣṇu and His incarnations had sacred spots of pilgrimage or *tīrthas* all over the country from Mathura and Devgarh to Rameswaram. The cults of Skanda and Varāha were popular in the Gupta age and those of Gaṇeśa and Nṛsiṁha appear to have gained in popularity in the post-Gupta age.

The doctrines and practices of these sects and cults may be seen in the *Purāṇas, Āgamas* and *Saṁhitās. Viṣṇu, Vāyu, Mārkaṇḍeya,* and *Matsya Purāṇas* may be mentioned among the earlier *Purāṇas* dateable in the Gupta period. Some of the Āgamic *Saṁhitās* too belong to this period. *Viṣṇudharmottara, Bhāgavata* and the original or earlier parts of the *Skandapurāṇa* may be placed in the post-Gupta period from the 7th to 9th centuries. Many of the *Pāñcarātra Saṁhitās* and Śaiva *Āgamas* of the South and Kaśmīra may also be placed during the period.

These Smārta-Paurāṇic cults were flanked by the ritualistic traditional Vedic religion (*Śrauta-dharma*), on the one hand, and the growing devotional movement, mentioned above, on the other. The appeal of elaborate *Śrauta-dharma* was to the learned Brāhmaṇas and orthodox rulers like the Vākāṭakas and the Guptas; the *Smārtapaurāṇika dharma* appealed to all the classes and castes but still preserved the orthodoxy of a ritualistic faith, albeit newly fashioned. The religion of *Bhakti* had a still wider appeal and was radical in character.

Beyond the pale of the various aspects of the Vedic faith, new and old, lay the wholly heterodox sects of the Buddhists and the Jainas. The accounts of the Chinese travellers Fa-hsian, Hsuan Tsang and I-tsing give us a vivid picture of Buddhist monasteries and temples, learning and literature in the Gupta and post-Gupta ages. Although Buddhism had declined in the northwest and some of its traditional centres, it was still important especially in eastern India. Both Mahāyāna and Hīnayāna flourished and a distinguished galaxy of Buddhist philosophers flourished in unbroken succession from Vasubandhu to Dignāga, Dharmakīrti, Śāntarakṣita and Kamalaśīla. It was also the period when the Jaina canon had been finalized at Valabhi in the 5th century and a series of brilliant authors and philosophers made their appearance—Devanandin, Samantabhadra and Akalaṅka, Prabhācandra and Vidyānanda, Haribhadra and Jinasena. If Buddhism dominated eastern India Jainism was finding a firm foothold in the west. In the south both Buddhism and Jainism especially the latter contended with the new Vaiṣṇava and Śaiva *Bhakti* movements.

While the *Śrauta-dharma* emphasized ritual action as the essence of religion and even conceived society as held together as a ritual order, *Smārtapaurāṇic dharma* stood for a synthesis of ritual and devotion which would be helpful for happiness here and hereafter. The religion of pure *bhakti* was non-egoistic and undemanding. Jainism emphasized asceticism as did Hīnayāna Buddhism but both had also adopted the worship of the Saviour and the use of images and temples. Mahāyāna Buddhism had given a great fillip to the cult of the saviours called Bodhisattva but it also made a clear-cut distinction between popular and philosophical religion. Real religion for it was the pursuit of wisdom (*prajñā*) through dialetical reasoning, contemplation and silence, it recognized that wisdom and compassion were inseparable and hence emphasized a prolonged course of training and good deeds towards the salvation of all beings. The active ethos of Mahāyāna helped to turn Buddhism into a world religion.

The prevailing web of social ritual was substantially unaffected by the distinction of orthodoxy and heterodoxy except in the names of the gods propitiated or the religieux given veneration. As Udayanācārya remarked later on, 'the Vedic ritual order from conception to the last rites was performed by all the sects even though some described it as merely empirical: *'Nāstyeva tad darśanaṁ yatra sāṁvṛtametad ityuktvāpi garbhādhānādyantyeṣṭi-paryantām Vaidikīṁ Kriyāṁ nānutiṣṭhati janaḥ'.*[41]

The system of the four *varṇas* had been for some time increasingly encrusted by a fast-growing *jāti*-system.[42] The natural growth of new specializations and vocations and the growth of the essentially locally organized social groups in times of insecurity engendered by invasions and the breakdown of large empires led to the recognition of numerous *jātis.* This was specially true of the lowest state which depended on skilled or unskilled labour.[43] The second and third *varṇas* displayed an amazing social mobility in point of fact. Adventurers and invaders belonging originally to diverse social groups were declared to be Kṣatriyas or even Brāhmaṇas or *Brahma-Kṣattras.*[44] The old *varṇa*-order had been created within a Vedic ethos in which the position of the Brāhmaṇa depended on his monopoly of religious magic and the Kṣatriyas ruled by their support within a strongly traditional community. The growth of diverse strands of heterodoxy, of Śramaṇism, and of rulers with foreign and tribal origins, gradually paved the way for decline of the old order. Medhātithi, thus, declares that the word Rājan is applied not only to the Kṣatriya-jāti but also to a non-Kṣatriya ruler (*rāja-śabdascāyamakṣattriye' pi janapadeśvare dṛṣṭaprayogaḥ*).[45] This attests to the actual mobility of the Kṣatriyas which became indistinguishable from *rājan, rājanya,* or *rājaputtra.* It is during this period that the beginnings of the new ruling class called the Rajputs lie. Similarly the meaning of Śūdra came to be considerably extended. It came to include numerous kinds of artisans called *Śilpin, Kāru* or *Prakṛti* such as a carpenter, goldsmith, blacksmith, jeweller, barber, gardener, potter, weaver, shampooer, tailor, plasterer, painter, actor, washerman, distiller, fisherman, butcher, shoemaker, and fowler.[46] This vastly extended meaning of Śūdra to include diverse manual crafts and guilds has a dual significance. It shows an actual improvement in the economic condition of the Śūdras but at the same time a decline in the social status of the artisans. Various distinctions came to be made among the Śūdras as 'high', 'low' and 'middling' or 'good' and 'bad'. At the lowest level were the *Antyajas* who included certain low occupations as well as certain tribes. Thus *Cāṇḍālas, Mātaṅgas,* and *Śvapacas* were classed among them from ancient times. Now *Kirātas, Niṣādas, Pulindas, Bhillas* and even *Mlecchas* are regarded as *Antyajas* in some texts.[47] It may be noted that *Śreṇis* or guilds continue to be mentioned in the inscriptions but the *Smṛtis* increasingly tended to regard them as subcastes within the Śūdra-*varṇa*. On the other hand, at least in South India, merchants were organized in powerful guilds and corporations which could be local and called *nagarams* or could have an extensive inter-state spread unaffected by minor wars and revolutions. Such were the *Manigrāmam* and the *Nānādeśīs* or *Ainnurruvar*. 'The *Ainnurruvar*, often styled the Five Hundred Svamis of Ayyavalepur (Aihole), were the most famous of the South Indian merchant guilds'.[48] They were the protectors of 'the *Vira-Bananju-dharma* i.e., the law of the noble merchants.' This *dharma* was embodied in 500 *vīra-śāsanas*. They traded within the country as well as with distant foreign countries.

The age-old vocations of the Brāhmaṇas were to act as teacher and priest. Where necessity compelled them they could take on the occupations of the lower castes. They ran the village schools and pursued traditional learning and received grants for the purpose. Apart from *Brahmapuris*, *Ghatikās* and *Agrahāras*, the *mathas* played an important part in the cultivation of learning especially since the 9th century. Thus a 9th-century college in Kerala promoted the study of *Vyākaraṇa*, *Mīmāṁsā* and *Trairājya vyavahāra*. Nṛpatuṅga endowed several *maṭhas* and colleges where fourteen *Vidyās* were studied.[49] Buddhist monastic universities as of Nalanda were world-famous institutions. The vitality of the Brāhmaṇical and Buddhist systems of education is shown by the vigorous development of learning and literature in the age.

Science and superstition grew apace at the same time. The Gupta and post-Gupta ages were the golden period of Indian science when its great classics were produced in mathematics and astronomy, in medicine and alchemy and much progress was attained in grammar and rhetoric and in the systematization of the arts. Indian science was strongly empirical and traditional. In mathematics and medicine it was highly original but learned a good deal from the Greeks in astronomy, and in turn, it was the Indian science of this period which participated in the tutoring of the Arabs in their initial scientific efforts. Logic naturally grew up in this milieu.[50] Dignāga and Pakṣilasvāmin may be said to have been the pioneers in its systematization as an independent science which continued to develop becoming more and more formal and influenced the study of all the other disciplines in course of time.

Superstition was closely connected with the growth of ritualism and worship. There were a myriad saviours, human and divine.[51]

To avoid misfortune or to gain diverse personal ends through their intercession became the order of the day. *Yoga* and *Tantra* preyed upon this atmosphere of credulity, hope and fear.[52] The fact that Tantra seemed to give obvious psychic powers to some naturally gifted individuals, led others to hope for similar results. The relaxation of rigid social rules in the Tantric, Yogic and ascetic communities were possibly another source of their popularity. The writings of Bāṇa and Bhavabhūti and the *Bṛhatkathāślokasaṁgraha* are eloquent testimony of these tendencies.

Philosophically it was a golden age characterized by the proliferation of schools, of debate and controversy, of reinterpretation and increasing formalization. The philosophical schools were closely allied to religious sects as may be seen from the description of Bāṇa above, where no distinction is made between them. The fact is that philosophy in India was never satisfied by the indirect knowledge of truth, verbal and inferential. It always sought the direct vision of truth and sought to harmonize its logical enquiries with revealed truth. Doubtless there were exceptions such as the Lokāyata school. Even the orthodox Mīmāṁsakas had little sympathy with any kind of mystical enterprise and even the Nyāya-Vaiśeṣika, although they accepted the possibility of mystical vision, did not generally appeal to it in support of their doctrines. However, the Mīmāṁsakas as well as the adherents of Nyāya-Vaiśeṣika unreservedly accepted the authority of the *Vedas* especially in the context of moral and spiritual life. The Buddhists and the Jainas rejected the *Vedas* but believed in the authority of their own scriptures. All the schools advocated, thus, the moral and spiritual life enjoined in some authoritative texts belonging to their tradition.

Apart from the appeal to some kind of supernormal word or vision, the schools generally accepted the validity of both experience and reason. There did not obtain any sharp division between empiricism and rationalism. Indeed the primacy of experience was accepted by all. While this appeal to common experience and reasoning based upon it made it possible for the schools to engage in dialogue and debate, their differences with respect to religious scriptures and practice set a limit to the fruitful exchange of ideas. Such creative discussions were commoner where the opposite parties belonged to the same stream or school and the differences were relatively minor compared to their basic agreements. In such cases sub-schools multiplied and the tradition of the school underwent logical evolution. Where, however, the differences were wide-ranging with respect to religious matters the disputes took the form of contentious wrangling. Public debates aimed at the defeat and discomfiture of the opponent rather than the common discovery of truth were the rage of the day and tradition records several such debates with unfortunate consequences.[53]

Most of the important philosophical schools of the time as may be gleaned from the writings of Kumārila, Śaṅkara or Śāntarakṣita were quite ancient and had centuries of history behind them. In fact, it has been characteristic of Indian philosophy as contrasted with contemporary philosophy that it strongly emphasized its traditional character. The Buddhist schools appealed to Buddha's words and where necessary did not even scruple to invent them. The Vedāntins claimed to be reiterating the *Upaniṣads* even when they mixed their teachings with those of Mahāyāna. The Jainas believed that their canon as fixed in the 5th century A.D. was the same ancient one which was revealed a millennium ago. The Sāṅkhyas appealed to the *Ādi-Vidvān* Kapila, the Mīmāṁasakas to the eternal word of the *Veda*. None of the great masters claimed individual originality believing that it would be too capricious and uncertain to leave the discovery of fundamental truth to merely the chance discovery made by individuals. As Vācaspati Miśra pointed out, while one might leave the confirmation of empirical and pragmatic truth to experience, it would be hazardous to say the least to leave beliefs about after-life in such a state.[54] Absolute certainty is needed with respect to them and it cannot be obtained merely with the help of individual experience and reasoning. An authentic and unimpeachable tradition is necessarily required by any philosophy which does not claim that its primary function is to doubt and rest content with common sense, uncontradicted by science in all practical matters. A philosophy which claims to support some moral or spiritual way of life has to appeal to a tradition grounded in something deeper than individual fancy or surmise, however acute or seemingly logical.

The ancient traditions of the philosophical schools, thus, were closely connected with specific moral and spiritual insights and came to develop them in terms of specific philosophical attitudes and cultures. It is the neglect of the 'culture' of the schools which led to much fruitless debating, though their occasional cross-fertilization led to brilliant synthesis.[55]

Such was the epoch of Śaṅkara who stands between the classical and the post-Classical ages. He also represents the meeting point of two streams, orthodox and heterodox, Brāhmaṇical and Śramaṇic. The cultural history of India could be conceived in terms of its changing spiritual values.[56] The Vedic Age, thus, could be characterized by the primacy of *Karman* as ritual action, the Classical Age from the Buddha to Śaṅkara by its acceptance of *Jñāna* as the supreme value, the medieval age by the exalted position it gave to *Bhakti*, the modern age by its renewed emphasis on *Karman*, deritualized and demythicised.[57] It has, of course, to be remembered that cultural change in India has rarely been radical, violent or sudden. It has often preserved many past elements substantially. Old values, symbols and institutions have been continually reinterpreted and readjusted so that it is not always clear whether the continuity is illusory or the changes.[58] The concept of *Dharma* or the institution of caste would illustrate this.

Śaṅkara like the Buddha represents a turning point in the development of Indian Culture. The ancient Vedic Age was characterized by the general acceptance of that positive outlook towards life within the bounds of the moral and ritual order called *Ṛta*,[59] which Manu has described as *Vaidika Karma-Yoga*.[60] The Age of Buddha saw the emergence of diverse movement of revolt and reform against the Vedic ethos as interpreted by the priestly orthodoxy.[61] Whether Śramaṇic or Āgamic, all of them questioned the authority or adequacy of the *Vedas*, the efficacy or desirability of sacrifices and the position of the priestly class. What is more, they tended to adopt a negative outlook towards wordly life now conceived as *saṁsāra*. They were also generally more favourable to the spiritual eligibility of the common people. The new class of Śramaṇas or other ascetics competed with the Brāhmaṇical establishment for spiritual guidance.[62] A cross-section of these heterodox schools may be seen in the *Brahmasūtras*.[63]

In the long and crowded millennium which followed the Buddha, these two traditions, orthodox and heterodox, often clashed but as often attempts were made to synthesize them in diverse ways. The epics and the *Smṛtis*, the Āgamic *Saṁhitās* and the *Purāṇas* illustrate the process of reconciliation.[64]

It has been said that the flowering of Indian Culture in the Gupta Age was the result of this spirit of synthesis which is illustrated by the poetry of Kālidāsa and the art of Ajantā. One could say that the Classical Age which followed the Vedic Age was the result of an interaction between orthodoxy and heterodoxy and of the reconciliation of the ideals of *Pravṛtti* and *Nivṛtti* at the social and religious levels even while the intellectual debate between the protagonists of *Jñāna* and *Karman* continued, though it also produced attempts at their syntheses such as the theistic systems.

At the end of the Gupta Age when the Classical period was on the wane a sense of social despair and decline came to be voiced and the concept of the Kali Age was elaborated. The sense of *vanitas vanitatum* came to be expressed frequently in the epigraphs.[65] A marked ambivalence became noticeable in the attitude towards life which was characterized by asceticism and sensuality, superstitious faith and logical argumentation. It is this transitional phase to which Śaṅkara belonged. With him the supremacy of *Jñāna* was assured over *Karman* in the Vedic tradition, and a philosophical basis was provided for the synthesis of the practical religion of Purāṇic-Tantric cults within the aegis of Vedānta as a philosophical religion.

REFERENCES

1. Vide *Age of Imperial Kannauj, Struggle for Empire* (Vidya Bhavan Series); H.C. Ray, *Dynastic History of Northern India*, 2 vols.; Nilakanta Sastri, *History of South India* (1931).
2. Cf. Dr. Beni Prasad, *The State in Ancient India*, pp. 282, 400.
3. Cf. *Harṣacarita*, pp. 58-60; cf. Devahuti, *Harsha*, pp.153, 154 ff, 163 ff.
4. Cf. Watters, *On the Travels of Yuan Chwang* I, p.177; Devahuti, *op.cit.*, pp. 167, 169.
5. *Ibid.*, p.169.
6. Attempts have been made by some historians with Marxist leaning to interpret this system of land-holding on the analogy of medieval European feudalism e.g., R.S. Sharma *Indian Feudalism* (1965); Such an interpretation, however, is highly misleading; cf. Coulburn, *Comparative Studies in Society and History*, Vol. X. p.356, G.C. Pande, *Foundations*, Vol. II, pp. 91-93, D.C. Sircar (ed.), *Land System and Feudalism in Ancient India* (Calcutta, 1966), Om Prakash, *Early Indian Land Grants and State Economy*, D.N. Shukla, *Uttar Bharat Ki Rajasva-Vyavastha*.
7. For the general features of feudal society in the West, Cf. Marc Bloch, *Feudal Society*, Vol. II, p.446.
8. On *Sāmanta* Cf. Devahuti, *op.cit.*, pp. 163-65; Lallan Ji Gopal, *JRAS*, 1963, pp. 21-37.
9. Cf. *Age of Imperial Kannauj*, pp. xvi-xix.
10. See below.
11. J.M. Derrett, (ed. and tr.) *Bhāruci's Commentary on the Manusmṛti*, 2 Vols.
12. E.g. the well known charter of Viṣṇusena, *EI*, Vol. 30.
13. Cf. Lallan Ji Gopal, *The Economic Life of Northern India*.
14. D.C. Sircar, *Sudhakar Chattopadhyaya Memorial Lectures*.

15. Cf. Nilakanta Sastri, *A History of South India*, pp. 331-33.
16. Cf. *Ślokavārtika-Vyākhyā of Umveka-bhaṭṭa* (Madras, 1971): Preface and Introduction; Kane, *Hist. of the Dh. S.* Vol. I.
17. *Yājñavalkyasmṛti with Bālakrīḍā of Viśvarūpa*, (ed. Ganapati Sastri), Pt. I. p. 200.
18. *Ibid.*, p.186.
19. *Ibid.*, p.85.
20. Cf. Jolly, *Institutes of Viṣṇu*, Intr. pp. xxvii ff.
21. Cf. G.C. Pande, *Foundations*, II, Chap. 8.
22. D.C. Sircar, *Sudhakar Chattopadhyaya Memorial Lectures*, Visvabharati.
23. Rahul Sankrityayan invented the term '*Siddha-Samanta Yuga*'.
24. *Harṣacarita* (Nirnayasagar) (1937), p.60.
25. 'Pārāśarya-Śilālibhyām Bhikṣu-naṭa-sūtrayoḥ'. (Pāṇini, 4.3.110) Cf. Kaviraj, *op.cit.*, pp. 1-2.
26. *Harṣacarita*, p.80.
27. *Ibid.*, '*Saṁsārasārāsāratva-kathana-kuśalā brahmavādinaḥ*', first referred to by Kaviraj ji, *op.cit.*, p.58, fn.
28. *Harṣacarita*, p.236.
29. *Maskarī* signified generally an ascetic holding a staff but also the *Ājīvikas*, the followers of Maskarī Gosāla, in particular. V.S. Agrawal interprets the term as referring to the Pāśupatas—*Harṣacarita—Ek Samskritika Adhyayana*. p.191.
30. Their identification is not clear. Dr. Agrawal identified them with the *Ājīvikas* but gives no reason, *op.cit.*, p.190.
31. It is worth noting that this use of 'Jaina' for Buddhist seems to be followed in the *Mādhavīya*.
32. The Commentator Śaṅkarācārya explains *Aiśvarakāraṇikas* as *Naiyāyika*. It may be recalled that the great author of the *Nyāyavārtika*, Uddyotakara was styled a *Pāśupatācārya*. So was *Bhāsarvajña*.
33. Beal, *Travels*, II. pp. 23a ff; Cf. R.S. Tripathy, *History of Kannauj*, pp. 150-60; on Harṣa's partiality to Hsuan Tsang and the punishment of the heretical conspirators, cf. *Ibid.*, pp. 164-65.
34. Thus Harṣa called himself *Parama-māheśvara* but was favourable to Buddhism as is clear in *Harṣacarita* as well as Hsuan Tsang's account. Harṣa's brother was a Buddhist, his father a worshipper of the sun.
35. Cf. Kane, *History of the Dharmasastra*, Vol. II, pt. II.
36. This may be seen in the representation of the ascetics in the *Nāṭyaśāstra* as well as in classical plays e.g., in Mahendra-Varman's *Matta-vilāsa-prahasana*.
37. Cf. V.S. Pathak, *The Smarta Religious Tradition*.
38. Cf. Nilakanta Sastri, *op.cit.*, pp. 422 ff.
39. Cf. Susmita Pandey, *Birth of Bhakti in Indian Religions and Art*, *Divyaprabandha*, 4 Vols. (Visvabharati), *Draviḍāmnāya-divya-Prabandha-vivarta* (Bombay, 1958).
40. Cf. N. Veezhinathan, *Sankara-Vijaya of Anantanandgiri*.
41. *Ātmatattva-viveka*, p.417.
42. Vide G.C. Pande, *Foundations of Indian Culture*, Vol. II, pp. 228 ff.
43. The *Śreṇis* tended to be merged in the *Jātis*, largely of the Śūdra *Varṇa* by the 11th century, *ibid.*, p.240.

44. The long-standing debate on the origin of the Rajputs may be referred to here. Manu is well known to have counted foreign tribes as *Vrātya-kṣattriyas*, Dashrath Sharma, *Lectures on Rajput History & Culture*, pp. 5 ff.
45. Medhātithi, *ad Manu* 4.84.
46. Cf. '*Śreṇyo rajakādayo' ṣṭādaśa hīnajātayaḥ*' (*Vīramittrodaya*), quoted in Kane, *Hist. Dh. Ś.* II. pt. I. Kane interprets it as the social rise of the lower castes, *History of the Dh.S.*, Vol. II, pt. I p.70.
47. Cf. Halāyudha, p.67.
48. Nilakanta Sastri, *op.cit.*, p. 331.
49. *Ibid.*, pp. 322-23; R.K. Mookerji, *Ancient Indian Education* 19, 367 ff; A.S. Altekar, *History of the Rāṣṭrakūṭas*, pp. 401 ff.
50. Cf. S.C. Vidyabhusana, *History of Indian Logic*.
51. Cf. *Harṣacarita*, p. 153.
52. On the prevalence of Tantricism in the Buddhism of this period Cf. *Age of Kannauj*, pp. 258 ff.
53. E.g., in Paramārtha's *Life of Vasubandhu*, Hsuan Tsang's *Si-Yu-Ki*, Mādhavas', *Śaṅkara-digvijaya*, Merutunga's *Prabandha-Cintāmaṇi*.
54. *Nyāya-Vārtika-tātparya-ṭīkā* ad. NS. 2.1.68 (=*ND*, pp. 565 ff.).
55. M.M. Gopinath Kaviraj has especially emphasized this, vide G.C. Pande, *M.M. Gopinath Kaviraj* (Sahitya Akademi).
56. Cf. G.C. Pande, *Meaning and Process of Culture*.
57. G.C. Pande, *Bharatiya Samskriti ke Mūla Svara*, pp. 124 ff.
58. G.C. Pande, *An Approach to Indian Culture and Civilization*, pp. 39 ff.
59. G.C. Pande, *Foundations of Indian Culture*, Vol. I, pp. 24-27.
60. *Manusmṛti*, 2-2: *Kāmātmatā napraśastā nacaivehāstyakāmatā Kāmyo hi Vedādhigamaḥ Karmayogaśca vaidikaḥ//"*
61. G.C. Pande, *Studies in the Origins of Buddhism*, pp. 327 ff.
62. For a detailed account of Śramanas, see C.G. Pande *Śramana Tradition*.
63. *Brahmasūtras*, 2.1.2. Sāṅkhya and Yoga were originally Sramanic, see, G.C. Pande, *Origins of Buddhism*, 305 ff.
64. G.C. Pande, *Foundations*, Vol. I, pp. 164 ff.
65. Cf. V.S. Pathak, *Smarta Religious Tradition*, pp. 18-20.

4

Early Life and Legend

As noticed before, according to the tradition the first biographical accounts of Śaṅkara were produced in the first two centuries of the death of the Master at the instance of his immediate or remote disciples.[1] According to the Kāñcī Tradition Citsukha was Śaṅkara's contemporary while Ānandajñāna or Ānandagiri was the disciple of Śuddhānanda and the 7th *ācārya* of the Kāmakoṭi Pīṭha who belonged to the spiritual lineage of Sarvajñātma Muni, the disciple of Sureśvara, but this tradition has been questioned.[2] These works unfortunately have not survived except in excerpts and apocrypha. The second wave of writings appears to have consisted of *Purāṇic* and semi-Pūraṇic legends, rewritings of older works and the originals of works like the *Vyāsācalīya* and the *Anantānandagirīya*, apparently at the instance of authors seeking to refurbish and popularize the memory of the Master and to meet the challenge posed by Islam and non-Advaita Vedānta. The next wave consisting of extant works commenced after the reorganization of monasteries, which began in the 14th century. The Kāñcī and Śṛṅgerī Maṭhas built up their own traditions of pontifical succession going back to Śaṅkara. While these works claim to give precise information and utilize earlier traditions, they are not wholly congruent and are also occasionally influenced by the motive of exalting the *maṭha* and *pīṭha* to which they belong. Besides, they seek to strengthen faith by weaving pious legends into poetic biographies. Their direct relevance, thus, is limited to the legend of Śaṅkara, though they all presuppose a broadly common framework which seems to echo more ancient writings.

It is clear that at least three major factors helped shape the growth of the Śaṅkara legend. The first was the belief that Śaṅkara was an incarnation of Śiva destined to eradicate the forces of heresy. This deification was expressed powerfully in Purāṇic apocrypha found in *Mārkaṇḍeya Saṁhitā*, *Skandapurāṇa*,

Kūrmapurāṇa, Saurapurāṇa, Liṅgapurāṇa, Bhavisyottara Purāṇa and the *Śivarahasya.*[3] The second factor was the reorganization of the monasteries and their need of 'authentic' tradition to support their claims spiritual and social. The third factor was the growing polemic of Advaitic and non-Advaitic schools, which tended to highlight Śaṅkara's *digvijaya*. The total tendency of these factors was to inculcate a sense of faith and reverence in the founder of the monastic traditions organized at several centres. It emphasized Śaṅkara's connection with miracles, cults and monastic establishments as well as his disputations. How far this emphasis stemmed from the realities of Śaṅkara's historical career needs to be examined, though any final conclusion would hardly be possible in the present state of evidence.

The traditional accounts of Śaṅkara's birth begin with a celestial prologue where it is conceived as a divine incarnation intended to restore the Vedic faith that had become corrupted by the rank growth of heterodox beliefs and practices. This conception appears to have been first adumbrated in the semi-Purāṇic works like *Śivarahasya* in the early medieval period,[4] although the idea that God incarnates Himself to restore Righteousness goes back to the *Gītā*. Śaṅkara's preface to his commentary on the *Gītā* underlines the importance of this idea.[5] Commenting on *BS* (III, 3.32) he mentions a class of great men (*adhikārikas*) who are born in order to fulfil a divinely ordained mission. Śaṅkara, however, is so modest and impersonal that he does not appear to speak of himself at all in his writings. Nor do Śaṅkara's immediate disciples speak of him as an incarnation, although they refer to him with the highest reverence and admiration for his surpassing qualities of head and heart. The testimony of Sureśvara who had been a mature person and a famous Mīmāṁsaka before his conversion is specially valuable in this context.[6] Padmapāda, indeed, refers to him as '*apūrva-Śaṅkara*', expressing the idea of Śaṅkara's divinity in a playful and metaphorical manner. It is clear that while Padmapāda does not regard Śaṅkara as an incarnation, he regards him to have been so extraordinary that he could well have been an incarnation.[7] Vācaspati Miśra too does not speak of Śaṅkara as an incarnation.[8] Nor does Sarvajñātma Muni in the *Śaṅkṣepa-śāriraka.*[9] Thus the idea that Śaṅkara was an incarnation could only have arisen after the early 9th century A.D. but not much after because the Purāṇic texts like the *Kūrmapurāṇa* could not be later than *c.* A.D. 900 even in their present form. On the other hand, from the references to him by his disciples, it is clear that he was recognized as an extraordinary individual who became the source of a new and distinct tradition within the Vedānta. The extraordinary reverence with which he was regarded comes out most clearly from the fact that he was regularly referred to as *Bhagavat* or *Bhagvatapāda*. This epithet of singular veneration is to be found in the colophons of his genuine works. In the 9th century even in the far southeast of Asia his fame had spread and he appears to have been referred to as *Bhagavat*.[10]

Some legendary accounts relate that the background for Śaṅkara's birth was provided by an acute struggle between heterodoxy and orthodoxy. It is said that at first King Sudhanvā favoured the 'Jainas'* but was converted by Kumārila and turned against them.[11] The King is not known to history but it seems to be a fact that during the Pallava rule there was a vigorous Hindu revival and many tales are told of religious persecution. Thus it is said Mahendravarman I persecuted the Śaivites until his conversion when he turned against the Jainas. The celebrated Śaiva saint Sambandar is said to have converted a Pāṇḍya ruler who then persecuted the Jainas. Even some Vaiṣṇavite rulers and saints are said to have persecuted the Jainas and the Buddhists.[12] These tales which remind one of the Buddhist stories about Puṣyamitra cannot, however, be taken at their face value.[13] The political tradition was normally tolerant and so was the religious ethos despite sectarian rivalries. While the intolerance of occasional rulers cannot be excluded a priori, it does need to be established by firmer evidence than late legends. At the same time it must be remembered that by the time of Śaṅkara, a gentle and popular religion of *Bhakti* was sweeping over the south and it hardly needed political violence to establish itself.

There is a general agreement in the traditional accounts that Śaṅkara was born in the village of Kalati or Karati in the state of Kerala, although in some manuscripts of Anantānandagiri's *Śaṅkaravijaya* he is said to have been born at Cidambaram.[14] That Śaṅkara was a Southerner is proved by the contemporary evidence of Sureśvara who says in the *Naiṣkarmyasiddhi* (4.44) *Evaṁ Gauḍair Drāviḍair naḥ pūjyair arthaḥ prakāśitaḥ*. Here *Gauḍa* seems to refer to Gauḍapāda and *Drāviḍa* to Śaṅkara. It is notable, however, that in the writings of Śaṅkara all the geographical

* The word also meant 'Buddhist', see Chap. 2.

allusions are to northern India. Thus there are references to Mathurā, Srughna, Pāṭaliputra, Magadha, Gaṅgā, and the Himalayas.[15] This could be due to the fact that the texts he had before him had originated in the north and the 'examples' he mentions could have been drawn from a commentarial tradition relating to these texts. Or, more plausibly, it could have been due to the fact that Śaṅkara spent most of his time in the north, especially during the years he wrote his celebrated works.

It may be concluded reasonably that while Śaṅkara was born in the south, he came to the north and stayed there at least during the period of his literary activity. As to his birthplace, Kalati in Kerala may be accepted as the most likely. Ātmabodha in the *Suṣamā* mentions a rival tradition, apparently in favour of Cidambaram, and explains it as due to a confusion between Ādya Śaṅkara and Abhinava Śaṅkara.[16] Such a confusion between different persons styled Śaṅkarācārya is not implausible.

Kerala has been justly famous for its greenery due to its woodlands dense with trees and creepers.[17] Aśoka had already noticed the Ketalaputas beyond his borders, the *Periplus* included Cerobothra within Damirike and Ptolemy refers to Cerobothra as ruling Karoura.[18] The Epics and the *Purāṇas* regularly mention Kerala along with Cola and Pāṇḍya. Kerala was, thus, an ancient *janapada* which provided an inland mart for a flourishing oceanic trade. Quilon was the most important port on the Malabar Coast. Chinese as well as Arab ships halted there in their journeys further west or east.[19] It has, however, been argued that the relative share of Indian shipping in oceanic trade declined from this period owing to the rise of Arab and Chinese shipping and other factors. It has also been argued that Indians tended to concentrate increasingly on coastal trade and inland distribution.[20] On the other hand, literary romances of the time regularly refer to oceanic trade between Quilon and South-east Asia. The trading guilds of the Manigrāmam and the Nānādeśīs were justly famous.[21] The hypothesis of the decline of Indian trade in this period still rests largely on an interpretation of negative evidence.

Whether the presence of Arab traders on the Malabar Coast meant any dissemination of Islamic ideas in Kerala, remains a mere supposition.[22] It must, however, be remembered that Syriac Christianity had reached India much earlier and found a home in Kerala.[23] Even a Jewish merchant community is said to have been established in Quilon.[24] The Semitic idea of monotheism, thus, could have reached Kerala in diverse ways from quite ancient times.

During the dark period which followed the Sangam Age, the heterodox sects of the Buddhists and the Jainas seem to have gained influence in the South. According to the *Keralotpatti* and the *Keralamāhātmyam* 'the rulers of the land had to be imported from neighbouring countries and they assumed the title of Perumal. Possibly the Vaiṣṇava saint Kulasekhara Alvar was one of these Perumals.'[25] As mentioned before, from the 6th to the 9th century A.D., the Age of Śaṅkara, South India witnessed a struggle for power between the Cālukyas of Badami, the Pallavas of Kāñcī and the Pāṇḍyas of Madura; political anarchy, however, did not obstruct cultural efflorescence. The development of Vaiṣṇava and Śaiva devotionalism checked the tide of Buddhism and Jainism. During the days of the Pallava Renaissance there was a close interconnection between the learned Brāhmaṇas of Kerala and the Pallava court at Kāñcī. It is worth noting that Cheraman Perumal who could have been a contemporary of Śaṅkara or of his disciples is said to have taken an interest in diverse religious faiths including Christianity and Islam. A story even relates his conversion to Islam and pilgrimage to Mecca. He is also said to have partitioned Kerala in deference to Śaṅkara's prescriptions.[26]

It has been said that "...Kerala represents a land of isolation where ancient customs have been preserved and where immigrants soon lost contact with their homelands and made strange adaptations to the customs of the native populations, thus themselves adding to the peculiarities of the land."[27] Against this, however, it must be remembered that towards its south end Kerala was always in continuous contact with the Dravidian heartland. Besides, the sea joined the land with other coastal areas and distant lands. Nor should the role of PalGhāt be forgotten.

Kalati is said to have been a village situated on the northern bank of the river Marudvṛdhā or Cūrṇi or Pūrṇā now called Alvae.[28] The village is at a short distance from the railway station of Alwaye and Angamalai on the Kochin Shoranur railway line.[29] Many Brāhmana families known for their learning are reputed to have been settled there. The temples of Sri Govinda and Sri Vṛṣādrinātha were well known local temples. Apart from the fact that it adjoined a river, had two temples and a settlement of Nambudiri Brāhmaṇas, not much is known of the home village of Śaṅkara. It may be assumed that it subsisted on agriculture and had a population consisting of different castes and classes. It may be recalled that among the Nambudiris it was the duty of the oldest son to marry and rear a family. In the *Govindanāthīya* and the *GVK* stress is laid on the preeminently Brāhmaṇa population of the village. Rājacūdāmaṇi describes Kalati as an *agrahāra*, which implies that the first charge on the village revenues lay with the temple and some family or college of learned Brāhmaṇas. One Vidyādhirāja is said to have been the grandfather of Śaṅkara. Vidyādhirāja's son was named Śivaguru who was himself a learned person. He was married to the daughter of a scholar named Makha who according to a local legend is said to have belonged to a place called Melapalur, about 40 km from Ernakulam. Śivaguru and his wife called Āryā or Āryambā generally were, however, without a child for a long time. It is said that to secure a child they performed a penance and worshipped Śiva who favoured them at last.[30] Their son was Śaṅkara. Śaṅkara, thus, belonged to a prosperous, learned and pious family of Nambudiri Brāhmaṇas of the Atrigotra, belonging to the *Taittrīya-śākhā*.[31]

As mentioned before some works like *Br. S. V.*, *Prā Śivarahasya*, *Puṇyaśloka Mañjarī* and *Suṣamā* give the date of Śaṅkara's birth or death in the Kali or Yudhiṣṭhira era. The authenticity of these dates is more than doubtful. On the other hand, the astronomical details of *tithi* etc., are not incredible because the tradition of memorial verses normally included such details. But the tradition is not unanimous even in this respect and several different astrological charts of Śaṅkara's birth are consequently current.[32] It is said that he was a precocious child who learned quickly and far beyond his age. In particular, his extraordinarily retentive memory has been the subject of praise in traditional accounts. It is said that he was an *eka-śruti-dhara* i.e., one who retained what he heard but once.[33] As will be seen later, the survival of *Pañcapādikā* has been attributed to this quality of Śaṅkara. He is said to have started speaking in his first year and to have learnt writing in the second year. By the third year he is said to have memorized a good deal of poetry, legend and history. His *Cūḍākarman* or Tonsure was formally performed in the third year.[34] In the next two years he is said to have learnt a good deal of the secular learning current among the Brāhmaṇas of the time. This included generally grammar, rhetoric and logic.[35] Such stories of child prodigies are not unknown to legend or history. The childhood accounts of many famous ancient *ācāryas* are full of such tales. On the other hand, history too attests that some famous men have been child prodigies. For example, John Stuart Mill is known to have acquired fabulous learning while yet a child. At the age of five Śaṅkara's father initiated him into Vedic study by performing his *Upanayana* but died even before the son could proceed to the home of the teacher for formal study. It may be mentioned that there is divergence in the traditional accounts at this point. According to one version Śivaguru performed the *Upanayana* of Śaṅkara and then left the mortal coil. According to the other version Śivaguru died while yet intending to have the *Upanayana* performed. The two versions may be reconciled by assuming that while Śivaguru initiated the process, he could not live to complete it.[36]

Education in the villages has been traditionally Sanskritic as well as popular. "The three Rs' were taught in village schools which met under the shade of a tree or in the verandas of temples and the village teacher (*vatti* or *akkariga*) was among the regular village officials who held assignments of land from the village on the condition that they fulfilled specified duties."[37] Recitations from epics and *Purāṇas* provided another dimension of education just as the wandering mendicants provided a third. Temples and monasteries, orthodox and heterodox, provided centres of more specialized education. Gifts of land and houses were made to Brāhmaṇas to induce them to settle and pursue learning. They were sometimes organized into corporate colleges called *Brahhmapurīs* and *Ghaṭikās*. The inscriptions of Rāṣṭrakūṭa and Cola rulers from the 9th to 11th centuries provide ample evidence about the existence of richly endowed colleges of learning.[38] Thus an inscription of the 9th century Rāṣṭrakūṭa ruler Nṛpatunga mentions a college at Bahur, near Pondicherry where the fourteen *vidyās* were studied. Inscriptions speak of the students and teachers of the *Veda*, of Pāṇini, of the two schools of Pūrvamīmāmsā, Nyāya and Vedānta, of the *dharmaśāstra* and of medicine.[39] It is clear that in the 8th and 9th centuries Sanskritic education in the different *śāstras* was spread far and wide in the South and was maintained by royal munificence as well as organized local support.

Nor must it be supposed that this general picture leaves out Kerala on account of its geographical isolation. As a matter of fact the rulers of the imperial dynasties made repeated claims to include Kerala within their sway.[40] More directly a grant of the Ay King Karunandadakkan in the middle of the 9th century mentions the endowment of a college and a hostel for the maintenance of 95 Vedic students who were admitted after an entrance test in *Vyākaraṇa, Mīmāṁsā, Paurohitya,* and *Trairājya-Vyavahāra* which has been understood as the law and usage of the three states, perhaps Pāṇḍya, Cola and Kerala. The college was located in a Viṣṇu temple at Pārthivasekharapuram in South Travancore.[41]

In view of these general conditions of education in his times it is plausible to assume that when Śaṅkara went to school he could expect to meet competent scholarship in diverse *śāstras,* although no historical details about his particular school are available. In the school or *gurukula* Śaṅkara is said to have mastered the *Vedas* along with the six *Aṅgas* in two years. Although he himself belonged to the tradition specializing in *Yajurveda* of the *Taittirīya śākhā,* he studied all the four *Vedas.* He is also said to have acquired proficiency in the orthodox systems of philosophy.[42] In the eighth year he returned to his home and spent some time studying the *Vedas* and performing Vedic ritual. Even while at the *gurukula* Śaṅkara is said to have instructed pupils on his own and the fame of his precocious learning is said to have spread far and wide.[43] It is said that a King Rājaśekhara wished to invite him to his court but as Śaṅkara declined to comply with the request, the king himself travelled to meet the child prodigy and is said to have recited his three plays before him. It was to the unfailing memory of Śaṅkara that the plays owed their recovery and survival after they had been accidentally destroyed in later years.[44]

The historicity of this legend, mentioned only in some biographies, is however, questionable since it is difficult to identify the king. Perhaps there has been a confusion between the royal name Kulaśekhara and that of the famous dramatist Rājaśekhara. Or the ruler in question could have been some local magnate who is unknown to history but who is said to have built the local temple of Candramaulīśvara and paid homage to Śaṅkara.

At the age of eight Śaṅkara wanted to renounce the world but could not do so immediately in deference to the wishes of his mother to whom he was greatly attached. A peculiar incident is said to have helped him out of the predicament. Bathing in the river he was one day seized by a crocodile and cried out to his mother to release him for renunciation in view of his imminent death: such a renunciation is called *Āpatsannyāsa.* The mother agreed in this crucial hour and miraculously enough Śaṅkara was released by the crocodile.[45] He then left home as a peripatetic mendicant in search of a preceptor after promising to his mother that he would be with her at the hour of her death and perform her last rites. He left his mother in the care of his relations who became the heirs of his ancestral property.

Several miraculous stories are related about the childhood of Śaṅkara. The traditional biographies are not unanimous about them and even when some of them agree about the incident as a whole, they give varying details. It is said that once when as a child he was required to worship the family deity in the absence of his father and the temporary disability of his mother, he insisted that the goddess should actually partake of the offering and leave something for him. It is said that the goddess was touched by his sincerity and having eaten up the whole offering proceeded to pacify the child crying at this outrage by giving him milk from her own breast. A line in the *Saundaryalaharī* has been interpreted by commentators to refer to this incident.[46] Whether the incident is real or only the mythical expression of the idea that to learn is to be breast-fed by the goddess of learning, remains a matter of faith. Similar stories have been recounted about some other saints also such as Nāmadeva.[47] There is a surmise that *Devī-bhujaṅga-stava* was composed by Śaṅkara on the occasion.

Again, it is said that once while begging as a student in the *gurukula* he met a poor woman who gave him an *āmalaka* in the absence of any other possession. Śaṅkara was touched and prayed for her prosperity. The prayer was promptly accepted and the woman's house was filled with gold.[48] It may be recalled that this motif of a rain of gold is not unknown in ancient myth and legend.[49] The composition of the *Kaṇaka-dhārā-stotra* has been surmised to belong to the occasion.

Tradition avers that Śaṅkara's mother found it difficult to go to the river Cūrṇi daily owing to her frailty. Śaṅkara by the magic of his prayer, then, made the river slightly alter its course and flow nearby.[50] This change in the course of the river is said to have led to its being known as the Ambā river. Perhaps this was one of the names by which the river was known, and this fact became the occasion of the mythical legend which sought to explain it. The change in the course of the river could well be accidental too.

As for the story of the crocodile, its real significance is to bring home the point that Śaṅkara was destined to live in the world for only eight years. The voluntary acceptance of *sannyāsa* which is tantamount to dying for the world, gave him a further lease of life as totally dedicated to the mission of helping the spread of a spiritual way of living.

It is reported that on the eve of his departure from home he saw the vision of Vāsudeva, in which the latter told him that his *śilā-vigraha* in the nearby temple was in imminent danger of being washed away by the river of which the course had changed owing to Śaṅkara's intervention. Śaṅkara is then said to have had the stone image shifted to a safer place.[51]

Leaving his village home Śaṅkara proceeded towards the north.[52] Perhaps he followed some peripatetic bands of mendicants, or pilgrims, or moved in the wake of some trading caravan wandering far from home. Leaving home while still very young, in search of spiritual enlightenment, has not been unknown in India. Svami Dayananda, for example, ran away from home while still a young boy and during his peregrinations met a Yogin in the Vindhya region. Al-biruni mentions the vogue of pilgrimage and names Varanasi, Puskara, Mathura, Kuruksetra, Kashmir and Multan as famous places of pilgrimage.[53] Varanasi was pre-eminent among these. Perhaps Śaṅkara set out for Varanasi or the distant Himalayas in search of spiritual wisdom.

What route Śaṅkara could have followed in travelling north is not easy to determine because the available descriptions of routes seem to leave out the land-routes from Kerala. As it is unlikely that Śaṅkara travelled any distance by sea, he could either have proceeded towards Kāñcī via the extreme south or towards Karnataka and Konkana. According to Al-biruni there was a route running from Mandgir on the Godāvari to Alispur and thence to Namavur on the bank of the Narmadā. Another route ran from Tana, the Konkana capital on the sea-coast, to 'Maharatta-desh' and thence to the valley of Namiyya, 7 *farsakh* from Dhar.[54] There is a suggestion that Śaṅkara proceeded through the realm of the Kadamba or Vanavasi rulers and passed through Śṛṅgerī on the Tungabhadrā.[55] It may be recalled that according to one legendary version it is from Śṛṅgerī that Śaṅkara had later on proceeded to Kalati to meet his dying mother.[56] It may also be mentioned that in the accounts of Śaṅkara's *digvijaya* the towns of the south which find special mention are Gokarṇa, Sriparvata, Śṛṅgerī, Kāñcī and Rāmesvaram. There is also mention of his sojourn in Maharastra. The routes from the north through Central India to Maharastra and Konkana or Kāñcī and Rāmesvaram were well known and Śaṅkara must have met one of these routes. He could have availed of the route passing through the PālGhāt or Coimbatore pass in Karnataka and moved up across the Godāvari to Narmadā. Both of these rivers were famous for their religious sanctity. Godāvari had the earlier name of Gautamī, and Bhavabhūti, most probably a contemporary of Śaṅkara, praises the river most eloquently.[57] Nasik, Pañcavaṭi and Govardhana were famous *tīrthas* on it. According to one version Śaṅkara passed through Gokarṇa where his erstwhile classmate Viṣṇuśarman joined him on Narmadā where Onkāreśvara or Onkāra Mandhata was the most famous *tīrtha*. It is regarded as the site of one of the *Jyotirliṅgas* and is located near Khandwa. It has been identified with Mahismati which Patañjali locates at a distance of a limited journey from Ujjayini[58] and which Kālidāsa describes as surrounded by the Revā or Narmadā. The background of Śaṅkara's meeting with his *guru* is provided by the holy waters of these rivers and the rugged beauty of the Vindhyās described so brilliantly by Bhavabhūti. Śaṅkara's journey probably lay through Palghāt, Śṛṅgerī and Gokarṇa[59] to Onkāreśvara. It is generally believed that Śaṅkara met Govindapāda on the bank of the Narmadā in a narrow cave near Onkāreśvara, though there are versions which locate Śaṅkara's meeting with his preceptor in Kāśī or in the far north at Badarī. Śaṅkara met his teacher in his ninth year and studied the various *śāstras* with him till he was twelve. Govindapāda presumably expounded to him the Vedāntic tradition as received from Gauḍapāda and at last advised him to proceed to Kāśī and write a commentary on the *Brahmasūtras*.

A miracle performed by Śaṅkara during his stay with Govindapāda finds a prominent mention in the tradition. It is said that Narmadā began to be flooded by rains and its swollen waters threatened to enter the cave where Govindapāda was seated in deep meditation. All the disciples were frightened by the imminent threat for the teacher. Śaṅkara solved the problem by placing a charmed pot before the mouth of the cave, which attracted within it the overflowing water of the river and contained it.[60] This story evidently belongs to the tradition of stories connected with Yogic miracles. In fact, Śaṅkara is said to have thus proved his eligibility to become a disciple of Govindapāda.

Śaṅkara's relationship with Govindapāda and Gauḍapāda is well attested by his own writings. In the colophons of his works he is described as the disciple of *Govinda-bhagavatpūjyapāda* who is given the title *Śrīmatparamahaṁsa-parivrājakācārya*. The teacher of Govindabhagavatpāda is believed to have been Gauḍapāda. At the end of the *Māṇḍūkyopaniṣatkārikābhāṣya*, Śaṅkara bows to his teacher's teacher but does not name him, which was in accordance with the accepted proprieties. In the *Śārīrakabhāṣya* too he quotes him twice but refers to him as Master of Tradition without naming him. Thus commenting on *B.S.* 1.4.14 he says '*Tathā ca sampradāyavidovadanti*:

Mrllohavisphuliṅgādyaiḥ sṛṣṭiryā coditānyathā Upāyaḥ so avatārāya nāsti bhedaḥ Kathañcana//' The verse quoted corresponds to *Āgamaśāstra* 3.15. Similarly commenting on *BS*2.1.9 he says, '*Atroktaṁ Vedāntārthasampradāvavidbhir ācāryaih. Anādimāyayā supto yadā Jīvaḥ prabudhyate/ Ajamanidraṁ asvapnam advaitam budhyate tadā*// This corresponds to *Āgamaśāstra* 1.16. Again in *Upadeśasāhasrī*(II 18.2.) he bows to his teacher's teacher: '*Pramathya vajropama-yukti-sambhṛtaiḥ śruterarātīn śataśo vacobalaih/Parokṣa-Vedārthanidhiṁ Viśāladhīrnamo Yatīndrāya gurorgarīyase*//' Here Gauḍapāda is described as the defender of the Vedic treasure against its detractors and as the chief of mendicants.

Thus even though the authenticity of Śaṅkara's *Māṇḍūkyopaniṣadkārikābhāṣya* is not beyond dispute,[61] it is clear that Śaṅkara claimed to belong to an ancient Vedāntic tradition which reached him through Gauḍapāda and his disciple Govindapāda. In the introductory verses to the *Taittirīyopaniṣadbhāṣya* he says that his exposition is based on the grace of his teachers (*ācārya-prasādataḥ*) and bows to his teachers as having expounded Vedānta earlier in accordance with grammar, exegesis and logic (*pada-vākyapramāṇataḥ*). Thus although Śaṅkara is totally silent about his worldly parentage and upbringing, he clearly indicates his spiritual and intellectual lineage. Obviously he regarded that alone as important. Whether Gauḍapāda was the name of one individual or merely refers to a school of teachers from Gauḍa has been questioned. Max Walleser's opinion, however, has not found much favour with scholars.[62] It seems more in accordance with the evident belief of the ancients to accept Gauḍapāda as referring to an individual. Whether that individual belonged to *Gauḍa*, remains a moot point.[63] In determining the date of Gauḍapāda we have to reckon with the fact that it appears likely that he is quoted by Bhāvaviveka who was a senior contemporary of Dharmapāla and whose work was translated into Chinese about A.D. 630.[64] This would place Gauḍapāda in the second half of the 6th century. He would then be nearly a century earlier than Śaṅkara and it would mean that he could not have been the immediate teacher of Śaṅkara's teachers. On the other hand, we have to remember that Gauḍapāda is regarded a Yogi and Govindapāda an alchemist and Yogi. Like some other such persons, they could have lived very long.[65] It is thus possible that a long time elapsed between Govindapāda, his teacher and his disciple.[66]

Tradition avers that Gauḍapāda was a disciple of Patañjali who cursed him to be a *brahmarākṣasa*.[67] He was released from the curse when he met Candra whom he taught the *Mahābhāṣya*. Again, having been released he became a disciple of Śuka, the son of Vyāsa and became known as Gauḍapāda. This Candra is said to have had several sons one of whom was Bhartṛhari. Again, this Candra is said to have been named as Govindapāda after he was initiated into *sannyāsa* by Gauḍapāda.[68]

The historicity of these traditions is highly doubtful. Patañjali, belonging to the 2nd century B.C., is too far removed from Gauḍapāda who could not have been earlier than the 6th century A.D. Again, Bhartṛhari is now placed in the 5th century A.D. and hence could not be posterior to Govindapāda who probably lived in the 7th century A.D. Again, there is nothing in the known works of Gauḍapāda to connect him with the grammarians except that some of them like Bhartṛhari followed a distinctive school of monistic thought. Gauḍapāda's monism, however, is quite different.

Apart from the *Āgamaśāstra* or the *Māṇḍūkya Kārikās* several other works too have been ascribed to Gauḍapāda. Among these may be mentioned the *Uttara-gītā-bhāṣya* and the *Subhagodaya* as also a commentary on the *Nṛsiṁhatāpanīya* and *Śrī Vidyāratnasūtra*. These ascriptions, however, cannot be authenticated.

Even less is known about Govindapāda of whom no definitely ascribable work exists. A work *Rasahṛdaya* is supposed to have him as its author. It is said that he was a great Yogi and adept whose body defied age. His chief title to historical memory is that he acted as the link between Gauḍapāda and Śaṅkara. He is said to have dwelt on the Narmadā where Śaṅkara met him. He initiated Śaṅkara formally into *sannyāsa* and the Advaita tradition. Śaṅkara is said to have spent two years with him according to *Br. S. V.* (T.S. Narayana Sastri, *op.cit.*, p.63). Śaṅkara was then directed to go to Kāśī. In order to reach Varanasi from Mahismati Śaṅkara presumably followed the age-old route through Vidisa, Bharhut and Prayaga or Kausambi.

As Al-biruni has stated Kāśī was the *tīrtha* par excellence where the anchorites wish to stay till death. It was said that even a murderer was cleansed of his sins by entering Varanasi.[69] It was as famous for its orthodox learning as for its holiness. It is near Varanasi that Buddha had started his teaching and Sarnath had been a famous centre of Buddhist art. By the 7th century, however, orthodoxy had asserted itself. Hsuan Chwang says, 'The country. . . is densely populated. The families are very rich and in the dwellings are objects of rare value. The disposition of the people is soft and humane, and they are earnestly given to study. They are mostly unbelievers, a few reverence the law of the Buddha. . . There are about thirty *sanghārāmas* and 3000 priests. They study the little vehicle according to the Sammatīya school. There are a hundred or so Deva temples with about 10,000 sectaries. They honour principally Maheśvara. Some cut their hair off, others tie their hair in a knot, and go naked, without clothes (*Nirgranthas!*) they cover their bodies with ashes (Pāśupata), and by the practice of all sorts of austerities they seek to escape from birth and death. . . In the capital there are twenty Deva temples, the towers and halls of which are of sculptured stone and carved wood. The foliage of trees combines to shade (*the sites*), while pure streams of water encircle them.The statue of the Deva Maheśvara, made of Teou-shih (native copper), is somewhat less than 100 feet high. Its appearance is grave and majestic, and appears as though really living."[70] Another description of Kāśī not far removed from the time of Śaṅkara may be gleaned from the Kashmiri poet Dāmodaragupta who belonged to the court of King Jayāpīḍa (A.D. 779-813 or 751-82. We have to remember that during the 8th century King Lalitaditya Muktāpīḍa had invaded the Madhyadeśa and won a resounding victory over the ruler of Kannauj. There was a fairly brisk contact between the scholars of Madhyadeśa and Kashmir where the Court provided them patronage and set critical standards. The Varanasi of Damodaragupta is in line with the later reputation of the town. It was at once a city steeped in holiness as well as worldliness. Its temples, monasteries, priests, scholars and ascetics of diverse shades proclaimed its religious importance while its tall and decorated buildings, flourishing business, festive sounds of dance and song, and bold hetaerae proclaimed its wealth and secular attachment. '*Asti Khalu nikhila-bhūtalabhūṣaṇa-bhūta vibhūti-quṇa-yuktā/ Yuktābhiyukta-janatānagarī Vārāṇasī nāma//*'[71] It was a second Amarāvatī on earth. It is in this city of orthodoxy, ritualism, sectarianism and ascetic vagaries that Śaṅkara now took his abode.[72] Either before or after the completion of his magnum opus Śaṅkara is said to have journeyed to the Himalayas.[73] He is said to have gone to Badrīnātha and to have restored the worship of Badrīnārāyaṇa there.[74] He is said to have stayed in *Vyāsa-guhā* and to have visited Kedāranātha and Uttarakāśī. It is said he was once virtually carried off by the swift Alakanandā but was saved by Sanandana. He is also credited with the discovery of a hot-water spring.[75] According to one version it is in the Himalayas that he was inspired with the mission of being a preacher of Advaita.[76]

In Kāśī Śaṅkara is said to have stayed near the Manikarnika Ghāt, worshipped Śiva and instructed a growing band of disciples which included the celebrated Sanandana who had come from the banks of Kāveri in the Cola country.[77] Śaṅkara was then twelve years of age. Whether the writing of the famous commentaries was accomplished in Kāśī or in Badari in the far North, is disputed in different traditions.[78] In any case it is generally agreed that the writing of the commentaries was completed when Śaṅkara had attained the age of sixteen.

While he was staying at Kāśī a startling incident is said to have occurred and pointed the way to the far North for Śaṅkara. One day while he was proceeding towards the river with his disciples he met a Cāṇḍāla on the way and asked him to move away. The Cāṇḍāla, however, promptly pointed out the contradiction between the Vedāntic idea of spiritual unity and the caste notion of untouchability. Śaṅkara was quick to realize his error.[79] Whether the Cāṇḍāla was Śiva himself in human form or whether Śaṅkara realized that the Cāṇḍālas like all beings could not be anything other than Śiva, are merely the same fact presented mythically or philosophically. The incident could hardly be a fabrication of later times when such a repudiation of untouchability or caste-inequality was unthinkable within orthodoxy. It is said that it was the Śiva as Cāṇḍāla who directed Śaṅkara towards Badari where he was to write the commentary on the *Brahmasūtras.*

Another story relates that after Śaṅkara had completed his commentary on the *Brahmasūtras,* he was once accosted by an old man who was sceptical about the young Master's understanding of the *sūtras.* A long debate ensued at the end of which the Brāhmaṇa revealed himself to be none other than the author of the *sūtra* work itself. It is said that the sage Vyāsa blessed Śaṅkara with another lease of life for a further sixteen years.[80] An alternate version makes Vyāsa merely bless Śaṅkara without there having been any argument between them.[81]

Thus Śaṅkara entered the second half of his life which he is said to have spent as a debating peripatetic while organizing a new order of mendicants at the same time. It is difficult to arrange the various traditional accounts of these years in any definite chronological order. The incidents consist of his pilgrimages and peregrinations to different parts of the country, the establishment of monastic seats, debates with scholars and teachers of other schools and sects and the training of a growing band of devoted students and disciples who began composing further commentaries and expositions of the Master's works.

At some point in this period occurred the demise of Śaṅkara's mother.[82] According to one version Śaṅkara was able to reach her before she died and thus fulfilled his earlier promise to her.[83] He is also believed to have himself performed her last rites. As this was opposed to the established code of behaviour for a *sannyāsin* he was ostracised by his kinsmen and villagers.[84] This incident is another instance of the Master's disregard of mere conventions. The people of the village, however, were treated by posterity as accursed on account of their attitude to the Master, an interdiction which was lifted only some time back.

As will be seen from the legendary accounts mentioned above, Śaṅkara's life falls into two distinct parts. The first sixteen years constitute the years of education and principal literary activity. Whether this constitutes half of his life depends on the view taken of the total length of his life. According to the tradition he lived for only thirty-two years, although there is a slightly divergent tradition also.[85] On the other hand, some modern critics have questioned these traditions.[86] These views would be discussed later as also the question of the total literary output of Śaṅkara.

It seems incontrovertible on the basis of contemporary evidence itself that Śaṅkara was a Southerner by birth but familiar with the North, a Brāhmaṇa of the *Atri-gotra* who had renounced the world and became a mendicant, and that he was the disciple of Govindapāda and the grand-disciple of Gauḍapāda. That he came from a Namboodiri family from Kalati, that he met Govindapāda on the banks of the Narmadā, while hardly nine years of age, and that he composed the celebrated *Brahmasūtrabhāṣya* by the age of sixteen in Kāśī or in the Himalayas near Badrīnātha, are averments made more or less unanimously in the traditional accounts. The incidents narrated about the meeting with the Cāṇḍāla in Kāśī or the death and last rites of the mother have probably a historical basis because they are too untraditional to have been fabricated in later times. The story about Śaṅkara's meeting with Vyāsa can only be regarded as mythical. Whether Śaṅkara met Gauḍapāda would normally seem most unlikely except for a curious passage in the *Chāndogyabhāṣya*, which has been interpreted to mean that Gauḍapāda was still alive while Śaṅkara was writing.[87] The interpretation is not impossible if Gauḍapāda could be supposed to have lived for more than a hundred years like Tailang Swami or the 'ageless' Devraha Baba.

According to tradition Śaṅkara was originally destined to live for only eight years but got a further lease of eight years when he died the voluntary death of *sannyāsa*. It is said that at sixteen when he had completed the writing of the *Bhāṣya*, Vyāsa was so pleased with him that he gave him a further lease of sixteen years so that he could adequately teach and spread the doctrine expounded by him. It has been suggested by a recent author that these extensions in the longevity of Śaṅkara should be understood to indicate three different phases in his life. 'Completion of study marked the first phase. His initiation into the *sannyāsa* way of life was the second phase. He became a social reformer in the third phase.'[88] Although this interpretation cannot be said to reveal the conscious intention of the legend-makers, it does point to critical turns in the life of the Master. When he took *sannyāsa* under the shadow of imminent physical death, he did die for the world as a possible householder and was reborn as a seeker of transcendental spirituality. When he turned to be a preacher for the world at large, it was a return from withdrawal, a *Katabasis* in the Platonic sense. He was no longer a merely self-absorbed seer or a cloistered intellectual but an active missionary. This too may be deemed as a kind of rebirth.

Before we proceed to consider the mission of Śaṅkara, we might critically review his achievements during the first half of his life. These consist mainly of his intellectual and spiritual learning and his literary output. The general intellectual and educational culture of his age as probably accessible to him has already been briefly sketched and so has the tradition about his precocious and prodigious learning. A clearer and authentic understanding of the question may be gained by an examination of Śaṅkara's own writings.[89] In his commentary on the *Brahmasūtras,* he quotes from the following works:

(*a*) *Vedic literature: Ṛgveda-saṁhitā, Atharvaveda-saṁhitā Aitareya-Brāhmaṇa, Ārṣeya-Brāhmaṇa, Śatapatha-Brāhmaṇa, Kauṣītaki-Brāhmaṇa, Kāṭhaka-Brāhmaṇa, Chāndogya-Brāhmaṇa, Maitrāyaṇī-saṁhitā, Pañcaviṁśa-Brāhmaṇa, Ṣaḍviṁśa-Brāhmaṇa, Taittirīya-Brāhmaṇa, Vājasaneyi-saṁhitā, Tāṇḍyamahā-Brāhmaṇa, Aitareya-Āraṇyaka, Aitareya-Upaniṣad, Īśopaniṣad, Kenopaniṣad, Kauṣītaki-Upaniṣad, Muṇḍakopaniṣad, Praśnopaniṣad, Taittirīyāraṇyaka, Taittirīyopaniṣad, Śvetāśvataropaniṣad, Jābālopaniṣad, Paiṅgirahasya-Brāhmaṇa; Yāska's Nirukta, Kātyāyana Śrautasūtra, Āśvalāyana Śrautasūtra, Kauṣikasūtra;* (*b*) *Epics, Purāṇas, and Smṛtis: Mahābhārata, Rāmāyaṇa, Āpastambadharmasūtra, Pāraskara-gṛhyasūtra, Mānavadharmaśāstra, Bhagavad-gītā, Mārkaṇḍeya-Purāṇa;* (*c*) *Sūtras and Philosophical works; Kāpila-Śāṅkhyasūtra, Jaimini-sūtra, Yoga-sūtra, Nyāya-sūtra, Vaiśeṣika-sūtra, Pāṇini's Aṣṭādhyāyī,* Gauḍapāda's *Kārikās,* diverse commentaries on the Mīmāṁsās such as of Śabara and Upavarṣa, and Vedāntic teachers like Dravidācārya, Bodhāyana, Brahmadatta, Bhartṛprapañca, Sundara Pāṇḍya. Among heterodox philosophies Śaṅkara is aware of the Lokāyatas, the Buddhists, the Jainas, the Pāñcarātras and the Pāśupatas. He seems to refer to some Buddhist texts which appear to go back to the Sautrāntikas and the school of Dharmakīrti. His awareness of contemporary or near-contemporary philosophers like Dharmakīrti, Kumārila and Maṇḍana Miśra is undeniable.

In the *Bṛhadāraṇyakopaniṣadbhāṣya* additional references to the following works have been pointed out: (*a*) *Vedic: Bahvṛca-Brāhmaṇa, Kaṭharudropaniṣad, Māṇḍūkyopaniṣad, Mahānārāyaṇopaniṣad, Nāradaparvrājakopaniṣad, Nṛsiṁha-Pūrva-tāpanīyopaniṣad, Nṛsiṁhottaratāpanīyopaniṣad,* (*b*) *Smṛtis and Purāṇas: Baudhāyana dharmasūtra, Gautama dharmasūtra, Śivapurāṇa, Vāyupurāṇa, Viṣṇupurāṇa, Vāsiṣṭhasmṛti.*

The *BGB* also refers to the *Baudhāyanadharmasūtra* and *Smṛti.*

Thus Śaṅkara appears to have been well versed in the traditional fourteen branches of learning (*Vidyās*), viz., the four *Vedas,* the six *Vedāṅgas* (*Śikṣā, Chandas, Vyākaraṇa, Nirukta, Jyotiṣa* and *Kalpa*), *Purāṇa, Tarka, Mīmāṁsā* and *Dharmaśāstra.* What knowledge he had if any of *Āyurveda* to which he refers, or of *Dhanurveda, Gāndharvaveda* and *Arthaśāstra,* we do not know. The story about the claim to 'omniscience' or the *sarvajña pīṭha* which required

Śaṅkara to learn even erotics suggests that the ideal of learning in those days was to be acquainted with all the *śāstras.* Śaṅkara's primarily philosophical and spiritual interest as well as his strong distaste of irrelevance in thought and activity militate against his having exercised his mind or spent his time in merely utilitarian and empirical studies with no moral or spiritual relevance. Śaṅkara had acquired the traditional learning expected of a well-educated Brāhmaṇa teacher of the *śāstras.* He was also familiar with orthodox and heterodox schools of philosophy. At the same time he was a well-travelled and wide-awake person, aware of his social surroundings and possessed of vigorous common sense. He was essentially an original thinker who, though well-read, used his learning lightly and only when necessary.

As to Śaṅkara's spiritual education this question is partly tied up with the view we take of the authenticity of the various works ascribed to him. He had an orthodox and Brāhmaṇical education but gave up ritualistic religion when he took up *sannyāsa* and the wandering life of a mendicant. Govindabhagavatpāda must have initiated him into the spiritual tradition of Vedānta, of which some texts claim to give an account. How deep was his interest and training in *Yoga* and *Bhakti* or *Tantra* would be discussed below.

REFERENCES

1. Cf. Baldev *Upadhyaya, op.cit.,* pp 11 ff.
2. It has been argued that Ānandajñāna in his *Aitareyopaniṣadbhāṣya* is said to quote from the *Dīpikā* of Vidyāraṇya and should thus be later than the 14th century. Similarly it has been argued by T.A. Gopinath Rao that Sarvajñātmamuni's teacher Deveśvara should not be identified with Sureśvara but with the disciple of Devānanda who was the disciple of Śreṣṭhānanda as mentioned in the *Pramāṇalakṣaṇa* which was written by Sarvajñātmamuni. R.K. Aiyar and K.B. Venkataraman. *The Truth About the Kumbakonam Mutt,* pp. 87-89; contra T.S. Narayan Sastri, *op.cit.,* p.227; Baldev *Upadhyaya, op. cit.,* p.222; N. Veezhinathan, *The Saṅkṣepa-śārīraka of Sarvajñātman,* pp. 3-5. The fact that Madhusudana Sarasvati and Ramatirtha accept the Deveśvara-Sureśvara equation is strong evidence for it.
3. Vide *supra* Chapter 1, many supporters of the Śṛṅgerī tradition question the authenticity of these works, e.g., Aiyar and Venkataraman, *op.cit.,* p.17. What they really oppose is the support these works occasionally tend to the claims of Kāñcī as an *āmnāyamaṭha.* However, the absence of critically edited texts for these works makes it difficult to decide the authenticity of specific lines or passages.
4. *Śivarahasya* (9th Aṁśa, 16th Chapter). *Varṇāśrama-paribhraṣṭān adharma-pravaṇān janān/Kalyabdhau majjamānān stān dṛṣṭvānukrośatombike//*

Madaṁśa-jāto Deveśi Kalāvapi tapodhanam/Keralesutadā vipraṁ janayāmi maheśvari//—Jainā Bauddhā buddhiyuktā mīmāṁśāniratāḥ kalau/ Veda-bodhaka-Vākyānām anyathaiva prarocakāḥ/ ... Teṣām utpāṭanārthāya sṛjāmīśe madaṁśataḥ"; Kūrmapurāṇa, (27.31-32)" *Kalau Rudro Mahādevo lokānām īśvaraḥ paraḥ/Tadeva sadhayen nṝāṁ devatānāṁ ca daivatam// Kariṣyatyavatāraṁ svaṁ Śaṅkaro Nīlalohitaḥ/Śrauta-smārta-pratiṣṭhār the bhaktānāṁ hita-Kāmyayā; "Mārkaṇḍeya-saṁhitā (Khaṇḍa 72, Parispanda 7*): *"Lokānugraha-tatparaḥ para-śivaḥ samprārthito Brahmaṇā Cārvākādi-mata-prabheda-nipuṇām buddhim sadā dhārayan, Kālaṭyākhya-purottame Śiva-gurur Vidyādhināthaśca yaḥ tat patnyaṁ śivatārake samuditaḥ Śrī-Śaṅkarākhyāṁ Vahan//"*

5. *Gītā-bhāṣya, Upodghāta—"adharmeṇa abhibhūyamāne dharme pravardhamāne ca adharme jagataḥ sthitim paripipālayiṣuh sa ādikartā Nārāyaṇākhyo viṣṇuh bhaumasya brahmaṇo brāhmaṇatvasya rakṣaṇārthaṁ Devakyāṁ Vasudevāt aṁśena Kṛṣṇaḥ kila sambabhūva."*
6. Sureśvara in the *Naiskarmyasiddhi* describes Śaṅkara as the great teacher whose excellence was unsurpassed (*Yasmād vyāvṛttās tambhādayaḥ,* 1.2.), as the omniscient sage established in Brāhmaṇa (*Sarvajñam brahmasaṁstham,* 4.76), and as the teacher of teacher (*guru-guru*) who used reason to illumine the disciples (*nyāya-śalākayaiva,* 4.77). In the *Bṛ. Vārtika* he describes Śaṅkara as one who had faithfully followed his teachers (*guravo' nuvṛttaguravaḥ*). In the *Tai. vārtika* he describes Śaṅkara as famous all over, full of compassion for the suffering populace and as the terror of mere logicians (1.2.). He is again described as the Prince of Mendicants (*maskarīndra*), as the leader of the caravan of spiritual seekers, and as bearing the name of Śiva (*bhava-nāma-bhṛto yateh,* 3.10.48-49).
7. Padmapāda's verse uses *double entendre* brilliantly—*Namāmy abhogi-parivāra-sampadaṁ Nirasta-bhūtim anumārdha-vigraham Anugram unmṛdita-kāla-lāñchanam vinā Vināyakamapūrva-Śaṅkaram/* i.e., 'I bow to the New Śaṅkara (Śiva) who does not have the rich entourage of snakes (or worldlings), who does not smear ashes (but who has extinguished the cycle of rebirth), whose other half is not Umā (but logical inference), who is not fierce, who has eradicated the stigma of time, and who is without Gaṇeśa (or who has set aside the Buddhists).' It is curious that in explaining this verse the commentators seem to miss the obvious equation of *Bhūti* and *Bhava.*
8. Vācaspati Miśra in the *Bhāmatī* describes Śaṅkara as gifted with pure knowledge and abundant compassion (*natvā viśuddha-vijñānaṁ Śaṅkaram Karuṇāniddim*).
9. *Sarvajñātman says, 'Vaktāramāsādya yam eva nityā Sarasvatī svārtha-samanvitāsīt/Nirasta-dustarka-kalaṅka-paṅkā namāmi taṁ Śaṅkaram arcitāṅghrim//* (1.7) i.e.,' I salute Śrī Śaṅkara whose feet were worshipped by all, and on obtaining that exponent the eternal speech—the *Veda*—became possessed of its true import, as from it the fallacious reasoning, metaphorically, the dirt and loose clay, has been removed.' (Veezhinathan's tr.)
10. Cf. '*Yenādhītāni śāstrāṇi Bhagavat-Śaṅkarāhvayāt/ Niḥśeṣa-sūri-mūrdhāli-mālā-līḍhā-ṅghri-paṅkajāt//*' (*Inscription du Cambodge,* ed. G. Coedes, I. pp. 36-46).
11. *M,* Canto I, Tirumala Dīkṣita, *Śaṅkarābhyudaya,* Canto I.

12. Cf. Burton Stein, *Peasant State & Society in Medieval South India*, pp. 80-81.
13. Cf. Nilakantha Sastri, *A History of South India*, p.424.
14. *AA* (ed. Veezhinathan), Preface, pp. iii-v. The quotation from *AA* in Acyutaraya Modaka's Comy. confirms the authenticity of the text being Kalati. *Prācīna* 32.1: '*Kālatyākhya-grāmavarye keralālaṅkṛtikrte*, quoted, Narayana Sastri, *op.cit.*, p.272).
15. Cf. Alston, *A Sankara Source Book*, Vol. I, p.44.
16. *Suṣama* ad RMS, 17: '*Nava-Śaṅkarendra-vibhorasyābhedagraheṇa janma-digvijaya-niryāṇa-pramukheṣu sthaleṣu tayordvayor api vṛttam ekataḥ saṅkulīkṛtya nibabandhuḥ—Katipaye kavava ityavagantavyam.*'
17. *GVK*, 1.32-36, contains a lovely descriptoin of Kerala.
18. Asoka, *RE* XIII and II; vide B.C. Law, *Historical Geography of Ancient India*, p.164.
19. Lallanji Gopal, *The Economic Life of Northern India* (700-1200 A.D.), pp. 147-48.
20. *Ibid.*, pp. 125 ff.
21. Cf. Nilakanta Sastri, *op.cit.*, pp. 331-32.
22. Cf. Tara Chand, *Influence of Islam on Indian Culture.*
23. An Alexandrian merchant, Cosmas travelled to South India in A.D. 522 and founded Nestorian Church at Quilon. A copper-plate grant to Malabar Christians goes back to A.D. 774. Nilakanta Sastri, *op.cit.*, p.440.
24. *Ibid.*, p.163.
25. *Ibid.*, p.145.
26. Cf. *IA* 1887, pp. 160-61.
27. Irawati Karve, Quot, Burton Stein, *op.cit.*, p.58 fn.41.
28. *GVK*, 1.37: *Kāraṭī* as a primarily Brāhmaṇa village; Rājacūḍāmaṇi *Śaṅkarābhyudaya*, 1.11: *Kālaṭī* as an *agrahara*; Govindanatha gives an admirable description, 2.9.12: '*Nilā Marudvṛdhā ceti tatra nadyau virājataḥ/ Nilāyāṁ Śambara (Śaṅkara) Kroḍam bhāsate śāsturāsadam/ Nānā-kṣetraṁ catasyā hi tīre dīvyati muktidam/ Bhavanam Padmanābhasya bhuvana-trayapāvanam// Cūrṇīti Cāpaī khyātā tīrayor ubhayor nadī/ Atisvaccha-jalā dhatte puṇyān api surālayān// Ṛddhimān uttare tīre tasyāḥ pāvana-pāthasaḥ/ Kaścid deśo mahān asti Kālaṭī ti suviśrutaḥ//*

    Cidvilāsīya (5.4-8) describes Kāraṭī as a prosperous city on the bank of the Cūrṇi, near Dakṣina-Kailāsa or Vṛṣācala. According to *M.* Canto II, on the bank of the river Pūrṇā Śiva descended as a *svayambhū-liṅga* at Vṛṣācala. The King Rājaśekhara had a temple constructed there. Nearby was the *agrahāra* of Kalati.
29. Cf. '*Pazurpanai Illam* in the neighbourhood of Trichur, has been in all Kerala understood to be the family to which Śaṅkara's mother Āryāmbā belonged. . . The specified place where he (Śaṅkara) took his birth is now crowned with a shrine dedicated to him. . . The place where Śaṅkara conferred his benediction to a poor lady by singing his '*Kanakadhārā stotra*' still continues to bear the name '*swarnathu manaikal*' owned by a Nambudiri, who claims to be a lineal descendent of the lady.' (T.S. Narayana Sastri *op.cit.*, pp. 275-76).
30. *Vyāsācalīya*, cantos II-IV, treats of the circumstances leading to the penance elaborately. Purusottama Bharati's *Śaṅkaravijayasangraha* makes out Śaṅkara to be a posthumous child. This tradition was utilized by some followers of Madhva to cast aspersions on the legitimacy of Śaṅkara's birth. According

to the Kāñcī tradition it was not Ādya Śaṅkara but Abhinava Śaṅkara who was posthumous.

31. Śaṅkara has been called *Atri-Kulodbhava*, Sureśvara, *Br. B.V.* His family Veda is said to be *Taittirīya-śākhā*. Dhanapati Sūri's *Diṇḍima* ad M.II.6.

32. According to a quotation from *Prācīna-Śaṅkaravijaya*, Śaṅkara was born 'in the fourth (*Karkata*) *Lagna* under the constellation of Punarvasu, in the month of Vaiśākha... in the year Nandana.' A quotation from the *Bṛhat Śaṅkaravijaya* confirms the year Nandana, the month of Vaiśākha and the Punarvasu *nakṣatra*, and adds that it was a Sunday and the *tithi* was *Śukla pañcamī*. The Dvārakā Mutt also accepts Vaiśākha *Śuklapañcamī* as the birth-*tithi* of Śaṅkara. According to the horoscope accepted by the Śṛṅgerī Maṭha Śaṅkara was born in the *Ārdrā Nakṣatra* and the *Mithuna lagna*. An anonymous tradition places the birth of Śaṅkara in *Vaiśākha śukla daśami* in the year *Vibhava*. (T.S. Narayana Sastri, *Age of Sankara*, pp.217, 237, 239, 256 265, 273; K.B. Pathak in *I.A.* 1882).

33. E.g. *M.IV.* 1 ff 'Within his first year this child... showed himself proficient in languages. By the second year, he could recite all books and showed an untaught mastery of *Kāvyas* and *Purāṇas*. Hearing once, he could learn anything" (tr. Tapasyananda), *Vyāsācala*, *IV* 31, *GKV*, II. 2-4.

34. *M.IV.* 5; the same verse occurs in *Tirumala*, III 13. G.K.V. II 5; *Govindanātha*, III. 2-4 here the knowledge of reading, writing etc. is placed after the *Caulakarman* in the third year. So also *Cidvilāsa*, VI. 24 ff.

35. Cf. *Govindanatha* (114) '*Kāvyāni cetihāsāñśca purāṇānyakhilāni ca*', *Cidvilāsa (VI.* 36-37: he studies *Kośas, stotras, Kāvyas, Chandas, alaṅkāras* and '*gīta-vāditra-nṛtyādi-śāstra-tattva-Vicāravit*.'

36. The first tradition about Śivaguru having performed the *Upanayana* and then dying is found in *RSM, BSV* and *PSV* also in *Cidvilāsīya*. Thus *RSM*, 17 runs. '*Upanīya divaṁ gate sva-tāte*', *BSV* has '*Śivagurur upanīya Śaṅkarāryam*' (quoted *Suṣamā*), *PSV* has '*Caulaṁ Karma Samāpya copanayanaṁ tāte divaṁ prasthite* (*Quoted Suṣamā*), *Cidvilāsīya* (VII. 10) has '*Ataniṣṭopaṇītiṁ sa samastair bandhubhiryutaḥ*'. On the other hand, *M.* (IV11) describes Śivaguru as '*upaninīṣita-sūnu*', while dying, so Govindanā also '*Pañcamābde nijam putram upanetumanā dvijaḥ / Pañcatvamagamat sadyah*' (III. 6). Vyāsācala has '*Tam Pañcamābda upanetumānassa eva pañcatvamāpa*' (IV.32), so also *GVK* (I. 6-7). The *Suṣamā* seeks to support the earlier version. Radhakrisna Sastri suggested the reconciliation mentioned in the text, *SVM* p.51.

37. Nilakantha Sastri, *op.cit.*, p.321. The state of education in pre-British India was far from being dismal as made out by Macaulay, vide Dr. Dharmapal's most significant work, *The Beautiful Tree* (1983), R.K. Mookerji's *Education in Ancient India* sketches the state of education in Cālukya, Rāṣṭrakūṭa and Cola times on the basis of epigraphic evidence. That is the background accepted here.

38. Nilakantha Sastri, *The Colas*; A.S. Altekar, *The Rāṣṭrakūṭas*, pp. 400-405.

39. R.K. Mookerji, *op.cit.*, pp. 367-70.

40. E.g., D.C. Sircar, *Select Inscription*, Vol. II, pp. 448, 453, 459, 474, 484, 545 etc.

41. Nilakantha Sastri, *History of South India*, pp. 323-24.

42. Thus (*M* IV. 16) he studied the four *Vedas* along with the six *aṅgas*; *M.* (V. 20) '*Ānvīkṣikyaikṣi Tantre paricitir atulā Kāpile Kāpi lebhe Pītam*

pātañjalāmbhaḥ paramapi viditam bhāṭṭa-ghaṭṭārthatattvam, "GVK (1.8) = "avāpa Vidyāh/Aṣṭādaśevanayanāni vikasvarāṇi// The 18 Vidyās are specified by Yājñavalkya thus—" Aṅgāni Vedās' Catvāre mīmāṁsā nyāyavistaraḥ/ Purāṇam dharmaśāstraṁ ca vidyā hyetāścaturdaśa// Āyurvedo dhanurvedo gāndharvam cārthaśāstrakam/, Rājacūḍāmaṇi, I. 36-37; Tirumala, II. 14-20.

43. *M*, V. 31-33, *Tirumala*, II. 71.
44. *GVK* (I. 9); *M*, V. 10-30; Rājacūḍāmaṇi, I. 39.40, *Tirumala*, II. 68-70.
45. *M*, V. 61 ff; Rājacūḍāmaṇi, I. 43-51; *Govindanāthīya*. III. 13-20; *Cidvilāsīya*, VIII. 14-21; *GVK*, II. 13. It is worth noting, however, that Tirumala does not mention the story but attributes the permission of the mother to the expostulation of sages-II. 78 ff.
46. Several commentaries of the *Saundaryalaharī* such as *Saubhāgyavardhini, Aruṇāmodinī Ānandagirīyā and Padārthacandrikā* mention the story in connection with the verse *Tava stanyam manye* etc.
47. *Hindi Padāvalī* of *Namadeva*, ed. Callewaert and Lath (Delhi 1989) p.17.
48. *M* IV. 21 ff.
49. E.g., Kālidāsa, *Raghuvaṁśa*, V.
50. *M*. V. 75, *Govinda*, III. 11-12.
51. *M*, V. 76 ff.
52. *M*, V. 90; but Cidvilāsa(VIII) 38 places it in Badari. Govindanātha places it in Kāśī, Canto III. 20.
53. Al-biruni (tr. Sachau), II. pp. 146 ff.
54. *Ibid.*, Vol. I. pp. 208-209.
55. Baldev Upadhyaya, *op.cit.*, pp. 60-61.
56. *M* 14. 28-29; *GVK* 2.61.62, makes Śaṅkara go to his mother from the banks of Revā.
57. *Uttararāmacarita*. 2.23.24.
58. Cf. B.C. Law, *op.cit.*, under Māhiṣmatī.
59. T.S. Narayana Sastri, *op.cit.*, pp. 39-40.
60. *M*, V. 138.
61. See below.
62. Max Walleser, *Der ältere Vedanta, Geschichte, Kritik Und Lehre*, Heidelberg, 1910. The question is also discussed by Belvalkar, *S.K. Shree Gopal Basu Mallik Lectures on Vedanta Philosophy*, Pt. I, Poona, 1929. Against these doubts, see. *IA*, Oct. 1933, pp. 122-23.
63. Cf. *Naiṣkarmyasiddhi*, 4.43-44, which says '*Evam Gaudair Drāvidaiṛ naḥ Pūjyair arthaḥ prakāśitaḥ.*' This reference does not imply two schools but only two venerated individuals.
64. Cf. Vidhusekhara Bhattacarya, *Āgamaśāstra*, Intr. p.76.
65. Cf. G.N. Kaviraj, *op.cit.*, p.20.
66. But see below on Gauḍapāda.
67. There are two main sources of the traditional account of Gauḍapāda, viz., Rāmabhadra Dīkṣita's *Patañjali-Caritam* and Harimiśra's *Gauḍapādollāsa* which has been quoted in *Suṣamā* and of which a MS was once said to be available in the Oriental College Library, Lahore. In the *RSM* it is stated '*Abhiyuñjad ayārcya-pūjyapādān apalūnyādiniṣāka-Siddhanetṝn/Atha Gauḍapadān Phanīśabhāṣya-prathamācāryakapaṇḍitān prapadye//.* "(v. 10) *Suṣamā* comments" *Abhiyuñjatā vivādāya ātmānam upanirundhatā*

Ayārcyeṇa tadabhidhena Himālaya-śṛṅgavarti-Buddha-siddha-sabhā-nāyakena Pūjyau sevyamānau pādau yeṣāṁ tān. Apalūnyaḥ tadākhyaḥ kaścit. Ādiḥ mukhyam yeṣām teṣām niṣāka-siddhānām Aparāntyayoginām prāvṛti-prabhṛtīnām netṝn anuśāsitṝn Phaṇīśa-bhāṣyasya Patañjali-bhāṣyasya Prathamācāryake ādya-pravacane candraśarmaṇaḥ iti śeṣaḥ paṇḍitān... Gauḍapadān... Ayaṁ kila Gauḍapādaḥ purā svayameva śeṣarūpam avatiṣṭhamānena bhagavatā Patañjalinā procyamāne svakṛta-mahābhāṣye tacchiṣyeṣvanyatamaḥ pravacana-sthalān nivṛttya nirdagdheṣvavagaṇitācārya-nideśeṣu apanīta-javanikeṣu ativiṣama-viṣama-viṣānalena niravaśeṣeṣu sabrahmacāriṣu prakṛtim āpannasya paścāttāpino guroh śāpād avāptabrahma-rakṣobhāvaḥ paran tasyaiva praṇipāta-prasanna-mānasaḥ sadṛśādhikārisampraveśita-sva bhāṣya-sampūrṇa-pravacanāvadhir astvasau śāpa ityanugṛhītaḥ samucitādhikāriṇe praṇigadya Candra-Śarmaṇe pātañjalaṁ mahābhāṣyam avamuktah śāpād āruhya Himālayādri-śṛṅgamavalokita-śukarṣi-prasāda Samāsādita-saṁyamācāronavaratam anusaṁsthānam ātma-yāthātmya sakāśa eva kva cid durge samākalitasaṁsthānānām Takṣaśilādhīśa-śākya-prāvṛti-pramukhair Apalūnya-Damīśādya-Āparāntya-Yogi-saṅghaiśca sevyamā-nānām Ayārcya-pramukhānām anugata-Śauddhadanikādadhvanām abhiyogataḥ pravisṛṣṭadurmata-durabhiniveśānām punar āpatitasya prācya-śiṣyasya Candraśarmaṇaḥ svasmād eva gṛhītasaṁyamasya samāśliṣṭa-Govinda-nāmnaḥ ca pratyahamupadiśyamāna-paramādvaitavidyā-sampradayaściraṁ sukham uvāseti Harimiśrīya Gaudapadollāsa-Patañjali-vijayādau nirūpyamāṇa-Kathātrānusamdheyā.

According to the *Patañjali-Vijaya* Patañjali used to teach the *Mahābhāṣya* to his disciples from behind a curtain so that his thousand-headed dragon-form should remain invisible. It was incumbent on the disciples not to lift the curtain nor to get up from the lesson without reciting the *Śāntipāṭha*. Once the students broke the first rule out of curiosity and were promptly burnt down: *'dadhur atha sadṛśīs tanūḥ smarena'*. Gauḍapāda, who was one of the students, had meanwhile gone out without permission or *Śāntipāṭha*, he was for this reason cursed to become a Brahmarākṣasa. But Patañjali later relented and modified the curse to endure only so long as a suitable student for the *Mahābhāṣya* was not found by passing the test of correctly indicating the past participle of the root *pac*. Such a person was at last discovered by Gauḍapāda as a *Brahmarākṣasa* in a Brāhmaṇa named Candraśarman who then learnt the *Mahābhāṣya* and thus freed Gauḍapāda from the curse.

The story narrated by *Suṣamā* tells us that after his emancipation from the curse Gauḍapāda went to the Himalayas, was instructed by Śuka, and converted Buddhist sages like Ayārcya and seekers from the West Coast like Apalūnya, Niṣāka etc. He then taught the Advaita doctrine to Candraśarman who came to have the name, Govinda.

The legends appear to freely combine bits of history with free fancy. Gauḍapāda could not have had any historical connection with Patañjali who probably belonged to the 2nd century B.C. Perhaps the connection was invented on the assumption that as the author of *Mahābhāṣya* was also the author of *Yoga*, it indicates that he was a master of *Yoga*. That the study of the *Mahābhāṣya* was revived by the efforts of one Candrācārya and Bhartṛhari seems a historical fact. The legend further seems to suggest that Gauḍapāda had some contact with Buddhist Masters of Taxila and some philosophers from the West Coast. This could be a fact. Indeed, the names Ayārcya and Apalūnya suggest non-Indian Greek or Tokharian originals. That Gauḍapāda had Buddhist contacts is certain and that Buddhist Masters included the natives of Bactria and Sogdiana is also certain. It may also be mentioned that according to Ānandagiri's comy. on the *Āgamaśāstra "ācāryo hi purā Badarikāśrame Nara-Nārāyaṇādhiṣṭhite. Nārāyaṇam bhāgavatam abhipretya tapo mahadatapyata. Tato bhagavān atiprasannah tasmai vidyām prādāt it."*

68. *RMS: Hari-talpa-harāṅghri-nūpura-kṣmādhara-Saumitra-Balatrinetra-lakṣmā/Jayatād uparevam āttadhāmā Jayagovindamuniḥ sa candranāmā//* (VII).

According to *Suṣamā* the first line mentions the title by which Candra was named. These indicate that he was the incarnation of Śeṣa and was Patañjali himself. It quotes *Prācīna-Śaṅkara-Vijaya: Govindam āśrayad ahīndra-mahāvatāram. Ārāt tuṣāra-kara-deha-bhuvas taṭinayāḥ / Apyātmajenagalitātma-bhavābhimānenārādhitam ca Hariṇā niyamā-śritena.//'* It has also been claimed, though without evidence, that Gauḍapāda wrote *kārikās* on the *Brahmasūtras,* and that he was known as Draviḍācārya. (T.S. Narayana Sastri, *op.cit.,* pp. 54-55). Nor is there any reason to identify our Gauḍapāda with the commentator of the *Uttaragītā* or the *Śāṅkhyakārikās.* He stayed near the river Narmadā (*Uparevam*).

Govindapāda was called 'Jaya Govinda' since he was in the habit of saying 'Jaya Govinda' but remained silent otherwise. *Suṣamā,* again, quotes the *PSV* to support it. *'Satatam nigadan rasena yo sau Jaya Govinda Jayeti Sūktimekām.' RSM* goes on to pay homage to Hari or *Bhṛtḥari* as the son and dear disciple of Govinda. Hari had renounced his kingdom and attained perfection. *Suṣamā* says *'candraśarmaṇa eva sutaḥ Bhartṛhari-Vikrama-Bhatti-Vararucaya iti vṛddhāḥ'* and also identified Bhartṛhari with Bhartṛprapañca, which would seem unlikely since Śaṅkara is very critical of Bhartṛprapañca.

According to the *Patañjali-Vijaya,* Candra married four wives of four different *varṇas* at Ujjayini and taught *Mahābhāṣya* to students there. After his four children had been educated he adopted renunciation and repaired to Kāśī first and then to Badarikāśrama to meet Gauḍapāda once again.

He is said to have authored *Yoga-tārāvalī, Advaitānubhūti* and *Brahmāmṛtavarṣini* (Narayana Sastri, *op.cit.,* pp. 61-67) but the ascription has nothing to recommend it. Nor is there any reason to suppose that he was the author of the text *Rasahṛdaya.* According to a tradition current in spiritual circles Govinda-bhagavatpāda is said to be an ever-young Mahāyogī (G.N. Kaviraj, *op.cit.,* p.20).

69. Al-biruni, II. p.146 ff.
70. Hsuan Chwang, tr. Beal, Vol. III pp.291 ff.
71. *Kuṭṭanīmatam.*
72. Sadānanda, *Śaṅkara-digvijaya-sāra* (canto III, pp. 18 ff) gives a picturesque description of Śaṅkara's visit to Kāśī.
73. Rājacūḍāmaṇi, I, 63-65, Vyāsācala, IV, 65-66 *M* VI. 56 ff. Govindnātha, III, 58 Cidvilāsa, VIII-38.
74. *GVK,* 3-38.

75. *Ibid.*, 2-28.
76. *Cidvilāsīya*, XII, 2-5.
77. *M* VI, according to *Cidvilāsiya* X he was born in Ahobala, was the son of Mādhava and Lakṣmi who obtained him as son by the grace of Nṛsiṁha. His original name is said to have been Viṣṇuśarman. Śaṅkara gave him the name Sanandana. According to the *Govindanāthīya* IV, he was born in Kuṇḍagrāma in Kerala and was the son of Somaśarman. Having been very poor at first he amassed wealth through business but left it when his Caravan was plundered in a forest once.
78. *M* (VI. 60) and *Brahmānandīya* place it in Badari, *Cidvilāsīya* in Kāśī. *Govindanāthīya* (II) 59-60 also places it in Badari.
79. *M* VI 21-40; Nilakantha, *Śaṅkarabhyudaya*, IIII 10 ff; Tirumala, III. 65 ff. The same idea is expressed in *Maniṣā-pañcaka* attributed to Śaṅkara Cf. K. Sacchidananda Murti, *Sankara Jayanti Mahotsava Lecture*, 1989.
80. *M* VII.
81. Rājacūḍāmaṇi, *op.cit.*, II.
82. *M* 14.29 ff.
83. Vyāsācala, IV. 76 ff.
84. *Vyāsācalīya*, IV. 100-103, Rājacūḍāmani, III; *M* 14-29 ff. According to T.S. Narayana Sastri there is no reference in the *BSV* and *PSV* to any opposition to Śaṅkara's performing the funeral rites of his mother; *op. cit.*, p. 109, fn. 101.
85. Cf. The Oft-quoted verse—*Aṣṭavarse caturvedī dvādaśe sarvaśāstravit/ Śodaṣe Kṛtavān bhāṣyam dvātriṁśe munir abhyagāt//*" occurs in K.S. Pathak's MS as also in *Āryavidyāsudhākara*.
86. The *Keralotpatti* gives Śaṅkara an age of 38 years. G.N. Kaviraj, *op.cit.*, p. 24; Cf. Nakamura, *op.cit.*, so Prof. K.S. Murty too favours a much longer life for Śaṅkara.
87. Vide S.L. Pandey, *op.cit.*
88. Kulakarni, *Ādi Śaṅkara*, p.134.
89. Paul Deussen, *The System of the Vedānta*, pp. 479-500; Thibaut, (tr) *Vedāntasūtras with Śaṅkara's Commentary*, Vol. II pp. 421-30; Mādhavānanda (tr) *Br. Up. Bhāṣya*, pp. XXI-XXII; S.L. Pandey, *op.cit.*, pp. 84-86.

5

Śaṅkara's Literary Activity

Traditional Account of Śaṅkara's Literary Work

Citsukha's *BSV* is said to detail the various literary works of Śaṅkara along with the occasions when they were composed. Thus it is said that he composed the *Devī-Bhujaṅgastava* of 28 verses while he was hardly five. The *Kanaka-dhārāstotra* is said to have been composed while he was seven on the occasion of the rain of golden *āmalakas*. *Bāla-bodha-saṅgraha* is said to be another work composed while Śaṅkara was in the *gurukula*. The *Acyutāṣṭaka* is said to have been composed on the eve of his departure from home and commemorates the re-establishment of the image of Kṛṣṇa at a place safe from the ravages of the river Cūrṇi. The authorship of the *Vedānta-Pañca-prakaraṇī* or *Māyā-vivaraṇa* is also attributed to Śaṅkara at this stage. While Śaṅkara was staying with Govindapāda he is said to have composed the following works: *Narmadāṣṭaka, Prātassmaraṇa, Sādhana-Pañcaka, Yati-Pañcaka, Vākyavṛtti, Viveka-Cūḍāmaṇi, Daśa-ślokī, Ātmānātma-viveka, Ekādaśottaraśata-vākya-grantha, Pañcīkaraṇa* and *Bālabodhinī*. Of these the first four are small poems. The next three are popular philosophical expositions. *Pañcīkaraṇa* has a commentary attributed to Sureśvara. While in the Himalayas he is said to have composed the *Ṣaṭpadī, Hari-stuti, Śataślokī, Svātma-nirūpaṇa, Paramārtha-sārasaṅgraha, Prauḍhānubhūti Prakaraṇa, Parā Pujā, Dakṣiṇāmūrti-stotra,* and the *Dhanyastotra*. Then followed the commentaries *Māṇḍūkyopaniṣad-Kārikās, Viṣṇusahasranāma* and *Sanatsujātīya*, and later the commentaries on the *Gītā*, the *Upaniṣads* and the *Vedānta-sūtras*. He is said to have composed at the request of Viṣṇuśarman *Adhyātmasannyāsa-vidhi* and *Vedānta-diṇḍima*, followed by *Mahāvākyavivaraṇa*. For the sake of his dying mother he is said to have composed the *Tattva-bodha* and the *Kṛṣṇāṣṭaka*. The *Mātṛi-stuti* was composed on her death. *Ātmabodha* is said to have been specially composed for the benefit of Sanandana. While going to Prayāga he is said to have composed *Gaṅgāṣṭaka,*

Prayāgāṣṭaka, Yamunāṣṭaka, Lakṣmī-nṛsiṁha-ratna and *Vedasāra-Śiva-Stotra. Tattvopadeśa* is said to have been composed for the benefit of Prabhākara. *Kāśī Pañcaka, Annapūrṇāṣṭaka, Maṇikarṇikāṣṭaka* and *Kāla-Bhairavāṣṭaka* are attributed to his stay at Kāśī, *Manīṣāpañcaka* was the result of the encounter with the Cāṇḍāla. *Gurvaṣṭaka* is said to have been composed on the occasion of the death of his *guru. Ekaślokī* was composed for the benefit of Udaṅka. *Ānandalaharī* is said to have been composed while reviving a dead boy at Kausambi or Gokarna and *Saundaryalaharī* is said to have been received in the Himalayas from Śiva Himself or to have been composed in whole or part in Kashmir.

This account is based essentially on the report of T.S. Narayana Sastri who claimed to have a fragmentary copy of the *Bṛhat-Śaṅkara-Vijaya,* and has been followed by Dr. Antarkar and Radhakrishna Sastri. The *Mādhavīya* does not speak of Śaṅkara's childhood works except that the *Kanakadhārā stotra* is referred to (V I.93). It speaks of his writings when he visited Badari, 'he wrote in his twelfth year his most profound and attractive commentary on the *Vedāntasūtras* of Bādarāyana. He also wrote commentaries on the principal *Upaniṣads,* beginning with the *Īśa.* Next he commented on the *Bhagavad Gītā,* which forms the core of the *Mahābhārata,* as also on the *Sanatsujātīya, Nṛsiṁhatāpanī* and *Viṣṇusahasranāma.* He also produced many treatises like *Upadeśasāhasrī*' (VI. 61-63). Dhanapati Sūri mentions only ten *Upaniṣads* in his commentary here. It is worth noting that the *Upadeśasāhasrī* is conspicuous by its absence in the *BSV* tradition. The *Mādhavīya* does not speak of other *prakaraṇas* or *stotras* on other occasions except that it mentions Śaṅkara's praise of the Devi at one place and of Nṛsiṁha at another where Dhanapati Sūri quotes the *Lakṣmī Nṛsimha stotra.*

The *Guruvaṁśakāvya* (II. 25) at first follows *M* but then adds that Śaṅkara composed also the *Saundaryalaharī, Prapañcasāra, Subhagodayapaddhati* and the *stotras* of all the popular gods (*Ibid.,* 26). Tirumala speaks of the commentaries including the one on *Viṣṇusahasranāma.* Govindanātha speaks of the commentaries as fifteen in the summary at the end. *Cidvilāsīya* mentions that Śaṅkara was directed to comment on the *Brahmasūtras,* the ten *Upaniṣads,* the *Gītā, Sahasranāma* and the *Rudrādhyāya* (IX. 52). Śaṅkara is said to have composed these as also the *Saundaryalaharī* and *stotras* (X. 2-5). Rājacūḍāmaṇi mentions the commentaries on

Viṣṇusahasranāma, Prapañcasāra, Subhagodayapaddhati, hundreds of *stotras* especially *Saundaryalaharī,* commentaries on the *Upaniṣads,* and finally on the *Brahmasūtras* (I. 51-65). Some of the *stutis* are included in the text itself.

The commonly accepted tradition thus seems to be that Śaṅkara wrote his major commentaries in the Himalayas near Badarīnātha, and that he also composed some other smaller tracts as well as diverse *stotras* on different occasions. His major period of writing is generally placed around his twelfth year but perhaps it may be more reasonable to place it between his twelfth and sixteenth years. No clear chronology of his writings can be said to survive since the tradition supposed to be preserved in *BSV* finds no confirmation in the other texts. In particular the absence of any such tradition in the commentaries on the *M* or even in the *Suṣamā* casts doubt on its genuineness though it does not constitute a disproof. What is more likely is that these traditions might have been associated with some of the *stotras* owing to their contextual appropriateness. Thus the *Kanakadhārā stotra* could be easily imagined in the context of the rain of golden *āmalakas.* The incident itself could be an imaginative reification of the poetic context of the *stotra.* Similarly the *Acyutāṣṭaka* and the *Kṛṣṇāṣṭaka* could be easily connected with the worship of Kṛṣṇa by Śaṅkara's mother. The *stotras* to Narmadā, Kāśī, Gaṅgā, Prayāga, Yamunā etc., could be easily connected with Śaṅkara's visits to those places. Similarly the *Mātṛpañcaka* and the *Manīṣā-pañcaka* suggest their contexts appropriately. The question, however, is of the authenticity of these writings. If they were authored by Śaṅkara, it would be fairly reasonable to suppose that their apparent context could also have been their real context. It is, however, necessary to emphasize that despite disagreements on detail, traditional accounts unanimously credit Śaṅkara with the writing of not only commentaries but also *prakaraṇas* and *stotras.*

The question of determining the authenticity of the writings ascribed to Śaṅkara is complicated by the fact that too many writings have been ascribed to him. This coupled with the small number of years traditionally ascribed to Śaṅkara creates a strong suspicion about the genuineness of the traditional list of writings. The diversity in the character of these writings is another cause of scepticism about them. Modern critics, thus, tend to move to the other extreme and are reluctant to admit anything more than three or four writings of Śaṅkara as genuine.

It is necessary at the outset to face the fact that there are no universal norms about how much, how early or how quickly one may write. Geniuses have been known to flower very early. The epoch-making writings of Galois, Ramanujam, Keats and Shelley belong to their early twenties. Even a work of vast factual scholarship such as *Der Untergang des Abendlandes* was produced in the thirties of the author's life. Some of Tolstoy's great novels presupposing vast knowledge and experience belong to the same age. Wittgenstein's *Tractatus* was first published at thirty-two, Ramsey died at twenty-six. Jñāneśvara had a shorter life. Vivekananda died at thirty-nine. Systematic research may reveal more pertinent facts but it is clear that major works of significance have been produced by geniuses in their twenties or thirties and that significant creative writing may belong to the late teens. If, then, the period of Śaṅkara's major writings were to be placed after his 16th year rather than before it, credibility would not be strained at all. It is quite possible that Śaṅkara left home at twelve rather than eight and that except for spontaneous poetry he may have started serious scholarly and philosophical writing at sixteen rather than at twelve. Indeed, the tradition by supposing that all his writings were completed by sixteen provides a long period simply for debating and organizational work. There is no contradiction in supposing that Śaṅkara continued to write during the period. In any case, it sounds more credible to suppose that he began teaching and scholarly writing at sixteen rather than at twelve. Nor is there any indisputable evidence on the other side except a legendary tradition.

The primary thrust of Śaṅkara's writings is on the logical consideration of revealed and current beliefs. As already mentioned, for this purpose Śaṅkara had acquired adequate traditional learning before he started writing his major works. This also points to the late rather than the early teens for the commencement of such writing. At the same time Śaṅkara's writings spring from his ratiocinative energy rather than from the weight of his learning or from any extensive factual knowledge. Indeed, the background of factual knowledge in Śaṅkara is quite limited and is expressive more of the acuteness of his observations rather than of their breadth or extent. The assumption that the period of Śankara's major writings commenced from about his sixteenth year would provide just enough time for the maturity of the intellectual powers or genius and also a period of nearly a decade for the acquisition of adequate traditional learning. It would also provide several years of *Wanderjahre* for acquiring basic acquaintance with the world and its diversity.

How much Śaṅkara could have written in the fifteen or twenty years available to him, is not easy to estimate. Some works take a long time to be produced and represent the thinking of a life time. Such is the *Kritik der reinen Vernunft* and such presumably were the *Pramānavārtika* or the *Abhidharmakośa*. Gaṅgeśa's *Tattvacintāmaṇi* or the works of Pāṇini and Patañjali are other examples of such works. But a thinker like Thomas Aquinas produced not less then 10,000 double columned folio pages including the twenty-one volumes of the *Summa* which is far more complicated, extensive and ambitious than the *Abhidharmakośa* with *Sphuṭārthā*. And the major works of Aquinas belong to the last twenty years of his life which ended before he was fifty. Hegel is another example of a philosopher who was as prolific as profound. As for Śaṅkara the corpus of his work accepted in the Vani Vilas Press edition falls short of 5000 pages. Most of the works in this corpus are fairly repetitive. Śaṅkara did not propound any vast or detailed syntheses like Hegel but he had, like Hegel, certain general ideas which he used in different contexts. Most of the writings attributed to him are either commentaries on given texts with an earlier tradition of commentaries where the task of Śaṅkara is mostly critical and elucidatory, or small independent tracts which summarise or briefly argue his point of view. The largest number is filled by brief poetical works and there are a few works like *Prapañcasāra* which select and summarize. It will, thus, be seen that in considering the authenticity of works attributed to Śaṅkara it is not the case that an impossibly large corpus has been ascribed to him since there is no compelling reason to suppose that he finished writing at twelve or sixteen. The real doubt arises from another fact which has not been sufficiently emphasized. It was unusual for authors in that age to write so much or for those writings to survive in such large numbers. Good writing tended to be quintessential and concise. And at least in the northern plains large scale destruction of books took place from time to time during foreign invasions. Such was the destruction of the great Buddhist monastic libraries in the 12th century. Apparently it was the Śaṅkarite monasteries of the South which helped preserve the writings of Śaṅkara in contrast to the fate which had overtaken the writings of his predecessors in Vedānta. Thus although the survival of Śaṅkara's writings is understandable, one cannot avoid the impression that of many of these writings attributed to him quite a few are dull and repetitive. It seems *prima facie* that what we have here is for a good part a gradual accumulation of works by the successors of Śaṅkara whose works have been ascribed to him through confusion. The uneven quality and stylistic differences of some of these works also suggest that their authorship is not uniform. Even differences in beliefs and attitudes are discoverable and it is this which has attracted the most attention in recent discussions. As for style, it must be pointed out that no thorough stylometric studies have so far been carried out. As for beliefs and attitudes, identifying the author through these often precipitates a *petitio principii.* It also assumes that the ideas and attitudes of an author must remain unchanged and be wholly consistent. Such an assumption cannot be unconditional, nor can variation be assumed arbitrarily.

It is only definitive external evidence that can prove that a certain work ascribed to Śaṅkara is really his. For example, the authenticity of the *Brahmasūtrabhāṣya* universally ascribed to Śaṅkara is definitively confirmed by the fact that his own disciples so regarded it and commented upon it. On the other hand, the unauthenticity of a work ascribed to Śaṅkara can be definitively proved by clear anachronisms in it. Considerations of language, style and ideas can be of help especially when they are unambiguous and convergent, or systemetically quantified. At least a couple of unpublished dissertations are reported to have attempted a limited stylometric analysis.[1] From what has been published of such work it seems that formal and semantic criteria are not kept apart in it. The reliance on semantic criteria is total in the work of Hacker and Mayeda discussed below. On mixed criteria of language, style, ascription, commentators and ideas several older scholars like Mahamahopadhyaya G.N. Kaviraj, Baldev Upadhyaya and S.K. Belvalkar have commented on the authenticity or otherwise of works ascribed to Śaṅkara. The work of Dr. Belvalkar is the most systematic and has been largely followed by Baldev Upadhyaya.

Different catalogues ascribe nearly four hundred works of different kinds to Śaṅkara and it is generally agreed among modern scholars that most of them are apocryphal. Under the inspiration of Śṛṅgerī a twenty-volume edition of Śaṅkara's writings had been published by the Vani Vilas Press. A revised edition has since been brought out in ten volumes by the Samata Books. These include the commentaries on the *Prasthānatrayī*, five minor commentaries, thirty-three *prakaraṇas*, sixty-five *stotras* and the *Prapañcasāra*. Among the *Upaniṣads* it includes the *Nṛsiṁhapūrvatāpinī*, in the minor commentaries those on *Viṣṇusahasranāma, Sanatsujātīya, Lalitā-Triśatī, Hastāmalakīya* and the *Āpastambīya Adhyātmapaṭala*. The total number of works thus amounts to one hundred and seventeen. Against this Belvalkar admits the authenticity of only twenty-four which includes eleven commentaries, five *prakaraṇas* and eight *stotras*.

It will be noticed that the differences are largely with respect to the *prakaraṇas* and the *stotras*. Among the commentaries the authenticity of the *Brahmasūtrabhāṣya* is universally admitted. It has been commented upon from the time of Śaṅkara himself, when Padmapāda planned the first commentary on it, to the present day and remains the unquestioned *magnum opus* of the Master. Among the Upaniṣadic commentaries a similar status is generally recognized for the *Bṛhdāraṇyakabhāṣya* to which the *Vārtika* of Sureśvara remains a standing tribute. Since Sureśvara commented similarly on the *Taittirīyabhāṣya* its authenticity deserves a similar recognition. Some difficulty is, however, presented by the introductory verses in this *bhāṣya*. From the earlier two commentaries mentioned above it would seem that it was not the style of Śaṅkara to begin with such benedictory verses. It is, therefore, possible that these preliminary verses in the *Tai-bhā*, at least the third one, have been added by someone at a later date, some time before Ānandagiri. The third verse, indeed, occurs in the *Vārtika* of Sureśvara which is its obvious source. The authenticity of the *bhāṣya* itself remains unaffected as attested by the contemporary *Vārtika* of the most famous and learned of Śaṅkara's disciples.

Doubts have also been raised on the commentary on the *Māṇḍūkyopaniṣad* and the *Māṇḍūkyopaniṣat-Kārikās*. Here we have two introductory and three final verses. Not only is the very presence of these verses suspect but their indifferent quality and metrical and even grammatical lapses appear strange. The obvious connection of its preamble with that of the *Nṛsiṁhatāpanīya* is also a cause of suspicion. Jacobi was the first to voice this suspicion in 1913 principally on grounds of logical style.[2] V. Bhattacharya, Kaviraj, Belvalkar and Upadhyaya have also expressed doubts.[3] T.R. Chintamani tried to defend the authenticity of the work[4] and recently Mayeda has argued elaborately in favour of the authenticity of the work.[5] The principal argument of Mayeda is that certain crucial terms are used in the same way in the *Gauḍapādīyabhāṣya* as in the *Brahmasūtrabhāṣya*. These eight terms are *avidyā, nāmarūpa, māyā, Īśvara, ānanda, vivarta, Śiva* and *Vyāsa*. 'Śaṅkara shows his peculiarities in those terms to such an extent that Śaṅkara's genuine works can be distinguished from even those of his direct disciples with considerable certainty'.[6] Another argument in support of the authenticity of the work in question is said to be that like the *Brahmasūtrabhāṣya* it quotes the *Br.* most frequently and so the *Gītā* among *smṛti* texts. It may be conceded that as far as the conceptual structure and language of the *MKB* are concerned they are consistent with Śaṅkara's strict usage in his *BSB*. Mayeda must be deemed equally successful in rebutting some of the arguments of the sceptics. It is true that Śaṅkara never quotes the *MU* in the *BSB* but he does quote the *MK* and as for V. Bhattacharya's doubt about the apocryphal character of the *MU* itself, Mayeda decisively points out that Sureśvara quotes *MU*, 6, as *Māṇḍūkya-śrutivacas*. Besides, Śaṅkara himself appears to unify the *MU* and the *MUK* into a single '*Vedāntārtha-sāra-saṅgraha-bhūtam idam prakaraṇacatuṣṭayam*'. As for the argument that Śaṅkara appears to misunderstand Buddhist terms in *MUK*, which would be surprising for the author of *BSB*, Mayeda's reply is that Śaṅkara deliberately misinterprets the text at places in order to give an orthodox Vedāntic construction to what was in reality genuinely Buddhistic. This is paralleled by Śaṅkara's efforts in his commentary on the *BG* as well as the *BS* where his stress on pure knowledge or simple non-duality is hardly in the spirit of the texts themselves. Perhaps, instead of deliberate misinterpretation one should speak of an orthodox reinterpretation. As for the benedictory stanzas Mayeda points out that the *BGD* and the *Upadeśa* also have such stanzas. As for the metrical and grammatical defects Mayeda appeals to the absence of a critical edition.

While Mayeda's comments on the ideas and interpretations of the *MUKB* are plausible and establish the high probability of its authenticity, his comments on the benedictory verses are wholly unsatisfactory. In fact, he does not quite realize what is wrong with the verses. While the grammatical lapses could be removed in an emended text, the metrical irregularity plainly shows that the author has no sense of versification at all and none of poetry. It is hard to accept that Śaṅkara could be responsible for such bad verses which would put a novice to shame. Sound and rhythm, words and phrases, imagery and sense, in every respect the verses are without merit and clumsy. If, then, the *MKB* is authentic, its benedictory verses must be regarded as clumsy additions.

The *Kenopaniṣad* has two commentaries, *Padabhāṣya* and *Vākyabhāṣya*. Several scholars have argued that the *Vākyabhāṣya* could not be authentic because it contradicts the *Padabhāṣya* at several places (2.2, 4.4) and offers less plausible explanations or readings.[7] On the other hand, Mayeda has argued that both the *bhāṣyas* are authentic. It is true that there are no significant doctrinal differences between them but, as pointed out above, there are differences in textual readings and explanations at several places. This does raise a doubt about the *Vākyabhāṣya*.

The commentaries on the *Śvetāśvatara* and the *Nṛsiṁha Pūrvatāpanīya* have generally been held to be apocryphal. The latter presupposes the *MKB* and *Prapañcasāra*. In fact, the author declares himself to be the author of *Prapañcasāra*, quotes from *MU* and uses *vivarta* in an apparently technical sense. Traditionally *Nṛsiṁha-bhāṣya* is sometimes supposed to be the first composition of Śaṅkara but the work itself would have us believe that he had already written the *Prapañcasāra* and the *MKB*. The *Śvetāśvatara-bhāṣya* gives long quotations, which is not Śaṅkara's style. These quotations include those from late *Purāṇas* like *Liṅga* and *Viṣṇudharmottara* and even the *Yoga-Vāsiṣṭha*. Besides, it speaks of *Śuka-Śiṣyaḥ Gauḍapādaḥ* which is not only lacking in courtesy but in strong contrast to the way in which Śaṅkara refers to his teacher's teacher in *BSB*.

Commentaries on the *Kauṣītaki, Kaivalya, Maitrayaṇīya, Gopālatāpanīya, Mahā-Nārāyaṇa, Paramahaṁsopaniṣad, Śākaṭāyana* and *Maṇḍala-Brāhmaṇa-Upaniṣad* have also been attributed to Śaṅkara. On these, however, even traditional scholars have expressed their doubts and even the Vani Vilas Press edition of Śaṅkara's works excludes these. The traditional biographies of Śaṅkara also speak of his commentaries on ten *Upaniṣads* only, although Śaṅkara refers to many more *Upaniṣads* in his *BSB* and *BGD* such as *Kauśitaki, Jābāla, Nṛsiṁha-pūrva* and *Uttaratāpanīya* etc. Thus among the authentic commentaries on the *Upaniṣads* which are vouched for by Sureśvara and Ānandajñāna may be counted those on the ten classical *Upaniṣads*, viz., *Īśa, Kena, Kaṭha, Praśna, Aitareya, Taittirīya, Muṇḍaka, Māṇḍūkya, Chāndogya* and *Bṛhadāraṇyaka* with the rider that the commentary on the *Māṇḍūkya* was really on *Māṇḍūkya-Kārikās* as constituting the four *prakaraṇas* and that the benedictory verses in *TUB* and *MKB* are to be regarded as spurious. The *Kena-Vākya Bhāṣya* too has a doubtful status. It would be noticed that none of the Upaniṣadic commentaries has any benedictory verses except for the spurious ones in *TUB* and *MKB*. Perhaps these works were originally delivered as expository lectures to students. Or perhaps Śaṅkara felt no need for *maṅgala-śloka*, '*vipat-pratīkāra-pareṇa maṅgalam niṣevyate bhūti-samutsukena vā / Jagaccharaṇyasya nirāśiṣaḥ sataḥ kimebhir āśopahatātmavṛttibhiḥ//*'

Turning from the *śruti-prasthāna* to the *smṛti-prasthāna* we find the following commentaries attributed to Śaṅkara, viz., on the *Bhagavad-gītā, Uttaragītā, Śiva-gītā, Sanatstujātīya, Viṣṇusaha-sranāma, Lalitā-Triśati-Bhāṣya, Lalitā-sahasranāma-bhāṣya, Brahma-gītā, Sūta-saṁhitā, Adhyātma Paṭala* of *Āpastamba dharma-sūtra, Gāyatrī-bhāṣya* and *Sandhyābhāṣya*.

About the authorship of the *Gītābhāṣya* some doubts have been expressed. However, most critical scholars like Faddegen, Ingalls, Raghavan and Mayeda have supported the authenticity of the work.[8] An important piece of external evidence is the fact that Bhāskara who is not far removed from Śaṅkara appears to refer to his *Gītābhāṣya*. The colophons clearly ascribe the work to Śaṅkara-bhagavat rather than to the more ambiguous Śaṅkarācārya. The tradition is unanimous in ascribing the work to him. Ānandagiri has written a commentary on Śaṅkara's *Gītābhāṣya* and speaks of its author as *Bhagavān-bhāṣyakāra*. It may be recalled that Ānandagiri is traditionally regarded as the fifth pontiff at Kāñcī[9] and may be expected to have been aware of the tradition. The language and style of the *BGB* are characteristic of Śaṅkara, fluent and lucid, simple and profound, always focused and relevant, without any rhetorical flourishes or pedantry, logical in reasoning but without any scholastic formalism. As in the *BSB* Śaṅkara indicates his main theme concisely in the preface, briefly elucidates the text, argues against any ritualistic or dualistic interpretations. The ideas and arguments in the *BGB* are generally consistent with those expressed in the *BSB*.

Following Hacker, Mayeda has attempted a detailed comparative analysis of the use of certain characteristic terms of Śaṅkara in the *BGB* and *BSB*. He finds that the *BGB* uses *Avidyā* without materializing it as was done by the followers of Śaṅkara, *nāmarūpa* as the matrix of the world, *māyā* much less frequently than *Avidyā*. The term *Īśvara* is used commonly, *ānanda* is not used to characterize the *Brahman,* and Vyāsa is not confused with Bādarāyaṇa. The *BGB* shows the same preference for quotations from the *BU* as does the *BSB.* Mayeda, thus concludes that the *BGB* is, on the whole, consistent with *BSB* in its use of characteristic Śaṅkara concepts.

As for the fact that the *BGB* begins with a verse, apparently serving the function of benediction, it has to be remembered that it is really a quotation which is not inappropriate to the work. As Nārāyaṇa becomes the opening word, the verse becomes an appropriate benediction for the commentary on the *Gītā.*

Thus of the commentarial works of Śaṅkara belonging to the *Prasthānatrayī* twelve may be deemed authentic with more or less certainty and these include the ten *Upaniṣads,* the *Gītā* and the *Brahmasūtras.*

There are hardly any serious advocates of the authenticity of the commentaries on *Uttaragītā, Śiva-gītā, Brahma-gītā, Lalitā-sahasranāma, Sūta-saṁhitā* and *Sandhyā-bhāṣya. Gāyatrībhāṣya* has been fairly popular under the name of Śaṅkara but the ascription remains debatable. *Lalitā-triśati-bhāṣya* is a wholly Tantric work of which the commentary begins with four benedictory works such as were common in later times. Apart from the fact that the last of the verses lacks felicity, such benedictory beginnings are not characteristic of Śaṅkara even if we assume that he was the author of Tantric works. The commentary on the *Viṣṇusahasranāma* is widely believed to be the genuine work of Śaṅkara. Sometime it is even believed to be the first commentary composed by him. The work, however, begins with three benedictory verses and quotes the *śrutis* and *Purāṇas* at great length. Both of these features are uncharacteristic of Śaṅkara. Long quotations are especially suspicious since they constitute a stylistic feature. The *Sanatsujātīya-bhāṣya* shows similar features though to a lesser extent. Its second sentence, '*Svataścidānandādvitīyabrahmasvarūpo' pyātmā svāśrayayā svaviṣayayā vidyayā svānubhavagamyayā svābhāsayā*' etc. characterizes *Ātman* by *ānanda* and invokes a possible distinction about the *āśraya* and *viṣaya* of *avidyā*- which became significant in these very terms in the school of Śaṅkara after him. Both these works, thus, appear to be apocryphal as Hacker-Mayeda criteria go and also stylistically.

On the other hand, the *Adhyātma-paṭala-bhāṣya* has been regarded as a genuine writing of Śaṅkara by several modern critics. In its ideas, style of argument, directness and simplicity of language, preference for brief quotes from ancient works, concept of *doṣa* and *jñāna*, absence of benediction etc., the work is consistent with the authentic writings of Śaṅkara. It is interesting to reflect on why Śaṅkara chose this particular text for commenting. One of his principal preoccupations in his writings was to combat the orthodox tradition which laid an exclusive emphasis on good works and ritual. In this work he not only argues against the theory of works but also expounds the spiritual ethics needed for right knowledge. It could have been one of his earlier works where the primary interest is not metaphysical but ethical. It may be contrasted with the *MKB*.

Commentaries in several works ascribed to Śaṅkara himself or to his disciples have also been attributed to Śaṅkara. For example he has been credited with a commentary on a short work attributed to Hastāmalaka. Since the latter was a young disciple of the Master and the work in question is simple and effusive there is no plausibility in holding that Śaṅkara thought it worthy of his own commentary. Besides, it begins with benediction and seeks to explain why its absence in the original text itself may be excused. It refers to Hastāmalaka as *ācārya*. *Hastāmalakīyabhāṣya* may, therefore, be confidently excluded from the writings of Śaṅkara, although among the mendicants of the Śaṅkarite orders it is believed to be authentic and is included in the Samata edition.

The spuriousness of the following commentaries hardly needs to be argued—*Aparokṣānubhava-vyākhyā, Amaruśataka-ṭīkā, Ānandalaharī-ṭīkā, Ātmabodha-ṭīkā, Uttara-gītā ṭīkā, Upadeśasāhasrīvṛtti, Ekaślokī-vyākhyā, Dakṣiṇāmūrtyaṣṭaka-ṭīkā, Pañcapadī-prakaraṇa-ṭīkā, Pañcīkaraṇa-prakriyā-vyākhyā, Brahmagītā-ṭīkā, Bhaṭṭikāvya-ṭīkā, Laghu-vākya-vṛtti ṭīkā, Śataślokī-Vyākhyā, Śiva-gītā-vyākhyā, Ṣaṭpadī-ṭīkā, Sankṣepa-śārīraka-bhāṣya, Sāṅkhya-saptati-ṭīkā, Jayamaṅgalā*. Most of these are commentaries on works ascribed to Śaṅkara himself. *Amaruśataka* does not have any real connection with Śaṅkara except a mythical ascription. *Bhaṭṭikāvya* is hardly a work of Śaṅkara to comment on. *Saṅkṣepa-śārīraka* post-dates Śaṅkara. Mm. G.N. Kaviraj has argued that *Jayamaṅgalā* was not the work of Śaṅkara but of a different scholar named Śaṅkarārya who has written similarly named commentaries on other texts also.[10]

Three commentaries ascribed to Śaṅkara relate to *Yoga* - *Rājayoga-bhāṣya*, on *Maṇḍala-Brāhmaṇopaniṣad, Vijṛmbhita-Yoga-sūtra-bhāṣya,* and *Yoga-sūtra-bhāṣya-vivaraṇa.* Of these the authenticity of the last one has been argued by many competent scholars since it was published in 1952. The editor, Sri Rama Sastri argued that the ascription in the colophon is supported by the opening which is paralleled in the *CUB* and the *Adhyātma-paṭala-bhāṣya*.

Śaṅkara cannot be said to have been really hostile to Yoga. In fact, he refers to the *Yogaśāstra* at several places in the *BSB* respectfully. He points out that the Vedāntic rejection of Yoga is partial, not total. '*Samyagdarśanābhyupāyo hi yogo Vede vihitaḥ*. . . *Liṅgāni ca Vaidikāni Yogaviṣayāṇi sahasraśaḥ upalabhyante*.'[11] This harmony of Yoga and Vedānta was further elaborated by Vācaspati Miśra who pointed out that the heart of Yoga does not lie in its dualistic and realistic Sāṅkhyan principles but in its practical methods which are necessary for spiritual illumination.[12]

The fact is that the *Vivaraṇa* is not written from an orthodox Sāṅkhya-yoga point of view. It questions the concept of *Pradhāna* as well as the plurality of the Selves. It modifies the Yoga concept of *Īśvara*.[13] Thus the *Vivaraṇa* appears to be an attempt to understand the *Yogaśāstra* in conformity with Vedānta.

Paul Hacker has applied his usual tests of authenticity to the *Vivaraṇa* and concluded that it passes the test and could well be the work of Śaṅkara.[14] From this he surmised that Śaṅkara probably began his career as a *Yogin* of the Patañjala school and later became a Vedāntin, 'retaining, however, some traces of his former affiliation, especially in peculiarities in his doctrines of Nescience and of the Self'. Hacker supposes that it was the *MKB* which mediates between Śaṅkara the *Yogin* and Śaṅkara the Vedāntin. The definite change came with the *TUB*. It is in these earlier works that Śaṅkara retains some benedictory verses which he later abandons. Mayeda agrees that 'it is very probable that Śaṅkara is the author' of the *Vivaraṇa*.[15] Nakamura also agrees that there is no bar to the recognition of the authenticity of the work. He has argued rightly that it is not necessary to suppose that Śaṅkara changed his doctrinal affiliations. He could have written the *Vivaraṇa* as a Vedāntin.[16] Leggett and Alston too favour the authenticity of the text.

One stylistic feature in which the work differs from the principal writings of Śaṅkara is the presence of benedictory verses both at the beginning and the end of the work. The last of these verses is clearly spurious since it seems to be modelled on a verse of Padmapāda. At least one other verse appears similarly spurious. Even if the other verses be genuinely a part of the commentary they are stylistically much better than the verses in the *MKB*. The general style of the *Vivaraṇa* is, however, not characteristic of mature Śaṅkara.

It must also be remembered that Śaṅkara is invariably described in the traditional accounts as a great *Yogin* who had immense *vibhūtis*. His teachers Govindapāda and Gauḍapāda are also famed as *Yogins* and have also been traditionally connected with Patañjali. It is thus probable but not certain that the present work—*Vivaraṇa*—is a genuine work of Śaṅkara.

Vijṛmbhita-Yoga-sūtra-bhāṣya has not been published and is said to be a commentary on the *Rāja-yoga-sāra* or *Yogatārāvalī* which is said to have been attributed to Govindapāda by Citsukha or more usually to Śaṅkara himself. *Yogatārāvalī* has been published in the Samata edition and is a small work in verse containing twenty-nine stanzas in a polished language. It advocates *Kevala-kumbhaka* as the prime method of Yoga. Such a *Kumbhaka* leads to *Unmanī*, a state of pure, objectless consciousness. The text claims to prescribe a special method for attaining this condition: '*Unamanyavasthādhigamāya vidvann upāyam ekaṁ tava nirdiśāmaḥ/ Paśyann udāsīnatayā prapañcam saṅkalpam unmūlaya sāvadhānaḥ//*' It leads to '*Saṁvinmayīṁ tāṁ sahjāmanaskām*.' In this respect the work is reminiscent of Gauḍapāda's *Asparśa-yoga*. However, the penultimate verse speaks of the longing of the author to meditate in the Śrī-śaila mountain and the last verse recalls what may be called the 'Bhartṛhari option' of being either lost in *samādhi* or in the love of lovely women. It may be recalled that according to the traditional legend Bhartṛhari was one of the four sons of Govinda as Candraśarman. Both of these verses, however, are uncharacteristic of Śaṅkara, especially the second. Whether the work was authored by Govindapāda is difficult to say since so little is known about him. Under the circumstances the ascription of the *Vijṛmbhita-bhāṣya* to Śaṅkara would appear highly doubtful. It seems to expound some kind of *Kuṇḍalinī-Yoga*. It may be recalled that two different but not unconnected interpretations of Yoga developed in this period, one of them emphasized psychic spontaneity, the other strenuous effort which could be physical or in terms of the use of *mantras* or both. From the standpoint of Śaṅkara the only relevant kind of Yoga would be the withdrawal and transmutation of consciousness on the basis of understanding or knowledge.

We may now conclude about the commentaries on the *Prasthāna-trayī*. On the *śruti-prasthāna* Śaṅkara commented on the ten principal *Upaniṣads* including the *MK* in all probability although he quotes many other *Upaniṣads* in his authentic writings. It is possible that he may have informally commented on them in his lectures to students and some of his later followers may have composed apocryphal commentaries on some of them. On the *smṛti-prasthāna, Viṣṇusahasranāma* and the *Sanatsujātīya* contain late features despite their popular ascription. The ascription of the *Adhyātma-paṭala-bhāṣya,* however, now appears certain. On the *nyāya-prasthāna,* the *BSB* is the most certain of Śaṅkara's work and the *Yoga-sūtra-bhāṣya-vivaraṇa* is quite likely.

At this point it is necessary to call attention to the fact that there seem to be no really critical editions of any of these works. The result is that in some of these there are occasionally grammatical lapses. Thus *Ch-B* has *samāpayitvā, BSB* has '*Prāsaṅkṣyet*', *Kena-B* '*Namitum*', *Katha-B* '*Triḥkṛtvā*' etc.[17] This makes the application of linguistic criteria uncertain in marginal cases.

If we turn to the independent tracts or *Prakaraṇas* attributed to Śaṅkara, we find a large and indefinite number ascribed to him. Kaviraj lists 76 which are ascribed to *Govindabhagavatpāda-śiṣya-Śaṅkara.* Upadhyaya seems to accept the authenticity of about 39 *prakaraṇas.* Belvalkar accepts the authenticity of five *prakaraṇas* and doubts the authenticity of eight. Western critical opinion rejects the authenticity of all the *prakaraṇas* except the *Upadeśa-sāhasrī* which passes the tests devised by Hacker and applied by Mayeda. *Upadeśa,* however, hardly needed these tests except perhaps for the verification of the tests themselves because it was apparently known to Sureśvara in whom references to it may be seen. Vedāntadeśika's reference to the *gadya-prabandha* testifies to the authenticity of the prose portion of the text also which, in any case, resembles the *BSB* closely but appears to be later since it contains some refinements over it.[18] It is quite probable that the *Upadeśa* is a collection of several, originally independent tracts. The *tattvamasi-prakaraṇa,* thus, has benedictory verses both at the beginning and the end. But the whole work too has such verses and it is possible that although composed independently on different occasions, the idea of collecting these compositions was conceived by Śaṅkara himself.

Belvalkar accepts the authenticity of *Aparokṣānubhūti,* a brief tract consisting of 144 stanzas in the *Anuṣṭubh,* ascribed to Śaṅkara-bhagavat the disciple of Govindabhagavatpūjyapāda. The work begins with a benedictory verse in which the author bows to Sri Hari. The work has several old commentaries one of which is attributed to Vidyāraṇya but the ascription is not certain. The text itself is simple and consistent with the doctrines of Śaṅkara and does not have any noticeable features which could be considered late or uncharacteristic of Śaṅkara. In fact, its preference in quoting *Br.* is characteristic of Śaṅkara. It is also characteristic of Śaṅkara that the work should speak of Brahman as eternal consciousness rather than as bliss. It also speaks of Māyā non-materially as a kind of transcendental trickery. On the whole, the work has a fair claim to be considered genuine.

Ātmabodha is another short *prakaraṇa* which has been popular among Vedāntins and which is accepted as genuine by Belvalkar and Baldev Upadhyaya. It has several old commentaries. One is by Bodhendra who was the disciple of Gīrvānendra, the head of an Advaita monastery. Apart from Śaṅkara himself Madhusudana Sarasvati's commentary is mentioned on it. Its thirteenth verse is quoted in the *Vedānta-paribhāṣa*. This evidence of recognition in classical Advaitic tradition is a significant piece of external evidence supporting the ascription. Its style and contents are on the whole compatible with Śaṅkara's authorship. As for Hacker and Mayeda's rejection, it is true that the text does not fulfil all their criteria. It clearly characterizes Brāhmaṇa in terms of *Ānanda* and speaks of *avidyā* as *anādi* and *anirvācya*. However, in these respects the criteria of Hacker and Mayeda are themselves unconvincing. For example, the *BSB* clearly speaks of *Adhyāsa* as *anādi* and also identifies *Adhyāsa* and *Avidyā*, from which it follows that *avidyā* is *anādi*.[19] Similarly in the recognition of the phenomenal world as neither *sat* nor *asat*, the recognition of its indeterminability is clearly implicit and the concept of *anirvacanīya* is the same as that of *avyakta* or *avākṛta* of Śaṅkara. Again, the conception of Brahman as *ānanda* is quite clear in the *Upaniṣads* and in the *Brahmasūtras* and also in the Advaita tradition from the direct disciples of Śaṅkara himself. As for Śaṅkara's own view it is expressed most clearly in his *BUB* 3.9.28, as well as *BSB* 1.1.12-19. In the former he says explicitly '*Tasmāt 'vijñānam ānandam iti svarūpākhyāna-paraiva śrutiḥ, nātmānandasaṁvedvatvārthā.*' In the latter he says '*Yā tu Bhārgavī vidyā' ānando brahmeti vyajānāt iti tasyām mayad aśravaṇāt. priya-śirastvādyaśravaṇācca yuktam ānandasya Brahmatvam*'. Śaṅkara could not and did not deny that

Brahman is of the nature of *ānanda*. What he wanted to avoid was the impression that this *ānanda* was at par with empirical happiness and that it could be conceived as some kind of 'experience' or its content, implying duality and change. Even the ancient Buddhists had distinguished *sukha* from *sukhasaṁvedana*. Śaṅkara may not have in his commentaries habitually spoken of *avidyā* as *anādi* or *anirvacanīya* or of Brahman as *ānanda*. It does not follow that he could have any objection to such usage in principle or that he could not have followed such usage occasionally. Indeed, if he frowned on such usage, it is not intelligible how his immediate disciples could indulge in it in his own lifetime. Hacker and Mayeda have not shown that these instances constitute a real conceptual departure among the followers of Śaṅkara. As for stylistic characteristics one cannot rule out some variation in different works of different kinds and occasions.

Pañcīkaraṇa or *Pañcīkaraṇa-prakrīyā* is a short prose text in eight brief paragraphs. It has been held in high regard traditionally and has been honoured by several commentaries. Svayamprakāśa, the disciple of Gopāla Yogīndra, has commented on it. So has Ānandagiri. There is another commentary called *Tattvacandrikā*. Even a *Vārtika* is attributed to Sureśvara on which Śivarāma Tīrtha has a *Vivaraṇa*, and on the *Vivaraṇa* there is a further subcommentary called *Ābharaṇa*. The authorship of the *Vārtika* by Sureśvara has been doubted on the ground that the work is 'redolent of Tantra', which assumes without any reason that Advaitins kept away from Tantra.

Belvalkar accepts the work as of Śaṅkara tentatively but remarks that 'there is nothing in the work itself to warrant its ascription to Śaṅkarācārya, except that it has called forth such extensive commentarial activity.' He fails to see the peculiar position of the work in the writings of Śaṅkara. Śaṅkara avoids cosmological discussions in his commentaries in order to highlight the central truth of Advaita. And yet cosmology is not really avoidable even in the context of spiritual practice because cosmological 'back-tracking', as it were, is a familiar method of spiritual meditation. As has been shown by Hari Harananda Aranya, it was essential to Sāṅkhya and is well recognized in Tantra, as, for example, in Śrīvidyā. *Pañcadaśī*, itself starts with cosmology. What the *Pañcīkaraṇa-prakaraṇa* sets out to do is to explain the *Pāramahaṁsya-vidhi* and in this context relates the different *upādhis* of the Self to the stages of cosmogenesis as well as the elements of *Praṇava* as analysed in the *Māṇḍūkya*. This brief description of Śaṅkara, thus, became one of the sources of later Advaitic metaphysics and meditation.

Śataślokī has a commentary ascribed to Śaṅkara himself but there is one by Ānandagiri. According to Belvalkar 'The work is remarkable for the easy familiarity with which it marshalls forth Vedic and Upaniṣadic texts in support of Advaitic conclusions'. He rightly remarks that 'The last stanza does not appear genuine.' It is the 101st stanza and since the work concludes itself with the 100th stanza ending with 'Vāsudeva', it is unnecessary. Besides, it is a distinctly poor verse in comparison with the general standard of the whole work. Despite occasional lapses in *Yati*, the versification in the work is fluent and the marshalling of phrases (*padaśayyā*) generally admirable. It is not merely a philosophical work in verse but a veritable philosophical poem. Its third verse seems to summarize the prologue of the *BSB*. It is true that it violates the Hacker-Mayeda criteria by speaking of the blissful nature of the self and by using the phrase *māyopādāna*. But the texture of thought is on the whole consistent with that of Śaṅkara. The text as published, however, does not seem to be free from corruption as it contains solescisms like *samviditvā, rodamāna, aikṣat*. Verse 29 has *Yaḥ Purodhāḥ samāteḥ*, which seems to contain some mistake. Perhaps it should be *Yośamāteḥ purodhāḥ*.

Belvalkar mentions a work named *Ātmajñānopadeśavidhi* and says that it claims to possess commentaries by Ānandagiri, Pūrṇānandatīrtha and Rāmacandrasarasvatī. Hacker questions its authenticity from the colophon itself, which is a good argument although not decisive. Along with this *Māyāpañcaka* and *Upadeśapañcaka* are included by Belvalkar in works which are usually but not convincingly attributed to Śaṅkara. Both of these are non-descript doctrinally but effectively phrased. *Laghu-Vākyavṛtti* has a commentary ascribed to Śaṅkara and another to Rāmānanda Sarasvatī. Its use of the distinction of *savikalpaka* and *nirvikalpaka* and of *cidābhāsa* as a prominent concept are said to make it suspect but its interest is not in metaphysics but rather in advice on spiritual practice. Besides, Śaṅkara does use *caitanyābhāsa* in *Ch. U.B.*[20]

Vākyavṛtti is a short tract of 53 verses, explaining how self-knowledge may be gained from the Vedāntic *Tattvamasi*. It begins with obeisance to Viṣṇu and the teacher and is a lucid work in chaste language and verse. Among its commentaries are listed those by Ānandagiri, Rāmānanda Yati and Viśveśvarapaṇḍita who was the disciple of Yogī Mādhava Prājña. Although it violates the Hacker-Mayeda criteria by emphasising *ānanda,* it could well be a genuine work, showing the limitations of those criteria.

Vākya-sudhā or *Dṛgṛśya-viveka* is in all probability falsely attributed to Śaṅkara by the commentator Munidāsa. The commentator Brahmānanda Bhāratī believes that it was the joint work of Bhāratītīrtha and Vidyāraṇya although the commentator Viśveśvara holds it to have been the work of Vidyāraṇya alone.

Vivekacūḍāmaṇi is perhaps the most popular of the *Prakaraṇas* attributed to Śaṅkara. Although Hacker thought it genuine, Mayeda thinks it apocryphal on Hacker's criteria.[21] Ingalls has also argued against its genuineness on the ground that its doctrinal content does not fully agree with Śaṅkara's unquestioned works. Thus it is said to equate the waking and dream states in the manner of Gauḍapāda while Śaṅkara is said to distinguish the two carefully. Similarly it is said that it violates the Hacker-criterion on *avidyā* which is described as *anādi* and *anirvacanīya* here. It also violates the Hacker-test on *ānanda* since it describes the *ātman* in terms of *ānanda.* In this context it must be pointed out that the *Viveka* draws the parallelism of dream and waking to illustrate the power of the mind and point a way to spiritual equanimity. It does not intend any metaphysical or cosmological equality between them. Similarly the *Vivekacūḍāmāṇi* does not draw any technical distinction between *avyakta, avyākṛta* and *anirvacanīya.* In fact, Śaṅkara never does. For Śaṅkara the falsity of the empirical world consists in its being misunderstood as other than Brahman. The attempt to clarify the epistemic and logical status of the empirical world thus conceived as *vyāvahārika* rather than *pāramārthika,* necessarily led to the concept of *anirvacanīyatā-khyāti* as distinct from the other views on error. Śaṅkara does not designate the rival *khyātis* but that does not mean he was unaware of their precise nature. Similarly what he describes as his own view that the empirical world is a pragmatically efficient but misunderstood appearance of absolute reality implies that the empirical world is neither absolutely real nor absolutely unreal and that is precisely what is meant by *anirvacanīya-khyāti.* That Śaṅkara does not use the term *anirvacanīya* in this context in the *BSB* does not mean that he could not have used the term elsewhere. Nor is there any developmental relation between the use of *avyakta* in the cosmological or metaphysical context and that of *anirvacanīya* in the logical context since Śaṅkara accepts the Brahman as the cause of the world but also that the world is an illusory appearance of Brahman. This tends to give a duality to *avidyā*. What is *avyakta* as causal matrix in one context, is *anirvacanīya* or logically indeterminate in another, and the two contexts are not distinguished in the *Viveka*. Nor should the word *anirvacanīya* in the text be invested with all the technicality it conveyed later. As for the description of *avidyā* as *anādi*, it has already been pointed out that such a use does not contravene Śaṅkara's ideas or usage. The present text goes further to describe *avidyā* as the material source of the world, which again contravenes a Hacker-criterion that *avidyā* should not be materialized. *Viveka* describes *avidyā* as *triguṇātmikā*, as the power of *āvaraṇa* and *vikṣepa*, as *avyakta*. Such a description is not really contrary to Śaṅkara's known ideas. It fully asserts the sole reality of Brahman as immanent and transcendent. *Avidyā* is an illusive power but to explain the origin and diversity of the world the Sāṅkhyan notion of *Prakṛti* is implicitly adopted and identified with *Avidyā* or *Māyā* following the lead of the *Śvetāśvatara*. *Viveka* remains Vedāntic though it uses Sāṅkhyan ideas sanctified by the *Upaniṣads* to explain creation and diversity in a systematic creativist metaphysic in which the principle of *avidyā* could not remain a simply psychological principle as in Buddhism. Śaṅkara could have avoided such a situation in the *BSB* where he mentions his illusionism in the Preface and follows orthodox creationism in the text. The need to relate *avidyā* as the principle of illusion with the principle of creation or world causation was unavoidable in any systematic statement. What is found in the *Viveka* simply follows the direction in which alone Advaita metaphysics could formulate itself. There is no reason to suppose that faced with the task of teaching *Advaita*, Śaṅkara took no steps in this direction. Indeed, he is traditionally supposed to have been familiar with the writings of his own disciples Sureśvara and Padmapāda. And this is in consonance with common sense. His probable Yoga background may also be recalled.

The characterization of Brahman as *ānanda* was, as argued earlier, quite orthodox and not unacceptable to Śaṅkara. If in his commentaries he was keen not to encourage an empiricistic misconstruction of *ānanda* as applied to Brahman, in his more popular work he would certainly have felt the need to emphasize the axiological aspect of *Brahman* to attract its seekers. Hacker, Mayeda and others, indeed, assume not only that Śaṅkara's *prakaraṇas* should be consistent with his commentaries but that he must express in certain cases precisely the same ideas in the same manner. This does not allow for any change of emphasis or development even in the direction in which such change certainly took place historically within Śaṅkara's own lifetime. If, as is likely, the more polished, vital *prakaraṇas* like *Viveka* are later than the commentaries and, in any case, more systematic, it is not unlikely that they should reflect the need for development required by systematization and logical discussion unavoidable in teaching and actually evidenced in the works of the immediate disciples like Padamapāda.

The major argument against the authenticity of *Viveka* however, is its use of the concept of *prāgabhāva* which, as Belvalkar had pointed out, Śaṅkara has rejected in *BSB*. However, it is worth noting that *prāgabhāva* is used as a *dṛṣṭānta* to illustrate the destruction of *avidyā* as of something which never was. In the *BSB* *prāgabhāva* was rejected as an element of *asatkāryavāda* and illustrated by the *Vandhyāputra*. There *satkāryavāda* had been assumed. Here it is used within the higher standpoint of illusionism to illustrate an impossibility. It cannot be said to have been accepted in the context of real causality. For Śaṅkara the prior non-existent is ever non-existent and has no illustration in reality. Such is the world illusion which appears and ceases after apparently having been. However, *Vivekacūḍāmaṇi*, whether actually authored by Śaṅkara or not, is traditionally held to voice his views authentically. Even Ramana Maharṣi was inspired to translate it. It is written in a simple, clear and chaste style and its language and verse, despite an occasional lapse like *vimocitum*, are fluent and effective. It expounds briefly and exhorts, and thus, to some extent simplifies and underlines.

Ekaślokī in one stanza is ascribed by colophon and tradition to Śaṅkara. There is also a comment on it by Svayamprakāśa Yati. The stanza gives a beautiful poetical expression to a well known idea in the *Br.* and is worthy of Śaṅkara.

Prabodhasudhākara in 257 elegant *āryā* verses appears to be a later composition since its primary emphasis is on *Kṛṣṇabhakti* after the manner of *Bhāgavata* rather than on *Jñāna*. Its distinction of *Māyā* and *Avidyā* as belonging to Brahman and *Jīva* respectively is also suspect as is the fact that it violates the Hacker criteria on *ānanda* and *Māyā*.

Svātmaprakāśikā in 68 verses too appears apocryphal because it seems to use *vivarta* technically and has an elaborate concept of *ābhāsa*.

Manīṣāpañcaka in five verses seems to have an appropriate connection with the context of the meeting of Śaṅkara with the *Cāṇḍāla* in Kāśī. It is a sublime composition worthy of Śaṅkara and despite its reference to beatific bliss held suspect by Hacker should be genuine in all probability.

Nirvāṇāṣṭakam is more effective as verse than *Advaita-pañcaratna,* although both have the same theme. The refrain *Cidānanda-rūpaḥ śivo'ham' śivo'ham'* has gained immense popularity, but whether it is genuinely Śaṅkara's is doubtful. Perhaps it is an apocryphal version of the *Daśa-ślokī* which has strong claims to be regarded as genuine owing to the honour given to it by the great Advaitin Madhusudana Sarasvati. It is also consistent with the Hacker criteria.

Advaitānubhūti and *Brahmānucintana* are similar and non-descript and violate the Hacker criteria. *Praśnottararatnamālīka's* reference to *Yāvāni Bhāṣā* shows that it belongs to a period when Muslim rule had been established and the learning of *Yavana-Bhāṣā* had become a real temptation. *Sadācārānusandhāna* with its distinction of *vṛttivyāpyatva* and *phalavyāpti* is plainly apocryphal.

Like *Dhanyāṣṭaka, Jīvanmuktānandalaharī* is full of poetical exultation but it has occasional grammatical mistakes like *raman* and *gāṇāpatya. Yatipañcaka* too has *ramantah. Anātmaśrīvigrahana* forcefully reviles the achievements of the world. Its refrain *Tatah Kim* is as famous as *Śivaḥ kevalo'ham.*

Tattvopadeśa is a brief tract which is partly similar to *Vākyārtha* but adds the *Ch.* illustration of Return to Gandhāra in an elaborate manner. It fails the Hacker tests about *ānanda* and *anirvacanīya*. Otherwise it is commonplace. *Prauḍhānubhūti* is a poetic expression of Advaitic experience in 17 fluent *sragdharā* verses. *Brahma-jñānāvalīmālā* is simplistic and trite. *Nirvāṇamañjarī* is a short poem exulting in 'What I am'. *Svātmanirupaṇa* has 154 polished *āryās* in a distinctive style which does not seem to be Śaṅkara's. It is in a class with *Prabodhasudhākara.*

Among these *prakaraṇas* it may be noted that style and theme show much variation. *Upadeśasāhsrī* is unique in having a primarily logical focus and its language and metre are generally correct but rarely poetic. *Vivekacūḍāmaṇi* is more systematic and poetic but states and expresses rather than argues. *Śataślokī* gives doctrinal advice but is written in elegant verse. *Manīṣāpañcaka, Ekaślokī* and *Daśaślokī* are spontaneous poems expressive of spiritual experience. It would seem that Śaṅkara was capable not only of writing logical philosophy in prosaic verse but also of writing elegant or sparkling philosophical poetry expressive of spiritual experience. It would be unfair to the traditional memory of Śaṅkara and to the evidence of the works which may be ascribed to him to limit his authorship only to versified logical philosophy. He has also been remembered as a great religious and spiritual leader, not merely as a philosophical commentator.

The largest of the well-known *prakaraṇas* is *Vedānta-sāra-saṅgraha*. It has been accepted in the Vani Vilas Press edition. Kaviraj and Upadhyaya are favourable to it, though Belvalkar thinks it not-genuine. The work has a clear, systematic and elegant style free from errors of language and metre. It recalls the context of several other writings of Śaṅkara especially the *BSB*. It violates Hacker's tests by characterizing Brahman as *ānanda* and by speaking of *Avidyā* as *anādi* and *anirvacanīya* in the manner in which Padmapāda speaks of it. It is broadly similar in scope and style to *Vivekacūḍāmaṇi*. It begins with three benedictory verses, to Govinda the teacher, the Self, and Gaṇeśa. Naming the teacher and mentioning Gaṇeśa are very unusual for Śaṅkara.

Apart from the *prakaraṇas* noted above and mostly included in the Vani Vilas Press edition of Śaṅkara's writings, there are numerous other such works ascribed to Śaṅkara. They are either "Philosophical compendia after the style of *Sarvadarśanasaṅgraha* or digests of Yoga and Tantrism. Still others deal with the life and conduct of ascetics and recluses, giving also rules for the various *maṭhas* as well as occasionally, moral instructions suitable to all classes of men. Others treat of Vedāntic topics like the *Ātman* or *Brahmana*, the meaning of the *mahāvākyas, Māyā, Nirvāṇa* etc."[22] Belvalkar says that most of these can be rejected because they contain grammatical mistakes or artificialities of composition, or contradict Śaṅkara's well known ideas, or are mediocre in thought and style, 'and the burden of proof must hence be on him who wishes to claim authenticity for any of these tracts, rather than of disproof on him who would *prima facie* deny such claim.' It is worth reflecting at this point that if the formal ascription of a work in its manuscript tradition is rejected as *totally* worthless, it would rarely be possible to ascertain the authenticity of any ancient work by internal evidence alone. The unending debate over the *Arthaśāstra* of Kauṭilya or the plays of *Bhāsa* may be recalled in this connection. The fact is, as mentioned earlier, that internal evidence can act as a check to confirm or disconfirm an ascription but can never be sufficient by itself to reach a positive identification. Hence, where the manuscript tradition is suspect in general, what is needed for reaching a definite judgement is some objective reason confirming or disconfirming the tradition. If the tradition were to be rejected outright and *a priori*, further discussion would be futile. Even scepticism has to be reasoned.

Among the *prakaraṇas* which Belvalkar treats as 'non-genuine' but which merit discussion, the following may be mentioned for comment:

(*a*) Regulations for ascetics and monasteries such as *Śaṅkara-smṛti* which is said to be current among the Nambudri Brahmins of Śaṅkara's native district, and the various *Maṭhāmnāya-vicāra.* While the authenticity of these may not be uncritically accepted, it needs to be historically investigated. The difficulty in this regard lies in the fact that these texts have never been critically edited. The *Maṭhāmnāya* texts exist in the monasteries and have been occasionally published but their mauscript history is unknown. An examination of the antiquity of the monastic tradition would be attempted below.

(*b*) Disquisitions on Tantra and Yoga including the *Prapañcasāra.* Some of these texts could be genuine as already discussed above with regard to *Yoga-sūtra-bhāṣya-vivaraṇa. Prapañcasāra* is considered below.

(*c*) Compendia of philosophy for different schools. For the rejection of *Sarva-siddhānta-saṅgraha,* which is excluded in Vani Vilas Press edition, Kaviraj Ji already gave a definite reason.

(*d*) Vedāntic manuals. Some of these have been discussed above. Most of these may be rejected on the ground that they are non-descript and banal and bear no trace of the genius, originality or style of Śaṅkara.

(*e*) Works containing the discussion of specific Vedāntic topics or *mahāvākyas.* Some of these like *Advaitānubhūti, Prauḍhānubhūti* and *Jīvanmuktānandalaharī* have been discussed above.

Turning now to the hymns or *stotras* attributed to Śaṅkara, there is first the opinion that he did not compose any. Since this is the expression of an *a priori* attitude or prejudice, it needs to be discarded. That, contrary to tradition, the *bhāṣyakāra* could not have been a *stotrakāra*, needs to be proved on objective grounds. Many philosophers and *Jñānīs* in India have been poets and devotees also. Madhusūdana Sarasvatī is an excellent example. Even Ramana Maharṣi wrote poems and hymns.

A more critical opinion has been expressed by Belvalkar who accepts as very probable the authenticity of the following eight *stotras—Ānandalaharī, Govindāṣṭaka, Dakṣiṇāmūrti-stotra, Daśaślokī, Dvādaśa-pañjarikā, Carpaṭa-pañjarikā, Ṣaṭpadī, Harim Īḍe' stotra*. He thinks the authenticity of the following three as plausible, though not certain: *Manīṣā-pañcaka, Sopāna-pañcaka* or *Upadeśa-pañcaka, Śivabhujaṅga stotra.*[23] H.R. Bhagavat finds the following authentic: *Advaitapañcakam, Ātmāṣṭakam, Upadeśa-pañcakam, Kāśī-pañcakam, Kaupīna-pañcakam, Carpaṭa-pañjarikā, Dakṣiṇāmūrti, Dvādaśa-pañjarikā, Dhanyāṣṭakam, Nirguṇa mānasa-pūjā, Nirvāṇa-mañjarī, Parā pūjā, Manīṣā-pañcaka, Vijñāna-naukā, Ṣaṭpadīstotram* and the *Harim Īde*.

Recently Robert E. Gussner has attempted to apply stylometric methods to the study of the *stotras.*[24] He studied the *stotras* affirmed by Bhagavat to be genuine by comparing the frequency of selected words in the *Upadeśa-sāhasrī* and these *stotras*. The words chosen are *Adhyakṣaḥ, ānandaḥ, avidyā, mālā, tathā, tu, duḥkham, dṛk, dṛśi, draṣṭā, brahma, bhaktiḥ, māyā, mokṣaḥ, yathā, yadvat-tadvat, śuddhaḥ, saṁsāraḥ, hṛd*. He finds that the frequencies are so different that there is hardly a chance in thousand that they could have a common authorship. He buttresses his conclusions by comparing the meanings in which *bhakti, ānanda* and *hṛd* are used in the two sets of works and finds the usage quite different. His conclusion is that except possibly for the *Dakṣiṇāmūrti-stotra*, the rest could not have Śaṅkara as their author. He generalizes that the *stotras* were the result of a medieval tendency to popularize Vedānta by bringing it near to the Bhakti movements.

The basic fault with this study is the premiss that the *upadeśa* is comparable with the *stotras* because both are in verse. As a matter of fact, the kind of verse which is found in the *upadeśa* or similar purely philosophical works such as the famous *Vārtikas* of Dharmakīrti or Kumārila or Sureśvara differs very greatly from the poetic verse which is found in the *stotras*. Having recognized the difficulty, Gussner curiously remarks 'But this difficulty in

Sanskrit verse is not as great as one would initially suppose—the difference between instructive couplet and *stotras* can be slight.' This remark needs considerable justification because *Sastraic* verse especially in *anuṣṭubh* would seem to have generally a prosaic and different vocabulary and style than poetic verse. In the second place, the variation in some of the words like *avidyā, dṛśiḥ, māyā, mokṣa* and *śuddha* attains a level of significance only of the order of one in hundred rather than of one in thousand. As for adverbial particles which constitute the heart of stylometry very few have been used. *Tathā* and *Yathā* should be significant but *tu* is generally frowned upon in poetic verse and *yadvat tadvat* hardly ever used. The semantic variation in *Bhakti, ānanda* and *hṛd* is only to be expected because the *stotras* are devotional works while *Upadeśa* is not. Gussner says that 'the words for the pure witness (*dṛk, drśiḥ, draṣṭā, adhyakṣah* and *jñātā*) are common in the *Upadeśa* but entirely missing in the *stotras* except for a few instances of *jñātā* and *Dṛśiḥ*'. He finds only eight occurrences of such words in the *stotras*. This is a very strange statement and statistics as will be seen from a random check of some of the *stotras—Harimide stotra* has *jña* five times, *sākṣin* once, *dṛśi* four times, *Kṣetrajña/viṣayajña/jñātā* in the sense of eternal witness five times, 'witness', by paraphrasis *dṛśyādanyaḥ/jñeyātītam jñānamayam/hitvā hitvā dṛśyam aśeṣam/sarvam vetti. . . na yaṁ vetti sarvaḥ/paśyan śuddhaḥ/ caitanyāṁśa,* has six occurrences. It would be clear that the idea of the witness occurs in this *stotra* of 43 stanzas at least 21 times. Similarly in the *Advaita pañcaratna* of five verses, the very first one is about the *Sākṣin*. It is not intelligible how Gussner lists a total occurrence of 35.

Thus Gussner's conclusions are vitiated as much by the failure to see the typal difference between *Upadeśa* and the *stotras* as by the assumption that Śaṅkara's conceptual emphasis must remain the same between the philosophical works and the *stotras*. It is also interesting to note that of the *stotras* listed by Bhagavat, Belvalkar recognizes only the *Dakṣiṇāmūrti, Carpatapañjarī* and *Harimīde*. Of these the first two fare well in Gussner's tests. The real difficulty with *Harimīḍe* is that it seems to recognize the authenticity of the *Sāttvata-tantras*. Śaṅkara, of course, could refer to the *Sāttvata-tantras* in *stotra* intended for the Vaiṣṇavas. Even in the *BSB* he recognizes that there are some good points in their doctrines. The pronounced rhythm of the *stotra* is suggestive of its being meant to be sung in a *kīrtana*. There are commentaries on it by Vidyāraṇya, Svayamprakāśa and Ānandagiri, which constitute strong evidence for its authenticity.

The *Dakṣiṇāmūrtistotra* has a striking sublimity of meaning and style. Kaviraj calls it undoubtedly Śaṅkara's. It has several commentaries by Vidyāraṇya, Svayamprakāśa, Nārāyaṇa Tīrtha etc. A *vārtika* called *Mānasollāsa* is also found on it and is ascribed to Sureśvara. Doubts have been expressed about its authenticity because it is tilted towards the Kashmir Śaiva point of view. It may, however, be recalled that according to one tradition Sureśvara was originally Maṇḍana Miśra who hailed from Kashmir.[25] Besides, as will be argued below, it is possible that in his last phase Śaṅkara came in contact with the varieties of Agamic and theistic monism which were current in Kashmir. While the basic philosophy of Śaṅkara and his monistic spiritual experience must be considered to have remained constant, it is quite possible that his acquaintance with and tolerance of diverse modes of *Upāsanā* became deeper with his years of peregrination and preaching to diverse groups of people.

Apart from the *Dakṣiṇāmūrtyaṣṭaka* there is also another *Dakṣiṇāmūrti-stotra* in eleven stanzas with *upajāti* verses. The hymn is simple but faultless.

Govindāṣṭaka has a commentary by Ānandagiri. It is moving and deeply devotional poetry which recalls diverse incidents out of the Kṛṣṇa legend. Whatever may be the controversy about the date of the Bhāgavata, there is no doubt about the relative antiquity of the Kṛṣṇa legend. It is worth remarking that there is nothing in common between this *stotra* and the *Upadeśa* in their thematic focus or style or language. The *stotra* emphasizes *bhakti* and *ānanda* but its basic philosophical assumptions are clearly Śaṅkara's:

> *Satyaṁjñānam anantaṁ nityam anākāśam paramākāśaṃ. . . Māyā-Kalpita-nānākāram anākāram bhuvanākāram, "Vaimalya-sphuṭa-cetovṛtti-viśeṣābhāsam anābhāsam Śaivaṁ Kevala-śāntam. . . buddham buddherantastham sattā-mātra-śarīram—"* etc.

For the author *saguṇa* and *nirguṇa* are not different, nor pure being from pure bliss.

Ānandalaharī (20 stanzas) is again highly devotional and sublime poetry where the lovely *Śikhariṇī* matches the sense. It describes the *devī* as *parama-brahma-mahiṣī* and emphasizes her majesty and compassion. *Ṣaṭpadī* is much shorter having only seven short stanzas which constitute one of the most beautiful prayers addressed to Viṣṇu. It reconciles a basic *advaita* with a kind of apparent duality required by *bhakti.* Its sense of sound and rhythm is exquisite. As many as six commentaries of the work have been mentioned, one by Śaṅkara himself!

Mohamudgara has justly attained wide popularity. It is a simple but moving poem exhorting dispassion from the attachments of the world. It seems to have been intended to be sung by wandering mendicants but is said to have been composed to enlighten an old grammarian.[26]

The *Śivabhujaṅga-stotra* in 40 faultless verses (except that it regards *prapañca* as neuter) is said to have been composed by Śaṅkara for the benefit of his mother in her last hour. It refers to the 36 *tattvas* of the Śaivas.

Among the other *stotras* which tradition especially ascribes to Śaṅkara may be mentioned—*Lakṣmī-nṛsiṁha-stotra* (there are two such *stotras*), *Acyutāṣṭaka, Nirguṇa mānasapūjā, Kālabhairavāṣṭaka, Narmadāṣṭaka, Yamunāṣṭaka, Gaṅgāṣṭaka, Maṇikarṇikāṣṭaka, Kāśī-pañcakam, Kanakadhārā, Annapūrṇāṣṭaka.*

In Śaṅkara's philosophy while *Jñāna* is the immediate means of liberation, it requires a prior purification of the mind of which *bhakti* is the prime means. God or *saguṇa brahma* figures quite prominently in his thought. It is, therefore, quite plausible that he may have given poetic expression to the devotion for Viṣṇu and Śiva, the two gods whose worship was then sweeping the South. Viṣṇu probably was the tutelary deity of his family and he shows a distinct preference for him over other gods in his commentaries. Śiva, on the other hand, was the deity *par excellence* of Kāśī where he spent some time. Narmadā, Gaṅgā, and Yamunā have a special connection with his own life. Lalitā was specially associated with Kāñcī and Śāradā with Kashmir. Hymns to these are, thus, not implausible, though we are offered so many that it is difficult to choose from among them.[27]

A crucial case is presented by the *Saundaryalaharī* which not only represents devotional poetry of a very high order combining sublimity with majesty and an unparalleled mastery of the *Śikhariṇī.* It is at the same time regarded as a *siddha-stotra* received by Śaṅkara from Śiva Himself in the Himalayas. Sometimes this honour is reserved for the first 40 verses. The *stotra* is written from the point of view of the Advaitic Śākta Āgama connected with Lalitā. There are over 35 commentaries on the work including those by Lakṣmīdhara, Bhāskara Rāya etc. Most of these commentators regard Śaṅkara as the author of the work. The 75th verse of the *stotra* has been held by many to refer to a story about Jñāna-Sambandara, the great Śaiva saint, who has been placed in the middle of the 7th century and could not have been far-removed from Śaṅkara himself.

Those modern scholars who think of Śaṅkara simply as a philosopher represented by the commentaries naturally regard the tradition of Śaṅkara's being an adept in the Tantras as a myth even worse than the one which makes him the author of devotional *stotras*. However, Hacker and Mayeda have had the courage of suggesting that Śaṅkara began as a worshipper of Viṣṇu and as a *Yogin*. Now tradition avers that in his last years Śaṅkara was at Kāñcī where he consecrated a centre of Tantric worship. An alternative tradition takes him to Kashmir which too was the home of Tantra. There is no inherent contradiction in Śaṅkara having acquired and given expression to Tantric learning since he recognized the need for preparatory *Sādhanā* and Advaitic *Āgamas* culminate in pure *Jñāna-mārga*.

The Tantric work *Prapañcasāra* has been attributed to Śaṅkara and according to the Tantric work *Śrīvidyārṇava* Śaṅkara was the founder of a line of Tantric worship.[28] It gives an account of Śaṅkara's Tantric teachers and disciples, a tradition which is claimed by some to be still surviving. This is strengthened by the fact that the worship of the *Śrīcakra* has been known in Śaṅkarite monastic centres and many famous *advaitins* have belonged to *Śrīvidyā sampradāya* as far as *Upāsanā* is concerned. Whether this tradition can actually be traced back to Śaṅkara depends on what view we take of the authenticity of *Saundaryalaharī, Prapañcasāra, Śrīvidyārṇava* and the monastic tradition.

On the *Prapañcasāra* which is a compendium of Tantric lore and practices a commentary has been attributed to Padmapāda. Its authenticity has been held suspect. According to the *Prayoga-krama-dīpikā* on this commentary Śaṅkara composed the work as a *sāra-saṅgraha*, culling out essentials from the old tradition of *Prapañcāgama*.[29] It was not an original composition of Śaṅkara who made the collection while he was staying in Kashmir. The great Vedāntic commentator Amalānanda (ad. *Bhāmati* on *BS* 1.3.33) has also attributed *Prapañcasāra* to Śaṅkara. Śaṅkara's connection with *Prapañcasāra*, thus, is a distinct possibility, though not a certainty at present.

To sum up, twelve of the commentaries on the *Prasthānatrayī* are generally and justly accepted as authentic while the *Yoga-sūtra-bhāṣya-vivaraṇa* could also possibly be counted as one. Of the *prakaraṇas* only the *Upadeśasāhasrī* has received general acceptance, although the authenticity of about half a dozen other works is arguable. Of the *stotras* the *Dakṣiṇāmūrtyaṣṭaka* has received the widest acceptance, although several others were also probably composed by him. Śaṅkara was also perhaps connected with the currency which Tantric works like *Saundaryalaharī* or *Prapañcasāra* gained. He could have been the author of the first and the editor of the second, if it be accepted that he was connected with Tantricism, as he seems to have been in his later years.[30]

It would be noticed that different kinds of criteria have been used by scholars in this context. Older scholars like Kaviraj and Belvalkar attached much importance to the recognition of a work by early commentators and authors. This must undoubtedly be a major consideration. From Sureśvara and Padmapāda to Ānandagiri a series of subcommentaries attest to the authenticity of the major *bhāṣyas* and some other works like the *Upadeśasāhasrī* or the *Dakṣiṇāmūrtyaṣṭaka*. Another criterion relied upon by the older scholars is their personal impression of the style of Śaṅkara. This is undoubtedly important but needs to be spelled out. One would like to suggest that it might be profitable to examine Śaṅkara's effective use of the desiderative, the balancing of sentences, the use of the optative and conditional moods, an even balance between passive and active constructions, the use of simple well known words, clear and logical expression, the sparing use of metaphor or imagery. These features, however, belong to Śaṅkara's prose style. It does not follow as assumed by Belvalkar, that it rules out any ornamentation, elaboration or 'artificiality' in verse also. Philosophical verse would keep close to prose but the devotional hymns could hardly disregard the established conventions of the poetry of the times.

As mentioned before, Hacker and Mayeda have proposed that Śaṅkara's use of certain words is characteristic of him:

(*a*) use of *avidyā* as meaning *adhyāsa* and not as a material cause which would be *jaḍa, bhāvarūpa, āvaraṇa* or *vikṣepa-śakti,* and not characterized as *anādi* or *anirvacanīya;* (*b*) *Nāmarūpa* as the matrix of the world and as *pratyupasthāpita,* etc., by *avidyā;*

(*c*) relatively infrequent use of the term *māyā* in comparison with *avidyā;*(*d*) frequent occurrence of the term *Īśvara;*(*e*) reluctance to accept *ānanda* as a positive characteristic of Brahman; (*f*) non-occurrence of the term *vivarta* in the sense of an illusory effect.[31]

These criteria are doctrinal rather than stylistic and, as pointed out earlier, while generally useful, they may mislead, especially (*a*) and (*e*), if understood to exclude the possibility of non-contradictory variations, refinements or elaborations in different works. In particular, there is no reason to assume that Śaṅkara did not take *Īśvara* and *saguṇopāsanā* seriously or to disregard his theistic religion.[32] It is with his Catholic theism and the context of *upāsanā* that Śaṅkaıa's *stotra* are connected.[33] He explicitly approves the religion of devotional worship.[34] Stylometric tests are unfortunately tied up with Hacker's view and, besides, seem to need extensive revision to prove themselves. Finally, it is unreasonable to suppose that Śaṅkara could only repeat his words and thoughts after the *BSB.*

The need for the edition of several texts and for the critical edition of most of those ascribed to Śaṅkara remains a major desideratum in the absence of which definitive stylistic judgements are not always possible. As the texts stand, many of them even contain occasional grammatical lapses which it would be hard to attribute to Śaṅkara himself. This could only reflect faulty publication or preservation.

REFERENCES

1. *JAOS,* 1976, pp. 259-60.
2. Jacobi, *JAOS,* Vol. 33, 1913.
3. V. Bhattacharya, *The Āgamaśāstra of Gauḍapāda*; Kaviraj, *op. cit.*; Belvalkar, *op. cit.*, p.218; Upadhyaya, *op. cit.*, p.154.
4. Chintamani, *Proc. Third Oriental Conference* (Madras, 1924).
5. Mayeda, *Adyar Library Bulletin,* Vol. 31/32 (1967-68), pp. 73 ff.
6. *Ibid.*, p.75.
7. Vide *Kenopanisad,* ed., Sridhar Sastri Pathak (Poona, 1919), *Prastavikam,* pp. 9-10 where as many as 12 differences are listed.
8. Ingalls, *ABORI,* 1952, pp. 1-14; Raghavan, *WZKSO* (1968-69), pp. 281-94; Mayeda *WZKSO,* 1965, pp. 155 ff.
9. This has been questioned, see Chap. 1.
10. Kaviraj, *op. cit.*, p.30.
11. *BSB,* 2.1.3.
12. See below Chap. 10.
13. Trevor Leggett, *Śaṅkara on the Yoga-sūtras,* Vol. I (1981), pp. xviii-xx.

14. Hacker, *WZKSO*, Vol. 12/13 (1968-69), pp. 119 ff.
15. Mayeda, *Encyclopaedia Brittanica*, 15th ed., under Śaṅkara.
16. Cf. Alston, *A Śaṅkara Source Book*, Vol. I, pp. 48-49.
17. *E.g., Ch.U.B.* 1.6.1, 8.8.4, 8-12-3, 8.15; *BSB* 3, 2-32; *Katha*, 1.17; Cf. D.R. Bhandarkar, '*Solescisms of Śaṅkara and Kālidāsa*' Indian Antiquary, 1912, p.214.
18. Cf. *Upadeśa*, (Prose), 2.
19. *BSB, Adhyāsa-bhāṣya.*
20. *Ch. U.B.* 6.3.2 = *Īśādi*, p.513.
21. See *JAOS*, 1965, pp. 178 ff.
22. Belvalkar, *op. cit.*, p.225.
23. *Ibid.*, p.223.
24. Gussner, *JAOS*, 1976, pp. 259-67.
25. See below.
26. Mahadevan, *Hymns of Śaṅkara*, p.33.
27. Cf. Gaurinath Sastri, *Sārasvatī Suṣamā*, 1986-87, pp. 33-37.
28. *Śrīvidyārṇava*, Vol. 1, p.3; Kaviraj, *op. cit*, pp. 51-55, Kaviraj, Intr. to Visvarupananda, *Vedāntadarśanam*, Vol. I.
29. *Prapañcasāra* (ed. A. Avalon, 1935, 1981) *Prayoga-krama-dīpikā*, p.382: "*Samastāgamāḥ sattva-sāgara-saṁhitādayaḥ teṣām saṅgrahaḥ prapañcāgamaḥ tasyāpi sāra-saṅgraha-rūpam iti prapañcasāra evāyam abhipretaḥ Kaśmira-maṇḍale... nivasatā ācāryeṇa ayaṁ granthaḥ kṛta iti tad anusmaraṇotpattiḥ*"; Kaviraj, *op. cit.*, pp. 30-31, fn.
30. See below, Chap. 12.
31. Hacker, *ZDMG*, 100 (1950), pp. 246-86; Potter, *Encyclopaedia*, III, p.115.
32. Śaṅkara's affiliation to Vaiṣṇava theism—Hacker, *WZKSO*, 9.1965, pp. 147-53; Cf. Vetter, *Lehre und Entwicklung Śaṅkaras*, pp. 16-19.
33. Cf. *Sārasvatī-suṣamā*, 86-87, pp. 93 ff.
34. *BSB*, 2.2.42 : "*Yadapi tasya Bhagavato' bhigamanādi-lakṣaṇam ārādhanam ajasram ananya-cittatayā-bhipreyate, tadapi na pratisiddhyate, śruti-smṛtyorīśvara-pradhānasya prasiddhatvāt*".

6

Śaṅkara and the Earlier Vedāntic Tradition

During the course of its long and continental history, Indian philosophy has assumed the most diverse forms. Yet, 'if we were asked to name the representative thought of India, we would not hesitate even for a moment to assert that it is Vedānta philosophy. No other form of thought has left such decisive and enduring impression on the whole of Indian culture.'[1] One would like to say that this pervasive influence of Vedānta and its dominant position in the Indian philosophical tradition are due to the fact that in Vedānta philosophy is able to provide rational meaning to religious faith and a deeply religious way of life to rational enquiry. Vedānta is at once a religion and a philosophy. Its leading concepts of *Vicāra* and *Jñāna* are at once religious and philosophical. It is true that there are many other systems which may be described as religious as well as philosophical. Nevertheless, it is the unique distinction of Vedānta that while its formal starting point is faith in the Vedic religious tradition, its real starting point is philosophical reflection over the nature of the self. It is, therefore, able to attract not only those who are brought up within the bounds of traditional faith but also those who are independent seekers of spiritual truth. Vedānta comes close to the ideal of being a philosophical and universal religion. Alternatively one could say that it comes close to realizing the ideal of a universal philosophy which can also fulfil the yearning of the religious heart. In all these respects the great rival of Vedānta was Buddhism which was conceivably even more rational and universal as a philosophical religion than Vedānta. Nevertheless, Vedānta selectively absorbed and replaced it in India and became the principal expression of its spiritual culture and philosophy.

That Vedānta became the golden thread of Hinduism and a sublime spiritual philosophy with a strong intellectual and universal appeal, may be traced to a fair extent to the life and work of Śaṅkarācārya. When his life was transfigured into a legend in medieval times, it was largely a recognition of his continuing and growing influence which has maintained its creative utility to our own days. The elevated insights of the *Upaniṣads* had been in course of time obscured by an overgrowth of ritualistic religion and even that religion was losing ground in favour of the Smārta-Paurāṇic religion in the Gupta Age. The popular mind was being captured by theistic cults where worship had a new ritual centring round images and temples. The philosophy of *Nyāya* had emerged as the champion of the theistic idea and engaged atheistic systems in debate. When the Mīmāṁsakas entered the arena of philosophical debate they did so as champions of Vedic ritualism, not of Vedānta. Thus by the end of the Gupta period while the principal philosophies were Buddhist and Jaina, Sāṅkhya, Nyāya and Mīmāṁsā, religion largely centred round ancient or recent ritual, anthropomorphic gods, divine incarnations or divinized prophets and heroes. Despite its ancient greatness Vedānta had become a minor voice scarcely to be discerned in the clash of orthodox ritualism and heterodox mendicancy, theism and atheism. In this situation the principal concern of Śaṅkara could be described to have been the restoration of Vedānta to its original meaning from which it had been distracted by misinterpretations. An ancient system of philosophical and spiritual wisdom, *ātmavidyā* and *brahmavidyā,* appeared to have been subordinated to a formal religion of ritual and worship. The influence of Mīmāṁsā tended to obscure the intimations of the glory of *Jñāna* and of the transcendence of *Brahman* in the *Upaniṣads.* At the same time a growing monotheism blurred their sharp monism, introducing dualistic shadows. Reinterpreting the Vedānta by combating the Mīmāṁsakas and many earlier commentators of the *Upaniṣads,* the *Brahmasūtras* and the *Gītā* by composing new commentaries on them, was the first and principal concern of Śaṅkara. Mādhava has well said,

> *Kudṛṣṭi-timira-sphurat-kumati-paṅka-magnām purā*
> *Prāśarabhuvā cirād budha-mude budhenoddhṛtām*
> *Aho bata jaradgavīm anagha-bhāṣya-sūktāmṛtairapaṅkayati*
> *Śaṅkaraḥ praṇata-Śaṅkaraḥ sādaram//*

i.e., in the days of yore Vedic teachings were sunk in the confusion of false opinions and views like an aged cow in a swamp at night.

It was the wise son of Parāśara who had rescued it from that plight for the delight of the wise. Now Śaṅkara with the blessing of Śaṅkara has cleansed the cow of all mud and mire adhering to it by the nectar of his faultless commentary.[2]

Despite appearances and ostensible claims, however, this attempt at the restoration of ancient Vedānta was not a mere revival or going back; 'it was, in fact, a profoundly original reinterpretation which as often as not introduced new wine in old bottles'.[3] What Śaṅkara achieved by the writing of his celebrated commentaries, something remembered in later tradition as an epoch-making event, was not merely the restoration of Vedānta to its rightful position but its reinterpretation as a coherent philosophy of monistic absolutism. In seeking to discover the meaning of the ancient texts Śaṅkara's hermeneutic is not simply formal but instinct with his own spiritual vision and logical conviction. In Śaṅkara's Vedānta revealed tradition fuses with an original philosophic rationality, reminiscent of the syncretic images which were then gaining popularity.

Several scholars have attempted to trace the development of Vedānta before Śaṅkara.[4] Such an attempt, however, needs to be supplemented by being placed in the changing context of the general history of Indian culture and thought. Chronological uncertainties too need to be faced in all such attempts. Although much has been written on the different textual sources of Vedānta, it remains a fact 'that the philosophy of the Vedānta school has yet to be fully examined from a historical viewpoint'.[5] What is being attempted here, however, is no more than the underlining of the succession of phases in Vedāntic history within certain broad cultural and intellectual trends in the history of ancient Indian thought within which the development of Vedānta lies. It must be remembered that if Advaita Vedānta in its modern form seems to begin from Śaṅkara, it had an early history of nearly two millennia.

While the literal meaning of the word *Vedānta* is a matter of some dispute, it has not been generally disputed that the *Upaniṣads* constitute the primary source of Vedānta. They may be considered as chronologically the latest portions of the Vedas and deal with matters of the greatest concern for human life i.e., with questions of ultimate reality and value (*paramārtha*). There can be no doubt that the *Upaniṣads* constitute a literature which evolved during several centuries. Indian scholars have generally placed the classical *Upaniṣads* before Buddha. That some of the *Upaniṣads* like *Bṛ.*

or *Ch.* are prior to Buddha has been generally conceded by all scholars but there is much difference of opinion about the relative and absolute dating of the Upaniṣadic corpus. The most detailed and critical work on the relative dating of the Upaniṣadic texts has been done by Belvalkar, on which the present author has commented elsewhere.[6] The absolute dating of Belvalkar places the *Upaniṣads* between 1200 B.C. - 500 B.C. This merely means that they are later Vedic and pre-Buddhistic, and the present consensus of Indian scholarship may be said to be generally favourable to it. On the other hand, we have the opinion of Nakamura, which places the *Upaniṣads* between 500 B.C. and A.D. 200.[7] While Nakamura recognizes that the older *Upaniṣads* are prior to Buddha and Pāṇini who in his opinion lived in the 4th century B.C., a view which is not generally accepted now. His attempt to trace a Buddhistic influence on some *Upaniṣads* like the *Kaṭha* too cannot be considered successful.[8] In any case, avoiding precise dates, it may be said that Upaniṣadic thought as represented by the classical *Upaniṣads* was the culmination of Vedic thought and generally pre-Buddhistic. Early Vedic thought may be said to be mythical in form, without 'myth' being understood in a pejorative sense. Middle Vedic thought had the form of ritualistic speculation. In the later Vedic age some of the Brāhmaṇas who appear to have repaired to forest hermitages developed a system of symbolic meditations as a replacement for material ritual. In continuation with ritualistic speculations these meditations were essentially cosmological. Just as in Greece, the First Upaniṣadic 'philosophies' were cosmological in character. Who fashioned the world? What was the material out of which the world was fashioned? These were the two major questions. About the first of these the *Upaniṣads* move away from the multiplicity of gods to the idea of a single sentient and cosmic principle described in various ways. The most pervasive of these came to be *Brahman*. About the second question, although a number of different 'first principles' like water, air, non-Being or Being were suggested by different thinkers, the prevailing view came to be that the cosmic creator or *Brahman* created the world out of Himself. Upaniṣadic cosmological reflections culminated in this theory of *Brahman* as the efficient and material cause of the world. As to the nature of *Brahman* it was regarded as pure being or knowledge or as the self in all beings. This last view which identified *Brahman* with *Ātman* was one of the most important in the *Upaniṣads*. It made the human self cosmic and divine and the cosmic principle sentient. This view of the *Brahman* as the creative matrix of the world and as identical with the individual self constituted the basic affirmations of Upaniṣadic *Advaita*.[9]

So far Upaniṣadic Vedānta was a continuation and development of the Vedic tradition. On this view the world is essentially divine and the intuitive apprehension of ultimate reality is conceived positively as the fulfilment of human seeking and aspirations. The limitations and dissatisfactions of human life including the fear of mortality are due simply to human ignorance, not to some necessary evil in the human self or the universe. To realize one's true nature is to be fulfilled in infinity and eternity. Such a fulfilment is described as a beatific experience.[10]

However, there appear to have been wandering groups of mendicants also in this age who rejected Vedic optimism, ritualism and theism. They believed in the doctrines of *saṁsāra* and *karman*. For them human life was a vale of tears and what the wise man aspired after was to be rid of the existential suffering entailed in human life itself. This required the giving up of desires and work and withdrawal into a lonely life of silent contemplation. This was the ideal of mendicancy in complete contrast to the traditional Brāhmaṇical ideal of an active and ritually punctuated social life. On this traditional view every man is born with three obligations. By studying the *Veda* in the First *Āśrama* he repays the obligation to the sages. By rearing a family and performing sacrifices in the second *Āśrama* he repays the obligations to the ancestors and the gods. It is only after repaying these obligations that man may legitimately repair to the forest in the third *Āśrama* and meditate over the mysteries of life and death. The ideal of mendicancy, on the other hand, disparaged the whole process of social life, regarding the notion of social obligation as dependent on egoistic desire and ignorance. The social origins of these mendicants called *śramaṇa* or *muni* are not clear. They could have been connected with the Harappan Civilization which is itself enigmatic.[11]

It seems that some Upaniṣadic thinkers like Yājñavalkya were acquainted with this kind of thinking which was characteristic of wandering mendicants or *Śramaṇas* and tried to incorporate the ideas of *Karman, Saṁsāra* and *Mokṣa* within the traditional Vedic thought. This implied a disparagement of Vedic ritualism and the recognition of mendicancy as an ideal.

Apart from the priests, hermits and mendicants, there was one other social group which contributed to Upaniṣadic thought and this included that of enlightened rulers or Kṣatriyas. They tended to generalize the concept of sacrifice as the immanent principle of human life, here and hereafter.

There were also Śūdra and *atiśūdra* teachers like Kavaṣa Ailūṣa of the Chāgaleya or Sayugvā Raikva. It is clear that the Upaniṣadic seers included Brāhmaṇical priests as well as other non-Brāhmaṇical groups. As illustrated by the story of Satyakāma Jābāla or the *Mbh* story of the birth of Vyāsa, social divisions were not yet based rigidly on birth. Freedom of thought accompanied this situation. The Jain work *Isi-bhāsiyam* also illustrates how thinkers of diverse origins and shades of thought commanded respect.

As the Vedic Age ends and we enter the Age of the Epics and the Sūtras (*c.* 600 B.C. - 100 B.C.) there is a considerable change in the social and intellectual scene. The age of migrations and settlement ended and we see now the rise of the *Mahājanapadas* and what has been called the Second Urban Revolution with emerging towns, trade and money. *Gaṇarājyas* and ancient monarchies are seen aspiring after universal sway, based on professional soldiers and administrators, whose point of view is reflected in the *Arthaśāstra*. The *Dharmasūtras* reflect the priestly attempt at the precise definition of the social law even while the actual divisions of society belie it. This age of widespread social, economic and political change is also the age of an unprecedented intellectual and religious ferment. We see numerous mendicant or *Śramaṇa* sects and schools such as the Buddhists, the Jainas, the Ājīvakas and the Sāṅkhya. While republican Kṣatriyas patronized the *Śramaṇas*, some ambitious rulers patronized the 'Secularists' (*Lokāyatikas)* and some others supported the old Kṣatriya tradition of a wisdom which sought to consecrate a life of action synthesizing Brāhmaṇism and Śramaṇism, Sāṅkhya and Yoga. The Brāhmaṇas were busy creating the various sciences including philosophy (*ānvīkṣikī*). The Buddhists speak of six different heterodox schools including materialism. In the *Mbh* we hear of five types of philosophy, viz., *Sāṅkhya, Yoga, Pañcarātra, Pāśupata* and *Vedāraṇyaka*. The *Arthaśāstra* speaks of *Sāṅkhya, Yoga* and *Lokāyata*.

Faced with challenges and alternatives the ancient Upaniṣadic philosophy seems to lose its centrality. There were challenges from ritualism, theistic movements, 'secularist' atheism and ascetic atheism. The age of growing science raised doubts and demanded conceptual clarity and rational evidence. Being an age of social change and mobility it was also an age of conflicting attitudes and values—*pravṛtti* and *nivṛtti, artha* and *kāma* versus *dharma* and *mokṣa.* It demanded reconciliation and a search for some ultimate value or law behind accidents and conventions. 'The ancient Vedic Age was characterized by the general acceptance of that positive outlook towards life within the bounds of the moral and ritual order called *ṛta,* which Manu has described as *Vaidika Karmayoga.* The Age of Buddha saw the emergence of diverse movements of revolt and reform against the Vedic ethos as interpreted by the priestly orthodoxy. Whether Śramaṇic or Āgamic (or Lokāyatic), all of them questioned the authority or adequacy of the *Vedas,* the efficacy or desirability of sacrifices and the position of the priestly class. What is more they tended to adopt a negative outlook towards worldly life conceived as *saṁsāra.* They were also generally more favourable to the spiritual eligibility of the common people. The new class of heterodox ascetics competed with the Brāhmaṇical establishment for spiritual guidance.[12] The half millennium between 600 B.C. and 100 B.C. represents an age of conflict between orthodoxy and heterodoxy, *āstikya* and *Nāstikya, Pravṛtti* and *Nivṛtti, Karman* and *Jñāna* and also the beginnings of a rapprochement between them.

The reformulation of Vedānta in this age was done principally by the *Bhagavadgītā* and the *Brahmasūtras* though the *adhyātmapaṭala* of the *Āpastamba Dharmasūtras* may also be noted here. The date and composition of the *Gītā* has been much debated. There was a tendency to date it in the post-Christian era. The argument had been based on linguistic, metrical and stylistic considerations as also on the dating of the *Mbh* itself. It tended to disregard the fact that the age of the *sūtras* was also the age of *Saṁhitās* which had little to learn from the classical Purāṇic verse or style. The fact that the *BG* struggles to reconcile *Jñāna* and *Karman* clearly shows that it is earlier than the *Purāṇas* where their reconciliation is taken for granted. A similar argument shows the antiquity of the *Mbh* which discusses all these moral, social and political issues which are already settled for Kauṭilya and Manu. The social scene in the *Mbh* too shows its antiquity.[13] Despite the fact that interpolation and additions were made to it between 200 B.C. and 200 A.D., the period of the composition of the *Mbh* should be deemed to have been basically completed by 200 B.C. Its original nucleus or *Jaya* being earlier than Pāṇini and Āśvalāyana goes back to the period before 600 B.C., though it underwent elaboration (*upabṛṁhaṇa*) between 600 B.C. and 200 B.C. principally through the interpolation of subsidiary stories or *Itihāsas* as also through repetitions and in some cases through revision. There is, however, no reason to suppose that it underwent any radical change of character in this process.

The *BG* called *Upaniṣad, Brhmavidyā* and *Yogaśāstra* constitutes the ideal focus of the *Mbh.*[14] Whether it also underwent elaboration with the *Mbh* is difficult to say. It is traditionally believed to be a unitary whole and the attempts to analyse it into its constructional phases have not commanded general acceptance. The connection of the *BG* with the *Upaniṣads* is obvious and close. Kṛṣṇa himself figures in the *Ch* and the doctrine which was taught to him there, is racapitulated in the *BG* which also summarizes diverse other teachings of the *Upaniṣads* relating to *Brahman* and *Ātman*. Its description of Yoga recalls the *Kaṭha* and the *Śvetāśvatara*. Its concept of *parā* and *aparā prakṛti* is particularly reminiscent of the *Śvet.* But the Upaniṣadic doctrines undergo a definite intellectual and emotional transformation in the *BG*. In the first place the *BG* perceives the apparent conflict of Vedic *Karmakāṇḍa* and the Vedāntic doctrine of *Jñāna*, which it assimilates to and calls *Sāṅkhya*. Creativity and hence action are not generally excluded from *Brahman* and hence from *Ātman* in the *Upaniṣads* and this point of view is continued in the theism of the *BG* where God creates and acts without desire and this is the model to be followed by the ideal man also. Nevertheless the *BG* perceives the conflict between the path of ritual and the path of knowledge as also between the transcendental and empirical dimensions of the spirit who is at once the detached witness and yet involved in action and experience. The *BG* goes beyond the older *Upaniṣads* in facing these contradictions intellectually and seeking to answer them in terms of its justly famous concept of *Niṣkāma Karman*. In this the *BG* represents a progressive adaptation of the Vedānta to the challenges of the Mahājanapada Age. In another respect too *BG* develops the Vedānta and that is as a devotional monotheism consistent with monism. The concept of incarnation was in particular a wholly new idea. It may be said to have been the orthodox answer to the cult of perfected (*Siddha*) and 'superhuman' (*Lokottara*) men current among the heterodox cults. Buddha, Jina, *Avatāra* equally provide a link between the common man and transcendent Reality.

In the ultimate analysis the *BG* reconciles *Karman* and *Jñāna* in terms of *Bhakti* and its ultimate term is the personal *Īśvara*

(*Puruṣottama*) rather than the neuter *Brahman*. It is the incarnation of the personal god who without directly fighting holds the balance in the struggle of Right and Wrong around which the story of the *Mbh* is woven. The *Mbh* with the *BG* may be regarded as a vast and stupendous, dramatic image of the Vedāntic philosophy in action.

It is well known that the *BG* and the *BS* refer to each other, which is best explained by the supposition that both have undergone some elaboration. Belvalkar has argued that in the beginning the *BS* were probably composed separately in different *śākhās* for reconciling the different parts of the *Upaniṣads* belonging to them.[15] Thus there appears to have been a *Chāndogya Brahmasūtra* underlying the present *BS* which could have grown as a *sarvaśākhīya* text through additions and elaborations. Once such a composite origin of the *BS* is accepted, it is easy to assume that in some form it could have been a much more ancient text than it seems to be on account of its references to Buddhist philosophy. On the basis of its knowledge of *Śūnyavāda*, Jacobi had dated the *BS* in the 5th century A.D.[16] According to Belvalkar the *prati-śākhīya Brahmasūtras* were earlier than the *BG* while the *sarvaśākhīya* text could have been of about 300 B.C. and the present elaborated text could date from about the beginning of the Christian era. Nakamura is in agreement with the manner and stages of the composition of the *BS*, though not with this dating. He says that in the first period synopses were composed in the schools belonging to the *Sāma-Veda*, centring on the *Chāndogya* and treating of the *Upaniṣad*. In the second period the theories of the *Upaniṣads* were taken up in the *Brahmasūtras* and the entire *sūtra* was notably enlarged. At the same time the *Sūtra* came to be adopted as the synopsis of the *Upaniṣads* for the Vedic schools in general. In the third period the entire *Sūtra* was unified and revised, logical refutation of other Indian schools appended and thus the present *BS* came to be formed. For Nakamura the beginnings of the *sūtras* would go back to the period of the *Kalpasūtras* while its present form could not be earlier than Vasubandhu, that is A.D. 400.[17]

That the *BS* have a special relation to the *Ch* is indubitable and had been pointed out by Deussen.[18] That it has assumed the present form after some revision and enlargement is plausible. That this was in three phases and that the work is of many authors, remain unproved hypothesis of which the tradition preserves no memory. The commentarial tradition went back to the ancient teacher Upavarṣa whose work was available to Śaṅkara. There were undoubtedly other Vedāntic works, perhaps called *Brahmasūtras* before the present one which refers to several ancient sages, but there is no reason to suppose that the present work has been constituted by their composition and elaboration. Pāṇini refers to a *Bhikṣu-sūtra* of Pārāśarya and this has been construed to be a reference to the present work which tradition ascribes to Pārāśarya or Vyāsa and which is concerned with the study proper to the fourth *āśrama*, clearly stated by Manu. Nevertheless the *BS* are not known as *Bhikṣu-sūtras*. As for implications of the doctrines refuted in the *BS*, the mention of Sāṅkhya, Yoga, Vaiśeṣika, Jainism, Pāñcarātra and Pāśupata, and much of Buddhism including the concepts of *skandha, santāna* and *pratītyasamutpāda* as well as the principles of Sarvāstivāda presents no real difficulties because they were current in some form before 300 B.C. As for the refutation of Vijñānavāda and Śūnyavāda, there is no real evidence that the *Sūtras* intend their refutation in their later systematic form. In fact as in the *Nyāya-sūtras* the *BS* do not distinguish Vijñānavāda and Śūnyavāda. What they seek to refute is the Buddhist denial of the external world as understood by common sense. Such a denial is quite ancient in Buddhism. The roots of Buddhist idealism are older than the Mahāyāna schools and scriptures of the Kuṣāṇa and Gupta periods and can be found in the Eighteen Sects which were fully developed between the Second and Third Councils i.e., by the 3rd century B.C. The Lokottaravādins, the Ekavyāvahārikas and the Prajñaptivādins denied the reality of external things in various ways. The concepts of *Śūnyatā* and *Kṣaṇikatva* are also found among various sects. It is true that owing to their anticipation of Mahāyāna some of these sects and ideas have themselves been dated late, but that is really begging the question. The *BS*, thus, could be placed between the 4th century B.C. and the 2nd century B.C. It is also possible that part of the refutation of rival systems was the result of a later revision which could be placed between the 2nd century B.C. and the 1st century A.D., the period of the early *Mahāyānasūtras* and of the classical development of Sarvāstivāda. Thus the original *BS* could be placed between 350 B.C. and 150 B.C. and their revised version which updated the critique of rival systems could have been completed before A.D. 100.[19] This would barely allow time for the pre-Śaṅkara commentators of the *BS* and the *Mīmāṁsā-sūtras*.

The Upaniṣadic and pre-Buddhistic period has been called the Creative Period of Indian philosophy. The age of the *Sūtras* (600

B.C.-200 B.C.) may be called the age of systematization when different disciplines and schools of thought received their first systematic formulation. The *BS* give to the philosophy of the *Upaniṣads* or Vedānta its first systematic form. They sum up the discussion of earlier thinkers and in their present form at least dispute the views of rival schools. Among the thinkers mentioned we find the names of Bādari, Jaimini, Āśmarathya, Ātreya, Kāśakṛtsna, Auḍulomi, Kārṣṇājini and, of course, Bādarāyaṇa who is generally credited with the authorship of the work. The major issues of discussion with these thinkers and reflected in the *BS* were '(1) the nature of creation and the first cause, (2) the relationship between the supreme spirit and the individual, and (3) the role of work and knowledge in relation to salvation'.[20] Some thinkers tended to interpret the first cause in a Sāṅkhyan manner, a tendency which Bādarāyaṇa rebuts sharply. On the relationship of *Brahman* and *Jīva* three important views were upheld. Āśmarathya believed that the relationship between the two was one of identity in difference and illustrated it by the example of fire and its sparks. Auḍulomi, on the other hand, regarded their identity to hold only after emancipation just as the river becomes one with the sea only when it joins the latter. Kāśakṛtsna affirmed the essential identity of *Brahman* and *Jīva*. On the path to salvation Jaimini held religious works to be necessary and Bādarāyaṇa did not regard work as irrelevant to salvation although he admitted the efficacy of knowledge. The need for meditation on the Upaniṣadic *vidyās* was generally upheld.

The *BS* have four *adhyāyas* with four *pādas* in each. Traditionally the *Sūtras* are grouped in thematic divisions called *adhikaraṇas*. It must be recognized that many of the *sūtras* remain in themselves obscure and ambiguous because of their laconic and elliptical style. The ancient commentarial tradition too has been lost. As a consequence we are left to understand the *sūtras* in the light of the later commentators who are apt to put new wine into old bottles. This was inevitably the case where the discussion related to heterodox schools. The later commentators could not afford to disregard the views and arguments of the later representatives of the heterodox schools to the extent they were known to them. Thus Śaṅkara reads the arguments of Vasubandhu and Dharmakīrti in the critique of Buddhism in the *BS*.

The first or *samanvayādhyāya* of the *BS* begins with the *Jijñāsādhikaraṇa* which discusses the presuppositions of Vedāntic study. The second or *Janmādyadhikaraṇa* defines *Brahman* as the source etc., of the world. The third or *Śāstrayonitvādhikaraṇa* declares *Brahman* to be the source of the *Veda* and knowable through it alone. The fourth or *Samanvayādhikaraṇa* argues that *Brahman* as the eternal real is the principal concern of the Vedāntic texts. The fifth or *Īkṣatyadhikaraṇa* is 'engaged in proving by various arguments that the *Brahman* which the Vedānta texts represent as the cause of the world, is an intelligent principle, and cannot be identified with the non-intelligent *pradhāna* from which the world springs according to Sāṅkhya.'[21] In these five *adhikaraṇas* the fundamental position with respect to the nature of *Brahman* stands defined. In the remaining sections it is argued that it is *Brahman* alone which has been diversely described in the Upaniṣadic texts as the golden person, the subtle ether, the vital breath, the light that shines within and without, the Inner Monitor, the Imperishable, the Highest Person to be meditated upon with the syllable *Oṁ*, or which dwells in the heart. Many such and other descriptions are merely representations of *Brahman* for meditational purposes.

The second chapter called *Avirodhādhyāya* seeks to refute rival schools—Sāṅkhya and Vaiśeṣika, Buddhist and Jaina and Pāśupata and *Pāñcarātra*. This would be of great historical value if only we could be sure of Bādarāyaṇa's date. The *adhyāya* goes on to discuss the derivation of the fundamental elements of Nature from *Brahman* and seeks to determine the nature of the soul which is considered intelligent and individual, an eternal aspect or part (*aṁśa*) of *Brahman* endowed with the power of will and action. It has been the considered opinion of Prof. Thibaut that Bādarāyaṇa's views on the subject are nearer those of Rāmānuja than of Śaṅkara.[22]

The third *adhyāya* discusses the course of after-life and various meditations, worshipful meditation being regarded the way to self-realization. The last *adhyāya* while continuing the earlier discussion takes up the subject of the result of Vedāntic practice and thus discusses the nature of emancipation. Liberation could be direct or gradual. The liberated souls do not acquire any power to run the world.

The *BS* are at once theistic and monistic. On the one hand, *Brahman* is conceived as the creator and lord of the universe through whose worship man can attain salvation. On the other, He is the sole reality with whom the universe and the individual souls are essentially identical. What man, then, needs is only the true knowledge of reality. Between these two views of *Brahman*, as the supreme Lord to be worshipped and as the only spiritual reality, there is a latent tension which was bound to come out in the works of subsequent commentators, some emphasizing unity, some duality and others seeking to reconcile them. These divergent tendencies had antedated the *BS* and they were by no means finally reconciled by the *sūtras*.

There can be no doubt that the *BS* give to Vedānta the form of a systematic philosophy stated in abstract conceptual terms and defended by logical arguments. It appeals to the *śruti* as the ultimate authority for the knowledge of *Brahman* and argues that mere reasoning cannot give certain knowledge about what lies beyond the ken of human experience. However, in arguing with those philosophies which reject the authority of the *Veda*, it appeals to rational arguments only and tries to show how these philosophies are logically inconsistent and inadequate to explain the facts of experience. In interpreting the *Veda* it follows the canons of *Mīmāṁsā*. In fact, there can hardly be any doubt that in this early period the two *Mīmāṁsās* were regarded as essentially continuous. The *Pūrva-mīmāṁsā* elaborated the canons of interpretation and sought to harmonize the vast system of rituals as the means of realizing *dharma*. The *uttara-mīmāṁsā* or Vedānta enquired into the nature of *Brahman* after this earlier enquiry into *Dharma*. *Dharma* and *Brahman* were the two major concepts of the later Vedic Ages and the two sections of Vedic literature, *Karmakāṇda* and *Jñānakāṇda*, corresponded to them. The two *Mīmāṁsās* were philosophical systematizations of these two sections.

The social reconciliation of these two ways of life—the practice of ritualistic *dharma* and the intellectual enquiry into spiritual reality or *Brahman*—was sought to be accomplished through the system of the four *āśramas* which the *Dharmasūtras* were formulating in this age. The social distinction between the Brāhmaṇical *bhikṣus* of the fourth *āśrama* and the *śramaṇas* would be blurred for the general public except that the former were orthodox and the latter heterodox. The Brāhmaṇical *sūtrakāras* emphasized this distinction to ostracise the *śramaṇas* from social patronage. For a long time, however, they fought a losing battle.[23]

An important distinction between the Brāhmaṇical *bhikṣu* and the *śramaṇa* was in relation to the caste system. The *śramaṇa* mendicants disregarded caste and came from all sections of society. The Brāhmaṇical authors did not permit, inconstantly enough, non-Brāhmaṇas to adopt mendicancy even though they accepted the fact that the mendicant has to give up caste-status! In the *Upaniṣads* we find seers from all castes and classes and even the *Gītā* threw open the doors of worship to the Śūdras. The *BS*, however, seek to restrict the knowledge of *Brahman* from the Śūdras. This *Apaśūdrādhikaraṇa* is at par with the similar section of the *Pūrva mīmāṁsā* where Śūdras are denied the right to perform Vedic ritual. The fact is there were enlightened sages like Bādari who upheld the religious rights of the Śūdras, which must have been reflected in social reality in an earlier stage. Perhaps it was the desire of the priests to preserve their leadership of the Vedic ritual in the face of the anti-Vedicism and anti-ritualism of the *śramaṇas* or even of the enlightened Brāhmaṇical seers or rulers which led to this restrictive and reactionary outlook. There is no doubt that a liberal view of caste and religious rights was current even within orthodoxy in this age as is proved by the *Mbh*. The *Sūtras* sought to counter this tendency. In the present instance we can also see additional evidence of the close relationship between the *BS* and the traditional, ritualistic *Mīmāṁsā*.

During the centuries which lie between Bādarāyaṇa and Śaṅkara the form of popular religion underwent a great transformation. Vedic gods were eclipsed and the more elaborate Vedic ritual remained a reality only for kings and learned Brāhmaṇas. For most people religion came to be defined by the *Smṛtis* and *Purāṇas* and came to mean reliance on superhuman saviours and incarnations to be worshipped through devotion, images and temples. While Vedic rites on principal occasions like birth, marriage and death remained important as also the minimum daily chore of *agnihotra* and *svādhyāya* for the Brāhmaṇas, the new and popular mode of worship relied basically on the anthropomorphically conceived aspect of the deity. Image worship was common to the orthodox as well as the heterodox sects which attracted wide following. While the *Purāṇas* sought to reconcile conflicts and diversity by simple syncretism, the philosophers passionately debated the question of what constitutes authority in relation to religious truth or the contradictions between impersonal Absolutism and personal theism, the path of pure knowledge and the path of action including devotional worship. The Buddhists in particular constituted a standing challenge, not only with their denial of the soul and God, but their description of the world as an illusion grounded in the non-dual Absolute. For attracting the popular mind they were able to put forward the idea of the *Bodhisattvas* as personal saviours who were fully human and could be pleased by faith and devotion. On the social side the *Smṛtis* from Manu to Nārada and Devala sought to adapt the concept of *Cāturvarṇya* to the conglomerate of heterogeneous social groups based on clan, region and occupation which then prevailed, by the concept of *Jāti*. The third *āśrama* had virtually disappeared in practice and the first *āśrama* could have survived only in a truncated form in some orthodox Brāhmaṇa families because of the exclusion of women from Vedic study and the vogue of early marriages. The departure of existing conditions from the older ideal was recognized as a settled fact and the concept of the *Kali* Age was gradually evolved. The Brāhmaṇas, however, strenuously strove to maintain the ideal of life lived by ritual, old and new, and placed increasing emphasis on the virtue of charity, a virtue which was emphasized equally by *Mahāyāna*. This was bound to lead to competition and conflict among the religieux of diverse orders.

The process of conflict and reconciliation between orthodoxy and heterodoxy at different levels—social, religious and intellectual—continued from the Śuṅga to the Gupta periods. It is to these centuries that the pre-Śaṅkara commentators of the *BS* belong. Among these many names are available—Upavarṣa, Bodhāyana, Draviḍācārya, Brahmanandin, Brahmadatta, Bhartṛmitra, Bhartṛprapañca, Ṭanka, Guhadeva, Bhāruci, Kapardi, and Sundarapāṇḍya. The original works of these are lost except for references to their views in Śaṅkara and later authors. Nor is anything definite known about their life or dates. There were also other teachers of monistic philosophy with which Vedānta was not unconnected. Among these one could mention Bhartṛhari and also monistic-monotheistic Śaiva schools.

Upavarṣa to whom Śaṅkara refers with reverence as Bhagavan Upavarṣa could have been the earliest of these as he appears to have preceded Śabarasvāmin.[24] Upavarṣa appears to have been the author of a celebrated *Vṛtti* on both the *Mīmāṁsās* and became famous as the *Vṛttikāra*. He appears to have been concerned with adopting some of the criteriological and epistemological principles generally associated with *Pūrva mīmāṁsa* in later times such as *svataḥ prāmāṇyavāda* and the six *pramāṇas*. He also defended the existence of the soul against Buddhist attacks by arguing that it is known introspectively in the very notion of 'I'. He is also supposed to have attacked the Buddhist denial of external reality as also the Grammarians' view of *sphoṭa*. He defended the view that the word is simply a succession of letters. On the 'self' he seems to have developed the notions of Yājñavalkya. The 'self' is self-luminous independently of thoughts. Nor can external objects be reduced to thought-forms.[25]

There are old traditions that Upavarṣa was the contemporary of Kātyāyana or the younger brother of Varṣa and thus should belong to the 4th century B.C. This does not seem probable at first sight and the Vedāntic commentator Upavarṣa could have been a different person, probably later, because he criticises *sphoṭa* and some Buddhist views. In view of the scarcely known earlier history of these views, however, the antiquity of Upavarṣa is not impossible. He was certainly prior to Śabara. Śaṅkara seems to have specially relied on Upavarṣa and the latter's reliance on Yājñavalkya harmonised with Śaṅkara's attachment to the *Bṛ*.

Bodhāyana was another famous *Vṛttikāra* who wrote a detailed work on the *BS* and also appears to have written on the *Mīmāṁsā-sūtras*. Just as Śaṅkara appears to be near to Upavarṣa, Rāmānuja claimed to follow Bodhāyana. For Bodhāyana the *BS* presuppose the *Pūrva mīmāṁsā* and the quest for *Brahman* the earlier practice of *dharma*. The two *Mīmāṁsās* appear to have been connected for him as one grand system. Bodhāyana appears to have been essentially a thiest for whom the soul and God are not wholly identical. God is for him the Infinity or *bhūman* for which the individual soul aspires.[26] *Bhakti* as service of God was apparently stressed by him.[27]

It is worth noting that both Upavarṣa and Bodhāyana were known as *Vṛttikāras* and although the general attitudes of Śaṅkara and Rāmānuja towards them are known, we cannot be sure that when Śaṅkara is rejecting a view attributed to a *Vṛttikāra* in later works that *Vṛttikāra* must be Bodhāyana. This produces a certain ambiguity about the views of the *Vṛttikāras* except where they are identified by name in some later work.

Rāmānuja has referred to Bhāruci, Ṭanka, Guhadeva, Kapardin and Dramiḍācārya. It has been suggested that the first four were posterior to Śaṅkara[28] but such an opinion is questionable.[29] Now since the commentary of Bhāruci on parts of *Manusmṛti* has been discovered it is clear that he was in all likelihood earlier than Śaṅkara.[30] Of the philosophical and Vedāntic interest of Bhāruci there is ample evidence in his commentary on Manu.

Practically nothing is known about Ṭanka, Guhadeva and Kapardin. Sometimes Ṭanka has been identified with Brahmanandin who is famous as the *Vākyakāra* on the *Chāndogya*.[31] Some of his views have been quoted in the *Saṅkṣepa-śārīraka* and its commentaries.[32] It seems that he held the causal process to be merely pragmatically real (*saṁvyavahāramātram*) and it has been said that he really upheld the concept of *Vivarta* in place of *Pariṇāma*. On the *Vākyas* of Brahmanandin one Dramiḍācārya is stated to have composed a commentary or *Bhāṣya* so that Dramiḍācārya is referred to as the Bhāṣyakāra.[33] He is stated to have emphasized the concept of *Nirguṇa Brahman*[34] and the eternal identity of the self and Brahman which he expressed through the famous parable of the prince brought up by a huntsman from childhood but who realized his true identity on being told of it. This parable is quoted by Śaṅkara and elucidates the idea of self-realization as the recollection or recognition of a pre-existent fact.[35] Śaṅkara refers to him as *Āgamavit* or *Sampradāyavit*.

Brahmadatta was another famous Vedāntic commentator on the *BS* or the *Ch* and supported a peculiar kind of monistic doctrine—'*ekam brahmaiva nityaṁ tad itaradakhilaṁ tatra janmādibhāg*'. Śaṅkara, Sureśvara, Jñānottama and Vedāntadeśika allude to his views.[36] The world as well as the individual soul both arise from *Brahman* and merge into Him. For such absorption it is necessary to follow the Upaniṣadic prescription or *niyoga*, viz., *Ātmā vā are draṣṭavyaḥ*,' '*atmetyevopāsīta*', etc. Having acquired the indirect knowledge of *Brahman* from the *śruti* it is necessary to meditate on it and realize its truth directly, even so, full liberation comes only after death. *Karman* must not be abandoned. Brahmadatta is thus a *Dhyāna-niyoga-vādin* as also *Jñāna-karma-samuccaya-vādin*. Sureśvara criticises him in *NS* 1.68-69. Sometimes *Prapañca-vilayavāda* and *Bhāvādvaita* have also been ascribed to him but the ascription has been questioned.

Just as Dramiḍācārya has been sought to be identified with the Alvar saint Sathakopa or Vakulābharaṇa, the great Ācārya Saundarapāṇḍya has been surmised to be the same as the Pāṇḍya king who was converted by the Śaiva saint Tiṛujñāna Sambandhar and found his place in the list of the Nāyanārs.[37] This identification however, has been questioned on the ground that there was a difference between the monism of the Śaivas and that of Śaṅkara. But this argument cannot be regarded as decisive because while Śaṅkara clearly criticizes dualistic theistic doctrines like those of the Pāśupatas, he does not criticize monistic Āgamic doctrine. His attitude to such Āgamic schools needs to be critically discovered in the light of the view taken of the ascription of the *Dakṣiṇāmūrti* and *Saundaryalaharī stotras.*

In his commentary on the *BS* Śaṅkara quotes some verses saying *apicāhuḥ.*[38] These have been ascribed to Saundarapāṇḍya by Ātmasvarūpa. Some more verses have been quoted from him by Amalānanda. It seems that Sundarapāṇḍya was clearly an Advaitin held in high regard by Śaṅkara who quotes his view to the effect that while the social self of man is 'secondary' or 'conventional' (*gauṇa*), the psychophysical or 'natural' self of man is 'unreal' or 'delusive' (*mithyā*). Nevertheless the empirical knower and the empirical means of knowledge remain valid till supreme knowledge. *'Dehātma-pratyayo yadvatpramāṇatvenakalpitaḥ/ Laukikaṁ tadvad evapramāṇam tvā 'tmaniścayāt//'* On this view the Absolute, though transcendent becomes the object of speech and thought through superimposition and negation (*adhyāropāpavādābhyām niṣprapañcamprapañcyate*).

Śaṅkara's greatest hostility was reserved for the ancient teacher Bhartṛprapañca who apparently commented on the *Kaṭha* and the *Bṛ*, and also on the *BS*. Śaṅkara and Sureśvara refer to his views.[39] Bhartṛprapañca believed in *bhedābheda, Brahmapariṇāma, Jñāna-karma-samuccaya* and *Pramāṇa-samuccaya.* Śaṅkara briefly summarises his view thus: "*anekātmakam brahma yathā-neka-śākho vṛkṣaḥ evam aneka-śakti-pravṛtti-yuktam brahma. Ata ekatvam nānātvam cobhayamapi satyam eva. Yathā vṛkṣa ityekatvam śākhā iti nānātvam. Yathā ca samudrātmanā ekatvam phenataraṅgādyātmanā nānātvaṁ yathā ca mṛdātmanā ekatvam ghaṭaśarāvādyātmanā nānātvam. Tatraikatvāṁśena jñānān mokṣavyavahāraḥ setsyati nānātvāṁśena karma-kāṇḍāśrayau laukika-Vaidikav vyavahārau setsyata iti.*"[40] This posits a real unity underlying a real diversity. The one becomes many without losing its unity.[41] *Brahman* is not a bare unity but is rich with infinite potentialities. Empirical knowledge and revelation both show different poles of reality and make action and realization possible respectively.[42]

The three analogies mentioned by Śaṅkara above correspond to three different views of the relation of *Brahman* to creatures, viz., tree and branches to whole and part, sea and waves to substance and mode, clay and pots to cause and effect. The analogy of the universal and the particular has also been adduced in this context and it has been said that the followers of Bhartṛprapañca developed his ideas into four different sub-schools. Bhartṛprapañca is also said to have differentiated *para* and *apara Brahman*[43] and to have outlined eight stages or aspects of creation, viz., *Antaryāmin, Sākṣī, Avyākṛta, Sūtra, Virāṭ, Devatā, Jāti,* and *Piṇḍa*. These are further classed into three sets or *rāśis,* viz., *Paramātma-rāśi, Mūrtāmūrta-rāśis* and *Jīva-rāśi. Antaryāmin* corresponds to the first, *Jīva* or *Sākṣī* to the second, *Avyākṛta* to *amūrta* and the rest to *mūrta.*[44] Bhartṛprapañca held that it is *avidyā* that limits the *Jīva* but distinguished between *Vijñānātman* and *Paramātman.*[45]

Bhartṛprapañca was undoubtedly a monist who sought to combine the ultimate unity of Brahma with the reality of the world and the relevance of religious life. Śaṅkara ridicules him as *Aupaniṣadammanya* quite unfairly, apparently because of the influence of Gauḍapāda on him.

Bhartṛmitra was another thinker prior to Śaṅkara. Whether he was only a Mīmāṁsaka, or also a Vedāntin, is not certain. Kumārila is supposed to have censured him as one of those who virtually converted Mīmāṁsā into a materialistic system (*lokāyatīkṛtā*). A statement attributed to Bhartṛmitra reads '*Nitya-niṣiddhayoı iṣṭāniṣṭa-phalaṁ nasti.*' This denial with respect to the *nitya-karman* is not difficult to understand but the denial with respect to *niṣiddha-karman* is enigmatic. That Bhartṛmitra is to be understood as a *Lokāyata* does not appear correct for he is described as a Mīmāṁsaka, apparently very unorthodox.[46]

Of all the pre-Śaṅkara masters of Vedānta Gauḍapāda remains the most significant not only because he was the grand-teacher of Śaṅkara but also because his works have survived and hence have continued to exert influence on posterity. Max Walleser has doubted whether Gauḍapāda was an individual at all and others have doubted whether the four chapters of the *Āgamaśāstra* had a single author.[47] Vidhushekhar Bhattacharya has expressed the opinion that the *Māndukyopaniṣad* itself was based on the *Āgamaśāstra.*[48] These doubts, however, cannot be said to have been well-founded. Śaṅkara refers to Gauḍapāda with reverence but without naming him. He is familiar with the *prakaraṇa-catuṣṭaya* even if we doubt the ascription of the *MKB* to him.[49] Sureśvara too is familiar with Gauḍapāda and his work.[50] Buddhist authors of the 8th century quote from him. There can be little doubt that he preceded Śaṅkara, composed the *Prakaraṇa Catuṣṭaya* and founded the kind of Vedāntic tradition which Śaṅkara followed.

It has been argued that Bhāvaviveka in his *Tarkajvālā* quotes four verses relating to Aupaniṣadic views, of which three are closely paralleled in the *MK* and the fourth is identical with *MK*, 3.5. This would suggest that Gauḍapāda should be placed earlier than Bhavya who was a senior contemporary of Dharmapāla and may be placed between A.D. 500 and 575 which would also be the latest period for Gauḍapāda. This would make it difficult for him to have been the teacher of Śaṅkara's teacher,[51] if Śaṅkara is placed in the 8th century. However, even the identical verse (*MK*, 3.5.) has been attributed by Vijñānabhikṣu to the *Viṣṇupurāṇa*.[52] The verses could have been drawn from or modelled upon some ancient source. They are concerned with a rather widely discussed analogy, viz., between the self and the sky, and do not articulate any characteristic idea of Gauḍapāda.

There has been a great deal of discussion about the relationship of Gauḍapāda to Buddhism and his role in the history of Vedānta. Of Gauḍapāda's familiarity with Upaniṣadic and Mahāyānic thought there can be no doubt. He not only alludes to and comments upon Upaniṣadic ideas but uses Mahāyānic terms, concepts and arguments quite explicitly. That he is well disposed towards Buddhism too is undeniable. He makes an explicit obeisance to the Buddha himself[53] and declares that Vedānta has no opposition to the Buddhist principle of *Ajāti*.[54] The Buddhistic contacts of Gauḍapāda have been repeatedly pointed out.[55] The question is, was Gauḍapāda a Buddhist? Was he a Vedāntin who adopted some Buddhistic ideas to bring out what he thought was essentially implicit in Vedānta? Was he a Vedāntin who merely wished to distinguish Vedānta from apparently similar but really different Buddhist views? The first of these three possibilities may be easily dismissed. Gauḍapāda is counted as a teacher belonging to the Vedāntic tradition by Śaṅkara, Sureśvara, Śāntarakṣita and Kamalaśīla, never as a Buddhist teacher. And Gauḍapāda's work takes an *Upaniṣad* as its starting point, not a Buddhist text. *Prima facie* he is a Vedāntin, and not enough evidence has been put forward to show that he was a Buddhist. He certainly bows down to Buddha in respect but that only shows that he was a Catholic and enlightened person. Similarly the view that Gauḍapāda was a Vedāntin who wrote these tracts to distinguish Vedānta from Buddhism does not stand to reason. Where was the need for this unusual exercise at that time? The *BS* and its commentators like Upavarṣa had already criticised Buddhism which on its part clearly distinguished its position from Upaniṣadic *Ātmavāda*. Indeed, Gauḍapāda's work gives the impression of non-difference rather than of difference between Buddhism and Vedānta. This, indeed, gives the clue to his intention. He deeply appreciates certain basic Mahāyānic ideas and uses them to present a new interpretation of Vedānta which is for him not merely a spiritual absolutism but an illusionistic absolutism. He identifies reality with *Brahman* as the eternal and indescribable absolute. He declares the empirical world to be a mere appearance projected by the illusive power of the mind and hence creation and causation to be essentially unreal. Empirical objects are for him rooted in mental construction just as are dream objects. The Upaniṣadic *Brahmavāda* becomes in Gauḍapāda a powerful *Māyāvāda* which appeals not only to Vedāntic texts and ideas but also utilizes the spiritual and logical insights of Mahāyāna especially *Vijñānavāda* and the Mādhyamika school.

The first or *Āgamaprakaraṇa* of the *MK* begins by recounting the four states of consciousness described in the *MU*, waking, dreaming and sleeping, their worlds and subjects which are grounded in the 'fourth' or transcendental consciousness. Although there are various theories of creation they are not really satisfactory. They presuppose the reality of empirical phenomena. A beginningless *Māyā* keeps the individual asleep. When he wakes up he finds reality to be an eternal non-duality. The phenomena being unreal can neither begin nor cease. Duality is an illusion, only non-duality is true '*Māyāmātram idam dvaitam advaitam paramārthataḥ*'. This duality which is mere *māyā* is termed *prapañca* or *vikalpa*. The rest of the first *prakaraṇa* is concerned with expounding *praṇavapāsanā*. The first three *mātrās* are identified with *Viśva, Taijasa* and *Prājña*. *Turīya* is *amātra* and is contemplated in silence alone. *Praṇava*, thus, corresponds to the lower (*apara*) as well as the higher (*para*) *Brahman*.

The second or *Vaitathyaprakaraṇa* is concerned with showing the falsity of the empirical world of duality. The waking world is essentially similar to the dream world and its objects are no more external to the mind than those of the dream-world. Both the worlds are *sāṃvṛta* and false.[56] It is the *Ātmā* which by its mysterious power (*māyā*) imagines itself diversely and apprehends diversity. '*Kalpayatyātmanātmānam ātmā devaḥ svamāyayā / Sa eva budhyate bhedān iti Vedānta-niścayaḥ //*'[57]

The first construction (*vikalpa*) of the divine Self is the empirical self (*Jīva*), 'which is the basis of all other construction'.[58] The empirical self thus may be described in Kantian language as the first of the transcendental presuppositions of experience.[59] The world of diversity is an illusion built upon it like a dream or hallucination. The truth is that there is neither creation nor destruction, neither bondage, nor release. '*Na nirodho na cotpattir na baddho na ca sādhakaḥ/Na mumukṣur na vai mukta ityeṣā paramārthatā//*' (*AS*, 2.33). The final end of man is to realize this non-dual (*advaya*) quiescence (*prapañcopaśama*). (*AS*, 2.35).

The third *prakaraṇa* entitled *Advaita* proceeds to establish non-duality in the context of the concept of non-creation (*ajātivāda*) and diverse Upaniṣadic statements. Duality and the possibility of meditation (*upāsanā*) arise only after creation but creation is not the real creation of duality. It is only an appearance. The 'sky' may appear to be divided into many if we consider the space inside each pot. The multiplication of Brahman is just like the multiplication of *ākāśa* into diverse *ghaṭākāśas*. The identity of *Brahman* and *Jīva* has been expressed in the *śruti* in many ways. When it speaks of creation on the analogy of clay and pots or of fire and its sparks, that should be considered only as expedients for easier communication (*upāyah sovatārāya*) with those of lesser spiritual calibre. These examples do not imply any duality. '*Advaitam paramārtho hi dvaitaṁ tadbheda iṣyate*'. Non-duality is real, duality only apparent and due to *Māyā*. How can the nature of anything change? How can the eternal and the immortal be subject to change and lose its real nature? Creation is a logical impossibility. Nevertheless what is real (*sat*) may appear to be born through an illusion (*māyā*). The apparent diversification of the real is like the projection of a dream. The world of duality is simply a mental objectification: '*Manodṛśyam idam dvaitam*'. When the mind becomes non-mind this world ceases—'*Manaso hyamanībhāve'dvaitam naivopalabhyate*'. The mind becomes non-mind when it ceases to construct or imagine (*na saṅkalpayate yadā*). When the objects are thus dropped, the quiescent consciousness realizes its oneness with the eternal *Brahman*. This state of the mind is different from that of sleep. It is free from words and thoughts, quiescent and motionless, luminous and secure: '*Sarvābhilāpa-vigataḥ sarva-cintā-samutthitaḥ/ Supraśāntaḥ sakṛjjyotiḥ samādhir acalo'bhayaḥ//*' (3.37). Such a state of *nirvikalpa-samādhi* is described by the author as '*asparśa-yoga*'. The mind should be detached and stilled but kept fully awake. Where the mind is not merged in darkness, nor distracted by objects, when it is motionless and imageless, then is *Brahman* realized '*Yadā nalīyate cittaṁ na ca vikṣipyate punaḥ/ Aniṅganam anābhāsam niṣpannam brahma tat tadā/ /*' (3.46).

The fourth *prakaraṇa* entitled *alātaśānti* is the most Buddhistic of the four. It begins with an unmistakable obeisance to Buddha, '*Sambuddhas taṁ vande dvipadāṁ varam*'. Buddha is described as one who awoke to the sky-like phenomena by a sky-like knowledge identical with them: '*Jñānenākāśakalpena dharmān yo gaganopamān/.*

Jñeyābhinnena sambuddhas taṁ vande dvipadāṁ varam/ /' (4.1). This indicates that knowledge and its objects are not different. In their eternal nature they are nothing except non-dual infinity. V. Bhattacharya interprets this verse as a statement of *Vijñāna vāda*. It looks equally like *Śūnya vāda*. The author then bows to him who preached the *Asparaśa yoga*. Here again, the efforts of V. Bhattacharya to identify this Yoga with *sañjñā vedita-nirodha* misunderstand the nature of that *Nirodha* which is a state of psychic suppression.[60] *Asparśayoga*, on the other hand, is the realization of noesis in its eternity. The term seems to be a new coinage of the author and its reference has many parallels in *philosophia perennis*. Causality and creationism are then dialectically refuted in the manner of Nāgārjuna and the author concludes: *Evaṁ hi sarvathā Buddhair ajātiḥ paridīpitā./*

The reality of external objects as well as of their ideas is then attacked dialectically. It is concluded that the Buddhas have taught causality only as a concession for those who believe in the existence of things on account of empirical knowledge and activity. It is for those who are afraid of *Ajāti*: '*Jātistu deśitā Buddhair ajāteḥ. trasatāṁ sadā*'. One may speak of the existence of things only in the same way in which one may speak of the magical elephant (*māyā-hastin*). The mind or *Vijñāna* is unborn, motionless, 'no-thing-ness' (*avaṣtutvam*), non-dual, quiescent, giving the appearance of universals, motion and things. Just as a moving fire-brand produces the illusions of luminous forms, so does the mind produce the illusion of the phenomenal world. All the forms which appear, all the phenomena are nothing except the mind in movement, *spandana*. The birth or causation of things is only an empirical truth (*samvṛti*), not an essential truth (*tattvataḥ*). It is like *māyā* which itself is not real. Since nothing is really produced, one cannot speak of eternalism or nihilism. Neither words nor distinctions can apply to the eternally unborn things. The duality of subject and object is merely the vibration of the mind which is in iteslf eternally detached and objectless. Appearances and causes are merely *samvṛti,* not *paramārtha.* About the three grades of knowledge and being one may learn from the *agrayāna* (=*mahāyāna*),[61] but reality is naturally luminous, pure and non-dual like the sky. That is why it is beyond speech and thought. Buddha has not spoken of anything at all. The author ends by bowing down to the profound condition of non-duality.

Any impartial reader is bound to wonder why this highly Buddhistic *prakaraṇa,* Buddhistic in terms as well as ideas, is included as a Vedāntic text. To say that it should be interpreted as an attempt to distinguish Vedānta from what the Buddha said, seems to require some forced constructions. Apparently the author would like Buddha to be listened to as a representative *Jñānin,* not as the founder of a sect. And he seems to find in the words of Buddha the best interpretation of the Vedāntic truth. He would like the *Upaniṣads* to be understood in the light of the best known principles of Mahāyāna which may be attributed to the insight of a *Jñānin* like Buddha. It should be noted that except for certain philosophical generalities consistent with Vedānta, the author does not allude to any Buddhistic principles. He does not speak of the 'four truths', *Pratītyasamutpāda, Nairātmya, Śūnyatā* or even *Vijñaptimātratā.* He only speaks of non-duality, illusionism, and the universality of consciousness. He distinguishes *samvṛta* causality and places truth beyond words and thought. His attempt is to highlight certain Buddhistic insights as affording a perspective for understanding and interpreting Vedānta. The Upaniṣadic tradition conceived *Brahman* as the creator or first cause of the world. Buddhists, however, had argued that for something to be a cause it must undergo change in time and that the causal chain cannot have a first beginning. How could *Brahman* be eternal and yet a cause, a cause and yet a first cause? Gauḍapāda finds the answer in the Mādhyamika critique of causation itself. Logically considered, causation cannot be real. It can only be something given in experience but illogical and hence unreal. *Brahmavāda* is thus, joined to *ajātivāda* and creation declared illusory. As a consequence multiplicity too is abolished and non-dualism established at the same time.

The *Upaniṣads* had declared *Brahman* as *sat.* For Gauḍapāda *sat* must be interpreted as beyond the distinction of being and non-being, *asti* and *nāsti,* because such a distinction cannot apply to the infinite No finite determinations or categories can, thus, apply to

Brahman which must be beyond speech and thought. *Brahman* must be regarded as the non-dual absolute where the mind is eternally silenced. Gauḍapāda's *Brahman* is far from the theistic God, the Supreme Person. It is indistinguishable from the Buddhist *Dharmadhātu*, and Gauḍapāda's *Brahman* is reminiscent of *Śūnyavāda*.

The *Upaniṣads* had conceived the self as consciousness but placed it beyond waking, dreaming and sleeping, beyond particular thoughts (*sañjñā*) and the distinction of subject and object. Gauḍapāda finds it similar to the Buddhist conception of a foundational and pure *Vijñāna*. The subject and the object are correlative and both are functions of the mind. What appears before the mind is merely phenomenal, not substantial or essential. The individuality and empirical determinations of the self are relative to the illusive functioning of the mind, not real. The individual self is one of the illusory modes of the Absolute which is the mind or consciousness in its infinite purity. Gauḍapāda's theory of the *Ātman* is difficult to distinguish from Buddhist *Vijñānavāda* in its absolutist interpretation.

In interpreting the Upaniṣadic concepts of *Brahman* and *Ātman* in terms of a non-dual spiritual absolutism, Gauḍapāda adopted the Buddhist theory of Two Truths, *paramārtha* and *samvṛti*. Without such a distinction there could be no logical reconciliation of real non-duality with empirical diversity. The explanation of diversity was sought not in the mysterious creative power of God but in the mysterious power of illusive projection or *Māyā* which belongs to the mind. In thus reformulating Vedānta Gauḍapāda relies not so much on revelation as on the dialectical critique of causality, a distinctive 'phenomenological' analysis of experience, and the testimony of spiritual illumination. The ultimate evidence for him is the self-evidence of the silent mind absorbed in *Asparśayoga*.

Gauḍapāda's interpretation of Vedānta is a logically plausible one and the logic derives from the Mahāyāna schools of Buddhism. The interpretation does not thereby become unauthentic. Only, it is essentially philosophical rather than theological. It brings Vedānta close to some aspects of Buddhism but does not identify them except to the extent to which the absolutes of different spiritual philosophies are hard to distinguish. Gauḍapāda's inculcation of the Yoga of silence and reliance on its testimony are quite distinctive. His emphasis on non-duality and on the centrality of foundational consciousness are directly traceable to the *Upaniṣads.* His denial of the empirical world of duality, change and causation takes the help of Buddhistic arguments but may be said to develop what is implicit in the *Upaniṣads.* His emphasis on silence and peace: *prapañcopaśama, śiva, śāntam,* rather than on *Ānanda* is reminiscent of Buddhism but not opposed to the *Upaniṣads.* His substitution of the context of cosmology by that of dialectic and the 'phenomenology of consciousness' was a great departure from the established tradition of Vedānta and gave it a new philosophical turn.

Some scholars have placed the *Bhāgavata* before Śaṅkara and even before Gauḍapāda. The *Bhāgavata* appears to be familiar with a variety of illusionistic Advaita, and Śaṅkara or Gauḍapāda, it is argued, could have drawn upon it as one of their sources.[62] Śaṅkara is said to have been echoing the *Bhāgavata* when he declared the Buddha to have possibly tried to delude the people by preaching false doctrines. The date of the *Bhāgavata,* however has not yet been satisfactorily settled. By the 11th century it was recognized as one of the eighteen *Mahāpurāṇas.* Its language has a marked archaism and some scholars have placed it as early as the 6th century A.D. Others have argued that it presupposes the *Bhakti* movement of the south and hence could not be earlier than the 10th century. Śaṅkara's non-mention of the *Bhāgavata* itself has been construed as an argument for placing it after him. That would, however, leave too little time for it to become one of the great *Purāṇas* before the 11th century. It has to be remembered that despite the popularity and renown of the Āḷvāras, it is the *Bhāgavata* that became the standard scripture for the Vedāntic *ācāryas* of *Bhakti* throughout the country. On the whole, allowing for minor additions and revisions later, the *Bhāgavata* might be placed in the late Gupta or early post-Gupta period, that is between the 6th and 8th century. That it should not be far from Śaṅkara, seems most probable. Nevertheless, there is no real reason to suppose that the *Bhāgavata* should be regarded as one of the sources of Śaṅkara. The *Bhāgavata* places the *saguṇa brahman* clearly above the *nirguṇa brahman,* conceiving ultimate reality as a Person to be loved rather than as the Absolute where personality is transcended. Even in his commentary on the *BG* Śaṅkara uses all his ingenuity to exhaust *Bhakti* into either *Karman* or *Jñāna.* His silence about the *Bhāgavata* can only be regarded as a case of wise discretion in the context of logical philosophy. It is the theistic Vedāntins who turned to the *Bhāgavata* increasingly.

The case of the *Yogavāsiṣṭha* being regarded as a source of Gauḍapāda and Śaṅkara is a much stronger one. Dr. Atreya has pointed out many similarities in thought and expression between the *Yogavāsiṣṭha* and the *MK.*[63] Both propound an illusionistic non-dualism and lay stress on the role of the mind or consciousness in projecting different worlds corresponding to its different states. The same basic kind of spiritual philosophy can be discerned in both the works. The difference between them is in their style and purpose. The *Yogavāsiṣṭha* is a work of high literary quality. Its language is more elaborate and it is full of long stories and parables. It is also didactic and repetitive. The *MK*, on the other hand, is succinct, logical and systematic. Its style is characteristically philosophical while the *Yogavāsiṣṭha* is reminiscent of Purāṇic and Āgamic works like the *Bhāgavata* or the *Tripurārahasya*. It cannot, however, be shown that the *MK* specifically draws on the *Yogavāsiṣṭha*. Both seem to exemplify a common tendency which tended to cut across the distinction between Vedānta and *Mahāyāna*. The *Laṅkāvatāra* is itself an illustration of such a tendency.

It needs to be mentioned that some scholars have dated the *Yogavāsiṣṭha* between the 11th and the 13th centuries. Against this it has been rightly pointed out that as the *Laghu-Yoga-Vāsiṣṭha* of Abhinanda may be dated in *c.* 900 A.D. the *Yoga-Vāsiṣṭha* would be earlier chronologically; thus, the priority of the work of Śaṅkara stands to reason. Nevertheless, as argued above, Śaṅkara's relationship is to the *MK* rather than to the *Yogavāsiṣṭha*.

Another source suggested for Gauḍapāda is Adiśeṣa's *Paramārthasāra* which was adapted by Abhinavagupta in the 11th century. Prof. Suryanarayana Sastri has pointed out a number of parallel verses between the *Parmārthasāra* and the *Āgamaśāstra*. These relate to the four states of consciousness, the transcendence of ultimate reality (*Paramārtha*), the detachment of consciousness, the notion of *māyā* etc. Vidhushekhar Bhattacharya has argued that in these instances it could be more plausibly argued that the *Paramārthasāra* is the borrower although he admits that the *Paramārthasāra* appears to depend on some independent Āgamic source also.[64] As a matter of fact the similarities between *Paramārthasāra* and the *Āgamaśāstra* do not prove borrowing by either from the other. They only show that Mahāyānic ideas constituted an influence over Vedānta as well as Kashmir *Āgamas*.

Besides the *Upaniṣads* must be presumed to have been equally available to Gauḍapāda as well as to the author of the *Paramārtha-sāra.*

Bhartṛhari is believed in some Advaitic traditions to have been the son of Śaṅkara's teacher Govindapāda when he was a householder under the name Candra. This would make Bhartṛhari prior to but not far removed from Śaṅkara. The earlier dating of Bhartṛhari in the 7th century which depended on his mention by I-tsing would seem to harmonise with this. However, recently it has been pointed out that Bhāvaviveka, Harisvāmī and even Dignāga seem to have known Bhartṛhari, which places him not later than the 5th century A.D.[65] That would place him distinctly earlier than Śaṅkara. It may therefore, be securely assumed that as one well-versed in *Vyākaraṇa* and Vedānta, Śaṅkara may be presumed to have been familiar with Bhartṛhari who was not only the greatest philosopher among the grammarians since Patañjali but also reputed as a Vedāntin or *Brahmavit.* Of the works of Bhartṛhari while the *Vākyapadīya* survives for the most part, the commentary called *Dīpikā* on the *Mahābhāṣya* survives only in some fragments. His *Śabda-dhātu-samīkṣā* has been lost although some stray quotations survive from it.[66]

The grammarians were orthodox thinkers who believed in the *Veda* as the sole source of our knowledge of *dharma.* The relationship of the *Vedas* to *Brahman* was, however, conceived in several different ways within orthodoxy. The *Mīmāṁsakas* conceived the *Veda* as an eternal set of *Varṇas* and to be the source of creation. In the *Upaniṣads* the *Vedas* are conceived as the prime emanation from *Brahman* or as the lower *Brahman* (*apara-brahman*). The *Vedas* are the eternal word or *logos* and may be described as the creative facet or aspect of *Brahman.* That the word is the creative power of ultimate reality is a view which may be traced to the *Vedas,* but it was flanked on one side by a realistic and pluralistic view of creation and, on the other, by a view which saw in creation nothing but false Names and Forms. The grammarians developed a non-dualism which was quite distinctive thought clearly Vedic and orthodox. Their analysis of language showed that the mutable diversity of linguistic forms are derivable from certain immutable originals. At the same time language, thought and meaning-objects are not separable. We cannot think without language and objects are meanings revealed by language. The primary unit of language too is not the isolated word but the sentence or judgement. And sentences or judgements constitute a unitary whole of which isolated sentences or thoughts are merely abstracted fragments, words as articulate sounds are only the physical and sense-perceptible expression of the mental word or intelligible symbol which is necessarily connected with its meaning or intended object. This mental word mediates between pure consciousness and the physical word and its corresponding. Pure consciousness is conceived as active and self-expressive, intuitive and universal. Although in itself timeless and eternal this consciousness remains the creative matrix of the world—subjective and objective. Although the common root of speech, thought and objects, it is called speech because of its intending, determinative and expressive or creative nature. It was called the seeing speech or *Paśyantī,* and the Manifestor or *sphoṭa*. 'The eternal *Brahman* or the imperishable word-principle manifests itself objectively to start the world-process—'*Anādi-nidhanam brahma śabda-tattvaṁ yad akṣaram / Vivartate 'rthabhāvena prakriyā jagato yataḥ / /*'.[67]

The principal tradition of Vedānta disagreed with several features of this non-dualism. It rejected the theory of *sphoṭa* and also tended to regard words as part of the phenomenal world. It placed *Brahman* beyond all kinds of *Nāmarūpa,* while the creativity of *Brahman* and the special role of the word were accepted, the identification of *Brahman* with the word was not accepted. Gauḍapāda's Vedānta went on to reject the notion of creation itself, replacing it by that of illusion. Thus with Gauḍapāda, who could not have been chronologically far from Bhartṛhari, the two non-dualistic traditions departed even further.

It has been argued that Bhartṛhari's non-dualism was realistic and that it used *vivarta* and *pariṇānma* synonymously. The created world is on this view a revelation, not a concealment of reality. This interpretation is, however, somewhat simplistic. There is no doubt that creative power is definitely attributed to speech in this theory of *Śabdādvaita* and also that creation by word and thought can only be understood as self-expression. It would, thus, seem that Bhartṛhari is committed to a realistic theory of the world. However, if we reflect over the nature of the meanings intended by words or the objects projected by thought, it is difficult to see how these could be called real. The objects of speech and thought can hardly be said to have any reality apart from their appearing to consciousness. The linguistic model of creation shows the purely phenomenal nature of the world far more clearly than the older

Vedāntic analogy of the clay and the pots made out of it. As far as the status of the objects is concerned, this linguistic model is quite close to the dream model to be found in Mahāyāna or Gauḍapāda, although there is a difference in the manner in which creativity is connected with its ground in the two cases. Dreaming or hallucination is not inherent in the nature of consciousness whereas expressiveness is necessary to speech. To explain the emergence of externality, differences, change and order Bhartṛhari has to take recourse to the concepts of *Avidyā* and Time. Between him and Śaṅkara the concept of *Pariṇāma-Vivarta* and *Avidyā* constitute connections which need to be judiciously analysed.

The identity of Maṇḍaṇa Miśra has been a matter of much debate. The traditional view identified Maṇḍana with Sureśvara but this has been questioned by competent modern scholars.[68] While the whole question would be critically examined later, there is no doubt that Maṇḍana Miśra was a Vedāntin who was a senior contemporary of Śaṅkara and held views which do not wholly agree with those of Śaṅkara. Whether he later on became Sureśvara and changed his views, may be disputed but there is no disputing the fact that the views he has expressed in *Brahmasiddhi* will always remain important in the Vedāntic tradition and contact between Maṇḍana and Śaṅkara could hardly be denied.

Maṇḍana is a monist but his monism is quite distinctive. For him monism affirms the oneness of the positive reality which is not inconsistent with the admission of another negative reality. He has, therefore, been called an exponent of *Bhāvādvaita* or *Śabdādvaita*. On this view the negation of the phenomenal world *prapañca* must be admitted as a revealed truth and that would imply the view resembles the theory of *Viparīta Khyāti* for which to mistake is to misapprehend. The error about the self is really transcendental but Maṇḍana assimilates it to a case of misapprehension since the self does not go unapprehended and is at the same time apprehended differently from what it really is. In this idea one could see the closeness of Maṇḍana to Kumārila, which tradition asserts.

In Maṇḍana also is to be found the view that the *Jīva* is the locus of error while *Brahman* is its object, a doctrine which was later espoused by Vācaspati Miśra and the *Bhāmatī* school. The point of closest contact between pre-Śaṅkara Vedānta and Mīmāṁsā was provided by the doctrine that salvation required both knowledge and works, *Jñāna* and *Karman*. Maṇḍana was a staunch exponent of this view. He believed that although a *sannyāsin* may obtain liberation, a householder could obtain it more easily. He reviews seven earlier theories about the relation of *Karman* and *Jñāna*: 'That all the injunctions in the ritualistic portion of the *Veda* turn men away from natural activities. . .; that all these injunctions are intended to kill desires through a process of enjoyment. . .; that the performance of *Karman* is necessary to discharge the three congenital debts (*ṛṇa-traya*). . .; that the activities prescribed in the *Karmakāṇḍa* have two distinct functions (*saṃyoga pṛthaktva*) by conducting to their respective fruits and also to the realization of the *Ātman*; that all *Karman* and *Jñāna* are fundamentally opposed to each other and have no interrelation whatever'.[69] Maṇḍana rejects all of these except two. He is favourable to the two views which regard *Karman* as giving fruits and leading to self-realization, *saṃyoga-pṛthaktvapakṣa*, and as purifying men for *Ātmajñāna*, *saṁskārapakṣa*. Thus the basic contribution of *Karman* is to make a person capable of the kind of meditation which alone can lead to supreme knowledge. A *sannyāsin* too may practise meditation and reach the end but he will toil for a long time compared to one who as a householder regularly performs the enjoined works. The former will be plodding on foot, the latter galloping on horse-back.

The Upaniṣadic *mahāvākyas* need to be intensely meditated upon before they can lead to the direct knowledge of the highest truth. Such meditation was called *prasaṅkhyāna* and led to *sākṣātkāra* or *prajñā*. Since meditation is itself a kind of mental activity, it may be easily seen how Maṇḍana felt the need for accepting *Karman* as necessary for the attainment of knowledge. 'Perhaps it could be argued that meditation on the self or the attributeless *Brahman* is more cessation of activity than activity but then the cessation seems to require at an earlier stage some kind of volitional effort or direction, at least of bringing the mind back from the world of finite and plural objects towards the self'.[70] The fact is that *Karman* and meditational inactivity, are different points in the same scale while *jñāna* is a thing apart. It is Śaṅkara who made this cardinal distinction between action and knowledge a central point for departure.

Excerpts from Pre-Śaṅkara Vedāntins

I. *Āśmarathya:, BS* 1.4.20 - *Pratijñāsiddher liṅgam Āśmarathyaḥ. Ratnaprabhā* comments.
ad *BSB*, 1.4. 20 "*Jīva-brahmaṇor bhedābheda-sattvāt*".

II. *Auḍulomi*: *Nyāya-nirṇaya*
ad *BSB* 1.4.21 - "*Muktāvevābhedaḥ saṁsāre bheda eva*":
Bhāmatī compares it to the *Pāñcarātra* view. Vide also *BSB*, 4.4.6.

III. *Kaśakṛtsna*: *BS* 1.4.22 - *Avasthiter iti Kāśakṛtsnaḥ;*
BSB, 1.4.22 - "*Asyaiva Paramātmano nenāpi Vijñānātma-bhāvena avasthāṇāt upapannam idam abhedābhi-dhānam iti Kāśakṛtsna Ācāryo manyate*".

Ib.
"*Āśmarathyasya tu yadyapi jīvasya parasmād ananyatvam abhipretaṁ tathāpi pratijñā-siddher iti sāpekṣatvābhidhānāt Kārya-Kāraṇa-bhāvaḥ kiyān apyabhipreta iti gamyate. Auḍulomipakṣe punaḥ spaṣṭam eva avasthāntarāpekṣau bhedābhedau gamyete. Tatra Kāśakṛtsnīyam matam śrutyanusārīti gamyate pratipipādayisitārthānusārāt 'tattvam asīt yādi śrutibhyaḥ.*"

IV. *Upavarṣa:*
"*Indriya-mano-rtha-sannikarṣo mithyā-jñānasya hetuḥ, duṣṭeṣu hi jñānam mithyā bhavati—Prayatnena anvicchanto na ced doṣam avagacehemahi pramāṇābhāvād aduṣṭam iti manyemahi.—Nanu sarva eva nirālambanaḥ svapnavat pratyayaḥ pratyayasya hi nirālambanatā-svabhava upalaksitaḥ svapne—na, svapne viparyayadarśanāt—anyatas tu svapnasya mithyābhāvaḥ viparyayād avagantavyah—sanidrasya manaso daurbalyād nidrā mithyābhavasya hetuḥ svapanādau svapnānte ca—*
Śūnyastu katham? Artha-jñānayorākāra-bhedaṁ nopalabhāmahe Pratyakṣā ca no buddhiḥ atas tad bhinnam artha-rūpam nāma na kiñcid astīti paśyāmah. Syād etad evam yadi arthākārā buddhiḥ syāt, nirākārā tu no buddhih, ākāravān bāhyorthaḥ. . .
Yadi Vijñānād anyo nāsti Kastarhi jānātītyucyate?. . . Icchayā ātmānam upalabhāmahe. Katham iti? Upalabdhapūrve hi abhiprete bhavatīcchā. . . Nahi asmartāra icchantītyupapadyate ... Na cāhampratyayo Vyāmoha iti śakyate vaktum bādhakapratyayābhāvāt...Sva-saṁvedyaḥ sabhavatināsāvanyena

śakyate draṣṭum, katham asau nirdiśyeta iti. (see note no. 25 below)

V. *Brahmanandī: Ātreyaḥ: Chāndogya-Vākya-Kāraḥ: Ṭaṅkaḥ*

a) *'Siddham tu nivartakatvād' ityāgama-vidām sūtram* (*MKB*2-32) (Cf. *Iṣṭasiddhi—"Siddham tu. . ." iti Coktam vākyakāraiḥ*)

b) *SS*, 3. 217-20:
Subodhinī cites: *"asatah aniṣpādyatvat, sattve pravṛttyānarthakyāt, abhivyaktyarthatvepi aviśeṣāt, pravrtti-nityatvāt, sadā abhivyakti-prasaṅgāt, samvyavahāra-mātraṃ kāryam".*
Vedānanda's *Sambandhokti* cites: *"Syācca bhojya-bhoktṛvibhāgaḥ na ca anyatvam. samudra-phenormi-budbudavat. Pariṇāmastu syāt dadhyādivat".*

c) *Śrībhāṣya* (Vol. I, p. 18): *"Vākyakāreṇaitat sarvam prapañcitam, "Vedānām Upāsanaṁ syāt tadviṣaye śravaṇāt iti. . . 'Upāsanam syād dhruvānusmṛtir darśanānnirvacanācca iti".*
IB p. 19-20. *"Vākyakāraśca dhruvānusmṛteḥ vivekādibhya eva niṣpattimāha 'Tallabdhir viveka-vimokābhyāsa-kriyā-kalyāṇānavasādānuddharṣebhyah sambhavānnirvacanācca. 'iti'. "Jātyaśraya-nimittaduṣṭād annāt Kāya-śuddhir vivekaḥ". . . "Vimokaḥ Kāmānabhiṣvaṅgahiti". . . "Ārambhaṇa-saṁśīlanam punaḥ punaḥ abhyāsa iti". . . "Pañca-mahāyajñā-dyanuṣṭhānam śaktitaḥ Kriyā", "Satyārjava-dayā-dāna hiṁsānabhidhyāh kalyāṇāni iti". . . "Deśa-Kāla-Vaiguṇyāt śokavastvādyanusmṛteśca tajjam dainyam abhāsvaratvam maṅasaḥ avasādaḥ" iti. . . "Tadviparyayajā tuṣṭir uddharṣaḥ" iti. . .*

VI. *Draviḍācārya*

(*a*) Story of the prince brought up by the hunter—*BSB*, and Sureśvara, *BSBV*, 2.1. 506-17; *Śrutisārasamuddharaṇa*, 206 = *Dravido'pi ca tattvamasīti vaco vinivartakameva nirūpitavān Śabarena vivardhita-rāja-śiśuḥ nija-janma vidukti-nidarśanataḥ//*

(*b*) SS', 3.221: *Antarguṇā bhagavatī para-devateti*
Pratyagguṇeti Bhagvānapi Bhāṣyakāraḥ//
Āha sma yattadiha nirguṇa-vastuvāde
Saṅgacchate na tu punaḥ saguṇa-pravade//

(The *bhāṣya* is said to be on *CV*8.1.1. (*daharavidyā*) on which the *Vākya* was *'Yuktam/tadguṇakopāsanād'*. The *bhāsya* is said to be "*Yady api sacitto na nirbhugna-daivatam guṇagaṇam manasānudhāvet tathāpi antarguṇām eva devatām bhajati.*" Rāmānuja concludes "*Tatrāpi saguṇaiva devatā prāpyate*")

(*c*) *Ad CU.* 1.6.6; *Vākya*—"*Syāt tad rūpam kṛtakam anugrahārtham/taccetasām aiśvaryāt/Rūpaṁ vā atīndriyam antaḥkaraṇa-pratyakṣanirdeśāt/*"

Bhāṣya—"*Navā māyāmātram/añjasaiva viśvaṣrjo rūpam/ Tat tuna cakṣuṣā grāhyam/Manasā tu akaluṣena sādhanāntaravatā gṛhyate/Na caksuṣā gṛhyate nāpi vācā manasā tu viśuddhena iti śruteḥ/Na hyarūpāyā devatāyā rūpam upadiśyate/Yathārthavādi hi śāstram/ Māhārajanam Vāsaḥ vedāham etam puruṣam mahāntam aditya-varṇaṁ tamasaḥ parastād iti prakaranāntaranirdeśāc ca sākṣiṇaḥ/*"

(*d*) "*Phala-samvitsayā Karmabhir ātmānam piprīṣanti sa prītolam phalāya iti śāstra-maryādā.*"

(*e*) ad. *BU* 3.8.9.

"*Asyājñayā dhāvati vāyuḥ/nadyaḥ sravanti/Tena krtasīmāno jalāśayāh samadā iva meṣa-visarpitaṁ kurvanti/*"

"*Tatsaṅkalpa-nibandhanā hīme lokā na cyavante na sphuṭante/Sva-śāsanānuvartinam jñātvā kāruṇyāt sa Bhagavān vardhayeta vidvān karma-dakṣaḥ/*"

(*f*) ad. *CU* 8.1.6.

"*Devatā-sāyujyād aśarīrasyāpi devatāvat sarvārthasiddhiḥ syāt*".

VII. *Bhartṛprapañcaḥ*

(*a*) *BUB,* 1.4.10; *Ib.* 5.1.1. (*Bhedābheda*)

(*b*) *BUB,* 3.8.12; *BUBV,* 1.4., 486, 1043, 1065, 1143, 1151; 1.5.207; 1.6.36-40; 1.4.487.

"*Īśvara-vyākṛta-prāṇa-virāḍ-bhūtendriyātmakam/ Navidyopāśrayam muktvā saṁbhāvyam pratyagātmani//*

(*c*) *BUBV,* 2.3.112-13: "*Racayanti tathāsādhvīm prakriyām nyāyavarjitām/Mūrtāmūrtātmako rāśih eko bāhyaḥ kileṣyate//*

"*Uttamah parmātmākhya-rāśir atrābhidhīyate/ Madhyamoyam tṛtīyastu tābhyāṁ rāśiḥ prayojakaḥ//*

(*d*) *BUBV*, 1.4.947:
"Ātma-śabdābhidheyerthe pratyakṣamanya-rūpake/ Antarbhavanti nikhilā viśesā iti kecana//"
Ib. 1.4.950: *"Bhāga-bhāgi-vibhāgena Nābhi-nemyaravat tathā/ Vyācakṣate mahātmānaḥ sampradāya-balāt kila//"*

REFERENCES

1. H. Nakamura, *op. cit.*, Vol. I, p.2.
2. G.C. Pande, *The Role of Śaṅkara* (Jaipur, 1989), p.7.
3. *Ibid.*,
4. S.K. Belvalkar, *op. cit.*; Kaviraj, *op. cit.*; S.L. Pandey, *Pre-Śaṅkara Vedānta*; Muralidhara Pandeya, *Śrī Śaṅkarāt prāg Advaitavādaḥ*; Nakamura, *op. cit.*, Max Walleser, *Der altere Vedanta*; Deussen, *The System of the Vedānta*; Thibaut, (tr), *The Vedāntasūtras* (Introduction); Kuppusvami Sastri, *Brahmasiddhi*; Hiriyanna, *Naiṣkarmyasiddhi* (Intr.).
5. Nakamura, *op. cit.*, *l.c.*
6. E.g. Belvalkar and Ranade, *History of Indian Philosophy*, Vol. II; *The Creative Period*; pp. 334 ff. G.C. Pande, *Origins of Buddhism*, pp. 290 ff.
7. Nakamura, *op. cit.*, pp. 35-41.
8. G.C. Pande, "The Upanisads and *Buddha-Vacana*" in Balasubramanian and Sibjivan Bhattacharya (ed.). *Freedom, Progress and Society.* (1986) Chap. 8.
9. On the evolution of Upaniṣadic Vedānta, see G.C. Pande, *Origins of Buddhism*, *l.c.* Belvalkar and Ranade, *op. cit.*; R.D. Ranade, *Constructive Survey of Upanisadic Philosophy*; Belvalkar, *Lectures on Vedānta Philosophy.*
10. E.g. Ch. 7, cf. G.C. Pande, *Foundations of Indian Culture*, Vol. I, pp. 51-53.
11. G.C. Pande, *Buddha Dharma Ke Vikasa Ka Itihas* (3rd ed.) Chap. 1.
12. G.C. Pande, *Role of Sankara*, p.1.
13. G.C. Pande, '*The Socio-cultural Milieu of the Mbh*' in R.N. Dandekar, (ed.), *The Mahabharata Revisited* (Sahitya Akademi, 1990).
14. Cf. Sukhthankar, *The Meaning of the Mahabharata.*
15. Belvalkar, *op. cit.*, Lecture 4; Cf. Karmarkar, *ABORI*, 1921-22, pp. 73-79.
16. Jacobi, 'The Dates of the Philosophical *Sutras*', *JAOS*, XXI, 1910, pp. 1 ff.
17. Nakamura, *op. cit.*, pp. 435 ff.
18. Deussen, *The System of Vedanta*, p. 31, fn. 21.
19. Cf. Kaviraj, *op. cit.*, pp. 2ff; G.C. Pande, *Bauddha Dharma Ke Vikas Kaltihas.*
20. G.C. Pande, *Foundations of Indian Culture*, Vol. I.p. 125.
21. Thibaut, *op. cit.*, p. xxxii.
22. *Ibid.*
23. Cf. G.C. Pande, *Sramana Tradiotion.*
24. *BSB* 3.3.28 quotes Upavarṣa against *sphoṭa*. *Ibid.*, 3.3.53 refers to Upavarṣ on the existence of the *Ātman.*
25. *Mimāṁsā-darśana*, (*AAS*) Vol I, pṭ I, pp. 25 ff (=Śabara ad 1.1.5) Śabara refers to Vṛttiāra elsewhere too *Mīmāṁsā* 2.1.32-33, 2.1.16.; on the Vṛttikāra grantha, Cf. G. Jha, *POC*, IV 1926; K. Chattopadhyaya, *G.N. Jha Cọmmemoration Vol.*

26. Cf. Śrībhāṣya 1.1.1; *Ibiḍ, 1.21; Ibiḍ, 1.3.7; Ibid.*, 1.3.32; Cf. Thibuat, *op. cit.*, Vol. I, pp. xxi-xxii; MM. Kuppusvami Sastri *POC*, III, 1924, ="Bodhāyana and Dramiḍācāra."
27. This would follow if we accept the claim of Rāmānuja and his follower that they followed the path upheld by Bhdhāyana, e.g., *Vedārthasaṅgraha* (Poona, 1956), pp. 128-29. But Van Buitenen is sceptical, *ibid.*, pp. 23-24.
28. S.L. Pandey, *op. cit.*, p. 178
29. Cf. Van Buitenan, *op. cit.*, pp. 25-29; Muralidhara Pandey, *op. cit.*, p. 132.
30. Derret, *op. cit.*, Vol. I.
31. Van Buitenan, *op. cit.*, l.c.
32. *Sankṣepa*, 3.217, 220.
33. Cf. '*Brahmanandi-viracita-Vākyānāṁ bhāṣyakartā Dravidācāryo'pi advaya-brahmaṇaḥ pratyag abhedo Vākyakārābhipreta iti Kathayati sma.*" (Madhusudanaon *Sanksepa*, quoted Muralidhara Pandey, *op. cit.*, p. 137).
34. *Saṅkṣepa*, 3.221 = *iha nirguṇ-vastu-vāde;* also this is the implication of '*siddham tu nivartakatvāt*' quoted by Śaṅkara in *MUKB, Vaitathya*; 32. It has been attributed to Draviḍācārya Ānandagiri but M.D. Pandey argues that it was really Brahmanandin's (*op. cit.*, p. 134ff.)
35. *BUB*, 2.1.20; Cf. *Śrutisārasamuddharaṇam*, 206—'*Dravido'pi ca tattvam asīti vaco vinivartakam eva nurūpitavān/Śabareṇa vivardhita-rājā-śiśoḥ nija-janmavid-ukti-nidarśanataḥ//*
36. Hiriyanna, 'Brahmadatta, an old Vedantin', *Jor*, 1920, pp. 1-9. Fragments from Brahmandatta occur in *Tattva-muktā-Kalāpa, BUBV, NS* etc.
37. Mm G.N. Kaviraj, *op. cit.*, pp. 17-19; MM Kuppusvami Sastri, *JOR*, 1927, Vol. I pp. 1-15.
38. *BSP.* 1.1.4.
39. M.D. Pandeya, *op. cit.*, p. 175.
40. *BUB*, 2.1.14; *BUB*, 5.1.1.
41. *BUB, l.c.*
42. *Ibid.* '*Evam Kila dvaitasya satyatve karma-Kāṇḍasya prāmāṇyam yadā punar dvaitam dvaitam ivāvidyākṛtam mṛga-tṛṣṇikāvad anṛtam advaitam eva paramārthas tadā kila karma-Kāṇḍam viṣayābhāvid apramāṇam bhavati.*'
43. *IBid.*, 1.4.10.
44. Kaviraj, *op. cit.*, pp. 8-10; the reevant texts have been quoted in M.D. Pandeya, *op. cit.*, pp. 183-187, mainly from Suresvara's *BUVB.*
45. *BUVB*, 3.5.14.
46. Cf. Kaviraj, *op. cit.*, pp. 10-11.
47. Max Walleser, *op. cit.*, 3 ff; V. Bhattacharya, *Āgamaśāstra, Intṛ, p.* 37-47; Kaviraj, *op. ciṭ, pp. 19-23; Belvalkar,* op. ciṭ, pp. 184 ff; Cf. T.M.P. Mahadevan, *Gaudapada*, pp. 5-6.
48. V. Bhattacharya, *op. cit.* Intr. p. 24.
49. Vide *supra.*
50. *NS* 41-44.
51. V. Bhattacharya, *op. cit.*, Intr. p. 45; Nakamura, *op. cit.*, p. 212.
52. V. Bhattacharya, *op. cit.*, p. 51.
53. *AS.* 4.1.
54. *IB.* 4.5.
55. V. Bhattacharya, AS. Intr. pp. 58, 95-96; *AS*, p. 226.
56. *AS*, 4.57, 58, 74.

57. *Ibid.*, 2.12.
58. *MVKB* ad *MVK* 2.12.
59. Vide. e.g., A.C. Mukerji, *The Nature of Self (Attached)*.
60. *Saṁnavedita-nirodha* see G.C. Pande, *Origins of Buddhism*, p. 537.
61. *AS*, 4.90.
62. Cf. *ABORI*, 1932-33, pp. 182-218.
63. B.L. Atreya, *The Philosophy of the Yogavasistha*.
64. Cf. V. Bhattacharya, *op. cit.*, Intr.
65. H.R. rangaswamy Iyenger, *JBBRAS*, 1951. Frauwallner, *WZKSO*, I, 1961, pp. 83 ff; Nakamura, *op. cit.*, p. 80; K.A. Subrahmanya Iyer, *Bhartrhari* p. 2.
66. K.A.S. Iyer, *op. cit.*, pp. 4 ff; M.D. Pandey, *op. cit.*, p. 203 fn.
67. *Vākyapadīya* (ed. Raghunatha Sarma), Pt. I, *Brahmakāṇḍa*; 1.
68. E.g., M.m. Kuppusvami Sastri, *Brahmasiddhi*, Intr.
69. *Ibid.*, p. 33.
70. G.C. Pande, *Foundations*, I, pp. 132-33.

7

Śaṅkara's Philosophy and Interpretation of the Vedānta: Ātman, Brahman, Avidyā

Social Background of Śaṅkara's Philosophy

Although an original philosophical genius of the highest order, Śaṅkara developed his ideas principally through a series or commentaries reinterpreting and reformulating ancient Vedāntic texts and traditions. While he founded a new and perhaps the most influential school of Vedānta, he also seized upon some of the central religious needs and tendencies of his age to give them a new and abiding ideological direction for the future. Thus Śaṅkara's interpretation of Vedānta was not only its philosophical renovation but also the basis of connecting it with the new ethos of the Smārta-Purāṇica religion. Śaṅkara's philosophy not only summed up and illumined the past but provided a firm beacon for the subsequent ages. While the historical background of Śaṅkara has been sketched earlier and the precise nature of his socio-ethical and religious ideas will be discussed later, it may be pertinent to enquire here whether the key of social history can render significant help in the decoding of his fundamental text. It may be recalled that the traditional mode of understanding Śaṅkara is in terms of his own commentators, a method which has been justly questioned by modern researchers. To interpret the text of Śaṅkara it would be at least necessary to place it in its own historical context. It is admittedly difficult to analyse the social influences which were at work in the shaping of Śaṅkara's philosophical ideas. It has often been said that the focus of his thought was on a pure and transcendental spirituality which totally negated the world and life.[1] It regarded the whole of social and cultural life as a product of Nescience. In the ultimate analysis no value may thus be attached to religious ritual or worship, social obligation or institutions because they all presuppose the false consciousness of duality. Since reality is non-dual, human experience and activity can only be unreal. If this were to be granted literally, one would like to ask: 'How could such a philosophy of Transcendence be the voice of any social group seeking or opposing some vested interest?'

Perhaps it could still be suggested that such a philosophy reflects bleak social despair and the standpoint of the institution of mendicancy, and it should also be admitted that it was hostile to the claims and interests of ritualistic religion and the priestly class which championed it. This, however, could not really be said because whatever might be the theoretical implications of illusionistic non-dualism it did not mean the repudiation of altruistic moral and spiritual life or of cultural creativity even within Buddhistic monasticism which reflected the Śramanic ethos in its purity. In the case of Śaṅkara his legacy was a mixture of Brāhmaṇism and Śramanism i.e., of the admission of an immemorial religious and moral tradition underlying and regulating social life for the good of man as well as of a denial of the ultimacy of the social life of action and experience tied together in an endless cycle. Śaṅkara has no doubt that *Dharma* and *Brahman* constitute the two focal concepts of the Vedic tradition and that the Vedic Dharma has two aspects, viz., *Pravṛttilakṣaṇa* and *Nivṛttilakṣaṇa*, the active pusuit of social, moral and religious good, on the one hand, and the quietistic withdrawal into the silence of eternity, on the other.[2] Śaṅkara's philosophy does not absolutely negate the world or social life but merely relegates them to a relatively lower place without depriving them of all value. This accommodation of the relatively real empirical world by the side of the non-dual absolute was made possible by the doctrine of two truths which the Buddhists had first developed and which had been adopted by Gauḍapāda. It also corresponded to a practical compromise between two orders of social life, monastic and lay. For Śramanas the acceptance of the laity was the acceptance of an inevitable consequence of human frailty. For the Brāhmaṇas, the acceptance of mendicancy had been the reluctant admission of an unorthodox ideal as merely the last stage of a man's life after he had amply performed his social and ritual duties. The basic opposition of the two ideals, thus, had been modified into a practical compromise on both sides, Brāhmaṇical as well as Śramanic, during the millennium which had passed since the Buddha. It is this attitude of social compromise and conceptual synthesis which is reflected in the philosophy of Śaṅkara rather than bleak despair or total rejection.

In fact, such a compromise or synthesis is taken for granted by Śaṅkara who is himself concerned, as will be discussed later, with theoretical refinement and spiritual reform in an age of syncretic confusion, decaying institutions and ascetic spirituality. He reflects that peculiar combination of orthodoxy and radicalism which is characteristic of the truly great reformer. He regretted the decay of ancient Vedic social institutions and routinely upheld the orthodox view about restricted social eligibility in a formal sense to the institutionalized life of renunciation. But he strongly criticised the exaggerated claims of the ritualistic priesthood, arguing that spirituality is rooted in inner illumination not a causal effect to be obtained from exterior ritual or social works. This tends to make the order of seers or mendicants superior to that of priests or the laity.

Śaṅkara is supposed to have come from an orthodox Brāhmaṇa family following ancient Vedic mores. His sympathetic appreciation of the traditional Vedic social order is, thus, easy to understand. This is clearly reflected in his many references to the *Dharmaśāstra*. On the other hand, he deliberately chose to become a homeless and casteless wandering mendicant while still extremely young. Now the mendicants even when orthodoxy constituted at least potentially an alternative religious leadership to that of the priests, and when organized into monasteries constituted a veritable alternative to lay society. Mendicancy not only rejected ritual and social works but also the institutions of private property and family for the sake of an ascetic renunciation of secular life. Mendicancy did not reject all social life because within its coenobitic or monastic form it accepted the ideal of a spiritual fraternity and tradition as also the value of pure and altruistic action but it rejected the value claims of egoistic and instinctive satisfactions, holding that wealth cannot satisfy man and pleasures can only strengthen his misery and bondage. What mendicancy stood for was a distinctive kind of religious or spiritual value which disagreed with common social values. Even if one could speak of a class conflict of Brāhmaṇas and Kṣatriyas in the earlier days of mendicancy one could hardly think of it as relevant to the age of Śaṅkara. The opposition of *Jñāna* and *Karman* which concerns Śaṅkara so much must be regarded as a reflection of the opposition of divergent spiritual values rather than of any conflict between social classes or castes. Śaṅkara's thought presupposes the validity of the traditional Vedic social order as defined by the *Dharmasūtras* and *Smṛtis* and as including the option of mendicancy. What Śaṅkara does is to revolutionize the relative importance of this option in the traditional scheme of social life, which elevated in practice the role of the Sannyāsin as compared to that of the priest in post-classical Hinduism.

It would be a mistake to think of the socio-historical background of Śaṅkara's philosophy in terms of the dialectic of social classes, which was in any case dampened if not wholly contained by the caste system. His philosophy should rather be connected with a phase of the dialectic of cultural values in the realms of morality, spirituality and religion. It is true that in traditional societies social relations not unoften expressed themselves in a religious mode. Thus even during the European Reformation the debate over the theoretical questions relating to the Indulgences, Sacraments, Faith and works etc., was clouded by considerations of practical abuses as well as vested interests and as a result the ensuing political conflicts had a religious label but could hardly be attributed to merely religious passions. In such cases, however, social, economic and political conflicts are at least as clearly visible as the divergence of religious faith and theology. In the case of ancient Indian culture, however, it is difficult to read the history of religious movements in this fashion even though it is true that great religious movements occurred in times of social change. The religious movements in terms of their permanent, surviving elements were mostly concerned with existential, not social questions. It is true that the Śramanic movements or the *Bhakti* movement did have a liberal social dimension but their focus was spiritual and their liberal social outlook was a social reflection of their spirituality. That is why they never produced violent social revolutions even though they did work in the direction of social transformation. It would seem that social changes provided the occasion for the religious movements without determining their ideational content. Violent conflicts over religion were as a matter of fact rare and tolerance of religious dissent was a part of the common social ethos. The caste system effectively cut across merely economic classes and displayed an amazing vitality and flexibility by absorbing all dissenting religious groups, invading tribes and new occupational as well as ethnic groups within it as so many *jātis*. The *Purāṇas* similarly absorbed endless local cults and deities into a vast religious syncretism which still needed some rational principle of synthesis. There was certainly no dearth of political violence inspired by petty interests but these conflicts do not appear as a rule to have acquired the form of ideological conflicts. Scholars, savants and seers appear to have carried on their debates over the fundamental questions of life and death undisturbed by such conflicts. In moving round the country Hsuan Chwang was occasionally bothered by bandits but not by rival kings or their troops. Śaṅkara would have been in the same situation with the additional advantage that he had no property to save from bandits and no interest in acquiring royal patronage.

To appreciate the thought of Śaṅkara, then, we do not need to read into it the echoes of unknown and forgotten social conflicts. Nor indeed is it possible to see any influence on his thought of the slow but definite growth of a 'feudal-federal' polity except that he did observe the changing conditions of his times and did not sympathize with it. On the other hand, he was deeply involved in the religious as well as the philosophical scene of his times. He participated in its polemic and development. He could not have been indifferent to its proliferating syncretism which badly needed a reforming synthesis.

Interpretative and Philosophical Methodology of Śaṅkara

Behind the text of Śaṅkara one cannot mistake at least two clear voices. One is that of the ancient Vedic Tradition which affirmed the unity and divinity of reality. The other voice is that of a spirituality which denies all reality to the world and human life in it.[3] This kind of spirituality had received a prominent development in Mahāyāna but was not unknown in the Vedic tradition especially in its post-Buddhistic development. One of the principal endeavours of Śaṅkara is to harmonize these two voices while purifying each from its internal contradictions and exaggerations. This endeavour is multidimensional and encompasses several different pairs of contraries such as creationism and illusionism, *nirguṇa* and *saguṇa-Brahman, Jñāna* and *Karman, Pravṛtti-lakṣaṇa dharma* and *nivṛttilakṣaṇa-dharma,* the unity of godhead and the multiplicity of cults. This endeavour may be said to have produced the ultimate purification and synthesis of *brahma-vidyā* and *śramana-vidyā*, a synthesis which became the basis of classical Hinduism.

A possible misunderstanding must be cleared at this stage. The diversity of voices and the endeavour to harmonize them referred to above, do not represent the manifest content of Śaṅkara's text. Ostensibly he is the exponent of a single unalloyed tradition, viz., the Vedāntic, and sharply disputes all rival traditions and positions. He does not seek to reconcile or synthesize but to negate everything which compromises the sacred non-dual absolutism. Śaṅkara himself felt his principal concern to be the restoration of Vedānta to its original meaning from which it had been distracted by misinterpretations. An ancient system of philosophical and spiritual wisdom appeared to him to have been subordinated to a formal religion of ritual and worship and Vedic monism blurred by shades of dualism. Śaṅkara proceeded to cleanse the Vedic tradition of accumulated misconceptions and false views in which it had been 'sunk like a cow in the mire.'[4] It should, thus, seem indisputable that as a staunch Vedāntin the sole task of Śaṅkara was to purify and defend Vedānta against internal and external enemies. It is, however, equally indisputable that the Vedāntic tradition contained from the very beginning divergent and even contradictory elements which subsequent development and controversies did nothing to lighten. Śaṅkara was not unaware of this situation and the very task of interpreting ancient texts made it imperative for him to reconcile their divergent tendencies. Nor was he unaware of the logical force of the arguments of rival schools and it was incumbent on him to strengthen the Vedāntic position by suitably interpreting it. And above all he could not avoid following the authority of his own experience or the tradition of his teachers especially Gauḍapāda. As a result, in interpreting the Vedāntic texts as a consistent system of spiritual non-dualism capable of facing logical objections, Śaṅkara was led to recognize two voices within the Vedāntic texts, one voice clearly and directly affirmed the central truth of Vedānta, the other spoke of a lower and relative truth relevant to those still engaged in religious worship, meditation or works. This mode of interpretative reconciliation became possible on account of the theory of Two Truths.

Thus despite appearances and ostensible claims, Śaṅkara's restoration of ancient Vedānta was not as a matter of fact a mere revival or going back; it was actually a profoundly original reinterpretation which as often as not introduced new wine in old bottles. 'It is not that Śaṅkara was deliberately or basically untrue to the intention of the *Upaniṣads*, but he seized upon one aspect of their many-sided and varied teachings, and developed it uncompromisingly in the light of the logical implications of *Advaita* and the spiritual ethos of *Nivṛttidharma* which had seen a many-sided development in the Śramanic tradition since the age of the *Upaniṣads* and with which the Brāhmaṇical tradition had been in considerable interactions.'[5] The *Upaniṣads* had been in some ways a continuation of the earlier Vedic thought focused on the gods and their worship for the sake of happiness here and hereafter even though they (*Upaniṣads*) developed a new focus in inner spirituality and the Self. As interpreted by Śaṅkara the Upaniṣadic Vedānta is now linked to a later and alternative mode of spirituality which began with the perennial existential anxiety of man in the face of mortality and transience. The ideas of *saṁsāra* and *duḥkha* are only exceptional in the *Upaniṣads* and the spiritual end is generally conceived as fulfilment, immortality, perfection or bliss rather than as the transcendence of all experience. Reality is more often conceived in personal than in impersonal terms and the approach to it does not exclude all works, especially in the form of meditation. Cosmology and eschatology are topics of great interest and this tradition is continued in the *Brahmasūtras*. Thus the *Upaniṣads* often begin the praise of some esoteric ritual or meditation which would lead to the fulfilment of desires. They often identify the deity with some particular cosmic or psychic principle. Their conception of deity remained fundamentally the same as in old Vedic thought, viz., the creator of the world. The identification of the Person creating the world with the Person in man did not at once lead to any change in the fundamental characterization of *Brahman* as the creator.

Before examining how Śaṅkara reconciles the non-*Advaitic* or quasi-ritualistic sections of the Upaniṣadic and other Vedāntic texts with strict *Advaita*, it might be well to glance at his conception of the kind of knowledge which he seeks to formulate and the method he follows. The Vedānta formulates *Brahmavidyā* or *Ātmavidyā* of which the central principle, according to Śaṅkara, is *Brahmātmaikatva-vijñāna*, the knowledge of the identity of *Brahman* and *Ātman*. The *Upaniṣads* which formulate this *vidyā* do so without as a rule caring for definitions, proof or systematization. This Upaniṣadic formulation is regarded as *Veda* or *Śruti* or revelation, which for Śaṅkara is the highest source of valid knowledge or *pramāṇa* and the only one which can give access to the highest spiritual truth consisting in the identity of the real self with the reality underlying the cosmos. Traditionally the *Veda* was regarded as one of the four principal sciences or *Vidyās* and was distinguished from *Ānvīkṣkī* or philosophy where logic was emphasized.[6] Although *Adhyātmavidyā*, the prime content of the *Upaniṣads*, came to be included within *Ānvīkṣkī* in course of time since *Ātman* was regarded as the principal *prameya*, the focus of *Ānvīkṣkī* continued to be on logic, i.e., on the examination of *padārthas, lakṣaṇas* and *pramāṇas*. *Veda*, then, came to be formally regarded as the overriding *pramāṇa* in transcendental or spiritual matters in the orthodox systems of logic. During the age of the development of critical philosophy and logic, a parallel development occurred within Vedic scholarship which essayed the task of critically and systematically investigating the meaning and purport of the *Vedas* and defending it against heterodox attacks. This enterprise came to be called Mīmāṁsā and the *Brahmasūtras* illustrate *Brahmamīmāṁsā* which may be described as the philosophical presentation of *Brahmavidyā*. *Brahmasūtras* and the *BG* constitute *smṛtis* or authoritative tradition based on the *śruti*.

Brahmavidyā with which Śaṅkara is concerned is in itself intuitive or direct. It is the same as the ultimate, transcendental knowledge (*parā-vidyā*) which cannot be distinguished from reality, eternal and absolute (*Brahman*). For Śaṅkara *Brahmavidyā* in this sense cannot be attained without the aid of the Vedic revelation understood with the help of tradition, '*Sampradāya*' or *Āgama*. Revelation and Tradition are valid sources of knowledge and constitute *Aparā-vidyā*, the Lower Science. Although it points to the ultimate truth, it belongs itself to the world of what is empirically true but ultimately false. That is so because as valid knowledge revelation has a linguistic and logical form and hence presupposes duality. This is not the peculiar fault of revelation but the general character of all empirical and rational knowledge. Whether perceptual, logical, or verbal, such knowledge presupposes the subject-object duality. It is discursive and determinative. It is incapable of directly revealing the infinity of non-dual truth.

Thus although the Vedic revelation is the sole *pramāṇa* for spiritual truth, it is still placed by Śaṅkara within Nescience or *Avidyā*. Although the prime means to attain to *parā-vidyā*, the revelation is at the same time *aparā-vidyā* as a branch of learning and placed within the world of *avidyā* since it presupposes duality. Thus Śaṅkara was concerned with the interpretation and exposition of Vedānta which was a part of the *Veda* and recognized as a distinct branch of knowledge or *Vidyā*. As a *śāstra* or systematic body of knowledge, Vedānta was required to be coherent and plausible. At the same time its distinctiveness was held to lie in the transcendent or supernatural character of what it sought to reveal. Śaṅkara makes a sharp distinction between what the Vedānta reveals and what the other parts of the *Veda* reveal. For him Vedānta is concerned with ultimate reality or *Brahman,* not with transcendent norms or *Dharma*. The Vedānta, thus, is essentially an area of cognitive enquiry and 'positive' knowledge, not a normative system of religious worship or socio-ethical conduct. As a cognitive enquiry (*Jijñāsā, Mīmāṁsā*) or science (*Vijñāna, Vidyā, śāstra*) Vedānta cannot be indifferent to the deliverances of reason even though 'dry' or 'unaided' reason or *tarka* is not adequate to the discovery of that spiritual reality which Vedānta reveals. And yet the Vedānta as a *śāstra* and *pramāṇa* must also be left behind in the course of the spiritual journey which has to culminate in direct experience (*anubhavāvasānam*).

The Vedāntic science with which Śaṅkara is concerned could be described as a scholastic theology in the sense that it restricts reason within the bounds of faith. It could also be described as a spiritual philosophy based on a specific tradition of religious experience. In the particular form in which Śaṅkara accepts the Vedānta, it could above all be described as philosophical 'autology' based on the analysis of the deepest and most universal features of human self-awareness. Thus Śaṅkara's Vedānta is principally *Ātmavidyā* which was primarily a part of *Trayī* but was also included within *Ānvīkṣkī*. It began by accepting *śruti-prāmāṇya* but also accepted the common principles of logic and interpretation developed by Mīmāṁsā. It was critical of *śuṣka-tarka* but favoured *śrutyanugṛhīta-tarka*. Although it placed implicit trust in the testimony of Revelation, it held the revealed truth to be accessible to a direct experience (*anubhava*) which is only the pure and unalloyed experience of the self freed from radical Nescience and all delusions of empirical delimitation. Śaṅkara's Vedānta begins and ends with self-consciousness. It begins with the paradox of empirical self-consciousness[7] and ends with the realization of eternal self-consciousness.

The obvious method which Śaṅkara follows is the scholastic one of interpreting the scriptural texts in the light of the principles formulated by Mīmāṁsā. These principles constitute a remarkable rational hermeneutics to which Śaṅkara added the principle of the multiplicity of interpretative standpoints. Śaṅkara also attached great importance to the hidden light of the personally transmitted spiritual tradition to which he belonged. The deep import of Revelation cannot be grasped without the help of such tradition, which explains why many interpreters have gone astray.[8]

By the side of this reliance on the scriptures and their interpretation in the light of reason and tradition,[9] Śaṅkara relied on the analysis of self-awareness. This analysis followed to a large extent the kind of 'discrimination' between the self and the non-self which was originally associated with the school of the Sāṅkhya philosophers although it was really a much more widely current method. Even the early Buddhists practised the discrimination 'I am not this', 'This is not mine'. For Śaṅkara the self is indubitable as it is presupposed in doubting too, and yet in empirical self-consciousness it is constantly characterized by false and changing identities. The search for the true self requires the rejection of these false identities. This method of discriminative disidentification—*ātmānātma-viveka*—has been the central element in what has been known as the Path of Knowledge (*Jñānamārga*). *Viveka* or discrimination is preceded by rational deliberation or *Vicāra* over the distinction between self and non-self.

As a whole, thus, the methodology of Śaṅkara may be said to reflect the inner structure of the *Advaitic* mode of self-enquiry. Beginning with faith in revelation it uses rational reflection not only to understand and interpret the revealed Truth but also to negate the instinctive and philosophical prejudices against it so that personal realization may become possible. Discriminative deliberation or 'meditation' over self-awareness, distinguishing its undeniable reality from its spurious identities, is an essential part of the process. Since this process discovers a contradiction in empirical self-consciousness and seeks to resolve it by discrimination and negation, it could also be called a process of spiritual dialectic. In the methodology of Śaṅkara, thus, we have a combination of exegetical and dialectical reasoning within the context of a transcendental ontology, which as a whole expresses the meaning of the three steps in the Vedāntic search for truth. To the first two correspond in Śaṅkara's philosophy the exegesis and interpretation of the texts and the critical or dialectical analysis of self-consciousness. As already mentioned in his exegesis of Vedāntic texts, apart from using traditional Mīmāṁsā canons and methods of interpretation, Śaṅkara relies on the concept of Two Truths or standpoints. Faced with scriptural diversity the Buddhists had originally drawn a distinction between *Nītārtha* and *Neyārtha sūtras.* In his exegesis of the scriptural texts Śaṅkara takes care to understand their meaning from the standpoint, empirical or absolute, from which they speak and within the context and level where they have relevance. In his independent exposition of Vedāntic principles or his criticism of rival philosophies he brings out the contradictions latent in empirical consciousness and existence. He appeals to two basic principles of which one is epistemological and the other is ontological. Epistemologically he holds that while all empirical knowledge presupposes the subject-object duality, the subject can never be the object and *vice-versa.*[10] Ontologically he holds that the real cannot be changed or sublated.[11] What a thing is, it could not be otherwise. If it alters, it could not be what it seems. Since empirical consciousness and existence violate these principles they are shown to be false.

This falsity is, however, compatible with pragmatic validity, and since it is grounded in *avidyā* it could be termed 'transcendental'. To these two must be added Śaṅkara's conviction that the self is immediate in all experience and thought which would be impossible without it.[12] The self cannot, thus, be denied or doubted without a contradiction. Descriptions of the self, however, can and ought to be doubted and examined for the discovery of its true nature.[13]

These principles constitute an ample basis for Śaṅkara's theory of the self. Physical, mental and social phenomena being objective cannot belong to the self, and being transient cannot be ultimately real.[14] Experience requires the self but does not really belong to it. Some original mistake seems to underlie the involvement of the self in experience. That the self is real, non-objective, and the non-empirical ground of experience, although mistakenly involved in experience, are conclusions which belong to Śaṅkara's philosophy simply on the force of a logical examination of experience.

The reality of the self is self-evident but its nature as the universal ground of all existence, the same as *Brahman*, one without a second, is a principle which Śaṅkara derives from Revelation. At the same time it follows on essentially dialectical grounds that causality itself can only be illusory in reality i.e., illusory from the standpoint of absolute reality. The one spiritual reality, *Ātman* or *Brahman*, thus, becomes the transcendental ground of a world illusion. Nevertheless, this does not question the reality of the external world at the empirical level.

The Structure and Elements of Śaṅkara's Philosophy

Śaṅkara's philosophical theory, thus, may be said to have three aspects. In one aspect it affirms on logical grounds the indubitable but non-objective reality of the self, which strongly resembles the *Śāṅkhya* view. In another, it identifies the self with *Brahman* as the sole reality on the basis of his interpretation of the *śruti*. In its third aspect while accepting the scriptural view of creation it also accepts the theory of illusion which is in any case required to explain the appearance of duality. What appears to be a real creation or differentiation is in reality only an illusive appearance. The theory of Two Truths is used finally to tie together the whole system in which *Sāṅkhyan,* Vedāntic, and Buddhistic elements have been forged into an original and abiding synthesis. It is because of its *point d'appui* of reflection over human experience in the light of logical principles and even more so on account of its final synthesizing rationality that the whole system can only be called philosophical or speculative even though it claims, and possibly has, dependence on Revelation in its central doctrine of the identity of the self with the cosmic ground. The intimate union of philosophical rationality with textual interpretation is a striking character of Śaṅkara's philosophizing. At the same time his conceptual system maintains a close relationship of relevance to a characteristic system of spiritual values and *praxis* (*sādhana*).

The Nature of the Self

The *Ātman* is one of the major themes of discussion in the *Upaniṣads.* The word *Ātman* denoted reflexively the self and also what was held to be one's self. The most popular notion was and has been the instinctive one that one's self is the individual being that is identical with the body through which one acts and experiences. This is the view which appealed to Vairocana and which has been supported by materialists and naturalists of all ages.[15] Such a conception of the self is of little consolation in disease, old age and especially in the face of death, '*asyaiva śarīrasya nāśam anveṣa naśyati nāham atra bhogyam paśyāmīti*'.[16] So the final boon which Naciketas asked of the God of Death was for him to reveal whether man survives death.[17] The *Upaniṣads* have no doubt that the self or Person survives death. He is described as the immortal spirit whose presence in the body means life and whose absence is death. Various descriptions are given of its nature and after-life or even reincarnation.[18] Such a conception of the *Ātman* is the familiar one of *Jīva* in later thought. The *Upaniṣads,* however, also describe the self as transcending the body and mind, as pure being or consciousness, and finally as *Brahman,* the Cosmic Being or Person. It is only the last view that regards the self as pure, non-dual, universal being or consciousness which Śaṅkara accepts as the really correct view.

This conception of the identity of the *Ātman* and *Brahman* needed to be defended against rival philosophical opinions. The materialists and the Buddhists denied the very existence of the *Ātman* as a distinct entity.[19] The materialists reduced it to the body explaining consciousness as a capacity or function dependent on the body. The Buddhists reduced the self to a psycho-physical complex where the essential part is played by the stream of ideas or consciousness. Diverse realistic schools like Nyāya-Vaiśeṣika, Mīmāṁsakas and Jainas regarded the *Ātman* as a real and permanent, individual substance which is non-material and non-mental but has the capacity of association with body and mind functioning as a person in terms of knowledge, feeling and will. In the Sāṅkhya the self is conceived as a pure subject, an eternal consciousness which is individual but non-objective. Śaṅkara, thus, needed to defend the reality of the self, the identification of its nature as eternal consciousness, and the universality of such consciousness to give philosophical tenability to the Vedāntic view in his age. Śaṅkara says, "Hence some have been deluded (some say) 'Consciousness is produced and destroyed every moment in the form of the representation of (objects such as) the pot etc., just as clarified butter (is transformed) by its contact with fire'. Others (say) 'on its ceasing (i.e. of consciousness) nothing remains, as it were'. Still others hold 'the consciousness of objects like the pot etc. is impermanent, arises and ceases but it belongs to an eternal *Ātman*'. The Lokāyatikas say 'consciousness is a property of matter'."[20]

Again, "The common man as well as the materialists (the Lokāyatas) believe the body alone to be the self possessed of sentience, others hold that the senses or the mind is the self. Some say it is merely momentary consciousness. Others say that it is the void, still others believe that there is a soul separate from the body, which transmigrates and is the agent and the experiencer. Some say the soul is a mere experiencer and not an agent. Some say that there is a god who is different from this soul and is omniscient and omnipotent. Others say that he is the self of the experiencer'.[21]

The denial of the *Ātman* had rested primarily on its non-perception. The materialists argued that only the body and its behaviour are perceptible and perception is the sole means of cognition. Hence there could be no reason to accept the existence of the *Ātman* apart from the body and its behaviour.[22] The Buddhists admitted the validity of inference as a means of cognition and argued that the mind was known as a distinct entity through introspection but it was known only as a flow of contingent experiences, not as an unchanging substance. The soul was not evidenced by any introspection which only revealed changing states of the mind.[23] For moral and eschatological purposes this 'stream of consciousness' was adequate. Hence the soul was neither perceived through introspection nor was it necessary to postulate it on moral or religious grounds.

Against such attacks the logicians had tried to prove the existence of the soul by inference.[24] Śaṅkara, however, did not look on such attempts with favour. He says, 'Unless there were a conviction of the existence of the self in another life after death one would not be induced to attain what is good and avoid what is evil in that life. Therefore, the scriptures proceed to indicate the existence of the self in a future life . . .'[25] And he quotes passages from the *Katha* at length and then goes on, '*objection*: Is it not a matter of perception? Reply: No, for we see contradictory opinions among the schools. Were the existence of the self in a future life an empirical fact the materialists and Buddhists would not oppose us, denying the self. For no one disputes a perceptible object such as a jar, saying it does not exist. Śaṅkara then makes the point that when there is a difference of opinion on matters amenable to perception in principle, such differences of opinion can ultimately be settled. He then says that the Buddhists, despite the fact that there is the ego-consciousness, persistently deny the existence of the self except that they admit another body after death (*dehāntara-vyatiriktasya*). Therefore, being different from objects of perception, the existence of the self cannot be proved by perception. Nor by inference.[26] An objection is raised that the *Śruti* itself points out certain grounds for the existence of the self and these depend on perception. Thus inference may validly be used to prove the existence of the self (*śrutyā ātmāstitive liṅgasya darśitatvāt liṅgasya ca pratyakṣa-viṣayatvāt*). While Śaṅkara admits that some kind of inference may be used to prove the existence of a self, it cannot be shown that such a self survives death (*janmāntara-sambandhasya agrahaṇāt*). When the existence of the self 'has been known from the *Śruti* and from certain empirical grounds cited by it, the

Mīmāṁsakas and logicians, who follow in its footsteps, imagine that those Vedic grounds of inference are the products of their own mind, and say that the self is knowable through perception and inference.[27] It may be recalled that in the *Nyāyasūtras* III. 1.1-27 an attempt has been made to prove the existence of the *Ātman* as something distinct from the body, the senses and the mind on the logical ground that the self must be a unitary and stable conscious being capable of experiencing and remembering the objects of diverse senses. Each sense is limited to the perception of a specific class of objects but the self as the perceiver is not so limited and is consequently different from the senses. If the functions of synthesizing the percepts, judgement, remembrance, volition etc., are all referred to the mind, it would be another name for the self. Actually the 'mind' should only refer to the internal faculty which perceives pleasure and pain and is used as a tool by the self in handling percepts etc. Such and similar arguments have been used to establish the self as a unitary being with conscious functioning distinct from the aggregate of the body, the senses, and the mind. It may be added that the Sāṅkhya has used a different kind of argument to prove the existence of the self. The body and the senses are so organized that they may fulfil certain purposes, which shows that there must be a distinct conscious being with reference to whom this organisation acquires meaning.[28] All these arguments are designed to prove the existence of the self as a conscious being who gives unity and meaning to the psycho-physical aggregate and its functioning. All of them have been questioned by the Buddhists and all of them may be suspected of involving a *petitio principii.* Even if the soul be considered to have been established in this way, its future existence and the law governing its future state will still need to be established by the authority of Revelation. It is only for guidance with respect to moral and ritual law connecting action in this life with retribution in after-life that it is necessary to believe in the soul as a permanent and individual conscious being who can be held responsible for his actions. If the person lacks consciousness or freedom or a permanent identity, moral and religious prescriptions would be pointless. For this reason as far as the life of action in this world is concerned, one must take recourse to the guidance of *Śruti* as *Karmakāṇḍa.*

But these prescriptions are needed only by one who seeks to engage in activity for gaining or avoiding something, and he can do so only by imagining himself to be an individual agent and experiencer. For Śaṅkara the reality and relevance of the self as *kartā, bhoktā* and *pramātā* is, thus, limited to the world of action which being the world of duality appears to be real only within Ignorance. For him the *saṁsāra* is an evil (*anartha*) created by *avidyā* through superimposition.[29] For Śaṅkara those who pursue the goods of the other world are at par with those who pursue the goods of this world. Both are equally deluded.

And the delusion is about the real nature of the self. If the materialists and the Buddhists commit a 'category mistake' by their physical or psychological reductionism, a similar mistake is made by the Naiyāyikas, Mīmāṁsakas and other realists by thinking of the Self as an immaterial or spiritual substance which is one individual object (*prameya*) among others being equally subject to the general categories of thought. The source of these misunderstandings is the failure to understand the nature of consciousness. Consciousness in the first instance is the subject, not the object in the knowledge situation, which is the reason why all objects must be insentient and the subject incomprehensible under the determinations which apply to objects. In other words, the knowledge situation involves a unique subject-object relation which is altogether unlike any inter-objective relation. The subject is the Ego that knows and consciousness is its essence. When the subject or consciousness is turned away from itself towards an object its content becomes the form or representation of the object. In the knowledge situation now we seem to have a triplicity. There is the object which is represented in knowledge, there is the subject or consciousness to whom the object is represented, and there is the representation which is at once a logical form and a psychic event. Now the notion of the self is the notion of the Ego as the subject of experience which can never be represented as an object. Yet, since the content of consciousness reflects some object or the other, there is an innate and inveterate tendency in the extroverted consciousness or Ego to identify itself with some of the more persistent objects in its experience. It is due to this association of consciousness with psychic representations and functions that it is difficult to grasp the pure nature of the self. '*Caitanya-vyatirekeṇa hi kalā jāyamānās tiṣṭhantyaḥ pralīyamānāś casarvadā lakṣyante. Ata eva bhrāntāḥ kecit*'.[30]

The essential nature (*svarūpa*) of the self or consciousness needs to be distinguished from its adventitious and accidental character (*Upādhi*) lent to it in the process of psychosis. The self or consciousness is luminous like light. While no object, not even the absence of an object, can have meaning except when presented to the self or consciousness, the latter is self-revealing and requires nothing else. Its being is consciousness, consciousness being.[31] Essentially it is immediate and non-relational. Consequently it is undeniable, presupposed in all knowledge and by all objects, but indeterminate because the categories by which objects are known do not apply to it *"aviṣayāntaḥpāti pratyag-ātma-bhūtam"*[32], *"samastasya viṣayajātasya pratiṣedhād aviṣayaḥ"*[33] It is known in every knowing (*Pratibodha-viditam*) and remains unknown as an object. In Śaṅkara's own words:

'Ātmā tu pramāṇādi-vyavahārāśrayatvāt prāgeva pramāṇādi-vyavahārāt siddhyati.'[34] *'Yaddhi karaṇa-gocaram tad anyasmā upadeṣṭum śakyam jāti-guṇa-kriyā-viśeṣaṇaiḥ. Na tajjātyādi-viśeṣaṇavad Brahman'.*[35] *'Sarve pratyayā viṣayībhavanti yasya sa ātmā sarva-bodhān pratibudhyate sarva-pratyaya-darśī cicchakti-svarūpa-mātraḥ pratyayair eva pratyayeṣva viśiṣṭatayā lakṣyate'.*[36]

Since the self is the unchanging witness of all the changing mental states it must be distinguished from the latter. The changeless consciousness is pointed out by the changing representations themselves or the very consciousness of change which would not be possible without it. *'sarva-pratyayadarśitve copajananāpāya-varjita-dṛk-svarūpatā nityatvaṁ viśuddha-svarūpatvam ātmatvam nirviśeṣataikatvaṁ ca sarva-bhūteṣu siddham bhavati.'*[37]

Thus Śaṅkara moves away from the standpoint of relational psychology to that of critical epistemology. He accepts the validity of the idea of the individual soul at the level of empirical activity but neither the empirical world nor the individual soul are ultimately real. Our indubitable knowledge of the self is given by the ego-notion which has reference to the subject of knowledge or experience. Although I cannot doubt that I am, the question is what is my nature? Is the ego a mere logical subject, an abstraction or a relational term, or is it a metaphysical entity? For Śaṅkara the subject to which the ego-notion refers is neither a logical abstraction nor the merely synthetic unit of psychic functioning. For him the subject is really the changeless, witnessing consciousness (*sarvapratyayadarśī cit-śakti-svarūpa*). Unless that were real, knowledge of any kind, whether as a logical synthesis or as a psychic process, would not be possible. The subject as consciousness cannot be regarded as the systematic unity of objective knowledge, actual or ideal, or some kind of psychic fact. Nor does it become for that reason a mere nothing, for even the absence of a thing has to be the object of consciousness. The whole mystery of the self or consciousness is that it is 'a thing apart', the most real and yet the most elusive.

The Paradox of Self-consciousness and the Nature of Avidyā

Self-consciousness, indeed, presents a paradox. 'The object and the subject, referred to by the notions of You and I, being as contradictory in nature as darkness and light, cannot be logically identified. It follows that their attributes too cannot be identified without contradiction. Hence the superimposition of the object and its attributes which are the referents of the notion of You, on the subject having the nature of consciousness and referred to by the notion 'I' should logically be false just as the reverse superimposition of the subject and its attributes on the object would be. Even so through the mutual identification and superimposition of their attributes, and thus through the non-discrimination of absolutely distinct entities and their characteristics, the instinctive empirical usage of 'I am this', 'This is mine', arises, coupling the real and the unreal owing to the working of false knowledge.'[38] That is to say, empirical self-consciousness presupposes the mutual superimposition of the subject and the object, consciousness and the inconscient, and reveals the self as something other than what it really is. This superimposition of one thing on another is termed as *adhyāsa* by Śaṅkara. Thus we are aware of the self under a false notion which is instinctive and is called Nescience or *avidyā*. As a result we regard the self as an agent or experiencer. Only when we make this mistake about the self do the means of proof and practical norms, secular or religious, become applicable.

It is worth noting that so far Śaṅkara's conception of self runs parallel to the *Sāṅkhya* conception. The *Sāṅkhya* also regards the self as the pure and eternal consciousness without reference to which mental modifications would not constitute experience. The subject in experience is nothing but this consciousness which despite its purity and eternity is, as it were, mixed up with mental representations. Just as a pure crystal assumes the hue of a coloured flower when in close proximity to it, so does the self even though it is pure consciousness, appear delimited by objective features. Thus in speaking of the contradiction of the subject and the object and the error of their confusion at the empirical level, and in regarding the self as pure, eternal consciousness which is only the witness of psychic life, Śaṅkara seems to echo the views of *Sāṅkhya*. Since Śaṅkara begins his celebrated commentary on the *BS* with the expression of such views some modern critics have naturally expressed surprise.[39] The repudiation of the *Sāṅkhya* is one of the acknowledged motives of the *BS*. Why should Śaṅkara begin with an apparently pro-*Sāṅkhyan* stance ?

We may begin by noting that there is an undoubted similarity between the *Sāṅkhya* and Śaṅkara as far as the discrimination of the Self and the non-self is concerned. This methodology of seeking to discover the self as the pure subject by negating all objects is common to both and the general notion of Nescience as implying confusion is also common. But the similarity stops here. For *Sāṅkhya* the self is individual and plural and the Non-self belongs to *Prakṛti* which is real, objective, changing, autonomous and insentient. For Śaṅkara the self is one with *Brahman*. The identity of *Ātman* and *Brahman* is the basic thesis of Śaṅkara and the Sāṅkhyan *Prakṛti* or the plurality of *Puruṣas* cannot be reconciled with it. The nature of the radical error or *avidyā* too is not the same in the two cases. Thus Śaṅkara differs from Sāṅkhya about the Self, the Non-self, and the exact nature of the error about them.

Śaṅkara's distinction of the subject and the object is reminiscent of the *Sāṅkhya* but while the distinction indicates a real duality for *Sāṅkhya*, for Śaṅkara it is valid only so long as the sense of duality is real. That Śaṅkara begins with an apparently *Sāṅkhyan* position is principally because the self-non-self discrimination represents the logical starting point for self-enquiry. Also perhaps it is because of Śaṅkara's early interest in Yoga which was traditionally based on *Sāṅkhya*. In the *YSBV* he comments that the *Sāṅkhya* distinction of *Puruṣas* is unintelligible because there is nothing to distinguish them.[40]

Thus when Śaṅkara begins with a consideration of empirical self-consciousness he does so for both logical and historical reasons. In empirical self-consciousness he finds the prime illustration of illusion or *avidyā*. Here the 'I' appears as 'You' and the 'You' as 'I', producing a double misidentification of the subject and object of experience, which is logically impossible but serves as the basis of all empirical life. It is through the negation of all superimpositions that the identity of the self with *Brahman* can be immediately realized. This identity negates the separate reality of the cosmos as much as that of the individual self or *Jīva*. This paradigm of illusion which applies to the individual as well as the cosmos is most vividly illustrated by dreams. In the dream while the dreamer really remains wholly unaffected, all the time he still appears to become a different person and acts in a world which is not real. What one sees of oneself or the world is relative to one's state of consciousness and that is why there is no commensurability between the experience of waking, dreaming and deep sleep. The experience of spiritual intuition negates all these. The *Māṇḍūkya* had specially stressed this spiritual phenomenology[41] and Gauḍapāda had made it the starting point of his monistic illusionism. Plurality is not the result of any real creation but an illusory projection which is eternally unreal.

The relativity of the ego and its world to the state of consciousness is a principle which was used by the Buddhists to formulate an idealistic philosophy of which one is reminded in Gauḍapāda. For the Buddhists the empirical egos and objects are merely projections of the mind which transforms itself into subjects and objects. Here too is an illustionistic non-dualism which bases itself on an epistemological and phenomenological analysis of experience, especially self-experience. Historically it is connected with Śaṅkara through Gauḍapāda. However, Buddhist idealism regards the subject and the object as correlative abstractions within the concrete reality of momentary experience. As a result their view appears to be tainted with a psychological subjectivism, at least that is how Śaṅkara understood them. For Śaṅkara, underlying the false empirical ego is the transcendental, noumenal consciousness which alone is the true self.

Thus while Śaṅkara's theory of the self has points of contact with the *Sāṅkhya* as well as with Buddhist *Vijñānavāda*, it remains distinctively Vedāntic. Like the *Sāṅkhya* his self is a mere witnessing subject of all experiences and is an eternal and pure consciousness but unlike the *Sāṅkhya* it is the only and universal consciousness and also the sole reality. As in Vijñānavāda, the empirical and individual ego belongs to a false world which is like a dream and there is no reality except consciousness but unlike Vijñānavāda the self as consciousness in Śaṅkara is eternal and universal.

That the self as the subject of experience cannot be an object but must be an unchanging consciousness and that the ordinary empirical ego-notion or self-consciousness arises from a radical or transcendental delusion which misidentifies the subject and the object, are conclusions which Śaṅkara reaches from a logical examination of the phenomena of consciousness, viz., the knowledge of objects, self-knowledge, memory and such hallucinative states as dreams etc. But the crucial points in his theory are the transitions from the individual to universal consciousness and from that to the unitive character of reality itself.

That 'I am' and that I cannot be any of the things with which I identify myself habitually and instinctively follows from the testimony of indubitable experience and reason. 'In so far consciousness is an object of consciousness, it is no longer consciousness.[42] That pure consciousness is not just an abstract idea, rests on the realization of its immediate character, a realization which is helped by meditation.

But how does one proceed from the notion of pure subjectivity or pure consciousness to that of universal consciousness ? It has been remarked that 'it must be in the highest degree improper to convert consciousness in general without more ado into a universal consciousness. We can have absolutely no right to transform the logical identity of type into a numerical identity of existence.[43] And yet this 'conversion' is essential to Śaṅkara. *Advaitic* meditation provides the key to this process. When all attributes are negated of the self, its individuality also stands negated. Although it becomes a 'no-thing', it does not become nothing. Since *Brahman* is already conceived as pure consciousness there remains no logical difficulty to the identity of the Self and *Brahman*. The answer to the logical objection raised above, thus, is twofold. Consciousness is not a 'type', nor does it admit of any distinction of universal and particular as class and number or greater or lesser formal abstraction simply because no category (*viśeṣaṇa-sambandha, vikalpa*) can apply to it. To the extent to which one is able to regard consciousness as an immediacy free from all objective determinations one would be able to see it as the unique reality which illumines all possible worlds. Apart from the logical necessity of the transcendental consciousness presupposed by mental phenomena, and its confirmation by meditational experience, Śaṅkara formally relies on the authority of Revelation. In fact, this is a general feature of the methodology of Śaṅkara in which the logical considerations of experience, intuitive or meditational, and scriptural authority are used jointly. Formally the identity of the *Ātman* and *Brahman* rests on scriptural evidence even though epistemological and 'transcendental' considerations prepare the ground for it. The scriptures contain statements to the effect that the *Brahman* is infinite being and consciousness, the sole reality, the same as the

Ātman. It is the source of the world which is nothing apart from it. In such statements we are given the nature of *Brahman* and its relationship to the Self and the world. The *Upaniṣads* had reached the concept of *Brahman* in several different ways.[44] They thought of *Brahman* as the First cause of the world and seeking to discover the essential nature of *Brahman* they found it in the integral perfection of reality, knowledge and value. In relation to man it was either conceived as identical with his real self or as his lord and goal. All these and similar statements were reconciled by Śaṅkara with the help of his theory of two standpoints. When the empirical self and the world are regarded as real, God or the *saguṇa Brahman* is regarded as the real creator of the world and the Lord to be worshipped by the *Jīva*. From the absolute standpoint, however, *Brahman* is the *non-dual* reality identical with the Self and lying beyond all descriptions or characterizations. Śaṅkara argues that all the terms like being, knowledge, bliss etc., when applied to *Brahman* have to be understood to be of negative import.[45] Even the *Ātman* has to be understood through the negation of the *Anātman*. Thus Śaṅkara reconciles the concept of the *nirguṇa Brahman* i.e., the non-dual absolute with Vedāntic theism by admitting the *saguṇa Brahman* in relation to the cosmos. The concept of *avidyā* or *māyā* now comes back as the mysterious power of God responsible for the world illusion.

The *Brahmasūtras* (1.1.1) begin by declaring, 'Now, therefore, the enquiry into *Brahman*'. Some commentators earlier than Śaṅkara had connected the enquiry into *Brahman* with the enquiry into *Dharma*. They had sought to regard the search for the knowledge of *Brahman* as God as coming after a life of religious works and worship. By effecting a necessary connection between religious activity and the knowledge of *Brahman* both were reduced to the same level of empirical reality. This would be an effective de-absolutization of *Brahman*. So Śaṅkara rejects such an approach and connects the enquiry into *Brahman* with the enquiry into the self with which he was concerned in his preface to the commentary. He felt such a connection necessary for another reason. The *Brahmasūtras* following the *Upaniṣads* had defined *Brahman* as the cause etc., of the universe. Now if *Brahman* as the cause of the universe were simply an object it would be wholly transcendent and unsuitable to be an object of enquiry. It is because *Brahman* is immediately manifest as the self, that it can become the object of enquiry. The reality of the self is undeniable but its real nature is a matter of dispute. The enquiry into *Brahman* is, thus, nothing but an enquiry into the real nature of the self. Thus *Brahma-jijñāsā* is taken out of the realm of religious activity into that of philosophical reflection.

The *BS* at the outset defines *Brahman* as that from which the origination etc., of the world takes place. Thibaut has pointed out that the *BS* apparently regard *Brahman* as the cause of the universe to be the same *Brahman* who is to be enquired into in Vedānta as proposed in the earlier *sūtra*. Such *Brahman* is obviously not the highest reality for Śaṅkara. So it would seem that the point of view of the *BS* is that of a theistic monism and does not agree with the illusionistic and absolutistic monism of Śaṅkara.[46] Thibaut interprets the monism of the *BS* to be a kind of *Brahma-pariṇāmavāda* which being *Cetana-Kāraṇa-vāda* is distinguished from the *Sāṅkhya* but still seeks to be monistic.[47] The word *māyā* occurs only once in the *BS* (III.2.3) in the context of the dreaming self and that too suggests that the *Sūtrakāra* would not call the context of waking as *māyā*.

There is no doubt that the general Upaniṣadic position and that of the *BS* regard creation as real and look upon *Brahman* primarily in the context of creation even though it was affirmed that the creation was not different from *Brahman* who is the sole reality. There is also no doubt that this position is not ultimately true for Śaṅkara even though he concedes it as a truth of the lower order. Some theistic philosophers even argued that the reality of *Brahman* can be logically proved from His being the cause of the world.[48] Still others argued that the concept of *Brahman* acquired meaning and relevance only in the context of certain practical injunctions about worship and meditation just as the gods are relevant to ritual prescriptions.[49] Here the nature or even the reality of *Brahman* becomes irrelevant. What is relevant is that certain prescribed meditations lead to the 'transcendent' result called *mokṣa*.

Śaṅkara rightly rejects the cosmological argument as providing a rational proof for the existence of God. Even though the world may be characterized as an effect there is no way of connecting it with a transcendent cause. 'If *Brahman* were an object of the senses, we might perceive that the world is connected with *Brahman* as its effect, but as the effect only (i.e. the world only) is perceived, it is impossible to decide whether it is connected with *Brahman* or with something else'.[50] it may be remarked that the Nyāya school developed the cosmological argument with great refinements to answer its criticism by the Buddhists and the Jainas.[51] Among Vedāntins even Rāmānuja refused to put faith in the cosmological argument.[52]

Similarly Śaṅkara rejects totally the view that *Brahman* is the object of some prescription or that *mokṣa* is an effect to be gained by some prescribed activity. The knowledge of *Brahman* does not arise from any activity or prescription. The 'true knowledge of all existing things depends on the things themselves, and hence the knowledge of *Brahman* also depends altogether on the thing, i.e. on *Brahman* itself.' But although *Brahman* is an accomplished real, it is not the object of perception or any other natural means of knowledge. *Mokṣa* too is not to be construed as a product (*Utpādya*) or an event. It is not a modification to be made (*vikārya*), nor an adventitious thing to be acquired (*āpya*). Nor is it a refinement or improvement to be effected (*saṁskārya*). It is only the realization of the eternal nature of the *Brahman or Ātman*.[53] It is like waking up to what has always been there.

Thus for Śaṅkara what the *Śruti* reveals of *Brahman* is that it is a reality, eternal and infinite, beyond empirical knowledge but given directly though in a distorted manner in self-consciousness. Can such a principle really be the efficient and material cause of the world ? It is easy to see the logical difficulties in the idea. The *Sāṅkhya* and the Nyāya-Vaiśeṣika had postulated an insentient principle other than the souls or God to explain the insentient nature of the world. But the *BS* holding on valiantly to the principle of non-dualism argue that *Brahman* may transform itself into the world without loss to itself or without violating its own sentient nature because there are many examples to show that the cause and the effect may have divergent natures (*vilakṣaṇa-pariṇāma*).[54] Thus the living body produces hair and nails and dung produces insects. Similarly milk becomes curd. There are also cases where being with supernatural powers create real things by the exercise of their will. The *Pariṇāmavāda* of the *Sūtras* appears to be simply the *Pariṇāmavāda* of the *Sāṅkhyas* with *Brahman* replacing *Pradhāna*.

To Gauḍapāda and Śaṅkara who were well versed in the dialectic of Buddhism, it was clear that these attempts to reconcile the reality of creation with the non-duality and eternity of *Brahman* could not logically succeed. Nothing can function as a cause which does not itself undergo change. There can be no 'unmoved mover'. And if something changes, it cannot be eternal. Buddhists had argued that whatever functions must be momentary. If *Brahman* is the cause of the world it cannot be eternal and if the world is really caused, duality becomes real because it is a pervasive feature of change itself. And how is pure intelligence to be the material cause of the insentient world in a real sense ?

Śaṅkara argues that within the empirical world *Satkāryavāda* or *Pariṇāmavāda* is more reasonable than *Asatkāryavāda* but that ultimately causation itself cannot be reconciled with reality. That is real of which the nature admits of no change. Since causation implies the alteration of the cause it follows that the operation of the cause cannot be real. In producing an effect the cause if real can only put on a false disguise and appear as what it is not, without really becoming something different.[55] It follows that *Brahman* can be the cause of the world only in the sense of projecting an illusion. *Brahman* is merely the ground of the world illusion. The *BS* adopted a straightforward theistic creationism without recognizing any contradiction between it and the thesis of non-duality. It agreed with the Sāṅkhyan explanation of causality as *satkāryavāda* or *pariṇāmavāda*, but did not recognize that that radical difference of Spirit and Nature made it impossible for the Spirit to function as a cause. Now Śaṅkara did recognize that the Spirit in its real nature being the changeless witness of changes and something wholly apart from any possible object could not really undergo any transformation or really function as a cause. Śaṅkara could reconcile his views with those of the *BS* only by adopting a two-stage or dual ontology. In the context of common experience the world is certainly real and *Brahman* its material and efficient cause. Śaṅkara argues that causality implies that the cause has the power to produce an effect where the power is not different from the cause and the effect from the power. '*Kāraṇasyātmabhūtā śaktiḥ, śakteśca ātmabhūtaṁ kāryam.*'[56] Without such a continuity between cause and effect it would be impossible to establish any necessary connection between them. It does not, however, mean that the cause and the effect are absolutely the same. *Atyanta-sāmye Ca prakṛti-vikārabhāva eva pralīyeta*'[57]. Nor can the identity of the cause and the effect be reversible '*Ananyatvepi kārya-kāraṇayoḥ kāryasya kāraṇātmatvam, na tu kāraṇasya kāryātmatvam.*'[58] If the cause and the effect were to be absolutely identical causality would itself be abolished. We would simply have an identical and persistent cause without any effect. By its very nature causality implies that the cause can differentiate itself from itself by producing an effect which remains substantially identical with itself even while it undergoes a partial modification as an effect. The effect, thus, is nothing except the cause but the same identity cannot be reversed. The cause has many potentialities of which the effect is only one. The effect is, thus, a limited and differentiated aspect or mode of the cause. Thus the aspect of *Brahman* which continues identically in the world is Being or Existence but the other aspects of *Brahman* like sentience or purity are concealed. The world is a limited manifestation of *Brahman.*

Such a view, however, is open to dialectical objections. The effect has either to be the same as the cause or different from it. It cannot be both without splitting up the unity of cause as well as effect. Even if we split up the cause as well as the effect, the dilemma will occur again. We must face the ultimate and inevitable dilemma, how can a simple cause produce a simple effect which can neither be identical with it nor different? An unresolved dilemma about a thing only indicates its unreality: *Vastuni ca vikalpasyānupapatteḥ.*[59] The solution which Śaṅkara adopts for this situation is to accept the effect as only an *appearance* of the cause, not its real transformation *'Mūlakāraṇam eva. . . naṭavat sarva-vyavahārāspadatvam pratipadyate.'*[60] Thus before its production the effect has being and that being is identical with that of the cause. The production of the effect is the assumption of a new name and form by the cause like the assumption of a disguise for a role by an actor. The identity assumed by the actor is real enough on the stage but ceases to be so outside it where only the underlying reality, viz., the actor himself obtains. For Śaṅkara, thus, causality is empirically real and *satkāryavāda* an empirically valid theory. At the same time causality is for him only phenomenal because reality in itself, in its noumenal or absolute nature, is changelessly eternal. When *Brahman* is understood in His true nature there is no more any question of a God lording over the world: *'Na ca paramārthataḥ . . . ātmani Īśitrīśitavya-sarvajñatvādivyavahāra upapadyate'.*[61] The empirical world of duality and activity itself disappears: *'Evam paramārthāvasthāyāṁ sarva-vyavahārā-bhāvaṁ vadanti Vedāntāḥ sarve.'*[62]

How this is to be reconciled with the scriptural descriptions of *Brahman* in the context of cosmology, would be an obvious question. Śaṅkara answers that *Brahman* has been described under two aspects *nirguṇa* and *saguṇa. 'Dvirūpaṁ hi brahma avagamyate'.*[63] Sometimes he is described as qualified by accidental properties (*upādhis*) of diverse Names, Forms, and Modifications (*nāma-rūpa-vikāra-bhedopādhi-viśiṣṭam*). At others He is described as transcending all 'accidents' (*sarvopādhi-vivarjitam*). These two aspects correspond to the levels of *avidyā* and *vidyā*. In the state of *avidyā* the world appears real and so too is its lord as God. Godhead, then, is relative to *Upādhis* through which qualifications are ascribed to God. *Īśitrīśitavya-bhāva*, thus, is *Vyāvahārika*. *Brahman* as God i.e., as the creator of the world and as the object of worship, with name, and qualities, is relevant only so long as the empirical world of duality is held to be real. It is only in this context that cosmological descriptions are relevant.

Towards cosmology Śaṅkara expresses his plain distaste. He is willing to admit that the scriptural passages do not always agree in their cosmological descriptions but he does not consider it a matter of moment: '*Bhaved api kāryasya vigītatvam apratipādyatvāt*.'[64] Such descriptions have no importance in themselves and the knowledge which they convey serves no useful purpose. '*Na hya ayam sṛṣṭyādi-prapañcaḥ pratipipādayiṣitaḥ. Na hi tat pratibaddhaḥ Kaścit puruṣārtho dṛśyate śrūyate vā*.'[65] The sole purpose of such descriptions is simply to affirm the identity of the cosmic principle with *Brahman*. Śaṅkara, indeed, clearly says that cosmological descriptions are merely hyperboles or mythical stories. 'All of this may be contradictory. No. Since what is being intended is nothing except self-knowledge, all these descriptions are merely a species of *arthavāda* and as such blameless. Better still, they may be regarded as stories (*akhyāyaikā*) told to convey that creation is the handiwork of the omniscient, omnipotent God having great magical power (*mahāmāyāvī*) just as a magician (might create a magical show).'[66] Elsewhere too Śaṅkara mentions two different models of creation'. It is plausible that the omniscient creates the world out of the material of Name and Form which are identical with His own self (as bubbles with water). Or just as a knowledgeable magician shows himself flying in the air without the aid of anything appearing as some one other than himself, so the omniscient, omnipotent God who has mysterious power (*mahāmāyā*) creates the world out of himself as something different.'[67] He says that the second alternative is more plausible, *Yuktataram*. Thus instead of a cosmological science following an ordered system, Śaṅkara prefers the idea of creation being a 'magical' spectacle (*māyā*). If it is a mystery to explain how the Eternal One became the Many involved in Change, the mystery is rooted in the original magic of God which projects the world illusion. From another angle it is the same as the Nescience of man.

Saguṇa or qualified *Brahman* is the same as the God of theists, the omniscient and omnipotent being who creates and regulates the world and whose worship under diverse names and forms leads to His grace. However, these attributes, functions and relations of *Brahman* do not belong to Him only *per accidens* (*upādhi-vaśāt*). What, then, is the essential nature of *Brahman*? There are some well-known Upaniṣadic texts in this context e.g., *Satyaṁ jñānam anantam Brahma* (*Tai*), *'Sadeva somya idam agra āsīd ekamevadvitīyam'* (*Ch.*), *'Vijñānam ānandam brahma'* (*Br.*). *'Yo vai bhūmā tadamṛtam'* (Br.) The primary characteristic of *Brahman* is being or *sat*. The *Ch.* passages describe *Brahma* as the original, non-dual being in which all created being is grounded, which pervades all creation. The original being articulates created or finite being by name and form. Only the original being is true, created being is mere name and form.

Śaṅkara explains that being now appears as 'This being', as so many definite objects of knowledge each with *its* own name and form, *Nāma-rūpa-viśeṣaṇavad idaṁśabdabuddhi-viṣayam'*.[68] With respect to these even the Vaiśeṣika recognizes that they exhibit the universal called 'being' (*sattā-sāmānya*) but that being or existence could not apply to anything before creation. Hence the Being before creation could not be the category of which the Vaiśeṣikas speak. The Vedāntic Being before creation is the immanent ground of 'This' or determinate objective Being. Pure Being is the sole reality, subtle, homogeneous, perfect, universal and whole: *'astitvamātraṁ vastu sūkṣmaṁ nirviśeṣaṁ sarvagatam ekam nirañjanaṁ niravayavam'*.[69] Pure Being is partless and distinctionless, universal and eternal. Determinate being is nothing except Pure Being under self-imposed limitations.

The assertion of Pure Being prior to creation negates the opposite view that there was nothing prior to creation. The meaning is that if all determinate beings or existents were to be taken away what remains would be pure being, not non-being or nothing. Śaṅkara points out that there can be no affirmation of pure non-being because the idea of non-being depends on relational perception. Non-being has meaning only in relation to some perciever: *'asattvamātrā-bhyupagamo'pyayukta eva. abhyupaganturanabhyupagamānupapatteḥ.*[70] Śaṅkara mentions another argument for identifying pure being with pure nothing. Whatever has being is known as having determinate being such as the pot etc. What does not have being is not so known such as the hare's horn. Now *Brahman* is not so known. Hence not having any determination it does not exist. This indeed is the argument which Hegel gives for identifying pure Being with pure Non-being. Against this Śaṅkara argues 'The non-existence of *Brahman* is excluded by its being the cause of *Ākāśa* etc. No effect can be produced from nothing.'[71] But Śaṅkara must admit that *Brahman* cannot be a cause *per se* or involved in real causality. *Brahman* is the cause of the world through the adjuncts of name and form' '*Tābhyāṁ copādhibhyāṁ jñāṭṛ-jñeya-jñānaśabdārthādi-sarva-saṁvyavahārabhāg Brahman'*.[72]

Nor is pure being to be confused with the original, indeterminate being of the Sāṅkhyas which is capable of transformation into determinate objects. Pure being is pure consciousness endowed with the capacity of self-determination. '*Sattaiva bodho bodha eva ca sattā*'. Being and consciousness cannot be distinguished in *Brahman*. Vedāntic Being is, thus, distinct from being as conceived by the Vaiśeṣikas or the Sāṅkhyas, but this very distinction would seem to make it difficult for it to be the cause of the world. How can a partless whole, a mass of sentience be the cause of the diversity of insentient objects constituting the world! How can 'forms' arise without the arrangement of parts ? Śaṅkara's answer is that *Brahman* like light manifests the world of forms and objects and that this world is essentially illusory '*Sarvasyaivāsya nāma-rūpa-kriyā-kāraka-phala-jātasya yā bhivyaktiḥsā brahma-jyotiḥ-sattā-nimittā yathā sūryādi-jyotiḥ-sattā-nimittā sarvasya rūpa-jātasya abhivyaktistadvat'*.[73] '*Niravayavasya satah kathaṁ vikāra-saṁsthānam upapadyate? Naiṣa doṣaḥ Rajjvādyavayavebhyaḥ sarpādisamsthānavatbuddhi-parikalpitebhyaḥ sadavayavebhyaḥ vikāra-samsthānopapatteḥ.' Vācārambhaṇaṁ vikāro nāmadheyam mṛttiketyeva satyam' evaṁ sadeva satyam iti śruteḥ. Ekamevādvitīyam paramārtha idam-buddhi-kāle pi'* .[74] Brahman is described as Being but all determinations are negated of it. It does not thereby become non-being because determinations are themselves dependent or negations or abstractions. Their denial is intended to affirm the infinite reality of *Brahman*. If being were to be understood merely as limited being and non-being as simply its negation, *Brahman* would have to be regarded as neither being nor non-being. Eternal non-duality is prior to all determinations such as 'being', or 'non-being'. What is conceptually determined should be regarded as unreal like the objects of a dream. Duality does not obtain before the constructs of 'is' and 'is not'.[75] Thus *Brahman* is calld *Sat* to show His reality and infinity obliquely, not to describe it as a finite object. To predicate existence of *Brahman* is simply to deny non-existence or finite existence to Him. *Brahman* must be realized as 'being', not 'non-being'. '*Astītyevopalabdhavyaḥ*'. As to the ground for affirming the positive reality of *Brahman*, although Śaṅkara refers to His causal relation to the world, that is only a manner of speaking since *Brahman* is for Śaṅkara the ground of the world illusion rather than the cause of a real world. The real ground for affirming the reality of *Brahman* is the immediate perception of this reality in the heart: '*Hṛdaya-guhāyām nihitaṁ tatpratyayāvabhāsa-viśeṣeṇa upalabhyamānam astītyevam vijānīyāt.*[76]

When it is said '*Satyaṁ jñānam anantam Brahma*', we do not have just a string of qualifying predicates but rather a demarcating characterization of *Brahman.* Merely qualifying predicates distinguish an object from others of the same class, a 'blue' lotus, for example, from a 'red' lotus. 'Such qualifications are meaningful when there are many substances of many classes to which many adjectives could be applied but not when the object is singular'. In the present case as *Brahman* is singular the adjectives refer not to general qualities but function severally and obliquely as a set of markers of *Brahman. Satyaṁ* is that which it has been determined to be '*Satyam iti yad rūpenayan niścitaṁ tadrūpaṁ navyabhicarati tat satyam.*' What changes or is produced as a modification or alteration is untrue. '*Yad rūpeṇa yan niścitaṁ tad rūpaṁ vyabhicarad anṛtam ityucyate. Ato vikāro' nṛtam*'. Thus by calling *Brahman* as *satyam* all modifications or products are excluded from *Brahman.* '*Ataḥ satyaṁ Brahmeti Brahma vikārān nivartayati.*'[77]

This suggests that *Brahman* is the cause of the world or created being (*vikāra*) and hence itself involved in the causal function and insentient. To negate this the second demarcation or *Lakṣaṇa* as *Jñāna* is appropriate. *Brahman* is the real being underlying the world but it is of the nature of consciousness or knowledge regarded as something complete or accomplished in itself, not as the agent of the process or activity of knowing. '*Bhāva-sādhano jñāna-śabdo natu jñāna-kartṛ*'.[78] The agent of knowing will undergo a change of state and hence could not be true in the sense of being unalterable. Nor could it be 'infinite' because that is infinite which cannot be set apart from anything else. But the agent of knowing has to be distinguished from knowledge as well as the objects of knowledge, and hence cannot be infinite. '*Jñānakartṛtvena ca vikriyamāṇam kathaṁ satyam bhaved anantaṁ ca. Yad hi nakutaścit pravibhajyate tad anantam. Jñāna-kartṛtve ca jñeya-jñānābhyām pravibhaktam ityanantatā nasyāt*'.[79]

Brahman is knowledge but without any duality. It is without any temporal process or activity. Nor does it mean that there is any subject-object relation in it. Neither does the self as *Brahman* know anything other than itself nor itself as an object. So *Brahman* is called knowledge so that it may not be mistaken for an insentient cause or the agent of knowing. '*Jñānam brahmeti kartṛtvādi-kāraka-nivṛttyartham mṛdādivad acidrūpatā-nivṛttyarthaṁ caprayujyate.*[80]

Lest it might be presumed that *Brahman* as knowledge is determinate or limited after the manner of empirical knowledge, it is added that it is *anantam* or infinite. Thus the three adjectives *satya, jñāna* and *ananta* indicate *Brahman* by excluding their opposites—falsehood, insentience and limitation. At this point it may be objected that since the descriptions are purely negative and the referent unknown, the whole description could be of a non-entity (*śūnyārthatā*). This objection is ruled out by Śaṅkara on the ground that the terms *satya* etc., do not give up their meaning (*satyādīnāṁ svārthāparityāga eva*). Thus 'infinite' excludes finite referents and 'truth' and 'knowledge' retain their sense. '*Tatrānanta-śabdo antavattva-pratiṣedha-dvāreṇa viśeṣaṇam. Satya-jñāna-śabdau tu svārtha-samarpaṇenaiva viśeṣane bhavataḥ.*'[81]

Nor should it be supposed that even as an accomplished fact knowledge presupposes relation and activity and is hence liable to be impermanent or dependent. Knowledge is the nature of the self, not something adventitious which could be transient. It is only the mental representations or ideas of sense-objects which (representations) are the objects of the self but arise pervaded by self-consciousness and are hence confused with. '*Buddheḥ upādhi-lakṣaṇāyāḥ caksurādi-dvārair viṣayākāreṇa pariṇāminyā ye śabdādyākārāvabhāsāḥ te ātma-vijñānasya viṣayabhūtaḥ utpadyamānā eva ātma-vijñānena vyāptā utpadyante. Tasmād ātma-vijñānāvabhāsyāśca te Vijñāna-śabda-vācyāśca dhātvartha-bhūtā ātmana eva dharmā vikriyā-rūpā ityavivekibhiḥ parikalpyante.*'[82]

When *Brahman* is spoken of as knowledge, what is intended is the eternal nature of *Brahman,* not any quality, relation or activity. Here knowledge is the eternal nature of all things, undivided by space or time, itself the cause of time, *ākāśa* etc. Thus when applied to *Brahman* the term knowledge does not have the usual sense of activity or agent. Hence the application of the term which denotes a property of intelligence to *Brahman* can only be metaphorical. '*Jñāna-śabdena tallakṣyate natūcyate.*'[83] The same is true of the term *satya* which commonly denotes the universal common to external objects and can hardly apply to *Brahman* which lacks all particular determinations. Hence the terms *satya* etc. being used together limit each other and indicate *Brahman* by demarcating it from their usual references. Thus *Brahman* is indicated by words even while it remains unspoken, beyond speech and thought.

How does infinity apply to *Brahman* without contradicting the identity of everything with Him? Infinity has three senses—spatial, temporal and logical. Thus *ākāśa* is spatially infinite but not temporally because it is a created object. All created objects are temporally finite but *Brahman* has neither of these limitations. As to the differentiation of objects they are identical with *Brahman* because He is their cause. Nor does the relativity of cause and effect touch *Brahman* because the effects are not real. '*Anṛtattvāt kārya-vastunaḥ*'. Being the cause of even 'ākāśa, *Brahman* is spatially infinite. Not being an effect it has no temporal limitation. Since there is nothing apart from *Brahman,* it is infinite in essence. '*Ato niratiśayam ātmanaḥ ānantyam deśataḥ, tathā akāryatvāt kālataḥ, tadbhinnavastvantarābhāvācca vastutaḥ.*[84]

To conclude, Śaṅkara's discussion of the famous Upaniṣadic affirmation: *Satyam jñānam anantam Brahma* is to be understood in terms of reality and knowledge, both inseparably constituting His essential nature and both to be taken in an infinite or unlimited sense. *Brahman* is real without limitation with respect to space, time or qualitative determination. The entire universe of space, time, and causally or logically determinate objects is superimposed on *Brahman* whence alone it derives whatever reality it possesses. The reality of *Brahman* is not to be construed as the reality of an insentient object, whether cause or substance. Nor is it to be understood as the reality of a sentient subject who could be actively involved in the process of knowing objects other than itself. *Brahman* is neither a material nor a spiritual substance. He is the eternal light of consciousness without which there could be no manifestation of the world of objects.

The traditional understanding of *Brahman*, viz., in the cosmological context, made Him the supreme Person creating the world. This ran foul of Śaṅkara's ontology and epistemology. For Śaṅkara's ontology reality must be unalterable and hence causality and change can only be an unreal appearance. *Brahman* as *sat* is, thus, the ground of the illusory world appearance. Similarly Śaṅkara's epistemological analysis of self-consciousness shows that it divides into an eternal or changeless consciousness which witnesses the procession of the psychic representations of objects. The mutual superimposition of the two produces empirical self-consciousness. Just as the world is superimposed on *Brahman*, empirical objects are superimposed on the unchanging consciousness or self. From the principle of non-duality, which Śaṅkara accepts on the basis of Revelation, it follows that pure being, the ground of the world, and pure consciousness or the real self, must be the same and the illusion of the empirical self must be inseparable from world illusion. Thus Śaṅkara's logical reinterpretation of the concept of *Brahman* moves away from theistic cosmology to an illusionistic absolutism.

Not much attention has been given to the axiological aspect of Śaṅkara's theory in relation to his concept of *Brahman*. One part of his axiology is well known. Just as inconstancy, change and transience are marks of unreality, they are also marks of disvalue of *duḥkha* which pervades pain as well as pleasure. The cycle of empirical existence is, thus, to be ultimately transcended. That would be liberation or *mukti*. Since *duḥkha* or disvalue is neither pain nor pleasure nor moral evil, *mukti* too is not to be conceived in terms of happiness or moral goodness. *Mukti* is the eternal and pure nature of the self or *Brahman* who is beyond all dialectical opposites. The question, however, is that the Upaniṣads describe *Brahman* as *ānanda* and *mukti* as fulfilment, not merely liberation from disvalue. Hacker and scholars following him have argued that for Śaṅkara *Brahman* is not to be understood in terms of *Ānanda* at all.[85] Against the plausibility of this view must be placed the fact that the Vedāntic tradition before Śaṅkara as also after him including his followers clearly regards *Brahman* as *ānanda* and also regards *mukti* as positive fulfilment and bliss. His commentary on the *Tai* clearly shows that for him *ānanda* indicates the nature of *Brahman* as much as *satya* and *jñāna* though here too one must exclude the empirical features implying duality and change as in the case of Being and Knowledge. '*Ānanda*' is ordinarily used for happiness generally (*sukhasāmānyam*). It is experienced when the force of some past moral action momentarily clears the dark inertia (*tamas*) of the mind in which *ānanda* is expressed (*abhivyajyate*) in terms of some object like a 'son' or friend serving as its adjunct or *upādhi*. That is known as 'object happiness', *viṣaya-sukha*, and is transient. When the mind is purified by austerity, knowledge, chastity and faith, a characteristic happiness is manifested which is called *ānanda* or *rasa* and is superior to worldly enjoyment. This *ānanda* constitutes a subtle *upādhi* or *Kośa* called *ānandamaya* and although the highest and subtlest of the *Kośas*, it is still not to be confused with the pure transcendent nature of *Brahman*.[86] Śaṅkara, however, also states that since knowers of *Brahman* appear to be happy even without any external causes of happiness, it may be surmised that *Brahman* makes them happy in its aspect of bliss: '*Nūnam brahmaiva rasas teṣām Tasmādasti tat teṣām ānada-kāraṇam rasavad Brahma*'.[87] He distinguishes the *ānanda* of *Brahman* from *laukika ānanda*. Worldly *ānanda* is a fragment of *Brahmānanda* which is manifested within *avidyā* when its quality becomes purer. '*Laukiko pyānando Brahmānandasyaiva mātrā*.' It enables one to understand the *ānanda* of *Brahman* which is manifested in the pure mind from which objects have been abstracted: *Vyāvṛtta-viṣaya-buddhi-gamyaḥ*. This is the bliss which the desireless knowers of *Brahman* have. Śaṅkara here interprets *Brahmānanda* as the *ānanda* of *Brahman* as *Hiraṇyagarbha*: '*akāmahata-vidvac-chrotriya-pratyakṣo. . . yāvad Hiraṇyagarbhādyā Brahmaṇa ānandā iti*.' When all duality is transcended there is only the perfect bliss which is non-dual being: '*niraste tu avidyā-kṛte viṣaya-viṣayi-vibhāge vidyayā svābhāvikaḥ paripūrṇa eka ānandaḥ advaito bhavati*'.[88] It is this innate, non-dual bliss that is the supreme self itself, not the pleasure produced by the subject-object interaction. '*Abhinnaḥ svābhāvika ānandaḥ paramātmaiva, na viṣaya-viṣayi-sambandha-janitaḥ*'.[89] Elsewhere commenting on '*Vijñānam ānadam brahma*' Śaṅkara says, '*Vijñāna* is knowing (*Vijñapati*) and that is the same as *ānanda* which is not infected with pain like the knowledge of objects (*viṣaya-vijñāna*) but is rather tranquil, peaceful, incomparable, devoid of all strains, eternally self-sufficient, homogeneous. In ordinary usage the word *ānanda* denotes empirical felicity (*samvedye ca sukhe*). . . It is true that the word *ānanda* is applied to *Brahman* in the scriptures but they reject experience in *Brahman* by affirming His unity. . . Other philosophies of *mokṣa* too hold diverse opinions. Sāṅkhya and Vaiśeṣika reject the experience of pleasure in *mokṣa*. Others assert the experience of infinite bliss. There cannot, however, be any experience in *mokṣa* because no causal process survives death when the final *mokṣa* is attained. In the absence of bodily support there cannot be any experience. If experience could arise even in the absence of the body, there would never be any need of resorting to causal instruments. The theory of causality would be contradicted. If Brahman were held to be experiencing His own bliss ceaselessly the very distinction between experiencing and non-experiencing, would be pointless. That distinction is relevant only if the object of experience is something other, as one says 'He knows himself and another.' For example, if one attends to an arrow intently one could not speak of his uninterrupted experience or otherwise.'[90] In the case of *Brahman*, too, there is no other, nor any interruption. One cannot, therefore, speak of any experience, or the experience of bliss in *Brahman*.

Thus Śaṅkara distinguishes three kinds of felicity or *ānanda*. There is, first, the felicity of worldly enjoyment which is temporarily produced when a desire is satisfied by an object in a state of mind relatively free from *tamas*. This is *laukikānanda* or *Viṣayānanda*. Next, there is the felicity of the desireless knower of *Brahman*. This is called *Brahmānanda*. Finally there is the *ānanda* belonging to the non-dual nature of *Brahman*. This *ānanda* is not a felicific sensation or experience (*saṁvedana*) of any kind. It is the innate value or axiological self-sufficiency of *Brahman*. Value or happiness at all other levels is but a faint reflection of this innate value or *svābhāvika ānanda* just as all reality or knowledge on the empirical plane is but a reflection of *Brahman*. *Brahman* is not merely foundational being and consciousness but also foundational value (*Paramārtha, niḥśreyasa*). Cosmologically *Brahman* is the source of the world. Axiologically He is the end. The end is often described as *mukti* or freedom but although Freedom is the absence of *duḥkha* it is not a mere absence. It is the nature of *Brahman* and is the same as *ānanda*.

It is true that unlike his predecessors or Bādarāyaṇa himself Śaṅkara is clear that the *Ānandamaya-kośa* too is essentially external to *Brahman*. But he himself admits that *Rasovaisaḥ* does not refer to *Ānandamaya*. In fact he says categorically that '*Yā tu Bhārgavī Vāruṇī Vidyā 'ānando Brahmeti vyajānād'iti tasyām mayaḍ aśravaṇāt priya-śirast-vādya-aśravaṇāt cayuktam ānandasya Brahmatvam'*. Thus the distinction between *Brahman* and *Ānandamaya* does not mean for Śaṅkara that Brahman is not *Ānanda*.[91]

We may raise the question: is their anything in the basic conceptual framework of Śaṅkara which produces an asymmetry between *sat, cit* and *ānanda* so that the last of these cannot be admitted to the same status as the first two? In the case of *sat*, and *cit* Śaṅkara distinguishes between their empirical and transcendental meanings so that even while these terms remain meaningful and applicable to *Brahman* their application does not contaminate its pure transcendence. *Sat* and *cit* have a universal and transcendental meaning. Human experience cannot be understood without them and their reference can be apprehended in immediate experience, without necessarily requiring any duality. Now the suspicion about *ānanda* is that it may necessarily presuppose desire and hence duality and ignorance. This suspicion, however, cannot be said to have any basis in Śaṅkara who clearly distinguishes between the felicity dependent on desire and the felicity of those who are free from desire. What is more he distinguishes the *ānanda* which is an experience from that which is the natural essence of transcendent being. It cannot, therefore, be said that there is any asymmetry between *ānanda* and the other two terms, viz., *sat* and *cit*. Just as *sat* has no necessary reference to determinate objectivity or *cit* to mental representations, similarly *ānanda* has no necessary reference to subjectivity or hedonic experience. *Ānanda* is not essentially or necessarily the enjoyment of an object by a subject but the intrinsic value belonging to being itself. Indeed, even in the enjoyment of a *heteros, ānanda* supervenes only as a manifestation to the extent to which duality is transcended in a moment of lucidity.

Mayeda and Hacker, however, appear to base their opinion not on logical but statistical grounds, viz., that Śaṅkara does not usually refer to *Brahman* as *ānanda*. This is true of the commentaries and the *Upadeśa*. In the former Śaṅkara follows the texts, the latter is written primarily from a metaphysical point of view. Even Śaṅkara's religion primarily followed the path of knowledge (*Jñāna-mārga*). Nevertheless, his religious hymns do admit *ānanda* and it would be a *petitio principii* to exclude them just on this ground.

If the knowledge of *Brahman* as the cause of the world is descriptively indirect and in any case does not relate to the essential nature of *Brahman*, the direct acquaintance of *Brahman* is made by everyone as his own self. *Brahman* is either known or unknown. If He is known there would be no point in enquiring about Him. If He is unknown how could we enquire about Him? The answer is *Brahman* is by nature ever pure, enlightened and liberated, all-wise, endowed with all powers. This follows etymologically from the word '*Brahman*' which being derived from the root *Bṛh* indicates constant purity etc. And the reality of *Brahman* is known from His being the self of all: (*sarvasyātmattvācca Brahmāstitva-prasiddhiḥ*). Everyone knows himself to exist, not to be non-existent. And the self is *Brahman*. Hence we are constantly aware of *Brahman* in being aware of ourselves. Only our awareness is clouded by an illusion.

On the subject of the relationship of the individual soul and *Brahman*, Śaṅkara refers to these earlier views. Āśmarathya asserted that the soul is not absolutely different from the highest Self and yet there is a certain relation of cause and effect between them. Vācaspati Miśra explains that this view was known as *bhedābheda-vāda* and conceived the relationship of *Brahman* and *Jīva* on the analogy of that between fire and spark. Auḍulomi held that the difference and non-difference of the two depend on difference of condition. They are different before emancipation but non-different after emancipation—Vācaspati Miśra calls it *satya-bheda-vāda*. The difference is real but there is an assimilation after emancipation. Kāśakṛtsna, on the other hand, believed that the highest Lord himself is the individual soul, not anything else. Śaṅkara concludes that of the three opinions the one held by Kāśakṛtsna accords with the scripture, because it agrees with what all the Vedānta texts such as 'That art thou' teach. He argues that it is only on the view of Kāśakṛtsna that immortality can be viewed as the result of the knowledge of the soul. If the soul were a modification or creation of the Self it would be liable to lose its existence by being merged in its causal substance. Similarly if name and form were to really abide in the soul as they do in the case of rivers etc., the same difficulty would arise. As a matter of fact they really abide in the *upādhi* (limiting adjunct) and are ascribed to the soul in a figurative sense only. For the same reason the origin of the souls from the highest Self, to which the scriptures refer in some places as similar to the coming out of sparks from fire, ought to be seen as based only on the *upādhis* (limiting adjunct) of the soul.[92]

Those who postulated a difference between the *Jīva* and *Brah-*

man were swayed generally either by the cosmological texts which showed that *Brahman* as creator could not be the *Jīva* or by the texts which made *Brahman* a goal to be attained by the *Jīva* through worship etc. Śaṅkara argues that the cosmological texts intend only to teach the absolute oneness of *Brahman.* '*Mṛdādi-dṛṣṭāntair hi sato brahmaṇa ekasya satyatvam vikārasya cānṛtatvam pratipādayachāstraṁ notpattyādi paraṁ bhavitum arhati*'.[93] As to why the cosmological texts should be held subordinate to those which deny all difference rather than *vice versa,* Śaṅkara says that the texts which negate all differences lead to the cessation of all desire, for when the absolute oneness, permanence, and purity of the Self are once apprehended, the highest end of man is attained and hence there is no scope for any further desires. In support of this the following texts could be recalled 'what delusion, what sorrow can there be for him who beholds unity? (*Īśa.* 7), 'You have reached fearlessness, O Janaka' (*Br.* IV 2.4) etc. This also follows from our observing the experience of contentment in the wise and from the fact that the scriptures blame the false notion (of the reality) of effects, *Vikārānṛtā bhisandhyapavādācca*), 'From death to death does he go who sees here any difference' (*Katha* II. 4. 10). The texts negating all difference cannot, therefore, be understood as subordinate to other texts. Those texts, on the other hand, which speak of the origination of the world etc. cannot help the cessation of all desire. At the same time it is evident that they have another meaning (*anyārthatvam*).[94] Thus the famous passage of the *Tai* on which the *sūtra,* '*Janmādyasya yataḥ*' is based intends to teach the sole reality of *Brahman* on the knowledge of which desires and fears cease.

Similarly the texts which speak of the *Jīva* 'going' to *Brahman* cannot be made the basis of a dualistic theory. If absolute identity seems to stand in the way of such 'going', real difference too would be unhelpful. In the case of real difference the soul could not reach *Brahman* and be united with it without losing its specific identity or essential nature. '*Sarveṣveteṣu pakṣeṣvanirmokṣa-prasaṅgah Saṁsāryātma-tvanivṛtteḥ. Nivṛttau vā svarūpa-nāśa-prasaṅgah.*'[95] Besides if the soul is different from *Brahman* 'it must be either of atomic size (*aṇu*), or infinite (*vyāpī*) or of middling size (*madhyama-parimāṇa*). If it is all-pervasive, it cannot go anywhere. If it is of some middling size, it will be impermanent. If it is of atomic size, it will not experience over the whole body.'[96] If on the other hand, the soul is to be regarded as different and non-different from

Brahman as its part (*avayava* or *aṁśa*) or effect (*kārya, pariṇāma, vikāra*), the difficulty of explaining how the soul goes to or attains *Brahman* remains unchanged. The part cannot 'go' to the whole except in the sense in which it always belongs there. Nor can the effect go back to the cause except by self-destruction. Besides, if the whole does not enter *saṁsāra* how can a part of it do so? And if the effect is real, how can the cause escape *saṁsāra*?

In all these three theories texts such as 'Thou art that' become futile. Because these texts require the realization of a pre-existing and total identity. There are, however, some schools which speak of liberation without the realization of such identity. They hold that the liberation of the soul consists in its isolation (*kaivalya*) which is gained when the soul abides in its own nature (*svarūpāvasthāna lakṣaṇam*). Such a liberation may be obtained by performing *nitya and naimittika* duties but avoiding prohibited or merely desire-prompted actions. Thus the force of past actions will be exhausted and there would be no further cause of rebirth. Hence after death liberation would occur even without the knowledge of the identity of the soul with *Brahman*. To this Śaṅkara's reply is, 'All this is false because there is no proof in support of it. . . It is assumed that because the *saṁsāra* depends on *Karman*, it will cease when there is no *Karman* but the absence of causes cannot be definitely ascertained (*nimittābhavasya durjñānatvād*).[97] That all causes of rebirth have been eliminated by suitable action or non-action, can never be definitely known.

Śaṅkara next considers another alternative which regards liberation as the elimination of the actual state of *saṁsāra* in the soul even though its nature and potentiality for *saṁsāra* remain unchanged. In the Nyāya-Vaiśeṣika, for example, emancipation occurs by the detachment of the soul from the mind. The soul is then isolated from all experience. The potentiality of the soul for action and experience remains but does not find the means for its actualization. Since it is this actualization that is evil, its elimination constitutes liberation from all painful existence. (*Kartṛtva-bhoktṛtva-kāryam anartho natac chaktiḥ*). Śaṅkara, however, points out that in the absence of true knowledge, the soul would naturally be an agent and experiencer and would not even desire *kaivalya*. What is more, so long as the potentiality exists it will inevitably produce the actuality.[98] Only the realization of the eternal identity of the soul and *Brahman* can lead to liberation.

What is the nature of the liberated soul? What powers does it enjoy? Those questions were discussed by earlier Masters. Jaimini held that the liberated soul enjoys the lordship of *Brahman*. Auḍulomi, however, opined that the liberated soul subsists only as pure consciousness or *citi*. The reference to purity etc. should be construed negatively as the absence of impurity etc. while the reference to powers should be deemed contingent on the presence of *Upādhis*. Bādarāyaṇa sought to synthesize the two views by holding that although the ultimate nature of the soul is pure consciousness, powers could be attributed to it in the sphere of relativity where a certain distinction will, however, inevitably obtain between the soul and God who is the lord of the universe, a power which cannot belong to any individual soul. Since Śaṅkara distinguishes between the spheres of relativity and absolute existence, this view of Bādarāyaṇa does not conflict with his own.

It was, however, incumbent on Śaṅkara to reconcile the unity of the pure, transcendent *Brahman* with the empirical diversity of the individual selves. Śaṅkara adduces the illustration of reflection, *ābhāsa* or *pratibimba*. '*Jīva* is only the reflection of the deity, caused by the contact with the material elements such as the *buddhi* etc., just as the image of a person may appear in a mirror or of the sun etc. in water. The deity has infinite power surpassing thought but through its contact with *buddhi* etc. there is reflected consciousness (*caitanyābhāsa*) which does not apprehend the real nature of the deity and thinks of itself as 'I am happy, unhappy, or uncomprehending'. Since the deity enters (the elements) only in the shadowy form of the soul, it remains untouched by bodily pleasure, pain etc., just as a man or the sun are not defiled by what their shadow enters.[99] The *Jīva* or individual soul is, thus for Śaṅkara essentially a phenomenal construct. He calls it the primary construct or *kalpanā*, on which all other illusory constructs are based.[100]

Thus while Śaṅkara bases the doctrine of the unity of reality and of the identity of the soul and *Brahman* on scriptural testimony, he provides the doctrine with logical support by the theory of a primordial illusion which superimposes the phenomenal on the real. This illusion produces the phenomenon of the empirical self, on the one hand, and that of the empirical world on the other. The concept of Illusion or Nescience is the logical lynchpin of the system of Śaṅkara because it serves to reconcile the reality of the pure non-dual Self with the appearance of a plurality of selves and objects in time.

This illusion or ignorance, called *avidyā* does not have an origin in time.[101] It is the precondition of the world of time and duality. It may, thus, be described as 'transcendental', in the sense that it is the innate condition of the empirical self and the world of phenomena in which it finds itself placed. Being the uniform precondition of phenomenal experience, *Avidyā* remains neutral as far as the phenomenal distinction of truth and falsity is concerned. In other words, although false from the noumenal point of view, *avidyā* is not false from the phenomenal point of view. *Avidyā*, thus, is beginningless or 'transcendental', empirically real but noumenally false. It is an innate tendency of the human mind, of the structuring, and, from a noumenal standpoint, distorting empirical consciousness. Although ultimately illusive, *Avidyā* is the power which projects empirical reality. It is the *bījaśakti* residing in *Brahman* and projecting *nāmarūpa*. As there is a distinction of true and false within phenomenal experience, *avidyā* is not to be confused with any empirical illusion. Śaṅkara concedes a relative or pragmatic reality to the phenomenal world. Beginningless and transcendental *avidyā* is invoked by Śaṅkara in two contexts, individual and cosmic.

In both the contexts the nature of *avidyā* remains the same, viz., a superimposition of the unreal over the real. Śaṅkara refers to various theories of error current in his days. 'Some think of error as the superimposition of the characteristics of one object over another.' These may be identified with the *Anyathākhyātivādins* such as the *Naiyāyikas*. Even *Ātmakhyātivādins* have been supposed here. 'Some regard error to be based on the non-perception of the difference that obtains between that which is superimposed and the substratum of the superimposition'. These are obviously the *Akhyātivādins* such as some *Mīmāṁsakas*. 'Still others say that it is the fictitious assumption of attributes contrary to the nature of that thing on which something else is superimposed.' This has been identified with the *asatkhyāti* of the *Mādhyamikas*. For Śaṅkara the normal meaning of an empirical illusion is 'the apparent presentation in the form of remembrance to consciousness of something previously observed, in some other thing.' He observes that the different theories of error agree insofar as they represent superimposition as the apparent presentation of the attributes of one thing on another thing. Thus the mother-of-pearl appears like silver and the moon, although one only, appears as if she were double. What happens in such cases is that the substrate reality is misapprehended in terms of a distorted appearance superimposed upon it.

The problem, however, must be faced that there is an incommensurability between any empirical illusion and the 'transcendental' illusion. An empirical illusion presupposes duality of the subject and the object and of the object and its attributes. The Self, on the other hand, is a non-dual reality. At the empirical level the subject mistakes one object for another. So 'how is it possible that on the inner Self which itself is not an object there should be superimposed objects and their attributes.' Śaṅkara replies first by arguing that the Self is not a non-object in an absolute sense since it is given immediately and is the object of the notion of the Ego. One could object that this forgets the fact that the self could become such an object only when Nescience were to produce the Ego-notion. If the illusion about the self presupposes the Ego-notion, the latter presupposes the illusion. In fact, the *Ahampratyaya* is *mithyāpratyaya* and the Self can be its object only owing to the working of *avidyā*. The ego-notion is, indeed, its prime construct the first step as *Jīva-Kalpanā*. So Śaṅkara turns to a second reply and says that it is not an exceptionless rule that objects can be superimposed only on such other objects as are before us. The unwise, thus, superimpose blueness on the sky which is not in itself presented as an object. This point is specially clarified in the *Upadeśasāhasrī*.[102] In the ego-notion the self and the non-self are not objects of distinct apprehension. They are always the objects of an undifferentiated knowledge. Hence the real justification of the superimposition of the non-self over the self is not that the self too is somehow an object, but simply the power of *avidyā* which does not follow the rules of empirical illusion.

By mutually superimposing the self and the non-self and creating the ego-notion, *avidyā* or Transcendental Nescience underlies the illusion of the empirical self. The world illusion is parallel to it. In both cases the ground is the same, viz., pure *Ātman* or *Brahman* and the nature of *avidyā* a power of *Brahman*. He also uses the term *māyā* more or less synonymous with *avidyā* but especially in the cosmological context. Although Śaṅkara has little interest in cosmological details, his general position is clear. *Avidyā* produces the presentations of *Nāma* and *Rūpa* which form, as it were, the stuff of the world.

Śaṅkara himself raises the inevitable question,—where is *avidyā* located, in the *Jīva* or *Brahman*'. *Brahman* being eternally effulgent cannot have any place for *avidyā*, while the *jīva* already presupposes it. So who is subject to *avidyā* and has his vision warped thereby! Śaṅkara says that *avidyā* obviously belongs to a person who is bothered about it and asks the question.[103] What Śaṅkara means is that *avidyā* belongs to the empirical subject. *Avidyā* is not to be conceived as a cause or a temporal antecedent but as an immanent condition of phenomenal experience. *Avidyā* is of the nature of obscuration inherent in empirical consciousness and its function is to cover or obstruct the light of pure consciousness: *tamaso hi pratyaya āvaraṇātmaktvād avidyā.*[104] This obscuring function of *avidyā* is threefold. It may produce a contrary idea, or a doubt, or non-apprehension. This triply obscuring power affects the instruments (*karaṇa*) of empirical consciousness, not the pure subject.

The terms *avidyā* and *māyā* go back to the *Upaniṣads* where *avidyā* had the sense of spiritual ignorance and *māyā* that of a mysterious, magical power, especially of God whereby He creates. The assumption that Śaṅkara's use of these terms derives from the *Upaniṣads* only is simplistic. These terms were used by the Buddhists and Gauḍapāda and are clearly in line with the Buddhistic tradition. It needs to be remembered that the concept of *avidyā* was common to most philosophical schools and stood principally for the misapprehension of the soul as the psycho-physical being. It did not, however, imply, as for Śaṅkara the unreality of the non-self. For Śaṅkara *avidyā* has a cosmic role also and the concept of *māyā* is peculiarly relevant to this context. It has, however, been pointed out that Śaṅkara uses *avidyā* more commonly than *māyā*.

Śaṅkarạ's theory of self, knowledge and reality is, thus based on a duality of standpoints. He says that the distinction between the absolute truth and the relative truth, between *paramārtha* and *vyavahāra*, must be admitted by all thoughtful persons. The hallmark of the absolute is eternity and invariance, non-duality and the transcendence of all objective determinations. In other words, eternity and infinity are the characteristics of absolute reality. The phenomenal world including the empirical ego and knowledge are not real in this sense but they are not absolutely unreal. So long *avidyā* is not removed, empirical phenomena are real enough for all empirical purposes. When *avidyā* is removed phenomenal experience is contradicted by right knowledge. This liability to contradiction constitutes the falsehood of the empirical world. This contradiction is not simply the ultimate cancellation of the empirical illusion by the vision of the absolute (*anubhava*) but is also something pointed out by reason and revelation.

REFERENCES

1. This used to be standard criticism of the Christian missionaries which Ram Mohun Roy had to face when he presented Śaṅkara's Vedānta for the first time in Bengali and English, and has been repeated since in may ways.
2. *BSB*, 1.4.23; *BGB*, *Upodghāta*.
3. On these two modes of spirituality, vide G.C. Pande, *Foundations of Indian Culture*, Vol. I pp. 60 ff., *Bharatiya Sanskrti ke Mūlasvara*; *Ātmānaṁ viddhi*.
4. G.C. Pande, *The Role of Śaṅkarācārya*, p.7.
5. *Ibid.*, l.c.
6. Cf. Vātsyāyana's *Nyāya-bhāṣya* (*ND*, pp. 4ff).
7. Cf. A.C. Mukherji, *The Nature of Self.* Although undeniable the self appears as an object. The attempt to avoid pan-objectivism tends to lead to agnosticism.
8. S. emphasises the role of the teacher who can reveal the meaning of the tradition e.g., *Īśādi*, p. 744 (*BUB*, 2.1.20) *BSB* 1.4.14; 2.1.9.
9. On the *Pramāṇas* in Advaita, vide D.M. Datta, *Six Ways of Knowing*, K. Sacchidananda Murthy, *Revelation and Reason in Advaita Vedānta.* The standard classical discussion is to be found in the *Vedānta-paribhāṣā.*
10. It is Yājñavalkya who appears to have first voiced this in the famous Maitreyī Brāhmaṇa of the *Br* and Śaṅkara begins the *BSB* with it. It is a well known principle in Sāṅkhya.
11. Oft-expressed by Śaṅkara, e.g, *BSB*, 2.1.11: *eka-rūpeṇa hyavasthito yo' rthaḥ sa paramārthaḥ; BGB* 2.16: *yad viṣayā buddhirna vyabhicarati tat sat, yadviṣayā vyabhicarati tad asat'.*
12. E.g., *BGB*, 2.18: *ātmanaḥ svataḥ siddhatvāt, siddhe hi ātmani pramātari pramitosoh pramāṇānveṣanā bhavati.'*
13. E.g., *BSB*, 1.1.1, *Sarvo hyātmāstitvam pratyeti tato jñātam eveti ajijñāsayatvam āpannam, na, tad viśeṣam prati vipratipatteḥ.'*
14. Advaitic tradition regarded the social self of man as secondary (*gauṇa*) and the 'psycho-physical self' as false (*mithyā*). Śaṅkara quotes *'Gauṇa-mithyātmano sattve putra-dehādi-bādhanāt'* (*BSB*, 1.1.4). The verses have been ascribed to Sundara Pāṇḍya.
15. *CUB* 8.8.4-5.
16. *Ibid.*, 8.9.1.
17. *Katha*, 1.1.20.
18. Cf. G.C. Pande, *Studies in the Origins of Buddhism*, pp. 290-95 where the development of the various Upaniṣadic views about the *Ātman* is delineated.
19. The Buddhists mention diverse views about the *Attā* in the famous *Brahmajāla-Sutta* and the *Sāmaññaphala-sutta* in the *Dīgha*; so the Jainas

mention diverse views in the *Sūyagadaṁga.*

20. *PUB,* 6.2—'*At eva bhrāntāḥ kecit. Agni—saṁyogena ghṛtam iva ghaṭādyākāreṇa caitanyam eva pratikṣaṇam jāyate naśyatīti Tannirodhe śūnyam iva sarvam ityapare, Ghaṭādi—Viṣayaṁ Caitanyaṁ cetayitur nityasya ātmano'nityaṁ jāyate vinaśyatī-tyapare caitanyaṁ bhūta-dharma iti Lokāyatikāḥ*'(*Īśādi,* p. 133)
21. *BSB*1.1: *Dehamātraṁ caitanya-viśiṣṭam ātmeti prākṛtā janā Laukāyatikāśca pratipannāḥ. Indriyāṇyeva cetanāny ātmety apare. Manaity anye. Vijñāna-mātraṁ Kṣaṇikam ity eke, Śūnyamity apare. Asti dehādi-vyatiriktaḥ Saṁsārī Kartā bhoktety apare. Bhoktaiva Kevalaṁ na Kartetyeke, Asti tad Vyatiriktaḥ Īśvaraḥ sarvajñaḥa sarva-śaktir iti Kecit. Ātmā sa bhoktur ityapare.*
22. Vide *Sarvadarśana-saṅgraha* (ed. Abhyankar), pp. 7-12.
23. E.g., *Kathāvatthu: Puggala-Kathā; Milindapañho* (p. 30) where the famous verse of Vajira is quoted; *Abhidharma-Kośa,* 9th chap; Stcherbatsky, *The Soul Theory of the Buddhists.*
24. *Nyāya sūtras,* 3.1.1-27 (as in *Nyāyadarśanam,* CSS) and its series of Commentators—*Vātsyāyana* (*Bhāṣya,* CSS, pp. 114-28), Uddyotakara (*Vārtika,* CSS, pp. 335-70) Vācaspati Miśra, (*Tātparya ṭikā, CSS,* pp. 496-518). Udayana discusses some pertinent issues in *Nyāya Kusumāñjali,* CSS, pp. 74-75 and more elaborately in *Ātma-tattva-viveka, CSS,* pp. 320-75.
25. *BUB,* Preface.
26. *Ibid.,* l.c.
27. *Ibid.,* l.c. *Āgamenatvātmāstitve' vagate Veda-pradarśitalaukika-linga-viśeṣaiśca tadanusāriṇo Mīmāṁsakā stā rkikāśca vadanti pratyakṣa-ścānumeya-ścātmeti.*'
28. This argument from *Pārārthya* has been questioned by the Buddhists, e.g., see *Nyāyabindu* 3.47.
29. *BUB,* Preface.
30. *PUB,* l.c.
31. Cf. *BSB,* 3.2.21, '*Sattaiva badho bodha eva ca sattā*'
32. *BSB,* 3.2.22.
33. *Ibid.,* l.c.
34. *BSB,* 2.3.7.
35. *KUB,* (Pada), 1.3
36. *Ibid.,* 2.4.
37. *Ibid.,* l.c.
38. *BSB, Upodghāta.*
39. Daya Krishna, *Indian Philosophy,* pp. 156ff.
40. Vide infra 'Debate with other School-*Sāṅkhya*'.
41. Cf. Sibajiban Bhattacharya in *Phenomenology & Indian Philosophy* (ed. D.P Chattopadhyaya etc.), pp. 44 ff.
42. A.C. Mukerji, *op. cit.,* p. 122 (quote from Gentile).
43. *Ibid.,* p. 75 (quote from A. Seth Pringle Pattison).
44. Cf. G.C. Pande, *Origins,* l.c.
45. E.g. TUB, 2.1. '*satyādīnāmanṛtādi-dharma-nivṛttiparatvād-Īśādi* p. 284), cf. *TUBV* (Balasubramanian), pp. 321-22.
46. *BSB* (Tr. Thibaut), Vol. I, p. xcii.
47. *Ibid.,* pp. xciv-xcvi.
48. *BSB,* 1.1.2, reference to the view of *Īśvara-Kāraṇinah.*

49. *Ibid.*, 1.1.4: *Upāsana-vidhi-śeṣatva* or *pratipatti-vidhi-viṣayatā*.
50. *Ibid.*, l.c.
51. Udayana's *Nyāya-Kusumāñjali* represents the high watermark of such argumentation.
52. *Śrībhāṣya*, I.1.5.
53. *BSB*, 1.1.4 (=*SG*, Vol. VII p.24); *BUB* 3.3.1 (=SG, Vol. X p. 386) = '*Utpattyāpti-Vikāra-saṁskārā hi Karma-sāmarthyasya viṣayāḥ*'.
54. *BSB*, 2.1.6.
55. E.g., *BGB* 18.48 (*SG, VI*, p. 530) = *Sāṅkhyasyāpi yaḥ pariṇāma-pakṣaḥ sopi apūrva-dharmotpatti-vināśāṅgīkaraṅāt Vaiśeṣika-pakṣāt naviśiṣyate—Pāriśeṣyāt sat ekam eva vastu avidyayā utpatti-vināśādi-dharmaiḥ anekadhā naṭavat vikalpyate iti.*
56. *BSB*, 2.1.18 (=*SG*, VII, p. 320).
57. *Ibid.*, 2.1.6 (=*SG*, VII, p. 245).
58. *Ibid.*, 2.1.9 (=*SG*, VII, p. 299).
59. *Ibid.*, 1.4.14 (=*SG*,VII, p. 250).
60. *Ibid.*, 2.1.18 (=*SG*, VII, p. 324).
61. *Ibid.*, 2.1.14 (=*SG*, VII, p. 316).
62. *Ibid.*, l.c.
63. *Ibid.*, 1.1.4 (=*SG*, VII, p. 49), Cf. *BSB*, 4.3.94: *BUB*, (Īśadi, pp. 664 ff, 668-69).
64. *Ibid.*, 1.4.14 (=*SG*, *VII*, p. 252).
65. *Ibid.*, l.c.
66. *AUB* 2.1. (=*SG*, VII, p. 580).
67. *Ibid.*, 1.2. (=SG, VII, p. 559).
68. *CUB*, 6.2.1 (=*SG*, IX, p. 341).
69. *Ibid.*, l.c.
70. *Ibid.*, p. 343.
71. *TUB*, 2.6. (=*SG*, VII, p. 697).
72. *Ibid.*, p. 699.
73. *BSB*, 1.3.22 (=*SG*, VII, p. 182).
74. *CUB*, 6.2.2 (=*SG*. IX, p. 347).
75. *MUKB*, generally.
76. *TUB*, 2.6 (*SG*, VII, p. 704).
77. *Ibid.*, p. 666.
78. *Ibid.*, p. 667.
79. *Ibid.*, l.c.
80. *Ibid.*, p. 668.
81. *Ibid.*, l.c.
82. *Ibid.*, pp. 669-70.
83. *Ibid.*, p. 670.
84. *Ibid.*, pp. 673-74.
85. Hacker, *ZDMG*, 100 (1950), pp. 246-86.
86. TUB (SG, VII) pp. 691-92.
87. *TUB*, 2.7 (Īśādi, p. 303).
88. *Ibid.*, p. 712-13.
89. *TUB*, 2.8.5 (=*SG*,VII, p. 717).
90. *BUB*, 3.9.27 (*SG*, X, pp. 486-90).
91. *BSB*, 1.1.19 (=*SG*, VII, pp. 61-62).
92. *Ibid.*, 1.4.20-22 (=*SG*, VII, pp. 262-68).

93. *Ibid.*, 4.3.14 (p. 498, Nirnayasagar, ed., text only).
94. *Ibid.*, l.c.
95. *Ibid.*, l.c. (p.499).
96. *Ibid.*, l.c.
97. *Ibid.*, p. 500.
98. *Ibid.*, p. 501.
99. *CUB*, 6.3.2 (Īśādi, p. 513).
100. *MUKB*, 2.16 (Īśādi, p. 513).
101. Thus *adhyāsa* is called *anādi* in *BSB, Upodghāta*, = *BSB*, (Nirnayasagar, text only), p. 4.
102. *Upadeśa*, Prose, Chap. 2.
103. *BGB* (MLBD) pp. 195-96.
104. *Ibid.*, p. 192.

8

Śaṅkara's Philosophy: Dharma, Naiṣkarmya and Mukti

Śaṅkara and Dharma

The empirical self-consciousness of man is mediated by a graded complex of adjuncts or vehicles termed *upādhis.*[1] These may be summed up as mind and body. As a psycho-physical organism man is subject to the force of instincts, desires and past impressions which involve him in a ceaseless cycle of actions and experiences. At the same time since he is of the nature of pure consciousness he cannot find peace in this cycle. Insofar as man acts by his natural impulses and faculties he cannot avoid existential suffering and the fear of death. Śaṅkara fully accepts the old Śramanic standpoint of *saṁsāravāda*. Life is a vale of tears, an unending cycle of birth and death, constantly stalked by the fear of mortality. The wise man does not run after pleasures but rather seeks his real good. The fool does not take note of the Revelation about after-life and holds that this world alone is real, there is no other world.[2] This is the standpoint of naturalism, the Lokāyatika philosophy. It prefers the pleasant to the good, *preyas* to *sreyas,* and it is unmindful of after-life or the law of *Karman* and rebirth.[3] The immortality of the soul, which underlies the notion of after-life and is indeed the basis of all religion, cannot be reached by mere reason but only with the help of the scriptures and a wise teacher.[4] Again, it is only from the scriptures that one can learn the distinction between right and wrong actions.[5] However, even though scriptural and traditional this religion of ritual and worship and of the performance of prescribed social obligations is still unable to distinguish between the pleasant and the good. It is a religion of works and can only lead to transitory results.[6] Man's real good is not a part of the acquisitive life which the unwise pursue. The real good or the ultimate end of human life is something immortal or eternal. Now nothing eternal can be gained by any transient means.

'*Na hyadhruvaiḥ prāpyate hi dhruvam tat.*'[7] And all works and actions are essentially transitory. Even when ritually and morally correct they are inadequate for the highest good of man. The highest end of man is liberation through self-knowledge.

The life of natural activity or *pravṛtti* is, thus, to be distinguished from that of Right or *Dharma*. Within *Dharma* again, the religion and morality of works (*pravṛttilakṣaṇa-dharma*) needs to be distinguished from the life of renunciation and wisdom (*nivṛttilakṣaṇa-dharma*).[8] Within the world of religious beliefs current in his age Śaṅkara generally takes for granted the rejection of a purely naturalistic idea of life in favour of its religious notion. The immortality of the soul, the reality of after-life and rebirth, and the law of *Karman* were generally accepted by all schools of thought. It is true that the Buddhists rejected the soul itself but they accepted the continuity of the individual stream of experience which ensured the continuity of the moral agent and experiencer. Śaṅkara attacks them metaphysically but does not question their rejection of the world as a vale of tears. He attacks the rationalists like the Naiyāyikas for believing that the metaphysical basis of morality in terms of the existence of God and soul could be established rationally.[9] It is the Orthodox Mīmāṁsakas and allied Vedāntins who remain his principal target of attack for believing that ritual and works constitute the prime duty of man and the sole means of his reaching the *summum bonum*.

However, as in his metaphysics so in his axiology, ethics and social philosophy Śaṅkara accepts a duality of standpoints. The ultimate value or *Puruṣārtha* is the realization of *Brahman* '*Brahmā vagatir hi puruṣārthaḥ.*'[10] And the only means for this is knowledge or *jñāna* which may be awakened in the spiritually eligible person by his contact with the Vedic tradition. For those, however, who are still attached to the world and believe in its reality the Vedas have laid down the prescriptions and obligations of *dharma* for happiness here and hereafter.[11] For the common man in the ordinary course of his life thus, Śaṅkara accepts the traditional Vedic faith as the only correct guide. For the spiritually enlightened or heroic person, however, he believes the ideal course of life to lie beyond the pale of all prescription. In Śaṇkara's philosophy, thus, we can see a precarious balance of orthodoxy and heterodoxy! It has conservative as well as revolutionary social implications, as will be seen below. In medieval times it is the conservative implications which were emphasized and helped the growth of a stable Hindu society and religion. In modern times, however, the emphasis is changing.

Dharma and Brahman

The natural means of human knowledge are limited to sensible phenomena. They cannot give any knowledge of noumenal reality or *Brahman*, nor about the moral law or *Dharma* of which the real subject is the individual soul migrating from life to life. Since the moral law operates over the destiny of the soul here and hereafter, its operations are transcendent to human sense perception and reasoning based on it. *Brahman* is man's real or noumenal being and constitutes his highest value, viz., freedom. '*Brahma-svarūpatvānmokṣasya*'.[12] *Dharma*, on the other hand, is the law of phenomenal actions and experiences and is revealed as a system of prescriptions and prohibitions. *Brahman* has to be known, *Dharma* has to be practised. The knowledge of *Brahman* has nothing to do with actions, prescriptions and prohibitions or with a man's social position. *Dharma*, on the other hand, relates essentially to action and is relative to a man's social position.[13]

It is important for Śaṅkara that the spiritual quest for freedom should not be confused with the moral or religious quest for virtue or for happiness in after-life. It is true that both *Brahman* and *Dharma* are *atīndriya* or supersensuous and that our guidance about both of them derives from the Vedas. Nevertheless, it must be recognized that the Veda has two distinct sections. One of them relates to action and lays down prescriptions. The other reveals the ultimate truth for knowledge. It must not be supposed that the knowledge of *Brahman* requires the performance of *Dharma* or that it is itself an obligation enjoined by the Veda.[14] Śaṅkara here distinguishes sharply between the life of spiritual freedom or philosophical wisdom, on the one hand, and the practical life of morality and religion, on the other. 'The knowledge of *dharma* leads to *abhyudaya* or empirical well-being but it depends on the performance of the duties. The knowledge of *Brahman* on the other hand, has for its result *niḥśreyasa* or absolute well-being which does not depend on the performance of any actions. When *dharma* is enquired into, it is only an ideal to be realized but not real at the time of enquiry. Its realization depends on human effort. Hence *Brahman* that is to be enquired into is given as real and being eternal does not depend on human effort.'[15] Thus, insofar as the scriptures reveal *Dharma* they are normative in character but when they reveal *Brahman* they are analogous to positive science. Practice implies options and all options are relative to the notions of men. On the other hand, the knowledge of the real nature of a thing depends on the thing itself. The knowledge of *Brahman*, thus, is necessary and objective, not relative to human attitudes.

An important consequence follows from this distinction. Since unlike *Dharma*, *Brahman* is not a matter of prescription but a matter of fact, it should be knowable by any relevant means, not necessarily by scriptural texts which can only impart information about something independent of them. Śaṅkara grants this possibility and accepts intuitive experience or *anubhava* as a means of knowing *Brahman*: '*Śrutyādayo 'nubhavādayaśca yathāsambhavamiha pramāṇam anubhavāvasānatvād bhūta-vastu-viṣayatvācca Brahma-jñānasya*.'[16] However, this does not amount to admitting that there is any other *pramāṇa* for *Brahman* except the Vedas. *Anubhava* being non-dualistic transcends the phenomenal duality implied in *pramāṇa*.[17] As real, self-dependent and non-dual, *Brahman* is beyond any natural means of knowledge. Although the Veda gives an intimation of it, its only possible knowledge is through identity i.e., in self-knowledge. What *śruti* says is that *Brahman* is to be known as the self.[18]

Value and Values

Following the Vedāntic tradition Śaṅkara conceives value in two ways. It is the ultimate end or goal of human seeking: *artha* or *puruṣārtha*.[19] It is also the infinity of being (*bhūman*, *ananta*) or intrinsic bliss (*Ānanda*).[20] It is to *Ātman* or *Brahman* that value belongs in both these senses. What is ultimately real is also the foundational value since all objects are desired or sought for its sake, all sense of value or felicity is reflection of this ultimate value.[21] No finite object can really satisfy human longing.[22]

In the realm of value as in that of being or knowledge Śaṅkara faces the problem of duality. Although self-realization constitutes the absolute value or *niḥśreyasa* men seek diverse empirical ends while still subject to *avidyā*. When the attainment of such ends constitutes well-being and happiness it may be termed *abhyudaya*. There is a characteristic difference between these two kinds of value, absolute and relative, transcendental and empirical. *Niḥśreyasa* is characterized by freedom from desire and seeking, pleasure and pain. It is beyond the dialectic of action and experience, good and evil. *Abhyudaya*, on the other hand, is of the nature of satisfaction which is necessarily limited in duration, scope and degree. It belongs to a process of seeking, activity, experiencing. If *niḥśreyasa* is autonomy, *abhyudaya* is necessarily heteronomous, a binding and tempting chain.[23] To attain *niḥśreyasa* it is necessary to retreat from external activity into self-knowledge. This is the path called *nivṛttilakṣaṇa dharma*. To gain *abhyudaya* it is necessary to follow the path of virtuous action and religious worship. This is the path called *pravṛtti-lakṣaṇa dharma*. For Śaṅkara Vedic *Dharma* is constituted by both of these.

Two Types of Dharma

Corresponding to the two types of reality, thus, we have two types of value and corresponding to them two kinds of *dharma* or means. 'Having created the world and seeking to maintain it, God created in the beginning the *Prajāpatis*, Marīci etc., and made them accept the law of Activistic Life (*Pravṛtti-lakṣaṇa dharma*) as prescribed by the Veda. Then He created others like Sanaka and Sanandana and made them accept the Law of Retreat from Activity (*Nivṛtti-lakṣaṇa dharma*) characterised by knowledge and dispassion. Thus the Law prescribed by the Veda is twofold, inculcating activity or renunciation. *Dvividho hi Vedokto dharmaḥ pravṛtti-lakṣaṇo nivṛttilakṣaṇaśca*.'[24]

Dharma, thus, is the essential and primordial law of creation, activistic and spiritual, revealed by God through the Veda. '*Dharma* is that which is the cause of the maintenance or stability of the universe and directly instrumental to the relative and absolute good of living beings. It is practised by the 'estates' (*varṇas*) and 'stations' (*āśramas*) like the Brahmanas etc., insofar as they seek their good'.[25] *Dharma*, thus, is the law which maintains the cosmos and at the same time the law which maintains human society. Like the medieval Christian concept of natural Law, *Dharma* is at once cosmic and moral. However, insofar as it is discovered, not by reason but by Revelation it is akin to canonical law.[26] This identification of the natural law of man and the universe with the revealed law certainly opens it to the charge of dogmatism but it does place it beyond the Humean charge that reason can only apprehend the connection of 'ideas', it cannot legislate with respect to values or ends.[27] The argument for connecting the human order with the cosmic order is based on the Law of *Karman*. God has created the world so that the law of *Karman* may be fulfilled and men may reap what they have sown and also be guided in action. In the scriptures we find moral law revealed clearly and objectively. This requires life after death, the action of God who reveals the moral law and supervises its operation, and the harmonious ordering of human life and the universe. Human life is not an accident in a non-moral and Godless universe, nor human society the product of merely natural instincts and reason, conflict and convention.

It should be noted that the role of these natural factors was fully appreciated in ancient Indian social and political thought. It contemplated the state of nature both as a condition of peace as well as of the war of each against all.[28] It realized that what requires the formation of the state as a coercive organization is human evil in the form of ignorance, egoism and the acquisitive passion. Nevertheless, it was recognized that what must guide the ruler can only be Law, not as a mere fiat, but as the voice of wisdom, the wisdom of seers and ultimately of God. In the ultimate analysis social and political life must be guided by *Dharma.*[29]

It is true that the ultimate authority or *pramāṇa* for *Dharma* is the Veda but subject to this ultimate authority there are other means also for recognizing *Dharma.* Tradition, example and conscience are these other sources.[30] Conscience is what the heart says, (*antaḥkaraṇavṛtti, hṛdayānujñā*), an inner faculty of discrimination (*viveka*).[31] It is this inward discrimination which corresponds to the morally legislative faculty of 'reason' in the idealistic tradition of Western thought. *Viveka, buddhi, prajñā* have a wide range in Śaṅkara. Discrimination begins with that between good and evil, *arthānarthau,* and culminates in that between the Self and the Non-self, *Ātmānātma-viveka.*[32] This goes to show that although the *Veda* was recognized as the source of *Dharma,* this did not amount to sheer dogmatism or formalism. There is a moral reason in man which may develop into full spiritual vision. Such a man or *sthitaprajña* would be a law unto himself, *svarāṭ* and yet a help rather than a danger to society.[33]

It may be objected that this can be true only of *dharma* as inward morality consisting of virtuous dispositions, feelings and motives. How can it be true of *Dharma* as socio-ethical or ritual norms? That there is a duality in the conception of *Dharma* is undoubted. On the one hand, it consists of practical norms and is *Codanā-lakṣaṇa.*[34] This applies primarily to *śrauta-dharma* and *Varṇāśrama-dharma.* Social and ritual conduct requires detailed institutional rules which need codification and interpretation. This is what the

Dharmaśāstra and the *Mīmāṁsā* do.[35] *Dharma* in this sense is subsumed by Śaṅkara under *pravṛtti-lakṣaṇa dharma.* On the other hand, *sādhāraṇa dharma* stands for moral virtues. Manu, thus, speaks of the *dharma* of ten characteristics (*daśa-lakṣaṇaka dharma*): '*Dhṛtiḥ kṣamā damosteyaṁ śaucam indriya-nigrahaḥ/ Dhīr vidyā satyam akrodho daśakam dharma-lakṣaṇam//*.'[36] These virtues lead to the highest good or freedom. For Manu the quest for freedom requires the practice of this *Dharma,* the fulfilment of social obligations, the hearing of Vedānta, and finally, the renunciation of active life but not of the *Veda.*[37] While Śaṅkara agrees with the cultivation of spiritual virtues as part of the *nivṛttilakṣaṇa dharma,* he does not agree with the concept of absolutely necessary social obligations or the permanent relevance of the Veda.[38]

As moral order, thus, *dharma* reflects the law of *karman* and the will of God. As rules of external conduct it is the social and religious law. As inner morality it is part of the universal path of spiritual liberation. For Śaṅkara the first two are bound up with the pursuit of the lower or relative good (*abhyudaya*), the third alone is necessary for the pursuit of the highest good (*niḥśreyasa*). It is, however, not the case that *pravṛtti-lakṣaṇa dharma* leading to *abhyudaya* is totally unconnected with *nivṛtti-lakṣaṇa dharma.* If the duties of *Varṇāśrama* etc., are practised in a detached manner out of a sense of surrender to God, such practice leads to the purification of the mind, and this purification makes the person fit for the awakening of spiritual knowledge and thus for the attainment of the highest end, viz., liberation. *Dharma* is essentially of the nature of *Karman;* it regulates all through obligation and serves as a means to the attainment of the good. '*Tacca Karma dharmākhyaṁ sarvān eva kartavyatayā niyantṛ puruṣārtha-sādhanaṁ ca.*'[39] When it is performed disinterestedly it prepares the way for spiritual knowledge and freedom.[40]

Karman and Jñāna

It is well known that Śaṅkara rejects *Karman* for *Jñāna* as the means for man's highest good. The close relationship with the *Dharmaśāstra* tradition which Śaṅkara and the Vedāntic tradition had, has not, however, received sufficient attention. Not only does he frequently quote *Dharmaśāstra* texts, he has commented on at least one, viz., *Āpastamba dharmasūtra adhyātmapaṭala.*[41] Even before him Bhāruci Vedāntin had commented on Manu.[42] His own disciple Viśvarūpa commented on Yājñavalkya.[43] Thus despite the fact that Vedānta taught the way of knowledge for the highest good, it is not the case that it neglected moral and social regulation of common life in accordance with the Vedic tradition. This is true of Śaṅkara also although his clear preference for a life of philosophical wisdom and his trenchant critique of mere ritualism or egoistic social life can create an exaggerated impression about his indifference to social life or action. The fact is that Śaṅkara's critique stems as a defence of the view that wisdom alone is sufficient for liberation. The *Dharmaśāstra* tradition, followed by Mīmāṁsakas and most Vedāntins, was hostile to the view that knowledge by itself was sufficient to lead man to liberation. It believed that man is necessarily subject to social, ritual and cultural obligations and is also burdened by the weight of past deeds and sins. As a result he cannot obtain liberation without the performance of social and religious duties.[44] A popular form of this was the *Jñāna-karma-samuccaya-vāda* which held that the performance of duties is not in itself sufficient for liberation. Nor is knowledge by itself sufficient. It is a combination of the two that is necessary.[45] It has to be recalled that the conflict which had begun historically as one between Brāhmaṇical orthodoxy and Śramanic heterodoxy was in course of time internalized as a conflict between the protagonists of *Karman* and *Jñāna* within the Vedic tradition. The *BG* is the most important example of this conflict and attempts a synthesis. It is in this context of earlier history and tradition that the point of view of Śaṅkara needs to be understood. He himself refers to an earlier interpretation of the *BG* based on *Jñāna-karma-samuccaya-vāda.*[46]

As the *pūrvapakṣa* for Śaṅkara one may note the standpoint of Manu, the most authoritative of the *smṛtikāras.* Manu declares that although it is not desirable to run after desires, desires as such are not banned in the Vedic *Karma-yoga.*[47] Ritual and moral practices presuppose will and desire. If one acts rightly one obtains felicity here and hereafter. Action preceded by desire but guided by scriptures is the way to the good (*śreyas*). Again, of all the *āśramas,* the second or *gṛhasthāśrama* is the most meritorious.[48] Bhāruci says, 'Since this householder's stage is called 'best'. . . one is entitled to conclude that having recourse to other orders (or stages) must be in conflict with the Veda. . . However, the position is this: there are three other stages of life available. . .'[49] Bhāruci, thus, explains both *aikāśramya* and *Cāturāśramya* in which *vikalpa* is permitted. Manu's intent is in favour of *Āśrama-samuccaya* for he says '*Anena karma-yogena parivrajati yo dvijaḥ* etc.'[50] He is also clearly in favour of *Jñāna-karma-samuccaya.* As Bhāruci explains, '*Sarvāśrameṣvayam Jñāna-karma-samuccayo brahmatvaprāpti-hetur vijñeyaḥ.*'[51] He explains Manu's '*vaidikaiścaiva karmabhiḥ*' as either referring to *agnihotra* etc., or to '*Vedānta-codita-pramātmopāsanā*'.[52] For Manu Veda is never to be abandoned even by a *Sannyāsin.*[53]

For both Manu and Yājñavalkya the highest end of man and the goal to which the practice of *dharma* leads is the knowledge of *Ātman* or *Brahman.* They accept the Vedāntic position that the Self is the sole and cosmic reality. But they do not believe that the human, social or cosmic worlds are all illusory. It is the spirit in man that is the highest reality. In its human embodiment it is weighted down by sins and obligations but the practice of *dharma* purifies it. So purified it can attain to self-realization through Vedāntic meditation.

For Śaṅkara the highest good (*niḥśreyasa*) of man is his only real good (*śreyas*) and it does not in any way depend on the pursuit of the lower good (*abhyudaya*). The two pursuits are in fact contradictory: 'the pursuit of liberation requires the renunciation of the life of action in search of diverse empirical goods. Action binds, it does not liberate. Only knowledge can liberate. To talk of the synthesis of action and knowledge is senseless. It is necessary for the person who seeks liberation to renounce all works: '*mumukṣoḥ sarvakarma-sannyāsa-vidhānāt.*'[54]

These views proceed from how Śaṅkara conceives liberation and action. Liberation is not a product, nor a modification, nor is it an improvement or refinement, nor something to be attained.[55] Liberation, therefore, dose not depend on any kind of causation action or movement. It is simply the nature of *Brahman* and is eternal and independent. Śaṅkara himself mentions a very sensible objection to this as follows. It might be said that release could be a quality of the Self which is hidden and becomes manifest when the Self is purified by some action; just as the quality of clearness becomes manifest in a mirror when the mirror is cleaned by means of the action of rubbing. This objection puts in a nutshell the whole theory of purification through the performance of prescribed actions, ritual or moral. Śaṅkara, however, considers this objection invalid, because the Self cannot be the substratum of any action. There can be no action which does not alter its substratum. Hence if the Self were modified by an action it would become impermanent.[56] Hence no action can abide in the Self. Nor can the Self be purified by an action abiding in something else since it has no relation to anything else. A further objection is natural here. If the Self cannot be affected by any action, all purifying ritual would be useless, which would contradict the scriptures. Śaṅkara answers that what is purified by such ritual is only the embodied, empirical self i.e., the Self insofar as it is under the power of *Avidyā*.[57] It is only the principle of the Ego (*ahaṁkārtṛ*) that is the agent in all cognitions, accomplishes all actions and experiences their results.[58]

The point of Śaṅkara's argument is that action belongs to the empirical self while liberation belongs to the real self. Action can only bind the empirical self, not liberate it. Action springs from desires and egoism and is subject to causal determinism as well as moral retribution. Actions can make the empirical self better or worse, happy or miserable but they keep it revolving in the beginningless cycle of *saṁsāra*. There can be no liberation unless one knows one's own true nature. One has to realize that one has been suffering from a radical mistake about oneself. To be liberated is *to know* oneself and *to be* what one really is. It is not *to do* or *to become* something.

In the earlier Vedic tradition will or the ability to act is an essential and precious possession of man who recognizes the ideals of a ritual and moral order. By his volition and resolve, *saṅkalpa* and *kratu*, man can make himself better and realize his ideals. His actions embody his freedom and responsibility. Man is in a deep sense a social and religious being who continues the tradition of his ancestors and teachers and worships the Gods. On this view, if one so desires, one may exercise this very power of the will to control the mind and attain the highest end. '*Ayam tu paramo dharmo yad yogenātma-darśanam*.'[59] It sees a kind of continuity between the lower and the higher good, between transient and everlasting felicity. Originally heavenly felicity after death was imagined on the model of felicity in this life. Later as *Brahman* came to be conceived as the one God behind all the gods and inner worship or meditation came to supplement and partly substitute external ritual, the highest end as the union with *Brahman* was conceived as the result of such worshipful meditation. 'Going to the world of some god or gods' (*devaloka*) was 'union with *Brahman*' (*Brahma-sampatti*). At the same time, since the idea of Rebirth and *Karman* had already been imbibed, it was added that man would be 'released' from its toil by attaining to *Brahman* which would be possible if he is freed from the force of his past deeds and acquires meditative vision of *Brahman*. Thus to the performance of obligatory duties and ritual were added meditation and ascetic detachment as constituting the way to the highest good. It should also be noted that in this process an ambiguity came to envelop the word *Karman*. To its old Vedic sense of being something good and valued, a new pejorative sense came to be added from the context of *saṁsāra*. *Karman* is an expression of freedom and also of bondage, a means to human betterment and happiness through the favour of the gods or God and also a barrier to the transcendence of the human condition and time.

This orthodox Vedic point of view which synthesizes the ancient Brāhmaṇical and Śramanic ideas and values is fully reflected in the *Brahmasūtras* and the *Bhagavadgītā*. The *BS* (II. 3.33-39) maintain that the Self is an agent: *Kartā śāstrārthavattvāt*. Since this disagrees with Śaṅkara's view he argues that the Self is an agent only when connected with the instruments of action like *buddhi* etc., but it ceases to be so when it is disassociated from them.[60] He justifies this interpretation by interpreting *BS* (II. 3.40): 'Just as the carpenter acts in both ways:' to mean 'Just as the carpenter works so long as he wields his instruments, and rests after having laid them aside.' The *sūtra*, however, more naturally means that the carpenter has the power to act or not to act. This would indicate that the soul has the essential capacity of action. In the stage (*āśrama*) of mendicancy when prescribed ritual etc., are excluded, meditation is enjoined and knowledge is regarded as the source of the highest good. Nevertheless the actions enjoined by the scriptures are to be respected because they are conducive to the rise of knowledge. In the *BG* similarly it is insisted upon that prescribed obligations should not be neglected even though mere ritual and actions are considered inadequate.[61]

From this state of the Vedāntic tradition two different but not unconnected questions arise for Śaṅkara. There is the theoretical question. Is it possible for the Self to act? Can action lead to liberation? And there is the practical question. Are prescribed duties obligatory for all? Is their performance relevant to the seeking for liberation? On the theoretical side Śaṅkara clearly returns a negative answer. Its force, however, is modified by the fact that what is impossible for the noumenal Self is nevertheless possible for the empirical Self. Thus although action as such cannot directly lead to liberation, it can still be prescribed for the empirical self. As for the relevance of such action to liberation, Śaṅkara admits an indirect kind of relevance. He remarks 'knowledge when produced requires nothing else for its result (*phala siddhi*) but it does require something else for its own production.'[62] In support of this he quotes a telling *smṛti* passage 'Actions lead to the working out of defilements (*kaṣāya pakti*) but knowledge is the ultimate goal. When the defilements have been 'matured' knowledge begins.' '*Kaṣāye karmabhiḥ pakve tato Jñānaṃ pravartate.*'[63]

Śaṅkara distinguishes between two aspects of the performance of works. One aspect of *Karman* is the practice of moral duties and virtues, another is the performance of prescribed religious ritual and worship. Now the seeker of knowledge must possess calmness of mind, must subdue his senses and so on. These are required even if sacrifices etc. should not be required. Actually sacrifices etc. are also required because the scriptures enjoin them. Thus we have *Yajñena vividiṣanti* etc. It is true that this is not as such an injunction but in effect it could be argued that it should be taken to be so because the connection of sacrifice with the search for knowledge is something new, not the restatement of something already known.[64] This shows the relevance of sacrifice etc., for the seeker of knowledge.

Śaṅkara brings in the evidence of the *BG* here. *Smṛtis* like the *BG* 'explain that sacrifices and the like if undertaken without desire for results become means of knowledge for those who seek *mokṣa*.'[65] Hence sacrifices and the like, on the one hand, and calmness of mind and so on, on the other are to be viewed as means of knowledge. The former, however, should be regarded as remote or indirect means while the latter should be viewed as approximate or direct means of knowledge. '*Tasmād Yajñādīni śama-damādīni ca yathāśramaṁ sarvāṇyevāśrama-karmāṇi vidyotpattāvapekṣitavyāni. Tatrāpyevamvid iti vidyā-saṁyogāt pratyāsannāni vidyā-sādhanāni śamādīni vividiṣā-saṁyogāttu bāhyatarāṇi yajñadīnīti vivektavyam.*'[66]

As far as sacrificial works are concerned their results have no connection with the result of knowledge. They are only connected with the origination of knowledge. They are not a subordinate means cooperating with the principal means towards its fruit. The ritual obligations are, in fact, not necessary. They are relevant only for those who are subject to them as part of their *Āśrama* obligation.

Action is essentially a function of the will which flows into speech and physical activity. Its egoistic presupposition places it within *avidyā*, its association with desire and feelings gives it a moral dimension and produces 'transcendent' results, its physical embodiment gives it causal power. Śaṅkara rejects the analysis of action as proposed by Sāṅkhya, Buddhism and Vaiśeṣika. For the Sāṅkhya action is the outcome of the ceaseless changes of the *guṇas*. For the Buddhists the action and the agent are the same. For the Vaiśeṣika the Self sometimes acts, sometimes remains inactive. The true Vedāntic view, on the other hand, is that action as change, causation and motion is something superimposed on the Self by Nescience. So long the Self is subject to egoistic illusion it cannot abandon action radically. When it is freed from the illusion it sees itself as actionless.

In what sense, then, does action serve the process of self-realization? The real view of Śaṅkara is that ultimately action cannot serve but can only hinder such a process. Nevertheless, one cannot give up action simply by formal renunciation or forcible inactivity. As one performs duties without desiring any advantage for oneself, one's mind is gradually purified of the taint of desires and attachments. What is more, the disinterested performance of duty reduces the burden of past sins. Besides, even if ritualistic obligations have to be formally renounced in some *āśramas*, one is not thereby freed from all duties because in those *āśramas* purely moral duties are recognized such as practising continence, austerities, truth, peace of mind, control of the senses and non-violence. The cultivation of such virtues is part of practical life and leads to the purification of the mind. Then there is the practice of meditation (*Upāsanā*) and devotional worship (*bhakti*) which are also of the nature of action. These are directly helpful in the rise of knowledge. They purify the mind, destroy past sin and fit the mind for enlightenment. It may be remarked here that the purification of the mind in this context is the eradication of sinful and worldly desires, the reduction of the obstructive force of past *karman*, and the containment of the habitual distraction of the mind.

A man may act out of merely natural impulse in disregard of Vedic injunctions. This brings him degradation after death. He may engage in ritualistic activity in pursuance of desires or may practise other good actions in a similar state of mind. He would then gain happiness and advancement in his future life. If he acts without desire out of a sense of duty, his mind is gradually purified. When his mind has been purified and he is without desire for what is external, transient, associated with ends and means, and resulting from the impressions of past acts, the desire to know the Self arises in him.

Practically, then, Śaṅkara modifies his extreme position, or rather, it would be truer to say that he frames his extreme position to contradict the extreme position of those who hold that action leads to liberation or is at least a *sine qua non* for it. Against them Śaṅkara points out that liberation is not an effect to be produced, that action has no direct connection with liberation and that knowledge has no necessary connection with action. At the same time Śaṅkara accepts the moderate position that in common practice action of a certain kind—desireless, meditative, purely moral helps to reduce the obstacles to the rise of knowledge. In this sense alone a certain combination of action and knowledge is possible. '*Jvara-maraṇa-kāryayor api dadhi-viṣayor guḍa-mantra-saṁyuktayoḥ tṛpti-puṣṭi-kārya-darśanāt. Tad vat karmaṇopi jñānasaṁyuktasya mokṣa-kāryopapatteḥ. . . Jñānasyaiva hi prāpakaṁ satkarma praṇāḍyā mokṣa-kāraṇam ityupacaryate.*'[67]

The nature of meditation and its relevance to knowledge and liberation need to be specially examined since it was a common belief even among the Vedāntins that meditation is necessary for self-realization. Śaṅkara, on the other hand, is quite emphatic that meditation falls within the realm of action and although it may be helpful and even required in some cases, it is not logically necessary for the rise of self-knowledge. He points out that *upāsanā* is the repetitive continuity of the same idea: '*upāsanaṁ nāma samāna-pratyaya pravāhakaraṇam.*'[68] It is the same as *nididhyāsana* and is a process of action in which the same idea is repeated continuously. '*upāsanam nididhyāsanam cetyantarṇītāvṛtti-guṇaiva kriyā-bhidhīyate.*'[69] For Śaṅkara this *upāsanā* or *nididhyāsana* may or may not be required to follow *śravana* or *śravaṇa* and *manana* depending on the degree of obstruction present in the mind to the realization of the Advaitic idea. Speaking of *dhyāna-yoga*, again, he says that it follows *karma-yoga* as a more internal process. If one practises *karma-yoga* in the right spirit of detachment one may easily approach *dhyāna-yoga*, because the secret of *dhyāna-yoga* is inner tranquillity (*śama*), ultimately not-acting or not-thinking. '*nakiñcid api cintayet' eṣa yogasya paramo vidhiḥ.*'[70] Owing to its suppression of desires, undistracted tranquillity and withdrawal from external objects *dhyāna-yoga* is near to *Jñāna* but it is still a kind of action since its content is still a mental idea or *pratyaya* which is maintained as a uniform flow through steady effort (*dhṛti*). The whole process of *karma-yoga*, thus, begins with desireless action and culminates in the 'actionless' effort of *Dhyāna-yoga, Nididhyāsana* or *Upāsanā*. The whole process purifies the mind and prepares it for the rise of knowledge.

While action depends on the human will which is free to follow or disregard natural impulses or prescribed norms, knowledge has a necessary character depending on the nature of its object. Knowledge, thus, is fundamentally different from action which is part of an objective and causal process. The relationship between action and its result is causal while the relationship between knowledge and its object is the timeless, one of revelation and its content. Knowledge arises when its subject is brought into contact with its object by the mediation of a valid means of knowledge or *pramāṇa*. It is the function of *pramāṇa* to remove the obscuration of the object. The result of this occurs to the subject who is the proper source of illumination.[71] The radical distinction between the subject and the object is not observed in empirical knowledge and hence a transcendental error infects all empirical knowledge. This, however, does not affect the empirical validity of such knowledge, which depends only on the proper functioning of valid means of knowledge or *pramāṇa*. There is, thus, a distinction between the unnegatable truth of absolute knowledge which is non-dual, non-temporal, non-relational and non-discursive, on the one hand, and the fallible truth of empirical knowledge which is particular and relational. Although even valid empirical knowledge is within transcendental error it is still possible for it to indicate the rule of that error and to point out self-critically the truth beyond it in a unique manner. Thus, according to Śaṅkara, although the revealed Word is within Nescience, it is still a valid means of knowledge and the only one which can intimate the truth of non-duality. As an example of how something within an illusion may be a pointer to something real beyond it, Śaṅkara refers to the fact that a dream though illusory may still contain portents of a real future.[72] The famous modern example of the chemist Kekule may be mentioned here.[73] Śaṅkara again, mentions a different kind of example when he says that symbols like written characters are able to communicate sounds through a false identification. 'This is *a* etc.'[74] Both these examples contain the seeds of profound arguments. That some elements in an illusion may point beyond it, suggests that within the illusion divine grace has constituted the Vedic revelation so that men could be awakened from the illusion. The Great

Magician has left a clue for those who are not satisfied with the magical show. The other example points out that a symbol is false as 'name and form' but may have a real significance. The role of the revealed word in relation to reality is symbolic in this sense. It is part of the world of Name and Form but reveals the real beyond it. "Nor can the truth of the principle of non-duality be impugned on the ground that the *mokṣa-śāstra* itself belongs to the world of unreality. It is reasonable to regard the entire world of phenomenal existence (*Vyavahāra*) as true as long as the knowledge of *Brahman* being the Self has not arisen, just as the dream world is considered to be true until one awakes. . . It is, moreover, known from the experience of scientific observers (*anvaya-vyatireka-Kuśalānām*) that such and such dreams are auspicious, others inauspicious. Also it is a matter of experience that the knowledge of the real syllables *akāra* etc., is reached by means of the lines which are not the real (syllables) but constitute the written letters (*rekhānṛtākṣara-pratipatteḥ*).'[75]

It is a fact that the hearing and study of the *Vedas* have been prescribed as a means to the knowledge of the Self and knowledge actually follows the practice of such prescriptions. Such knowledge cannot be described as useless or false since it destroys Nescience. This finally disposes of the problem of how the *Vedas* falling within the world of illusion can be the source of true knowledge. As Śaṅkara says elsewhere '*Na hi dṛṣṭe anupupannaṁ nāma.*'[76]

A common view found among other Vedāntins was that the mere hearing of the Vedāntic *Mahāvākyas* like *Tattvamasi* does not lead to the direct knowledge of the Self. They argued that statements like '*Ātmetyevopāsīta*' or '*Ātmāvā are draṣṭavyaḥ*' etc., contain practical injunctions and require that meditation—*upāsanā* or *nididhyāsana*—on their meaning must be practised so that direct knowledge may arise.[77] This requirement of the combination of intellectual and practical methods was another expression of *Jñāna-karma-samuccaya-vāda*. Three different versions of it were propounded by Brahmadatta, Maṇḍana and Bhartṛprapañca. Sureśvara summarizes the view of Brahmadatta thus 'Some declare on the strength of their tradition that the knowledge of the form 'I am *Brahman*', which arises from the Vedāntic statement, does not eradicate Nescience by its mere arising. That comes about only by its practice over a long time when the accumulated force of *bhāvanā* eradicates *ajñāna*.'[78] Śaṅkara too refers to this view: '*Apare varṇayanti upāsanena ātma-viṣayaṁ viśiṣṭam vijñānāṇantaram bhāvayet, tenātmā jñāyate, avidyā-nivartakam ca tadeva, nātma viṣayaṁ veda-vākya-janitaṁ vijñānam iti.*'[79] Bhartṛprapañca being a believer in *Bhedābheda* naturally tended to accept *jñāna-karmasamuccaya.*[80] Maṇḍana too supported the need of meditation or Prasaṅkhyāna. He interprets Vedāntic texts like '*Vijñāya prajñāṁ kurvīta*' as meaning that having obtained indirect knowledge (*parokṣa-jñāna*) from the Vedic statements one should practise meditation which leads to direct realisation. It is an inherent limitation of verbal knowledge that it is relational (*saṁsṛṣṭa-viṣaya*) and indirect.[81]

Śaṅkara rejects all those alternatives—*śravaṇādi-vidhi, dhyāna-niyoga, prasaṅkhyāna.* For him in '*Ātmetyevopāsīta*' or *śrotavyaḥ*' etc., no injunction of any kind is involved, neither original nor restrictive. 'The sentence, 'The Self alone is to be meditated upon', is not an *apūrva-vidhi* (original injunction). Why? Because apart from the knowledge arising from the affirmation of the nature of the self and the denial of the non-Self, there is nothing left to be done, either mentally or outwardly.' An injunction (*vidhi*) is relevant where after hearing it, an additional activity on the part of a man is required as in such sentences as 'one who desires heaven must perform the new and full moon sacrifices'. But in the case of statements such as, 'Not this, not this', there is no scope for human activity as in the case of the new and full moon sacrifices etc., because that knowledge removing ignorance puts an end to all activity. *'Naca tan nivṛttau pravṛtti-rupapadyate.'*[82] However, Śaṅkara does admit elsewhere a limited *niyama-vidhi,* though Sureśvara seeks to explain it away.[83]

Knowledge, thus, is not the subject of any injunction. Nor does it require any meditative practice since it arises simply from hearing the Vedāntic statements, *mahāvākyas.* But can verbal knowledge be immediate? Śaṅkara and many of his followers believe that it can be so provided the knowledge is of the knower himself. Self-knowledge is essentially immediate. In the state of *avidyā* it is covered by object-knowledge and becomes object-mediated. The *mahāvākyas* enable one to recover one's true identity and discard the illusion from which one had been suffering. Since the Self is always present immediately, its recovery from the midst of an illusory self-identity may be effected by verbal intimation. The story of the prince brought up by the huntsman related by Draviḍācārya has been referred to by Śaṅkara.[84] Sentences like *'Daśamastvamasi'* also illustrate a situation where words give immediate recognition.

Even if verbal knowledge may sometime be immediate, can words give knowledge of the Self or *Brahman*? Is not language confined to empirical objects, finite and relational? Śaṅkara's answer is that while language cannot describe or define *Brahman*, it can indicate it obliquely by a process of negation. Thus terms like 'being' or 'knowledge' may indicate *Brahman* when they are freed from all limiting determinations. *Brahman* is to be reached through the negation of all determination i.e. as what is properly infinite. That words as used do not lead to merely abstract knowledge is ensured by the fact that *Brahman* is immediately given in the ego-notion. It is the negation of the delimitations of the empirical Self that leads to the infinite Self or *Brahman*. Thus words can give the knowledge of the Self or *Brahman* obliquely through negation. *Brahman* is indicated by words, not stated (*lakṣyate na tu ucyate*).[85]

How does the *mahāvākya* convey its meaning? Later philosophers tried to define the precise nature of *lakṣaṇā* here in terms of a *jahad ajahal lakṣaṇā*.[86] Śaṅkara says, 'The sentence '*Tattvamasi*' teaches that the meaning of the term '*tvam*' is identical with that of 'tat'. Now the latter term denotes the subject of the present context, viz., the real and sentient *Brahman* (*sad Brahma īkṣitṛ*) which is the cause etc., of the world, and which is well known from the scriptures such as 'Brahman is Truth and knowledge infinite' (*Tai* II.); 'Brahman is knowledge and bliss' (*Br.* III. 8. 11); 'unseen seer' (*Br.* III 8. 11) 'unknown Knower' (*Ibid.*) 'unborn' (*Mu* II. 1.2); 'unaging, deathless' (*Br.* IV. 4.25); 'Neither gross, nor subtle, neither short, nor long'(*Br.* III 8.8). In these texts terms such as 'unborn' exclude existential alterations such as 'coming into being' etc.; such terms as 'not gross' exclude the properties of substances such as grossness; and by such terms as 'knowledge' etc., is stated its sentient and luminous nature. This entity which is free from all the features characteristic of *saṁsāra* and is of the nature of experience (*anubhavātmaka*), and called *Brahman*—is known to those learned in the Vedānta, as the meaning of the term *Tat*. Similarly the import of the term *Tvam* is the inward self (*pratyagātman*), the hearer, of whom the nature on reflection beginning from the body is ultimately determined as consciousness.[87] Thus having understood that *tat* refers to the transcendent Brahman and *tvam* to ones own Self, the identity of the two has to be understood in terms of pure intelligence from which all superimpositions have been negated. The ego is superimposed on the Self. "This *adhyāsa* or superimposition (of the ego on the Self) is negated on the evidence of 'Not this, not this', as if this presented itself as a reality (*prāptavat*). After that no *adhyāsa-vidhi* can be reasonable. Just as blueness (*mala*) is superimposed on the sky and negated by the unwise, so is the superimposition (of the ego) on the Self and its negation from it.'[88] The superimposition (*Adhyāsa, adhyāropa*) which is negated is *ab initio* false. This process of superimposition and negation, *adhyāropa* and *apavāda*, enables, as it were, a bridge to be built between the empirical and the transcendental, between what the words denote and what they indirectly indicate. Words and concepts denote objects only, not the pure Self. Now the ego and its characteristics are the superimpositions to which words apply directly. The ego, however, is proximate to the Self so that the two are mutually confused. Since *jāti, karman* etc., belong to the ego, words too apply to it. They cannot apply to the Self because such categories do not belong to it. The ego is a reflection of the Self. Words denote this reflection (*ābhāsa*) directly and indicate the Self only indirectly. 'The Self, its reflection (ego) and the place of the reflection (*buddhi*) are like the face, its reflection and the mirror. They are known from the scriptures and reasoning and so is the unreality of the reflection.'[89]

As mentioned above it was felt by many before and even after Śaṅkara that the mere hearing of the *mahāvākyas* does not actually produce immediate self-knowledge which requires in addition meditative practice. Śaṅkara, however, says that if 'the knowledge of *Brahman* being the Self cannot arise on hearing a text once only, it will not arise even when it is heard repeatedly. For if a text such as 'Thou art That' does not produce the true notion of *Brahman* if heard once, what hope is there that the intended effect should be produced by its repetition?'[90] If it is said that words need to be supported by reasoning to enable us to intuit *Brahman*, then too repetition would be useless. It may perhaps be said 'that the sentence and reasoning together produce only the knowledge of the general nature of the object not of its specific individual character'. For example, when you hear that someone is in pain you only have a general knowledge of the fact, not a specific and vivid intuition. If this is so, Śaṅkara argues, no amount of repetition or meditation would be of any help. The specific character not cognized in the first instance would not be cognized by any repetition of the same sentences or reasoning which were available in the first instance.[91]

Thus, for Śaṅkara the knowledge of the Self arises from hearing the *mahāvākyas* and requires nothing more than their proper comprehension. Such comprehension generally requires ratiocination also which enables one to discard one's false identification with the ego and thus reach the Self. Meditation on the meaning of the *mahāvākyas* is not necessary but may be a help in the case of those persons for whom the meaning of the terms is obstructed by ignorance, doubt, and misconception. Various misconceptions may need successive acts of attention and comprehension. Thus a successively progressive cognition of truth may take place through a process of meditation on the meaning of the *mahāvākya*. All this is, however, not necessary for one who is quick-witted.[92]

About the relationship of action and knowledge, thus Śaṅkara himself qualifies his principal opinion. It is knowledge arising from the hearing of the *mahāvākyas* which leads to liberation and requires neither action nor meditation. Nevertheless, the disinterested performance of duties helps the rise of knowledge and meditation too can be a help. With reference to texts like '*vijñāya prajñāṁ kurvīta*' *Śaṅkara* even admits as mentioned before, a *niyama-vidhi*. Thus although a rigorous *jñānamārgī*, Śaṅkara admits the practical relevance of *karman* and the validity of prescriptive *śāstras*. The question really is of the moral and intellectual eligibility of the seeker of knowledge. It is not a question of social or ritual eligibility, but of inward fitness. These conditions of eligibility for enquiry into *Brahman* are 'discrimination of what is eternal and what is non-eternal, the renunciation of all desire to obtain the results of one's actions both here and hereafter; the requirement of tranquillity, self-restraint and the other means, and the seeking of final release.' *Viveka, vairāgya, śama, dama, uparati, titikṣā, samādhi* and *śraddhā*, and *mumukṣutva*, these constitute the principal moral or rather spiritual virtues necessary for one who would enquire into *Brahman*. The person who seeks liberation has to cultivate the very virtues which are perfected in the liberated person. For Śaṅkara this is a rule of spiritual science.[93]

Bhakti

Although liberation comes from knowledge and the rise of knowledge is facilitated by disinterested work and the cultivation of spiritual virtues, it has been felt from the age of the *Upaniṣads* and emphasized by the *Gītā* that the grace of God and loving devotion to Him constitute a prime means of the rise of liberating knowledge. Śaṅkara accepts that knowledge may come from the grace of God and that devotional meditation, and contemplation may lead to the realization of the Self.[94] Just as Śaṅkara seeks the real nature of God in the pure, unqualified Self, he identifies *Bhakti* ultimately with pure knowledge (*paramārtha-jñāna-lakṣaṇa*).[95] *Bhakti* in its preliminary form comprises worshipful and meditative action which was called *gauṇi bhakti* in later treatises. Śaṅkara calls it *karma-lakṣaṇā bhakti*. In this form *Bhakti* is the greatest purifier of the heart[96] and culminates in surrender to God. The highest kind of *Bhakti*, however, is *jñāna-lakṣaṇā* by which one knows God as the pure sky-like consciousness free from all duality. In Śaṅkara's interpretation, thus, it is only in its lower form that *Bhakti* has the meaning of service or surrender to God. What Śaṅkara calls the highest *Bhakti* has no relationship to personal God at all. It is simply another name for non-dual self-knowledge, impersonal and absolute.[97]

It seems thus, that Śaṅkara does not see the new meaning of *bhakti* as pure love of God without any other motive as intended in the *Bhagavad-gītā*. This can only be attributed to the compulsive force of his absolutistic philosophy. The doctrine of *bhakti* as the highest means of spiritual realization, even as the highest end, appears to presuppose a metaphysics in which the spirit is not an unqualified non-duality but rather a 'Community' of Persons. It is true that an attempt was made in later times to give *bhakti* a place of honour within *Advaita Vedānta* itself. Nevertheless, it is a fact that Śaṅkara evaluates *karman* and *bhakti* in his commentaries from the standpoint of strict non-dualism as relevant only so long as Ignorance persists in some form. He identifies non-dual being with knowledge and excludes action and love from it except to the extent that love of God is interpreted as action for the Lord or as self-knowledge. If we were to interpret eternal self-knowledge as eternal self-communion or the eternal and infinite love by which God loves Himself, one could find a place for *bhakti* in Śaṅkara. But apparently Śaṅkara never personalizes the Absolute and never elevates love as the supreme value. In these respects he appears much closer to Buddhism than to theism.

Nevertheless, it is arguable that the system of Śaṅkara is not so watertight as to exclude an interpretation in favour of *bhakti* as an ultimate spiritual verity. The *Upaniṣads* had declared the *Ātman* to be the object of the greatest or real love. '*Ātman* is dearer than the son, dearer than possession, dearer and nearer than all objects.' 'The husband is not loved for the sake of the husband, he is loved for the sake of the Self. Nor is the wife—nor children loved for their sake, they are loved for the sake of the Self.'[98] Śaṅkara says, 'Since love of other objects is only a means for the love of the Self, all such love is secondary (*gauṇī*); love of the Self alone is primary.'[99] These passages suggest that the Self is the original, real or sole object of love. And is not Self (*Ātman*) convertible with person (*Puruṣa*)? The essence of personality is self-consciousness and that cannot be taken away from the Self.

The non-duality of the Self means that the Self is not an object to itself as another but its very being is consciousness which is wholly itself, turned away from everything else towards itself. The realization of the 'qualityless' Self is not the transcendence of all that constitutes the unique value of personality or humanity but rather its culmination in terms of self-realization which should be understood as self-communion, the fulfilment of man's original and highest love, esctatic and rapturous. 'Like one resting in ecstacy',[100] 'Like one embraced by his beloved and forgetting everything. . .'[101], 'This is the highest end, the highest fulfilment, the highest world, the highest bliss. All other engagements are merely fragments of it.'[102] Śaṅkara says, '*Eso'sya parama ānandah nityatvāt yo vai bhūmā tatsukham'iti śrutyantarāt.*'[103] The attainment of the Self is, thus, the attainment of what is loved in a non-dual experience which has been compared to that of ecstasy. How is this love and bliss of the infinite Self to be distinguished from the loving communion with God? The pure Self is conceived as infinite (*bhūman, ananta*), beatific (*ānanda, rasa*) and the sole object of love and valuation.

The Self is also conceived as the source of grace. He is the inner witness and monitor of the deluded empirical ego. All freedom belongs to the Self, the ego acting like a mechanically controlled doll. It is to this free or divine Self that man must turn to in complete self-surrender. Thus the idea of surrender to a spiritual reality which is infinite, beatific and gracious does find a place in Śaṅkara and that is what constitutes the heart of the path of *bhakti*.

It could be objected that these ideas in Śaṅkara are merely an *anuvāda* of some scriptural texts, not central to his system. For him the Self is transcendent rather than beatific. In fact, he underplays the very notion of *ānanda*. Similarly, it is the idea of renouncing the instinctive love for the non-self that is important in Śaṅkara, not the idea of the love for the Self. Self-realization is conceived by Śaṅkara as an example of knowledge rather than of love or communion. His Absolute signifies not the perfection of qualities and values but their transcendence.

Nevertheless, there is no denying the fact that Śaṅkara gives a place to both *Sādhana-bhakti* as well as *parā bhakti* in his system and that this fact has been insufficiently emphasized in some of his modern interpretations. The worship of *saguṇa brahman* as *Īśvara* or *devatā* is logically coherent with his system in which the superimposition of *upādhis* of diverse grades enables *Brahman* to function in a cosmic or religious capacity. The two principal *upādhis* of *Nāma* and *Rūpa* figure in the processes of *avidyā* as well as *Vidyā*. Their use in devotional worship is well known. It is the concept of *upādhi* that enables the non-duality of *Brahman* to be reconciled with the endless variety of the gods and their modes of worship. The *stotras* of Śaṅkara testify to the importance which may be attached to the devotional cults in his system. Indeed, in later tradition Śaṅkara has been described as *Ṣaṇmata-sthāpanācārya*. *Bhakti* as worship of the Gods is simply the diversified expression of the worship of God and insofar as this devotion is selfless it purifies the heart and leads to the gracious revelation of the divine person within the worshipper as his own eternal Self. While as a means of spiritual seeking *bhakti* is selfless worship and surrender, its perfection or consummation is in the inner experience of the realization of God as the Self.

Does *bhakti* require that God should be other than the self and that the vision of God should be one of emotional rapture or ecstasy? To say that the object of love must be an 'other' is to forget that love transcends 'otherness'. '*Madhuripuraham iti bhāvanaśīlā*.'[104] This is the truth of the Vedāntic dictum '*Ātmanastu Kāmāya sarvam priyam bhavati*', that the true object of love is the Self, is not the elevation of selfishness into a philosophical principle. When queen Mallikā said the same thing, Buddha is believed to have supported her.[105] The self that is the real object of love is not the ego. The ego must, indeed, be sacrificed at the altar of the universal or divine Self as a prerequisite of what Śaṅkara calls the devotion ripened into knowledge. 'To enter the mansion of love one must make an offering of one's own head.'[106] Nor, indeed, can it be said that the love for an object must be meditated by the name, form, appearance or qualities of that object. Such love can only be superficial. *'Na khalu bahir upādhīn prītayaḥ saṁśrayante'.*[107] True love must be centred in the unalterable being or self of its object, and that self cannot be really other than that of the subject of love. The whole mystery of love is that of a self-transcending self-communion. It cannot, therefore, be admitted that there is any radical incompatibility between Advaita and the philosophy of *bhakti* as love.[108] It is true that Śaṅkara does not emphasize emotional rapture or ecstasy in his commentaries but some of his probably authentic hymns do evince these in ample measure.

It is important to stress that the distinction of aspect between *Brahman* and *Īśvara, nirguṇa* and *saguṇa,* should not be regarded as a difference in reality. *Īśvara* is not "*Brahman* as merely viewed by the *jīva* in reference to himself and the world."[109] The creativity of thought (*īkṣā*) 'belongs to *Brahman* and is not simply referred to Him allegorically by the *jīva,*' though 'His creativity is like that of the magician, as the creativity of absolute appearance.' *Īśvara* has a dual form. He wields the *Māyā-śakti* and is immanent in the world. He is also the transcendent *Brahman. Īśvara* is 'not a false idea of the *jīva,* a mere symbol adopted for his *upāsanā* (worship).'

It is true that Śaṅkara's Vedānta is a religion of *jñāna* but 'This knowledge is itself understood as an intuition which amounts to ecstasy and does not in any sense mean a supersession of *bhakti.*' Although Śaṅkara's emphasis on *jñāna* is partly conceived as a protest against the doctrine of *karman* especially as ritualism, it is in 'no sense a protest against the religion of *bhakti.*'

Liberation

There is a peculiar paradox in Śaṅkara's concept of liberation. On the one hand, it is an eternal verity, the very nature of the Self or *Brahman* and in this sense cannot be a goal to be achieved. It is not something that can come to be in time. On the other hand, the bondage of man is the very starting point of all spiritual religion. If it is denied, the edifice of religion will be robbed of its foundations. Man seeks freedom but is eternally free. The classic solution of the paradox is in terms of knowledge which can be an event in time and yet reveal an eternal fact as its content. In the case of self-knowledge it means the dispelling of an illusion viz., the illusion of bondage. It cannot, however, mean the annihilation of nature and man, not even of one's own psychophysical personality and past history. The world is not an illusion of the individual soul but the magic of God. If from one point of view spiritual awakening is a recovery of what was never really lost, it is also from another point of view, a transformation or rather transmutation of the historical, empirical personality of the human seeker. *'Ahimiva kuvalaya-mālām.'* The concept of a human being who is both liberated and yet living in the world of men as a *Jīvanmukta* is a concept peculiar to such non-dualistic systems as Vedānta and Buddhism. From the identity of appearance and reality in the absolute it follows that what is phenomenally existent from one point of view is also an aspect or mode of eternity from another. *'Saṁsārasya na nirvāṇāt kiñcid asti viśeṣaṇam.' 'Sarvaṁ Khalvidam Brahma', 'Avajānanti mām mūḍhā mānuṣīm tanum āśritam param bhāvam ajānanto mama bhūta-maheśvaram* / /[110]

Between the spiritual seeker and the liberated person there is a continuity of qualities and aspects. The seeker assiduously practises the virtues which come naturally to the realized person. The description of the *sthitaprajña* in the *BG*, thus, falls in line with the conditions of eligibility for the seeker like *viveka, vairāgya* etc., mentioned earlier. Once spiritual knowledge dawns, *avidyā* with its inbuilt subject-object duality is understood to be illusive. Man is, thus, liberated from the bondage of all practical obligations, social and religious. He is free from desire and hatred, fear and anger. He is imperturbable and equanimous under all circumstances.

'Although the morality of imperatives and norms applies only to the empirical ego subject to transcendental or instinctive ignorance and not to the liberated person, it does not follow that Śaṅkara's *Advaita* is indifferent to morality. In the *Upadeśa-sāhasrī* (2.18) and the *Naiṣkarmyasiddhi* (4.62-69) the possibility of licence has been specifically refuted.'[111] *Na ca niyogābhāvāt samyagdarśino yatheṣṭaceṣṭā-prasaṅgaḥ. sarvatrābhimānasyaiva pravartakatvād abhimānābhāvācca samyagdarśinah.'*[112] The practice of the *sādhana catuṣṭaya* and its perfection in the liberated person excludes the possibility of any egoistic or anti-social conduct. 'The liberated person transcends *dharma* as prescription or prohibition but illustrates the ideal virtues of egolessness and universal compassion, detachment and desirelessness, peace and harmony as illustrated by the description of the *sthitaprajña* in whom the moral will is transmuted into the spontaneity of the holy will. Such a person must regard the others as the same as himself and cannot make any invidious distinctions. Although he has no personal ends to serve he must inevitably help any genuine seeker of truth. This is the characteristic kind of service which belongs to the *Jñānin*.'[113] '*Upadekṣyanti te jñānam jñāninas tattvadarśinaḥ*.

It is clear that the liberated person cannot be immoral because he is free from egoism, desires and passions and is endowed with self-restraint, tranquillity, forbearance, discrimination, non-violence, friendliness, compassion etc. The virtues which constitute the universal morality of the heart are found spontaneously operative in him. Far from being indifferent to morality he is in fact the paragon of spiritual morality. At the same time, it is equally clear that since the liberated person does not perceive himself in terms of any social roles or relations he cannot feel bound by the practical conventions of religious and social morality. He is not anyone's kin or foe, nor dependent on anyone. He expects nothing and feels no bondage or obligations. He has renounced social and religious life from within. Nevertheless, his condition does not amount in practice to a total renunciation of society since he depends on the institution of mendicancy. Even physical living requires some kind of activity. '*Śarīra-yātrā pi ca te no prasiddhyed akarmaṇaḥ*.' Nor is the liberated person without a social role even though that role cannot be reduced to a stereotype. The liberated person presents a living example of how saintliness may be practically realized and thus functions as a source of idealistic inspiration. He also functions as that rare kind of teacher who helps the continuation of the tradition of spiritual wisdom. This may be described as *lokasaṁgraha* at the highest level.

Social Ideas

Śaṅkara's social ideas tended to be generally orthodox. The system of *Varṇāśrama-dharma* as described in the *smṛtis* was believed by him to represent an ideal order but he noted with regret that it was not followed in practice just as the ideal polity of the universal ruler was nowhere to be found in his contemporary reality. Although Śaṅkara accepted the traditional social system and its ideals for the common man he perceived that the force of social obligations depends on man's acceptance of the social persona, roles and relations. It is only within the framework of socially defined identities that institutional norms acquire their moral force. For Śaṅkara all these identities, relations and norms presuppose a basic ignorance about the Self. Man is not a 'species being', a bundle of social relations, 'a system of appercipient systems'. Assuming a social persona, identifying himself with a social image, man misses his real Self and leads an unauthentic existence. He needs to rediscover himself by turning away from the familiar patterns of religious and social activity. Śaṅkara, thus, combines a traditional reverence for the Vedic social system with a thorough-going rejection of social relations and actions from the essential being of man and this comes out most clearly in his critique of the doctrines of the Mīmāṁsakas. Śaṅkara's rejection of the Mīmāṁsaka standpoint on *Karman* has too often been represented as a technical rejection of certain abstract conceptions. It has, 'however, far-reaching religious and social implications. It is the rejection of a ritualistic and formalistic religion in favour of a spiritual and philosophical religion. The obligatory character of religious ritual and its unseen supernatural efficacy constituted a characteristic doctrine of the priestly class. The life of the upper castes was regulated by a traditional ritual pattern ordained by the scriptures which claimed to lead man to felicity here and hereafter. The priestly philosophy did not distinguish between ritual, moral and social order.'[114] In its *smārta-paurāṇika* version renunciation was accepted as an *āśrama* but various rules were prescribed for being eligible for it and for duties which were imposed on it. *Sannyāsa* was not conceived as release from all prescriptions. Thus Medhātithi says, 'It may be argued that for one who has turned away from the world and has renounced *Karman,* there are no scriptural prescriptions. This, however, is not the intent of the scriptures. What constitutes renunciation is simply the abandoning of 'I' and 'Mine'.[115]

Now Śaṅkara rejects the ritualistic conception of human ends and means. The highest human end is not satisfaction but freedom which can be attained only by seeing things *sub specie aeternitatis,* not by any kind of action. He argues that the obligatory character of ritual duties is conditional on one's radically false identification with social rules, or *Varṇāśramādyabhimāna.* Such social identification rests on an instinctive delusion or *avidyā.* Ritual duties, thus, have no force for the authentic or enlightened person or *jñānin.* That this idea did not actually become a solvent of the ritualized religious order was only because the *Jñānin* was expected to be detached from the common run of social life and the mode of social existence held appropriate for him was that of *Sannyāsa* or renunciation which isolated him from the common run of social life. In a way thus, the *Jñānin* was expected to be indifferent to social or ritual claims intent only on his lone, spiritual quest.[116]

Varṇāśrama-dharma signified the ritual-social order which regulated action on the basis of role-identities (*abhimāna*) defined in terms of estate (*varṇa*) and life-station (*āśrama*). For Śaṅkara this order is divinely revealed through the Vedas and the Vedic tradition is the means for the realization of what is really good for man. Man may, doubtless, seek what he deems to be his good by devising means in accordance with his own wishes and fancies, or experience and calculation. Such an order in which men are moved entirely by their own instincts, perceptions and reason without the aid of revelation will not be a 'right' or stable order. Such a society will be an order of *artha* and *kāma* without *dharma* and *mokṣa*. There will be no place for men with a godly nature (*Daivī sampad*) in such a society. It can only be the society of the ungodly (*āsurī* and *rākṣasī sampad*). 'Such men believe in the body being the soul, pursue the principle of 'eat, drink and be merry', and lead a violent and predatory life.' 'They deny that the world has been created by God, assert it to be without any moral law, and believe the world process to be accidental.' This point of view is that of naturalism or materialism (*lokāyatikadrṣṭiriyam*).[117] 'Abandoning the revelation and acting by self-will' man cannot hope to reach real happiness. To the two types of humanity (*bhūta-sargau*), godly (*daiva*) and ungodly (*āsura*), correspond two contrasted ways of life, and the distinction is reminiscent of St. Augustine's distinction between *Civitas dei* and *Civitas terrena* where the earthly City is marked by the love of self, the heavenly by the love of God.[118] In Vedāntic terms, it is necessary for the social order to be regulated by *Dharma* if humanity is to be fulfilled.

When Śaṅkara speaks of the order of *Varṇas* and *Āśramas* he has in mind the revealed and divinely ordained institutions, not the actual state of society in his times. The actual conditions diverged considerably from the original ordinances. The *Varṇa* system was largely submerged under the ever-proliferating *jātis*, and the *āśramas* were in disarray or obsolete. While Śaṅkara notes the decline of *dharma* he shows no interest in the *jātis*. He accepts the *Varṇa* system as the classification of human nature and functions into basic types so that the roles could be correctly determined for social action which in its ultimate nature is sacrifice or worship offered to the Gods. The social order thus, becomes essentially a ritual order. '*Brahmaṇā sṛṣṭāh varṇāḥ karmārtham.*'[119] The creator has ordanined the *Varṇas* for the sake of work.

Thus while the ungodly are sunk in the degrading cycle of egoistic and acquisitive activity, the life of moral and religious activity in accordance with *dharma* constitutes the beginning of the life of the godly. But beyond these two types of human order, appetitive (*pravṛtti*) and ritual (*pravṛtti-dharma*), there is the saintly order. The wise (*Jñānins*), liberated by their wisdom, renounce the life of action and keep aloof. They eschew all social relations and worldly pursuits. In Buddhism and Jainism monastic orders had been created for the support and organization of all those who wished to pursue the life of wisdom. In Vedic tradition the fourth *āśrama* was meant for the cultivation of wisdom after the formal renunciation of works. In the Vedic tradition even this *āśrama* for the wise or the seekers of wisdom was subjected to many rules and restrictions. As a matter of history the concept of this *āśrama* did not originally belong to the Vedic tradition which insisted that Vedic study and ritual should not be given up. However, the popularity of the ideal of mendicancy owing to its support by heterodox sects led to its gradual acceptance in the Vedic tradition as the fourth station of life. In the Vedic ethos *Karman* as ritual action or ritualized social action was the prime principle of good life, and originally the estates and stations all represented the subdivisions of cooperating roles in social activity conceived ultimately as a sacrifice. The ungodly do not sacrifice, they do not give up their egoistic claims and possessions. For the godly, life is a perpetual sacrifice. In the Śramanic ethos the ritualistic conception of *Karman* was substituted by a purely moral law, superior to all human laws and independent of religious prescriptions or the will of gods. At the same time the human good was conceived not as the maximization of happiness but as complete freedom from pain. Since even moral *Karman* leads to pleasure not unmixed with pain, all *Karman* is of the nature of bondage and ultimately evil. To attain the ideal of freedom (*mukti*) and non-action (*naiṣkarmya*), it is necessary as a preparation to abandon social ties, duties, possessions, and lead a life of reason (*viveka*), dispassion, tranquillity, *askesis*, self-sufficiency, fortitude etc. It implies the renunciation of all domestic life, religious ritual, economic and political activities. The seeker of freedom must lead a life of non-violence, chastity and non-possession. Ultimately he must gain pure spiritual knowledge so that his practice of the life of renunciation may become a spontaneous realization. Thus *Śrāmaṇya* stood for an ideal which lay outside the original conception of the *varṇas* and *āśramas* but this ideal was incorporated in the classical *Varṇāśrama-dharma*. It is this later classical version which Śaṅkara has in mind and in the light of which he interprets the ancient texts. In this version the social order is tied by the ritual law and lies between the ungodly and the saintly human conditions but while it strenuously opposes the former, it accepts the aloofness of the latter as an ideal condition valid for those who are willing to renounce the world.

Mendicancy and Monasticism

This concept of *śrāmaṇya*, *mauna* or *sannyāsa* is reminiscent of the Cynic concept of *apathia* and the associated attitude of withdrawal and protest towards the religious and public life of the *Polis*. The concept of a universal natural law superior to the conventional laws of the polis emerged with the Stoics. Even in the Age of Philosophers in China the concept of Wu-Wei emerged as a counterweight to the ideas of *Li* and *Fa*.[120] In India too the clear emergence of the ideal of *śrāmanya* and *sannyāsa* belongs to the age when the later Vedic *janapadas* gave place to the *mahājanapadas* and the Second Urban Revolution. In the actual institutionalization of the ideal a number of factors joined hands. The breakdown of the clans and the rise of the cities implied the emergence of a class of persons dispossessed of their traditional means of livelihood. This swelled the ranks of labourers, slaves, destitutes, and beggars. Some of these doubtless turned to mendicancy also. The old *āśrama* or *brahmacarya* meant a way of life subject to the vows of chastity, obedience, poverty and Vedic study. The Śramanic sects adopted *brahmacarya* without Vedic study and as a final, not as a preparatory, station of life. Numerous detailed rules were adopted for the mendicants in the different sects, Śramanic or Brāhmaṇic. Although the ideal of mendicancy meant the renunciation of social life, this renunciation itself came to be clearly converted into a social institution.[121]

Traditionally the *sannyāsa āśrama* enshrined an essentially eremetical ideal which contrasted strongly with the coenobitism of classical Buddhist organization of monastic life. Buddhist monasticism constituted what might be called an alternative society which devoted itself entirely to the pursuit of higher culture and spirituality, though it depended for its existence on lay patronage.

The wise lived far and away from worldly concerns but performed a regular educative function for the lay society which supported them.

Now Śaṅkara has been traditionally created with introducing the Buddhist model of monastic life into the Brāhmaṇical tradition but the belief needs to be critically examined. For Śaṅkara the essence of *sannyāsa* or *Parivrajyā* consists in the knowledge of non-duality and the consequent giving up of all works (*karman*). The real *sannyāsin* is none other than the really enlightened person who has attained to *Jñāna and Naiṣkarmya. 'Tasmāt Vedānta-pramāṇa-janitaikatvapratyayavata eva karma-nivṛtti-lakṣaṇam pārivrājyam Brahmasaṁsthatvaṁ ceti.'*[122] It follows that since even a householder may attain such a knowledge he too would qualify for *Parivrajyā 'Etena gṛhasthasyaikatva-vijñāne sati pārivrājyam arthasiddham.'* Nevertheless, Śaṅkara insists that such a person cannot be confined to remain in anyone of the first three *āśramas* in which works are compulsorily prescribed. The *Jñānin* or *Parivrāḍ* must renounce works and in this sense can only belong the fourth *āśrama*. For Śaṅkara it is only the person with the Vedāntic knowledge of unity who may rightly renounce works for mendicancy. The Sāṅkhyas, the Buddhists or the merely indolent do not have such right because they lack the qualifying knowledge. As for the rules and formalities prescribed for the fourth *āśrama*, Śaṅkara does not set much score by them *'Vedoktam pārivrājyaṁ na yajñopavīta-tridaṇḍa-Kamaṇḍalvādi-parigrahaḥ.'*[123] This is reminiscent of the quotation from the *Mbh* found in *Vedānta-Kalpataru-parimala-'Kaṣāya-dhāraṇam mauṇḍyam triviṣṭabdhaṁ kamaṇḍalum/Liṅgānnyannārtham etāni na mokṣāyeti me matiḥ./'*

The staff, single or triple, was an oft-mentioned sign of the *sannyāsin* while *kamaṇḍalu, pātra, śikya,* and *pavitra* too find mention. *Yajñopavīta* finds mention in connection with the class of *Kuṭīcakas.* Various appurtenances are permitted for *Kuṭīcakas* and *Bahūdakas.* It is the *Paramahaṁsas* for whom there are no encumbrances or restrictions.[124] For Śaṅkara they alone seem to meet the idea of the *sannyāsin.* In disparaging the obvious insignia of the *sannyāsin* in terms of the staff or water-gourd, he actually seeks to identify the *sannyāsin* not with a formally recognisable group of persons but with those who have actually attained wisdom or *Jñāna.* He is to be identified with reference to his actual spiritual attainment, not his formal membership of a social group.

Now if *sannyāsins* are to be so defined, how can *sannyāsa* be institutionalized? The fact, however, remains that although Śaṅkara regards the essence of *Pārivrājya* to be *Jñāna* and *karma-nivṛtti*, he does not reject the current formal institution of mendicancy. In a way Śaṅkara maintains a clear distinction between the two because while the question of social eligibility does not arise for knowledge, it does arise for *sannyāsa* as an *āśrama*. Śaṅkara supports the view that it is only the Brāhmaṇas who are entitled for *sannyāsa*,[125] a view which is rejected by his own pupil Sureśvara who points out that tradition regards all the three upper castes eligible for *sannyāsa*.[126] Curiously Viśvarūpa supports the more orthodox view which creates a problem about his identification with Sureśvara.[127] It follows that although for Śaṅkara real *sannyāsa* is only the *vidvat-sannyāsa* of the *Paramahaṁsa*, he still accepted the institution of *vividiṣā-sannyāsa* as defined in the *dharma-śāstra* tradition. It may be concluded, thus, that Śaṅkara's conception of *sannyāsa* is consistent with his seeking to organise it institutionally with a view to reforming it in the light of its essential nature. But the question is, did Śaṅkara institute Vedāntic *maṭhas* as organized institutions of residence, education, preaching etc., for the *sannyāsins* of his school? The word '*maṭha* seems to have originally meant simply a hostel or residence for students and others. It is in this sense that it occurs in *Baudhāyana dharma-sūtras, Pañcatantra, Amara-Kośa* and *Daśakumāra Carita*. It did not have the specific sense of a monastery as the Buddhist *Vihāra* had.'[128] As mentioned above the *dharma-śāstra* tradition strongly emphasized the eremitical rather than the coenobitical mode of life for the Vedic mendicants. However, Śaiva and Pāśupata sects came to use *maṭhas* as residences and schools for ascetics, generally attached to temples, at least from the 6th century A.D. For the monastic idea thus Śaṅkara need not have gone to the Buddhists or the Jainas. There are, however, no specific epigraphic references to the *maṭhas* of Śaṅkara's followers anywhere near his times. The earliest epigraphic reference to a Śaṅkarārya who apparently belonged to the tradition of the great Śaṅkara and was a monastic pontiff near Kāñchī has been dated in A.D. 1111.[129] In the 14th century Vidyāraṇya refers to monastic residence as a possibility for the *Jīvanmukta*.[130] It is only from the 16th century with Madhusūdana Sarasvatī that we clearly know about the Daśanāmī sects said to have been founded by Śaṅkara.[131]

That the followers of Śaṅkara should have lived in *maṭhas* following the example of the Śaivas, Pāśupatas, Bauddhas and

Jainas though more or less obscurely as befitted a new sect without royal patronage, is not at all unlikely. What Śaṅkara is supposed to have contributed to their organization could be gleaned from the *Mahānuśāsana* attributed to him. What it inculcates is a sense of discipline and also the sense of a mission. The country is divided into a number of regions and the monasteries grouped accordingly. They are expected to preach the spiritual and religious principles and to cooperate among themselves. Whether Śaṅkara established four or five principal monasteries in the four corners of the country and appointed his principal disciples to each one of these, is quite uncertain since the traditions of these monasteries do not go beyond the medieval age. It is, however, quite plausible that Śaṅkara established some centres of worship, study and preaching in the course of his own pilgrimage to some of the famous holy places of his times and it is certain that his own example of a life dedicated to high spirituality, scholarship, teaching and debating served to inspire his followers as is attested by the history of his school in the subsequent centuries. While we cannot be certain of organizational details, there is no doubt that the tradition of Advaitic scholarship and saintliness continued vigorously after Śaṅkara. This illustrious *Vidyā-sampradāya* could not have grown without a distinctive and ample basis of social support and that does point to a growing all India monastic institutionalization during subsequent centuries which must owe its first inspiration of Śaṅkara himself.

Śaṅkara's view that the socio-ritual order based on *avidyā* is fraught with revolutionary potentialities. Just as this view questioned the spiritual value of the narrow institutions of family and private property, it could endanger the ritualized caste order by regarding it as unreal for the *Jñānin*. The Buddhists and Jainas had already protested against it and a similar protest may be found in the *Mahābhārata*. For Śaṅkara although the eligibility for Vedic study depends on caste, there is no such dependence on caste or *āśrama* as far as *jñāna* is concerned. It is true that Śaṅkara accepts the traditional rejection of the rights of the Śūdras to Vedic study and ritual but he accepts that Śūdras could actually be *jñānins* and had at any rate right to acquire knowledge from *Itihāsa* and *Purāṇa*.[132] It must also be remembered that in commenting on the classical texts Śaṅkara is necessarily bound by their plain views and the *Smṛtis* by his time clearly expressed discriminatory views as far as the rights of the Śūdras to Vedic study and ritual were concerned. At the same time there is some reason to suppose that Śaṅkara's attitude towards caste discrimination underwent a change as is brought out in the dramatic story of his meeting with the Cāṇḍāla in Vārāṇasī. The differentiation of Brāhmaṇa and Cāṇḍāla cannot apply to the body, *bhidyate annamayato' nnamayaṁkim'*; nor can it apply to the soul: '*Brāhmaṇa-śvapaca-bheda-vicāraḥ pratyagātmani kathaṁ tava yuktaḥ*'. The distinction of *dvija* and *śvapaca* is thus simply a false prejudice (*mithyāgraha*). The same truth is affirmed in the *Manīṣā-pañcakam*.[133]

Whether the anecdote of the meeting with the Cāṇḍāla is history or mere legend, cannot be ascertained but if the anecdote were unhistorical it would be difficult to explain its fabrication in later times. The very fact that it was accepted even as part of the Śaṅkara legend is not without significance.

Śaṅkara's doctrines of the *avidyāvad-viṣayatva* of *karma-kāṇḍa*, of *Varṇāśramādyabhimāna* as well as of the *Jīvanmukta* as a living example of the gracious teacher for suffering humanity, put together do imply that everyone worth his salt must seek the knowledge of truth and liberate himself from egoistic social and ritual bondage. Heavily insulated by technicalities and compromised by a latter day monastic tradition, this current of a purely spiritual religion failed to reach the masses till they were taken up by some medieval saints and reformers like Kabīr or modern crusaders like Vivekānand.[134]

Part of the containment of the revolutionary potential of Śaṅkara's moral and social ideals may be attributed to his own tendency to compromise with tradition. This followed naturally from the basic duality in Śaṅkara's thought between the two standpoints of *Vyavahāra* and *Paramārtha*. What he regards as the real truth, thus, gets balanced by a contrary conventional or 'practical' truth. He rejects *Karman* in favour of *Jñāna* but then admits *Karman* in various ways as a preparatory necessity for the common man. He does not admit that there is any question of social eligibility for *Jñāna* but also accepts that *Jñāna* in some sense requires the Vedic revelation and its study requires social eligibility. Śaṅkara's championship of non-dual knowledge is combined with his allegiance to the orthodox Vedic tradition, intellectual as well as social. At the same time while advocating the sole reality of the transcendent Absolute he also accepts the manifestation of God in diverse names and forms, and thus the validity of numberless sects and modes of worship varying from the philosophical reflection over the Self (*Ātmavicāra*) to Tantricism. Śaṅkara's thought is at once purist and catholic, revolutionary and traditional. For this very reason it was able to span two ages, the past and the future.

REFERENCES

1. Cf. *BSB* (Nirnayasagar, text only), pp. 43, 63, 67, 81, 96, 42, 112, 113, 114 etc.
2. *Katha*, 1, 2, 5-6.
3. *Ibid.*, 1.2.1-2.
4. *BUB*, Intr.
5. *BSB*, 3.2.35; ff. *BGB*, 16.24.
6. E.g., *Ibid.*, 2.43.
7. *Katha-B.* 1.2.10.
8. *BGB*, Intr.
9. E.g., *BSB* 1.1.2, *BUB*, l.c.
10. *BSB*, 1.1.1.
11. Cf. *Ibid.*, 3.4.40.
12. *Ibid.*, 1.1.4.
13. *Ibid.*, 2.3.20; 3.4.40.
14. *Ibid.*, 1.1.1-2, *Ibid.*, 1.14.
15. *Ibid.*, 1.1.1.
16. *Ibid.*, 1.1.2.
17. *Ibid.*, Intr: *Pramāṇa* as *avidyāvad-viṣaya*; *MKB*, 3.35-45.
18. Cf. *Upadeśa, Tattvamasiprakaraṇa*, vv. 57-58, 203.
19. *Katha-B*, 2.1.
20. *CUB*, 7.24.1; *TUB*, 2.9.
21. *BUB*, 2.3.5.
22. *CUB*, 7.23.1.
23. *Katha-B*, 2.3.
24. *BGB*, Intr.
25. *Ibid.*, l.c.
26. *Dharma*, in fact, will apply to all the four types of law formulated by St. Thomas Aquinas.
27. The Humean or positivistic view of reason seems to identify it with logical reasoning. By itself that cannot give knowledge of empirical facts or moral values.
28. Cf. *Mbh Śāntiparvan*, (*rājadharmaparvan*).
29. Cf. A.K. Coomaraswamy, *Spiritual Authority and Temporal Power in the Indian Theory of Government*, New Delhi, 1978).
30. *Manu*, 2.6; Viśvarūpa, *Bāla-Krīḍā*, pp. 12 ff.
31. Cf. *Medhātithi* on *Manu*, l.c.
32. *Katha B*, 2.1-2; *BSB* 1.1.1 *Brahma-jijñāsā* presupposes *nityānitya-vastu-viveka* and culminates in *Ātmānātma-viveka*. The story of Naciketas illustrates it vividly.
33. See below.
34. *BSB*, 34, 40.

35. Thus Manu includes in *dharma* all kinds of conventional and institutional law by his dictum—*'Jāti-Jānapadān dharmān* etc.'(8.41).
36. *Manu*, 6.92.
37. *Ibid.*, 6.95-26 ' *Vedam ekaṁ na saṁnyaset*'.
38. See below.
39. *BUB*, 1.4.15.
40. *BGB*, Intr.
41. See above, Literary Activities of Śaṅkara.
42. See ablove, l.c.
43. *See below*, Last Days.
44. A view repeatedly criticised in *BGB*.
45. *BGB*, 3, intr., (= *SG*, VI p.76).
46. *Ibid.*, l.c.
47. *Manu*, 2.2; *Ibid.*, 12.87.
48. *Ibid.*, 3.78.
49. Bhāruci, *Commentary on the Manusmṛti* (ed. J.D.M Derrett) Vol. II p. 89.
50. *Ibid.*, Vol. I. p. 45.
51. *Ibid.*, p. 43.
52. *Ibid.*, l.c.
53. Manu, 6.95-96; Bhāruci, *op. cit.*, Vol. I, p. 45: *Na hi Vedasya sannyāsosti śāstra-virodhāt'*.
54. *BGB*, 3. Intr. (=*SG*, VI, p. 78).
55. *BSB*, 1.1.4.
56. *Ibid.*, p. 17 (Nirnayasgar, text only).
57. *Ibid.*, l.c.
58. *Ibid.*, l.c.
59. *Yājñavalkya-smṛti*, 1.1.8.
60. *BSB* 2.3.40 (= *SG*, *VII*, pp. 465 ff.).
61. *BGB*, 18, 5-7.
62. *BSB*, 3.4.26 (= *SG*, VII, p. 737).
63. *Ibid.*, p. 738.
64. *Ibid.*, p. 739.
65. *Ibid.*, l.c.
66. *Ibid.*, pp. 739-40.
67. *Ibid.*, p. 792.
68. *Ibid.*, p. 783.
69. *Ibid.*, p. 766.
70. *BGB*, 6.25.
71. I.e., *Pramāṇa-phala* accrues to *caitanya*.
72. *BSB*, 2.1.14.
73. Kekule, German scientist, discovered the structure of the Benzene—ring in a dream-like vision in 1865.
74. *BSB*, 2.1.14.
75. *BSB*, 2.1.14 (Nirnayasagar text, pp. 198-99).
76. *BSB*, 4.1.2.
77. *BUB*, 1.4.7 (= *SG*. X, pp. 106 ff).
78. *NS*, 1.67 ff. Ānandajñāna on *Vārtika* ad Br. *BUB*. 4.4. 786-91; Hiriyanna, *POC* (3rd), pp. 440-50.
79. *BUB*, *SG X*, p. 108.

80. *Ibid., SG* X, p. 687-92); *BSB,* 3.1.4;9—*NS* (ed. Hiriyanna), Intr. pp. xxvi-xxx.
81. *MBS* pt. I, pp. 35, 134-35, 154.
82. *BUB,* (= *SG, X.,* p. 108).
83. *BUB,* (= *SG, X.* p. 113).
84. *Ibid.,* (=*SG,* X, p. 259).
85. TUB= (*Īśādi,* p. 285).
86. Cf. K. Sacchidananda Murti, *op. cit.,* pp. 88 ff.
87. *BSB,* 4.12 (p. 462 Nirnayasagar text only).
88. *Upadeśa-sāhasrī, 'tattvamasi',* vv. 21-22.
89. *Upadeśa,* 18.43.
90. *BSB,* 4.1.2.
91. *Ibid.,* l.c.
92. *Ibid.,* l.c.
93. *BGB,* 2, 54 = *'Sarvatraivahi adhyātma-śāstre Kṛtārtha-lakṣaṇāni yāni tāny eva sādhanāni upadiśyante yatna-sādhyatvāt.*
94. *BSB,* 2, 3.41 = *Tad anugraha-hetukenaiva ca vijñānena mokṣa-siddhi-r bhavitum arhati; Ib.* 3.2.24.
95. *BSB,* 12.20 (=*SG,* VI, p. 354); *Ibid.,* 18.55 (*SG, VI* pp. 541-42).
96. *Vikeka-Cūḍāmaṇi, 'bhaktir eva garīyasī'.*
97. *Cf. BGB* 18.55: *pratyagātma-viṣaya-pratyaya-santāna-karaṇā-bhiniveśaśca jñāna-niṣṭhā.*
98. *BUB* =(*Īśādi,* p. 666, 759).
99. *Ibid.,* p. 760 =*ātma-prīti-sādhanatvād gauṇī anyatra prītir ātmani eva mukhyā.*
100. *Ibid.,* p. 730.
101. *Ibid.,* p. 891.
102. *Ibid.,* p. 900.
103. *Ibid.,* p. 901.
104. *Gītagovinda,* 6.6.
105. *Saṁyutta, Mallikāsaṁyutta.*
106. Attributed to Kabir.
107. *Uttara-rāma-carita.*
108. Cf. my *Bhakti-darśana-vimarśaḥ* (Varanasi, 1991).
109. K.C. Bhattacharya, *Studies in Philosophy,* p. 117.
110. *BG,* 9.11.
111. G.C. Pande, *The Role of Sankara,* p. 12.
112. *B.S.B,* 2.3.48.
113. G.C. Pande, *op. cit.,* p. 13.
114. *Ibid.,* p.10.
115. Medhātithi, ad *Manu,* 6.32.
116. G.C. Pande, *op. cit.,* p. 11.
117. *BGB, XVI,* 8.
118. *Daivā-suram* was an ancient mythical-cosmological idea. The *BG* uses it as a psychological-ethical idea while St. Augustin would seek to discover it as operative in history.
119. *BUB,* 14.15 (*SG,* X, p. 151).
120. Cf. Fung Yu-lan, *History of Chinese Philosophy,* Vol. 3 I, pp. 330-35.
121. Cf. G.C. Pande, *Bauddha Dharma Ke Vikas ka Itihas.*
122. *Īśādi,* p. 408 (*CUB* 2.23=*SG,* IX, pp. 128-29).

123. *Ibid.*, l.c.
124. Vide Kane, *Hist. of the Dh-S.* Vol. II, pt. II pp. 930 ff, esp. pp. 935-41.
125. *BUB*, 3.5.1, *Ibid.*, 4.5.15.
126. *Vārtika* ad *BUB* 3.5.1.
127. *Bālakrīḍā*, ad Yājñavalkya, 361. Cf. Kane, *op. cit.*, p. 944.
128. G.C. Pande, *Role of Śaṅkara*, pp. 6-7.
129. See below, Last Days, where details of the inscription are given.
130. *Jīvanmukti-Viveka*, quoted Kane, *op. cit.*, p. 950.
131. Cf. Farquhar, *JRAS*, 1925, pp. 479-86.
132. *BSB*, *Apaśūdrādhikaraṇa*, Govind Chandra Pande, *Sankaracarya-Vicara Aur, Sandarbha* (1992), pp. 80 ff.
133. Cf. K. Sacchidananda Murty, *Śankara-Jayanti-Mahotsava-Vyakhyana*, 1989.
134. G.C. Pande, *op. cit.*, p. 12.

9

Digvijaya: Śaṅkara and Buddhism

The relationship of Śaṅkara to Buddhism has been the subject of considerable debate since ancient times. He has been hailed as the arch critic of Buddhism and the principal architect of its downfall in India. At the same time he has been described as a Buddhist in disguise. Both these opinions have been expressed by ancient as well as modern authors—scholars, philosophers, historians and sectaries.[1] It is proposed to analyse briefly the various aspects of the problem, historical as well as philosophical, and to show that while the historical facts are clear enough, the difference of opinion in question really arises from certain ambiguities in Śaṅkara as well as Mahāyānic philosophies.

Śaṅkara's writings clearly show his acquaintance with at least three schools of Buddhist philosophy, viz., the Sarvāstivādins, the Vijñānavādins and the Mādhyamikas.[2] Of individual Buddhist authors he certainly shows acquaintance with Dharmakīrti.[3] He criticises Buddhist doctrines and speaks disparagingly of the Buddha himself.[4] These facts tend to lend evidence to the legendary accounts in his biographies which show him disputing with Buddhists.

On the other hand, it is not disputed that Śaṅkara was the disciple of Govindapāda who in turn was the disciple of Gauḍapāda. Now Śaṅkara quotes Gauḍapāda and refers to him with reverence.[5] He is even said to have written a commentary on the *Kārikās* attributed to Gauḍapāda, although, this is more than doubtful.[6] It is, however, undoubted that Śaṅkara should have known and been influenced by Gauḍapāda just as the latter may be plausibly supposed to have known and been influenced by Mahāyāna.[7]

It seems thus that while Śaṅkara's direct acquaintance with Buddhism did not predispose him favourably towards it, he did imbibe unwittingly certain Mahāyānic ideas by virtue of his belonging to a tradition of Vedāntic interpretation inspired by

Gauḍapāda. Vedānta and Buddhism, in fact, may be said to form a subtle counterpoint within the complex harmony of the essential Indian spiritual tradition, or more abstractly, of the *philosophia perennis*.

Let us first turn to Śaṅkara's criticism of Buddhist philosophy to ascertain the extent and depth of his opposition to it. Although this criticism occurs in several of his works, it is taken up most systematically in the *SB.*[8] Following the *Sūtras* he takes up for criticism the common Buddhist ideas of momentariness, non-selfhood and causality as dependent origination, as also some specific doctrines of the three Buddhist schools mentioned before. Now the Buddhist principle of *momentariness* implies that all things are subject to change, that change takes place every moment, and that all change implies total destruction without any room for survival or persistence (*niranvayavināśa*).[9] In its fully developed form at the hands of Buddhist logicians this principle was grounded on the analysis of the concept of existence itself and formulated as a *svabhāvānumāna.*[10] Existence was conceived as instantaneous causal function (*artha-kriyākāritva*), causation as ordered succession of moments (*niyataprāgbhāvitva*), things as process (*santāna, pravāha*). The principle had, however, originated in existential concern and passed through several phases. It was the perception of human mortality and the evanescence of experience which led to the disparagement of the attachment to personal existence. The denial of the individual soul as a permanent spiritual substance was developed as its metaphysical support and corollary.[11] Individual existence, thus, came to be conceived as an aggregate, a stream of transient factors. In this earlier phase the doctrine of momentariness was essentially a doctrine of the transience of psychic states without any permanent substratum. It did not mean in this early phase the unqualified denial of all substantive entities. Later when the schools ramified, the concept of momentariness was formulated at least as early as the age of Aśoka.[12] It was elaborated in *Abhidharma* and the *Mahā-Vibhāṣā* and the *Abhidhamakośa*[13] record detailed debates on the nature of Time. In Mahāyānic texts the momentariness of things became the momentariness of the states of mind or experience. Logicians like Ratnakīrti gave the doctrine its finished logical form.[14]

The Sarvāstivādins to whom Śaṅkara alludes do admit a large number of *dharmas* which function momentarily but subsist through time. This is what gave them their name. It is true that substance, quality and mode are rolled into one in the *dharmas* but they do have persistent natures or characters i.e. *svabhāva* or *lakṣaṇa*.[15]

Now Śaṅkara's major critique of momentariness occurs in the context of Sarvāstivāda, apparently in its Sautrāntic version.[16] Śaṅkara thus attacks the doctrine of momentariness as inadequate to explain the facts of identity, especially personal identity, and the fact of causation itself. 'Those who maintain that everything has a momentary existence only admit that when the thing existing in the second moment enters into being the thing existing in the first moment ceases to be. On this admission it is impossible to establish between the two things the relation of cause and effect, since the former momentary existence which ceases or has ceased to be, and so has entered into the state of non-existence, cannot be the cause of the later momentary existence.'[17] Nor could it be assumed that the former momentary existence when its process has reached a mature conclusion and it is still in a positive state, is the cause of the later moment (*bhāvabhūtaḥ pariniṣpannāvasthaḥ pūrva-kṣaṇa uttara-kṣaṇasya heturiti*).[18] This would imply that the finished positive product becomes active once again and gets connected with the next moment. Nor would it help to assume that the mere existence of the antecedent moment constitutes its causal efficiency because it still remains unconnected with the succeeding moment.[19] If the nature of the cause does not influence the nature of the effect, the two cannot be called cause and effect (*hetusvabhāvānuparaktasya phalasyotpattyasambhavāt*).[20] If the nature of the cause persists in the effect, as that of clay in the pot, the principle of momentariness would be given up. If, on the other hand, the nature of the cause were to be assumed not to colour the nature of the effect at all, one would be able to affirm the causal relation arbitrarily (*Vinaiva vā svabhāvoparāgeṇa hetuphalabhāvam abhyupagacchataḥ sarvatra tatprāpteratiprasaṅgaḥ*).[21] Again, the production, and destruction of a thing being held to be simultaneous, how are they to be connected with its own nature or being? The three could not be identical, else the three terms would become synonymous. Nor could the three be distinguished as different states of the same thing because then one moment will in effect be trifurcated.[22] Nor could the production and destruction of a thing be different from its being because in that case its being would be untouched by them and become perpetual. Nor finally could the production or destruction of a thing be merely their perception or non-perception which being subjective will leave the object untouched and make it eternal once again.[23] Indeed, since the antecedent moment ceases before the rise of the subsequent one, the effect would appear to arise without a cause which would contradict the Buddhist belief in causality. If the antecedent moment is held to last till the subsequent moment arises, cause and effect would become simultaneous, and the principle of momentariness too would be falsified.

In the *Bṛhadāraṇyaka-bhāṣya* (ad *Br.* 1.2.1) too Śaṅkara attacks the concepts of production out of nothing and momentariness on several grounds: '*mṛdādi-kāraṇānām ghaṭādyutpattau Piṇḍādi-nivṛttāvanuvṛttidarśanāt—anumānābhāsāt sādṛśyādikalpanā-nupapatteḥ*' (*Śaṅkaragranthāvalī*, Vol. X, p. 15). Recognition or the perception of similarity would both be impossible if everything is momentary.

Śaṅkara's critique of the Buddhist principle of momentariness here appears to be based on a dynamic conception of causality of which the paradigm may be said to be the case of intelligent will transforming some material according to a design. Such is God's creation of the world (*īkṣāpūrvaka-sṛṣṭi*) as also of the potter's making of pots. Śaṅkara essentially identifies cause and effect, regarding causation as nothing but transformation.[24] The Buddhist view in contrast resolves causality into the invariance of succession where the cause is devoid of any motion or influence. '*Na gatir yasmāt saṁskṛtam kṣaṇikam*' (*Abhidharma* 4.2). The Buddhist model of causation is not the production of commonsense objects like pots, but the infinitesimal process of becoming as illustrated in the stream of consciousness.[25]

As for Śaṅkara's difficulties about the reconciliation of the three aspects of becoming in a single moment, this difficulty was raised and considered at length in the *Abhidharma*. The Sautrāntika answer was that the *saṁskṛta-lakṣaṇas* belong to the sequence or *pravāha*.[26] Static common-sense objects need to be replaced by continuous processes or flux. The identity of an object is defined by its characteristic function which must express itself instantaneously and cease. As a new function emerges a new object must be held to have been produced.[27] However, the indiscernibility of similar successive moments and functions leads to a sense of persistent identity in sequence.[28] While Buddhist momentariness reduces identity into an illusory construct, Śaṅkara views change as illusory modes or appearances of the changeless ground.[29] For the Buddhist to be is to change (*arthakriyākāritvaṁ sattvam*); for Śaṅkara to change is the sign of being unreal.[30] Śaṅkara ridicules the Buddhists as Vaināśikas or Nihilists, the Buddhists disparage Vedānta as Śāśvatavāda or Eternalism. Thus Buddhism and Śaṅkara appear to be mutually opposed as *Asadvāda* and *Sadvāda*.

This, however, does not represent the true position. The Buddha had expressly ruled out both eternalism (*śāśvatavāda*) and nihilism (*ucchedavāda*).[31] Hence to accuse his doctrine of nihilism could only be based on misunderstanding. The Sarvāstivādins accept the enduring reality of the *dharma-svabhāvas*, the Vijñānavādins regard *Vijñaptimātratā* as the foundational or noumenal reality underlying the phenomena, the Mādhyamikas clearly distinguish *śūnyatā* from non-existence or unreality. No Buddhist school except the Sautrāntikas considers *Nirvāṇa* negative.[32] The fact is that the Buddhist doctrine of momentariness is intended to attack the common sense belief in the stability or reality of the empirical world including the empirical self. It considers the true nature of things (*dharmatā, dharmadhātu, dharmasvabhāva*), or *Nirvāṇa* as timelessly real and quiescent. Buddhist philosophy, thus, formulates a dual criterion of reality. It finds empirical reality characterized by instantaneous action but posits a timeless and infinite reality as the ultimate object of human endeavour. This duality of conception goes back to Buddha himself. What Śaṅkara attacks is the Buddhist analysis of empirical reality by pointing out that change in the empirical world is unintelligible without endurance. When he attacks *Nirvāṇa* it is only in its Sautrāntika version.

On the other hand, in characterizing the real as eternal Śaṅkara condemns the empirical world of time and change as unreal. For him cause and effect, substance and mode are real only within the bounds of empirical reality, that is to say, they are unreal transcendentally. He defends *satkāryavāda* against *asatkāryavāda* of different kinds but the real import of his *satkāryavāda* can only be understood in terms of what later on came to be called *Vivartavāda* as distinguished from *Pariṇāmavāda*.[33] Śaṅkara like the Buddhists disparages the empirical world as transient and evil and like them posits the infinite and eternal as the goal of human aspiration. Both distinguish *Paramārtha* and *Vyavahāra* and agree that the former is timeless, the latter fundamentally impermanent and insubstantial. They differ in their analysis of empirical things and causality.

The fact is that in the Buddhist proposition 'All things are momentary', the term 'all things' ('*sarvam*', '*sarve dharmah*') needs clarification. It has been explained as meaning 'all composite things or synergies' (*saṁskṛta-dharmas, saṁskāras*) or as 'the twelve spheres or *Āyatanas*.[34] Clearly the *asaṁskṛta dharmas* are excluded. Again, the separate *dharmas* imbued with distinctive essences are clearly not exhausted as subsistent potencies and so a reasonable distinction was made between *dharma-svabhāva* and *dharma-lakṣaṇa*. In other words, although the composite objects of common sense are momentary in the sense that they become different every moment, and although their ultimate constituents or *dharmas* appear and disappear every moment, it has still to be admitted that these *dharmas* have or rather are distinct timeless characters which are exhibited by entitatively different phenomena. Sarvāstivāda, thus clearly posits a system of timeless, intelligible essences underlying the momentary phenomena of the empirical realm. Nor is substance itself denied by Sarvāstivāda in every sense since the *dharmas* themselves are called *dravyasat*.[35] To be substantively, is to have an essence, which may be contrasted with momentary phenomenal appearance in which case being is doing and dying. Thus Buddhist ontology as reflected in Sarvāstivāda does imply a distinction between timeless, and momentary being. Śaṅkara's criticism does not take note of this distinction. Indeed there is a striking similarity between Sarvāstivāda and Sāṅkhya especially as expounded by Vyāsa in his Commentary on the *Yoga-sūtras*.[36] Śaṅkara is clearly not aware of this.

So far we have seen that Śaṅkara's critique of the Buddhist principle of momentariness relates to the Buddhist analysis of empirical reality, not to its formulation of transcendental reality. His critique of Buddhist *Nairātmyavāda*, however, has been represented as a counterblast to the Buddhist critique of *Ātmavāda*, and the two, *Ātmavāda* and *Nairātmyavāda*, have been represented as forming two fundamentally different streams of thought within the Indian tradition.[37] For Śaṅkara the Buddhist denial of the *Ātman* means that the person is to be understood as merely an aggregate (*samudāya, saṅghāta*) of psycho-physical elements and the individuality of the person as no more than the distinctiveness of a stream of consciousness (*santāna*). The self is not to be construed as a permanent or simple spiritual substance which is the subject of knowledge and action. For the Buddhists material atoms are aggregated into the physical body and that along with the other four *skandhas* into the person. Śaṅkara argues that the Buddhists are unable to explain how the aggregates are brought about.[38] Material aggregates are said to be formed from constituents which lack intelligence (*acetana*) and the kindling of intelligence (*cittābhijvalana*) presupposes an aggregate such as the body. The Buddhists do not admit any other permanent intelligent being, such as either the experiencing individual soul or the ruling Lord who could bring about the aggregation of atoms (*anvasya vā kasyacit cetanasya bhoktuḥ praśāsitur vā sthirasya saṁhantur anabhyupagamāt*). 'Nor can the atoms and *skandha* be assumed to enter on activity on their own account, for that would imply their never ceasing to be active.' In short, the self-conscious unity of personality cannot be understood as the result of a fortuitous concourse of atoms and elements. It is the unity of self-consciousness which holds together the elements of a personality. Some Buddhists had perceived this and formulated the concept of *Ālaya-vijñāna*[39] to explain the unity and continuity of the stream of consciousness. Śaṅkara argues that the *Ālaya* can neither be identified with nor distinguished from the particular cognition. Besides, if it is also momentary it will fail to serve as a unifying centre. If not, it would be the self under another name. It is interesting to note that Śaṅkara here uses the same kind of arguments as were used by most of the Buddhists against the conception of the *Pudgala* held by the Vātsīputrīyas and the Sāmmitīyas.[40]

Śaṅkara then attacks the notion of *Pratītya-samutpāda* as explaining the origin and regulation of the *santāna* without the intervention of any conscious agent. The Buddhist formula 'does not intimate an efficient cause for the formation of the aggregates.'[41] The various causal factors beginning with *avidyā* presuppose the stream of consciousness for their operation. In its absence they cannot operate to create it since that requires an intelligent being who can perceive and coordinate ends and means. The various elements of the causal series have only a limited causal force with respect to their immediate effects. They need the appropriate collocation of circumstances (*Hetupratyayasāmagrī*) before they could effect the meaningful aggregation of factors on which the stream of consciousness depends. Momentary atoms cannot by their separate movements produce the purposeful self-conscious unity of the psycho-physical aggregate. If the stream of aggregates is held to be beginningless, it would either mean the regular continuity of similar aggregates or else an erratic and chaotic change from one kind of aggregate to another without any determinate law. Neither possibility accords with the regular change of the aggregates in accordance with moral law in the course of *saṁsāra*. Further, not only is it impossible to derive personality aggregates from unguided atomic particulars, the hypothesis of such aggregates will fail in its purpose in the absence of an abiding self. If the stream of personal life consists of nothing but particular moments of consciousness, pain and pleasure would be self-experiencing and not the objects desired or sought to be avoided by any self. The same would be the case with bondage and release. Indeed, the notion of emancipation is hard to reconcile with that of the self as a mere stream of consciousness. The Buddhists conceive of emancipation as an attainment of cessation through knowledge.[42] Since each moment of the stream exists by producing an effect, the stream could never cease by itself. If the destruction is only of a moment in the stream, that would be nothing more than its normal fate. Again, if cessation is attained through knowledge, it would cease to be uncaused, which would violate the Buddhist principle of spontaneous destruction. The Buddhists further describe the cessation not only as a non-entity but also as eternal. This is contradictory (*avastunityam ceti vipratiṣiddham*).[43]

A fundamental difficulty raised by Śaṅkara and other Brāhmaṇical thinkers to the Buddhist denial of the self as a permanent substance is the impossibility of satisfactorily explaining the facts of memory and recognition in that case.[44] Memory implies the continuity of the subject between past experience and present remembrance. Recognition implies also the continuity of the object between its past experience and its present perception. The Buddhists seek to explain these phenomena on the basis of the inheritance of past impressions (*vāsanā*) by subsequent moments in the stream of consciousness and also by postulating that the non-discernment of similars leads to the illusion of identity and recognition. Against the first Śaṅkara relies on the self-evident identity of the self in memory and against the second he points out that the recognition of identity is distinct from the perception of similarity. In any case to perceive the similarity of the past and the present, the self must persist in time.

This polemic clearly illustrates how debate aims at victory rather than truth. Śaṅkara does not examine the reasons which the Buddhists advanced in support of their position and without which the significance of their position can hardly be grasped. Instead Śaṅkara adopts the expedient of pointing out how some of the implications of the Buddhist position are at variance with 'facts and logic'. The principles and facts he relies on are basically two. Purposive wholes cannot be formed without reference to some intelligent being as subject, creator and disposer. Secondly, we recognize persistent identities among objects as well as in our selves. The first principle which attributes the formation of purposive wholes to the working of some intelligent agency is widely used by Śaṅkara in his criticism of Sāṅkhya and Vaiśeṣika also. It is really a matter of philosophical faith which the Buddhists are supposed not to have shared. In fact, the Buddhists have been credited with the rejection of the animistic outlook towards the bio-psychic organism in favour of a naturalistic one.[45] The classic Buddhist argument against a transcendent soul is strikingly Human. When we introspect we only perceive certain mental states but no soul apart from them.[46] Towards the mind itself the Buddhists adopted an analytical outlook (*Vibhajyavāda, abhidharma*) and treated it as a causally determined objective phenomenon. So far the Buddhist view of the human person may be justly described as simply naturalistic and empiricist. Some interpreters have indeed gone so far as to describe Buddhist philosophy as a species of positivism.[47] However, the fact is that Buddhism is no more positivistic than Śaṅkara. For Śaṅkara too the mind is not the self and no more than an object. It is, moreover, constituted out of matter.[48] For both Śaṅkara and Buddhism the mind is not the self and the empirical self-consciousness viz., the ego-consciousness 'owning' the mind and body, an illusive phenomenon arising out of transcendental Ignorance or Error.[49] Both Śaṅkara and Buddhism describe the ego as a reflection or *pratibimba*.[50] For both, the instinctive belief in the selfhood of the body and mind is a primal error. Although illusive, the empirical self or ego is for both morally responsible and continues from birth to birth with changing endowments and circumstances. Buddhism admits this *saṁsāric* continuity of the empirical self as an individual and unbroken stream of consciousness (*vijñānasantāna*). For Śaṅkara it is the *buddhi* that carries the reflection of the self in the ego-consciousness and wanders from birth to birth as the *liṅga* with *vāsanā*.[51] It is true that the emphasis in the conception of the empirical self is different in the two systems. Buddhism emphasizes the falsehood of the ego-consciousness which maintains the illusion of permanence and selfhood in a stream of changing factors none of which can be the self because they are impermanent and involved in suffering.[52] Śaṅkara emphasizes the falsehood of the ego-consciousness because it arises from the mutual superimposition of the self and the non-self.[53] For Śaṅkara, thus, the ego-consciousness is implicitly not wholly unreal. Searching the true nature of the self obscured by ego-consciousness one may thus hope to discard the unreal non-self and reach the real self. The discarding of the non-self is advocated by the Buddhists also. The question is, do the Buddhists advocate simple annihilation?

To this one can return a positive answer which is totally different from what Śaṅkara would have us believe and on the basis of which he sought to attack Buddhism vehemently. Buddha declared his position to be different from both eternalism and annihilationism.[54] He declared the non-selfhood of *saṁskāras* without categorically denying or affirming the self.[55] But he did affirm a reality which is infinite, eternal and beyond thought and speech.[56] It is this reality the attainment of which constitutes the *summun bonum* of life and the end of *saṁsāra*. *Nirvāṇa* is revealed by intuitive wisdom and this knowledge puts an end to the illusion of the ego and the separateness of being.[57]

Of all the Buddhistic schools it is only the Sautrāntikas who conceive *Nirvāṇa* negatively[58] and unfortunately it is their description which Śaṅkara regards as representative of the Buddhists. If such a one-sided view were deemed adequate, why not regard the Pudgalavādins who clearly affirmed the soul as representatives of Buddhism? In fact, they have a stranger claim because as the account of Hsuan Chwang shows, it is the Sāmmitīyas who were the most numerous among Buddhists in the 7th century A.D.[59]

For both Śaṅkara and Buddhism the emancipating vision of infinite reality is obscured by egoistic attachment. The Buddhists do not call this reality the self because they look upon the self as the egoistic principle.[60] Śaṅkara calls it the self but divests it of all individuality and limitation. For both the end of the journey is liberation from individuality and absorption in eternity through knowledge. The Buddhists emphasize the need for the transcendence of the ego, Śaṅkara for self-realization but both affirm the end of individual existence. This is a far-reaching agreement which differentiates Śaṅkara from systems like Sāṅkhya-yoga, Nyāya-Vaiśeṣika, Mīmāṁsā and Dualistic Vedānta. All the systems agree in seeking detachment from egoistic life but it is only Śaṅkara and Buddhism who regard the very individuality of the empirical self as ultimately unreal. The relationship of Śaṅkara's *Ātmavāda* with

Buddhist *Ānātmavāda*, thus, can hardly be regarded as one of total opposition.

If we now turn to Śaṅkara's criticism of Mahāyāna schools a new dimension of similarity can be glimpsed beneath the clash of dialectical arms for now to the illusoriness of the empirical individual is added the illusoriness of the world itself. In criticizing Vijñānavāda at length[61] Śaṅkara follows a procedure different from the one he followed in attacking *Sarvāstivāda*. He concentrates on the Vijñānavāda denial of the external world but begins by a careful exposition of the principal arguments used by it. Apparently he has in mind principally the version of Vijñānavāda as found in Vasubandhu, Dignāga and Dharmakīrti.

The roots of Vijñānavāda go back to the most ancient Buddhist canonical writings where *Vijñāna* is described as infinite, wholly luminous, invisible or formless.[62] It is by climbing the mansion of *prajñā* that Buddha became enlightened and viewed common humanity with compassion. It is true that *Vijñāna* was also used in the sense of empirical cognition mostly and it is recorded that Buddha condemned those who sought to cling to these transient flashes of consciousness as a permanent soul. Nevertheless, the idea of an infinite and transcendent knowledge was clearly expressed by him. The idea is definitely reminiscent of some Upaniṣadic utterances. Some of the early *Hīnayānic* sects continued this notion of the mind as pure and effulgent.[63] In the Mahāyāna *sūtras* especially the *Laṅkāvatāra, Vijñānavāda* may be seen in its ful-fledged form. Already the *Aṣṭasāhasrikā Prajñā Pāramitā* had sought to bridge the gap between the empirical and transcendental *Vijñāna* by speaking of the condition 'where the mind becomes non-mind' (*Yatra cittam acittam bhavati*). The development of the concept of the three Bodies tended in the same direction bridging the gap between transcendent reality, mental radiance and physical appearance.[64] Buddha had declared the mind to be sovereign and primary.[65] The Mahāyāna took it up as its key formula. Vijñānavāda and Śūnyavāda were at first merely two aspects of the same Mahāyānic philosophy.[66] The *Upaniṣads* had shown the parallelism of dream consciousness and waking consciousness. Mahāyāna *sūtras* held the dream consciousness to be paradigmatic of the waking because it enabled one to realize clearly the subjectivity and transience of experience. The external objects of waking consciousness have the same kind of reality or unreality as dream objects. Their basic character is the same viz., being objects presented to consciousness. This is the basic ground for asserting their falsehood because being immediately presented to consciousness they could not be anything apart from it, but since they do appear apart, they could be no more than appearances as in a dream.[67] Another argument which Vasubandhu mentions in favour of Vijñānavāda is a *reductio ad absurdum* of external reals and rests on a critique of atomism.[68]

A further argument was apparently developed out of the Sautrāntika critique of Vaibhāṣika realism. Owing to momentariness and the successiveness of cause and effect the immediate object of cognition could not be the real external object itself.[69] The acceptance of the representative theory of knowledge (*sākāra-vijñānavāda*) also suggested that the assumption of an external object apart from the form represented in knowledge would be logically superfluous. To the argument from *sārūpya* was added the famous argument from *shopalambha-niyama* which is found in Dharmakīrti.[70]

To explain the diversity of experiences in the absence of external objects the concept of *Vāsanā* was invoked quite early. The Buddha himself had proclaimed desire to be the architect of empirical existence of which the impressions in turn strengthened the force of desire, and this forms a beginningless series. Just as in a dream the impressions of desire and memory invent a world of experience so also is the waking of *saṁsāra*.

Śaṅkara attacks these arguments from the standpoint of common sense realism. The external objects are real because they are plainly perceived. Unless they were real, how would representation be possible? How else to explain the diversity of cognitions, for cognitions are differentiated only by their objects. It is true that cognition and object are apprehended together but they are not apprehended as identical. Curiously Śaṅkara does not raise any objection from the public character of the external objects, an objection which Vasubandhu had anticipated and answered. But Śaṅkara does raise another objection which Vasubandhu had sought to answer and, that is, that dream objects are sublated by waking experience and hence are not comparable to the stable objects of the waking world. Vasubandhu had answered that the sublation of dream objects occurs only after one has ceased to dream.[71]

Śaṅkara raises the further objection that if the cognition and its object are identical, each momentary cognition would be exhausted by its own self-cognition and there would be no possibility of any comparison of ideas. None of the Buddhist doctrines could then be established. Even more serious is the assumption that an idea may cognize itself and thus the subject and the object may become one. The fact is that the act of cognition reveals as its content an object different from itself and the cognitive act itself is apperceived by the witnessing consciousness or the self. To the natural Buddhist objection that this self-luminous witnessing consciousness or *Sākṣin* is simply another name for the Buddhist *Vijñāna,* Śaṅkara replies that the Buddhist 'ideas have the attributes of originating, passing away, being manifold, and so on' while the Vedāntic Self is one and eternal.

This sudden turn in discussion shows how near Śaṅkara and Buddhism are, separated by a wall of glass, as it were. It is worth noting that in discussing *Vijñānavāda* Śaṅkara eschews the discussion of what constituted the higher truth of that system. As in the case of Sarvāstivāda he is content to attack the Buddhist theories of empirical existence from his own empirical standpoint. He does not consider the principle of *Vijñaptimātratā* which represents the ultimate truth for the Vijñānavādin. *Vijñaptimātratā* is non-empirical, non-dual consciousness beyond the scope of particularities or conceptual thought.[72] It is, however, the ground which gets dirempted into the illusive distinction of subject and object and their multifarious diversities. This is surely comparable to the Adavaitic doctrine of *Brahman* as knowledge and the ground of the world illusion including subjective individualities.[73] It needs to be noted that since the *Vijñaptimātratā* is identified with *Tathatā* and the *Dharmakāya* it must be deemed timeless.

The Buddhists themselves noted the similarity of their doctrines to the Upaniṣadic Advaita. Śāntarakṣita declares that the Upaniṣadic view rightly regards the world as the manifestation of knowledge but 'Errs a little' in speaking of it as eternal. How can the eternal be the ground of an ever-changing diversity of manifestation?[74] This criticism misses the fact that the world is an illusion superimposed on Brahman, not its causal transformation for Śaṅkara. The fact is that both Śaṅkara and the Buddhists criticise each other from logical principles they hold appropriate for empirical existence and from which they exempt their own ultimate truth or *paramārtha*.

Śaṅkara gives short shrift to the Mādhyamika doctrine which he interprets literally as the doctrine 'that everything is empty (i.e., that absolutely nothing exists)'. This 'is contradicted by all means of right of knowledge, and therefore requires no special refutation. For this apparent world, whose existence is guaranteed by all the means of knowledge, cannot be denied, unless someone should find out some new truth (based on which he could impugn its existence.)'[75] It deserves to be noted that Śaṅkara is here speaking entirely from the empirical standpoint because otherwise he himself regards the world as illusory as also all the 'right means of knowledge' including the scriptures as part of the realm of Error.[76] Since the Śūnyavādins themselves concede pragmatic reality to the empirical world, his criticism has hardly any force. In fact, it was the Śūnyavādins who first made systematic use of this distinction of two standpoints, absolute and empirical, which is found in Śaṅkara also.[77] As is well known even the dialectical method propounded by Nāgārjuna found a favourable echo in some of the later followers of Śaṅkara.

As for the wholly nihilistic interpretation of Śūnyavāda, it is difficult to find sufficient justification for it. Buddha himself declared that he advocated the Middle way which avoids both being and non-being, and he identified it with *Pratītyasamutpāda* which meant that nothing could be or could be conceived without dependence on something else.[78] This was a doctrine of the relativity of all phenomena (*dharmāḥ*). The counterpart of *Pratītyasamutpāda* was *Nirvāṇa* which was inconceivable and hence beyond such categories as being and non-being. Nāgārjuna claims to follow the Middle way and identifies it with *Pratītyasamutpāda* and *Śūnyatā*.[79] It is clear that *Śūnyatā* is not to be understood as non-existence in the empirical sense. *Śūnyavāda*, thus, is clearly not to be construed as nihilism in the ordinary sense. *Śūnyatā* is absolute quiescence, *prapañcopaśama*. It cannot be expressed as a view or opinion (*dṛṣṭi*).[80]

In conclusion we may seek to sum up the similarities and dissimilarities between Śaṅkara and Buddhism. Śaṅkara agrees with the Buddhists in holding a duality of standpoints, absolute and empirical (*pāramārthika* and *vyāvahārika*). He agrees with Mahāyānic schools in holding empirical reality to be illusive from the absolute standpoint. He agrees with them in holding reality to be non-dual and beyond the application of any categories of discursive thought. He agrees with the Buddhists in denying ultimate reality to the empirical individual. He also agrees with them in holding that liberation from *Saṁsāra* is also the transcendence of all particularity and individuality. Śaṅkara's philosophy is, like that of Mahāyāna, a kind of impersonal and non-dual absolutism. On the whole, Śaṅkara is nearer the Mādhyamikas than the Yogācāras.

On the other hand, Śaṅkara rejects the Buddhist theory of change and causality applicable to empirical existence, favouring the Sāṅkhyan views in such matters up to a point. He also rejects the Buddhist reduction of the individual person to an insubstantial stream of consciousness. He rejects the Sautrāntika account of *asaṁskṛta dharmas,* Yogācāra epistemology and Mādhyamika logic. He perceives in Buddhism not only indefensible but dangerous philosophical theories such as *Anātmavāda.*

Thus while Śaṅkara and Mahāyāna have a distinct affinity in their broad spiritual vision for which empirical existence is illusory and reality non-dual, they differ sharply in their conceptual analysis of the logical problems relating to common experience.

From Śaṅkara's disparagement of the Buddha and Buddhist thought as known to him, it is also clear that he was their opponent and did not consciously borrow from them. On the other hand, certain basic ideas such as that of the world as illusion, of the unreality of the empirical individual, and of reality as the non-dual, transcendent ground of the illusion of empirical existences, and of the duality of standpoints, have too strong an affinity with Buddhism to have developed without some interaction between the Vedāntic and Buddhist traditions at some stage. The Upaniṣadic standpoint as expounded by Bādarāyaṇa clearly views *Brahman* as God, the supreme personal creator. The world is viewed as a real transformation (*pariṇāma*) of *Brahman.* Nor is the individuality of the *Jīva* clearly regarded as illusory. Now Śaṅkara's point of view being quite different from this kind of Vedāntic tradition, he has to begin his commentary with the celebrated preface on illusion and in the course of the commentary he has to fall back on the theory of Two Standpoints to reconcile his own ultimate views with those plainly expressed in the *sūtras.* It may perhaps be argued that it was possibly Gauḍapāda from whom Śaṅkara derived these Buddhistic ideas. That Gauḍapāda's work bears unmistakable traces of Buddhistic influence in ideas as well as terminology has been forcefully argued by M.M. Vidhushekhar Bhattacharya. That Śaṅkara had reverence towards Gauḍapāda is also unmistakable. On the other hand, it is, of course, true that there were other

Advaitic writers of whom we know practically little. They may have developed illusionistic ideas on the basis of Upaniṣadic intimations independently. In that case we would have to suppose that there was a far greater influence of the *Upaniṣads* on the Mahāyāna *sūtras* than what is supposed till now.

REFERENCES

1. Cf. Mādhava, *Śaṅkaradigvijaya* (ed. B. Upadhyaya, Haridwar), Canto I where the main thrust of attacking the Buddhists is attributed to Kumārila as a precursor of Śaṅkara; G.N. Kaviraj, *Introduction to Ratnaprabhā* (Acyuta Granthamala), pp. 46-47; Baldeva Upadhyaya, *Sri Śaṅkarācārya* (1963); on the other hand, Bhāskara, Vallabha, Vijñānabhikṣu, Yāmuna and Rāmānuja accuse Śaṅkara of Buddhistic leanings—Nakamura, *History of Vedanta Philosophy*, Vol. I, pp. 121, 125. The charge arose particularly on account of the concept of *Māyā*. Several modern scholars have repeated it with reference to Gauḍapāda while others have sought to refute such a charge—e.g., S.L. Pandey, *Pre-Sankara Advaita Philosophy*, p. 310 ff; Cf. Potter (ed.) *Encyclopaedia of Indian Philosophy*, Vol. III, pp. 20-21; S.N. Dasgupta, *History of Indian Philosophy*, Vol. I, pp. 423, 493-494; Radhakrishnan, *Indian Philosophy*, Vol. II, pp. 463 ff; Cf. Jacobi, *JAOS*, Vol. 33, pp. 51 ff, V. Bhattacharya, *The Āgamaśāstra of Gauḍapāda*, pp. cxxxii-iii; S.S. Roy, *The Heritage of Sankara*, pp. 5ff; A.C. Mukerji, 'Nāgārjuna and Śaṅkara' in *Allahabad University Studies*, 1938; Louis de la Vallee Poussin, 'Vedanta and Buddhism', *JRAS*, 1910; "Is the Advaita of Sankara Buddhism in Disguise", *QJMS*, Vol. 24, no. 1-2, 1933; C.D. Sharma, *Critical Survey of Indian Philosophy*, Chap. XVII; V. Bhattacharya, 'Evolution of Vijnanavada', *IHQ*, 1934; T.R.V. Murti, *Central Philosophy of Buddhism*; T.M.P. Mahadevan, *Gauḍapāda* (1954).
2. E.g., Comy ad B.S. 2.2 18-33.
3. *BSB* 2.2.28 has '*sahopalambha-niyamād abhedo*' which is part of the verse continuing as '*nīla-taddhiyoḥ/ Bhedaśca bhrāntivijñānair dṛṣyetendāvivādvaye*' // The first line has been traced to *Pramāṇaviniścaya*, the second to *Pramāṇavārtika*; *SB* ad *BS* 2.2.28 has '*yadantarjñeya-rūpaṁ tad bahirvad avabhāstate*' which is Dignāga's verse as quoted by Kamalaśīla ad *TS* 2082-84; *Upadeśa-sāhasrī* 2.18.24: '*Abhinno' pi hi buddhyātmā viparyāsitadarśanaiḥ/Grāhya-grāhka-saṁvittir bhedavān iva lakṣyate*'. It has been traced to *Pramāṇa-viniścaya* and corresponds to *Pramāṇavārtika* II. 354; *Upadeśa* 2.18.143; '*Bhūtir yesāṁ kriyā saiva kārakaṁ saiva cocyate*' is oft-quoted. *Bodhicaryāvatārapañjikā* (9.6) gives the full verse, the first line being—'*Kṣaṇikāḥ sarva-saṁskārāḥ asthirāṇāṁ kutaḥ kriyā/*'. With this may be compared *SB* ad *BS* 2.2.20—'*atha bhāva evāsya vyāpāraḥ*'.
4. Ad *BS* 2.2.32: '*Sugatena spaṣṭīkṛtam ātmano's sambaddhapralāpitvam, pradveso vā prajāsu viruddhārthapratipattyā vimuheyur imāḥ prajā iti.*'
5. Commenting on *BS* 1.4.14 Śaṅkara refers to Gauḍapāda as *sampradāyavidaḥ* and quotes a verse corresponding to *Āgamaśāstra* 3.15; again, on *BS* 2.19 he

again refers to him as *Vedāntasampradāyavidaḥ ācāryaḥ* and quotes a verse found in *Āgamaśāstra* 1.16. A reference may also be seen in *Upadeśa sāhaśri* 2.18.2. If the *Māṇḍūkyopaniṣad-kārikā-bhāṣya* is accepted as authentic, no further evidence would be needed.

6. The verses in the *Māṇḍūkya-kārikā-bhāṣya* contain metrical and grammatical errors and the style lacks Śaṅkara's characteristic felicity—Kaviraj, *op. cit.*, pp. 29-30, Upadhyaya, *op. cit.*, p. 154; SS. Surayaṇarayana Sastri, *Life and Teachings of Sankaracharya* (2nd ed. Madras), p. 43, *Collected Papers of Suryanarayana Sastri* (Madras, 1961), pp. 262-71; Hacker and Mayeda have defended the authenticity of the work—Potter, *op. cit.*, p. 309.
7. V. Bhattacharya, *The Agamasastra of Gaudapada*—Intr. § 15.
8. E.g., Comy on *Br.* § 1.2.1., 4.3; *Upadesa* 2.18; *Gita* 18.50; *BS 2.2.18-33.*
9. Its classical form may be seen in Ratnakīrti's *Kṣaṇa-bhaṅgasiddhi*, see *Six Buddhist Nyaya Tracts* ed. by H.P. Shastri, Calcutta, 1910.
10. *Yat sat tat kṣaṇikam yathā ghaṭaḥ santaścāmī vivādāspadibhūtāḥ padārthā iti svabhāvahetuḥ"* (*Ibid.* p. 54)
11. Cf. G.C. Pande, *Studies in the Origins of Buddhism* (2nd ed.), pp. 482ff; *Pramānavārtika* (Varanasi, 1968), I 219-21: *Yaḥ paśyatyātmānaṁ Tatrāsyāham iti śāśvataḥ snehaḥ Ātmani sati parasañjña, svaparavibhāgāt Parigrahadveṣau/ /*
12. E.g., *Kathāvatthu,* 22.8.
13. *Abhidharmakośa,* (Varanasi, 1971) Vol. II, pp. 568 ff; *Ibid.*, Vol. III, pp. 803 ff.
14. E.g. Ratnakīrti, *op. cit.*; *Tattvasaṅgraha* (Varanasi, 1968) Vol. I, pp. 166 ff.
15. Cf. *Abhidharmakośa,* 3.27.
16. This is suggested by the wholly negative construction put on the *asaṁskṛtas.*
17. Thibaut's tr. of the *SB* in SBE Vol. I. p. 407.
18. *Śaṅkara-granthāvalī,* Vol. VII (2nd ed. Samata), p. 385.
19. Cf. *Upadeśa,* 2.18.143.
20. *Śaṅkara-granthāvali,* Vol. VII (2nd Ed. Samata), p. 385.
21. *Ibid.*, l.c.
22. *Ibid.*, p. 306; *'evam apyādyanta-madhya-kṣaṇa-traya-sambandhitvād vastunaḥ kṣaṇaikatvābhyupagama-hāniḥ'.*
23. This objection would become significant in the context of the Sarvāstivādin distinction of *dharma-lakṣaṇa* from *dharmasvabhāva* - Cf. Stcherbatsky, *op. cit.*, p. 42.
24. Although Śaṅkara often adopts a point of view similar to Sāṅkhyan *Pariṇāmavāda* at the empirical level and although he does not distinguish the terms *pariṇāma* and *vivarta,* his real view on causality is what came to be called *vivartavāda* later. In the Comy on *BG. Śaṅkara criticises the Sāṅkhya view also, see below fn. 29.*
25. Cf. Stcherbatsky, *Buddhist Logic,* Vol. I, pp. 106 ff.
26. *Abhidharmakośa,* Vol. I, pp. 1 255-62.
27. *'Viruddha-dharma-saṁsargāddhyanyad vastu', Nyāyabinduṭīkā,* quoted by Stcherbatsky, *Central Conception,* p. 38 fn. 3.
28. Cf. *Tattvasaṁgraha,* vv. 446 ff.
29. Comy ad *BG* 18.48 (*Śaṅkara-granthāvali,* Vol. VI, p. 530); *'Sadekam eva vastu avidyayā utpatti-vināśādi-dharmaiḥ anekadhā naṭavad vikalpyate'*; Comy ad *Ch. 2.2* The effect is the cause with a superimposed illusory form.
30. *BG.*, p. 27: *'yat viṣayā buddhirna vyabhicarati tat sat, yadviṣayā vyabhicarati*

tadasat.'

31. One might recall, for example, the famous sermon to Katyayana in the *Samyutta* and is alluded to by Nagarjuna also.
32. Vide G.C. Pande, *op. cit.*, pp. 444-50.
33. Cf. Supra fn. (29); Comy ad *ch.* 6.2.2. (=*Śaṅkara-granthāvali, voli,* Vol. IX, p. 347); Cf. *Śrutisārasamuddharanam,* (Pune, 1936), 140 which uses the same illustration of the actor *Nāmarūpamatto api kāryamatho abhidhāpi naṭasya pṛthagviditā/ Na Pṛthaktvam upaiti naṭah kimiti prativācyam avaśyam idaṁ kuśalaiḥ/ /.*
34. Cf. Stcherbatsky, *Central Philosophy*, p. 5.
35. Cf. *Ibid.*, p. 26.
36. *Ibid.*, pp. 43 ff; G.N. Kaviraj, *op. cit.*, p. 26 fn.
37. Cf. T.R.V. Murti, *Indian Cultural Heritage,* Vol. III.
38. *Śaṅkara-granthāvali,* Vol. VII, p. 382 (ad *BS.* 2.2.18).
39. E.g., *Laṅkāvatāra* (Kyoto, 1956), pp. 46 ff etc.; *Vijñaptimātratāsiddhi-triṁśikā* (Paris, 1925) pp. 33 ff; Cf. A.K. Chatterjee, *The Yogācāra Idealism* (1975), pp. 88 ff; Suzuki, *Studies* in the *Laṅkāvatāra* passion.
40. *Abhidharmakośa,* Vol. IV, pp. 118 ff. Pudgalaviniścaya, sometimes called the 9th *Kośasthāna.* Cf. Stcherbatsky, *Soul Theory of the Buddhists.*
41. ad *BS* 2.2.19 *(= Śaṅkaragranthāvalī,* Vol. VII, pp. 383-84).
42. *Ibid.*, pp. 387-88.
43. *Ibid.*, p. 389.
44. *Ibid.*, pp. 389-91; Comy ad *Br.* 1.2.1 (= *Śaṅkaragranthāvalī,* Vol. X, pp. 15-16).
45. Cf. Rhys Davids, *American Lectures, Hibbert,* Lectures; Jayatilleke, *Buddhist Theory of Knowledge.*
46. *Kathāvattu-aṭṭhakathā, Puggalakathā* (kv. 1.1); Cf. Hume, *A Treatise of Human Nature* (Pelican Classics), p. 300; 'For my part, when I enter most intimately into what I call *myself,* I always stumble on some particular perception or another, I never can catch *myself. . .'* So the Buddhist argument for the non-existence of the *Pudgala* from its non-perception (*anupalabdhi*) in the mass of mental states (*śuddha-saṅkhārapuñja*).
47. Jayatilleke, *op. cit.*, where the silence of Buddha is attributed to the meaninglessness of metaphysical questions.
48. Comy ad *ch.* 6.5.1 (= *Śāṅkaragranthāvalī*—Vol. IX, p. 362): *'Tataśca annopacitatatvān manaso bhautikatvam eva.'*
49. Comy ad *Māṇḍūkyopaniṣatkārikā* 2.17 (*Śaṅkara-granthāvali,* Vol. VIII, p. 439): *Tatra jīva-kalpanā sarvakalpanāmūlam ityuktam'. Ibid.*, p. 522. *Jīva. . . avidyamāna eva citta-vikalpanāmātra ityarthaḥ'.*
50. Comy ad *Ch.* 6.3.2. (= *Śaṅkara-granthāvali,* Vol. IX, p. 354): *Jīvo hi nāma devatāyā ābhāsamātram-ādarśa iva praviṣṭaḥ puruṣa-pratibimbaḥ' Ibid.*, Vol. X (=Br. 1.4.7.) pp. 98-102, which discusses the meaning of *anupraveśa* critically but ultimately does use the image of *pratibimba* (*Ibid.*, p. 102).
51. Ad *Br.* 4.3.7. (=*Śaṅkara-granthāvali,* Vol. X, pp. 526-30); *Ibid.*, pp. 286-93 (=*Br.* 2.3.6).
52. Thus in canonical texts *anitya* and *duḥkha are held to indicate anātmā.*
53. E.g., In the *adhyāsabhāṣya: 'mithyājñāna-nimittaḥ satyānrte mithunīkṛtya 'aham idam' 'mamedam' iti naisargiki' yam loka-vyavahāraḥ'.*
54. Cf. G.C. Pande, *Origins of Buddhism,* pp. 422 ff, *Saṅyutta* (PTS ed.) II. 17; Cf.

Mādhyamika-kārikā, XV.7.

55. *Ibid.*, pp. 485 ff; Cf. The *Vatsagotra sūtra* referred to in *Abhidharmakośa* (Varanasi ed.) Vol. IV, p. 210.
56. *Ibid.*, pp. 473-75; *Itivuttaka, sutta 43*; *Udāna, sutta 73*; *Majjhima* (PTS) I. 173.
57. *Ibid.*, pp. 460-65.
58. *Ibid.*, p.447; *Abhidharma*, Vol. II, pp. 324-25.
59. *Si-yu-ki*, tr. Watters; Cf. G.C. Pande, *Bauddha Dharma ke Vikas ka Itihas*, p. 299.
60. Cf. G.C. Pande, *op. cit.*, pp. 500-1; Cf. N. Dutt, *Aspects of Mahayana*, pp. 142-43.
61. Comy ad *BS* 2.2.28-31; *Br.* 4.3.7; *Upadeśasāhasrī*, 2.18.
62. E.g., *Majjhima* I, p. 329; G.C. Pande, *op. cit.*, pp. 494-98; G.C. Pande, *Bauddha Dharma Ke Vikas ka Itihas*, chap. 11.
63. *Ibid.*, p. 288.
64. *Ibid.*, p.353; see also N. Dutt, *op. cit.*
65. E.g., *Dhammapada* 1st verse.
66. Cf. G.C. Pande, *Bauddha Dharma ke Vikas ka Itihas*, p.402.
67. Vedānta too regards *dṛśyatva* as the sign of falsity—e.g., vide *Advaita-siddhi*.
68. *Vijñaptimātratāsiddhi, Viṁṣikā* (ed. S. Levi), pp. 6-8.
69. Cf. *Sarvadarśanasaṅgraha* (Pune, 1978), pp. 33 ff.
70. Supra fn. 61.
71. *Viṁśikā*, p.9 '*Svapne dṛgviṣayābhāvān nāprabuddho' vagacchati*'.
72. *Triṁśikā*, 29-30 '*Acitto 'nupalambho' sau Jñānaṁ lokottaraṁ ca tat/ Āśrayasya parāvṛttir dvedhā dauṣṭhulya-hānitaḥ Sa evānāsravo dhātur acintyaḥ kuśalo dhruvaḥ Sukho vimuktikāyosau dharmākhyo' yam mahāmuneḥ//*' On this Sthiramati says '*Tatra grāhaka-cittābhāvād grāhyārthānupalambhācca acitto' nupalambho' sau dhruvo nityatvād akṣayatayā sukho nityatvādeva*'; Cf. Hsüan Chwang's *Siddhi* (Tr. Poussin) Vol. II, pp. 606, 693; V. Bhattacharya, *IHQ*, 1934, p.1 ff.
73. Cf. *Māṇḍūkyakārikā*, 2.16 and Śaṅkara's Comy on it.
74. *Tattvasaṅgraha*, pp. 330-32.
75. *Śankara-granthāvali*, Vol. VII, p. 402.
76. *Ibid.*, p.3; '*Tam etam avidyākhyam. . . adhyāsam puraskṛtya sarve pramāṇa-prameya-vyavahārā laukikāḥ pravṛttāh sarvāni ca śāstrāni vidhi-pratiṣedha-mokṣa-parāṇi*'.
77. E.g., *Madhyamaka* 24.8: *Dve satye samupāśritya buddhānām dharma-deśanā / Lok-samvṛti-satyaṁ ca satyam ca paramārthataḥ //* Cf. G.N. Kaviraj, *op. cit.*, pp. 24-75.
78. The famous *Kātyāyanāvavāda* of *Saṁyukta* is quoted by Nāgārjuna, *Madhyamaka*, 15.7.
79. *Ibid.*, 24.18.
80. Cf. *Ibid.*, 13.8.

10

Digvijaya: Śaṅkara and Mīmāṁsā

Close Connection of the Two Mīmāṁsās

As has been mentioned before the *Pūrva-mīmāṁsā* and the *Uttara-mīmāṁsā* or Vedānta had been closely connected since very ancient times since they represented two branches of learning which aimed at systematizing the meaning of the Vedas. The *Pūrva-mīmāṁsā* was concerned with the elucidation of the concept, content and practice of *dharma* and developed the principles of Vedic exegesis in this context. The *Uttara-mīmāṁsā*, on the other hand, was an enquiry into the nature of *Brahman*. The two *mīmāṁsās*, thus, were *dharma-mīmāṁsā* and *brahma-mīmāṁsā*. *Mīmāṁsā* as a form of enquiry or *jijñāsā* grew up out of the discussions and debates which took place between priests during and after sacrificial sessions. Although the two *mīmāṁsās* reached their classical form in the *sūtras* of Jaimini and Bādarāyaṇa as distinct systems, their close connection continued. The great teachers Bodhāyana and Upavarṣa, thus, appear to have commented on both of them but unfortunately their works have been lost. After the *sūtras* themselves, it is the commentary of Śabara that remains the earliest authoritative work of *Mīmāṁsā*. The *sūtras* as commented upon by Śabara have twelve *adhyāyas* but it is sometimes believed that originally they included four more *adhyāyas* designated *Saṅkarṣa-Kāṇḍa* or *Saṅkarṣaṇa-Kāṇḍa*. Together with the four *adhyāyas* of the *Brahmasūtras*, this corpus of twenty chapters was even held to constitute a unified work. 'The *Mimāṁsā-śāstra* consists of twenty chapters in which sixteen constitute the first part, the *Pūrva-mīmāṁsā-śāstra*, devoted to the discussion of *dharma* and authored by Jaimini. The other four chapters constitute the *Uttara-mīmāṁsā-śāstra* which is devoted to the discussion of *Brahman* and is authored by Vyāsa.'[1] The commentary of Bodhāyana sometimes called *Kṛtakoṭi* and that of Upavarṣa are said to have encompassed this whole corpus of twenty chapters.

As is well known Rāmānuja followed Bodhāyana. He says that *Karma-mīmāṁsā* and *Brahma-mīmāṁsā* constitute a single *śāstra* in which the *Śārīraka* is joined to the *Jaiminīya* of sixteen chapters.[2] The close connection between the two *śāstras* may also be seen from the fact that of the twelve teachers mentioned in them six are common to both.[3]

Apart from Śabara we find references to the commentaries of Devasvāmī and Bhavadāsa. The date of Śabara-svāmī has been suggested by Prof. R.G. Bhandarkar to have been in the Gupta period on account of the use of the honorific *svāmin* in which Scythian influence has been suspected.[4] On the other hand, Śabara has been placed earlier in the 2nd century A.D. or even earlier than Patañjali.[5] The popularity of *Śabara-bhāṣya* which alone has survived of the ancient commentaries, is attested by the fact that there are many sub-commentaries on it. It is said that there was a commentary on it by Bhartṛmittra, and Kumārila, Prabhākara and Murāri Miśra have written upon it. The most famous of these is the commentary of Kumārila Bhaṭṭa in several parts. Prabhākara is said to have been a rebel disciple of Kumārila. He was in all probability a contemporary of Kumārila since neither refers to the other directly which would not have been the case if one were distinctively earlier than the other. Attempts, however, have been made to trace reference to Kumārila in Prabhākara and vice-versa.[6] Maṇḍana Miśra, again, is said to have been a disciple of Kumārila. He is clearly critical of Prabhākara. What is the relationship of Maṇḍana to Śaṅkara and Sureśvara, has been an enigma for modern scholarship. That Kumārila, Prabhākara, Maṇḍana Miśra, Śaṅkara and Sureśvara, all belong to the 7th-8th centuries is more or less certain as is the fact of interaction between them.

Jaimini begins the *Mīmāṁsā* as an enquiry into *dharma* and discusses the sources of its valid knowledge in the first chapter. The second chapter is mainly concerned with primary normative rules *utpatti-vidhi*. The third chapter deals with 'ancillaries' especially the famous six criteria of interpretation, viz., *śruti, liṅga vākya, prakaraṇa sthāna,* and *samākhyā*. The fourth, fifth and sixth chapters consider various matters relating to ritual such as Prayoga, Krama and Adhikāra. The seventh and eighth chapters deal with Atideśa, the ninth with Ūha, the tenth with Bādha, the eleventh with Tantra, the twelfth with Prasaṅga.

Of these the first *pāda* of the first chapter is called the *tarka-pāda* and constitutes the philosophical backbone of the *Mīmāṁsā*. Here

Jaimini has sought to define *dharma,* indicate the means of its valid knowledge, explain and defend the nature of the *Veda* and discuss the nature of language and imperative statements. From the fragments of Upavarṣa presented in Śabara it seems that it was Upavarṣa who introduced here a full-scale discussion of epistemological and metaphysical questions. He discussed the six *pramāṇas* and criticised rival philosophical views including the idealistic and nihilistic views of the Buddhists and the theory of *sphoṭa* upheld by the grammarians. As Upavarṣa was a revered teacher of Vedānta also his views tended to form a part of the heritage of Śaṅkara. Kumārila's *Ślokavārtika* is a detailed philosophical excursus on the *tarkapāda,* to which Prabhākara's *Bṛhatī* and the lost *Laghvī* provide alternatives in some respects.

Despite common teachers like Upavarṣa the two systems of *Mīmāṁsā* and *Vedānta* remained different though connected. *Mīmāṁsā* enquired into the nature and structure of ideal norms or *Dharma, Vedānta* into what is eternally real or *Brahman. Dharma* is a system of prescribed ritual which needs to be performed, *Brahman* a matter of fact to be known. The performance of *Dharma* requires a social position and means. Much of it requires, in particular, being married and having some property. The search for *Brahman,* on the other hand, was generally conceived in the context of transcending social and worldly life. Just as the performance of *Dharma* had a special connection with the householder's life, the quest of *Brahman* was connected with mendicancy. These differences do not amount to any contradiction and are compatible with an over-all unification in which the performance of ritual in the stage of the householder may be followed by the quest for *Brahman* in the stage of the mendicant. Both the systems are strictly orthodox and rely on the sole authority of the Veda for the revelation of the good and have a similar point of view towards the *pramāṇas* in general. This closeness of the two systems comes out strikingly in the dictum '*Vyavahāre bhāṭṭa-nayaḥ*'.

However, in their defence of Vedic othodoxy against the attack of the Buddhists the *Mīmāṁsakas* tended to draw the battle lines deeply and comprehensively and this formulation of Mīmāṁsā as a full-fledged philosophical system such as may be found in Kumārila and Prabhākara is incompatible with *Vedānta,* whether of the *Maṇḍana-prasthāna* or of the *Śāṅkara-prasthāna.* This contradiction is expressed most vividly in the *Mādhavīya Śaṅkara-digvijaya* as the debate between Maṇḍana and Śaṅkara. The

Mīmāṁsakas adopted a realistic and pluralistic metaphysics along with a ritualistic and hedonistic ethics. In all these respects *Vedānta* held a contradictory position.

Of the purely Mīmāṁsā teachers Śaṅkara clearly names Jaimini and Śabara. It is, however, generally believed that he was a junior contemporary of Kumārila and sometimes it is also supposed that he refers to Prabhākara and even converted his son well known as Hastāmalaka. Whether historical or not the traditional account of the debate between Maṇḍana and Śaṅkara certainly does recall the traditional notion of the conflict between *Maṇḍana* and *Śaṅkara.*

Traditional Account of Śaṅkara-Maṇḍana Debate

According to the *Mādhavīya,* while Śaṅkara was at Prayāga he heard that Kumārila, who at one time established the superiority of the Vedas by jumping down from a mountain, and by whose efforts the Vedic cult of sacrifices was re-established, was about to enter into a fire made of paddy husk as an act of expiation for his sin of betraying his teacher. A master of the Vedas, a deep scholar in all branches of learning, and an accomplished dialectician, the wheel of his fame was revolving in all the three worlds.[7] That Kumārila had a thorough knowledge of Buddhist teaching especially of Dharmakīrti or rather Dignāga, is testified by the *Ślokavārtika.* Śaṅkara too quotes Dharmakīrti and could not be far removed from Kumārila whom his direct disciple Sureśvara criticises severely. That Śaṅkara met Kumārila briefly during the last days of the latter is, thus, historically probable. The picturesque circumstances narrated in the *Mādhavīya,* however, cannot be relied upon although there is nothing impossible in them. Self-immolation at Prayāga had a long tradition going back to the *ṚK-pariśiṣṭa.* There is epigraphic evidence of the Gupta ruler Kumāragupta immolating himself in the 6th century at Prayāga[8] where Hsuan Chwang too speaks of religious suicide. These references would not be far from the time of Kumārila. Whether he actually immolated himself and for the reason alleged, remains an unconfirmed possibility.

The legend in the *Mādhavīya* has it that Śaṅkara met Kumārila while he was already seated on husk fire. The great Mīmāṁsaka, however, is said to have seen and appreciated Śaṅkara's commentary and regretted that it was too late for him to compose a *Vārtika* on it as he would have wished to do. He, however, suggested that Śaṅkara should convert his great disciple Maṇḍana.

Bhagavān Śaṅkara now left Prayāga, and travelling through the sky, reached the city of Māhiṣmatī. After resting a while he started for Maṇḍana's place along the road before it was noon. He was informed on the way that where caged parrots discuss abstruse philosophical problems, that would be the gate of Maṇḍana's house. Entering a towering mansion, he got into the hall where Maṇḍana was seated but Maṇḍana was terribly annoyed to note that the newcomer was a *sannyāsin*.[9] After a dual of words and wits Śaṅkara proposed a debate by saying that his mission in life was to establish the truth of *Vedānta* by defeating in debate all who held an opposite view.[10] Maṇḍana having readily agreed Śaṅkara fixed his abode at a temple on a river bank amidst a grove of palms. The debate began the next morning with Maṇḍana's wife elected as the umpire. Śaṅkara announced his position 'Brahman, pure Existence-Consciousness-Bliss is the one ultimate Truth. It is He who appears as the entire world of multiplicity owing to the thick cover of ignorance, just as a shell appears as a piece of silver. Through the knowledge of *Brahman* the whole world is dissolved into its substratum, which is the same as one's own *Ātman*. This is supreme liberation and is the cessation of future births. The crown of the Vedas—the *Upaniṣads*—is the authority in support of this proposition'. Maṇḍana then announced his position, 'The *Vedāntas* or the *Upaniṣads* cannot be a proof for *Brahman* as Pure consciousness. For, words can have no application there. Therefore, the earlier part of the Veda, dealing with effects produced by works, is the real *Śabda-pramāṇa* (verbal testimony). In the light of it, actions alone lead to *Mokṣa*, and embodied beings have to perform action (*Karman*) till the end of their lives.'[11]

Śaṅkara relied on the import of the Vedāntic statements like '*tat tvam asi*' ('That thou art') but Maṇḍana argued that all Vedic sentences are injunctions prompting man to actions, and those which are not so apparently, are allied to actions and have to be interpreted that way. There are in the Veda no purely descriptive sentences about pre-existing facts intending to give mere information unconnected with action. Where such sentences appear to occur they have to be interpreted as statements ancillary to some injunction or imperative. Such descriptive sentences could, thus, be merely eulogistic (*arthavāda*) intended to attract one to some action or they could have a metaphorical or secondary significance. Hence *tat tvam asi* and such other Vedic passages are *vidhi-śeṣas*, ancillary to some injunction. Śaṅkara's reply was that the doctrine of *Vidhi-śeṣa* has no validity beyond the *Karma-Kāṇḍa* of the Vedas. *Tat tvam asi* can hardly be regarded a praise of the sacrificer. Maṇḍana then brought forward another alternative interpretation. *Tat tvam asi* could be for the purpose of meditation. When a sacrificer meditates 'I am That' and superimposes divinity on himself it enhances his power. *Tat tvam asi* would then be parallel to such symbolic meditations as 'Meditate on *Āditya* as *Brahman*.' To the objection that '*Tat tvam asi*' has the verb in the indicative mood while 'Meditate on *Āditya*' etc. has the verb in the imperative mood and thus the two are radically different, it is answered that to be a *śāstra,* Vedāntic passages, apparently descriptive, should be interpreted as veiled inducements to action or commandments. Such passages should be interpreted as *Jñāna-vidhi.* 'That thou art' would then mean 'If you want the fruit of *Mukti,* become *Brahman* through meditation concerning *Brahman* and *Ātman*.' It would be similar in import to more explicit passages such as '*Ātmā vā are śrotavyo mantavyo nididhyāsitavyaḥ*.'

Śaṅkara objects that by such an interpretation *Mokṣa* will become an effect of an action. For, meditation is a mental action. The implication of making *mokṣa* an effect is to make it impermanent like *svarga* and all attainments generated by human activity. In meditation you impose one entity on another by an assertion of the will and generate a new effect which did not exist before. *Brahma-vidyā* is not an activity like that of converting *Ātman,* which was not *Brahman* before, into *Brahman* by mental assertion. *Brahma-vidyā* is knowledge and not an activity like that of converting *Ātman,* which was not *Brahman* before, into Brahman by mental assertion. *Brahma-vidyā* is knowledge and not meditation. Knowledge is a mental mode of 'being what one has always been' and not of 'becoming something that was not before'. The text 'that thou art' declares the eternal nature of things.[12] Upaniṣadic passages looking like commandments such as '*Ātmā vā are śrotavyaḥ*' etc. are only for removing the obstacles to knowledge.

At this Maṇḍana is made to adopt a new position, viz., that what the *Mahāvākya* asserts is not the identity but only the similarity of the individual and supreme spirits, but there is no warrant for it in the *Mahāvākya* itself. The debate now shifts from the formal character of the Upaniṣadic statements to the nature of the truth which they reveal. It is now a debate between the assertion of the unity of *Ātman* and *Brahman* and the assertion of their difference. It is argued that difference cannot be proved by perception, inference or scriptural testimony. Differences are known only in and through the adjuncts or *Upādhis.* The differences are only apparent. The Vedic passages affirming the unity of being are not in any way affected by passages relating to the divisions and distinctions of empirical reality. For, while the non-dualistic passages give a kind of knowledge which cannot be obtained through other means, the dualistic passages teach difference which can be known through other means of knowledge also.[13] The Veda is unique among the means of valid knowledge in that it gives knowledge that cannot be derived from any other means.

Having thus won the argument Śaṅkara is then said to have explained the Jaimini's emphasis on action is relevant to the preparatory discipline of self-purification so that one may be able to move towards self-knowledge. Jaimini's rejection of God too is explained to be the rejection of the rationalist's God who is sought to be proved on the basis of the cosmological argument. This preserves the relevance and relative truth of the *Pūrva-mīmāṁsā.* Maṇḍana having been ultimately defeated and converted is said to have become a disciple of Śaṅkara and to have adopted *sannyāsa* under the name of Sureśvara. The *Mādhavīya* also identifies Maṇḍana with Viśvarūpa and Uṁveka.

The debate of Maṇḍana and Śaṅkara said to be recapitulated in the *Mādhavīya* is plainly not historical since it does not represent the views of Maṇḍana as known from the works attributed to him. The most famous of Maṇḍana's works is *Brahmasiddhi* which reveals him as an *advaitin* and a *Vedāntin* rather than as a *Mīmāṁsaka* though it is true that like many other pre-Śaṅkara Advaitins he had a close link with *Mīmāṁsā*. The reported debate, on the other hand, relates to the standard *Mīmāṁsā* position refuted by Śaṅkara in his works where he maintains that the Upaniṣadic *mahāvākyas* are revelatory of truth and have nothing to do with any injunction of practice. Since the Upaniṣadic truth is eternal and non-dual no action can be directly relevant to it, nor can any kind of duality have ultimate reality. Thus while the *Mādhavīya* correctly delineates the point of view of Śaṅkara vis-a-vis the Mīmāṁsakas generally,[14] it does not do justice to the famous *Vedāntin* named Maṇḍana.

The identity of Maṇḍana has been a matter of considerable controversy since his works have been published and studied. The age-long belief in the Śaṅkarite monastic tradition has been that Maṇḍana was identical with Sureśvara. The tradition recorded in the *Mādhavīya* has been referred to above. Similar views are recorded in other traditional biographies of Śaṅkara. Thus according to Anantānandagiri's *Śaṅkaravijaya* Kumārila informed Śaṅkara that Maṇḍana was his brother-in-law and that it would be advisable for Śaṅkara to debate with him and secure his conversion. This Maṇḍana later came to be a *sannyāsin* under the name of Sureśvara and was placed in charge of the monastery at Śṛṅgeri. The account given in Cidvilāsa's *Śaṅkaravijaya* is similar. It identifies Maṇḍana and Sureśvara. In Vyāsācala's *Śaṅkaravijaya*, however, the account is somewhat different. Here the scholar with whom Śaṅkara holds his debate is identified as Viśvarūpa. He is distinguished from Maṇḍana who is described as a householder whom Śaṅkara meets on the way to Viśvarūpa. In Govindanātha's *Śaṅkarācārya-carita* too, there is no reference to Maṇḍana Miśra while the debating adversary of Śaṅkara whom he meets on the advice of Kumārila is described as Viśvarūpa. This account finds partial confirmation in Lakṣmaṇa Śāstrī's, *Guruvaṁśakāvya* which represents the Śṛṅgeri tradition. Here too we find it stated that it was Viśvarūpa with whom Śaṅkara debated on the advice of Kumārila and that it was Viśvarūpa who became converted to *Sannyāsa* and came to be known as Sureśvara. It is, however similar to the *Vyāsācalīya* tradition in that it mentions Maṇḍana Miśra as a person whom Śaṅkara met and blessed on his way to Viśvarūpa.[15]

In these accounts we find two distinct traditions and also their conflation. According to one tradition Śaṅkara worsted Maṇḍana who become a *sannyāsin* under the name of Sureśvara. According to the other tradition it is Viśvarūpa with whom Śaṅkara debated and who became Sureśvara after assuming *sannyāsa*. The memory of Maṇḍana as well Viśvarūpa appears to have persisted in both traditions so that sometime the two were identified, at others Maṇḍana regarded as a distinct but independent scholar who was a householder and with whom Śaṅkara had a meeting. We have thus three distinct possibilities. Either Maṇḍana was Sureśvara and Viśvarūpa was a different person. Or Viśvarūpa was Sureśvara and Maṇḍana was a different person. Or Maṇḍana was Sureśvara as well as Viśvarūpa.

The traditional biographies of Śaṅkara give support to each one of these possibilities. The identity of Maṇḍana and Sureśvara strongly believed in by the monastic tradition has come in for heavy criticism recently so much so that the weight of scholarly opinion today may be said to be against it. The question, however, cannot be said to have been finally decided. Prof. M. Hiriyanna first challenged it on the ground of doctrinal divergences between Maṇḍana and Sureśvara.[16] He pointed out three principal doctrinal differences. Maṇḍana's views regarding the locus of *avidyā*, the concept of *bhāvādvaita*, and the special value of meditation (*upāsanā*) in transmuting the Brahma-knowledge arising from the *mahāvākyas* into Brahma-realisation, are different from the views of Sureśvara. Prof. Hiriyanna thus, tended to favour the tradition mentioned in the *Guruvaṁśakāvya*. Prof. S. Kuppuswami Sastri has carried the argument much further. 'A careful study of Maṇḍana Miśra's *Brahmasiddhi* in comparison with his other known works all of which are now available in print, and with the known works of Sureśvara and Śaṅkara and in the light of the works of Vācaspatimiśra, Vimuktātman, Prakāśātman, Ānandabodha, Prakaṭārthakāra, Citsukha, Amalānanda, Ānandagiri, Vidyāraṇya, Madhusūdana Sarasvatī, Brahmānanda Sarasvatī and several others representing the Advaita system, and a careful consideration of the references to Maṇḍana contained in certain important work of Mīmāṁsā, Nyāya, Dvaita Vedānta and other systems have made it possible to assemble here several data of overwhelming cumulative weight, which would be quite sufficient to kill the common belief in the *Maṇḍana-Sureśvara* equation, and to exhibit Maṇḍana and Sureśvara as two different individuals maintaining strikingly divergent views within the purview of Advaitism.'[17]

The arguments marshalled by Prof. Kuppuswami are as follows: Maṇḍana followed the *Sphoṭavāda* and *Śabdādvaita* of Bhartṛhari and thought it consistent with *Brahmādvaita*. He argued that the identity of *Praṇava* with *Brahman* indicates this unity. The imperishable word is the matrix of all phenomena and is the same as *Brahman*. Now Śaṅkara rejects the *sphoṭa*-doctrine and Sureśvara ignores it.

Maṇḍana gives an honoured place to the Bhāṭṭa theory of *Viparīta-khyāti* or *anyathākhyāti* as an explanation of error. The theory of the Advaitins, on the other hand, is *anirvacanīyatākhyāti*. Sureśvara refutes *anyathākhyāti* cavalierly. Maṇḍana, again recognizes two kinds of *avidyā* viz., non-apprehension (*agrahaṇa*) and misapprehension (*anyathāgrahaṇa*). He utilizes this distinction in explaining the relevance of meditation in his scheme of attaining liberation. Sureśvara specifically refers to Maṇḍana's view regarding *avidyā-dvaividhya* and argues against it.

Maṇḍana argues that *Jīva* is the locus (*āśraya*) of *avidyā* while *Brahman* is its object or *Viṣaya*. Sureśvara is against such a distinction and holds that *Brahman* is both the locus and object of *avidyā*. These two views served as the basis of the later distinction within *advaita* between the *Bhāmatī* school and the *Vivaraṇa* school going back respectively to Maṇḍana and Sureśvara.

Maṇḍana holds that since verbal knowledge is relational and mediate, the knowledge gained merely from the Upaniṣadic *mahāvākyas* is not the direct realization of *Brahman*. Meditation on this indirect knowledge is necessary to convert it into realization. This is called the doctrine of *Prasaṅkhyāna* and was in line with similar earlier views held by some Vedāntins. Sureśvara refers to this earlier tradition to which Maṇḍana belonged and rejects the idea that meditation is necessary for the realization of *Brahman* or that word can only give indirect knowledge. Maṇḍana's interpretation of the *Īśāvāsya* text '*vidyāṁ cāvidyāṁ ca* etc. is entirely different from those of Śaṅkara and Sureśvara. Maṇḍana has two different explanations but he seems to argue that it refers to the eradication of nescience by the practical realization of eternal self-knowledge. Sureśvara differs from even Śaṅkara and is keen that the verse is not so interpreted as to give any ground for bringing in the combination of action and knowledge (*jñāna-karma-samuccaya*).

On the relationship of *Karman* and *Jñāna* Maṇḍana holds a position strikingly different from that of Śaṅkara and Sureśvara. Maṇḍana notices as many as seven theories on this question. Of these he supports only two, viz., that the activities prescribed in the *Karman Kāṇḍa* are bi-functional in their character and have two distinct functions (*saṁyoga-pṛthaktva*) by conducing to their respective fruits and also to the realisation of *Ātman*. Or, that all *karman* is intended to purify men and make them fit for *ātma-jñāna*. Maṇḍana thus favours a peculiar variety of *Jñāna-karma-samuccaya* such as is implied in the *saṁyoga-pṛthaktvapakṣa* and the *saṁskāra-pakṣa*. In his opinion '*agnihotra* and such other obligatory rites form a highly valuable accessory to the repeated contemplation (*abhyāsa*) on the content of the verbal cognition (*śabdajñāna*) arising from the *mahāvākyas* of the *Upaniṣads*, in bringing about the final manifestation (*abhivyakti*) of the eternally self-luminous light of *Ātman*. . . That those who have chosen to enter the religious order of *sannyāsa* can and do come by *Ātman*-realisation, exclusively through the tranquillising, self-effacing, soul-centred, non-possessive contemplative discipline, wihout the performance of scriptural rites and that the meditative discipline which brings about the manifestation of the pure *Brahma-vidyā*, when implemented by the prescribed *Yajñas* and such other rites, enables one (presumably a *gṛhastha*), to get at the final goal far more quickly than otherwise, when *Karman* is not comprised in the means employed.'[18] The progress of the householder who performs obligatory and purifying ritual and also engages in meditation over the Vedāntic truth is much faster than that of the mendicant just as a person on horse-back gallops quickly to the goal compared with one who plods on foot.[19] For Śaṅkara and Sureśvara, on the other hand, the performance of ritual is not compatible with the knowledge of *Brahman*.

Maṇḍana's conception of *Jīvanmukta* differs from that of Śaṅkara and Sureśvara. The difference relates to the role of *Prārabdha-karman*. For Śaṅkara the *Prārabdha-karman* of the *Jīvanmukta* has to work itself out, it cannot be stopped like an arrow shot from the bow. The state of the *Jīvanmukti* would be inevitable in all such cases and Śaṅkara illustrates them by the *Sthitaprajña* of the *Gītā* or the *Ādhikārikas* like Apāntaratamas, Sanaka, Vasiṣṭha etc. Maṇḍana, on the other hand, holds *sadyomukti* to be perfectly logical and consistent with *smṛti* and *śruti*. He admits, however, that *pārabdha-karman* may continue to produce effects for some time and that this would be the state of *Jīvanmukti* but he contests Śaṅkara's examples by regarding the *sthitaprajña* and the *ādhikārikas* as merely evolved *sādhakas*, not *siddhas*. *Jīvanmukti* is a temporary state resulting from the persistence of some trace of nescience (*avidyā-saṁskāra*).[20]

Maṇḍana believed in what has been called *bhāvādvaita* or *sadadvaita*. 'According to this view there is only one absolute reality of a positive kind, viz., *Brahman*. . . the realisation of *Brahman* as the only absolute reality brings about the removal of nescience (*avidyā-nivṛtti*); the negation of the world and the removal of nescience are negative realities and do not come into conflict with the monism of Advaita, which excludes only a second positive reality (*bhāva*) and is quite compatible with the recognition of a negative reality other than *Brahman*, in the form of *prapañcābhāva* or *avidyādhvaṁsa*.'[21] Although Maṇḍana does not use the term *bhāvādvaita* such a view is associated with his name in later Advaitic and Dvaita classics and may be supported from his own writings. Although the doctrine continued to exert influence on subsequent Vedāntins, Sureśvara rejects it categorically as inconsistent with the very nature of negation which cannot have a negative locus.

While Sureśvara was a devout and avowed follower of Śaṅkara, Maṇḍana gives the impression of being an independent thinker who differs from and criticises Śaṅkara as a rival philosopher. Maṇḍana's interpretations of scriptural passages such as *'oṁ iti Brahma', ' Vijñāya prajñāṁ kurvīta', Vidyāṁ cāvidyāṁ ca', ' Tattu samanvayāt', 'Sarvapakṣe ca yajñādiśruteraśvavat', ' Vedānta-vijñāna-suniścitārthā. . .'* etc. illustrate his divergence from Śaṅkara and Sureśvara.

Prof. Kuppuswamy says, 'In none of the available authoritative works on the *Advaita* system, Maṇḍana Miśra is identified with Sureśvara, while in many Vedāntic works of the Advaita and Dvaita schools, Maṇḍana and Sureśvara are distinguished as two different *advaitins*'.[22] Thus Sureśvara himself criticises Maṇḍana's views. Sarvajñātmamuni distinguishes Maṇḍana's *prasthāna* from that of Śaṅkara. Prakāśātman speaks of the *Brahmasidhikāra* without identifying him with Sureśvara. Similarly Ānandabodha refers to Maṇḍana's views and distinguishes them from Sureśvara's. Citsukha attributes these references to *Brahmasiddhikāra.* Pratyaksvarūpa differentiates Maṇḍana from Sureśvara. Ānandānubhava distinguishes Viśvarūpa from Maṇḍana clearly and identifies Viśvarūpa with Sureśvara. Ānandagiri states that Sureśvara rejects the views of Maṇḍana. Amalānanda too draws attention to the contrast of Maṇḍana's views with those of Śaṅkara and Sureśvara. Vidyāraṇya too identifies Viśvarūpa and Sureśvara while distinguishing between him and Maṇḍana. Appayadīkṣita too generally distinguishes between the views of *Brahmasiddhikāra* and *Vārtikakāra* even though he mixes them up at one place. The distinction may be found again in Madhusūdana Sarasvatī, Brahmānanda Sarasvatī, and the commentators of the *Saṅkṣepaśārīraka.* The *Dvaita* philosopher Vyāsatīrtha too treats Maṇḍana and Sureśvara differently.

Prof. Kuppuswamy concludes, '*firstly* that Maṇḍana, the author of the *Brahmasiddhi,* was not identical with Sureśvara and represented an *advaitic prasthāna* different from *Śāṅkaraprasthāna; secondly* that Sureśvara who was known as Viśvarūpa in his *gṛhastha* and came to be known by the name of Sureśvara when he became a *sannyāsin* and a disciple of Śaṅkara;. . . and *thirdly* that Maṇḍana should have written his *Brahmasiddhi* after seeing

Śaṅkara's *bhāṣyas,* more particularly the *Brahmasūtra bhāṣya.*[23]

That there are doctrinal differences between Maṇḍana and Sureśvara may be taken to be unquestionably established. But can that be taken to be a sufficient reason to regard them as different persons? As Prof. Kunhan Raja has rightly pointed out even the work of the same author may show strikingly different opinions.[24] For example Prabhākara is known to be responsible for both the *Vivaraṇa* as well as the *Nibandhana,* which contain distinct views. One could adduce many other examples here. Bertrand Russel or even Wittgenstein could be recalled here. Such changes in opinion come easily to authors who are independent thinkers or who come under the influence of a new school or personality. In the case of Maṇḍana both of these factors undoubtedly operated. He had a strongly independent turn of mind. Even as a Mīmāṁsaka he differed from both Kumārila and Prabhākara. At the same time he was also a Vedāntin and as a Vedāntin he differed from Śaṅkara and followed another tradition. With such antecedents if he were to be converted one would expect him to undergo some change of opinion. This has been emphasized by several scholars like Prof. P.P. Subramanya Sastri and Prof. Balasubramanian.[25]

An important factor on the side which argues in favour of the identity of Maṇḍana and Sureśvara is the identity of a number of arguments in substance as well as words in the *Brahmasiddhi* and the *Sambandhavārtika.* If the authors were different these striking correspondences would be quite puzzling. Somehow this fact escaped Prof. Kuppuswamy Sastri. Rama Krishna Kavi says that the similarity is such that it could be the basis of a charge of plagiarism against Sureśvara. 'Works of Maṇḍana and Sureśvara have many common thoughts, arguments and even expressions. If their identity is denied similarity in thought and expression may border upon Sureśvara's plagiarism as he lived a few decades later than Maṇḍana. It may particularly be noted that a series of arguments in the *Sambandhavārtika* of Sureśvara appears to be the mere paraphrase in verse of the second and third chapters of Maṇḍana's *Brahmasiddhi.* In two or three places common verses occur without any alteration. This commonness prompted later readers to identify them instead of attributing plagiarism to Sureśvara.'[26] The explanation which is suggested by R.K. Kavi is that the *Sambandhavārtika* was intended to continue the polemic of Maṇḍana against Prabhākara. Śālikanātha had rebutted Maṇḍana's charges and Sureśvara 'had to write his preface in which repeating all the arguments of Maṇḍana he supplemented his own to defeat Śālikanātha. This phase of development was long forgotten by later scholars who were naturally reluctant to attribute plagiarism to Sureśvara and imagined his identity with Maṇḍana.'[27] As Prof. Balasubramanian says this explanation is not satisfactory. The *Sambandhavārtika* has a genuine connection with the introduction of the *Bhāṣya* itself. As to the wholly hypothetical history reconstructed by R.K. Kavi, Prof. Balasubramanian pertinently remarks, 'How Kavi came to know of this phase of development, we do not know; nor has be furnished any evidence in support of his contention.'[28]

Prof. Suryanarayana Sastri has given a different explanation of the common thoughts and expression between Maṇḍana and Sureśvara. He argues that 'what is good enough to be appreciated is also good enough to be appropriated', seems to have been the maxim of the time.'[29] Thus although Sureśvara borrowed a good deal from Maṇḍana we should not charge him (Sureśvara) with plagiarism in view of the conventions of the time. It is not clear where Prof. Sastri found the evidence for formulating such a convention. Prof. Balasubramanian rightly remarks 'It is not a case of common ideas, similar arguments and identical expressions which are found in a limited number of verses, say half a dozen or so. The entire sequence of arguments and turns of expressions closely packed and briefly stated in nearly four pages of terse prose in the *Brahmasiddhi* are found restated in the *Sambandhavārtika* in more than sixty verses.'[30]

As for the difference noticed by some Advaitic authors between the views of Maṇḍana and Sureśvara and the references made to them as distinct authors, it is worthy of note that the distinction is always made between either the *Brahmasiddhikāra* and the *Vārtikakāra* or between the *Maṇḍana-prasthāna* and the *Śāṅkara-prasthāna* or between certain views stated in the *Brahmasiddhi* and those stated in the *Vārtika* or the *Naiṣkarmyasiddhi.* There certainly is a difference in the opinions expressed by Maṇḍana in the *Brahmasiddhi* and those expressed by Sureśvara in the *Vārtika* or *Naiṣkarmyasiddhi* and this difference is noticed by later writers. The identity of Maṇḍana and Sureśvara does not thereby stand impugned because the earlier views of Maṇḍana in some respects still evoked a favourable response in later writers. Maṇḍana was admittedly an author of established fame and authority before his conversion and the tradition which he represented and to which he had contributed did not wholly die out even after his conversion.

Some scholars like M.M. Ananta Krishna Sastri have argued that the doctrinal differences between Maṇḍana and Sureśvara were after all not so great.[31] Thus it has been questioned that Maṇḍana believed in *Bhāvādvaita*. Maṇḍana's *viparītakhyāti* is not much different from *anirvacanīyatākhyāti*, a point conceded by Prof. Kuppuswami Sastri also. The views of Maṇḍana and Sureśvara on liberation and on the alternatives of *Karman* and *Jñāna* are capable of reconciliation.

There is no doubt that there are similarities as well as differences between the writings ascribed to Maṇḍana and Sureśvara but their identity is not proved by the similarities just as it is not disproved by the differences. If the internal evidence is not sufficient to decide their identity, the external evidence consisting of the traditional biographies of Śaṅkara or of the references in Advaitic writers collected by Prof. Kuppuswamy Sastri too is insufficient to pronounce decisively on the question. Maṇḍana could well be the same as Sureśvara but we cannot be certain because the tradition of their identity dates only from medieval times and we cannot be sure about the lost ancient sources on which it claimed to base itself. On the other hand, the more fashionable view which makes out Maṇḍana and Sureśvara to be different persons confuses the historical identity of persons with the identity of views. If adequate external evidence is lacking, no question of identity can be satisfactorily settled merely by considerations of views or even style. Considerations of 'internal evidence' cannot be definitive. And in the present case they give contradictory indications.

On the identity of Viśvarūpa and Sureśvara, however, the evidence is distinctly better but not without contradiction. Not only is it attested by several of the traditional biographies of Śaṅkara, some ancient references too seem to support it. Mādhavācārya in his commentary on the *Parāśara Smṛti* quotes a verse from the *Bṛhadāraṇyaka-vārtika* and ascribes it to Viśvarūpa.[32] Brahmānanda Bhāratī in the *Puruṣārthaprabodha* attributes the *Naiṣkarmyasiddhi* to Viśvarūpācārya. The *Nyāyaratnadīpāvalī* clearly distinguishes between the works written by Viśvarūpa as *gṛhastha* and those written by him as a *sannyāsin* when he was known as Parivrājakācārya Sureśvara.[33] Vidyāraṇya in his *Vivaraṇaprameyasaṅgraha* quotes Sureśvara under the name of Viśvarūpācārya.

It would be sufficiently definite from these references that

Viśvarūpa was probably the civil name of Sureśvara before he became a mendicant disciple of Śaṅkara. Whether Viśvarūpa was also called Maṇḍana, however, remains uncertain. It may be mentioned here that an attempt has been made to explain Maṇḍana as an honorific. At the same time, it needs to be noted that Viśvarūpa and Sureśvara differ over the eligibility to Sannyāsa.[34]

Maṇḍana himself does not give any definite information about himself. He refers to the views of Kumārila as well as Prabhākara. He is aware of Dharmakīrti, and he has been criticized by Sureśvara and Śālikanātha. This makes him more or less a contemporary of Śaṅkara. That he was a famous Mīmāṁsaka and also a Vedāntin aware of the pre-Śaṅkara tradition are well established facts. Whether Maṇḍana became a disciple of Śaṅkara is not certain but that he came in contact with the works of Śaṅkara and reacted to them with characteristic independence in the philosophical arena by accepting as well as criticising his views in the *Brahmasiddhi* is most probable. Kuppuswamy Sastri, Tilmann Vetter and Allen Thrasher have pointed out a number of passages in Maṇḍana which seem to refer to Śaṅkara and criticise his views.[35] Some ancient commentators like Amalānanda too have seen a reference to Śaṅkara's views in Maṇḍana. Thus irrespective of whether there was a formal debate between Maṇḍana and Śaṅkara or whether Maṇḍana was finally converted into Sureśvara or not, the fact remains that Maṇḍana was challenged by Śaṅkara's ideas into trying to refute them or rather critically resynthesize them, but ultimately lost in the struggle for primacy within the circle of non-dualistic Vedāntins not only because of the influence of Śaṅkara but in particular because of Sureśvara's critique of his (Maṇḍana's) ideas, presumably at the behest of Śaṅkara. It may be recalled that there was an old tradition to the effect that the disciples of Śaṅkara at first doubted whether Maṇḍana could faithfully interpret the Master's ideas. *Brahmasiddhi* could well create such doubts. It is only the *Naiṣkarmyasiddhi* that set the doubts at rest.

Since Maṇḍana was apparently the most important representative of the Mīmāṁsā as well as of pre-Śaṅkara Vedānta in the age of Śaṅkara, his views would serve to highlight what Śaṅkara and Sureśvara refuted. Maṇḍana's works on Mīmāṁsā are the *Mīmāṁsānukarmaṇikā*, the *Bhāvanāviveka* and the *Vidhiviveka*. His *Sphoṭasiddhi* tends to follow the path shown by Bhartṛhari, *Vibhramaviveka* discusses the nature of error and *Brahmasiddhi* is his major work on Vedānta. The *Bhāvanāviveka* seeks to develop

Kumārila's exposition of the concept of *ārthī bhāvanā* which is defended against the grammarians' theory which subsumes *bhāvanā* in the meaning of the roots as the mere production of an effect, not as volitional effort. In a prescriptive sentence the mood of the verb expresses its activating or instigative intention and is called the *śābdībhāvanā* while the verb in its generic sense signified the action to be motivated. Prescriptive or imperative statements contain the intention of the speaker or an impersonal impulsion as well as a motivation for the addressee. Broadly *śābdībhāvanā* and *ārthībhāvanā* correspond to this distinction. By its very form the imperative statement contains a normative or directive intention or force which requires to be connected with motivation for its realization. An imperative like '*svarga-kāmo yajeta*' impels a person to the voluntary performance of a sacrifice. The impelling force of the words is the *śābdībhāvanā* while the voluntary action to which the person is motivated is the *ārthībhāvanā*.[36] What is the nature of the activating force in ritualistic or moral prescriptions was a matter of much discussion. The Mīmāṁsakas especially Prabhākara tended to be formalistic while the Nyāya tended to be utilitarian.[37] Maṇḍana attempts in effect a reconciliation which would be relevant to the Vedāntic position too. The Mīmāṁsakas had tended to restrict the scope of the signification of Vedic statements to action only, thus regarding the Veda simply as a body of practical prescriptions. All descriptive statements were then held to be ancillary to action or else eulogistic or metaphorical. This would contradict the Vedāntic stand that the *mahāvākyas* are primarily revelatory of truth.

In the *Vidhiviveka* Maṇḍana maintains that the impelling force or *pavartanā* conveyed by the mandatory affixes in a Vedic prescription consists ultimately in the realization that the action being indicated is a means to the satisfaction of some desired good (*iṣṭasādhanatva*). 'Nothing leads a man to action except the means to what is desired. This impulsion is called the activating *dharma*.'[38] Man engages in action only to realize some good, viz., some desired end and adopts a course of action which he understands to be a means to it. The Vedas reveal the means like sacrifice etc. by which men may attain to their good and thus Vedic statements induce men into engaging in ritual etc. The followers of Prabhākara had held that Vedic statements are of the nature of command—*Niyoga*—which obliges men into directed activities.[39] This notion of the unconditionally obligatory character of a command represents a perennial kind of formalism to be found in theories of law and morals. Maṇḍana rejects this way of thinking by arguing that the sense of some obligation depends on its being recognized as contributing to one's good. Even if one were to accept that the Veda invariably enjoins some activity, 'the Upaniṣadic texts could be maintained to be purposeful and valid, in as much as they lead to the highest kind of *pravṛtti* in the form of meditation on the Absolute *Brahman* as the only reality, such *upāsanā* being indispensable for transforming the indirect knowledge of *Brahman* arising from the *mahāvākyas* into direct Brahma-realisation and such *pravṛtti* being directed towards the highest end of human endeavour viz., *Brahman*-realisation concomitant with complete liberation from bondage (*mukti*).'[40]

The *Brahmasiddhi* of Maṇḍana is his only known avowedly Vedāntic work. Its continuity with the *Sphoṭasiddhi* gives it a slant different from that of Śaṅkara who rejected the idea of *sphoṭa* following the lead given by Upavarṣa. In Śaṅkara *avidyā* is the creative power (*bīja-śakti*) of *Brahman* which projects *nāmarūpa* or phenomena. It is not simply the Ignorance located in the *Jīva*. Maṇḍana, on the other hand, is constrained to regard the phenomena as the manifestation or transformation of the World which in its eternal nature is the same as *Brahman*. He thus locates *avidyā* in the *Jīva* and makes *Brahman* its object. For him the word is creative as also normative and revelatory. Maṇḍana's preoccupation with the nature and role of the word arose from his connection with both the grammatical and the Mīmāṁsaka traditions. He never fully realized the difficulties of combining these traditions with Vedāntic non-dualism and the kind of Nescience which that requires. It would seem that Maṇḍana was originally a Mīmāṁsaka who never gave up his concern with the role of the Vedic word in the context of the active human search for the good. He appears to have been converted to non-dualism under the influence of Bhartṛhari. The influence of Śaṅkara led him into Vedānta firmly but he sought to weave a new and original synthesis in which elements of Mīmāṁsā, Bhartṛhari, pre-Śaṅkara and Śaṅkara Vedānta were put together. It has been assumed that the epithet 'Pre-Śaṅkara Vedāntin' is sufficient to explain his relationship to Śaṅkara. In fact, 'Pre-Śaṅkara Vedānta' did not constitute a single school and while Maṇḍana and Śaṅkara were both acquainted with earlier commentators and Masters, our own knowledge about them is extremely scanty. Although some later Advaitins referred to the tradition to which Maṇḍana belonged, Maṇḍana himself does not avow allegiance to any Master or school in the *Brahmasiddhi*, neither Śaṅkara nor another. His reliance even on the *Brahmasūtras* is but slight since they are referred to only five times in the *Brahmasiddhi*. He relies principally on the *Upaniṣads* especially, the *Bṛhadāraṇyaka*, though he refers to *Mīmāṁsā* works more frequently. The difference between post-Śaṅkara and pre-Śaṅkara Vedānta rests essentially on the fact that the coordination between the two *Mīmāṁsās* underwent a basic change as a result of Śaṅkara's influence. Although Maṇḍana does not wholly succumb to this influence he is not untouched by it.

Maṇḍana begins the *Brahmasiddhi* with a defence of the view that *Brahman* is of the nature of ānanda. Śaṅkara's reluctance on this point has been remarked. Commenting on '*Vijñānam ānandam brahman*' (*Br.* 3.9.7), he mentions and rejects a number of views, maintaining that *ānanda* refers to the nature of *Brahman* not to its experienceability in *Brahman—'tasmād vijñānānandam iti svarūpānvākhyānaparaiva śrutiḥ natvānanda-saṁvedyatvārthā*.'[41] Maṇḍana discusses the problem and the view of Śaṅkara without any explicit reference. Like a bold *Vārtikakāra* he admits the essential truth of Śaṅkara but adopts a refinement. *Ānanda* is not experienced as an object but it is not inexperienced since it is the nature of self-consciousness. '*Tasmāt saṁvedyam ātmaprakāśatvāt, asaṁvedyam ca viṣayavat karmabhāvābhāvāt*.'[42]

Concerning *avidyā* Maṇḍana describes it as '*nātyantam asatī nāpi satī evam eveyam avidyā māyā mithyāvabhāsa iti. . . tasmād anirvacanīyā*.'[43] This is essentially within the position of Śaṅkara who describes *avidyā* as *adhyāsa* and *adhyāsa* as *mithyāpratyaya-rūpa*. *Avidyā* constructs *nāmarūpa* and these are *anirvacanīya*. As to the distinction between the *viparītakhyāti* held by Maṇḍana and the position of Śaṅkara, the distinction is not substantial. Śaṅkara refers to the *khyātis* without designating them and without proposing a new one called *anirvacanīya-khyāti*. He says that all the views must accept that error involves the appearance of one thing as another—*anyasyānya-dharmāvabhāsatām*.' What is essential to Śaṅkara's position is the rejection of Mīmāṁsaka realism with which Maṇḍana too cannot agree. The question of error had been discussed in classical systems earlier but the emergence of illusionism within the orthodox fold was a phenomenon which had been initiated by Gauḍapāda and completed by Śaṅkara. The views of Maṇḍana in the *Brahmasiddhi* are intelligible only in this context. It has been said that Maṇḍana distinguishes two aspects of *avidyā*, viz., *agrahana* and *anyathāgrahana.*[44] Śaṅkara notes that distinction without making it fundamental. Thus he says *avidyā* may be *'viparītagrāhakaḥ saṁśayopasthāpakah vā agrahaṇā-tmakovā.'* There are thus *three* forms of *avidyā—avidyātrayam.*[45] As to the locus and object of *avidyā* Śaṅkara rightly discusses it in a dialectical manner. The attempt to dogmatize the answer as in Maṇḍana and later disciples of Śaṅkara only shows that they were later systemizers.

Maṇḍana says that the diversity of the *Jīvas* is due to *avidyā—'kalpanādhīno hi jīva-vibhāgaḥ.'* This really goes back to Gauḍapāda who says *'Jīvam Kalpayate pūrvam.'* Śaṅkara follows it and declares *'Tatra Jīya-Kalpanā sarva-kalpanā-mūlam.'*

Again as regards the relationship of cause and effect Maṇḍana says *'Nahi prakṛti-vikārayor atyantam availakṣanyam, prakṛtivikāra-bhave eva na syāt.'* This is similar to Śaṅkara's *'atyantasārūpyeca prakṛti-vikāra-bhāva eva pralīyeta.'*[46] Maṇḍana argues that *Brahman* and *Jīva* being like *bimba* and *pratibimba* are not different but the reflection acquires the impurities of the reflective medium.[47] This is similar to Śaṅkara who says *'jala-sūryādi-pratibimba-vad ātma-praveśaḥ.'*[48]

Maṇḍana argues that even something false in itself can convey a real meaning. *'Nāyam niyamaḥ-asatyaṁ na kasmaicit kāryāya bhavati. Bhavati hi māyā prīter bhayasya ca nimittam asatyam ca satyapratipatteḥ yathā rekhāgavayo lipyakṣarāṇi ca'.*[49] Śaṅkara too argues similarly—*'Tathākārādi-satyākṣara-pratipattirdṛṣṭa-rekhānṛtākṣara-pratipattiḥ.'*[50]

Again Maṇḍana's distinction of *Brahman* and *prapañca* even though not identical is clearly reminiscent of Śaṅkara. Maṇḍana says *'Brahmaṇona sarvātmatā, sarvaṁ tu brahmātmakam.'*[51] Śaṅkara says, *'Brahma-svabhāvo hi prapañco na prapañca-svabhāvam brahma.'*[52]

On the other hand, when Maṇḍana formulates the *Pūrvapakṣa* as *'Tasmān nāvagata-brahmātma-bhāvāt prāgiva sāṁsārika-dharma-bhāk, yastu tathā nāsāvavagata-brahmātmā iti,'*[53] he is clearly quoting Śaṅkara who has *'Tasmān nāvagata-brahmātma-bhāvasya yathāpūrvam saṁsāritvam, yasya tu yathāpūrvam saṁsāritvam nāsāvavagata-brahmā—tma-bhā vaityanavadyam.'*[54] It should also be noted that in the course of this *pūrvapakṣa* which asserts that *'Dvaita-viṣayam karma advaitaviṣayam jñānam,'* the arguments mentioned by Maṇḍana seek to summaize those used by Śaṅkara.

The main difference of Maṇḍana from Śaṅkara lies in the former's acceptance of the need of meditative action even after the hearing and understanding of the *mahāvākyas* and of the relevance of works to the life of spiritual seeking. Even after one has understood the *mahāvākyas* false perceptions arising from past habit continue and to remove them meditative practice is needed. Prescribed ritual too helps by removing the force of past actions. '*Tan nivṛttaye astyanyad apekṣyam, tacca tattvadarśanābhyāso loka-siddhaḥ, yajñādayaśca śabda-pramāṇakaḥ abhyāso hi— pūrva-saṁskāram pratibaddhya sva-kāryam santanoti Yajñādayaśca kenāpyadṛṣṭena prakāreṇa.*'[55]

As mentioned earlier Maṇḍana accepts the role of *Karman* in the attainment of knowledge as *samyogapṛthaktva* and *saṁskāra*. He admits the concept of *Āśrama-vikalpa* and hence the possibility of the attainment of knowledge without the performance of ritual works as in the case of those who do not enter the householders' life. But he holds that the practice of ritual duties makes the attainment of knowledge faster. He does not, however, accept the Mīmāṁsā contention that the Upaniṣadic statements have to be construed as injunctions or unconditional commands to some kind of practice except that the right knowledge about *Brahman* obtained from such statements may lead to meditative practice for its perfection. The Upaniṣadic statements are not practical injunctions or categorical commands, nor do they convey any meaning in terms of some action or norm. They give the knowledge of what is a fact. This knowledge can be the basis of further voluntary practice, in this case, of meditation.

Thus although Maṇḍana has repudiated a number of Mīmāṁsā presumptions about the interpretation of Upaniṣadic statements in the light of the concepts of *bhāvanā* and *niyoga*, he has not wholly sundered the connection between the two *Mīmāṁsās*. The Upaniṣadic word is not a prescription or command but the revelation of a fact; nevertheless, it prepares the ground for meditation. The *coup de gras* to this retention of a *mīmāṁsaka* attitude is given by Sureśvara in his *Naiṣkarmya-siddhi* which seeks to establish that *jñāna* is the sole means to *mokṣa* and that *karman* needs to be renounced in the process.

The Mīmāṁsakas conceived *mokṣa* in a purely negative fashion as the cessation of *saṁsāra* and no more. The means of achieving this comprise abstention from desire-prompted or immoral deeds (*kāmya* and *pratiṣiddha-karmans*), and strict adherence to the performance of obligatory works (*nitya-karmas*). Having thus presented the *pūrvapakṣa* Sureśvara points out that *karman* itself is rooted in *avidyā* which is the real cause of *saṁsāra*. The *nitya-karmans* or socio-religious obligations presuppose *varṇāśramādyabhimāna* which proceeds from *avidyā*. *Avidyā* can be eradicated by *vidyā* or knowledge only. Now both the *Mīmāṁsās* are agreed that this knowledge can come only from the Veda. The Prābhākara school had held the extreme position that language is necessarily pragmatic and hence Vedic statements can only relate to works. Kumārila accepted that there could be descriptive statements but held them to be logically secondary in the Vedic context. Thus descriptive statements about the Self do not reveal anything new since the Self is known introspectively. Such statements do not constitute any valid and original source of knowledge such as the Veda is expected to be. These statements, thus, are to be interpreted as secondary to the injunctions to action. The Vedāntins did not accept this because the nature of the Self as non-dual and identical with *Brahman* is not known from any other source and this knowledge is itself the final end. It is not preliminary to any further action or end.

At this point, however, the earlier Vedāntins had mutual differences. Sureśvara refers to three such views which advocated diverse ways of combining *Jñāna* and *Karman*.[56] The first of these views advocating *samuccaya* has been attributed to Brahmadatta. According to it the *Upaniṣads* advocate meditation on the *Ātman*. '*Ātmetyevopāsīta*' is thus primary while '*Tat tvam asi*' furnishes the theme for the meditation prescribed by the former. Emancipation really comes from this practice. In the meanwhile the obligatory works must be performed. The second view attributed to Maṇḍana is similar except that it regards emancipation to follow from the direct knowledge which comes from the practice of meditation. The third view was ascribed to Bhatṛprapañca and advocated *Jñāna-karma-samuccaya* on the basis of a doctrine of *bhedābheda*. All these views are rejected by Sureśvara who holds that the Upaniṣadic statements are capable of giving direct knowledge. *Śruti* is the sole and sufficient source of self-knowledge. It is the nature of knowledge that arises from the *Pramāṇa* and conforms to its object. It does not depend on any volitional effort or action. On the other hand, it is not denied that action or meditation has an indirect relevance as a preparation before the actual dawn of knowledge which can come only from the Vedic word as *Pramāṇa*. What is implicit in this view is a theory of graded spiritual eligibility.

Sureśvara's critique of the Mīmāṁsakas in his *Naiṣkarmyasiddhi* was composed at the instance of the Master himself who had already argued his position extensively. For example in his comments on the *sūtra 'Tat tu samanvayāt,'* Śaṅkara presents several alternatives argued by the Mīmāṁsakas and rejects them in detail. Jaimini has the *sūtra āmnāyasya Kriyārthatvād ānarthakyam atadarthānām'* (1.2.1). 'Because the Veda is concerned throughout with action, the Vedāntic parts which do not contribute to that end are useless.' It follows that the *Upaniṣads* should be construed either as auxiliaries to some injunctions (*Kriyā-vidhiśeṣatvam*) or as throwing light on the nature of the agent of the sacrifice or of the presiding deities or other factors in it. Or else they could be taken to be enjoining meditation. Thus their relevance would be to show the symbolic significance of the presiding deity and other elements in the sacrifice.[57] If the Upaniṣadic texts are purely informative they would be practically useless or else embody some implicit recommendation for some enjoined action. As merely descriptive the Upaniṣads cannot lead by themselves to the highest good.

Against this Śaṅkara argues that the *Upaniṣads* plainly claim to inform us about the nature of *Brahman*. Why should this plain intention be disregarded? As for enjoined acts like the sacrifices the *Upaniṣads* repudiate their necessity for the person with wisdom. *Brahman* is undoubtedly a fact, but it is not accessible to any empirical source of knowledge. Nor is this fact of any practical value to man because its knowledge alone can destroy all suffering. Nor can it be argued that the Upaniṣadic statements about the Self constitute an injunction about meditation or that an injunction is required to know the Self. The Self is known by hearing the Upaniṣadic statements and this knowledge is itself the final end. No injunction for any action is involved here. If the very hearing of a statement were to require a prior injunction, there would be an infinite regress because the hearing of that prior injunction would require still another. The fact is that injunctions belong to a practical context, not to a purely cognitive context.

It has been said that Śaṅkara's opposition to the Mīmāṁsakas 're-enacts the opposition of the forest-sages of the Upaniṣadic period to the ritualists of the small towns and villages of their day'. Actually Śaṅkara's critique represents the ancient tradition of mendicancy which protested against the 'materialism' which was accommodated by the ritualists. Śaṅkara advocated a catholic and philosophical religion of pure spirituality against an orthodox religion of works tied to social roles and relations.

REFERENCES

1. *Prapañcahṛdaya—'Tad idam Viṁśatyadhyāya-nibaddham. Tatra ṣoḍaṣādhyāya-nibaddham Pūrva-mīmāṁsā-śāstram pūrva-kāṇḍasya dharma-vicāra-parāyaṇam Jaimini-kṛtam. Tad anyad adhyāya-catuṣkam uttara-mīmāṁsā-śāstram, uttara-kāṇḍasya Brahmavicāra-parāyaṇam Vyāsa-kṛtam.'* (quoted, *Yudhisthira Mīmāṁsaka, Mīmāṁsā-Śabara-bhāṣyam,* Vol. I, p.3).
2. *Śrībhāṣya, 1.1.1—'Vaksyati ca karma-Brahma-mīmāṁsayor eka-śāstratvam. Saṁhitam etac chārīrakam Jaiminīyena śodaṣa-lakṣaṇena iti śāstraikatva-siddhiḥ'.*
3. Yudhisthira Mimamsaka, *op. cit.*, p.10.
4. R.G. Bhandarkar, *Peep into the Early History of India.*
5. Cf. Kane, *op. cit.*, Vol. I.
6. Cf. *Ślokavārtika-vyākhyā-tātparya-ṭīkā* (Madras, 1971), Intr. pp. xxxi-xxxvi.
7. *M,* 75-76.
8. Fleet, *CII, III, Aphsad Ins.*
9. *M,* 8.14.
10. *Ibid.*, 8.37-38.
11. *Ibid.*, 8.61, 64.
12. *Ibid.*, 8.76, 85.
13. *Ibid.*, 8, 86-91, 112-30.
14. Śaṅkara's critique of *Pūrva-mīmāṁsā* may be seen in *BSB,* 1.1; *Ibid.*, 1.1.4; *Ibid.*, 3.4.8-14; *Ibid.*, 3.4.21-24; *Ibid.*, 4.3.14 (=*SG,* VII, p.837) which seems to report and rebut the views expressed by Kumārila in *SV, Sambandha*; 108ff); *TUB,* (-*SG, VIII,* pp. 612-14).
15. *M,* 7.111-17; *Ibid.*, 8.32, 63, 131; *Ibid.*, 10.74-75, 104-6; Vyāsācala, 5.36, canto 6; Cidvilāsa, 18.44-45; Govindanātha, 5-25; *Ibid.*, 6.1.
16. Hiriyanna, *JRAS,* 1923, April; *Ibid.*, 1924 Jan.
17. Kuppuswami Sastri, *MBS,* Intr. xxvi.
18. *Ibid.*, pp. xxxiii-xxxiv.
19. *Ibid.*, p. xxxv.
20. *Ibid.*, p. xxxvii.
21. *Ibid.*, p. xli.
22. *Ibid.*, p. l.
23. *Ibid.*, p. lvii.
24. *SV* (Madras, 1971), Intr. x-xi.
25. *MBS,* Foreword; Balasubramanian, *JAOS,* 1962, pp. 522-32.
26. Rama Krishna Kavi, *JAHRS,* 1931, Vol. V pt. III, pp. 187-92, quoted Balasubramanian *op. cit.*
27. Quoted Balasubramanian, *op. cit.*, p. 530.
28. *Ibid., l.c.*
29. *Journal of the Madras University,* 1939, Vol. XI, no. 1, pp. 30-40, quoted Balasubramanian, *op. cit.*
30. Balasubramanian, *op. cit.* p. 531.

31. Anantakrishna Sastri, *MBS* (Madras, 1963), Intr.
32. Kane, *HDS*, Vol. I.
33. Quoted *MBS* (1937), Intr. p. li.
34. Cf. Kane, *HDS*, Vol. II, pt. II.
35. Cf. *WZKS*, 23 (1979), pp. 117-39.
36. Cf. *Mīmāṁsā-nyāya-prakāśa* (Benares, 1949), pp. 3-4.
37. Cf. S.K. Maitra, *Hindu Ethics*, p. 36.
38. E.g., *Vidhiviveka* (Varanasi, 1978), 173; *Ibid.*, pp. 215-17.
39. Cf. *Ibid.*, p. 192.
40. *MBS* (1937), Intr. lxi.
41. *Īśādi*, pp. 849-50.
42. *MBS* (1937), p.4
43. *Ibid.*, p. 9.
44. *Ibid.*, l.c.
45. *BGB.*, XIII. l.
46. *BSB*, 2.1.6.
47. *MSB* (1937), p.11.
48. *BUB* 1.4.7 (=*Īśādi*, p.658).
49. *MSB* (1937), p.13.
50. *BSB*, 2.1.14.
51. *MBS*, p.20.
52. *BSB*, 3.2.21.
53. *MSB*, p.34.
54. *BSB*, 1.1.4.
55. *MSB*, p.35.
56. See above.
57. *BSB*, prefatory remarks on 1.1.4.

11

Digvijaya: Śaṅkara and Sāṅkhya and Yoga

The *Vedānta sūtras* consider the *Sāṅkhya* to be a heterodox system and devote painstaking attention to its refutation especially because it apparently sought to interpret Upaniṣadic passages in the light of its own philosophy. Following this tradition Śaṅkara describes the *Sāṅkhya* as the 'principal rival' (*pradhānamalla*). However, that Śaṅkara had a specially close relationship to Sāṅkhya-Yoga has been suggested by several modern scholars. As pointed out before, Hacker, Mayeda, Nakamura and Leggett believe that Śaṅkara was in all probability the author of *Yoga-Sūtra-bhāṣya-vivaraṇa*. Hacker and Mayeda have devised certain terminological criteria which when applied to this work indicate the consistency of its ascription with its authenticity. Hacker has argued that Śaṅkara was originally a Yogin who later turned to Vedānta retaining 'many traces of his former affiliation, especially in peculiarities in his doctrines of Nescience and of the Self, which distinguish the thought of S 'from that of other Advaia Vedāntins.'[1] Prof. Nakamura accepts the probable authenticity of the work but suggests that there is no need to postulate a Yogin Śaṅkara prior to the Vedāntin Śaṅkara. The Vedāntin Śaṅkara could have equally well commented on the *Yoga-bhāṣya*.[2] Leggett too tends to follow these scholars generally. On the other hand, later Vedāntic tradition does not seem to be aware of this work as an authentic writing of Śaṅkara, and it has been suggested by M.M. Gopinath Kaviraj that the work could be the work of a late 14th century author Śaṅkarārya.[3]

That the work should have been neglected by later Advaitic scholars is understandable in view of the later atmosphere of scholastic controversies and purism, especially if Śaṅkara had been a Yogin before becoming a full-fledged Vedāntin. The Śaṅkara legend certainly preserves the memory of Śaṅkara as a wonder-working Yogin. Even his teacher Govindapāda is said to have been an accomplished Yogin. Govinda's teacher Gauḍapāda has an undoubted relationship to *Yogācāra* as well as *Yoga* of which he defines the variety designated *Asparśa-Yoga*. Śaṅkara himself makes many references to Yoga, *Yoga-vibhūtis* and Yogins and expresses appreciation and reverence towards them.[4] It is, therefore, reasonable to accept that Śaṅkara was familiar with the theory and practice of Yoga. The contents of the *vivaraṇa* attributed to him are in many respects consonant with his authorship of it though its style is not characteristic of Śaṅkara as it is more diffuse than of his more famous commentaries.

It must, of course, be remembered that Yoga as a spiritual methodology is not the prerogative of the *Sāṅkhya* but a common possession of all the spiritual ideologies in India.[5] It is, thus, quite possible that Śaṅkara as Yogin need not have owed allegiance to the *Sāṅkhya*. In fact, even *vivaraṇa* which follows the *Yoga-bhāṣya* in many respects, shows unmistakably that its author does not subscribe to the peculiar tenets of *Sāṅkhya*. At the same time he seeks to expound the *Yoga-śāstra* and expresses his critical familiarity with *Sāṅkhya*.

In the *BSB* (2.1.3), Śaṅkara says, 'By this refutation of the *Sāṅkhya-smṛti*, the *Yoga-smṛti* too should be deemed refuted. These two principles are assumed in contradiction to the scriptures such as *Pradhāna* as an independent cause and its effects like *Mahat* etc., which are unknown to experience or Revelation.' A special reference is made to Yoga because '*Yoga* is prescribed in the Vedas as the means of right knowledge (*samyag-darśanābhyupāyo hi yogo vede vihitaḥ*)'.[6] This may be seen in the prescription about 'hearing, reasoning and meditating on the Self' and also in the elaborate reference to Yoga in the *Śvetāśvatara*. Thousands of Vedic indications about Yoga can be found. The *Kaṭha*, for example, speaks of Yoga and *Yoga-vidhi*. Śaṅkara then quotes an aphorism from some *Yoga-śāstra* to the effect 'Now Yoga is the means of realizing the Truth (*tattva-darśanopāyo yogaḥ*)'.[7] This is apparently from some ancient text other than that of Patañjali. '*Sāṅkhya* and Yoga are well known to people as the means to the realisation of the highest end, they are accepted by the cultured and supported by scriptural indications.' Hence their deviations from scriptural truth are all the more dangerous and need to be guarded against. 'They have to be refuted in as much as the knowledge of *Sāṅkhya* or the path of Yoga, when independent of the scriptures, cannot lead to the highest end. Except for the Vedic knowledge of the unity of the Self, Revelation excludes other things from being the means to the good. Now the *Sāṅkhya* and Yoga are dualists, they do not see the unity of Self.' '*Dvaitino hi te sāṅkhya yogāśca nātmaikatva-darśinaḥ.*' Śaṅkara points out that the words *Sāṅkhya* and *Yoga* in Vedic texts, should be understood to mean Vedic 'knowledge' and 'meditation' respectively. At the same time where the *Sāṅkhya* and *Yoga* systems are not opposed to the Vedic truth they may be accepted. Thus the *Sāṅkhya* doctrine of the pure transcendence of the Self is really Vedic. Similarly the *Yoga* advocates mendicancy which too is Vedic.[8]

It is clear that in Śaṅkara's time *Sāṅkhya* and Yoga were highly respected and Śaṅkara too gave them respect. He also accepted them in parts. What he rejected, following Bādarāyaṇa, was the heterodoxy connected with them and their advocacy of a dualistic philosophy. The Mīmāṁsakas were orthodox but ritualistic and hence overlooked the real significance of Vedāntic texts. *Sāṅkhya-yoga* was anti-ritualistic but originally heterodox and hence overlooked the Vedāntic texts as the original and sole source of spiritual knowledge. Both, therefore, came within the attack of Śaṅkara who opposed ritualistic orthodoxy as well as heterodox philosophy.

On the nature, origins and history of *Sāṅkhya* system many divergent views have been expressed by scholars. 'According to Garbe, the *Sāṅkhya* philosophy did not undergo in the course of its long history any essential modifications. We may thus take the classical *Sāṅkhya* of the *Kārikās* to represent in the main the original *Sāṅkhya* also. Further, the *Sāṅkhya* of the epics and of the *Upaniṣads* is the product of a combination of this *Sāṅkhya* with Vedāntic ideas. Consequently, the *Sāṅkhya* was originally heterodox, i.e., non-Vedic. Jacobi disagrees with Garbe chiefly in positing the existence of a "pre-classical" from of *Sāṅkhya*. . . Oldenberg sees the origin of *Sāṅkhya* in the *Kaṭha* and especially the *Śveta* and thinks that Epic *Sāṅkhya* far from being a contamination of classical *Sāṅkhya* with Vedānta, represents, on the contrary, an independent line of development taken by original *Sāṅkhya*.'[9] Frauwallner believes that there is a thread of continuity from the dialogues of Yājñavalkya to the final summary in the *Sāṅkhya-kārikās* of *Īśvara Kṛṣṇa*. The Epic *Sāṅkhya* is then said to be a development of the original thread relieving the *Puruṣa* of all active and cosmic functions by emphasizing its transcendence.[10] Still another stage in the development of *Sāṅkhya* arose with the systematization of an evolutionary cosmology which would supplement the transcendence of the spirit. This stage has been sought to be connected with Pañcaśikha and Vṛṣagaṇa. Larson, thus, distinguishes *Proto-sāṅkhya* of the *Upaniṣads* and the Epics, *Pre-Kārikā Sāṅkhya* of lost texts and teachers like *Ṣaṣṭhitantra, Pañcaśikha, Vārṣagaṇya,* Paurika, Pañcādhikaraṇa, Vidhyavāsa and Mādhava, and *Kārikā-Sāṅkhya.*[11]

Despite the researches of Oldenberg and Frauwallner it seems to us that the essential continuity and heterodoxy of *Sāṅkhya* ought to be conceded. Reconstructing philosophical history from fragmentary references from several works is an undoubtedly hazardous procedure in which it is difficult to decide between alternative hypotheses. What is certain is that the *Sāṅkhya-Kārikā* of Īśvara Kṛṣṇa gives the classical version of the origin and development of the *Sāṅkhya* tradition. This tradition does not derive itself from the Vedas but condemns the Vedic tradition for involvement in ritual. It derives itself, on the other hand, from the primordial teacher Kapila. The Vedic tradition or *nigama* claims to be impersonal and beginningless. In contrast the *Sāṅkhya* represents a definite personal and historical tradition—*pauruṣeya āgama.* Kapila is said to have founded it and to have communicated it to Āsuri whence it came to Pañcaśikha who was responsible for creating a diversified system or *tantra.* Apparently Pañcaśikha was the author of the *Ṣaṣṭhitantra* which was probably the standard text or collection, not merely a designation of the system. This seems to be implied by Īśvara Kṛṣṇa's claim that the seventy *Kārikās* summarize the essential principles of the *Ṣaṣṭhitantra,* leaving out only the 'stories' and 'debates with rival systems'. It is reasonable that during the course of its long history the *Sāṅkhya* tradition should have been diversely interpreted especially in the course of controversies with rival systems. In these controversies diverse refinements could have been proposed and attempts made at the synthesis of *Sāṅkhya* with Vedāntic principles. It is also true, as Śaṅkara has pointed out, that the terms *Sāṅkhya* and *Yoga* were also used in more general and non-technical sense. This need not be supposed to have altered its basic principles which may be said to be threefold, viz., a radical duality between *Puruṣa* and *Prakṛti, satkāryavāda* or *pariṇāmavāda* as the basis of cosmology, and *apavarga* or liberation through discrimination (*viveka*) and dispassion (*vairāgya*). *Sāṅkhya* is at once a contemplative phenomenology of experience, as well as a soteriological religion.[12] '*Sāṅkhya-Yogau pṛthag bālāḥ pravadanti napaṇḍitāḥ.'* It sought liberation from the travails of existence through spiritual discrimination and the adoption of a mendicant's life.

With these general aims of *Sāṅkhya* and Yoga Śaṅkara was in full sympathy. That liberation comes from knowledge alone and that knowledge requires the renunciation of works and the adoption of a mendicant's way of life, were as much a part of Śaṅkara's Vedānta as of *Sāṅkhya*. For both the liberating knowledge is the knowledge of the spirit or Self but while for Śaṅkara it is the knowledge of unity, for *Sāṅkhya* it is the knowledge of difference since the Spirit is a thing apart. 'For both the real nature of the "self" is pure consciousness. Both make a fundamental distinction between object-knowledge and consciousness of Self. All object-knowledge is relational, determinate, temporal and dependent. All these features are negated in pure consciousness.'[13] While both Sāṅkhya and Vedānta as interpreted by Śaṅkara hold the Self to be pure consciousness and regard all objects including the mind and ego to be non-self, the former concedes reality to both the Self and the non-Self while the latter does not accept the ultimate reality or independence of the non-Self. For Śaṅkara the Self is not merely the transcendent ground of the world-illusion but is the self-conscious wielder of the Power of Illusion, the same as God, the sole cause of the phenomenal world. Like *Sāṅkhya,* Vedānta stresses the opposition between subject and object so that the hard shell of the Ego may be broken. But unlike *Sāṅkhya,* Vedānta gives a different description of the ultimate reality and status of things. Consciousness is the sole reality and if anything appears different, the appearance of difference must be a false appearance. In fact, consciousness is being while appearing is for it and can only be described as pseudo-being. In this sense appearance is identical with unreality. When we think of the necessity or ground of appearance we think of its reality which is identical with consciousness. On the other hand, when we think of appearance as a determinate and finite object which has a distinctive nature of its own, our thought is really enmeshed in a self-constructed net of unreality.[14] *Sāṅkhya* contradicts Vedānta by maintaining the plurality of the *Puruṣas* and the independent reality of *Prakṛti.* Śaṅkara attacks it for the dualism of its theory of the Self and its atheistic cosmology.

Vedāntic cosmology going back to the *Upaniṣads* holds that the world is the effect of a First Cause which is sentient and divine. This

Cetana-Kāraṇa-Vāda or *Puruṣa-Kāraṇa-Vāda* is in full contradiction to the *Acetana-Kāraṇa-Vāda* or *Pradhāna-Kāraṇa-Vāda* of the *Sāṅkhya*. *Pradhāna* or *Prakṛti*, commonly translated Nature, is conceived by the *Sāṅkhya* as a non-spiritual principle which has three essential and constituent aspects, viz., the three *guṇas* or strands. These are *sattva, rajas* and *tamas*—recognized by their characteristic functions of plasticity or luminosity, motion and inertia respectively. They are also defined in terms of pleasure, pain and dullness or obscurity. These *guṇas* or strands are always present together but in varying degrees. Constituted of these triple strands Nature is an insentient energy which is the autonomous cause and stuff of the world, material and mental. When the 'strands' are in equilibrium Nature may be said to be in a state of undefined, unmanifest potentiality (*avyakta*). When there is disequilibrium owing to the force of the unseen potential or past *Karman* maturing in time, creation begins with the successive manifestation or emanation of a series of principles, viz., *Mahat* or Cosmic Intelligence, *Ahaṁkāra* or Egoity, eleven senses including the mind accompanied with five types of sensuous objectivity (*tan-mātra*), and finally five types of matter. These along with the *Avyakta* and *Puruṣa* constitute the twenty-five elements (*tattvas*) of the *Sāṅkhya*. *Puruṣa* is conceived as sentient and eternal, *Prakṛti* whether unmanifest or manifest as insentient but incessantly changing. The causal process which is immanent in Nature is a process of autonomous transformation or evolution, *pariṇāma*. Cause and effect are essentially continuous, causation being nothing but manifestation. The effect is not a new emergent, it has a prior though unmanifest existence latent in the cause.[15]

Although Nature is insentient the world process is automatically so geared as to provide creatures with experiences suited to their deeds. In a way it is the force of human action that powers Nature. Now human consciousness arises from the failure of the Spirit to distinguish itself from the ideas and experiences which it witnesses. Although in reality a detached witness constituting the deepest prior condition of the possibility of experience, the Spirit or Self finds itself under the delusion of an empirical constitution in terms of the body and the mind where the root of the illusion lies in the non-discrimination of the Self as subject from the modes of experience which derive their light from it and represent objects.

While *Sāṅkhya* and Vedānta are both spiritual philosophies and religions, *Sāṅkhya* largely derives its principles from rational reflection over experience. Its two basic insights are that knowledge shows the union of a changeless consciousness with a changing manifold of representations, and that objective being is a process of constant becoming or transformation. Thus on the basis of perception and inference *Sāṅkhya* establishes the reality of its twenty-five principles. It accepts the authority of the testimony of those who know as adequate to validate the tradition originating in Kapila. But for this communication from the First Seer the fact of liberation as realizable would not be known except as a desired ideal. But for this recognition of a spiritual communication from one who is beyond the empirical world, *Sāṅkhya* would become a rational philosophy of Nature joined to an epistemology which makes the Self unknowable.

In his critique of *Sāṅkhya* Śaṅkara not only attacks its principles and arguments logically but also defends the rival Vedāntic principles against the counter-attack of *Sāṅkhya*. Although Śaṅkara rejects the claims of rational theology, he is equally critical of the rational atheism of *Sāṅkhya*. The basis of the atheistic cosmology of *Sāṅkhya* is provided by its theory of causation which postulates an essential identity between cause and effect. The First Cause would thus be like the natural world an insentient, causally functioning matrix, indeterminate in itself like potential energy. *Brahman*, on the other hand, is a sentient and eternal principle and could not be the cause of the world which is insentient and changeful and hence the opposite of *Brahman*. Against this Śaṅkara argues that the very reality of the causal relation presupposes that the cause and the effect are not totally identical, otherwise causation itself would disappear. '*Atyanta-sāmye ca prakṛti-vikāra-bhāva eva pralīyeta.*' Between cause and effect there is a real but covert identity which is overlaid by manifest differences. It is the *sat* aspect of *Brahman* from which the world derives its relative existence. The other aspects of *Brahman* become dormant and in the obscurity of *Avidyā* the kaleidoscopic phantasmagoria of 'Name and Form' is manifested. Creation takes place under the magical veil of the Lord's illusive power. It does not involve the transformation of *Brahman* but only a mysterious veiling of reality and the unveiling of appearance. For the *Sāṅkhya* the paradigm of creation is the transformation of the clay into pots or the evolution of seeds into plants. For Śaṅkara it is the projection of a dream world or a magical show.

It needs to be noted that Bādarāyaṇa is as realistic as *Sāṅkhya* and defends the idea of heterogeneous transformation (*vilakṣana-pariṇāma*) on grounds derived from empirical observation. We do find in practice that effects differ from their causes. The living spider produces the non-living net and the non-living cowdung produces the living worm, milk produces curd and so on. Śaṅkara defends this at the empirical level. When the *Sāṅkhya* argues for a First Cause similar to the observed world it goes beyond what can be ascertained empirically. While Śaṅkara prefers *satkāryavāda* to *asatkāryavāda,* he does not regard it as faultless—the fact is that causation does not measure up to the demands of reason. Causality implies the identity as well as the difference of cause and effect, a logically inconsistent position. For Śaṅkara, therefore, causality or creation is essentially illusive or miraculous, depending on whether one adopts a philosophical or religious point of view.

Śaṅkara's defence of Vedāntic cosmology against the attack of *Sāṅkhya,* thus, takes place at two levels. Assuming the empirical reality of causation there is no reason to suppose that *Brahman* cannot be the cause of a world which is of a different nature than itself. However, at a deeper level causation itself is illusive and the eternal *Brahman,* the sole reality, does not admit of any change.

On the other hand, the *Sāṅkhya* attempt to infer Nature as the self-sufficient cause of the world cannot be considered rationally just. Bādarāyaṇa says 'That which is inferred (by the *Sāṅkhya,* viz. the *Pradhāna*) cannot be the cause (of the world), on account of the orderly arrangement (of the world) being impossible (on the hypothesis)'. (Thibaut's rendering) Śaṅkara explains the reasoning of the *Sāṅkhya* thus, 'Just as the variations like the jars, dishes, etc., are accompanied by their clayey nature and hence are seen to have clay in general as their prior cause, so it would be reasonable to suppose that the diversity of external and internal things which are constantly accompanied by the characteristics of pleasure, pain and dullness presuppose pleasure, pain and dullness in general as their prior cause. Pleasure, pain and dullness together constitute a common principle characterized by three *guṇas* and called *Pradhāna.* Insentient like the clay, the *Pradhāna* evolves by its own nature into diverse products to realize the purpose of the sentient spirit.'[16] Against this the Vedāntic argument is that it is nowhere observed in the world that anything non-intelligent should serve the purpose of a person without being guided by any intelligent being. We find that houses, places and the like are fashioned by intelligent workmen. But even the best of them cannot understand the complexities of this infinitely ordered world. How can one assume that a non-intelligent principle like the *Pradhāna* is able to fashion it![17] The fact of purposive structures or teleology in nature, thus, suggests that the First Cause should be intelligent because in all known instances such structures arise only from Intelligent causation. The *Sāṅkhya* appeals to the instances of milk flowing spontaneously to nourish the young or water flowing to benefit mankind but the appeal is rejected as not proving the non-association of intelligence with natural causation.

It is admitted that motion can be observed only in material or insentient objects. Nevertheless an intelligent being would seem to be required to act as the unmoved mover in the first instance. Without an external cause how would Nature change its original condition of equilibrium and non-manifestation? The three *guṇas* being of equal power it would be impossible for their equilibrium to change without an external cause. If 'natural' transformations were assumed to be unintelligently spontaneous or mechanical, they would not be adapted to the realization of any purpose.

To obviate such difficulties the *Sāṅkhya* assumes that Nature and Spirit are connected like the blind and the lame so that the former acts while the latter guides. Such an assumption, however, has to show how Nature and Spirit can get into any relation at all if they are totally heterogeneous. The *Pradhāna* being non-intelligent and the soul indifferent, and there being no third principle to connect them, there can be no connection of the two. If we attempt to establish a connection on the ground of natural fitness (of objectivity in the *Pradhāna*, of subjectivity in the Spirit), the permanence of such a natural relation would imply the impossibility of final emancipation.[18]

It would be seen that Śaṅkara's critique of the atheistic, naturalistic cosmology of Sāṅkhya rests on two major points. The structure of the created world shows an unmistakable purposiveness or the adaptation of means and ends. This points to the role of consciousness or intelligence without reference to which the patent teleological ordering of the world would be meaningless. The second major point is the fact of motion or causation itself which needs an intelligent mover or fashioner. Even if motion or causation were assumed to be automatic and mechanical it would be ceaseless and uniform and fail to produce any purposively ordered variety. Śaṅkara does not advance rational teleology as a sufficient proof of the divine creation of the world, for which he relies on the scriptures alone. He advances rational teleology as simply of enough weight to counter any rational atheism or naturalism, though in the *Vivaraṇa*, an early work, he does seem to advocate a rational theology.[19]

Apart from the doctrine of Natural Evolution or *Pradhāna-pariṇāma-vāda*, the other *Sāṅkhya* doctrine which came in for sharp criticism from Śaṅkara is that of the plurality of the souls. Even in the *Vivaraṇa* he questions the *Sāṅkhya* conception on the ground that there is really nothing by which the *Puruṣas* may be essentially distinguished—'*svarūpeṇa bhedo duravabodha eva*'.[20] Śaṅkara accuses the *Sāṅkhyas* of being inconsistent. They rightly regard the Self as devoid of agency but wrongly attribute subjectivity or *bhoktṛtva* to it. They do not see that there is no fundamental difference between being an agent or being an experiencer. Both *kartṛtva* and *bhoktṛtva* are modes of changeableness, *vikriyā*. The emergence and passing away of experience in the Self cannot leave it unchanged if it is really the experiencer. The *Sāṅkhya* argues that the Self being pure consciousness is by its nature the subject of experience but does not become anything other than pure consciousness merely by being the subject of different experiences. It is the changeless subject of changing experiences. Śaṅkara, however, points out that to the extent the Self is regarded as really experiencing it must be regarded as undergoing a change of state, some kind of modification in its being which would have to be placed in time as a succession of 'experiences' or *bhoga*. If the Self really owns the experiences in time its own being cannot be wholly timeless. '*Atha bhoga-kāle pi cinmātra eva prāgvat puruṣa iti cet na tarhi paramārthato bhogah puruṣasya*.'[21]

Again, according to the *Sāṅkhya* there are many all-pervading *Ātmans* consisting of pure consciousness without any qualities. For their sake there exists a common *Pradhāna*, through which they gain both the bondage of experience and release from it.[22] Now since there is no difference between the *Puruṣas* with respect to their proximity and non-activity in relation to *Pradhāna*, it is impossible to see why the *Puruṣas* are not connected with the same experiences in exactly the same way. The *Sāṅkhyas* argue that Nature acts in a differentiated manner towards each Self so that it could be helped towards liberation but such an assumption cannot be supported by any proof within the *Sāṅkhya* system. The *Sāṅkhya* argument that the plurality of the souls is proved by the fact that Nature serves the various interests of others fails to see that the being-for-another (*Pārārthya*) of Nature is grounded in the existence of the spirit as a principle separate from Nature, not on the presence of distinctions between a plurality of differentiated individual souls.[23]

The only basis on which the *Sāṅkhya* can distinguish one *Puruṣa* from another is their association with the different streams of experiences. If there were only one *Puruṣa*, it might be objected, the experience of each mind would affect all the persons. But does not *Sāṅkhya* regard these experiences to belong to the mind rather than the Self? And the experiencing by the Self is made possible only by an original Nescience. Since this association and the resultant sense of empirical identity are illusory, not real, it follows that it is only the empirical and deluded selves which can be distinguished, not the real Self which is untouched by empirical conditions. Śaṅkara endorses the *Sāṅkhya* contention that the subject and the object of experience cannot be the same but holds that this is not a reason for believing in a fundamental ontic duality. It is, on the other hand, a sufficient reason for holding that phenomenal experience and empirical individuality are self-contradictory and illusive. The subject and the object cannot be identical and yet their identification is the basis of all empirical life. *Ergo,* empirical life is founded on an illusion. *Bhoktṛtva,* like *Pramātṛtva* and *Kartṛtva,* cannot belong to the Self really. The *Sāṅkhya* errs by attributing to the Self what belongs to non-self.

The basic error of the *Sāṅkhya* lies in regarding the causal matrix of the objective world as a reality and as independent of the spirit. Śaṅkara admits antecedent causal conditions before the creation of the world but such a state is dependent on the highest Lord, not independent. Such a causal matrix must be admitted so that the Lord may be conceived as creator and it also makes it possible that the release of the souls should be final. 'For *Avidyā* is the causal matrix of the world, and is rightly designated the unmanifest (*avyakta*). It is an illusive power and its ground is God. It is a universal sleep in which lie all the transmigrating souls devoid of self-knowledge.'[24] The *Sāṅkhya* concept of a real Nature (*Prakṛti*) is substituted in Vedānta by the illusionistic concept of Māyā. *'Avyaktā hi sā māyā tattvānyatva-nirūpanasyāśakyatvāt.'*[25] *Avyakta, Avidyā, Māyā, Bīja-śakti* are identified.

It is the rationalistic bias of *Sāṅkhya* that lands it into trouble where the ultimate spiritual verities are concerned. It perceives that experience presupposes an eternal consciousness and the world must require an objective, changeable, insentient cause. These two principles must also be different since they are the subject and the object of experience. So far *Sāṅkhya* is unexceptionable but it errs in not realizing that the world has no reality apart from the eternal consciousness which is one and universal. It is misled by the fact that consciousness within experience appears to be individual while the objective world appears to be independent of this individual consciousness. Since it has no access to the Vedic revelation it does not know that the eternal consciousness is not individual and that there is nothing apart from it. The whole phenomenal panorama of individual selves and the objective world is rooted in the mysterious illusive power of the Lord.

The *Yoga-sūtras* of Patañjali and their celebrated commentary ascribed to Vyāsa are known to follow the basic features of the Sāṅkhya system although several scholars have tried to point out subtle differences between the Pātañjala Yoga and *Sāṅkhya*. There is at least one well known difference, viz., the acceptance of God in Yoga as a perfect *Puruṣa* who has a soteriological but no cosmological function. However, in the *Yoga-sūtra-bhāsya-vivaraṇa* this limitation is initially set aside. The *Yoga-sūtras* seek to give a rational proof of the existence of God. A gradation of knowledge can be discerned in the world, which indicates that there must be a being where knowledge reaches perfection in omniscience. In the *Vivaraṇa* the argument is generalized and the structure of objects in the world is adduced as evidence of a supreme and infinite intelligence.[26] 'The sole efficient cause for the fashioning of the body and senses is someone knowing all their purposes. . .' The order of the world is not merely natural, it must have a cause and it must be connected with a purpose 'namely to provide experience for living beings, like order in a palace'. So 'the movement of the moon and stars is not natural, just because it is a movement, like the movement of us human-beings'. If these movements were natural 'they ought always to be the same, like the heat of fire' which has no inherent drive to attain any purpose for itself. Purposive activity requires dependence on some external subject.

The *Vivaraṇa* not merely uses arguments from purposive structures in nature and the existence of motion to prove the reality of an omniscient and omnipotent God but also appeals to Vedāntic scriptures and common belief. The rational arguments are similar to those used in *BSB*. The appeal to common experience runs thus,

'Everyone, including women and cowherds, does turn to God, under names like Śiva and Nārāyaṇa.'

The basic argument is that with the development of the seeds (potentialities) of power and omniscience, an ultimate must be reached, as with any measure. As with all measures, the limitations of the measure come to an end in the self or in universal space or the like.[27] Unless an unlimited principle is accepted, there would be no certain basis for the postulated characteristics of the knowability of objects.[28] But the *Vivaraṇa* does not seek to establish the existence of God merely as the existence of one *Puruṣa* among others but of a unique and universal Self. 'The Lord experiences everything through the sense-organs of all the living beings, into which the inmost self, itself without sense-organs, has entered as into a house. There is nothing without the living Inner Dweller,'[29] as the *Br.* points out, God is in touch with everything and illumines every object. Time and Measure do not apply to Him.

Although the leanings of the *Vivaraṇakāra* are towards *Advaita*, he cannot help admitting that the *Bhāṣya* distinguishes between God (*Īśvara*) and the individual soul (*Kṣetrajña*) but that is an inevitable situation in the context of devotion. Elsewhere Śaṅkara admits that even though the ocean and the wave are the same, it is the wave that finds its nature in the sea, not *vice-versa*.

Thus as far as the concept of *Puruṣa* in *Yoga-śāstra* is concerned, the acceptance of God as the Inner Monitor takes it far from *Sāṅkhya* atheism and pluralism. The *Sāṅkhya Puruṣa* who as the *bhoktā* is the empirical individual now seeks salvation by devotion to God, the perfect Person, the Self of all selves. This is the way in which Śaṅkara reconciles the apparently Sāṅkhyan manner in which the *Gītā* speaks of '*Puruṣaḥ prakṛtistho hi bhuṅkte prakṛtijān guṇān*' and then goes on to speak of the *Maheśvara* and '*puruṣaḥ paraḥ*'. In other words, the introduction of the concept of God radically alters the Sāṅkhyan basis of Pātañjala Yoga and makes it reconcilable with Vedānta as illustrated by the *Gītā*.

The supposedly realistic concept of *Prakṛti* forms the other stumbling block in the Vedāntic appropriation of Yoga. However, it is not at all clear that the followers of Pātañjala Yoga were really wedded to any realism. Thus Vārṣagaṇya declared that the ultimate nature of the *guṇas* is transcendental while what comes within experience is a mere illusion—'*māyaiva sutucchakam*'. This is used by Vācaspati Miśra to show the consistency of Yoga and

Vedānta.[30] Similarly Mādhavācārya quotes the *sūtra* '*Kṛtārthān prati naṣṭam api anaṣṭam tadanya-sādhāraṇatvāt* ' to show that this contradicts any realistic interpretation of *Prakṛti*—'*Tacca tan mithyātve' vakalpate*'.[31] In fact, Vyāsa himself says of the unmanifest nature that it is neither real, nor unreal, nor not-unreal (*na san nāsan na nirasad*). It is, thus, not difficult to understand *Prakṛti* as the mysterious phenomenal matrix which could be identified with *Avidyā* and *Nāma-rūpa* as Śaṅkara does in his commentary on the *Gītā*.

In fact, in the commentary on the *Gītā* Śaṅkara also expounds the conception of Yoga as spiritual practice. He explains that the essence of Yoga lies in the relinquishing of all thoughts and in the spontaneous focusing of the mind on the Self so that self-awareness may dawn.[32] The regulation of conduct, the surrender of all actions to God and the practice of the stillness of body and mind are preparatory aspects of Yoga.

It may be concluded that Śaṅkara accepts Yoga as a practical discipline for the realization of Truth and sees no contradiction between Yoga and Vedānta.

REFERENCES

1. *WZSKO*, 1968/69, Vols. 12/13, pp. 119-48; Leggett, op. cit., p. xviii.
2. *Ibid., l.c.*
3. Kaviraj, *op. cit.*
4. *BSB*, 1.2 18; *Ibid.*, 1.3.27; *Ibid.*, 1.4.1; *Ibid.*, 2.1.1; *Ibid.*, 12.1.3.
5. Thus Hiraṇyagarbha is said to have founded Yoga, *Ahirbudhnya-saṁhitā*, quoted Kaviraj, *op. cit.*, p. 66. So *Bhāmatī*, *BSB*, 2.1.3.
6. *BSB*, 2.1.3.
7. *Ibid., l.c.*
8. Vācaspati Miśra proposes a detailed reconciliation of Yoga and Vedānta—*Bhāmatī*, 2.1.3.
9. G.C. Pande, *Origins of Buddhism*, p. 305.
10. Frauwallner, *History of Indian Philosophy*, Vol. I, pp. 218 ff.
11. *Encyclopaedia of Indian Philosophy*, Vol. IV, pp. 9-15. For quite different interpretations, see the works of Udaya Vira Sastri and Adya Prasad Misra. U.V. Sastri, *Sāṅkhya Darśana Kā Itihāsa*, A.P. Misra, *Sāṅkhya Darśana Ki Aitihasik Paramparā* (1967). Also cf. G.C. Pande, Review of Hulin's *Sāṅkhya Literature* in *History and Archaeology*, Vol. I, p. 363.
12. The most authoritative modern exposition of *Sāṅkhya* may be seen in the writings of Hariharananda Aranya collected in *Pātañjala-Yoga-Darśana* (Calcutta University); also see K.C. Bhattacharya, *Studies in Philosophy*, G.C. Pande, *Foundations of Indian Culture*, Vol. I, pp. 83-103.
13. G.C. Pande, *op. cit.*, pp. 90-91.

14. *Ibid.*, p. 92.
15. *BSB*, 2.2.1.
16. *Ibid.*
17. *Ibid.*, l.c.
18. *Ibid.*, 2.2.7.
19. *Yoga-sūtra-bhāṣya-vivaraṇa*, 2.25; Cf. *BVB*, 3.8.9.
20. *YSVB*, 3.41.
21. *PUB*, 16.3.
22. *BSB*, 2.3.50.
23. *MKB*, 3.5.
24. *BSB*, 1.4.3.
25. *Ibid.*, l.c.
26. Cf. Leggett, *op. cit.*, pp. 83-125.
27. *Yoga-sūtra-bhāṣya-vivaraṇa*, p. 58.
28. *Ibid.*, p. 66.
29. *Ibid.*, p. 69.
30. *Bhāmatī*, and *BSB* 2.1.3.
31. *Sūta-saṁhitā-tatparya-dīpikā* quot. *YSBV*, pp. xviii-xix.
32. *BGB*, 6.

12

Digvijaya: Debate with other Rival Schools

The early history of the Vaiśeṣika is lost in obscurity. It was presumably one of the many traditions of naturalistic philosophising which began in the later Vedic age and were clearly noticeable in the Age of Buddha. The *Upaniṣads* themselves give evidence of speculations similar to the naturalistic philosophies of the pre-Socratic Age. Air, water, ether, being, non-being, the mind, all these were speculatively regarded as the *archê* of the world. The *Lokāyatas* and the *Svabhāva vādins* reduced the world to original material elements independent of any conscious or divine creator. Peripatetic mendicants like Pakudha Kaccāyana formulated the doctrine of a few utterly distinct elements as the source of the world. Buddhist scriptures mention the doctrine of Six Basic Elements (*dhātus*). Early Jaina texts too contain echoes of naturalistic philosophies. It has been suggested that when the *arthaśāstra* speaks of Yoga as one of the three branches of *Ānvīkṣikī* it really has the ancient Vaiśeṣikas in mind.[1] By the time of Āryadeva the Vaiśeṣikas were certainly well-established and this is only confirmed by Bādarāyaṇa taking up their system for criticism. This should reflect a situation not later than the second century A.D. Apart from the *Vaiśeṣika-sūtras* and the *Daśapadārthaśāstra,* lost in the original, the *Praśastapādabhāṣya* represents the most ancient surviving text of the system.[2]

The system appears to have been originally a cosmology based on a speculative physics. It acquired a distinctive character by its doctrine of atomism of which it remained in later times the best known example in Indian philosophy. The emergence of the concept of six basic categories and a self-conscious theory of causation completed the basic structure of the system as an atheistic and rationalistic philosophy of nature which challenged the spiritualism of Vedānta as also the organicism of *Sāṅkhya.* Both

Sāṅkhya and Vedānta were philosophies of salvation while Vaiśeṣika appears to have based itself on common-sense observation and scientific inference. In this it lay between the pure empiricism of the *Lokāyata*, on the one hand, and the *Sāṅkhya* and the Vedānta, on the other, which accepted the testimony of spiritual tradition as a third means of knowledge over and above perception and inference. It is in this 'atheistic' form that the Vaiśeṣika is criticised by Bādarāyaṇa and following him by Śaṅkara.[4] As is well known at a later date the Vaiśeṣika and Nyāya became allied as a joined system in which the former gave the principles of atomism, causality and the six categories while the latter gave the principles of logic, epistemology, theism and soteriology.

Bādarāyaṇa's critique of the Vaiśeṣika begins with a refutation of the Vaiśeṣika charge that *Brahman* cannot be the cause of the world. He argues: '*Mahaddīrghavadvā hrasva-parimaṇḍalābhyām*', i.e., the world may originate from *Brahman* in the same manner in which finite magnitude and extension arise from infinitesimal extension and 'sphericity' (in the Vaiśeṣika system). Śaṅkara explains that this rebuts the Vaiśeṣika charge by pointing out a contradiction within that system. The Vaiśeṣikas argue as follows: The qualities which inhere in the causal substance produce qualities in the substance which constitutes the effect. Thus white threads produce white cloth. Hence if the intelligent *Brahman* were the cause of the world, intelligence should be found to inhere in the world.[5] Against this argument of the Vaiśeṣikas the *sūtra* points out that they themselves accept the production of effects which do not have qualities similar to those in the cause. It is true that when simple atoms produce *dvyaṇukas* or binary compounds, the latter are similar in colour etc., to the former but the magnitude of the compounds is admitted not to be of the same genus as that of simple atoms. Thus simple atoms have 'sphericity' (*Pārimāṇḍalaya*) or infinitesimal magnitude while the *dvyaṇukas* or binary compounds have a finite magnitude and extension which are minimal. These are called *aṇutva* or 'minuteness' and *hrasvatva* or 'shortness'. Again when binary compounds produce *caturaṇukas* (quaternary compounds) the magnitude of the latter is no more 'minute' and 'short' but 'big' and 'long'; *mahat* and *dīrgha*.[6] Thus just as from atoms characterised by *pārimāṇḍalya* binary compounds are produced which are minute and short and ternary compounds which are big and long, but without *pārimāṇḍalya*; or as from binary compounds, which are minute and short, ternary compounds etc. are produced which are big and long, not minute and short, so this non-intelligent world may spring from the intelligent *Brahman*. We have, thus, three levels with heterogeneous qualities despite the relationship of cause and effect between them. The *Paramāṇus* have *pārimāṇḍalya*, the *dvyaṇukas* which are their effect do not have *pārimāṇḍalya* but have *aṇutva* and *hrasvatva*, the *catunaṇukas* which are the products of *dvyaṇukas* have *mahattva* and *dīrghatva* in place of *aṇutva* and *hrasvatva*.

Against this it may be argued by the Vaiśeṣika that when the dyad or the quaternary is produced it already has a magnitude which excludes the reproduction or furtherance of the magnitude of the causal atom or dyad as the case may be. Since the dyad or the quaternary have the magnitudes of *aṇutva* or *mahattva* they cannot have *pārimāṇḍalya* or *aṇutva* respectively. But the world does not have such a positive and contrary nature to that of *Brahman*. The world simply shows the negative fact of the absence of intelligence, which by itself cannot be held to have prevented the reproduction of intelligence in the world.

Śaṅkara argues that this defence is not really relevant. What is relevant is that the cause produces an effect which does not show the quality inherent in the cause. That a cause may produce an effect with a heterogeneous inherent quality having been admitted in the Vaiśeṣika it cannot bring that argument against *Brahmavāda*. What is more, *aṇutva* or *mahattva* are said to be produced by such causal factors as number and accumulation. Why then does *pārimāṇḍalya* or *aṇutva* fail to produce qualities similar to what they are? And to argue that the effect has a magnitude which excludes the magnitude as the cause, is to forget that the effect neither has any magnitude before being produced nor even in the first moment of its life. The Vaiśeṣikas believe that every substance which is produced remains without any quality for a moment. There would then be every opportunity for the magnitude inherent in the cause to produce another of the same genus in the effect and there would be nothing in the effect at that time to inhibit its assuming the quality which the quality of the cause would seek to invest it with. That *pārimāṇḍalya* or the infinitesimal dimension of the atom is not reproduced in the effect cannot be due to the fact that the effect is characterized by its own contradictory dimensions because these dimensions arise after the effect has been produced and remained without any qualities for a moment. Besides the dissimilar dimensions in the effect arise from something other than the dimensions of the cause. Thus the fact that the infinitesimal dimension or *pārimāṇḍalya* of the simple atoms does not produce similar qualities in the effect is due[7] to their very nature (and not to the operation of any external cause).

The fact is that the Vaiśeṣika formulation of causal laws does not bespeak of any necessity. There is no universal law that causes should produce effects which have a nature similar to their own. For on the *Vaiśeṣika* view *saṁyoga* or contact is an attribute and is seen to produce substances when atomic compounds come into contact, which belong to a different category and are therefore by nature different from 'contact'. The fact is that having adopted the *asatkāryavāda* concept of causality, the Vaiśeṣika is forced to formulate a 'law' to account for the similarity of inherent qualities between cause and effect, and then to further modify this rule to account for the emergence of heterogeneous magnitudes. Śaṅkara rejects the whole concept of *ārambhavāda* on the grounds which were classically adduced by *Sāṅkhya*. Turning to Vaiśeṣika atomism a number of arguments are urged against it. Some of these could have been taken over from Vasubandhu's critique of Vaibhāṣika atomism. How can one atom be conjoined with another? If the conjunction is partial the atoms would cease to be partless wholes. If the conjunction is total, the atoms would coalesce into a single atom once again and the binaries would not be produced. Again, since the atoms are credited with a finite magnitude, however minimal, they should be capable of directional alignment. But such an orientation would reintroduce 'parts' into them.

The major criticism of the atomic theory from the Vedāntic point of view, however, lies in the difficulty of explaining their motion of atoms especially in the context of cosmology. For the Vaiśeṣika all substances having parts must be regarded as the product of the combination of parts as its causes. The jar, for example, is an effect produced by the combination of its two halves. This process of division and subdivision must reach a limit and that is the atom where subdivision is no longer possible. After dissolution and before creation the atom lie in a state of separation since creation is nothing but the process of the combination of atoms and dissolution of their separation. Now the question is, once the atoms are in a state of separation, how are they to be combined? Their combination must require motion and motion being an effect needs an occasioning factor (*nimitta*). Such a factor could either be an act of the will or an impulsion or impact of another body in motion. The former is impossible because in the absence of the body the soul is not associated with the mind and hence cannot have the quality of volition or effort. Nor are there ex hypothesi any moving bodies at the moment of creation. The Vaiśeṣikas argue that the first motion arises in the aerial atoms and is occasioned by *adṛṣṭa*. But the question is, where does *adṛṣṭa* inhere? If in the soul, it being devoid of contact with the mind is devoid of consciousness at that time and the atoms are ex hypothesi insentient. So is *adṛṣṭa* also. No relationship of insentient entities can by itself initiate motion without the intervention of a sentient being. If it is supposed that the atoms are in contact with the souls in which *adṛṣṭa* inheres and hence the atoms are moved by the force of *adṛṣṭa*, such motion would be perpetual because such a relationship would be perpetual. It follows that in the absence of a specific occasioning factor no motion would be produced and hence no conjunction of atoms or cosmic creation would arise. Similar difficulties will arise in the process of cosmic dissolution. There too no definite occasioning factor can be discovered. Even *adṛṣṭa* would be powerless there for it may account only for *bhoga*, not for *pralaya*.

There is another difficulty latent in this account of cosmic causality. The higher products like the binaries are supposed to be totally different from the causal entities like the primary atoms. However, the binary atoms being effects inhere in the atoms which are the causes. Now this relation of inherence (*samavāya*) being different from the two terms which it relates, would itself require another relation of inherence, and this would lead to an infinite regress. In fact, the Vaiśeṣikas themselves require the relation of conjunction (*saṁyoga*) to be related to the two conjuncts by a separate relation of inherence and argue that conjunction being a 'quality' (*guṇa*) is to be treated differently than inherence. This distinction between an external and accidental relation like *saṁyoga* and an internal or essential relation like *samavāya* is declared by Śaṅkara to be irrelevant insofar as both are relations and must be similarly connected with the relata in that capacity. The fact is that the whole causal theory of the Vaiśeṣikas depends on the assumption of a basic difference between cause and effect and yet their indissoluble connection (*ayuta-siddhi*) is undeniable. The Vaiśeṣikas attribute a separateness to objects which are merely distinct in understanding. The whole and parts, substance and quality or cause and effect, cannot be pulled apart without destroying the whole. But the Vaiśeṣikas regard the whole to be an effect inhering in the cause and hence to account for their apparent identity in difference they postulate a peculiar relation of inherence between them. Since this relation is not logically tanable the whole theory of causality as *asatkāryavāda* fails and with it the atomistic conception of cosmology.

There is still another difficulty in atomistic causality. If we assume a natural motion or motionlessness in the atoms it will either be favourable to creation or unfavourable to it, or both or neither. In the first two cases either creation will be perpetual or dissolution would be perpetual—the two tendencies being contradictory cannot coexist. If the inherent motion or motionlessness in itself favours neither creation nor dissolution, a further cause would be needed to determine it in favour of either. If such a cause were *adṛṣṭa* etc., it would be either perpetually connected or disconnected with the atoms and would hence lead to perpetual motion or motionlessness.

The Vaiśeṣikas believe in four ultimate kinds of atoms corresponding to the four material elements, viz., earth, water, fire and air. Now since the atoms possess the qualities of colour etc., they should themselves have further causes. Common experience teaches us that anything which possesses colour or other qualities is, compared to its cause, gross (*sthūla*) and unstable (*anitya*). A piece of cloth, for instance, is gross compared to the threads of which it consists, and is impermanent; and the threads again are impermanent and gross compared to the filaments of which they are made. Hence the atoms too which the Vaiśeṣikas admit to have colour etc. must have causes compared to which they are gross and unstable.[8] Since the atoms may be presumed to have a cause from which they derive their sensible qualities, they cannot be permanent.

The argument here is somewhat obscure. Apparently the sensible qualities are regarded as a sign of grossness implying dependence on a causal process. Just as the gross sensible objects require minute atomic causes, the latter would require further causes if they have similar qualities. The classical distinction between 'primary' and 'secondary' qualities may be recalled here since that too regards the sensible qualities like colour etc., as dependent on material causes characterized only by metric and inertial qualities. In the alternative versions of atomic theory current in ancient India, the atoms of matter free from all or some sensible qualities found a place. The Vedānta does not regard sensible qualities as ultimate qualities inhering in an eternal species of material being. Matter and sensible qualities are both derived from transcendent being enveloped by *Avidyā* and their reality is derivative as well as impermanent.

Śaṅkara then attacks the various reasons adduced by the *Vaiśeṣika-sūtras* for the eternity of the atoms. Thus it cannot be said that all positive entities which are without a cause must be eternal. Similarly, it cannot be said that the atoms must be eternal because without something being eternal we would not be able to speak of non-eternal objects meaningfully since no factual conclusions can be reached merely from the consideration of verbal usage. Nor can it be said that destruction can arise only from the separation of parts. This would be true only if the material cause were conceived as discrete atoms but Vedāntins conceive of it as a continuous and evolving matrix.

Similarly, the five elements contain an increasing number of qualities. Hence the substances in which they inhere must show a gradation of complexity. The atoms of the elements thus could not be simple and indivisible. If we assume that some kinds of atoms have more numerous qualities, it follows that their limited size (*mūrti*) will be increased thereby, and that implies their being atoms no longer.

Bādarāyaṇa's critique of the Vaiśeṣika is largely concerned with its atomistic cosmology and what he attacks is the idea that the cosmos may be traced back to eternal material atoms. Such atoms cannot be eternal and they cannot create the universe without the intervention of a sentient principle. In the course of this criticism some peculiar Vaiśeṣika tenets such as the production of *dvyaṇuka* etc., and the conception of *samavāya* are also criticised as indefensible hypotheses. Śaṅkara, however, goes beyond this criticism and attacks the concept of the atom as well as the Vaiśeṣika view of causality itself. He also criticises the Vaiśeṣika concept of eternity as also that of the six categories or *padārthas*. Against the doctrine of the *padārthas* he argues that it involves a contradiction. The *padārthas* are regarded as totally different entities with entirely distinct concepts (*atyanta-bhinnān bhinna-lakṣaṇān abhyupagacchanti*). Being different in nature and existence, the *padārthas* ought to be independent. And yet the Vaiśeṣikas regard all of them as necessarily dependent on *dravya* or substance!—*dravyādhīnatvaṁ śeṣāṇām abhyaupagacchanti*. This is contradictory. It is commonly observed that wholly different entities are not mutually dependent. If 'quality' is wholly different from 'substance' it should be independent. But if 'quality' is found only when there is 'substance' and is absent when the 'substance' is absent, it should be regarded merely an aspect of 'substance'. Nor can one perceive the 'quality' as dependent on but apart from 'substance' as one can perceive the smoke dependent on but apart from fire. On the contrary, as common usage recognises, the quality is seen as a qualification of the substance. The quality, thus, is identical with the substance as its mode. The same is true of motion, universal, particularity and inherence.

Suppose it is argued that the quality is held to depend on the substance because the two can exist only when mutually related. The notion of inseparability (*ayutasiddhatā*) would then need to be analysed. It may mean the denial of separate location in place or time or of having a separate nature. None of these alternatives is tenable. Inseparability in space would contradict the Vaiśeṣika assumptions that the quality like whiteness of a substance like cloth is located in the substance but the substance itself is located in its causal material, the threads. Thus whiteness is located in the cloth but cloth is located in the threads and the two locations are not the same because the cloth and the thread are different substances and the whiteness of the cloth is different from the whiteness of the threads. Inseparability in time would simply become simultaneity like that of two horns and their essential mutual dependence would not thereby be established. Inseparability in nature would contradict the very idea of the difference of categories.

Nor can the Vaiśeṣika view that separable objects are related by contact while the inseparable ones are related by inherence, be maintained. A cause, for example, must precede the effect and exist when the latter is not produced. Nor can the non-existent effect have any relationship to the cause.

There is also nothing to support the Vaiśeṣika doctrine that contact or inherence could exist apart from the terms. The same reality may be conceived and named in various ways. Although one only Devadatta forms the object of many different names and notions according to whether he is considered in himself or in his relations to others; thus he is thought and spoken of as man, Brāhmaṇa, learned in the Veda, generous, boy, young man, old man, father, son, grandson, brother, son-in-law etc. So again, one and the same line in writing (*rekhā*) is spoken of and conceived as meaning either ten, or hundred, or thousand etc. according to the place it occupies. Similarly two connected things are not only conceived and denoted as connected things, but in addition constitute the object of the ideas and terms, 'conjunction' and 'inherence', which, however does not prove that these ideas are themselves to be regarded as separate entities.[9]

Śaṅkara's critique of the Vaiśeṣika categories basically amounts to saying that they are logical distinctions but not entitatively separate. Besides the peculiar category of *samavāya* has to be imagined owing to the difficulties caused by the assumption of non-separable but essentially different entities. The concept of *asatkāryavāda* violates common sense and has to distinguish between diverse kinds of non-existence, which would convert it into some kind of positive existence. The Vaiśeṣika conception of the soul reduces it to a mere substance which is insentient by itself, many in number but pervasive, and uses the mind for its tool, which is also unconscious but atomic. Through the conjunction of these two substances—soul and mind—nine peculiar attributes of the soul like desire etc., arise. These inhere in the souls and their ultimate non-production constitutes liberation. Śaṅkara objects that there is no way of limiting the contact of a given mind to just one soul and thus of keeping the life-histories of the souls apart. The fact that minds are connected with different bodies is of no avail because the all-pervasive souls would be equally connected with all the bodies. Nor indeed can the souls be distinguished in themselves because they have the same character. Their distinctions arise from their association with particular minds and bodies, but the souls being essentially similar and all-pervasive one cannot see how they can have distinctive lives and destinies.

The fact is that the Vaiśeṣika concept of the Self does not make any ultimate distinction between the subject and object of knowledge. The soul is one among many objects, being a kind of substance. It has the peculiar capacity of acquiring consciousness but that is contingent on its contact with the mind and body. Nor is consciousness self-conscious. Pleasure etc., are said to inhere in the soul but are different from cognition. How would pleasure be cognized? And if the attributes of the soul are contingent in origin and different from the soul, why should they not belong to another soul or another mind? The Vaiśeṣika view of the Self is yet untouched by the insight of *Yājñavalkya—'vijñātāraṁ vā are kena vijānīyāt?'*

Debate with Pāśupatas

Several schools advocated plainly dualistic monotheism in which God is regarded as merely the efficient cause or supervisor of the world. They distinguish between God, the souls and nature or matter. God merely moves and regulates the world process of creation and dissolution in which the souls fulfil their destiny. Śaṅkara attributes such a view to several schools listed as the Sāṅkhya-Yoga, Māheśvaras, and some Vaiśeṣikas.[10] The Sāṅkhya-Yoga apparently refers to the kind of Yoga which perhaps Śaṅkara himself has described in the *Yoga-sūtra-bhāṣya-vivaraṇa* and which was later developed in what was called *Seśvara-Sāṅkhya* but which had been earlier adumbrated in the *Mahābhārata*. The Vaiśeṣikas meant here could be the Naiyāyikas who had adopted the older doctrines. Thus the famous Vārtikakāra Uddyotakara was a *Pāśupatācārya*. The Mahēśvaras constituted like the Bhāgavatas an ancient stream of religious beliefs and practices with many subdivisions. The *Śvetāśvatara* may be said to be the most ancient source of the sect. Among the seers who founded later schools within this broad sect the names of Śrīkaṇṭha and Lakulīśa are the most famous.[11] Lakulīśa is generally regarded as the founder of the *Pāśupata* sect and to have lived about the second century B.C. The Pāśupatas were certainly flourishing in the Gupta period as attested by the Mathura P.I. of the time of Candragupta II. Bāṇa and Hsuan Chwang refer to the Māheśvaras and their antics. Although Śaṅkara refers to the Māheśvaras generally, Vācaspati Miśra explains that they included four major sects, viz., Śaivas, Pāśupatas, Kāruṇika-siddhāntins, and Kāpālikas.[12] Rāmānuja too calls them fourfold and lists them as follows: Kāpālikas, Kālāmukhas, Pāśupatas and Śaivas.[13] In the *Sarva-darśana-saṁgraha* there is a brief description of the schools of *Nakulīśa-Pāśupata, Śaiva, Pratyabhijñā* and *Raseśvara*. There is no doubt that among the earliest sects was that of the Pāśupatas of which the *Pāśupata-sūtras* were commented upon by Kauṇḍinya in his *Pañcārtha-bhāṣya*. The Śaiva *saṁhitās* were ancient and diverse and some of them were certainly existing in Gupta times.[14] By the 9th century the dualistic Śaiva *āgamas* of the south as also the non-dualistic *āgamas* of Kashmir were certainly in existence.

Although Śaivism like Bhāgavatism was a vast and manifold movement growing in Śaṅkara's own times, his own awareness of it at the time of the writing of the *BSB* appears to have been limited. He is content to regard them as essentially non-Vedic and criticises them as imperfectly theistic and implicitly or explicitly dualistic. His acquaintance with Śaivism appears limited to the doctrine of the *Pāśupatas*. The Māheśvaras maintain that the five categories (*Pañca Padārthāḥ*) viz., effect, cause, union, ritual, the end of pain, were taught by the Lord Paśupati for the sake of breaking the bonds of the animal (i.e., the soul). Paśupati is according to them, the Lord, the efficient cause. Śaṅkara criticises this kind of doctrine as logically inappropriate. God and the souls are held to be absolutely different but while God is absolutely free the souls are dependent. Now the souls are found in diverse states of experience, high, middling and low. God as the supervising or operating cause of the world, then, must be responsible for this inequality between the souls by prompting their actions and letting their actions bear fruit. Since He is absolutely free He must then be unjust and subject to hatred, passion and so on, and 'is hence like one of us, and is no real Lord'. If we assume that God is guided by the merit and demerit of creatures in effectuating their actions, He would no longer be fully independent and Lord since He would then prompt actions on being acted upon by them and His actions would be determined by something independent of Him. If it is assumed that the actions of souls and the prompting and actuations by God form a beginningless chain and hence there is no difficulty in assuming mutual interaction between them, even so the difficulty is not really removed because the chain would simply be like the chain of blind men leading the blind.

There is still another difficulty. As the Naiyāyikas argue, action proceeds from some imperfection. 'Experience shows that no one who is not motivated by defects engages in action for oneself or another'. Moreover even when working for others men are seen to be motivated by some end of their own. If God too works for the souls, He would be presumed to have a similar motivation. Finally since God is held to be a special kind of soul, He would be characterized by the generic features of all souls which is indifference or inactivity.

There is still another difficulty in conceiving God as the activating and supervisory cause. Such activity on the part of God presupposes a relationship between God, on the one hand, and the souls and Nature on the other. Since God, souls and Nature are ubiquitous and partless, there can be no relationship by way of contact between them. Since they are not related as support or being supported, they cannot be related by way of inherence. Nor can any other causal relation such as natural ability (*yogyatā*) be assumed because the very fact of being cause and effect by nature needs to be established. If it is argued that this defect would have to be faced by the Vedāntin also, there are two replies to it. In the first place, Vedānta proposes the relation of essential identity or *tādātmya* between God and the world. In the second place, Vedānta is not obliged to reason from empirical instances because it relies on the authority of the Vedas. Nor can a similar exemption be claimed by rational theism. Its founders could be accepted as omniscient authorities only if the traditions founded by them could be regarded as revealed.

And how would God work on Nature which has no perceptible form in its original state? Nor can God act on it in the manner in which the soul acts on the senses since that is an inference from the involvement of the soul in experience. No such involvement of God can be presumed or else God too would not be free.

Nor can one attribute any kind of body or senses to God because these cannot exist prior to creation. Or if they are presumed one would have to conceive God too on the model of *saṁsārins*. If God is held to be omniscient and infinite and at the same time Nature and the souls are also regarded as different but infinite entities, there would result an insoluble contradiction. 'Let us ask, then, whether the Lord has any determinate cognition of Nature or of the souls or of Himself as 'such and such', or whether He has not. In whichever way the question is answered, the conception breaks down. Suppose you accept cognition, then Nature, the souls and the Lord must necessarily be finite, as they would be determinable as 'such and such'. For this is what we find in worldly experience. Any object, like a cloth, which is determinately known as 'such and such', is seen to be finite. And following this rule, the Triad of nature, the souls and the Lord would have to be finite, as they would have been determinately known as 'such and such'. 'They are also limited from the point of view of number since they constitute a triad. As the Lord has definite knowledge of them they must be limited in their intrinsic dimensions. It would make the souls limited in number for God knows them in their totality. And this would lead to the possibility of all the souls being liberated one day and then Nature would be functionless and God without creatures or Nature to be lord of. On the other hand, if we stick to the infinity of Nature, souls and the Lord so that the Lord does not have a determinate conception of them, then His omnisciene would cease. It is thus impossible to reconcile the omniscience of God with the infinity of what is other than God and a finite other is irreconcilable with God's own absolute infinity and lordship.

Śaṅkara's critique is in this section consistently aimed against opponents whom he designates logicians (*tārkikas*) and the arguments he uses are largely dialectical. The attempt to prove the reality of God as distinct from Nature and the soul but as their lord by rational means is shown to be an impossibility because its speculative hypothesis and arguments tend to produce dialectical contradictions. How is the total independence and goodness of God to be reconciled with the total dependence and yet inequality and suffering of souls? How is the omniscience and infinity of God to be reconciled with the infinity and otherness of Nature and the souls? How can God act without using or being involved in natural means? Why should God act when He has nothing to achieve? The generally accepted explanation of creation and human destiny was in terms of *Karman* and the orthodox belief was that God is necessary for *Karman* to take effect. '*Kva karma pradhvastam phalati puruṣārādhanam ṛte.*' If God and the soul are totally different there is no way of reconciling the will of God with the will of man or *Karman*, and similarly if God and Nature be totally different, the infinity of the one cannot be reconciled with that of the other. The Advaitic concept of *tādātmya* alone offers a way out of the dualistic difficulties. Again, rationalistic theism must be content to throw doubt on rationalistic atheism; for a positive conclusion it must surrender itself to faith based on Revelation.

Debate with Bhāgavatas

Following the *Sūtras* Śaṅkara criticises the doctrine of the *Bhāgavatas*, or rather, it should be said that he interprets the *Sūtras* to mean a criticism of the doctrines which he attributes to the *Bhāgavatas* or the *Pāñcarātra siddhāntins*. On the other hand, Rāmānuja argues that their real doctrines are not attacked but approved, only some misinterpretations being removed. Even Śaṅkara approves many of the principles ascribed to the *Pāñcarātra Bhāgavata* school and disapproves only some of them, viz., the creation of the soul, the multiplicity of ultimate principles, and the insufficiency of the Vedas. He approves of their theism and devotional worship.[15]

The origins of the school go back to the later Vedic age. The sage Nārada is one of the illustrious teachers of the school and is famous in the *Chāndogya Upaniṣad*. Devakīputra Kṛṣṇa too is mentioned in the same *Upaniṣad*. The *Mahābhārata* counts the *Pāñcarātra* among the five famous sects of the time, viz., *Pāñcarātra, Pāśupata, Sāṅkhya, Yoga, Vedāraṇyaka*. It also gives an account of how Nārada discovered the worship of Nārāyaṇa. From the second century B.C. the famous Besnagar Inscription tells of Heliodorus of Taxila who had become a *Bhāgavata* devotee. Thus by the time of the *Brahmasūtras* the Pāñcarātra or Bhāgavata sect had attained considerable following. In the subsequent centuries the *Āgamas* or *Saṁhitās* of the school emerged in large numbers and influenced the Purāṇic literature as well as the songs of the Āḻvārs. Its philosophical systematization was attempted by Vaiṣṇava *Ācāryas* and culminated in Śrī Rāmānuja.[16]

According to Rāmānuja Bādarāyaṇa does not attack the system but supports it, and as Rāmānuja claims to follow the ancient *Bodhāyana-Vṛtti*, this must be an old commentarial tradition[17]. Śaṅkara's critique of the system is largely of its quasi-dualistic leanings which found their echo in Rāmānuja.

The Pāñcarātra-Bhāgavata sect began originally with disatisfaction towards the Vedic tradition on account of its emphasis on the worship of many gods by sacrifices involving the immolation of animals. Thus Nārada in the *Chāndogya* confesses that he had studied the Vedas but had not reached the end of sorrow. He had merely acquired learning in the hymns! Ghora Āṅgirasa teaches Devakīputra Kṛṣṇa a symbolic interpretation of the sacrifice. Kṛṣṇa himself gives a low position to the Vedas and Vedic ritualism in the *BG*. In place of a multiplicity of gods he preaches a strict monotheism. The *Nārāyaṇīya* section of the *Mahābhārata* says that the king Vasu Uparicara could have a vision of the deity since his heart was full of non-violence while Bṛhaspati, the arch-priest of Vedic ritual was deprived of it. Śaṅkara himself quotes from some Pāñcarātra text to the effect that Śāṇḍilya failed to reach the good through the Vedas. Against this Rāmānuja argues that such statements are not meant to disparage the Vedas but only to praise the *Pāñcarātra-Āgama*. The Vedas are vast and difficult to comprehend and the *Āgamas* are meant to express their essence in a simple manner. Besides, the Vedas are not accessible to all while the *Āgamas* are. In fact, this shows that at least part of the motivation of the cult must have been to side-step the spiritual monopoly of the priests.

It is the strict monotheism of the school which gave it the designation of *Ekāntika* or *Ekāyana vidyā*. Insofar as this meant the advocacy of a supreme person solely responsible for the creation of the world, Śaṅkara endorses it but he opposes the doctrine of the *Vyūhas*. According to the *Pāñcarātra* God manifests Himself in five ways: *Para, Vyūha, Vibhava, Antaryāmī* and *arcā*. In His supreme form God is *Nārāyaṇa* or *para-Brahman* and may be conceived as the perfection and unity of the six dualities or *Ṣādguṇya*, viz., *Jñāna, Aiśvarya, Śakti, Bala, Vīrya* and *Tejas*. The four *Vyūhas* are Vāsudeva, Sankarṣaṇa, Pradyumna and Aniruddha.Śaṅkara mentions two ways of understanding them and finds fault with both.[18] According to the first, Vāsudeva denotes the highest Self, Saṅkaraṣaṇa the individual soul, Pradyumna the mind (*manas*), Aniruddha the principle of the ego (*ahaṅkāra*). Of these four Vāsudeva constitutes the ultimate causal essence, of which the three others are the effects. Now Śaṅkara says that he does not controvert the doctrine that Nārāyaṇa is the highest Self, and the Self of all, reveals himself by dividing himself in multiple ways; for various scriptural passages, such as, 'He is onefold, he is threefold', (Ch. VII. 26.2) teach us that the highest Self appears in manifold forms. We, however, must take exception to the doctrine that Saṅkarṣaṇa springs from Vāsudeva, Pradyumna from Saṅkarṣaṇa, Aniruddha from Pradyumna. It is not possible that from Vāsudeva, i.e., the highest Self, there should originate Saṅkarṣaṇa i.e., the individual soul; for if that were the case, there would attach impermanence to the soul and all the other imperfections which belong to originated things. Hence release, which consists in reaching the highest being, could not take place, for the effect is absorbed only by entering into its cause. Another reason for which this hypothesis of the successive origination of the *Vyūhas* is rejected is that the instrument is not known to be produced from the agent. Observation never shows us an instrument such as a hatchet and the like, to spring from an agent such as Devadatta, or any other workman. But the Bhāgavatas teach that from an agent, viz., the individual soul termed Saṅkarṣaṇa, there springs its instrument viz., the internal organ termed Pradyumna, and again from this offspring of the agent another instrument viz., the *ahaṁkāra* termed Aniruddha.

This interpretation of the *Vyūhas* certainly finds support in the *Pāñcarātra Āgamas*. Thus Rāmānuja himself quotes the *Parama-saṁhitā* as the source of the view: '*Parama-Kāraṇāt para-brahma-bhūtāt Vāsudevāt Saṅkaraṣaṇo nāma Jīvo jāyate, Saṅkarṣaṇāt Pradyumnasañjakam mano jāyate, tasmād Aniruddhasañjño ahaṁkāro jāyate.'* But Rāmānuja says that the soul is really accepted to be eternal since Saṅkarṣaṇa etc. are presiding deities over *Jīvas* etc., and are only manifestations of *Brahman.*[19]

Śaṅkara then mentions the second interpretation of the *Vyūhas.* Saṅkarṣaṇa etc. may not be intended as *jīva* (individual soul) etc., but as *Īśvaras* endowed with knowledge, lordship, force, power, prowess and glory. Endowed with the *ṣāḍguṇya,* they are all Vāsudevas, free from faults or support (in anything else), without imperfections. Even so the doctrine is open to serious objection. If the *Vyūhas* are different but alike in their Godlike character, then they are superfluous and would also contradict the basic doctrine that Vāsudeva is the sole, ultimate reality. If on the other hand, the *Vyūhas* are regarded as the manifestations of the one Lord but equal and alike, there would again be a contradiction because it would mean the production of an effect from a cause which has nothing to distinguish it. How can Saṅkarṣaṇa be born from Vāsudeva, and Pradyumna from Saṅkarṣaṇa etc. when they are not only one but wholly alike? Śaṅkara complains that the Pāñcarātra does not distinguish between the *Vyūhas* on the basis of any gradation of the six qualities since all the *Vyūhas* are regarded as Vāsudeva without any distinction. And if one does distinguish grades of manifestation, why should one limit the manifestations to just four? The whole universe from *Brahmā* to the clump of grass is nothing but the manifestation of the Lord.

Rāmānuja, however, points out that this way of understanding the *Vyūha* theory is incorrect.[20] The Supreme Lord has manifested Himself in many forms for the convenience of worship. The ultimate form is the subtle or *sūkṣma* form which is that of Vāsudeva in Himself and consists in the perfection of the six qualities. The *Vyūhas* are deliberate manifestations for the convenience of meditation of all the different castes. The *Vibhavas* are the incarnations Rāma, Kṛṣṇa etc. Their images used for worship are called the *arcā* forms. Thus there is no contradiction in God manifesting Himself in diverse grades. It may be recalled that in the *Ahirbudhnya Saṁhitā* it is clearly stated that each of the *Vibhavas* shows the pre-eminence of two of the six divine qualities.[21] Thus although essentially divine, the *Vyūhas* are distinct manifestations.

The basic objection of Śaṅkara is not to the monotheism of the *Pāñcarātra,* which he praises. Nor is it to the concept of manifestation which he accepts in principle. The *Pāñcarātra* emphasis on the devotional worship of God is also approved by Śaṅkara. The *Pāñcarātra* devotion included visiting the temple (*abhigamana*), making offerings (*upādāna*), worship (*ityā*), recitation of holy texts (*svādhyāya*), and meditation. This mode of worship which combined the use of images, temples, meditation and devotion had become current in the Kuṣāṇa and Gupta times owing to the influence of the *Āgamas* and the *Purāṇas*. It virtually replaced the more austere and more exclusive Vedic ritual. Now feeling was held of more importance than mere ritual. And the new method of worship was open to all castes and women also. Śaṅkara's tolerant approval of the new mode is a revealing commentary on his own attitude towards the new religious tendencies of the age.

The basic objection of Śaṅkara really relates to the tendency of the *Pāñcarātra* to deviate from strict monism. If Vāsudeva is the sole reality, why have the *Vyūhas*? If they are to be regarded as mere manifestations of the divine reality, why not see its manifestation everywhere? The fact is that a monotheism which forgets absolutism is likely to compromise non-dualism in its devotional and theistic fervour. It is this danger that Śaṅkara is concerned with fighting.

Debate with Jainas

Śaṅkara's acquaintance with Jainism appears to have been slight. Except for the brief section in the *BS* where the Sūtrakāra discusses it, Śaṅkara hardly makes any reference to it. Part of the reason might have been that the earlier literature of the Jainas is in Prākṛta rather than Sanskrit. *Tattvārthādhigama-sūtra* was a well known text in Sanskrit, possibly of the 2nd century A.D. Siddhasena Divākara's writings belonged to the Gupta period. The major logical and philosophical writings in Sanskrit, however, date from Akalaṅka, probably in the 8th century. In Śaṅkara's times the Jainas were locked in a fierce practical conflict with the Śaivas in the south. Perhaps that could also be a reason for Śaṅkara's indifference to this variety of heterodoxy. It may be recalled that the Śaṅkara legend devotes much attention to the debates of Kumārila and Śaṅkara with with the 'Jainas' but it is probable that we have here a confusion between the Jainas and the Buddhas since the Buddha was also called Jina.

Jainism was a typical Śramanic doctrine, ascetic, atheistic, realistic and pluralistic.[22] Although Śaṅkara advocated asceticism in the sense of the renunciation of life, he did not particularly favour austere self-mortification. Atheism and pluralism were totally rejected by him and realism admitted only at the empirical level. Śaṅkara begins by giving a brief description of the Jaina doctrine. The Jainas acknowledge seven categories (*padārthas*) viz., soul (*Jīva*), non-soul (*ajīva*), the influx (*āsrava*), restraint (*saṁvara*), destruction (*nirjarā*), bondage (*bandha*), release (*mokṣa*). In brief it may be said that they acknowledge two categories, viz., soul and non-soul, since the other five may be subsumed under these two. They also set forth a set of categories different from the two mentioned. They teach that there are five so-called *astikāyas* ('existing bodies', i.e., categories) viz., the categories of soul (*Jīva*), matter (*Pudgala*), *dharma, adharma* and space (*ākāśa*). All these categories are further 'subdivided in various fanciful ways'. To all these things they apply the following method of reasoning, which they call the *Saptabhaṅgīnaya*: somehow it is, somehow it is not; somehow it is and it is not; it is indescribable; somehow it is and is indescribable; somehow it is not and is indescribable; somehow it is and is not and is indescribable. They apply this *Saptabhaṅgīnaya* even to such conceptions as those of unity and eternity.[23]

Only two items in the Jaina system receive critical attention viz., the doctrine of *Saptabhaṅgīnaya* and the concept of the soul having the size of the body. *Saptabhaṅgīnaya* has been diversely evaluated by modern philosophers but on the whole it has been well received as an example of profound philosophical insight and unusual logical possibilities. For the Jainas the basis of *Saptabhaṅgī* lies in the principle of *Anekānta*. Reality has a multitude of aspects and it is the limitation of human thought and speech that it is abstractive and hence partial. The truth of assertions and denials is thus dependent on the point of view from which they are made. The Jaina dialectic is essentially constructive and synthetic like the Hegelian. Its metaphysics is one of reality as characterized by an infinity of attributes. Although reality is infinitely many-sided, it may be grasped by an infinite, intuitive knowledge called *Kevala-jñāna*. Rational knowledge, however, is necessarily one-sided and can be misleading unless corrected by *Syādvāda*. This is particularly necessary for philosophy which is apt to be the prisoner of some limited point of view. The absolutization of a particular point of view is what *Syādvāda* seeks to eliminate.

Advaita, on the other hand, is an avowed absolutism and its opposition to the Jaina theory is thus natural. Śaṅkara charges the Jainas with plain contradiction. 'It is impossible that contradictory predicates such as being and non-being should at the same time belong to one and the same subject like hot and cold'—*nahyekasmin dharmiṇi yugapat sadasattvādi viruddha-dharmasamāveśaḥ sambhavati śītoṣṇavat.*' Although the illustration which Śaṅkara chooses is unfortunate because 'hot' and 'cold' are relative assertions depending on some standard of reference, Śaṅkara goes on to point out the basic difficulty in all unlimited relativism. It tends to be suicidal. Are there seven categories or more or less? 'The unlimited assertion that all things are of a non-conclusive nature is itself something, and falls as such under the alternative predications "somehow it is", "somehow it is not", and so ceases to be a definite assertion.' Since the means of knowledge, the object of knowledge, the knowing subject, and the act of knowledge, would all be subject to the same inconclusiveness how would Jaina doctrine be at all practicable or useful? Nor can one say that this really leads to the indescribability of the categories, 'for if they are so they cannot be described, but as a matter of fact, they are described so that to call them indescribable involves a contradiction.'[24] Inconclusiveness about the soul, after-life and salvation would reduce religion to mockery.

Śaṅkara rejects Jaina atomism as subject to the same defects as the Vaiśeṣika theory. The Jaina doctrine of soul is more elaborately attacked since it holds the soul to be neither atomic (*aṇu*) nor universally prevasive (*Vibhu*) but of a middling size (*madhyamaparimāṇa*). The size of the soul and its increasing and decreasing in different births to fit different bodies is attacked on the assumption that it must lose or gain parts and thus become essentially impermanent.

Śaṅkara's critique of Jainism is as unsatisfactory as perfunctory. Many-valued dialectical logics cannot be dismissed by a simple appeal to the law of contradiction or Excluded Middle. Even Advaita admits a variety of standpoints. The world is real empirically but unreal transcendentally. It is thus neither real, nor unreal, but indescribable. Only Advaitic dialectic seeks to dismiss the reality of the plural, empirical world in favour of a transcendent absolute but has to concede an indescribable status to the phenomenal. Similarly the relationship between the soul and its embodiment is one of apparent identity as that of the light of a lamp and the room it illumines. The narrowing or extension of the area illumined does not mean that light becomes merely discrete and loses or gains in its essential being.

REFERENCES

1. Phanibhushan Tarkavagisa, *Nyāya-darśana*, but contra, Kangle, *Arthaśāstra*, Vol. II, p.6 fn.; Datar (ed.) *Arthaśāstra*, Vol. I, Pt. I, pp. 124 ff.
2. Cf. *Encyclopaedia of Indian Philosophy*, Vol. II, p. 5.
3. Frauwallner traces the development of Vaiśeṣika as 'nature philosophy', *History of Indian Philosophy*, II, pp. 3 ff.
4. In *BSB*, 2.2.37, S. describes Vaiśeṣikas as believing in God as merely the *nimitta-kāraṇa* of the world.
5. *BSB*, 2.2.11.
6. '*Dve dvyaṇuke*' of the *Bhāṣya* has been amended to '*dvedve dvyaṇuke*'. Alternatively it has been said that Śaṅkara has in mind the doctrine of the old Vaiśeṣikas represented by the lost *Rāvaṇa-bhāṣyam*—vide *Bhāṣya-Ratnaprabhā* ad. *BSB* 2.2.11.
7. *BSB*, 2.2.11.
8. *Ibid.*, 2.2.16.
9. *Ibid.*, 2.2.17.
10. *BSB*, 2.2.37.
11. Vide e.g. V.S. Pathak, *History of Śaiva Cults in Northern India*; Kaviraj, *op. cit.*, pp. 63-68.
12. Cf. *Bhāmatī* and *Ratnaprabhā* ad *BSB*, 2.2.37.
13. *Śrībhāṣya*, Vol. II, p. 551.
14. Vide P.C. Bagchi, *Studies in the Tantras*.
15. *BSB*, 2.2.42-45.
    Śrībhāṣya, Vol. II, pp. 554-61.
16. Vide Susmita Pande, *The Birth of Bhakti*, pp. 92 ff.
17. *Śrībhāṣya*, Vol. II, p. 556.
18. *BSB*, 2.2.44.
19. *Śrībhāṣya*, Vol. II, p. 557.
20. *Ibid.*, pp. 556-57.
21. *Ahirbudhnyasaṁhitā*, 5.19-20.
22. G.C. Pande, *Origins of Buddhism*, p. 260; also *Śramana-Tradition*, generally.
23. *BSB*, 2.2.33.
24. *BSB*, 2.2.33 = '*Avaktavyāścennocyeran, ucyante cāvaktavyāśceti vipratiśiddham.*'

13

Last Years

Śaṅkara has been described as *parivrājakācārya*, peripatetic Master who was a mendicant traditionally expected to be wandering from place to place except during the rainy season.[1] Apart from the inherent dynamics of the eremitical model of Brāhmaṇical mendicancy, what led Śaṅkara to travelling far and wide in the country is said to have been his mission of refurbishing Vedic religion and Vedāntic philosophy through teaching, preaching and debating.[2] Pilgrimages to holy centres and the reform and reorganisation of traditional modes of worship are mentioned as aspects of his travelling.[3] So also the organisation of a new monastic system is said to have been a reason and consequence of these far-flung tours.

Śaṅkara's travels are said to have ranged from snowy peaks of Kailāsa to the *Setu* on the blue ocean, '*Advaitam ā-tuhina-bhūdharamā ca setoḥ*.'[4] The order of chronology of these travels or their exact extent, however, cannot be decided because the legendary biographies do not give any coherent account except that there is more or less unanimity about his visits to Kāśī and Badarī, Kāñcī and Śṛṅgerī, Purī and Dwārakā as also about his visits to Ujjain, Haridvāra, Śrīparvata and the extreme south. The traditions about his visits to Kashmir and Kailāsa are also quite strong. The overall picture is certainly that of an indefatigable preacher and pilgrim, wandering over the length and breadth of the vast subcontinent, '*pṛthvīm pṛthvīm paryaṭan bhāṣyakāraḥ*.'[5] Not much before him Hsüan Chwang, the Buddhist pilgrim from far distant China had traversed Central Asia after touring the whole of India and returned to China in a space of 16 years (629-45), the same as were available to Śaṅkara.

According to the *Mādhavīya* Śaṅkara proceeded to the south after his conversion of Maṇḍana at Māhiṣmatī. Wandering through Maharashtra he gradually moved eastward and reached Śrīśaila which is located in the Kurnool district.[6] It had been a famous centre of the Buddhist *Caityaka* sects[7] and was well known as a place for occult practices and attainments in the 7th century.[8] The *Śivaliṅga* called *Mallikārjuna* was located here and was one of the twelve *Jyotirliṅgas*. Śaṅkara is said to have spent time here on the banks of the river Krishnā teaching his disciples and debating with the Pāśupatas, Vaiṣṇavas and Māheśvaras.[9] The reference to the Vīraśaivas is clearly anachronistic. It is said that the Kāpālika leader Ugrabhairava belonged here and sought to persuade Śaṅkara to let himself be sacrificed. Śaṅkara is even said to have agreed to the proposal out of sheer selfless magnanimity but Padmapāda intervened by invoking the grace of the fierce deity Narasiṁha and frustrated the Kāpālika who was killed.[10]

From Śrīśaila Śaṅkara is said to have proceeded to Gokarṇa on the west coast near Goa where Mahābaleśvara is located.[11] The form of Śiva located at Gokarṇa was famous, from the days of the ancient epics, and even Kālidāsa refers to the 'Lord resident in Gokarṇa' ('*Gokarṇa-niketam-īśvaram*').[12] 'For three days and nights Śaṅkara stayed at that holy spot, performing with great devotion the worship of the Lord of Gokarṇa—the Being that transcends the *Guṇas*. . .'[13] From there the supreme Master, who was on a pilgrimage to all holy places, next proceeded to the temple of Hari-Śaṅkara which had a syncretic image. Thence he proceeded to the shrine of Mūkāmbikā where he is said to have revived a dead child.[14] From there Śaṅkara moved to the *agrahāra* called *Śriboli*.[15] Here he is said to have been met by the famous *mīmāṁsaka* Prabhākara whose son was apparently a retarded child. In Śaṅkara's presence, however, the child miraculously flowered into a spiritual genius and spontaneously broke out into Vedāntic verse. These twelve verses are famous as the *Hastāmalaka-stotra*.[16] The child now known as Hastāmalaka followed Śaṅkara as one of his principal disciples.

Śaṅkara now proceeded to Sṛṅgagiri or Śṛṅgerī[17] which has been famous for its temple of the goddess known as Śāradambā and has remained for long one of the premier places of Śaṅkarite monasticism. Here a dull but devoted disciple of Śaṅkara received the Master's grace to become the famous Toṭakācārya.[18] Apparently Śaṅkara is supposed to have stayed at Śṛṅgerī for a long time and the works of his famous disciples Sureśvara and Padmapāda were commissioned here.[19]

Padmapāda is said to have expressed a desire to proceed on pilgrimage from here.[20] The Master at first dissuaded him saying that the proximity of the Guru is the real place of pilgrimage. The washings of his feet are the holy waters (*tīrtha*). The perception of the *Ātman* through the Guru's instruction is the best vision of the gods. It is better to be near the Guru, serving him, than wander about from place to place. . . Travel causes distraction as one has to search for proper water, food and shelter. Instead of the *Ātman* one would be worrying about his food, shelter and safety.[21] Padmapāda, however, was not to be deterred. He argued that inconveniences need to be faced anywhere and convenience, in any case, can hardly be said to enhance spiritual attainments. Disease and death overtake one when fated. 'By resorting to holy places, one gains peace of mind; by seeing many places, one's outlook becomes inquisitive; and by contacts with holy men, one is saved from dangers.'[22] At this the Master revealed that he was only testing the disciple's determination. He also gave him some sound advice—'Always go along safe and frequented paths. . . Do not stay too long in any place. . . It is better always to arrive at one's destination as early as possible. . .Strangers should not be trusted too much.'[23] While Padampāda travelled to the north and then southward, Śaṅkara sojourned in Kerala.[24] Travelling towards the Setu he debated with the Śāktas.[25] From Ramesvaram he moved to Kāñcī through Cola and Pāṇḍya countries.[26] At Kāñcī he 'built a temple, instituted the worship of Bhagawati, with rituals that are in accordance with the Vedic traditions (*śruti sammata*) and suited to the attainment of supreme knowledge (*Parāvidyā*). He eschewed in those rituals, every trace of the Tantrika modes of worship.'[27] Then he travelled through the Andhra country to Vidarbha. From there he moved to Karnataka and his followers are said to have been violently attacked by Kāpālikas who had to yield to the superior occult powers of the Master. Śaṅkara then proceeded to the western sea at Gokarṇa and there defeated the Śaiva Master called Nīlakaṇṭha in disputation. He then moved through Saurashtra to Dvārakā where the Vaiṣṇavas held sway. Next he came to Ujjayini and met the Śaivas, Śāktas and Sauras. He is said to have debated with Bhāskara here. This is plainly apocryphal because although Bhāskara has criticised Śaṅkara's views he himself appears to have lived sometime after Śaṅkara.[28]

In Bāhlika Śaṅkara is said to have disputed the Jaina doctrines. There is obviously some mistake here because Śaṅkara's visiting Bāhlika is as unlikely as the existence of Jainism in that region. However, the word 'Jaina' also denoted the Buddhists. Śaṅkara is then said to have disputed 'the Jaina sect known as Mādhyamikas' in the Śūrasena region. He toured through the lands of Darada, Kuru, Pañcāla, and successfully debated with Prabhākara, Bhaṭṭa, Udayana, Khaṇḍanakāra. This is obviously due to historical confusion as Udayana was at least two centuries removed from Śaṅkara and Khaṇḍanakāra lived much later. However, a confusion between two Harṣas, the playwright and the poet, could have precipitated this error. So Śaṅkara is said to have debated with Abhinavagupta in Kāmarūpa, which is, again, a case of anachronism as well as misplaced geography.[29]

After debating with various sects and schools in eastern India and the Madhyadeśa, Śaṅkara is said to have proceeded to the famous temple of Śāradā in Kashmir where after successfully debating with rival teachers he ascended the Throne of Omniscience.[30] After this he went to Badarī and finally to Kedāra and then to Kailāsa from where he left the world.[31]

According to the *Mādhavīya*, thus, Śaṅkara went from Kāśī to Prayāga and Māhiṣmatī and then to the south moving from the west coast to the east, thence to Kerala, back again to the east coast, then to the west coast through Deccan, moving up again to Saurashtra. Coming back to central India, Madhyadeśa and Prācya, and finally to Kashmir, Badarī and Kedāra. He visits the Himalayan region twice as also the west coast and central India. The account belongs essentially to the Deccan and the south and betrays lack of familiarity with northern, especially remote northern regions and gross historical anachronisms which have resulted from the attempt to give dramatic reality to debates of which no real memory had survived for the author. But it does effectively project the image of Śaṅkara as a peripatetic teacher, pilgrim and debater.

As the *Guruvaṃśa-Kāvya* belongs to the Śṛṅgerī tradition it conforms in important respects to the treatment of Śaṅkara's peregrinations as described in the *Mādhavīya*. In *M.* Śaṅkara goes to Badarī from Kāśī and writes the commentaries there. In the *GVK* Śaṅkara goes to Badarī as a pilgrimage after writing the commentaries.[32] There after meeting Kumārila at Prayāga he goes to Viśvarūpa who is now placed in Magadha.[33] He meets Maṇḍana on the way.[34] Śaṅkara then hears of his mother's illness and proceeds to Kāraṭī.[35] There Padmapāda meets him after having lost his manuscript commentary on Śaṅkara's *BSB*.[36] Śaṅkara now proceeds to Madhyārjuna where Śiva declares the truth of Advaita thrice.[37] Śaṅkara then goes to Anantaśāyi-purī, Rāmasetu and Rāmeśvara.[38] He then proceeds to Raupyapīṭha, acquires Hastāmalaka and Toṭaka as disciples and also the disease of fistula.[39] Recovering he proceeds to Gokarṇa and to the source of the Tuṅgabhadrā. There he finds in Śṛṅgerī a place fit for himself.[40] Thence he goes to Śrīśaila, Śeṣācala, Narasiṁhagiri and Jagannātha.[41] Back to Varanasi he created the five monasteries for his disciples.[42] After staying for sometime he went to Kaśmīra to ascend the Throne of Omniscience. Here the goddess questioned him about the science of erotics and Śaṅkara acquired its knowledge by reanimating the body of King Amaruka. Śaṅkara then having satisfied the Goddess Śāradā requested her to accompany him to the *Ṛṣyaśṛṅga āśrama* on the Tuṅgabhadrā with which she complied.[43] Here Śaṅkara spent much time with his disciples.[44] He then asked Sureśvara to stay there and worship the Candramaulīśvara liṅga, Ratnagarbha, Gaṇeśa and Sarasvatī but himself went to Kāñcī.[45] There he helped construct two cities and established the image of Kāmākṣī.[46] He gave instructions of the six sects, viz., Śaivas, Śāktas, Vaiṣṇavas, Sauras, Gāṇapatyas and Kaumāras or Kāpālikas and then went to Badarī where he rescued the image of Nārāyaṇa and established its worship. He left Padmapāda in charge of its worship[47] and himself proceeded to Kāśī where he was accosted by a Bhairavācārya to gift his head but Padmapāda foils the Tantric.[48] Śaṅkara planned the city of Śrīnagara[49], and sent Padmapāda to the east to stay in the Jagannātha monastery. Hastāmalaka was sent to Dvārakā and Toṭaka to Jyotirmatha in the Badarī forest.[50] He then himself proceeded to Nepal to the shrine of Siddheśvarī and at the end, to the hermitage of Dattātreya.[51]

Despite differences this account agrees with that of the *Mādhavīya* in important respects. The southern journey takes place after the debate with Maṇḍana and in the same period when the death of Śaṅkara's mother occurs. It culminates in the establishment of the worship of Śāradā at Śṛṅgerī and the end comes in the Himalayan region. However, *GVK* has two journeys in the south, the second taking place after Śaṅkara's visit to Kashmir. Turning to the other tradition connected with Kāñcī, we may begin with the *Jagad-guru-ratna-mālā*. Here, after converting Maṇḍana Miśra in his *agrahāra* called *Padmavana*, Śaṅkara proceeds by stages to Badarī where he worships Gauḍapāda and then goes up to Kailāsa (*dhavalācala*) for the vision of Śiva.[52] Śiva bestows on him the Five

Liṅgas viz., *Yoga-liṅga, Bhoga-liṅga, Vara-liṅga, Siddhi-liṅga,* and *Vimukti-liṅga,* and commands him to return and complete his *digvijaya.* Ātmabodha explains that Śaṅkara had already completed the *digvijaya* in the north and now proceeded to the south.[53] He established the worship of Bhāratī at Śṛṅgerī on the banks of Tuṅgabhadrā and spent twelve years there.[54] Then he proceeded on a further tour to the south towards Rameswaram and then towards Kāñcī, visiting Veṅkatādri and Kalahastin or *Daksiṇa-Kailāsa.*[55] At Kāñcī old dilapidated temples were got restored and two more got constructed by him and the *Śrīcakra* was established and with that the worship of Kāmākṣī as a benign deity.[56] Śaṅkara now ascended the Throne of Omniscience at Kāñcī and in this context acquired the knowledge of erotics by reanimating another body.[57] He nominated his four disciples to the four monasteries, Pṛthvīdhara at Śṛṅgerī, Padmapāda at Dvārakā, Hastāmalaka at Jagannātha, and Ānandagiri at Badarikāśrama, and himself stayed at Kāñcī where he finally left the earth.[58]

It will be noticed that in this version there is no reference to Śaṅkara's visit to Western India or to Kashmir. While the importance of Śṛṅgerī remains unaffected, Kāñcī is made even more important and the death of the Master is placed there.[59]

In the *Vyāsācalīya* it is stated that after completing his Vedāntic studies, Śaṅkara, desirous of pilgrimage to holy places, went towards the north to Badarī and composed his commentary on the *BS* at the age of sixteen.[60] Here he met his first disciple Sanandana.[61] Having learnt of his mother's illness he went to his home village in Kerala but returned to Badarī and began roaming and preaching.[62] He reached Prayāga and the confluence of holy rivers and remembered his mother. There he met the great Kumārila who was immolating himself there in slow fire. Kumārila directed Śaṅkara to attempt the conversion of his disciple Viśvarūpa staying in Magadha.[63] It is said that another disciple of Kumārila called Maṇḍana met Śaṅkara at Prayāga and was instructed by him in *Advaita* for which the indirect relevance of ritual was accepted.[64] From Prayāga Śaṅkara went to Viśvarūpa and converted him by debating.[65] The travels and travails of Sanandana are described in detail.[66] As for Śaṅkara it is said he went to Srivali village and Gokarṇa, and then Kashmir where he ascended the Throne of Omniscience after successfully debating with rivals.[67] This account is clearly fragmentary but close to that of the *Mādhavīya,* which agrees with the suggestion that the original of the *Vyāsācalīya* was perhaps the same as the source of the present version of the *Mādhavīya*.

In the *Govindanāthīya* Śaṅkara stays with his teacher Govindapāda for some time at Kāśi and then seeks his permission for proceeding on *tīrthayātrā*.[68] The dialogue between Śaṅkara and his teacher is of the same kind as between Śaṅkara and Padmapāda as reported in the texts mentioned earlier. Perhaps Govindanātha reproduces the original situation while its transference to Padampāda could be a later version. Roaming over the northern regions Śaṅkara reached Badarīkāśrama and stayed there for a considerable time, composing his commentaries.[69] Then learning of his mother's illness he went to Kerala but later returned to Badarī.[70] He acquires Sanandana as a disciple,[71] meets Kumārila at Prayāga, proceeds to debate with Viśvarūpa and converts him as Sureśvara.[72] While proceeding to Gokarṇa Śaṅkara once stopped at the village Sivavihara where he gained Hastāmalaka as disciple.[73] In the course of his pilgrimages Śaṅkara visited Haridvāra and stayed there for some time.[74] Then he went to the south towards Rāmasetu.[75] He visited the holy spot called Kalahastin and the place called Southern Kailāsa. Then he reached Kāñcī.[76] Then he went to Puṇḍarīkapura and Śivagaṅgā.[77] Proceeding along the Kāverī river he reached Śrīraṅga and finally reached Rāmasetu.[78] Going back to Kāñcī[79], he went to Kashmir and ascended the Throne of Omniscience.[80] Once again he went to the south and reached Vṛṣācala. There at Dakṣiṇa Kailāsa he breathed his last.[81] At the end, however, the text contradicts itself by speaking of the ascent to the Throne of Omniscience at Kāñcī.[82] It also adds more reasonably that after the last rites of his mother Śaṅkara had come to Prayāga to offer the holy water to the departed soul. The text avoids reference to *Digvijaya* but rather emphasises pilgrimage—*nānātīrtha-niṣevaṇotsuka-matih* (final verses, V.6). It is also distinctive in as much as it places the death of Śaṅkara in Kerala.

In the *Cidvilāsīya* Śaṅkara is said to have met his teacher Govindapāda at Badarī[83] and after composing his commentaries and seeking to go on a pilgrimage at last got the permission of his teacher for pilgrimage,[84] but shortly he had to go to the south for the last rites of his mother,[85] from where he proceeded to Prayāga[86] where he stayed for some time and acquired Hastāmalaka as his disciple.[87] He then came to Varanasi where too he resided for some time.[88] He acquired great fame there and Viśvanātha attested to the truth of *Advaita*[89] Śaṅkara also acquired Toṭaka as a disciple.[90] He then went to Ruddhpura to meet Kumārila who was lying in a pyre of burning husk.[91] Kumārila directed Śaṅkara to his disciple Maṇḍana who is here placed in Kashmir.[92] After the debate with Maṇḍana Śaṅkara presses Maṇḍana's wife Sarasavāṇī for debate during which Śaṅkara is compelled to acquire a knowledge of erotics by entering the dead body of a king. He then persuades Sarasavāṇī to come with him to the south to Śṛṅgerī on the Tuṅgabhadrā.[93] Then he went to Kāñcī and established a new mode of worship.[94] He also ascended the *Sarvajñapīṭha* there. He then travelled to Venkatesvara and Śeṣācala, Cidambara, Madhyārjuna and finally Ramesvara.[95] He then turned back to Vakratuṇḍapurī, Madhurā, Anantaśayana, Vāsukikṣetra and Mṛdapura.[96] After seeing Gokarṇa and Mahabalesvara, he turned to Śrīśaila.[97] Then he went to the east to Jagannātha and established a monastery with Padmapāda at its head.[98] Then he went to Ujjayini and gradually to Dvārakā. He established a monastery there and put Hastāmalaka in charge.[99] Then he went north and passing through Mathurā reached Badarī and established a monastery there in charge of Toṭaka.[100] Then he met Dattātreya and went up to Kailāsa, his own abode.[101]

According to Anantānandagirī Śaṅkara had gone from Kālaṭī to Vyāghrapura where he was initiated by Govindapāda.[102] Having composed his commentaries and gathered disciples he roamed about the country debating with rival teachers and sectaries. From Cidambara he proceeded to Madhyārjuna where Śiva Himself manifested Himself for a moment and proclaimed the truth of *Advaita*.[103] Then he moved to Ramesvara and debated with a sect of the Śaivas.[104] Proceeding to Anantaśayanam he debated with six sects of the Vaiṣṇavas.[105] At Subrahmanyakṣetra he debated with worshippers of Skanda, at Ganavaram with worshippers of Gaṇapati. At Tulajapura he debated with Śāktas and attempted reform of different kinds of sectaries.[106] Then he proceeded to Ujjayini to confute still other sects including the Kāpālikas and their spokesmen.[107] He visited the towns of Anumalla and Marundha and then went to Magadha towards the north and then to Indraprastha, Yamaprastha and Prayāga. Going to Kailāsa Śaṅkara obtained the Five Crystal Liṅgas from Śiva and consecrated to *Mukti-liṅga* at Kedāra, then he proceeded to Badarīnārāyaṇa by way of Kurukṣetra.[108] Then he travelled to Dvārakā, Nīlakaṇṭha-kṣetra and in due course to Ayodhyā. Then he reached Gayā, Śrīśaila and Mallikarjuna. At Ruddhapura he met Kumārila who directed him to his brother-in-law Maṇḍana staying in the north at a place called Bijilabindu.[109] After his victory over Maṇḍana and Sarasavāṇī, he persuaded the latter to stay as the deity at Śṛṅgagiri on the Tuṅgabhadrā, where he established a monastery and school. He stayed there for twelve years appointing Padmapāda as its head and establishing the worship of the *Bhoga-liṅga* there.[110] He then went to Ahobila and Venkatagiri whence he finally reached Kāñcī. There he helped establish the towns of Śiva Kāñcī and Viṣṇu Kāñcī. He also consecrated the *Śrīcakra* and the *Yoga-liṅga* at Kāñcī and made Sureśvara its head.[111] He also established the Six Sects in mutual harmony.[112] It is at Kāñcī that he left the world. The *Mokṣa-liṅga* was instructed to be sent to Cidambara.

Anantānandagiri is chiefly concerned with the debates of Śaṅkara with rival schools and sects. Dhanapati Sūri in his commentary on the Mādhavīya quotes a great deal from the older and lost *Digvijayas* which has a similar purport. He also says that the *Digvijaya* started from Madhyārjuna with a journey towards the south. His knowledge of the geography of the north is poor.

The account in Tirumala Dīkṣita's *Śaṅkarābhyudaya* is incomplete but tends to agree with the *Mādhavīya*. Śaṅkara stays at Kāśī,[113] whence he goes to Prayāga[114] and then to Māhiṣmatī to meet Maṇḍana.[115] After the victory over his wife Śaṅkara persuades her to preside over the worship of her divine form at Śṛṅgerī.[116] Śaṅkara travels through Maharashtra to Mallikarjuna.

Rājacūḍāmaṇi Dīkṣita's *Śaṅkarābhyudaya* gives a similar account. After meeting Kumārila at Prayāga,[117] Śaṅkara goes to debate with Viśvarūpa in Magadha.[118] Then learning of his mother's illness he goes to Kālaṭī.[119] After her last rites Śaṅkara wandered through Kerala,[120] acquiring disciples and also the disease of fistula. In the course of his pilgrimage he visited Gokarṇa, Hari-hara-kṣetra, Mūkāmbikā-kṣetra,[121] Anantaśayana-kṣetra, Madhurā,[122] Ramesvara,[123] the bank of Kāverī, Śri-raṅga-kṣetra, and finally Kāñcī where he ascended the Throne of Omniscience.[124]

In the *Patañjalivijaya* too it is stated that having composed the commentaries Śaṅkara embarked on his *digvijaya* and ultimately settled in Kāñcī. In Nīlakaṇṭha Dīkṣita's *Śaṅkarābhyudaya* Śaṅkara, after converting Maṇḍana, proceeds on his *digvijaya*, going first to Mallikarjuna, then to Hariśaṅkara and Mūkāmbikā-kṣetra.[125] Meanwhile Padmapāda has been travelling on his own and has managed to get his own commentary burnt down by his vicious uncle.

Padmapāda meets Śaṅkara in Kerala to report his misadventures.[126] Śaṅkara then travels to Veṅkatādri and thence to the Vidarbha country. He is said to travel in the west to Dvārakā and Ujjain and in the north-west to Bahlika and in the east to Gauda and Kāmarūpa. He is made to debate many scholars who lived much after him. He ascends the Throne of Omniscience in Kashmir and finally disappears in the Himalayas.[127]

All these different accounts diverge in the details of Śaṅkara's travels. They do not agree over the places he visited, nor do they mention them in the same order. Some of the accounts betray gross geographical ignorance and they sometimes adopt the *deus ex machina* of Śaṅkara's travelling by miraculous powers. The accounts derive from lost sources as well as local legends, largely southern. Nevertheless they are generally agreed that Śaṅkara left his home to go to north India to acquire Vedāntic wisdom and meet his teacher, that he once returned to his home in Kerala for the last rites of his mother, that he spent some time in Kāśī, met Kumārila at Prayāga or Ruddhapura, and travelled much for the sake of *digvijaya* and *tīrthayātrā*. It is generally agreed that his debate with Maṇḍana/Viśvarūpa was the most memorable. It is also agreed that he visited Śṛṅgerī and Kāñcī in the south and also the Himalayas in the north. It is most probable that he spent some time in Kāñcī just as he did in Kāśī and Śṛṅgerī.

That Śaṅkara visited the Himalayas is attested unanimously by his legendary biographies as well as by the local traditions of Badarinatha, Nepal and Kashmir. According to one version Śaṅkara went to Badarikāśrama between his twelfth and sixteenth years, met Govindapāda and Gauḍapāda there, and composed his commentaries while staying there.[128] It is also said that he was responsible for the emergence of the hot water spring nearby, resuscitated the image of Badarī Nārāyaṇa which was lying sunk in the river water and had a temple constructed over it under the supervision of Padmapāda.[129] Finally, it is said that it was here that he received the Five *Liṅgas*,[130] and founded a monastic centre, though when, is not clear. According to another version he visited the Himalayas again towards the end of his life and it was here that he left the earth.[131] Some of the acts with which he is credited could well have taken place during the second visit.

That Śaṅkara had a renewed meeting with Govindapāda in the Himalayas seems unlikely as he is said to have directed Śaṅkara to take up his residence in Kāśī. That Śaṅkara actually met Gauḍapāda is highly improbable and that he met Vyāsa near Badarī can only be mythical. But he could have stayed in a cave hallowed by its legendary association with Gauḍapāda. As for his literary activity, Kāśī is more likely to have been its venue since his indubitable writings are mostly scholarly and would normally presuppose the availability of books and the company of scholars. The founding of a monastic centre, if historical, should also in all likelihood come later in his career. The early visit to the Himalayas could only be a part of his *wanderjahre* during the period of spiritual quest. Visiting a cave hallowed by its association with his teacher's teacher would be natural and the Himalayas have always been famous for their ancient sages whom a lucky person might by chance hope to meet. For spiritual practice too they are reputed to be ideal. The Himalayan journey of Śaṅkara could well have taken him to Kailāsa which had obtained fame in mythology much earlier.

Badarikāśrama or Badarikātīrtha finds mention in the *Mahābhārata* and the *Purāṇas.*[132] It was located on the *Gandhamādana*. Bāṇa recalls in the 7th century that Arjuna and Kṛṣṇa had visited it. Nara and Nārāyaṇa are supposed to have performed penances in this region which was thus held to be spiritually hallowed in Śaṅkara's age. The present temple of Badarīnāth is in Garhwal (ancient *Kedāra-Khaṇḍa*) near the source of the river Alakanandā. The larger region within which it lay, seems to have had the appellation of Brahmapura or Kartṛpura during the Gupta period. From about the 8th century the region appears to have been ruled by the Katyuri monarchs of Joshimath. The ancient pilgrimage route to Badarīnātha which Śaṅkara presumably followed lay through Haridvāra and Rishikesh along the Gaṅgā and the Alakanandā. From the traditional account it is clear that there was no Vaiṣṇava temple at Badari before Śaṅkara. It is widely held but unconfirmed that the image at Badari is really Buddhist. That Śaṅkara rescued the image of Nārāyaṇa from the Nārada-Kuṇḍa and started its worship is implicitly attested by the *Skanda Purāṇa* (II.5.24) which, however has not been critically edited and contains apocryphal material.[133] There is little so far known archaeological support for connecting the present temple and image with Śaṅkara. The fact that the priests of the temple are traditionally Nambudri Brāhmaṇas from Kerala has been emphasized as evidence supporting Śaṅkara's consecrating the image and founding its present tradition of worship.[134] Unfortunately the succession of these priests is not uninterrupted, nor can its beginning be traced with certainty.

If Badari belongs geographically to the Kedara Khaṇḍa, Kailāsa and Mānasarovara belong to the Mānasa-Khaṇḍa of *Skanda-purāṇa* of which the date has been debated. Here the route to Kailāsa has been detailed. It begins from Kūrmācala, passes through the confluence of Dhauli and Kali, to *Caturdanṣṭra* (= Candarsa) and *Vyāsāśrama* (=Byasa) whence it goes to *Gaurīgiri, Mānasarovara* and *Nandaparvata.* Śaṅkara, however, is said to have gone to Kailāsa from Badari. At the same time he is said to have brought back Five *Liṅgas* from Kailāsa. If that is accepted and also the common tradition that he finally disappeared in Kailāsa, two distinct visits to Kailāsa would have to be postulated.

Local tradition attests Śaṅkara's visit to Nepal and his restoration of the worship of Paśupatinātha there. For this worship he is said to have entrusted the responsibility to Nambudri priests from Kerala. The practice is said to be continuing and a Śaṅkara monastery is adjacent to the temple of Paśupatinātha.[136] Here again how ancient this tradition is, has not been made out with any degree of certainty.

Śaṅkara's visit to Kashmir is attested by both local legends as well as his legendary biographies but there is no corroborative evidence from the ancient historical chronicles of Kashmir, which could be due to the fact that his visit did not attract any royal attention and also because Kalhana's knowledge of events before the 8th century is very deficient. Śaṅkara's visit is attributed to his desire to go to the famous shrine of Śāradā where poets and scholars flocked. The legend about Śaṅkara reanimating the corpse of a dead king, sometime identified with Amaruka, to learn the secrets of the science of erotics finds its place in this context.[137] Presumably the legend arose from a misunderstanding. '*Kāma-Kalā*' did not merely mean erotics, but had a technical significance in *Tantra-śāstra* for which Kashmir was famous. This sense may be seen in *Kāma-Kalā-Vilāsa.* Śaṅkara could have acquired a knowledge of the strongly *Advaitic Tantra-śāstras* in Kashmir, which would fit in with the tradition that ascribes the *Saundarya-laharī* and the *Prapañcasāra* to him as also the fact of the currency of *Śrīvidyā* among his followers. A commentary of the *Prapañcasāra* records that the work was compiled by Śaṅkara in Kashmir.[138]

Śaṅkara's travels and sojourns in the Himalayan regions appear to have been motivated essentially by the desire to visit holy places and his visits appear to have sparked off new religious currents in those places as evidenced by the local legends of temples such as the Śaṅkarācārya' temple at Srinagar, Badarināth temple, and the Paśupatinātha temple in Nepal. This is not to say that the legendary attribution of the establishment of these temples Śaṅkarācārya is to be accepted as a proved historical fact in the present state of our knowledge. He, however, does seem to have travelled widely in these areas and his dynamic personality appears to have made itself felt in a lasting manner.

Śaṅkara's travels in the south, apart from the journey to see his mother in her last moments, appear to have been motivated as much by the desire for *digvijaya* as for *tīrthayātrā*. The starting point appears to have been the meeting of Śaṅkara with Kumārila who directed him to debate with his disciple Viśvarūpa. Now Maṇḍana or Viśvarūpa is said to have resided at Māhiṣmatī which is normally placed in Avanti on the bank of the Narmadā but at the same time Maṇḍana is said to have lived in Magadha and Mahiṣmati has been identified with Mahisi in the Saharsa district in Bihar on the basis of some Tantric works. Vijjalabindu and Padmavana are also given names of the place where Maṇḍana resided.[139] He is also said to have been a Gauḍa Brāhmaṇa who was born in Kashmir. His wife is said to have come from the banks of the Son in Magadha. Obvious complications are further introduced if Maṇḍana and Viśvarūpa are distinguished. In any case it is not possible to decide the place of residence of Maṇḍana or Viśvarūpa with definiteness. Perhaps Kashmir would be the most likely place since that would reconcile the confusion of debating in front of Śāradā in Kashmir with that of debating with the wife of Maṇḍana identified with Bhāratī.

Among the famous holy places in the south which Śaṅkara visited we find mention of those with Vaiṣṇava, Śaiva and Śākta shrines. Thus Anantasayana near Travancore,[140] and Venkatagiri or Veṅkaṭācala near Tirupati[141] were famous for Vaiṣṇava worship and sects which Śaṅkara disputed in only a qualified manner. Madhyarjuna[142] in the Tanjore district and Cidambaram[143] were famous Śaiva centres. Śaṅkara criticises the Śaivas also. Śrīparvata south of the Krishna was an ancient and famous Tantric centre. It is at Śṛṅgerī and Kāñcī, however, that Śaṅkara is said to have established his own monastic centres. It is not possible to reconstruct the exact order or extent of Śaṅkara's travels in the south. However, given his visits to Kerala, Śṛṅgerī and Kāñcī, it is probable that he visited other holy places, preaching and debating.

In the Deccan Gokarṇa finds special mention. It was a Śaivite holy place well known in *Mahābhārata, Rāmāyaṇa* and *Raghuvaṁśa.*[144] Towards the west Dvārakā and in the east Puri are said to have been selected by Śaṅkara for establishing his own monastic centres.[145]

While the itinerary of Śaṅkara cannot be made out in detail and no details of his debates against individual adversaries have been reportedly preserved except for Maṇḍana/Viśvarūpa, the tradition which associates him with religious reform and monastic reorganization needs to be examined because that by itself has important implications about his travels and debates. That Śaṅkara not merely established the *Advaita* in its purity but also established the Six Sects, for which he came to be known as the *Sanmata-sthāpanācārya,* is asserted in several legendary biographies of Śaṅkara such as Anantānandagiri's *Digvijaya,* and *Guruvaṁśa-Kāvya.* The tradition finds support in *Mārkaṇḍeya-saṁhitā* and also the lost *Prācīna-Śaṅkara-Vijaya* apparently quoted in Dhanapati Sūri's commentary on the *Mādhavīya.* Śaṅkara is said to have debated with the votaries of the different sects, persuaded them to abandon their defective philosophies and exaggerations in ritual and conduct but allowed them to continue with their characteristic and divergent modes of worship. The basic truth is spiritual non-dualism as upheld by the *Upaniṣads. Brahman* is the only reality and is identical with the *Ātman.* However, the one reality manifests itself in diverse names and forms and worshippers may choose different deities for the sake of convenience if they realize that the differences are merely superimposed for the convenience of worship, not real. The diversity of gods, images and modes of worship was thus admitted as consistent with strict philosophical monism. The *Gītā* had already prepared the ground for this and the *Upaniṣads* and the *Brahmasūtras* admit a variety of meditative symbols for the same ultimate reality. Śaṅkara's doctrine of *Upādhi-bheda* constituted its explicit philosophical justification.

The Six Sects mentioned in this context are *Vaiṣṇava, Śaiva, Śākta, Saura, Gāṇapatya* and *Kaumāra* or *Kāpālika.* It has been pointed out that in Śaṅkara's commentaries there are several indications of his personal preference for the worship of God as Viṣṇu and this finds corroboration in the biographical tradition which makes out Govinda or Kṛṣṇa to have been his family deity.

Some of the most authentic of his *stotras* like *Carpaṭa-pañjarikā, Viṣṇu-ṣaṭpadī,* and *Harimide* give expression to his devotion for Viṣṇu. *Govindāṣṭaka, Kṛṣṇāṣṭaka* and *Acyutāṣṭaka* also lay claim to authenticity and give expression to Vaiṣṇava devotion. While recalling Viṣṇuite mythology most of these hymns are clearly Advaitic and adore Kṛṣṇa as the sole God or Self. In his commentary on the *Brahmasūtras* too, as seen above, Śaṅkara accepts the truth of Bhagavatism insofar as it is consistent with the authority of Vedas and the authenticity of the Vedānta.

Śaṅkara makes hardly any reference to Śiva worship in his commentaries except that he criticises the dualistic theism of the Pāśupatas or Māheśvaras in the *BSB.* Among the *stotras* ascribed to Śaṅkara and having a Śaiva affiliation the only one which lays undoubted claim to authenticity is the famous *Dakṣiṇāmūrti stotra* with many ancient commentaries. The *stotra,* however, is essentially *Advaitic* rather than sectarian. That is even truer of the *Daśaślokī* which is an acknowledged masterpiece of *Advaitic* thought and sentiment. The fact is that Śaivism in Śaṅkara's times in south India was generally dualistic but non-dualistic Śaivism was also known especially in Kashmir. Śaṅkara's knowledge of this system and his influence on its subsequent development cannot be ruled out. In fact the *Dakṣiṇāmūrti-stotra* has echoes close to this system and it cannot be denied that the remarkable development of Kashmir Śaivism dates from the age of Śaṅkara.

The traditional interpretation of Śaṅkara insists that *Brahman,* the sole reality, is *nirguṇa* while the world is totally false. The reality of *Īśvara* too is relative to that of the world, and as for the explanation of the world it is due to *avidyā* or *māyā* which in turn is inexplicable and indefinable. There is enough warrant for this interpretation in the writings of Śaṅkara. Nevertheless, it cannot be denied that Śaṅkara assigns a central place to *Īśvara* in his *BSB* and regards *avidyā* or *māyā* as power (*śakti*) of *Brahman.* He likens God with His mysterious power of creation to a magician. Here his philosophy is essentially akin to the non-dualistic schools of *Pratyabhijñā* or *Tripurā-Jñāna-Khaṇḍa,* or even *Yoga-Vāsiṣṭha.* There is, thus, no basic difficulty in supposing that Śaṅkara was willing to extend support to non-dualistic *Śaktism.* Against this it has been argued that in the non-dualism of Śaṅkara, reality is wholly transcendent while the phenomena are simply illusory and the two are connected only by the inexplicable force of Nescience which defies definition or location. In non-dualistic theistic schools, on the other hand, reality has the inherent power of creatively manifesting itself in the phenomenal world. However, it cannot be justly denied that for Śaṅkara too real being or consciousness has the power of self-manifestation as phenomena. Reality is not merely transcendent but also immanent in phenomena. Whatever is, is *Brahman*. To see it as otherwise is Nescience. Śaṅkara never abrogates the creativity or divinity of *Brahman*, though from the non-dualistic point of view there is no distinction between Lord and creature. It is only in this sense that the concept of God is relative to the apparent reality of the world.[146] It is not a denial of divinity but of dualism from the ultimate point of view. The situation is similar in non-dualistic theistic systems, Śaiva and Śākta, for which too there is ultimately nothing except consciousness conceived as Śiva or Śakti. It is true that medieval *Advaitic* polemic tended to emphasize the unreality of the world in the sense that the knowledge of the world was held to be logically false because it was sublated, and was inevitably led into subtle and ingenious speculations about the nature of *avidyā* and *jīva*, from which Śaṅkara was free. However, despite its subtlety this attempt remains essentially scholastic and leaves enough room for an empirical reality which serves a practical purpose. At the same time the empirical and pragmatic relevance of theistic worship was never denied. The world and religion are practical realities. The transcendence of reality is an ideal of philosophical understanding, not a denial of practical religion or of practical life in general.

Thus the essential kinship of Śaṅkara's *Advaita* to *Śākta Advaita* cannot be denied even though at the level of polemic there is considerable difference. In any case it needs no effort to reconcile Śākta worship with *Advaitism*. Among the *stotras* devoted to Devī and making strong claims for authenticity one may mention *Ānandalaharī* and *Saudaryalaharī*. The former is a simple expression of devotion set in a mythological context but notable for its poetic effectiveness. The latter, on the other hand, is not only sublime poetry and surcharged with devotion but also full of esoteric and mystical meanings. There are various stories about its origin.[147] There are numerous commentaries on the *stotra*. The very exquisiteness and perfection of the work makes it difficult to doubt its authenticity. It breathes the spirit of non-dualism but is untouched with any illusionism.

The fact is that illusionism is relevant only as an antidote to philosophical or common-sense realism. In the context of Tantric

Upāsanā reliance on the supreme creative power of consciousness linking individual with universal being is itself the prime supposition. Mind and matter are but phenomenal manifestations of the same universal consciousness which in its real nature transcends them. Like the twenty-five *tattvas* of *Sāṅkhya*, the thirty-six *tattvas* of Śaiva and Śākta *Āgamas* found wide acceptance and need to be understood not so much as speculative constructions or theological dogmas as practical landmarks in Tantric *Upāsanā*. It will not then be correct to say that the status of the world in Śaṅkara's *Advaita* is inconsistent with that in Śākta *Advaita*. In both consciousness is the sole reality which manifests itself as the world through self-limitation. In both consciousness is the essential ground of all phenomena which have no independent reality. The world-illusion is for Śaṅkara comparable to the show put up by a magician or the creation projected by a Yogī, that is, the creation of the world by God is simply the projection of an appearance by Him by His miraculous power. It may be said that in Śākta *Advaita* consciousness is a dynamic reality while in Śaṅkara it is wholly actionless and passive. This, however, would be a misunderstanding. The 'power', 'freedom' or 'dynamism' of consciousness in Śākta *Advaita* is the spontaneity of its self-affirmation, it does not necessarily mean external or causal creativity.[148] What distinguishes consciousness from unconsciousness is its innate power of self-consciousness, *ātma-parāmarśa, vimarśa*. Śaṅkara cannot be said to deny this of consciousness or the self, though he is always mindful of the Yājñavalkyan query. In his commentaries Śaṅkara stops short of the categorical affirmation of pure self-consciousness or bliss though he denies their negation. In his hymns his devotional fervour overcomes his epistemological caution with respect to Brahman and he sings of the freedom and majesty, glory and beauty of divine reality, and there is no hymn in the whole range of Sanskrit literature which could match the *Saundaryalaharī*, except perhaps the *Mahimnastotra* of Puṣpadanta. If we keep in mind the place of Īśvara in Śaṅkara we can see his contact with monistic theism.

Śaṅkara's approval of Tantricism comes out more clearly in the authorship of the *Prapañcaśāra* which has been attributed to him traditionally, and the attribution has been ably supported by Prof. Baldev Upadhyaya. There is a commentary on it called *Vivaraṇa* which has been ascribed to Padmapāda. According to this commentary Śaṅkara composed *Prapañcasāra* as a summary of an older and vaster compendium of Tantra called *Prapañcāgama* (*samastāgama-saṅgraha-prapañcāgama-sāra-saṅgraha-rūpam*).[149] It is also stated by the author of the subcommentary *Prayoga-Krama-dīpikā* that the work was compiled by Śaṅkara while residing in Kashmir which is why he begins by an obeisance to the goddess Śāradā.[150] The commentator's account of the nature of the work and the circumstances of its origin appears convincing enough, and receives support from Raghava Bhatta, the commentator of *Śāradātilaka*, and Kalicarana, the commentator of *Ṣaṭcakranirūpanam*.[151] Even Amalānanda, the famous Advaitin, refers to *Prapañcasāra* as a work of Śaṅkara.[152]

It is, of course, possible to doubt the ascription of the *Vivaraṇa* to Padmapāda as much as that of the *Prapañcasāra* to Śaṅkara, but the scepticism too must be reasoned. Belvalkar summarily dismisses all tracts on Yoga and Tantra as inauthentic without further ado. Still more modern scholars doubt the authenticity of all works ascribed to Śaṅkara except the *BSB* and the *BUB*. The fact, however, remains that ascription to *Śaṅkara bhagavatpāda* supported by traditional commentaries and references to the work as of Śaṅkara, do constitute a *prima facie* reason for accepting the ascription unless there are stronger reasons for doubting it. Now it seems that Śaṅkara was interested in Yoga from the beginning while his interest in Tantra appears to date at least from his visit to Kashmir or, on the other hand, from his 'reconstruction' at Kāñcī. There is no convincing reason to suppose that he could not have compiled a compendium of Tantric lore which need not as such represent his own philosophy.

Śaṅkara's intimate connection with Tantric worship is also clear from the monastic traditions of both Śṛṅgerī and Kāñcī. Both the traditions are agreed that Śaṅkara established the worship of the Goddess Śāradā at Śṛngerī and of Kāmākṣī at Kāñcī, and that he constructed and consecrated the *Śrīcakra* which is the symbolic representation of *Śrīvidyā* which belongs to non-dualistic *Śākta-tantra*. About the establishment of the worship of Śāradā at Śṛṅgerī there are two traditions. According to the one recorded in *GVK* the Śāradā whom Śaṅkara persuaded to come with him to Śṛngerī was originally the same as the deity that presided over the famous Śāradā temple in Kashmir. This tradition is sometimes connected with that of Śaṅkara's ascending the Throne of Omniscience in Kashmir and is also consistent with the tradition recorded in the subcommentary *Dīpikā* on the *Prapañcasāra*. Local tradition in

Kashmir as noted by Prof. H.H. Wilson in 1828 held that Śaṅkara ascended the *Sarvajña-pīṭha* in Kashmir. The other tradition recorded in *Mādhavīya* makes the wife of Maṇḍana an incarnation of the Goddess Bhāratī or Śāradā and holds that she was persuaded by Śaṅkara to follow him and when she finally stopped and disappeared near Śṛṅgerī, he established a temple there where she presides in her real form as the Goddess Śāradā. According to the Kāñcī tradition too as recorded in *Jagadguru-ratna-mālikā* Śaṅkara established the abode of the Spouse of the Creator on the bank of Tungabhadrā and stayed there for some time in a monastery. According to Ātmabodha Śaṅkara stayed there for twelve years![153]

At Kāñcī again, Śaṅkara is said to have established the temples of Varadarāja or Hasti-Girīśvara and Ekāmranātha and also reformed the worship of the Goddess Kāmākṣī. She was earlier known as a fierce goddess but Śaṅkara invoked her as a peaceful goddess to preside over *Śrīcakra-yantra* which he established in the temple. Both the traditions are, thus, agreed that Śaṅkara established temples of the goddesses Śāradā and Kāmākṣī and set up the *Śrīcakra* for worship.

Thus while Śaṅkara seems to have been connected with Viṣṇu worship by family tradition, he appears to have accepted Śiva as another name of the Supreme Spirit following the *Śvetāśvatāra* tradition. He also actively supported the worship of *Śakti* as Śāradā or Kāmākṣī or Tripurasundarī especially as presiding over the *Śrīcakra* in accordance with non-dualistic *Tantras*. To these three great deities the *Smārta* tradition of *Pañca-devopāsanā* adds *Sūrya* and *Gaṇeśa*. Their worship normally is a necessary but preliminary constituent in all worship. As principal gods their cults were relatively minor. Nor did their cults inspire any original or major philosophies of salvation. In visiting temples and *Tīrthas* and looking upon diverse modes of religious worship as reconcilable within the umbrella of *Advaita*, Śaṅkara could have looked upon the cults of *Sūrya* and *Gaṇeśa* also with a favourable eye. As for the sun, it had an honoured place in Vedic religion and was an accepted symbol of *Brahman* in Vedānta. As such Śaṅkara could only have supported the worship of the sun. The Purāṇic cult of the sun, however, was essentially a form of *saguṇopāsanā* which sought to ensure health, freedom from diseases especially of the skin and the eyes, longevity, fame etc. The original Vedic cult of the sun appears to have been merged partly in the post-Vedic cult of Viṣṇu and partly with anthropomorphization in the Purāṇic cult of the sun in the development of which Iranian priests also appear to have been at least marginally significant.

The cult of Gaṇeśa grew up out of the elemental religious necessity of having a form of God on which one could rely for saving one from impediments to success. The peculiar form in which the deity was envisaged has yet to be satisfactorily explained. In opposition to the Brāhmaṇical tradition the Buddhists interpreted Gaṇeśa as the Lord of Impediments, an essentially evil spirit. Like the Fire in Vedic religion, Gaṇeśa is the first of the deities in Purāṇic worship but his worship is generally a part of the worship of some principal deity. As such the worship of Gaṇeśa appears to have become gradually acceptable in the post-Gupta age and would have appeared so to Śaṅkara too. The numerous Gāṇapatya cults mentioned in works like the *Ānandagirīya* are distinguished only by their strange customs and rites for which Śaṅkara could have had no sympathy.

As for the Kaumāras or Kāpālikas there is even less evidence of any positive attitude of Śaṅkara towards them. The cult of Skanda acquired undoubted popularity in the Gupta Age and also in the south and the *Skanda-Purāṇa* is a monument to it beginning from post-Gupta times. For Śaṅkara it could only have been a philosophicaly minor cult. It is worth noting that Śaṅkara describes Skanda as an incarnation of the sage Sanat Kumāra who was among the chiefest of sages.[154] The Kāpālikas were a fierce sub-sect of the Śaivas who have been immortalized by Bāṇa and Bhavabhūti, and their cult was certainly widespread in the 7th and 8th centuries.[155] They figure in the biography of Śaṅkara, seeking to secure the sacrifice of the Master himself as part of their gruesome rites. It is quite possible that in the course of his travels Śaṅkara should have met them and sought to reform them and that in some of these encounters his disciples might have had to oppose the Kāpālika reliance on violence, but to say that he encouraged the spread of a purer form of the Kāpālika cult can only be a baseless speculation. Even in the case of Kāmākṣī, when he expoused her worship, he transformed her into a goddess of benign and peaceful aspects.

To sum up, while Śaṅkarācārya certainly assumed the role of *Advaita-sthāpanācārya*, there is no reason to suppose that he deliberately set out to be *Ṣaṇ-mata-sthāpanācārya* also, though his religious outlook was one of sectarian tolerance, liberal reform and philosophical sublimity. He accepted the diversity of ways of worship and the multiplication of gods, images and temples consistently with the doctrine of one *Brahman* and many names and forms. His pilgrimages to diverse *tīrthas* doubtless included not only debates with sectaries but also reforming advice.

The *smārta-Purāṇic* religion of the age was working towards a vast religious synthesis. The saints of the south too sought the harmony of the Six Sects. Śaṅkara certainly contributed to this process. In this sense he could be described as *Ṣaṇ-mata-sthāpanā-cārya* or rather, as *Advaitāśrita-Nānā-mata-sthāpanācārya.* It may be noted here that the determination of the *matas* as six has been attributed to esoteric rather than to historical reasons but the distinction was well-known in Śaṅkara's times in the south.[156]

Apart from his attempt at the philosophical reconciliation and practical reform of sects and cults, Śaṅkara is also credited with having set up a new monastic organisation for the mendicants following his doctrines. He is said to have established four or five or even six principal monastic centres in different parts of country and to have organised ten different mendicant orders with different surnames, and he is also said to have laid down a charter of instructions for the monastic heads. Before examining the historicity or contradictions of these traditions, it would be well to briefly mention the tradition itself.

Ātmabodha quotes the *Prācīna-Śaṅkara-vijaya* thus:[157] On his return from Kailāsa Śaṅkara established a *pīṭha* or place of worship at the *jyotirmaṭha* in Badarikāśrama. Toṭaka was placed in charge of it. Hastāmalaka was placed in the *maṭha* at Jagannātha and Sanandana was sent to Dvārakā. In the *Śāradāmaṭha* beside the Tuṅgabhadrā he placed Pṛthvīdhava. To settle any doubts that might arise with respect to the *sampradāya, maṭha, pīṭha, ākhyāna, vākya* or *avadhi,* he laid down the *Āmnāya-setu.* Himself he stayed at the Kāmakoṭi Maṭha.

On this account there were five original *maṭhas,* out of which four were placed in charge of his disciples by Śaṅkara and he himself stayed in the fifth. According to the alternative tradition upheld by Śṛṅgerī there were only four original *maṭhas* there being at Kāmakoṭi an ancient *pīṭha* but no original *maṭha* established by Śaṅkara. A third but marginal view regards the Sumera *maṭha* at Kāśī as the fifth or sixth original *maṭha.*

According to Ātmabodha there are four *Pūrvāmnāyas,* one *Madhyāmamnāya* and three *Uttarāmnāyas.*[158] The former are—I (1) Name (*saṁjñā*) - *Paścimāmnāya,* (2) *Maṭha* - *Dvārakāmaṭha,* (3) *Pīṭha* - *Kālikāpīṭha* (4) *Kṣetra* - *Dvāravatī,* (5) *Tīrtha* - *Gomatī,*

(6) *Deva-Siddheśvara,* (7) *Śakti-Bhadrakālī,* (8) *Veda-Sāmaveda,* (9) *Sampradāya-Kīṭavāra,* (10) *Yogapaṭṭa-Āśrama* (11) *Brahamacārī-Svarūpabrahmacārī,* (12) *Mahāvākya - Tattvamasi,* (13) *Ācarya-Padmapāda;* II *Uttarāmnāya, Jyotirmaṭha, Jyotiṣmatīpīṭha, Badarikāśrama, Alakanandā (Tīrtha), Nārāyaṇa, Pūrnāgiri, Atharvaveda, Ānandavāra (sampradāya), Giri, Ānandabrahmacārī, 'Ayamātmā brahma', Toṭaka;* III *Purvāmnāya, Govardhanamaṭha, Vimalāpīṭha, Puruṣottama-Kṣetra, Mahodadhi, Jagannātha,* Vimalā, *Śukla-yajus, Bhogavāra, Araṇya, Prakāśa-brahmacārī, 'Prajñānam brahma'*, Hastāmalaka; IV *Dakṣiṇāmnāya, Śṛṅgagirimaṭha, Śārādāpīṭha, Rāmesvaram, Tungabhadrā, Varāha, Śāradā, Kṛṣṇa Yajurveda, Bhūrivāra, Bhāratī, Caitanya-brahmacārī, 'Aham Brahmāsmi', Pṛthividhava;* V *Madhyāmāmnāya: Maulamnāya, Śrisāradāmaṭha, Kāmakoṭipīṭha, Satyavarata-Kāñcī, Kampāsaras, Ekāmranātha, Kāmakoṭi, Ṛgveda, Mithyāvāra, Indrasarasvatī, Satyabrahmacārī, 'Om Tat Sat', Śaṅkarabhagvatpāda.* VI. *Uttarāmnāya: urdhvāmnāya, Sumeramaṭha, Māyāpīṭha, Kaivalya-Kṣetra, Manonāśam, Nirañjana, Māyā, Upaniṣadaḥ, Śrīkāśī, Satyajñānābhidhāna, Śuddhabrahmacārin, 'Soham', Maheśvara.*

Two other *āmnāyas, pratyag* and *Niṣkal,* are detailed but they are even more metaphysical than the last one which has some connection with reality only by the occurrence of the name *Sumeramaṭha.*

Ātmabodha takes pains to authenticate the claims of Śāradāmaṭha, Kāmakoṭipīṭha by quoting *Bṛhacchaṅkara-Vijaya* according to which Śaṅkara stayed at Kāmakoṭipīṭha in Śāradāmaṭha. He also clarifies that the name of the *pīṭha* is associated with that of the *Śakti.* Thus the *Śakti* at Śṛṅgerī is Śāradā while the *Śakti* at Kāñcī is Kāmakoṭi. He also quotes the *Setu* to the effect that the *ācārya* of *Śṛṅgerīmaṭha* is called *Bhāratī,* that of *Kālikāmaṭha Āśrama,* of Jyotirmaṭha *Parvata,* of *Govardhana Araṇya* and of *Kāmakoṭimaṭha Indrasarasvatī.*

Since the order of Śaṅkara's travels is indeterminate, the order in which the monastic centres should be supposed to have been founded, is also uncertain. From the Kāñcī tradition it seems that the Śṛṅgerī Maṭha was founded earlier than the Kāñcī Maṭha which came last. The founding of the Śṛṅgerī Maṭha itself should be placed after the debate with Maṇḍana and the visit to Kashmir. The founding of the other *maṭhas* could have taken place in the course of the *digvijaya* and *tīrthayātrā.*

There are, however, many contradictions in the different monastic traditions and the absence of corroboration by any contemporary or near-contemporary evidence raises doubts about the whole tradition which, it has been suspected, could have grown up sometime in the early medieval period. As for the contradictions, the names of the *ācāryas* who were put in charge of the monasteries are diversely mentioned in different records, the controversy between the Śṛṅgerī and Kāñcī *maṭhas* has continued unabated for over a century, and a good deal of monastic chronology is in conflict with accepted history. The names of the founding *ācāryas* are stated in the *Maṭhā-mnāya-setu* but its text shows significant variations and there is no universally accepted or critical edition. Thus for the Govardhanamaṭha we have the names of Hastāmalaka as well as of Padmapāda, for Śāradāmaṭha we have the names of Padmapāda and Sureśvara, for Śṛṅgerī Pṛthvīdhava or Hastāmalaka and Sureśvara. These contradictions, however, do not seem irreconcilable. There is unanimity that Toṭaka was in charge of the Jyotirmaṭha in the north. That Sureśvara was put in charge of the Śṛṅgerī Maṭha is claimed by the tradition of that place and there is no reasonable ground to dispute it. It has been suggested that if Padmapāda is placed in the Govardhanamaṭha and Hastāmalaka in the Śāradāmaṭha or Dvārakā we would have a rational assignment of the four *ācāryas* to the four *maṭhas* in accordance with the Vedas they professed and the quarters to which the Vedas are traditionally assigned.[159] Thus Padmapāda professing the *Ṛgveda* assigned to the east would be in Govardhanamaṭha, Sureśvara professing *Yajurveda* would belong to Śṛṅgerī in the south, Hastāmalaka, *sāmavedī* would be in the western *Śāradāmaṭha*, and Toṭaka professing *Atharvaveda* would be in the north in *Jyotirmaṭha*.

While the Śṛṅgerī tradition claims that Śaṅkara did not establish any monastic centre at Kāñcī, the Kāñcī tradition claims that not only did Śaṅkara establish a monastic centre there but he ascended the Throne of Omniscience there and stayed there till he left the world. For the Kāñcī tradition, the Kāñcī Maṭha is superior to all others. There is really no reason to suppose that if Śaṅkara established any maṭhas, he established only four *maṭhas* as *āmnāya-maṭhas* and no more, though four may have gained prominence at some date on account of their significant location. Nor is there any reason to doubt that for several centuries since Vidyāraṇya the monastery at Śṛṅgerī remained pre-eminent, though the oldest record comes from Kāñcī. There is little to substantiate the charges of fabricating records levied by some sympathisers of either side on the other, though in this process the full public exposure of records appears to have been adversely affected. The fact is that existing 'sources', whether biographical or monastic lists of teachers or mnemonic verses have grown up over several centuries and are based on earlier and lost records. Those earlier records having been lost or misquoted or even distorted, the later biographies too contain confusions and contradictions. As for the monastic lists they suffer from confusion between similar names. The mnemonic verses seem to have lacked any references based on absolute chronology, with the result that while lunar dates etc., were preserved the years were remembered only in terms of 'cyclic years'. Gross chronological confusions have arisen by impossibly early dates being claimed in terms of the Kali era. Since it enormously increased the time gap between Śaṅkara and the present day, it led to the multiplication of names in the lists of monastic teachers. Śṛṅgerī Maṭha had to assign 700 years to Sureśvara, the Kāñcī-Maṭha declared that there were several Śaṅkaras after the original one, one of them in the very period where the historical Śaṅkara most probably belonged!

From these confusions and contradictions, however, it does not follow that the monastic traditions are totally unreliable. Thus the list of pontiffs at Śṛṅgerī takes us back through Vidyāraṇya and Bhāratītīrtha to Vidyātīrtha in the 13th century with a fair degree of historical corroboration. At Kāñcī the famous grant of the time of a 'Vijaya Gaṇḍa Gopāla' has now been dated as early as A.D. 1111 and reveals the existence of a Śaṅkarite monastery at Kāñcī.[160] Sri Harṣa's supposed reference to the *Yoga-liṅga* is also brought forward to corroborate the Kāñcī tradition in this respect, which would take it back to the 12th century.[161] Of its list of pontiffs independent confirmation can be obtained of names as far back as the 16th century, that is, as far back as Mahādevendra Sarasvatī. Before that the inclusion of the name of Vidyātīrtha suggests that the Kāñcī and Śṛṅgerī traditions were not originally distinct. If Śaṅkara established four *maṭhas* corresponding to the four Vedas and quarters and himself stayed at Kāñcī for some time as he is said to have done at Śṛṅgerī, it would follow that the Kāñcī Maṭha, while important, was intended to have a somewhat different character than the other four. The fact that Sureśvara professing *White Yajurveda* was stationed at Śṛṅgerī while Śaṅkara himself professing *Black Yajurveda* was at Kāñcī, itself suggests a close and complementary connection between the two centres.

It seems that the nature of the Śaṅkarite monasteries underwent a great change with the emergence of the Vijayanagar Kingdom in the 14th century and the patronage it extended to these monasteries especially at Śṛṅgerī. These monasteries now acquired a new affluence and semi-feudal authority in addition to their traditional religious influence and prestige. In their earlier phase these monasteries could have been only straggling establishments providing shelter to *Advaitic* mendicants but able to maintain able schools, without however attracting significant royal patronage or exercising any impressive socio-religious role. That there were good Advaitic schools is clear from the fact that the tradition of Advaitic scholarship, authorship and polemic continued undimmed later and by the 12th century the school of Śaṅkara had acquired recognized eminence in philosophical circles. This does lend indirect support to the reality of a monastic tradition founded by Śaṅkara. Monasteries were well known in his age not only among the Buddhists and the Jainas but also among the Māheśvaras and the Pāśupatas. Some of these establishments are known to have expanded into networks ranging from Central India to the south in the 10th and 11th centuries.[162] That in the course of his wide-ranging travels, debates, preaching and instructions Śaṅkara should have felt the need of an organization which would facilitate the life of mendicancy and also ensure the continuity and development of the distinct intellectual and spiritual tradition which he had himself founded, is quite natural. Founding some monastic schools and residences and accepting some kind of coenobitism within mendicancy, did not, however, mean that Śaṅkara already conceived the monastic organization as an all India organization constituted by four principal co-ordinate centres as *āmnāya-maṭhas*. It is, however, a fact that such an idea had clearly emerged ready-made in early medieval times. If its origin is not to be traced to Śaṅkara, we would have to postulate among his unknown successors an amazing vision and tenacity over centuries. The history of the Buddhist Sangha or the Christian Church furnish interesting parallels.

It is true that for nearly four centuries after Śaṅkara there is no corroborative epigraphic evidence of his monasteries but this is an inconclusive *argumentum ex silentio*. There is an instructive parallel for this in Buddhist history. The Buddha established a monastic system but it is only from Aśoka that we get epigraphic or independent historical corroboration of the existence of Buddhist monasteries. Epigraphic evidence for monasteries is generally evidence of lay patronage. What the state of evidence in the present case suggests is that Śaṅkarite monasteries as such were not the recipients of any major royal grants for several centuries. One reason for this probably was that in the orthodox tradition grants were made generally to learned Brāhmaṇas, *agrahāras* and temples. It is generally only where the *maṭha* was a school attached to a temple, that there are records of grants. Among the Buddhists the temples were connected with and in charge of the *saṅgha* which was one of the Three Jewels. The *saṅgha* was the recipient of gifts and was conceived as a distinct entity. Non-Buddhistic *maṭhas,* on the other hand, were conceived as merely hostels for students in the earlier phase and later as boarding schools attached to temples.[163] It is the Brāhmaṇas who were regarded as the recipients of considerable gifts. The mendicants were held to deserve alms but no more. The original contribution of Śaṅkara apparently was to organize mendicants into orders and connect them with definite monastic centres in terms of residence, schooling and guidance. It apparently took a long time for this idea to be recognized in the context of gifts made for religious purposes, the general Brāhmaṇical ethos continuing to treat Śaṅkarite mendicants as individual ascetics or philosophers.

It does seem that what Śaṅkara primarily founded was a philosophical school and that came to be recognized soon. That in the sphere of religion he was interested in reforming the existing Vedic-Purāṇic faith within the broad precincts of Vedānta and a liberal orthodoxy is also undoubted. He was neither the founder nor the exclusive supporter of any particular religious cult or temple. He regarded the essence of religious life to lie in the cultivation of wisdom, which in his view required the life of renunciation. His practical efforts were thus directed to reform and organize mendicancy within the orthodox fold by creating 'orders' and 'monasteries'. His efforts seem to have created a new direction of religious existence, which bore socially and politically significant results only after some centuries during which the country had passed through a religious and political crisis. It is worth remembering that the emergence of a triumphant organization in both Buddhism and Christianity is separated from their respective founders by intervals of several centuries. In the case of Śaṅkara the four centuries which succeeded him saw a vast proliferation of Tantric cults, images and temples by the side of a continuing orthodox ritualism. Royal benefaction went to temples, *agrahāras* and ritualistic priests. Despite Śaṅkara's protest the religion of ritual—Vedic, Purāṇic and Tantric—continued to grow and flourish unabated. Could it not be that it is only when this religion appeared inadequate in public life before the onslaughts of Islam that a more personal religion of spirituality received emphasis in the 13th and 14th centuries, and it was then that the voice of Śaṅkara came to be heard effectively in the religious domain as distinct from that of mere philosophical debate or contemplation?

According to the *Maṭhāmnāya-setu* as preserved in the Kāñcī tradition the mendicant orders established by Śaṅkara are as follows—*Tīrtha* and *Āśrama* connected with the Dvārakā Maṭha, *Giri,* Parvata and Sāgara connected with the *Jyotirmaṭha* of Badarī, *Vana* and *Araṇya* of the *Govardhana-maṭha* or Purī, *Sarasvatī, Bhāratī* and *Purī* of the *Śṛṅgeri-maṭha,* and *Indra-sarasvatī* of the *Kāñcī Maṭha.* Metaphorical explanations of these are given in the *Maṭhāmnāya.* It is worth noting that these together make eleven when the recognized number is only ten as indicated by the term *daśa-nāmī.* One may conclude that this also strengthens the originally close connection of Śṛṅgerī and Kāñcī *maṭhas* in terms of organization too just as the designation of *Śāradāpīṭha* or *Śāradā-Maṭha* also suggests as also the connection of Sureśvara with both. Not much, however, is known about the early history of these orders. They are said to have developed into the militant groups of Gosains organized in Akhārās in later medieval times.[164]

The immediate disciples of Śaṅkara were excellent scholars and thinkers. The most famous of these were Sureśvara, Padamapāda, Hastāmalaka and Toṭaka. As discussed earlier, the identity and history of Sureśvara before he became a mendicant disciple of Śaṅkara is shrouded in mystery. According to the *Puṇya Śloka-Mañjarī,* and its commentary Sureśvara was a Gauḍa Brāhmaṇa born in Kashmir, the son of Himamitra and originally named Maṇḍana Miśra.[165] He lived in Kāñcī and composed the *Taittirīya-bhāṣya-vārtika, Bṛhadā-raṇyaka-bhāṣya-vārtika, Naiṣkarmya-siddhi, Mānasollāsa, Pañci-Karaṇa-vārtika* etc. Apart from these attributed to Sureśvara as such there are several works attributed to Maṇḍana and Viśvarūpa. Sarvajñātma Muni was an eminent disciple of Sureśvara. The Kāñcī tradition regards Sarvajñātman as the first head of the Kāmakoṭi Piṭha. Of his works *Saṅkṣepaśāriraka* is the most famous.[166] His disciple and successor was Satyabodha whose historicity is attested by the reference to him by his disciple

Jñānottama who assumed the title of Jñānānanda. His disciple Śuddhānanda is mentioned by the latter's disciple Ānandajñāna who holds an honoured place among the commentators of Śaṅkara.[167] He would be the seventh in pontifical succession from Śaṅkara at Kāñcī. So far the succession is well attested historically. Afterwards the need to fill up a chronological gap of nearly 1200 years, as required by the traditional chronology, seems to catch up. It also suggests that there was a time of crisis after the 11th century.

Padmapāda was another of the most eminent disciples of Śaṅkara. He came from the south and his earlier name is said to have been Sanandana or Viṣṇuśarman.[168] He is said to have become the pontiff of the Govardhana Pīṭha and was the author of a number of works, viz., *Pañcapādikā,* an incomplete commentary on Śaṅkara's *BSB, Vivaraṇa,* a commentary on the *Prapañcasāra, Vijñānadīpikā,* an independent tract on *Karman.*

Hastāmalaka or Pṛthvīdhava is said to have been originally the apparently retarded son of a person named *Prabhākara,* sometimes sought to be identified with the great Mimāṁsaka of that name. His sole work by which he is known is the *Hastāmalakastotra.*

Toṭaka was the fourth of Śaṅkara's great disciples who is also said to have been a very dull but devoted attendant of Śaṅkara whose grace made him a spontaneous poet and scholar. A work in Toṭaka verses is ascribed to him and is called *Śruti-sāra-samuddharaṇam.* It is said that he wrote a big work in prose which is no longer traceable.

Among the other disciples of Śaṅkara the name of Citsukha is worth mentioning because he is said to have been a constant companion of Śaṅkara and the author of the lost work *Bṛhacchaṅkaravijaya* which is claimed to be the source of many quotations in later works.[169]

Śaṅkara's advice to his disciples and the mendicant orders and institutions is said to be contained in the tract called *Mahānuśāsana.* They are advised to wander constantly and to preach and inculcate right conduct. Their wanderings were to be restricted to their area but they were not to confine themselves to their *āśramas* all the time. They were to maintain a high standard of moral conduct, scriptural scholarship and spiritual practice. The succession to the headship of the *pīṭha* should be undisputed without any division. The monks should themselves follow discipline fully and strive to help maintain the *Varṇāśrama*-dharma.[170]

How and when Śaṅkara reached the end of his earthly career is a matter of considerable controversy. The Kāñcī tradition maintains that Śaṅkara spent his last days in Kāñcī. He ascended the *Sarvajñapīṭha* there, made arrangements for his other *maṭhas,* spent time teaching and worshipping and finally passed away.[171] The other version accepted at Śṛṅgerī and more generally holds that Śaṅkara undertook his last journey in the Himalayas and disappeared towards Kailāsa.[172] The traditional biographies are divided on this question and it is impossible to reach a firm decision on it.

REFERENCES

1. *Baudhāyana,* 2.6.22; *Gautama,* 1.3.20 = the mendicant should not stay in the same village more than a night except for the rainy season.
2. His very birth is declared in his 'biographies' to have been part of a divine mission, and then Vyāsa and Śiva are said to have appeared before him and expressly laid this mission on him. Cf. *Jagadguru-Kathā-saṁgraha,* quoted in *Suṣamā* (p. 41).: *Liṅga-pañcakam āsādya Śambhor ājñā-vaśo vaśī / Nivṛttaḥ paramācārya-padam punar aśiśriyat. / /*
3. Pilgrimage or *tīrthayātrā* finds prominent mention in the *Mbh* and the *Purāṇas—vide* Kane, *op. cit.,* IV, pp. 562ff. Similarly the practice of *śāstrārtha* and scholarly *Digvijaya* finds mention in Buddhist works like *Paramārtha's Life of Vasubandhu* or the accounts of Chinese travellers.
4. *BSV,* quoted *Suṣamā,* p. 38.
5. *Vyāsācalīya,* 5.1.
6. *M.* 10.107-108.
7. *Cf.* D.C. Sircar, *Select Inscriptions,* pp. 225-452; Beal, IV. pp. 423ff.
8. Bāṇa, *Harṣacaritam.*
9. *M.* 10.113-15.
10. *Ibid.,* Canto 11.
11. *Ibid.,* 12.1.
12. *Raghu,* 8.33.
13. *M.* 12.6.
14. *Ibid.,* 12.21-24.
15. *Ibid.,* 12.39.
16. The *stotra* may be seen in Baldev Upadhyaya, *Śrī Śaṅkarācārya,* pp. 182-83.
17. *M.* 12.63.
18. *Ibid.,* 12. 70-86.
19. *Ibid.,* Canto 13.
20. *Ibid.,* Canto 14.
21. *Ibid.,* 14.2-5.
22. *Ibid.,* 14.16.
23. *Ibid.,* 14.21-27.
24. *Ibid.,* 14. 148.
25. *Ibid.,* 15. 1-3.

26. *Ibid.*, 15.4.
27. *Ibid.*, 15.5
28. *Ibid.*, 15. vv 6ff.
29. *Ibid.*, 15. 142-62.
30. *Ibid.*, 16. 55-87.
31. *Ibid.*, 16. 93ff.
32. *GVK* 2.27. '*Tīrthāni paryaṭitukāma—Badarikāśramam āsasāda.*'
33. *Ibid.*, 2.43-45, 50.
34. *Ibid.*, 2.48-49.
35. *Ibid.*, 2.61-65.
36. *Ibid.*, 3.2-5.
37. *Ibid.*, 3.6-7.
38. *Ibid.*, 3.8-9.
39. *Ibid.*, 3.10-19.
40. *Ibid.*, 3.20-21.
41. *Ibid.*, 3.22.
42. *Ibid.*, 3.23.
43. *Ibid.*, 3. 24-31.
44. *Ibid.*, 3.32.
45. *Ibid.*, 3. 33-34.
46. *Ibid.*, 3.35.
47. *Ibid.*, 3. 36-40.
48. *Ibid.*, 3. 48-54.
49. *Ibid.*, 3. 58.
50. *Ibid.*, 3. 59-62.
51. *Ibid.*, 3. 63-70.
52. *Ratnamālā*, vv. 22-23.
53. *Suṣamā*, ad v.24, '*Parameśvarājñayā Pratinivṛttena samāpita-sakalottara-digvijayena dakṣināpatham āseduṣā.*'
54. *Suṣamā*, ad v.25, quotes '*Abdān dvādaśa sotyavīvahad adhivyākhyāna-siṁhāsanaṁ śiṣyān svān vinayan sva-bhāṣya-saranau Śrītuṅga-bhadrā-taṭe/.*'
55. *Ratnamālā*, v.20.
56. *Ibid.*, vv. 27-28.
57. *Ibid.*, vv. 29-30. Ātmabodha mentions here the other tradition according to which the winning of debate with Bhāratī and the vicarious learning of erotics took place after the debate with Maṇḍana, but he says that the order of events in the *Ratnamālā* is correct and is supported by other texts like *Śivarabhasya, Bṛhacchaṅkara-Vijaya, Keralīya-Śaṅkara-Vijaya, Prācīna-Śaṅkara-Vijaya, Vyāsācalīya* etc. He rejects the story which speaks of the earthly incarnation of Sarasvati due to a curse of Durvāsas.
58. *Ratnamālā*, v.32.
59. It is worth noting that according to the *Prācīna-Śaṅkaravijaya* as quoted by Ātmabodha as *RM.* V.31, the victory over Maṇḍana Miśra took place in front of the *Sarvajña-pīṭha* when Maṇḍana Miśra was brought suddenly or inexorably from Prayāga.
60. *Vyāsācala*, 4.65-67.: '*Tirthānisevitumanāh sayayāv udicīm*' (66).
61. *Ibid.*, 4.92.
62. *Ibid.*, 4. 93-5.1.

63. *Ibid.*,5.10-36.
64. *Ibid.*, 5. 37-57.
65. *Ibid.*, Canto 6.
66. *Ibid.*, Cantos 7-8.
67. *Ibid.*, Canto 12.
68. *Govinda*, 3. 32ff.
69. *Ibid.*, 3. 58-60.
70. *Ibid.*, 4. 1-8.
71. *Ibid.*, 4. 9-40.
72. *Ibid.*, Canto 5.
73. *Ibid.*, 6. 6-26.
74. *Ibid.*, 7. 9ff.
75. *Ibid.*, 7. 28.
76. *Ibid.*, 7. 39.
77. *Ibid.*, 8. 2-5. The description suggests Chidambaram as Śiva is said to have danced here.
78. *Ibid.*, 8. 16-28.
79. *Ibid.*, 9. 1.
80. *Ibid.*, 9. 2-16.
81. *Ibid.*, 9. 18-19.
82. *Ibid.*, additional verses at the end, verse 9. Its authenticity has been doubted by the exponents of the Śṛṅgeri tradition.
83. *Cidvilāsa*, 8. 38-46. This is the only text which places Śaṅkara's meeting with Govindapāda in the Himalayas rather than on the banks of the Narmadā. It also states that it is Govinda, who gave Śaṅkara, the Candramaulīśvara and the Ratnagarbha Gaṇeśa. (9.53).
84. *Ibid.*, 1013ff; 10.27 : '*aṭitum kṣetratīrthānī*'.
85. *Ibid.*, 10.35.
86. *Ibid.*, 10.48; 11.1.
87. *Ibid.*, chap. 11.
88. *Ibid.*, chap. 12.
89. *Ibid.*, 12.40-41.
90. *Ibid.*, 13.20.
91. *Ibid.*, 16.1ff.
92. *Ibid.*, 16. 31. This is unusual but conforms to the statement in the Kāñcī tradition that Maṇḍana was born in Kashmir.
93. *Ibid.*, Chaps. 20-21; 24. 10-18 Śaṅkara, had a temple of Śāradā erected here, constructed the *Śrīcakra, Śrīmatha* and *Vidyāpītha*—*Ibid.*, 24. 21-32. Sureśvara was placed in charge—*Ibid.*, 24.33. Sureśvara is asked to create the ten orders—*sampradāyas* (*Ibid.*, 24.36) and to worship Candramaulīśvara and Ratnagarbha Gaṇeśa. (*Ibid.*, 24. 37-38).
94. *Ibid.*, 25.7ff. Śaṅkara had a new city planned with distinct parts as Śiva-Kāñcī and Viṣṇukāñcī and the temple of Kāmākṣī. There the Śricakra was constructed.
95. *Ibid.*, chaps. 26-27.
96. *Ibid.*, chaps. 28-29.
97. *Ibid.*, chap. 29.
98. *Ibid.*, 30.11.
99. *Ibid.*, 30.54; 31.6.

100. *Ibid.*, 31.28.
101. *Ibid.*, 31.50.
102. *Anantānadagiri*, p. 16. Vyāghrapura has been identified with Cidambaram.
103. *Ibid.*, p.17. Madhyārjuna has been identified with Tiruvidaimarudar.
104. *Ibid.*, p. 19. Śaṅkara spent his first *Cāturmāsya* here. Chaps. 5-6 deal with the controversies with the Śaivas.
105. *Ibid.*, p. 43 Chaps. 6-9 deal with diverse sects of Vaiṣṇavas.
106. *Ibid.*, chaps. 12-22.
107. *Ibid.*, chap. 23ff.
108. *Ibid.*, chap. 5.
109. *Ibid.*, l.c.
110. *Ibid.*, chaps. 56-62.
111. *Ibid.*, chaps. 63-65.
112. *Ibid.*, chaps. 67-72.
113. *Tirumala*, 3. 50ff.
114. *Ibid.*, 4.17.
115. *Ibid.*, 4.35.
116. *Ibid.*, 6.87-88.
117. *Rājacūḍāmaṇi*, 2.31.
118. *Ibid.*, 2.44.
119. *Ibid.*, 3-1ff.
120. *Ibid.*, 3.19.
121. *Ibid.*, Canto 4.
122. *Ibid.*, Canto 5.
123. *Ibid.*, Canto 6.
124. *Ibid.*, Cantos 7-8.
125. *Nīlakaṇṭha*, 5.1-62.
126. *Ibid.*, 5.110.
127. *Ibid.*, Canto 6.
128. *Brahmānandīya*.
129. *PSV* quoted T.S. Narayana Sastri *op. cit.*, p. 104; *GVK*, 2.28; *Ibid.*, 3. 38; 3. 40.
130. *Śivarahasya*, 9. 16. 43-45; *Mārkaṇḍeya-saṁhitā*, quote *AAG*, Preface, p. 5; *Ratnamālā*, p. 26; *AAG*, p. 172; *cf. GVK*, 3. 33.
131. *M.*, 16. 100ff; *GVK*, 3.70.
132. *Cf.* B.C. Law, *Ancient Indian Geography*.
133. *Skandapurāṇa*, II. 5. 24.
134. Baldev Upadhyaya, *op. cit.*, pp. 209ff.
135. *Vide Mānasa-Khaṇḍa*, ed. by Gopala Datta Pande, Varanasi, 1989.
136. B. Upadhyaya, *op. cit.*, pp. 139-40.
137. *Suṣamā*, pp. 29-30 argues that the learning of erotics was on the occasion of *sarvajña pīṭhārohaṇa*, not the debate with Maṇḍana or his wife, but it places the *sarvajña pīṭha* at Kāñcī.
138. See supra.
139. *RMS*, p. 25: *Padmavana*, *M.*, 8. 1; Māhiṣmatī; *AAG*, p. 174 : Bijalabindu.
140. The famous temple of Padmanābha belongs here, *Padma*, 6. 110-8; *Ibid.*, 6. 280.19.
141. *Garuḍa Purāṇa*, *Brahmakanda*, Chap. 16 has *Venkata-giri-māhātmya*, *Skanda*, *Vaiṣṇavakhaṇḍa* too has *Veṅkaṭācala-māhātmya*.

142. Known as *Agnīśvara-Kṣetra* in *Bhaviṣyottara-purāṇa*. B. Upadhyaya, *op. cit.*, p. 133.
143. The Śiva temple at Chidambaram was built over centuries but some of its inner parts are said to be of legendary antiquity and existed before the 10th century—Percy Brown, *Ind. Arch.*, p. 99.
144. *Vide* Kane, *Hist. of the DhS*, Vol. IV, pp. 733-34.
145. E.g., *GVK*, 3.59-62; *PSV*, quoted in *Suṣamā*, pp. 31, 32, 37.
146. Prof. K.C. Bhattacharya has pertinently remarked on the error of underplaying the concept of *Īśvara* in Śaṅkara's Thought.
147. *Vide* supra.
148. *Cf.* Padmapāda ad *Prapañcasāra* (ed. Avalon), 1.1 : '*Tarhi nityaika-rupiṇyāḥ Śāradāyāḥ adhiṣṭhatṛtvaṁ Kāraṇatvaṁ vā nāstītyā-saṅkya paramārthataḥ tadabhāvepi māyā-dvāreṇāsyā eva taḍ abhyupa gantavyam, Pakṣāntaretu evam-vidha-Kāranatvasyāpi anupapatteritya-bhipretyāha, Viśvayoneriti ataḥ cittādi-saṅghāta-vyatiriktāyāh cinmātra-vigrahāyāḥ Śāradāyāḥ sattvam tasyāḥ citta-śuddhi-vitarana-sāmarthyaṁ ca siddhaṁ*', p. 2.
149. *Ibid.*, p. 1.
150. *Ibid.*, p. 382. Prof. K.S. Murty tells me that the original Sāradā temple had its site in Pak-occupied Kashmir.
151. *Cf.* Kaviraj, *op. cit.*, p. 31.
152. Amalānanda, ad *Bhāmatī*, 1. 3.33.
153. *Suṣamā*, p. 27.
154. *BSB*, 3. 3. 32.
155. V.S. Pathak *History of Saiva Cults in Northern India.*
156. *AAG*,
157. *Suṣamā*, pp. 31ff.
158. *Ibid.*, l.c.
159. Baldev Upadhyaya, *op. cit.*, p. 192ff.
160. On Vijaya Gaṇḍa-Gopāla's epigraph, see N. Ramesam, *Kamakotipītha of Sri Sankaracharya*, T.A.G. Rao, *Copper Plate Ins. of Kamakotipitha*. *E.g.* XIII, pp. 194ff. See discussion below.
161. *Naiṣadhīya*, 12.38. Although the commentaries accept the reading '*Yāgeśvara*', '*Yogesvara*' would be a good reading but has little to recommend it text-critically. Even '*Yāgeśvara*' as *sphaṭika-liṅga* is here connected with Kāñcī and Kailāsa and in fact, unless there were a *sphaṭika-liṅga* or holy tank at Kāñcī, the verse would lose in its aptness and expressive perfection.
162. E.g., the famous *Golaki maṭha*—Malkapuram Ins., S.I.I. X, no. 315; *JAHRS*, iv, 1; *JBORS*, XIII; cf. Yazdani, *Early History of the Deccan.*
163. So *Bodhāyana-dharma-sūtra*, *Amarakośa*, 2.2.8 = *maṭhaśchātrādi-nilayaḥ*; So Daṇḍin, *Daśakumāra-carita*, *Pañcatantra.*
164. *Cf.*, J.N. Farquhar, *JRAS*, 1925, pp. 479-86; B. Upadhyaya, *op. cit.*, pp. 239-43.
165. *Punyaślokamañjarī*, pp. 2-3.
166. *Ibid.*, l.c. It gives the year 2737 of the Kali era as the date of death at the age of 119. But see Nakamura, *op. cit.*, pp. 55-56; Kaviraj, *op. cit.*, p. 26; Veezhinathan, *SS*, pp. 2-5.
167. This would place Anandagiri sometime in the 10th or 11th century but it has also been argued that he presupposes Vidyāraṇya's work, and hence could not be earlier than the 14th century.

168. Viṣṇuśarman is also given as the original name of Citsukha, *Suṣamā*.
169. *Ibid.*
170. Baldev Upadhyaya, *op. cit.*, 27. 8-39 where an attempt is made to reconstruct the 'correct' text of the small tract.
171-72. E.g., Kuppuswami, *Sri Sankaracarya and His connection with Kanchipura*, pp. 39ff; Raj Gopal Sharma, *Kanchi Kamakoti Matha—a Myth*, pp.47ff. The following is the text of the inscription of Sri Gaṇḍa Gopāla, the Cola ruler : *Soyam Sri Gaṇḍa-Gopāla-Cola-Kṣmāpatirātmanah/*
Pattābhiṣecanād ūrdhvam Varṣe Ca sati śodaṣe/ /
Tapodhanāya munaye Śiva-dhyāna-ratātmane/
Svātmārāmāya Viduṣe Pappilli-prathitātmane/ /

1. *Prathitatmane / Sri-Hasti-Śaila-Nāthasya-nilayāt*
2. *Paścime maṭhe / Nigamānta-rahasyārtham Śisyebhyah suvivṛṇa/*
3. *te1[/ /]Nityānna-dāna-vidhi-santarpitāma-dvijātmane[/]Śrī-śaṅka-*
4. *-rārya-gurave vatsare Khara-saṁjñite* [1.2*] *Prāpte Karka-*
5. *-ṭakam Puṇya-rāśim Kamala-bāndhave* [1*] *Mitra-daivata-na-*
6. *Ksattara-Yuktāyāṁ śukla-pakṣake* [13*] *Indor vāreṇa yu-*
7. *Ktāyām daśamyāṁ sumuhūrtake* । *Prathag vidha-rasope-*
8. *tairannairamṛta-sammitaḥ* [18*] *Nityamaṣṭa-śatā-nāñca*
9. *Toṣaṇāya dvijanmanām* । *Prāñcam Gṛddharapurāt Kāñcīpurāt*
10. *Pratyañcam uttaram* [115*] *Kaidaduppurato grāmāt Sirunanne-*
11. *-śca dakṣiṇam* । *Vegavatyuttara-tati-sumārāmai-ka-maṇḍan-*
12. *-m* [116*] *Nālikerāmranasa-tāla-hintāla-śobhitam nā-*
13. *bhūruha-vatānām puṣpa-saurabha-vāsitam* [116*] *Yairko-sthiya-*
14. *majasrendu-maila (=mauli) Kāruṇya-rakṣitam* । *Ambikāpura-nāma-nama(=m) grā-*
15. *-ma-cintāmaṇi(=i)rdadau* । [18*] *Bhūmer(=bhumer) -asyāḥ pradānena yāvaccandrārka-*
16. *Yoggatiḥ* । *Śrī-Hasti-śaila-nilayaḥ priyatām(=prīyatām) Parameśvaraḥ* [119*] *ittha-*
17. *muttungatayā bhaktyā nidhāya manasi (-si) śvare* [1] *Deva-Śrī-Gaṇḍa-Go-*
18. *-pāla-colas Śaṅkara-Yogine* [119*] *Bhu (bhū)-danā-śāsanaṁ svasya hasta-*
19. *-samlikhitākṣaram* । *Adādumata-dharmasya lābhāya śubha-cetasā* [11*]
20. *Dāna-pālanayormaye dānāt śreyonupā-*
21. *lanam* । *Dānāt svargam avāpnoti pālanādacyutaṁ padam* । [12*]

According to Sri N. Ramesam the inscription is of the Telugu Cola ruler Sri Vijaya Ganda Gopala and 'the date corresponds only to 17th July 1111 A.D.' Astronomical data are conclusive on this. The grant of the village Ambi is also implied in another stone epigraph on the walls of the temple as in Ambi and is dated in Śaka year 1436 (=1514 A.D.) of the time of Kṛṣṇadeva Rāya. In fact, several inscriptions of about the same time refer to Śaṅkarite *svāmis*. Thus a copper-plate inscription of Saka 1444 records the grant of two villages to Candracūḍa Sarasvatī, the disciple of Mahādeva Sarasvatī. Chandracūḍa is described as resident in Kāñcipura and a *māyāvādin*. *'mahādeva-sarasvatyāḥ [Śiṣyāya] śiva-cetase* । *Vya-khyātākhila-śāstrāya vikhyātāya mahātmane Kāñcīpura-nivāsāya māyāvādāmbudhīndave* । *Candracūḍa-sarasvatyai yatirājāya dhīmate.*' A grant of 1429 Śaka records the gift of two villages to Mahādeva Sarasvatī, the disciple of Sadāśiva Sarasvatī : *Parama-hamsa-parivrajakācāryaya mumkṣave Bhasmoddhūlita-gātrāya rudrākṣāvali-dhārine// Śītoṣṇādi-d··andva-duḥkha-vyatītāya mahātmane | Samasta-śāstra-pāṭhādhi-pāragāya tapasvine | Aṣṭāṅga-yoga-yuktāya Dayāśīlāya dhīmate | Sadāśiva-sarasvatyās sisyāyāmita-tejase/ Mahādeva-sarasvatyai gurave śiva-rūpine/.*' A series of later grants and documents attest the continued recognition of the Śaṅkarācāryas of Kāñcī in subsequent centuries. Documentary evidence, thus, takes back the antiquity of the Kāñcī Maṭha to the period earlier than the 12th century.

This conclusion is assailed by some scholars. They have doubted the genuineness of the Gaṇḍa Gopāla grant for no cogent reason. T.A.G. Rao apparently sought to identify the ruler with King Gaṇḍa-Gopāla of the 13th century but the details of epigraphic data do not tally with the proposed years 1231 or 1291 and the year 1351 suggested by H. Krishna Sastri would be too late. The argument against 1111 is that Telugu Colas rose into prominence only in the 12th century after the decline of the imperial Colas. This argument, however, is too general since the origins of the Telugu-Colas are obscure and there could be more than one Gaṇḍa-Gopāla or Vijaya Gaṇḍa-Gopāla. The evidence of a dated epigraph cannot be overruled by surmises and doubts based on imperfect evidence. While a ruler called Vijaya Gaṇḍa Gopāla certainly existed *c.* 1300, the Telugu-Colas *did* rule in the 11th century (cf. *The Struggle for Empire,* pp. 202-3, 219-20), obviously as feudatories of the Colas.

The antiquity of Śṛṅgerī easily goes back to the 13th and 14th centuries when Vidyātīrtha, Bhāratīkṛṣṇa and Vidyāraṇya flourished. Unlike the obscurity which surrounds the early history of Kāñcī, this initial epoch of Śṛṅgerī lies in the full blaze of history. The credit for organising the Śaṅkarite monastic system in the form in which it has been known for some centuries must really go to these early pontiffs of Śṛṅgerī.

It seems, thus, that the existence of some monasteries or *maṭhas* housing Śaṅkarite mendicants by the 11th century must be conceded at least in the south. At the same time, it is undeniable that there was an unbroken tradition of scholars who studied Vedānta following Śaṅkara since the days of Śaṅkara himself. Whether Śaṅkara himself established four or five *āmnāya-maṭhas* as an all India institution remains as uncertain as the existence of such an institution before the 14th century. But it is certain that there were monks studying Śaṅkara Vedānta and following the order of mendicancy as *Paramahaṁsa Parivrājakas,* who were *Eka-daṇḍin sannyāsins* without *śikhā, sūtra* or *tilaka.* Whether Śaṅkara himself divided them into ten orders or they came to be so divided later, remains uncertain.

It is only from the 14th century that Śṛṅgerī received the patronage of Vijayanagara empire and acquired the means to grow into a powerful and influential institution. The Daśanāmīs similarly acquired militant organisation and influence from the 16th century at least. The current monastic tradition of Śaṅkara, thus, is a medieval social creation around his ancient but spiritual lineage.

Epilogue

Unlike the poet, the historian cannot go beyond the critically acceptable testimony of his sources which must ultimately be derivable from eye-witness accounts. This limitation did not bother the medieval biographers of Śaṅkara who claimed to be poets and were men of deep faith. These extant traditional biographies of Śaṅkara, poetic and credulous, were composed between the 14th and 18th centuries under the aegis of the Śaṅkarite monasteries in the South. What they intended was to refurbish and popularize the legend of Śaṅkara as an incarnation and saint. What they succeeded in creating may be described as the medieval legend of Śaṅkara. It may be paralleled by the legend of Buddha as in the *Buddha-carita*.

However, these biographies did not normally intend to invent new facts but only to present in a new poetic garb in accordance with their faith and sentiments what they believed to have been based on more ancient tradition. That they describe miracles cannot be a proof of their falsehood because it is a common and inevitable feature of hagiography. Even the accounts of the New Testament which claim to derive from eye-witnesses are full of miracles. The modern historian may not believe such details but he cannot argue that such details show the falsehood or baselessness of the accounts. They only show the acceptance of the supernatural by the tradition and the need for its critical examination for purposes of earthly history.

The medieval biographies claim to be based on some older texts called *Prācīna-Śaṅkaravijaya* or *Bṛhat Śaṅkaravijaya* which are no longer extant but which claimed to derive from eye-witnesses. Agreements and common materials between the different extant 'biographies' as well as excerpts from the lost sources give credibility to this tradition. A Śaṅkara legend arose as early as the 10th century and was refashioned in the 14th century. If the traditior about ancient and lost texts is totally rejected, there would be no possibility of any kind of biography of Śaṅkara. But this is an extreme and unreasoned scepticism at par with those early views which rejected the historicity of Buddha and Christ. A more reasonable view is to search what material in these biographies seems to be common and derived from a more ancient source. The resultant data can be checked in certain respects from unimpeachable records. For example, Śaṅkara's writings give evidence of the kind of education he had, of his attitudes towards his teachers and rival scholars, of his perception of contemporary society. So Śaṅkara's disciples give some facts and personal impressions about him. A faint biographical outline of Śaṅkara is certainly possible. While certain broad features of his career emerge with fair clarity it is impossible to attest particular details precisely. We know about his birth and lineage, education, journeying to the north, meeting his teachers and engaging in literary activities. He did further engage in debates and pilgrimages but these cannot be detailed with any degree of reliability. The tendency to update the debates and pilgrimages in line with the expectations of a much later age played havoc with the older tradition. The later biographers were unwilling to leave out any later sects or temples from the ambit of Śaṅkara's activities! Another unfortunate fact was that in some respects the interests and controversies of monastic establishments intruded in these texts and have led to flagrant contradictions. Thus one version places Śaṅkara's *Sarvjña-pīṭhārohaṇa* and *Niryāna* in Kāñcī with which other versions disagree.

The image of Śaṅkara that emerges from these biographical records is not simply that of a young prodigy, scholar, philosopher, author, teacher, debator and wandering mendicant but also of a yogi, saint, Master of all sciences, including the science of worship or *Tantra*, devotional poet, wandering religious preacher, tolerant reformer and the organiser of a new school and monastic centres.* His excellent scholarship, and intellectual acumen are there for everyone to see. His spiritual knowledge is attested by the universal tradition of his disciples and followers. That he was a most

* A number of sculptures are said to give 'portraits' of Śaṅkara—one of these is from an 8th century Pallava shrine in Kanchipuram at Airavatesvaram, the other from Rajasthan in the 9th century, cf. Prof. Sivaramamurti in *India's Contribution to World Thought & Culture* (Madras, 1970), p.285.

formidable debator is implied in the tradition recorded by the Buddhist historian Tārānātha and the debate with Maṇḍana is a central event in his biographies which are not unoften called *Digvijaya* or *Vijaya*. Although the history of his pilgrimages cannot be reconstructed, there are local legends attesting his 'visits' in farflung parts of the country, Kashmir, Badarināth, Nepal, the Deccan and the South. Many of these could have grown up in medieval times but they do indicate a feature of the earlier tradition. His connection with Yoga as a doctrinal system is being admitted by some modern scholars. Now tradition thinks of Śaṅkara as a Yogi but not as a scholar of the Sāṅkhyan Pātañjala Yoga. There is, however, no real contradiction, for although Śaṅkara should have been a Vedāntic Yogi, not a Sāṅkhyan one, he could still have been interested in Sāṅkhya-yoga, some elements of which he admits in his system in a subordinate place. Thus beginning his career as a mendicant Yogi, Śaṅkara went on to restore Vedānta from the ritualistic morass into which it had sunk, to its purity and a new state of maturity in which it was able to more than absorb the challenge of Buddhism. Teaching, debating, wandering Śaṅkara became a moving religious force. His religious devotion is patent in his hymns which also evidence his religious open-mindedness. Some modern scholars tend to disagree with this traditional belief but then their scepticism does not seem to be based on adequate reasons. Śaṅkara's authorship of at least some of the *stotras* is generally admitted by reputed and knowledgeable scholars. Śaṅkara's Advaita was not inconsistent with his having been *Ṣaṇmatasthāpanācārya* since his doctrine of *Upādhi* enables one to see the same divinity under diverse names and forms leading to diverse sectarian modes of worship. Only the principle of *Advaita* needs to be preserved as Śaṅkara emphasizes in his critique of *Pāñcarātra*. That Śaṅkara was an accomplished Master of Tantra is a part of his traditional image but most modern scholars reject it as they exclude Tantric writings such as *Prapañcasāra* from the genuine corpus of his works. There is, however, an obvious *petitio principii* in such reasoning. *Prapañcasāra* is not Śaṅkara's writing because he was not a Tantric and he was not a Tantric because his genuine writings do not evidence Tantric principles! Śaṅkara's connection with Tantricism has been discussed before and it seems reasonable to believe that after his visit to Kashmir he made a collection of Tantric lore in *Prapañcasāra* and also established the Tantric worship of *Śrīvidyā* at Śṛṅgerī and Kāñcī. Here too there is no contradiction because the doctrine of *adhikāra-bheda* permitted *upāsanā*. Thus Śaṅkara's career shows him in its different stages as Yogi and *Jñānin, Bhakta* and Tantric Siddha, *Jīvanmukta* and *Karma-yogin*. It must be remembered that while Śaṅkara's major commentaries are in the context of *nirguṇa-brahma-vidyā*, his devotional writings belong to the context of *saguṇopāsanā*.

The most popular of beliefs about Śaṅkara is that he established four or five monastic centres called *Āmanāya-maṭhas* in the different parts of the country and also organized the *Daśanāmī* sects of mendicants. There are two major difficulties in accepting this tradition as such. In the first place tradition is not unanimous about the number of *Āmnāya-maṭhas* to be attributed to Śaṅkara and the subject has been fiercely debated within monastic circles without any agreement. The Kāñcī Maṭha has acquired great preeminence in the present century but its claims of antiquity have been disputed by some sympathisers of Śṛṅgerī which has the best attested history going back to the days when the great empire of Vijayanagar was founded. In the second place there are no universally acceptable ancient records mentioning these monasteries for centuries after Śaṅkara. The earliest record in this context is a grant which has been dated in A.D. 1111 and mentions Śaṅkarārya guru in Kāñcī, but the dating although most probable is not undisputed. From the grant it does seem that even before the 14th century Śaṅkarite monasteries were known. A Cambodian inscription implies that even at the beginning of the 9th century, teachers known by the designation Bhagavat Śaṅkara were famous. The succession of great names for several generations after Śaṅkara in his school does suggest that an effective organisation for the teaching and dissemination of Śaṅkara's teachings did exist. This organisation was certainly connected with the monasteries in later times but its connection with Śaṅkara himself is not definite. The *Maṭhāmnāya* and the *Mahānuśāsana* make Śaṅkara the author of an elaborate monastic system. What is more likely is that the system evolved gradually especially after the 14th century when it received powerful imperial patronage.* Its earlier shape is not known except that in all probability there must have been some centres of Advaitic study clustering around celebrated monks and

* The same happened to Buddhism and Christianity after Aśoka and Constantine respectively.

spread far and wide in the country. In this sense—as special centres of residence and study for monks professing Advaita—'Sankarite' monasteries could well go back to Śaṅkara but it is not definitely proved that he conceived just four or five *Āmnāya-maṭhas* and that these *maṭhas* go back to him in an uninterrupted succession. *Maṭhas* existed from earlier times as hostels for students or residences for mendicants. In Śaṅkara's age there were many Pāśupata *maṭhas* which developed far-flung chains of branch *maṭhas* in the subsequent centuries. The Buddhists and Jainas had a well-developed monastic organisation. It is thus not at all surprising that in the course of his peregrinations Śaṅkara might have felt the need of such coenobitic organizations where the monks of his school could stay and study. But in the absence of hard evidence we are unable to go beyond mere possibility. We know that such a system definitely emerged after a few centuries when a great empire decided to support it. The Daśanāmīs too clearly emerge into history only from the 16th century. That this monastic system should grow up gradually in the course of centuries is not surprising either. The Buddhist or Christian monasticism grew up in a similar manner. But in none of the three cases is the later organisational development totally unconnected with the ideas of the founder.

Despite detailed controversies the date of Śaṅkara must be held to be between A.D. 650 and 800. He is not earlier than Dharmakīrti and Kumārila, and he is not later than Bhāskara, Vācaspati Miśra or Śivasoma. His age seems to be the age of anarchy which succeeded the death of Harṣa in the north and the struggle of the Cāḷukyas and the Pallavas in the south. It was an age of Paurāṇic cults, rising Tantricism and declining Buddhism. It was the age of devotional fervour in the south. In the social arena *smārta* orthodoxy was contending with more liberal trends in the devotional and heterodox sects. In the intellectual sphere it was an age when the challenge of Buddhist and Jaina heterodoxy was being sought to be met by the Naiyayikas and the *Mīmāṁsakas.* It was also an age of scientific development.

Śaṅkara stands between the classical and the early medieval ages. The Classical Age had gradually evolved the synthesis of *Pravṛtti* and *Nivṛtti, Karman* and *Sannyāsa.* The Smārta-Purāṇic religion had joined the cults of numberless gods to the monotheism which had evolved out of the Vedic age. Śaṅkara's principles of *Upādhi-bheda* and *satya-bheda* provided these processes of synthesis with new intellectual tools. At the same time his exposition of the Higher Truth or Paramārtha could easily be understood as an encouragement to the ideal of ascetic otherworldliness, and it is thus that his doctrine became the basis of the monasticism within which Vedānta flourished in medieval times. However, whether philosophy alone provides an adequate basis for monasticism is a moot question.

That the ideas of Śaṅkara constitute a homogeneous system which he expressed without variation, is common ground between the traditional and most modern interpretations of his philosophy. Some scholars, however, have seen a development of ideas in Śaṅkara springing from the changing contexts of worship. Some have seen in him a precarious balance of incompatible tendencies. There can be no doubt that both of these contentions are substantially just. When Śaṅkara argues with the Mīmāṁsakas or some older Vedāntins he totally rejects any role for *Karman* in liberation which depends on knowledge and knowledge alone. On the other hand, he accepts the ancillary role of *Karman* in the contexts of *Varṇāśrama-dharma*, surrender to God or worship. He admits that while *Karman* does not directly lead to liberation, it is indirectly useful if it is practised as Karma-yoga. While Śaṅkara emphasises the lack of direct connection between *Karman* and *Mokṣa*, the indirect connection which he admits is in itself of immense significance in the social as well as the religious context, for it recognizes the spiritual value of action performed in the right spirit. On the other hand, insofar as *Varṇāśrama-dharma* regulated conduct by prescribing social and ritual duties, Śaṅkara's doctrine of the Renunciation of Works (*Naiṣkarmya*) is stridently critical of it but it is not a doctrine of indolent inaction. Although best known as the great champion of mendicancy which was later monastically organized, Śaṅkara accepts the relevance of *Karman* in spiritual life in more ways than one such as the disinterested performance of duty, practice of Yoga, devotional worship and social good (*lokasaṅgraha*).

Similarly while Śaṅkara establishes the falsehood of the world in the context of spiritual monism (*Brahmādvaita*), he argues for its reality in his debate with the Buddhists. Against the Vaiśeṣika he supports the evolutionism (*Parināmavāda*) of *Sāṅkhya*, but abandons it in the context of ultimate truth where all becoming is illusory and nothing is really created (*ajāti*). Continuing to use terms like *sat, cit* and even *ānanda* for *Brahman*, he discards their common empirical meanings, holding them to be significant in a unique and non-literal fashion. He denies the reality of differences but does not reduce reality to the abstraction of Hegelian *Sein*. Reality remains for him unique, partless and infinite.

Thus Śaṅkara's Truth is both transcendent and immanent. Being non-dual it transcends empirical and logical understanding but being non-dual nothing can be given which is not itself under some veil. Śaṅkara describes this veil over the real as the result of the power of obscuration dependent on reality itself and projecting Names and Forms as the matrix of finite creation. The empirical truth of common life, thus, contains a mutual superimposition of what is true and what is false. Śaṅkara's philosophy is one of reflective discrimination which would separate unitive truth from the divisiveness of error.

But it is more than a philosophy. It is also a religion of salvation. *Mukti* is determined as the goal, but it is not the negation of life as may be seen from the concept of *Jīvanmukti*. Unfortunately it is the negative image of Śaṅkara's doctrines which gained currency in medieval times when it devoted itself whole-heartedly to the waging of a polemical war against theistic Vedānta and upheld mendicancy and monasticism as the ideal forms of social life. During the modern Indian Renaissance there was a natural revulsion against this and an attempt has been growing to reinterpret Advaita and Śaṅkara. Ram Mohun Roy understood the *BSB* as a system of monotheism and even K.C. Bhattacharya protested against the attempt to downgrade *Īśvara* in Śaṅkara's thought. Vivekananda sought to recapture the dynamism of Śaṅkara's *Naiṣkarmya* and saw in *Advaita* a universal religion. Ramana Maharsi has rediscovered the practical meaning of *Advaitic* practice. Radhakrishnan and many others have sought to interpret its theory in the modern context using comparisons from Western philosophy. Apart from religious reformers and philosophers, historians too have sought to rediscover Śaṅkara in his original, pre-medieval form.

To conclude, the *Brahmādvaita* of Śaṅkara is not a 'Concealed form of Nihilism', nor is his *Ātmavāda* indifferent to enlightened human values, nor his Renunciation of Works a species of escapism. His negations are contextual and relative, not absolute and final. His philosophy is designed to lead man to the fullest self-realization, not to suicidal annihilation. The transcendence of differences only reveals the universal and infinite unity of ground reality. Even though a commonplace, it is worth recalling that Śaṅkara's own life is the standing refutation of the charges of nihilism, metaphysical and socio-ethical, against him.

'If Vedanta is the "national religion" of India and its universalism at the same time, and if its unique combination of spirituality and reason makes it a philosophical religion, it is to Śaṅkara, after the *Upaniṣadic* seers, that the credit should go.'*

* Vide the author's *Śaṅkarācārya-Vicāra Aur Sandarbha* (National Publishing House, New Delhi, 1991), p.116.

SELECTIVE SUBJECT INDEX

SELECTIVE NAME INDEX